Be My Disciples

Peter M. Esposito
President

Jo Rotunno, MA
Publisher

Anne P. Battes, M.Ed.
Associate Publisher

Program Advisors
Michael P. Horan, PhD
Elizabeth Nagel, SSD

GRADE TWO
TEACHER EDITION

"The Subcommittee on the Catechism, United States Conference of Catholic Bishops, has found this catechetical series, copyright 2014, to be in conformity with the *Catechism of the Catholic Church*."

NIHIL OBSTAT
Rev. Msgr. Robert Coerver
Censor Librorum

IMPRIMATUR
† Most Reverend Kevin J. Farrell DD
Bishop of Dallas
March 5, 2013

The *Nihil Obstat and Imprimatur* are official declarations that the material reviewed is free of doctrinal or moral error. No implication is contained therein that those granting the *Nihil Obstat and Imprimatur* agree with the contents, opinions, or statements expressed.

Acknowledgments

Excerpts are taken and adapted from the *New American Bible* with Revised New Testament and Revised Psalms, © 1991, 1986, 1970, Confraternity of Christian Doctrine, Washington, D.C., and are used by permission of the copyright owner. All Rights Reserved. No part of the *New American Bible* may be reproduced in any form without permission in writing from the copyright owner.

Excerpts are taken and adapted from the English translation of the *Roman Missal*, © 2010, International Commission on English in the Liturgy, Inc. (ICEL); *United States Catholic Catechism for Adults*, © 2006, United States Conference of Catholic Bishops, Washington, D.C.; *National Directory for Catechesis*, © 2005, United States Conference of Catholic Bishops, Washington, D.C. English translation of the *Catechism of the Catholic Church* for use in the United States of America, second edition, © 1997, United States Catholic Conference, Inc.- Liberia Editrice Vaticana; excerpts from the *General Directory for Catechesis*, © 1997, United States Conference of Catholic Bishops, Washington, D.C. All rights reserved. No part of these works may be reproduced in any form without permission in writing from the copyright owner.

Excerpts from *Dogmatic Constitution on Divine Revelation* [Dei Verbum]; *Dogmatic Constitution on the Sacred Liturgy* [Sacrosanctum Concilium]; *Decree on the Ministry and Life of Priests* [Presbyterorum Ordinis], from *Vatican Council II: The Conciliar and Post Conciliar Documents*, New Revised Edition, Austin Flannery, O.P., Gen. Ed., copyright © 1975, 1986, 1992, 1996 by Costello Publishing Company, Inc. Used with permission.

Excerpts and adaptations of prayers were taken from the book of *Catholic Household Blessings & Prayers*, © 2007, United States Conference of Catholic Bishops, Washington, D.C. All rights reserved. No part of the book of *Catholic Household Blessings & Prayers* may be reproduced or transmitted in any form or by any means, electronic or mechanical, including photocopying, recording, or by any information storage and retrieval system, without permission in writing from the copyright holder.

Toll Free   877-275-4725
Fax   800-688-8356

Visit us at www.RCLBenziger.com
and www.BeMyDisciples.com

20772 ISBN 978-0-7829-1641-6 (Teacher Edition)
20762 ISBN 978-0-7829-1635-5 (Student Edition)

1st printing
Manufactured for RCL Benziger in Cincinnati, OH, USA. April, 2013

Contents

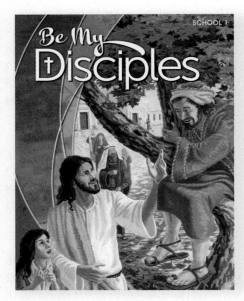

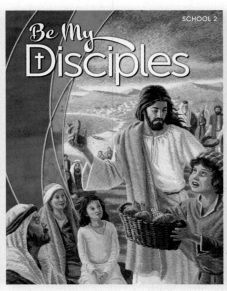

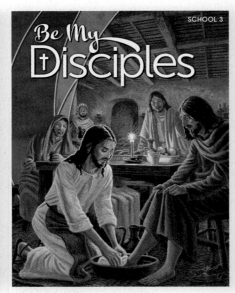

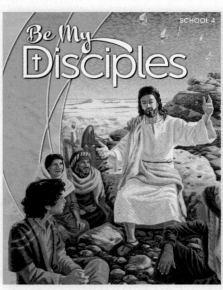

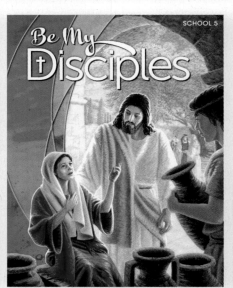

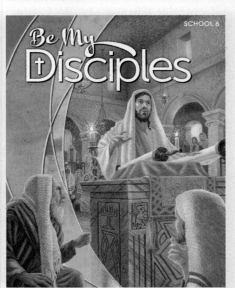

Be My ✝ Disciples

The innovative new program that leads Catholic children and their families to:

- grow in their conversion to Jesus Christ.
- develop the habits of discipleship.
- decide each day to choose life in Christ.
- live as active, committed members of the Catholic Church.

A Balanced Approach to Students' Catechesis

A BALANCED APPROACH

An innovative religion curriculum that empowers children and their families to answer Jesus' call to "Be My Disciples"

- **Invites** children to discipleship
- **Teaches** Scripture, Doctrine, and Celebration
- **Challenges** children to integrate faith and life

Invites
through its **Catechumenal Methodology**

Teaches
through its **Spiral Structure** of Scripture, Doctrine, and Celebration

Challenges
through Integration Activities and Faith Choices

A Child-Centered Catechesis

Be My Disciples shares the Christian story in a catechumenal methodology, using reflection on Scripture and doctrine, plus prayer celebration in every class and during all the major seasons of the Church year. It initiates children into the community of faith and challenges them to discipleship.

A Balanced Approach

- **Invites** students to discipleship through a dynamic methodology that incorporates the latest findings in brain research, psycho-social development, and emotional intelligence.

- **Teaches**, reinforces, and extends knowledge of Scripture, Catholic doctrine, and the Church year *every year in every grade* through RCL Benziger's unique **spiral structure**.

- **Challenges** students to a deeper integration of faith and life by leading them to higher levels of thinking and encouraging a weekly faith choice.

A Child-Centered Catechesis

Be My Disciples helps children know and live their faith through loving service to others. Week by week, students gather to:

- **Grow in Knowledge.** Through RCL Benziger's unique spiral structure, students are introduced to Scripture, Catholic Tradition, and the liturgical year, and reinforce and extend their knowledge year by year.

- **Connect Faith with Their Experience.** Through a process of presentation, application, reflection, and decision, students relate knowledge of the Catholic faith to their life experiences and commit themselves more deeply to the person and mission of Jesus Christ.

- **Practice the Skills of Discipleship.** By learning the gifts and qualities of discipleship and practicing its habits and virtues, students learn the skills required to follow Jesus.

BeMyDisciples.com

Unparalleled online resources for children, parents, teachers, and catechetical leaders invite and deepen discipleship.

Student Book Features

Innovative features develop religious literacy and invite the integration of faith and life.

The student's book is divided into six units of four chapters each. The structure of each twelve-page chapter invites the students to Explore, Discover, and Decide on a life-centered response to the lesson content.

Unit Opener

An opening Scripture story grounds the unit content in the Word of God. Each grade uses a unique art style to engage the student's imagination from year to year.

The second page activates the student's prior knowledge of the unit content.

EXPLORE

Chapter Opener

The Chapter Opener invites reflection on life experience and Scripture to engage the student's interest and ground the chapter content in the Word of God. A combination of word and image helps to illuminate the core concepts the child is learning.

The Church Follows Jesus

The second page tells the story of a Saint, holy person, or ministry of the Church that has made a difference in the world. By learning more about a person or group that has lived the values of Jesus, students begin to learn the habits of discipleship.

A key character formation feature teaching virtues, gifts, or qualities that build disciples

A question to connect the lesson topic with the life of a student

Scripture reflection

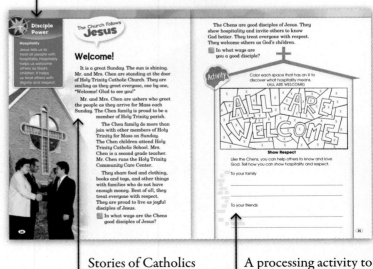

Stories of Catholics who have made a difference

A processing activity to help the students begin to integrate the faith concept into their lives

DISCOVER

A question predicting the key chapter teaching, plus clear definitions of chapter terms

Highlights a Catholic doctrine or practice to help build Catholic identity

Doctrinal presentations and Scripture quotations

A related Saint or holy person who models the way of discipleship

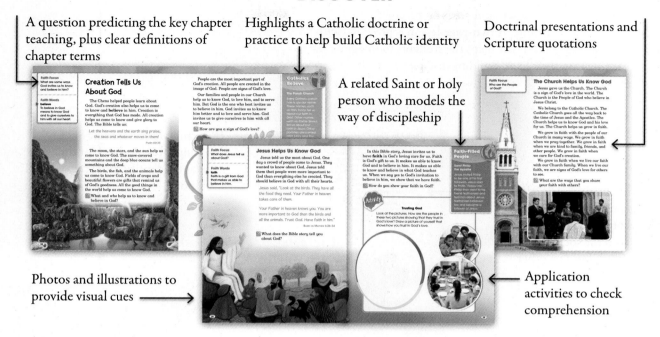

Photos and illustrations to provide visual cues

Application activities to check comprehension

DECIDE

I Follow Jesus

This response page summarizes the lesson teaching, provides an integration activity, and invites the child to make a faith choice.

An integration activity to connect faith and life

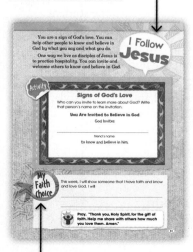

A weekly challenge to live as a disciple

CONCLUDING THE LESSON

A review to check understanding of key concepts

A variety of prayer styles to help students celebrate their faith

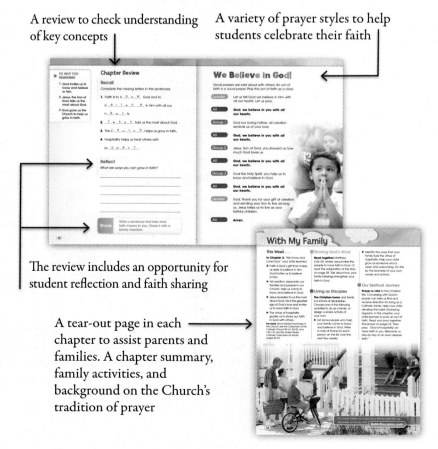

The review includes an opportunity for student reflection and faith sharing

A tear-out page in each chapter to assist parents and families. A chapter summary, family activities, and background on the Church's tradition of prayer

Catholic Social Teaching

Every unit ends with a lesson that focuses on one of the principles of Catholic Social Teaching. A two-page lesson is provided with an interdisciplinary approach that helps the students to integrate the social teaching into their lives. Building discipleship through service to others!

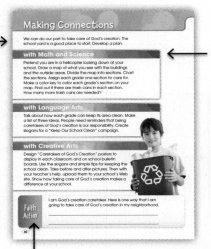

The principle is explained through a story format that will help the student begin to understand the social teaching and ways it is lived by other students their age

The principle of Catholic Social Teaching is highlighted for the student to identify the focus of the lesson

Photos and illustrations to engage the student and provide visual clues

A summary of the social teaching guides the students into the interdisciplinary activities

Three interdisciplinary activities are provided to help the student understand the social teaching from different perspectives. The student is invited to choose an activity that will engage their interest level and learning style.

Each student is invited to commit to a Faith Action in response to the Catholic Social Teaching that is highlighted in that lesson

WE LEARN AND CELEBRATE THE CHURCH

Special Features

Students and families are encouraged to learn and celebrate the feasts and seasons of the Church all year long. The special features in the back of each student book encourages students and their families to fully participate in the life of the Church, through the Liturgical Lessons, Catholic Prayers and Practices, We Celebrate the Mass, A Visit to Church for grades 1 and 2, and Key Teachings of the Catholic Church.

There are sixteen liturgical lessons celebrating the saving presence of Christ in the world. Each lesson lists the Scripture readings for the feast or solemnity in which students and families are encouraged to read together.

A processing activity helps the student understand the lesson while you check for understanding

The history and explanation of the feast or solemnity is provided to help the student understand the celebration at an age appropriate level

A challenge to live as a disciple of Jesus

An ending prayer to help the students grow in their relationship with Jesus Christ

Photos and illustrations provide students with visual clues

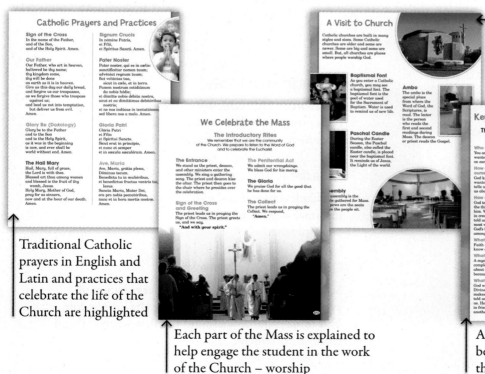

Young learners in first and second grade visually see the key places and objects in the church that help us celebrate as the People of God

Traditional Catholic prayers in English and Latin and practices that celebrate the life of the Church are highlighted

Each part of the Mass is explained to help engage the student in the work of the Church – worship

A summary of what we believe and celebrate as the Catholic Church

Build Religious Literacy

A variety of resources activates prior knowledge and measures the students' progress.

Unit Openers

The second page of the Unit Opener activates the student's prior knowledge of the unit content and forecasts key concepts and vocabulary.

Unit Reviews

In addition to the Chapter Reviews, the Unit Reviews offer variety of strategies help students to reinforce key concepts and identify their own faith discoveries.

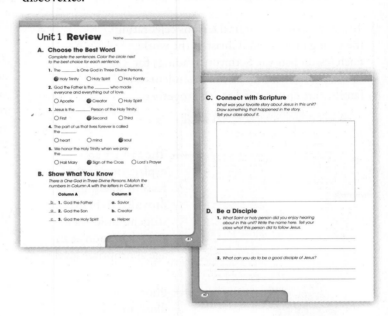

Assessment Tools

A resource of reproducible masters available in both print and online versions helps you create an assessment portfolio for each student.

Assessment Tools Booklet

It includes chapter and unit tests, and suggests other informal ways to assess the ongoing faith growth of your students.

Online Chapter Reviews

Student's interactive reviews for every chapter of every grade level are available at *BeMyDisciples*.com. This tool reinforces learning and invites parental and family involvement.

A Lesson Process That Works!

In **Be My Disciples** you will follow
a simple, effective three-part process for each chapter.

▶EXPLORE   ▶DISCOVER   ▶DECIDE

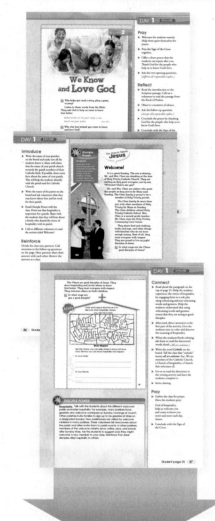

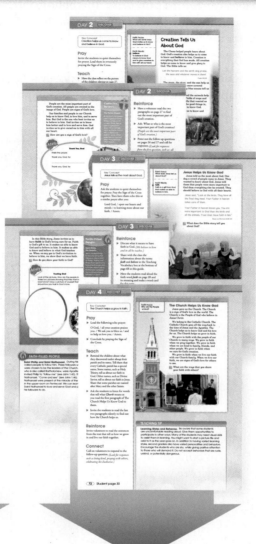

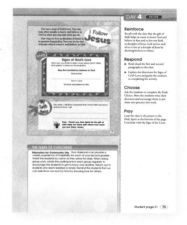

1. Explore

You will lead the class through an opening process that engages their life experiences, grounds the chapter content in Scripture, and invites reflection on it. A second and third page titled The Church Follows Jesus helps you share a story from the Church's Tradition about a Saint, holy person, or ministry that illustrates discipleship.

2. Discover

These doctrinal teaching pages are the building blocks of your lessons and will make the core doctrinal content accessible to the students. Each page of the teaching plan names the core concept for the page and provides you with simple teaching steps.

3. Decide

This page shows you how to assist the students in integrating the content with their own lives and making a clear faith choice for the coming week to continue their journey of discipleship.

Be My Disciples *Teacher Guides offer Front-to-Back Teacher Formation.*

From Day One

Your starting point for confident, capable, committed catechesis. This built-in interactive workshop, found on pages 18–36, will help you get the year off to a great start *from Day One*. It includes a correlation to related modules in the *Echoes of Faith* program for teacher/catechist formation.

A short theological essay, practical teaching advice, and quotes from Church documents focused on the chapter theme.

A clear focus and outline for each part of the lesson process, including materials you'll need and optional teaching tools

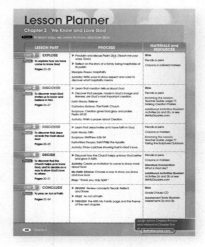

A concise point-by-point plan that leads you page by page through a creative teaching process

Additional background and teaching tips to bring greater confidence and creativity to your catechesis

Three optional activities to enrich or extend the learning for each chapter

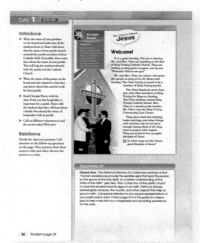

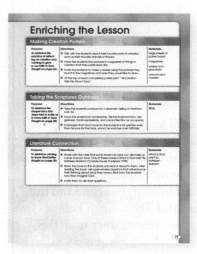

BeMyDisciples.com

CONCLUDING THE LESSON

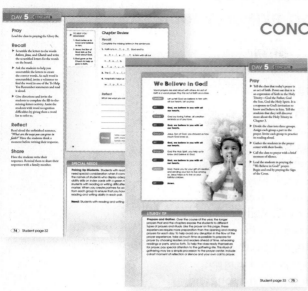

Chapter Review

Guidelines for leading the students in

- a brief review of chapter content through the To Help You Remember feature

- a Chapter Review activity with three sections: Recall, Reflect, and Share.

We Pray

Your lessons end as they began—with prayer. The lesson plan provides clear instructions for leading the prayer, along with ideas for involving the students and enhancing their prayer experiences.

With My Family

The With My Family page that ends each chapter assists the family in guiding faith formation at home. It includes:

- A summary of the chapter's doctrine concepts

- Suggestions for reading the Bible at home

- Ideas for family activities

- A spirituality feature to deepen knowledge of the Church's spiritual tradition and prayer practices for the home

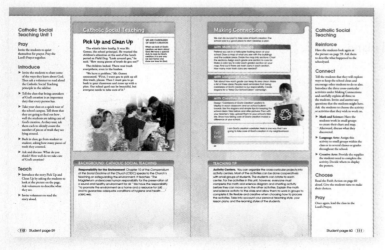

Catholic Social Teaching

At the end of each unit, a two page lesson is provided on one of the principles of Catholic Social Teaching. An interdisciplinary approach helps to integrate the social teaching into the various aspects of the students' lives.

Resources designed to enrich and extend your lessons!

A Complete Music Program for Grades 1–8

The *Be My Disciples* Music Program for Grades 1–8 was directed by well-known Catholic performing artist Steve Angrisano. A veteran musician, composer and youth minister who has been featured at six World Youth Days, several National Catholic Youth Conferences (NCYC), LA Congress, the March for Life Rally, and many diocesan youth conventions and conferences, Steve brings a fresh, youthful perspective to the *Be My Disciples* Music Program. He is the composer of the *Be My Disciples* theme song and is featured in several other tracks on each CD.

Eight Music CDs for Grades 1–8

Each music CD contains:

- A program theme song
- Six hymns (one for each unit) sung by young voices that help children build a musical repertoire of liturgical music as they advance through the grades
- Sung Mass parts reflecting the *Roman Missal*
- Instrumental music for classroom meditation

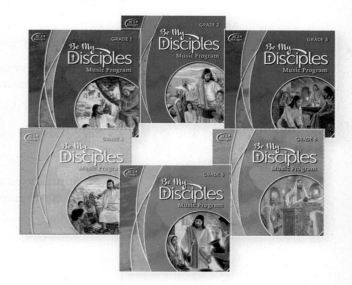

Music Accompaniment Book

Complete lyrics and accompaniment for guitar and piano complete the *Be My Disciples* Music Program.

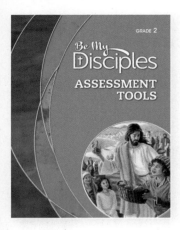

Assessment Tools Booklet

Use these reproducible masters to create an assessment portfolio with chapter and unit tests and other assessment instruments.

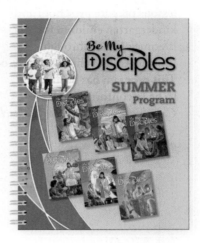

Be My Disciples Summer Program

A complete resource to help parish catechetical leaders adapt the ***Be My Disciples*** curriculum for use in a summer program format.

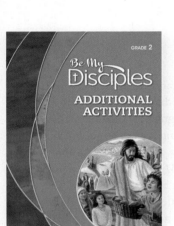

Additional Activities Booklet

Enhance your lessons with time-saving reproducible activities that extend learning in class or at home. Available in print or downloadable versions.

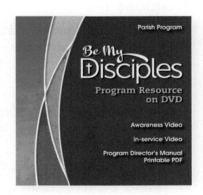

Program Director's Resource DVD

This accessible e-resource includes everything the principal and catechetical leader needs to implement ***Be My Disciples*** in your school, including ideas for training and parent/family support, meeting and retreat models, and much, much more.

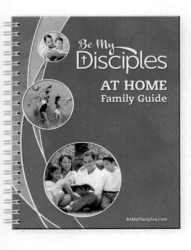

Be My Disciples At Home Family Guide

An at-home companion to the ***Be My Disciples*** program will help parents and families either teach or reinforce the content of the students' text. Suitable for homeschoolers as well.

Sow Seeds of Discipleship from Preschool through Grade 8!

*The **Be My Disciples** family of texts provides a comprehensive and complete program for parish religious education.*

Stories of God's Love for Children, Ages 3–5

Age-appropriate religion readiness lessons prepare preschool and kindergarten children for a lifetime of faith through an introduction to the Word of God. This program has been found to be in conformity with the *Catechism of the Catholic Church.*

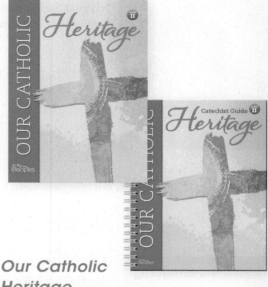

Our Catholic Heritage

This comprehensive and engaging two-level program for intermediate-age and junior high students is designed for older students who are just beginning formal catechesis on their journey of faith. It includes a number of features from *Be My Disciples* to prepare the students to enter the regular basal curriculum in the following year. It offers an appealing design for new, and older students.

Be My Disciples for Grades 1–6

A Christ-centered and balanced approach to catechesis focuses on an exciting exploration of our Catholic faith using a catechumenal methodology. Found to be in conformity with the *Catechism of the Catholic Church.*

Be My Disciples Junior High

Four semester texts make it easy for you to design your own two-year course of study—one that meets your scheduling needs. Each text treats a category of doctrine and also includes special Church History time-line that help students see how the development of doctrine has occurred within the history of the Church.

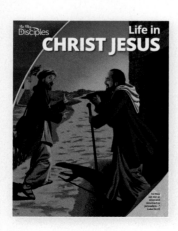

The bilingual Spanish edition mirrors the content of the English edition, however, the Life of Jesus and Glossary are designed in a consecutive style.

BeMyDisciples.com

BeMyDisciples.com offers the best possible support for students, families, teachers, and program directors.

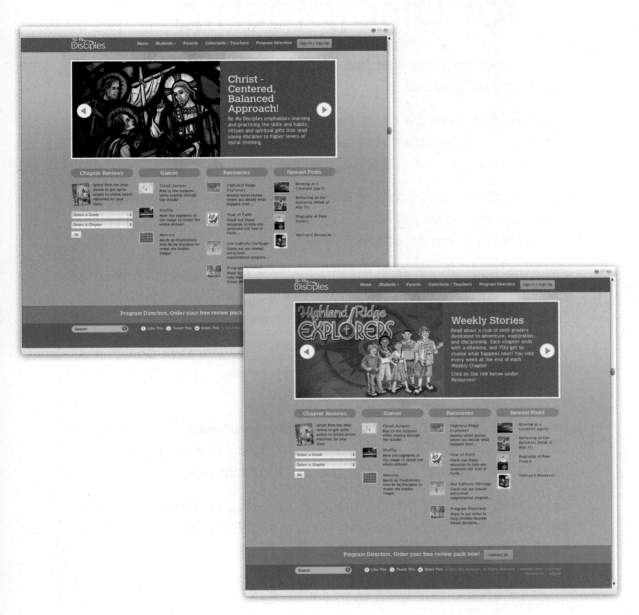

- Connections between the textbooks and the Web site enhance the learning experience in the classroom and at home.

- Social networking opportunities offer safe, faith-filled venues for sharing faith beyond the printed page.

- Easy access for catechists and program directors encourages the use of the extensive practical and creative resources.

- Downloadable activities and assessment tools support busy teachers, principals, and catechetical leaders.

A Teacher's Prayer for Discipleship

Lord, make me your disciple. Help me to bring the Good News to others as you did.

Give me the *courage* to answer your call, as Simon and Andrew and the other Apostles did, and to invite others to answer bravely too.

Give me the *wisdom* to see that following your Way brings blessings and true joy, and give me the words and actions to show this wisdom to others.

Give me your spirit of *forgiveness*, that I may never allow anger or judgment to enter into my relationship with my students. In this way, I will help them to be reconcilers too.

Give me the *reverence* to pray always, in my words and in my deeds. Help me to teach my students to pray, that they may grow ever closer to you.

Give me the gift of *creativity*, to bring your message of hope alive in the hearts of my learners, so that I can engage their hearts, heads, and hands in the work of the Gospel.

Give me a spirit of *generosity* and poverty, so that I will never become too attached to the world's goods. Help me to inspire my students to see the emptiness of material things.

Give me the *faith* of Martha and Mary, to find the balance between prayerfulness and my good works for the Gospel. In this way I will lead my students to greater works than my own.

Spirit of Love, help me to proclaim the *Good News* to all I meet, so that I can hasten the day when your Reign will come in its fullness. I ask this in the name of your Son, Jesus Christ. Amen.

From Day One

Your starting point for confident, capable, committed catechesis

Welcome to *Be My Disciples!*

Thank you for answering Jesus' call to discipleship! You have agreed to serve in the Church's ministry of the Word as a Catholic school teacher. Your decision is a sign of your faith commitment to the young people and their families, to your fellow teachers, and to your school and parish.

RCL Benziger not only wants to support you, but also to empower you with the knowledge, skills, and spirituality needed to be a confident, capable and committed teacher and catechist. From day one, as *Be My Disciples* was being developed, great consideration was given to the learner, the learning process, and to you—the teacher and catechist.

This built-in interactive workshop will help you get the year off to a great start *from Day One*. You'll also find a correlation to related modules in the Echoes of Faith program for teacher formation that will increase your confidence still further.

For Reflection

From Day One, think about the ways you have answered the call to discipleship and who has nurtured you along the way. Now think of the ways you can help the young people in your class to be engaged learners as they answer Jesus' call to discipleship.

Be Confident: You Are a Catechist!

As a teacher of religion, you are a catechist. You are joining a long line of dedicated believers stretching back through the ages who have answered God's call to share the Catholic faith with others. Like them, you have been touched by your experience of Jesus Christ and are unable to keep the Good News to yourself.

Dr. Thomas Groome speaks of the catechist as a "leading learner." This image can help you remember that you do not need to have all the answers. You are still learning yourself, and that process will continue for the rest of your life, as a teacher and as a Christian. But you are indeed a leader for the students in your care. They look to you for information, but even more, they look to you as a role model. This is both an honor and a great responsibility.

As important as your role is, it is not the most important one in the faith formation of these young persons. That role is reserved for their parents; your role is to support them. Ideally, the home is the "domestic Church" in which the Catholic faith is nurtured on a daily basis. In others, family pressures may get in the way and make your classroom the best experience the students have of the Church, at least for a time. The best attitude to have toward the families of your learners is to assume that, at heart, all parents want the best for their children and that they are grateful for your assistance.

Your role in the students' faith formation is to make more explicit for them the Scripture and doctrine of the Catholic Tradition and to give them opportunities to integrate their new knowledge into their daily lives. It is to help students celebrate the great events in the life of Jesus Christ, his mother Mary, and the great Saints of the Church throughout the year. In this role you are helping the students establish their Catholic identity.

For Reflection

How well equipped are you to be a "leading learner" in your catechetical setting? What do you see as your strengths and weaknesses? Discuss your assessment with your principal or catechetical leader. He or she can help you establish a growth plan for continued learning throughout the year.

Be Confident...The Six Tasks of Catechesis

[T]he definitive aim of catechesis is to put people not only in touch but in communion [and] intimacy with Jesus Christ.

On Catechesis in Our Time 5

Just as some actors play multiple roles in a drama, so will you in your role as teacher, the catechist. At times, you are a storyteller, at others a facilitator, a presenter, or a leader of prayer. At all times, you are a witness to your own faith in Jesus Christ. The Catholic Church defines six key tasks for you to fulfill in your role as a catechist.

The *General Directory for Catechesis*, published in 1987, guides the worldwide Church in its catechetical mission. It identified six important tasks of catechesis (*GDC* 85–87). These tasks are reiterated in the *National Directory for Catechesis*, published in 2005 (*NDC* 20). Reflect on the list on the next page and assess your abilities in each of these areas before you begin the year.

The Six Tasks of Catechesis

1. **Promoting knowledge of the faith.** Teachers introduce their learners to all that has been revealed through Jesus Christ by initiating them gradually into the whole truth revealed through Scripture and Tradition.

2. **Liturgical education.** As a catechist, you will help students understand the Church's sacramental life and give them an experience of the signs, symbols, gestures, prayers, and creeds of the Church.

3. **Moral formation.** Moral catechesis involves both the announcement of the Good News through your proclamation of the Gospel call to moral living and your presentation of what the Church's Tradition teaches about this message. The Disciple Power feature in every chapter helps you introduce the young people to the gifts, virtues, and habits of Christian living.

4. **Teaching to pray.** Every chapter begins and ends with prayer. *Be My Disciples* will provide you with a wide variety of prayer experiences to introduce the students to the Church's tradition of prayer. The last chapter in the student's book teaches and extends the young people's knowledge of the Our Father every year.

5. **Education for community life.** You are leading children into a way of life that you have already been privileged to experience. You invite them to join a loving community of faith, to live simply and humbly, to care for the poor and alienated, to forgive as they wish to be forgiven, and to join in common prayer. Your classroom will become a daily experience of Christian community for the students.

6. **Missionary initiation.** Catechesis prepares children to live the Gospel in daily life and to prepare the way for the coming of the Kingdom of God. *Be My Disciples* is filled with suggestions for outreach activities and service projects to help young people begin to participate in the Church's mission. Be sure to note the Catholic Social Teaching feature at the end of each unit.

FOR FURTHER STUDY

See the *Echoes of Faith Plus* "Roles of the Catechist" and the "Person of the Catechist" modules. Go to EchoesofFaith.com for more information.

For Reflection

For which task of catechesis do you feel most qualified? Which seems most daunting? Share with another teacher what strengths and concerns you bring to the catechetical vocation.

Be Capable…
The Be My Disciples Approach

A BALANCED APPROACH

An innovative religion curriculum that empowers children and their families to answer Jesus' call to "Be My Disciples"

- **Invites** children to discipleship
- **Teaches** Scripture, Doctrine, and Celebration
- **Challenges** children to integrate faith and life

Invites
through its **Catechumenal Methodology**

Teaches
through its **Spiral Structure** of Scripture, Doctrine, and Celebration

Challenges
through Integration Activities and Faith Choices

A Child-Centered Catechesis

You feel confident as a teacher when you know what your role is. You will feel more and more capable as you develop the skills to facilitate the catechetical process effectively. *Be My Disciples* uses a unique balanced approach to children's catechesis rooted in the mandate of the *General Directory for Catechesis* that all catechesis include formation as well as information, so that the life of the learner may be transformed (see *GDC* 29).

A BALANCED APPROACH that

- **invites** children to discipleship through a dynamic methodology that incorporates the latest findings in brain research, psycho-social development, and emotional intelligence.

- **teaches,** reinforces, and extends knowledge of Catholic doctrine and the Church's seasons *every year in every grade* through RCL Benziger's unique spiral structure.

- **challenges** children to a deeper integration of faith and life by leading them to higher levels of thinking and encouraging a weekly faith choice.

Be My Disciples helps students to know and live their faith through loving service to others. Here is what they will experience through the balanced approach.

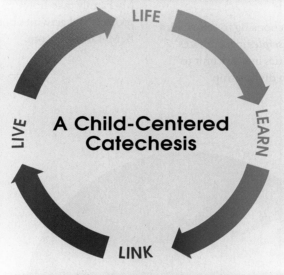

1 Begin with Life.
Each chapter begins with a question to relate the faith concepts to the child's experience. By following this question with a Scripture passage, the students can see that the Bible, too, is related to life. It reflects the life experience of people who came to see God as active in their midst.

4 Practice the Skills of Discipleship.
By learning gifts and qualities of discipleship and practicing its habits and virtues, students learn the skills of daily living required to follow Jesus, and are challenged to integrate them into their daily lives.

A Child-Centered Catechesis

LIFE

LEARN

LINK

LIVE

2 Grow in Knowledge.
Through RCL Benziger's unique spiral structure, students are introduced to Sacred Scripture, the four pillars of the *Catechism of the Catholic Church* and the celebrations of the liturgical year. Every year at every grade, their core knowledge is both reinforced and extended.

3 Connect Faith with their Experience.
Through a process of presentation, application, reflection, and decision, students relate knowledge of the Catholic faith with their life experience and commit themselves more deeply to the person and mission of Jesus Christ.

For Reflection

Which do you think is more important in catechesis—the teaching of the truths of the faith, or facilitating the integration of faith and life?

For which of these tasks are you the most qualified? What could you do to balance your strengths and challenges?

Be Capable... The Eight Human Methodologies

The *National Directory for Catechesis* describes eight methodologies, or avenues through which individuals come to faith. *Be My Disciples* incorporates these methodologies in a consistent way throughout the program.

1. Learning through Human Experience

We respond to God's invitation through our human experience. Every *Be My Disciples* chapter begins by engaging the child's interest and imagination and helping them relate the lesson concept to their experience.

2. Learning by Discipleship

We learn the Way of Jesus Christ by choosing to follow him and do what he asks of us. *Be My Disciples* incorporates New Testament reflection and activities in every unit to assist in the young people's growth in discipleship.

3. Learning within the Christian Community

The witness of the Church shows these young people how to believe, worship, and to take up the Gospel call to service. Each week, *Be My Disciples* invites students to make concrete faith choices for the Kingdom of God.

4. Learning within the Christian Family

The Christian family is often the first experience the child has of what it means to live in a Christian community. The family offers the first and best environment for growth in faith. *Be My Disciples* engages the family through the With My Family take-home pages, and through a variety of other projects and activities both within the text and online at BeMyDisciples.com.

5. Learning through the Witness of the Catechist

You will be a powerful influence on your learners' faith formation this year, both by the faith knowledge you will share with them and, most importantly, by your witness of the Catholic faith. Your words and actions model for the children what it means to live a Christian life. Your *Be My Disciples* Catechist Guide offers you front-to-back catechist formation to assist you every step of the way.

6. Learning by Heart

When we "learn by heart," we make knowledge or a skill our own. Memorization of key definitions, doctrinal formulations, and prayers plays an important role in building religious literacy and identity. *Be My Disciples* highlights faith vocabulary and reinforces key concepts in every chapter through student book sidebar features and Teacher Guide strategies.

7. Making a Commitment to Live the Christian Life

Our acts of commitment to live the faith, made again and again throughout our lives, are how we learn what it means to have faith. *Be My Disciples* invites young people to make a faith choice at the end of every chapter so that they can live the faith more deeply in the coming week.

8. Learning by Apprenticeship

Learning by apprenticeship allows us to learn from an experienced Catholic, a mentor, who can give us insight into the Christian life. You are such a person for your learners this year. *Be My Disciples* also provides activities at every grade level inviting young people to begin modeling for younger children actions of a disciple.

Look for a box in every chapter's lesson plan that will assist you in incorporating the human methodologies into your lessons. The boxes provide you with helpful background information, activities, and lesson strategies.

FOR FURTHER STUDY

Review the *Echoes of Faith Plus* Methodology module for grades 1 and 2. Look for activities and teaching techniques that utilize the eight human methodologies. Go to EchoesofFaith.com for more resources.

For Reflection

Which of the human methodologies has most helped you grow in faith? How will utilizing the different methodologies help you to be a more effective teacher and catechist?

Be Capable...
Getting to Know Your Second Graders

"Catechesis, therefore, is given by right on the basis of diverse and complementary age groups, on account of the needs and capacity of its recipients." General Directory for Catechesis 171

Second graders are striving to make sense of the world. They are friendly but can sometimes be reserved, moody, and self-conscious. *Order* is the word for the year—second graders need and want a sense of order because they tend to be worriers. Because of a need for structure, they also have a strong capacity for remembering details, especially stories and facts. They tend to prefer playmates of the same sex, playing with one friend or even alone. These young persons seek both love and attention from their teachers, families, and other key adults in their lives. They want to be liked by these important adults in their lives. Intellectually, these second graders work hard to ensure their work is complete and orderly. Problem solving and hands-on tasks through games, especially computer games, will assist second graders in their cognitive growth. Time limits only defeat these orderly, perfectionist learners! Most important, second graders enjoy conversations with adults, are becoming better listeners, and their vocabulary is dramatically increasing. You will enjoy a busy and active year filled with much love from these thought-filled, dramatic young learners.

Growing in Discipleship

On their journey of faith, second graders especially enjoy learning through Bible stories. This is exactly how Jesus taught people. When telling Bible stories, the use of puppets, gestures, art, and role-playing engages students to help them remember the story as well as the concept. They interpret the stories literally with little symbolic meaning. They embody a natural sense of wonder, which fosters sensitivity to the sacred. This is the perfect age to involve young learners in prayer services, processions, liturgical gestures, and blessings.

Their hearts are touched through prayer experiences, like short periods of quiet meditation and prayers of praise and petition. Ritual experiences provide that sense of order for these young ones. They have a strong spiritual sense about God and imagine God as a human person. As you nurture these young people, help them to know how special they are as children of God. This is an exciting time to watch children grow in their relationship with God as they learn to answer Jesus' call to *Be My Disciples*.

Physical Characteristics

Demonstrate ability to focus for longer periods of time

May have difficulty copying from the board due to difficulty reading at a distance

Enjoy physical activities, with increased gross and fine motor skills

Exhibit more aches and pains

Cognitive/Learning Skills

Learn through inquiry and repetition

Love stories

Have increased problem-solving capabilities

Are increasing their vocabulary skills

Enjoy one-on-one conversations with adults

Relationships

Need love and attention from key adults, especially teachers

Remain very family-centered

Thrive on encouragement

Need security and structure

Religious Growth

Delight in Bible stories and interpret stories literally

Appreciate prayer experiences, ritual, and ceremony

Experience life through wonder and awe

Recognize Church through the experiences of home and parish

Are growing in their understanding of community

Are growing in their religious imagination

Imagine God as human

For Reflection

- What do you remember about your experiences as a second grader? What are the similarities and differences between your experiences and today's second graders?
- How does this help you understand your second graders, to enjoy them, and to plan for your religion classes this year?

Be Capable... Helping My Second Graders Learn

For as in one body we have many parts, and all the parts do not have the same function, so we, though many, are one body in Christ and individually parts of one another.   Romans 12:4-5

God has given each of us a variety of spiritual gifts to help us to grow individually and in the community. Each gift is unique and each person and gift is needed. It is these diverse spiritual gifts that contribute to the one Body in Christ.

Learning Smart

A well-known educator, Howard Gardner, believes that each of us is born with at least eight different ways of processing and responding to new information that he calls multiple intelligences. All of us possess each of these kinds of 'smart' in one degree or another. The particular combination of these intelligences is what makes each of us unique; there is usually one or several of these intelligences dominant for each person. Refer to the "Eight Kinds of Smart" chart on the next page.

When you were in school, did you prefer just listening to a lecture, taking notes while you were listening, or did you keep your fingers or your feet tapping while you were listening? Do you prefer reading a novel or seeing a movie? Do you want just the facts or do you prefer open-ended questions with lots of possibilities? The answers to these questions tell a lot about the ways you prefer to learn and express yourself. You may prefer to learn by listening, by seeing, by imagining, or by doing. Students have these preferred ways of learning as well.

Digital Disciples

Young people today are also digital learners. They access information quickly from multimedia sources; primarily utilizing the Internet, laptops, and cell phones. Learning takes place through multitasking while processing pictures, sound, color, and video before text. Digital learners are graphic thinkers! They respond to learning that is relevant, instant, active, useful, and fun.

Learning Heart

How do you recognize your own emotions and how do they affect your thoughts and behaviors? How do you manage your emotions and adapt to change? How do you understand the emotions, needs, and concerns of other people? How do you develop and maintain good relationships and communicate clearly?

The research of Daniel Goleman on emotional intelligence is an important part of understanding who you are and who you are in relationship with others. The 'heart' must be a part of learning if the person is to be transformational. This is why *Be My Disciples* uses its balanced approach. The goal is formation and transformation as well as information.

As children grow in relationship with others and Jesus, they need to know how to express their own feelings and knowledge if they are to have common ground with their family, classmates, and people from other cultures and religions. *Be My Disciples* provides a variety of strategies that respect the many gifts of children as they learn smart, learning ways to grasp knowledge and to grow spiritually.

To assist you in engaging all your learners, look at the chart on the next page. Here are some activities related to the eight intelligences that support the different ways children can learn and express their relationship with God and one another.

FOR FURTHER STUDY

The "Methods for Grades 1 and 2" module of *Echoes of Faith Plus* will help you to provide activities that will assist many kinds of learners. See Echoes of Faith for more resources.

For Reflection

- Knowing your own gifts will assist you in helping your second graders discover their own gifts. How do you learn smart and what are your preferences for learning? How does this help you understand the young people in your class so that your catechesis will engage them more?

- How will you nurture and incorporate the emotional intelligence of the young people so that their faith response will be more authentic?

WordSmart

LogicSmart

ImageSmart

SelfSmart

8 Kinds of Smart

BodySmart

PeopleSmart

NatureSmart

SoundSmart

Language and Music-Related Activities

- Researching word meanings
- Word games and puzzles
- Reading and Bible search activities
- Storytelling and journal writing
- Learning hymns and Mass responses
- Writing prayers or songs
- Using background music for activities

Object-Related Activities

- Learning "how many?" of different categories
- Celebrating the liturgical seasons
- "You are there" activities such as placing oneself in the action of a Bible story
- Using maps and models
- Using or creating graphic organizers
- Posters and art activities
- Crafts and classroom dramas
- Using gestures with songs and prayers
- Expressing response through dance
- Nurturing plants and animals
- Creating gardens or nature areas

Person-Related Activities

- Cooperative learning activities
- Peer tutoring and sharing
- Teaching other students
- Games and simulations
- Quiet prayer times
- Writing and drawing in journals
- Creating autobiographies
- Self-assessment activities

Teaching Trends

- Build in more discovery.
- Put content in context.
- Pose problems first and teach second.
- Give fewer conclusions.
- Integrate digital learning.
- Utilize higher-level thinking techniques.

Be Capable . . . Designing the Environment

The most important task of the catechesis of children is to provide, through the witness of adults, an environment in which young people can grow in faith. National Directory for Catechesis 48E.2

The learning process can occur in any place, anywhere, at any time. Our Master Teacher, Jesus, taught while he was walking, sitting on a hillside, preaching in the synagogue, or conversing in a home. Jesus modeled a variety of ways to teach through telling stories, asking questions, offering compassion, and challenging others. He also knew that the physical needs of people must be met so they can focus on God's message. A caring, child-centered environment helps invite young people to discipleship. Since passing on faith is a sacred task, it deserves the creation of sacred space.

Prayer Space

Every learning environment should integrate a catechetical space that is focused around an age-appropriate prayer space. Here are some suggestions:

- Cover the table with an attractive cloth that matches the liturgical season.

- Place a crucifix at the highest point in the prayer space.

- Place a candle on the surface of the table as a sign of the light of faith. Light the candle only during the prayer service. Use an electric or flameless candle if school fire regulations require it.

- Enthrone an open Bible on the table. The opening lesson in your student book includes a prayer service for enthroning the Bible on the first day of class.

- Place a plant or other objects in the prayer space to symbolize the lesson theme or the liturgical season.

- You may want to consider placing a cell phone, laptop, or another type of technology in the prayer space. Make sure it is turned off! This can indicate to your learners that digital media, when used properly, can be used to communicate the Christian message.

Learning Space

Now it's time for careful consideration of the other aspects of your sacred learning space. How will you create a distinctive space for catechesis? Here are some questions to help you create a student-centered learning environment that will encourage faith reflection:

- Are chairs or desks arranged in such a way to promote cooperative learning? Is the arrangement flexible to allow for individual, small, and large group learning experiences?

- Can you easily transition the young people to the prayer space for a more solemn reading of Bible stories and prayer services?

- Can you adjust lighting during reflective activities or prayer services?

- How can you display student activities? Is there a way to use liturgical colors in the learning area beyond the prayer space?

- Do you have some reflective music available for use in prayer services and reflective activities? As you know, music can help to set the mood appropriately to signal that the class is moving into a more sacred time. Consider utilizing the *Be My Disciples* Music Program to enhance the learner's knowledge of liturgical music and experience of prayer.

Learning Materials

You will need the usual classroom essentials: pencils, pens, paper, and some art supplies. Here are a few other items you will want to have available to enhance your religion classes:

- Materials for the prayer space
- A class set of Bibles
- Maps of the Bible lands
- Photos and posters that match the lesson themes
- General literature titles connected to the lesson themes
- A DVD/CD player

How will you incorporate digital learning solutions to engage these young learners and where can they be incorporated into the physical space? Discuss with your principal or catechetical leader what resources are available and learn how to use them. If you have a smart phone or laptop and have Internet access in the classroom, there are many resources at BeMyDisciples.com that could enhance your classroom lessons. The Church asks us to "proclaim the Gospel to the world of youth with courage and creativity" (*General Directory for Catechesis* 181). Jesus used all the means available to him in his own time to invite others to conversion, and so should you!

FOR FURTHER STUDY

Take a look at the *Echoes of Faith Plus* module "Getting Started" for ideas on creating a positive environment for catechesis. Go to EchoesofFaith.com for more resources.

For Reflection

- What can you do to plan an effective sacred learning space for your lessons?

- How can you create an inviting climate for prayer that will deepen the experience for your learners?

Be Committed: Being A Person of Prayer

Liturgical formation . . . must explain what the Christian liturgy is, and what the sacraments are. It must also however, offer an experience of the different kinds of celebration and it must make symbols, gestures, etc., known and loved.

General Directory for Catechesis 87

To teach others to pray requires, first of all, that you are a person of prayer yourself. Your students look to you as an example of what a prayerful person looks like. Prayer is listening with openness to God's Word, and responding in faith, hope, and love. Our response involves a willingness to spend time with God, to ponder the words of Scripture, to discern God's message to us, and to respond with our whole selves—body, mind, and heart. Spending daily time alone with God in an attitude of openness and thanksgiving will transform you and prepare you to be the inspiration to the children that you hope to be and that they deserve.

Worship is simply the prayer of the Church. We gather together to lay our lives before God the Father, to praise him and give thanks for the gift of his love, and to join with his Son in offering our lives for his service. That is why the *Catechism of the Catholic Church* refers to liturgy as "the participation of the People of God in the work of God" (CCC 1069). Liturgical celebrations weave together signs and symbols drawn from our human experience—words and actions, singing and music, and sacred images. An artful blending of these elements produces a worship experience that can evoke for us the mystery of God and lead us to a fruitful response.

As the students experience such gestures as signing, anointing, blessing, and kneeling within the intimacy of your classroom setting, you will be preparing them to participate more fully in the worship of the whole community. Just as you have certain ways of praying with which you are most comfortable, you will find that children have their preferences too. The many approaches that are included in the **Be My Disciples** program will provide a true school of prayer for your learners.

How *Be My Disciples* Will Help You

- Beginning and closing prayer experiences in every lesson

- A rich variety of prayer experiences using the signs, symbols, and gestures of the Church's liturgy whenever appropriate

- An exposition of the rich variety of the Church's tradition of prayer, liturgy, and Sacraments

- Tips for enhancing the classroom prayer experiences

- A closing chapter on the Our Father that summarizes the year's Gospel message

FOR FURTHER STUDY

See the *Echoes of Faith Plus* "Prayer and Spirituality" and "Liturgy and Sacraments" modules. Go to EchoesofFaith.com for more resources.

For Reflection

- How do you create opportunities in your daily life to hear the voice of God speaking to you?

- What forms of prayer will you most enjoy leading for your learners?

Scope and Sequence | Grade 2

UNIT 1: WE BELIEVE, PART ONE

CHAPTER 1—The Bible
Faith Concepts:
- The Bible is the revealed and written Word of God.
- The Bible is made up of the Old and New Testaments.
- The Gospels tell us about Jesus.

Sacred Scripture: Hebrews 1:1–2 (God speaks to us through Jesus); Matthew 13:1–9, 19–23 (Parable of the Sower and the Seed); Psalm 119:14, 130, 160 (The Word of God); Colossians 3:16–17 (Let God's Word grow in you)

Disciple Power: Respect (capital virtue)

Faith Vocabulary: Bible, disciples. Psalms, Gospels

Faith-Filled People: King David

Catholics Believe: The Gospels

The Church Follows Jesus: A Saint Who Loved the Bible (Saint Jerome)

Prayer: A Listening Prayer

Catechism of the Catholic Church (CCC): 101–114

U.S. Catholic Catechism for Adults (USCCA): pp. 11–15

CHAPTER 2—We Know and Love God
Faith Concepts:
- God reveals himself in his creation.
- Jesus is the greatest sign of God's love.
- The Church helps us know God and his love for us.

Sacred Scripture: Psalm 25:4 (Teach me your ways); Psalm 69:35 (All creation sings God's praise); Matthew 6:26–34 (Jesus invites us to trust God)

Disciple Power: Hospitality (capital virtue)

Faith Vocabulary: Believe, faith

Faith-Filled People: Saint Philip the Apostle

Catholics Believe: The Parish Church

The Church Follows Jesus: Welcome! (belonging to a parish)

Prayer: We Believe in God (an Act of Faith)

Catechism of the Catholic Church (CCC): 50–67, 84–95, 142–175

U.S. Catholic Catechism for Adults (USCCA): pp. 50–53

CHAPTER 3—The Holy Trinity
Faith Concepts:
- God the Father is the First Person of the Holy Trinity.
- God the Son is the Second Person of the Holy Trinity.
- God the Holy Spirit is the Third Person of the Holy Trinity.

Sacred Scripture: John 14:25–26; Matthew 22:37, 39 (The Law of Love); Luke 11:13 (The promise of the Holy Spirit)

Disciple Power: Wonder (Gift of the Holy Spirit)

Faith Vocabulary: Holy Trinity, soul, Son of God

Faith-Filled People: Saint Patrick

Catholics Believe: Sign of the Cross

The Church Follows Jesus: Many Languages (praying in one's own language)

Prayer: The Sign of the Cross

Catechism of the Catholic Church (CCC): 232–260

U.S. Catholic Catechism for Adults (USCCA): pp. 51–53

CHAPTER 4—God, Our Father
Faith Concepts:
- God is the Creator, who created all things out of love.
- God is almighty and can do all things.
- Jesus taught us that God is our Father.

Sacred Scripture: 1 John 3:1 (We are God's children); Genesis 1:1, 7–12, 16, 20–21, 24–25, 27, 31 (God is the Creator); Genesis 1:31 (God found it good); Psalm 145:9 (God loves and cares for every creature); Psalm 89:9 (There is no one like God); Matthew 6:9 (Jesus taught the Lord's Prayer)

Disciple Power: Honor (capital virtue)

Faith Vocabulary: Creator, almighty

Faith-Filled People: Saint Bonaventure

Catholics Believe: The Lord's Prayer

The Church Follows Jesus: A Garden for Others

Prayer: The Lord's Prayer

Catechism of the Catholic Church (CCC): 268–274, 279–314, 325–349

U.S. Catholic Catechism for Adults (USCCA): pp. 50–54

Catholic Social Teaching — Unit 1 Caring for God's creation

UNIT 2: WE BELIEVE, PART TWO

CHAPTER 5—Jesus, the Son of God
Faith Concepts:
- The Covenant is a sign of God's love and mercy.
- God made covenants with Noah, Abraham, and Moses.
- The birth of Jesus Christ, the Son of God, is a sign of God's love and mercy.

Sacred Scripture: Isaiah 7:14, 9:5–6 (God's promise to his people); Luke 2: 4–7 (The birth of Jesus); Matthew 14:13, 15–20 (Jesus feeds the crowd)

Disciple Power: Mercy (capital virtue)

Faith Vocabulary: Covenant, Jesus Christ

Faith-Filled People: The Blessed Virgin Mary

Catholics Believe: Works of Mercy

The Church Follows Jesus: Brother Martin (Saint Martin de Porres)

Prayer: The Angelus

Catechism of the Catholic Church (CCC): 51–67, 456–560

U.S. Catholic Catechism for Adults (USCCA): pp. 77–87

CHAPTER 6—Jesus, the Savior
Faith Concepts:
- Jesus Christ is the Savior whom God promised to send us.
- Jesus suffered Death on the Cross to save all people from their sins.
- God the Father raised his Son, Jesus, from death to new life.

Sacred Scripture: John 13:34; 15:13 (Love one another); Matthew 1:20–23 (Joseph's dream about Mary and Jesus); Luke 23:33–34, 44, 46 (The Crucifixion and Death of Jesus); 1 Peter 2:24 (Jesus forgave our sins); Luke 24: 4, 6, 9, 11–12 (The women at the tomb); John 20:1–2 (Mary Magdalene at the tomb)

Disciple Power: Sacrifice (Fruit of the Holy Spirit as related to love)

Faith Vocabulary: Crucifixion, Resurrection

Faith-Filled People: Saint Mary Magdalene

Catholics Believe: The Crucifix

The Church Follows Jesus: Saint Elizabeth of Hungary

Prayer: Praise God (includes Memorial Acclamation C)

Catechism of the Catholic Church (CCC): 422–451, 456–478, 599–655

U.S. Catholic Catechism for Adults (USCCA): pp. 91–98

CHAPTER 7—The Holy Spirit

Faith Concepts:
- Before he returned to his Father in Heaven, Jesus promised the Father would send the Holy Spirit.
- The Holy Spirit came to the disciples on Pentecost.
- The Holy Spirit is our helper and teacher.

Sacred Scripture: 1 Corinthians 12:4–11 (The Holy Spirit gives us spiritual gifts); Luke 24:49 (The promise of the Holy Spirit); Acts 2:1–6 (The first Pentecost); Romans 8:26 (The Holy Spirit prays for us)

Disciple Power: Generosity (Fruit of the Holy Spirit)

Faith Vocabulary: Ascension, Pentecost

Faith-Filled People: Saint Luke

Catholics Believe: Gifts of the Holy Spirit

The Church Follows Jesus: Kids' Kitchen

Prayer: Come, Holy Spirit

Catechism of the Catholic Church (CCC): 687–741

U.S. Catholic Catechism for Adults (USCCA): pp.102–108

CHAPTER 8—The Church

Faith Concepts:
- The Church is the People of God who follow Jesus Christ.
- The Church is the Body of Christ.
- The Church is the Communion of Saints.

Sacred Scripture: Acts 2:42–47 (The early Church); Matthew 28:19–20 (Baptize all people); 1 Corinthians 12:12–13 (We have been baptized into one body)

Disciple Power: Goodness (Fruit of the Holy Spirit)

Faith Vocabulary: Catholics, Body of Christ, Communion of Saints

Faith-Filled People: The Faithful

Catholics Believe: Patron Saints

The Church Follows Jesus: Father Augustus Tolton

Prayer: A Litany of Saints

Catechism of the Catholic Church (CCC): 751–776, 781–801, 874–993

U.S. Catholic Catechism for Adults (USCCA): pp. 143–147

Catholic Social Teaching — Unit 2 We are all God's children

UNIT 3: WE WORSHIP, PART ONE

CHAPTER 9—We Celebrate God's Love

Faith Concepts:

Sacred Scripture: Psalm 100:1–2 (Shout with joy to God); Mark 5:22–24, 38, 41–42 (The healing of Jairus' daughter); Psalm 34:2 (Bless the Lord at all times)

Disciple Power: Piety (Gift of the Holy Spirit)

Faith Vocabulary: Worship, Sacraments

Faith-Filled People: Saint Mark

Catholics Believe: Sacramentals

The Church Follows Jesus: Blessed John XXIII

Prayer: We Bless the Lord

Catechism of the Catholic Church (CCC): 1066–1186

U.S. Catholic Catechism for Adults (USCCA): pp. 168–169, 295–298

CHAPTER 10—Our Church Welcomes Us

Faith Concepts:
- Baptism is the first Sacrament we receive.
- The Sacrament of Baptism joins us to Christ and makes us members of the Church.
- The words and actions of Baptism show that we share in God's life.

Sacred Scripture: Galatians 3:26–28 (You have been baptized in Christ); Acts 10:30–48 (The baptism of Cornelius and his family)

Disciple Power: Faith (Theological Virtue)

Faith Vocabulary: Baptism, deacon, grace

Faith-Filled People: Saint Paul the Apostle

Catholics Believe: Baptismal Candle

The Church Follows Jesus: Saint Kateri (Tekakwitha)

Prayer: Glory to God (a prayer of adoration)

Catechism of the Catholic Church (CCC): 1213–1284

U.S. Catholic Catechism for Adults (USCCA): pp. 183–187

CHAPTER 11—We Celebrate the Holy Spirit

Faith Concepts:
- Confirmation is received after the Sacrament of Baptism.
- In Confirmation, the Holy Spirit gives us spiritual gifts to help us love and serve God and one another.
- In the Sacrament of Confirmation, the Holy Spirit strengthens us to live our Baptism.

Sacred Scripture: 1 Corinthians 12:4–11 (There are different gifts, but one Spirit); Romans 12:5–6, 9–12, 18 (Use your gifts to share God's love); Galatians 4:6 (God sent the Holy Spirit to live in our hearts)

Disciple Power: Knowledge (Gift of the Holy Spirit)

Faith Vocabulary: Confirmation, spiritual gifts

Faith-Filled People: Saint Stephen

Catholics Believe: Sacred Chrism

The Church Follows Jesus: Gifted Saints (Saint Catherine of Siena and Saint Thomas Aquinas)

Prayer: Send Your Spirit

Catechism of the Catholic Church (CCC): 1285–1314, 1830–1845

U.S. Catholic Catechism for Adults (USCCA): pp. 203–209

CHAPTER 12—We Celebrate Forgiveness

Faith Concepts:
- Sin is choosing to do or say something against God.
- In the Sacrament of Penance and Reconciliation, we ask for and receive forgiveness for our sins.
- Contrition, confession, penance, and absolution are always part of Reconciliation.

Sacred Scripture: Luke 15:7 (There is great joy in Heaven for one who asks for forgiveness); Luke 15:11–24 (Parable of the Forgiving Father); John 20:19–23 (The Apostles receive the power to forgive sins)

Disciple Power: Forgiveness (capital virtue)

Faith Vocabulary: Sin, reconciliation, penance

Faith-Filled People: Zacchaeus

Catholics Believe: Act of Contrition

The Church Follows Jesus: Saint John Vianney

Prayer: Prayer of Petition

Catechism of the Catholic Church (CCC): 545–546, 587–590, 976–983, 1420–1484, 1846–1848

U.S. Catholic Catechism for Adults (USCCA): 234–243

Catholic Social Teaching — Unit 3 We Make Peace

UNIT 4: WE WORSHIP, PART TWO

CHAPTER 13—We Gather For Mass

Faith Concepts:
- The Mass is the most important celebration of the Church.
- Everyone at Mass has a part to play in the celebration of the Mass.
- The Introductory Rites of the Mass gather us and prepare us to worship God.

Sacred Scripture: Joel 2:15–16, 23 (Worship the Lord); Matthew 18:20 (Where two or three are gathered); Acts 2:42 (Jesus' followers gathered together); Psalm 100 (Shout with joy to God)

Disciple Power: Love (Theological Virtue)

Faith Vocabulary: Mass, assembly

Faith-Filled People: Saint Justin

Catholics Believe: The Lord's Day

The Church Follows Jesus: To Keep the Faith Alive (Father Petr Pit'ha)

Prayer: Praise God (Psalm 100)

Catechism of the Catholic Church (CCC): 1322–1332, 1346, 1348

U.S. Catholic Catechism for Adults (USCCA): pp. 215–218

CHAPTER 14—We Listen to God's Word

Faith Concepts:
- The Liturgy of the Word is the first main part of the Mass.
- The Gospel is the main part of the Liturgy of the Word.
- At Mass we listen and respond to the Word of God.

Sacred Scripture: Luke 11:27–28 (Blessed are those who hear the Word of God and keep it); Luke 13:18–19 (Parable of the mustard seed)

Disciple Power: Compassion (capital virtue)

Faith Vocabulary: Liturgy of the Word

Faith-Filled People: Saint Paul Chong Ha-sang

Catholics Believe: The Sanctuary

The Church Follows Jesus: Announcing God's Word (American Sign Language)

Prayer: Lord, Hear Our Prayer

Catechism of the Catholic Church (CCC): 1322–1332, 1346, 1349

U.S. Catholic Catechism for Adults (USCCA): p. 218

CHAPTER 15—We Give Thanks

Faith Concepts:
- At the Last Supper, Jesus gave the Church the Sacrament of the Eucharist.
- At the celebration of the Eucharist, the bread and wine become the Body and Blood of Jesus.
- We receive the Body and Blood of Jesus in Holy Communion.

Sacred Scripture: Psalm 35:18 (I thank you, Lord); 1 Chronicles 16:34 (Give thanks to the Lord); Luke 22:17–20 (The Last Supper)

Disciple Power: Thankfulness (Fruit of the Holy Spirit as related to generosity)

Faith Vocabulary: Liturgy of the Eucharist, Eucharist

Faith-Filled People: Saint Pius X

Catholics Believe: The Holy Sacrifice

The Church Follows Jesus: Thank You, Lord (The Franciscans)

Prayer: Blessed Be God

Catechism of the Catholic Church (CCC): 1345–1405

U.S. Catholic Catechism for Adults (USCCA): pp. 218–220

CHAPTER 16—We Live as Disciples of Jesus

Faith Concepts:
- At the end of Mass, we receive God's blessing to live as Jesus' disciples.
- The Dismissal sends us forth from Mass to glorify God.
- The concluding procession reminds us that we are people sent on a mission.

Sacred Scripture: Isaiah 6:8 (Here I am, send me); John 13:4–5, 13–14, 34–35 (Love one another as I have loved you)

Disciple Power: Courage (Cardinal Virtue)

Faith Vocabulary: Procession

Faith-Filled People: Saint Damien de Veuster

Catholics Believe: Washing of Feet

The Church Follows Jesus: Spreading the Gospel (Saint Francis Solano, Jean Donovan, Saint Frances Cabrini, and Saint Damien de Veuster)

Prayer: Here I Am, Lord

Catechism of the Catholic Church (CCC): 1333–1405, 1822–1823

U.S. Catholic Catechism for Adults (USCCA): pp. 220–227

Catholic Social Teaching — Unit 4 We Reach Out to People

UNIT 5: WE LIVE, PART ONE

CHAPTER 17—In God's Image

Faith Concepts:
- All people are to be honored and respected.
- Jesus taught that we are to live as children of God.
- The Holy Spirit helps us make choices to live as children of God.

Sacred Scripture: 1 John 3:1 (God the Father loves us); Genesis 1:27–28 (God created human beings in his image); Psalm 8:6 (The Lord has blessed us); Matthew 18:1–4 (Become like a little child); John 14:6 (I am the way and the truth and the life)

Disciple Power: Kindness (Fruit of the Holy Spirit)

Faith Vocabulary: Honor, grace

Faith-Filled People: Saint Teresa of Jesus (Saint Teresa of Ávila)

Catholics Believe: Fruits of the Holy Spirit

The Church Follows Jesus: The Little Flower (Saint Thérèse of Lisieux or Thérése of the Child Jesus)

Prayer: May God Bless Us

Catechism of the Catholic Church (CCC): 1699–1756, 1996–2016

U.S. Catholic Catechism for Adults (USCCA): 307–309, 351–354

CHAPTER 18—We Live as Children of God

Faith Concepts:
- Jesus teaches on his own authority.
- Jesus taught us the greatest Commandment.
- The Great Commandment tells us to love God and to love other people as we love ourselves.

Sacred Scripture: Psalm 25:4–5 (Lord, let me know your ways); John 14:9 (Whoever has seen me has seen the Father); Matthew 5:43–44 (Be kind, forgiving, and loving); John 7:16 (My teaching is not my own); Matthew 22:36–40 (The Great Commandment); 1 John 4:16 (God is love)

Disciple Power: Fortitude (Gift of the Holy Spirit)

Faith Vocabulary: Rabbi, Great Commandment

Faith-Filled People: Saint Peter

Catholics Believe: The Cross

The Church Follows Jesus: Saint Pedro (Calungsod)

Prayer: An Act of Love

Catechism of the Catholic Church (CCC): 2052–2055, 2083, 2196

U.S. Catholic Catechism for Adults (USCCA): pp. 307–309

CHAPTER 19—We Love God
Faith Concepts:
- God gave us the Ten Commandments to live happy and holy lives.
- The first three Commandments teach us to love and honor God.
- Proverbs are wise sayings that help us to love God and to live happy and holy lives.

Sacred Scripture: Psalm 119:1–3 (Happy are those who keep God's laws); Proverbs 3:5–6 (Trust God); Proverbs 3:9–10 (Honor God)
Disciple Power: Obedience (capital virtue)
Faith Vocabulary: Ten Commandments, proverbs
Faith-Filled People: Saint Scholastica
Catholics Believe: The Bishop's Motto
The Church Follows Jesus: Saint Benedict
Prayer: Come, Holy Spirit
Catechism of the Catholic Church (CCC): 2083–2136, 2142–2165, 2168–2188, 2194
U.S. Catholic Catechism for Adults (USCCA): pp. 341–369

CHAPTER 20—We Love Others
Faith Concepts:
- People who live the Ten Commandments help build a kind world.
- The Fourth through Tenth Commandments teach us to love, honor, and respect other people and ourselves.
- Jesus calls us to follow him by keeping the Ten Commandments and the Golden Rule.

Sacred Scripture: Matthew 7:12 (Treat others the way you want them to treat you); Mark 10:17–22 (Give what you have to the poor)
Disciple Power: Justice (Cardinal Virtue)
Faith Vocabulary: Covet, false witness
Faith-Filled People: Saint John Bosco
Catholics Believe: Almsgiving
The Church Follows Jesus: Caring for Others (St. Vincent de Paul Society)
Prayer: Trust in the Lord
Catechism of the Catholic Church (CCC): 2196–2246, 2258–2317, 2331–2391, 2401–2449, 2464–2503, 2514–2527, 2535–2550
U.S. Catholic Catechism for Adults (USCCA): pp. 375–455

Catholic Social Teaching — Unit 5 We Respect All People

UNIT 6: WE LIVE, PART TWO

CHAPTER 21—We Make Choices
Faith Concepts:
- It is important for us to make wise choices.
- Making wise choices will help us find happiness.
- The Proverbs can help us choose wisely.

Sacred Scripture: Joshua 24:15 (Choose to serve the Lord); Proverbs 16:3 (Trust in the Lord); Proverbs 12:24 (Work hard); Proverbs 15:15 (The gloomy and the cheerful person); Proverbs 15:22 (Say yes to good advice); 1 Thessalonians 5:16–18 (Rejoice every day); Proverbs 12:20 (Happy is the person who chooses to make peace)
Disciple Power: Humility (capital virtue)
Faith Vocabulary: Wise choices, Heaven
Faith-Filled People: Saint Clare of Assisi
Catholics Believe: Daily Prayer
The Church Follows Jesus: Saint Francis of Assisi
Prayer: A Peace Prayer (Lord, make us instruments of your peace)
Catechism of the Catholic Church (CCC): 1719–1724, 2825
U.S. Catholic Catechism for Adults (USCCA): pp. 315–317

CHAPTER 22—We Can Choose Right from Wrong
Faith Concepts:
- We are making wise choices when we choose to live as Jesus taught.
- Wise choices show we are forming and following our consciences.
- All of our choices have consequences.

Sacred Scripture: Deuteronomy 30:19 (Choose what is right); Sirach 15:14–15 (God gave us free choice)
Disciple Power: Joy (Fruit of the Holy Spirit)
Faith Vocabulary: Consequences, conscience
Faith-Filled People: Saint Philip Neri
Catholics Believe: Examination of Conscience
The Church Follows Jesus: Paula's Choice (Saint Paula Frassinetti)
Prayer: Be the Joy of My Heart (Saint Augustine)
Catechism of the Catholic Church (CCC): 1716–1724, 1730–1738, 1776–1794
U.S. Catholic Catechism for Adults (USCCA): pp. 314–315, 341–369

CHAPTER 23—We Share in God's Life
Faith Concepts:
- Grace is a gift from God.
- Sanctifying grace is the gift of God's life that he shares with us.
- The gift of peace helps us live a holy and happy life.

Sacred Scripture: John 1:14,16 (Jesus is the living Word of God); Matthew 25:36 (I was in prison and you visited me); Galatians 3:26 (You are all children of God); John 20:21–22 (Peace be with you)
Disciple Power: Trust
Faith Vocabulary: Sanctifying grace, mortal sin, venial sin
Faith-Filled People: Saint Monica
Catholics Believe: The Gift of Peace
The Church Follows Jesus: A Caring Ministry (prison chaplains)
Prayer: Hail Mary
Catechism of the Catholic Church (CCC): 1846–1869, 1996–2016
U.S. Catholic Catechism for Adults (USCCA): pp. 193, 328–330

CHAPTER 24—The Our Father
Faith Concepts:
- We pray the Our Father to show our love and adoration for God.
- The Our Father helps us to live as children of God.
- The Our Father helps us to prepare for the Kingdom of God.

Sacred Scripture: Matthew 6:9 (This is how you are to pray)
Disciple Power: Hope (Theological Virtue)
Faith Vocabulary: Kingdom of God, trespass, Lord's Prayer
Faith-Filled People: Saint Thomas Aquinas
Catholics Believe: Vocation
The Church Follows Jesus: A Life of Prayer
Prayer: Go Forth!
Catechism of the Catholic Church (CCC): 2777–2856
U.S. Catholic Catechism for Adults (USCCA): pp. 481–492

Catholic Social Teaching — Unit 6 We Take Part in Our Community

WE CELEBRATE THE CHURCH YEAR

See page 38 for a listing of the lesson titles.

Be My Disciples

Peter M. Esposito
President

Jo Rotunno, MA
Publisher

Anne P. Battes, M.Ed.
Associate Publisher

Program Advisors
Michael P. Horan, PhD
Elizabeth Nagel, SSD

GRADE TWO
SCHOOL EDITION

Contents

(5)

Welcome to Be My ✝Disciples!

A Few Facts About Me

My name is _____

My favorite story is _____

My favorite holiday is _____

I am good at _____

New Things to Learn

This year we will learn many new things about God. We will learn more about Jesus and how to celebrate with our Church family.

Play this game with a partner to begin to learn new things. As you come to each section, write the answer to the question.

Unit 1: We Believe, Part One
God is the Father and Creator. He made everyone and everything out of love, without any help.
Write the word that means only God has the power to do everything good. _____Almighty_____
Clue: Look on page 52.

6

Welcome

Creating an inviting environment is an important part of everything you do with the students. Before your first class, prepare name tags for the students. Greet each student as they arrive. This will help them feel safe and ready to learn. This first day of classes provide the opportunity for you to get to know the students. By setting realistic expectations, introducing them to their new books, and creating an atmosphere of prayer and hospitality, the students will know they are welcome.

Invite

Give each student a name tag with their name on it. You can find additional introduction activities at BeMyDisciples.com.

Discover and Involve

▶ Introduce the book and allow the students to look through it and find a favorite picture.

▶ Have them share their favorite picture.

▶ Tell the students that they will now join with a partner to complete the activity on pages 6 and 7. Let them know that you will help them.

▶ Read to the class the first question and clue in the activity. Have them turn to page 52 and find the word almighty. Then show them where to write the word.

- ► Read to the class the second question and clue in the activity. Have them turn to page 81 and find the name Jesus. Have everyone write the name Jesus in the New Things to Learn activity.

- ► Have the students read the third question and clue in the activity and turn to page 124 to find the word described by the clue.

- ► Work with the students on the fourth question and clue. Read the question, and help them find the bold-faced term on page 189. Then have the students write the term Alleluia in box four on page 7.

- ► Ask the students to work with a partner to discover a sign of how Jesus lived the Great Commandment. Remind them to look on page 246. Have them write the words The Cross in box 5.

- ► Have the students focus on the last activity and read the question. Have them turn to page 322 and discover the word that means "Yes it is true. We believe!" Give them time to write Amen in the final blank space on page 7.

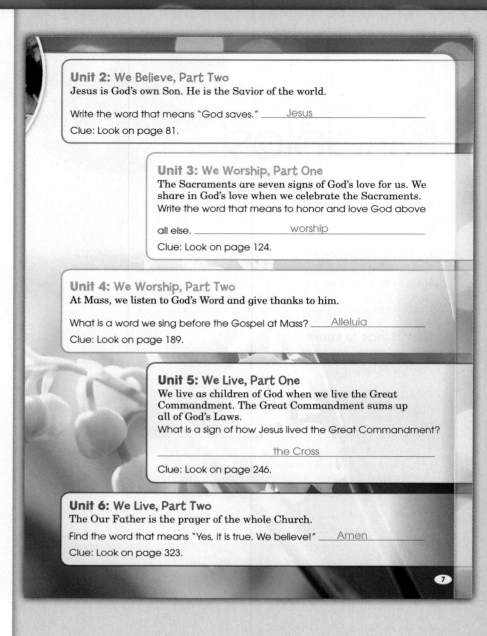

Unit 2: We Believe, Part Two
Jesus is God's own Son. He is the Savior of the world.

Write the word that means "God saves." _____Jesus_____
Clue: Look on page 81.

Unit 3: We Worship, Part One
The Sacraments are seven signs of God's love for us. We share in God's love when we celebrate the Sacraments. Write the word that means to honor and love God above all else. _____worship_____
Clue: Look on page 124.

Unit 4: We Worship, Part Two
At Mass, we listen to God's Word and give thanks to him.

What is a word we sing before the Gospel at Mass? _____Alleluia_____
Clue: Look on page 189.

Unit 5: We Live, Part One
We live as children of God when we live the Great Commandment. The Great Commandment sums up all of God's Laws.
What is a sign of how Jesus lived the Great Commandment?

_____the Cross_____
Clue: Look on page 246.

Unit 6: We Live, Part Two
The Our Father is the prayer of the whole Church.
Find the word that means "Yes, it is true. We believe!" _____Amen_____
Clue: Look on page 323.

7

Enough for Everyone

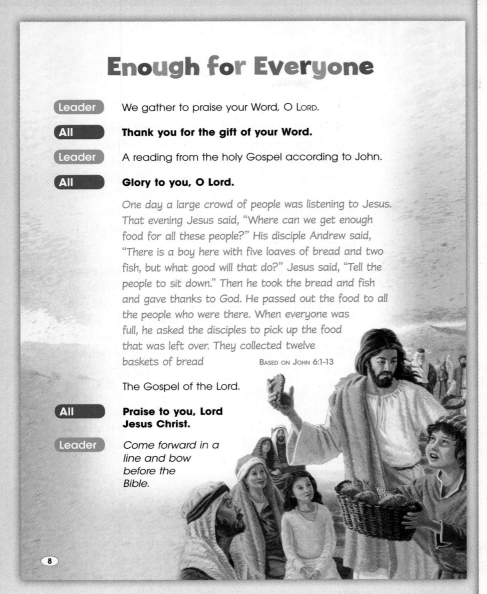

Leader   We gather to praise your Word, O LORD.

All   **Thank you for the gift of your Word.**

Leader   A reading from the holy Gospel according to John.

All   **Glory to you, O Lord.**

One day a large crowd of people was listening to Jesus. That evening Jesus said, "Where can we get enough food for all these people?" His disciple Andrew said, "There is a boy here with five loaves of bread and two fish, but what good will that do?" Jesus said, "Tell the people to sit down." Then he took the bread and fish and gave thanks to God. He passed out the food to all the people who were there. When everyone was full, he asked the disciples to pick up the food that was left over. They collected twelve baskets of bread   BASED ON JOHN 6:1–13

The Gospel of the Lord.

All   **Praise to you, Lord Jesus Christ.**

Leader   *Come forward in a line and bow before the Bible.*

8

Pray

▶ Invite the students to prepare for prayer. Reverently hold a Bible slightly above your head and lead them in procession to the prayer space.

▶ Teach the students to echo, or repeat after you, the parts of the prayer marked "All."

▶ After a moment of silence, pray the prayer. Use a hand gesture to invite the students to join in when you want them to echo their parts of the prayer.

▶ After the prayer, place the Bible on the prayer table and reverence it by slightly bowing your head. Invite each student to come forward and do the same.

▶ Invite them to experience the feeling of this sacred prayer space throughout all their classes and the coming school year.

TEACHING TIP

Creating a Prayer Space. Having a prayer space that is decorated in a special way will help the students realize the importance of prayer. Display the Bible in your prayer space in such a way that shows its importance. Talk about respecting the Bible. Always hold the Bible reverently when you proclaim God's Word. Before you pray together, allow a moment of quiet time and share with the class that God is with them.

We Believe

Part One

Objectives

In Unit 1, the students will learn that:

▶ The Bible is the written Word of God.

▶ Faith is knowing and believing in God with all our hearts.

▶ God is the Holy Trinity. He is One God in Three Divine Persons.

▶ God is the Creator who made everyone and everything because of his love.

Spiritual Insights

God makes himself known to us through Revelation in order to both give us something and to draw a response from us. Both this gift of God and our response to his Revelation are called faith. By faith, we are able to give our minds and hearts to God, to trust in his will, and to follow the direction he gives us (*United States Catholic Catechism for Adults*, Washington, D.C.: USCCB, 2006).

Living the Six Tasks of Catechesis

Promoting Knowledge of the Faith: Saint Robert Bellarmine (1542–1621)

Even as a young boy in Italy, Robert felt called to serve God as a priest. After years of study, he was ordained a Jesuit priest. His first assignment was teaching Greek at a boys' school. Robert was successful only because he first taught himself the language by staying one lesson ahead of his students in the textbook.

Robert had a gift for preaching. People traveled great distances to hear him explain the Scriptures and to defend the faith during the challenges of the Reformation. He also wrote two catechisms to help people grow in their understanding of the Catholic doctrine. Although he became a bishop and then a cardinal, he never lost his thirst for learning and teaching.

Cardinal Bellarmine lived a very simple life, even when he lived in a lavish apartment in the Vatican while serving as the Pope's official theologian. It is said that he took down the hangings that decorated his walls and donated the fabric to clothe the poor. When he was quizzed about his empty walls, he showed his sense of humor by declaring, "The walls won't catch cold."

Saint Robert Bellarmine is an excellent model for catechists. His life encourages us to know our faith well so that we can share it with our learners. He reminds us to be proud of our calling to profess our faith in Jesus and the Church.

Sharing Your Faith

Find a partner to work with: a spouse, a friend, a fellow teacher. Come together at the beginning or end of each unit for shared prayer and discussion. Use the questions below as a starting point. As an alternative, record your thoughts in a personal journal.

▶ What three words describe your journey of faith?

▶ How has God made himself known to you?

▶ What prompted you to become a religion teacher?

We Believe
Part One
UNIT 1

God's Chosen One
Jesus read God's Word from the Bible.

"God's Spirit is with me. God has chosen me to bring good news to the poor. God wants me to help blind people see and to help all people be free. God wants me to tell everyone that he will save all the people."

Jesus said. "I am the one God chose to make his words come true."

BASED ON LUKE 4:18–21

9

What I Know
What is something you already know about these faith concepts?

The Bible

_____

_____

The Church

_____

_____

Put an X next to the faith words you know. Put a ? next to the faith words you need to learn more about.

____ believe ____ disciples ____ Creator

____ faith ____ Holy Trinity ____ soul

Whose words do we listen to in the Bible?

_____

A Question I Have

What question would you like to ask about the Holy Trinity?

_____

_____

10

Unit 1 Opener

The unit opener pages help to assess the students' prior knowledge and growth in faith. The first page proclaims a Scripture passage. The second page continues the assessment of prior knowledge of key faith concepts.

Opening Page

▶ Invite the students to tell you what they see in the image on the page.

▶ Proclaim the Scripture story. Ask: "What did God want Jesus to do? Did Jesus do as God the Father asked him?" Accept their answers, but do not respond further at this time.

Getting Ready

As you process this page, do not correct the student's responses. You will invite them to return and self-correct themselves at the end of the unit.

▶ Have the students write their responses under What I Know, Faith Words, and A Question I Have. You may also do the exercises orally.

▶ Record the students' questions on a chart. Refer back to the chart as you progress through the unit and ask volunteers to respond when they can answer the questions.

▶ Ask the students to turn to the next page and begin Chapter 1.

The Bible

BACKGROUND

The Living Word of God

We cherish the Scriptures because they are the inspired holy Word of God. The words of Sacred Scripture tell the story of the many marvelous ways that God has spoken and continues to speak to us, drawing us to live in covenant and communion with him. The Scriptures are not just any group of stories. They are the living Word of God.

Interpreting Sacred Scripture

In familiarizing ourselves with the Bible, we do not strive merely to memorize chapter and verse, although it is always good to be familiar with particular Bible passages. We strive to understand the depth of God's message to us. To do this we employ three criteria for interpreting the meaning of Sacred Scripture.

First, we are attentive to the content and unity of the whole of Scripture. We avoid lifting a particular passage out of context. This means that we always read each passage and each book with regard to the whole of the Bible.

Second, we appreciate Scripture as part of the living tradition of God's people. The inspired books of the Bible are written less upon paper than they are upon the hearts of the People of God. Thus, only within the living body of the Church, guided by the Holy Spirit, can Scripture be interpreted, and the meaning of God's Word to us be truly discovered.

Third, we do not simply read the Bible as if it were like any other type of literature. We always remember there is a deeper message leading us into greater faithfulness to God.

Being Fed by the Word of God

When we proclaim, reflect upon, meditate over, or study the Scriptures, we are nourished by the Word of God, living and active among us.

. . . [T]he force and power in the word of God is so great that it stands as the support and energy of the Church, the strength of faith for her [children], the food of the soul, the pure and everlasting source of spiritual life . . . Easy access to Sacred Scripture should be provided for all the Christian faith.

Dogmatic Constitution on Divine Revelation (Dei verbum) 21, 22

As teachers who venerate and employ Scripture through all of our formational, liturgical, and educational endeavors, we constantly bring people to the table of the Word of the Lord. We invite people to be fed with the living Word of God.

For Reflection

What passage from the Gospel sheds a special light on Jesus Christ for me?

How does prayerfully reading Sacred Scripture provide strength for my faith and food for my soul?

Teacher to Teacher

A Good Start

You have accepted a wonderful opportunity to make a difference in the lives of a group of young children—each uniquely special and loved by God. Don't be surprised if the students are a little apprehensive as you begin—that's natural. Your relaxed, prepared, and friendly manner will go a long way toward making them comfortable and creating community. You will want to make sure the students know that they may express themselves freely and without fear of judgment or being wrong. And remember, the sooner that you are able to call each child by name, the more comfortable and accepted each student will feel.

Establish Rituals

At this age children love ritual and drama and will respond positively to the sense of awe and specialness created by you in the class. Establish a simple ritual for carrying and reading the Bible throughout the year. Teach reverence for the Word of God by your own deliberate and respectful actions when reading from the Bible.

The Church Teaches . . .

"Catechesis aims to bring about in the believer an ever more mature faith in Jesus Christ, a deeper knowledge and love of his person and message, and a firm commitment to follow him" (*National Directory for Catechesis,* 19A).

By living Christ's message and sharing his love, you hand on the gift of faith to the next generation.

Further Reading and Reflection

For more related teachings of the Church, see the *Catechism of the Catholic Church,* 101–133; and the *United States Catholic Catechism for Adults,* pages 21–23.

Teacher Prayer

Spirit of Wisdom, help me to share the Word of God wisely and generously with the students. Amen.

Lesson Planner

Chapter 1   The Bible

Focus To learn more about what is in the Bible

LESSON PART	PROCESS	MATERIALS and RESOURCES
DAY 1 EXPLORE **Focus** To explore how God speaks to us through the Bible **Pages** 11–13	▶ Proclaim and discuss Hebrews 1:1–2 (God speaks to us through Jesus). **Disciple Power:** Respect ▶ Learn the story of Saint Jerome and how he helped people know the Sacred Scripture. **Activity:** Illustrate a Bible story and solve a puzzle about the importance of paying attention to the Bible.	Bible Pencils or pens Crayons or colored markers
DAY 2 DISCOVER **Focus** To discover what the Bible tells us about God **Pages** 14–15	▶ Learn that the Bible is God's loving Word to us. ▶ Learn that the two main parts of the Bible are the Old and New Testaments. ▶ Learn that those who follow and learn from Jesus are his disciples. **Faith Words:** Bible, disciples **Catholics Believe:** The Gospels **Activity:** Review the Bible story through sequencing and understanding the concept.	Bible Pencils or pens Markers **Enriching the Lesson:** Teacher Guide, page 61 The Listener Game
DAY 3 DISCOVER **Focus** To discover the Book of Psalms **Pages** 16–17	▶ Discover that the Psalms are the Word of God we can sing. **Faith Words:** Psalms **Faith-Filled People:** King David **Activity:** Write and sing a prayer.	Pencils or pens Crayons or markers **Literature Connection:** *The Listening Walk*
DAY 4 DECIDE **Focus** To decide on a way to help others know about God **Pages** 18–19	▶ Discover that each of the four Gospels tells us about Jesus. **Activity:** Draw a picture of one way to tell people about Jesus. **My Faith Choice:** Choose to read the Bible this week. **Pray:** "Thank you, Holy Spirit."	Pencils or pens Crayons or markers **Enriching the Lesson:** Teacher Guide, page 61 Proclaiming God's Word **Additional Activities Booklet:** Activities 1a and 1b or see *BeMyDisciples*.com
DAY 5 CONCLUDE **Focus** To listen and pay attention with a Scripture prayer **Pages** 20–22	▶ **REVIEW** Review concepts: Recall, Review, and Share ▶ **PRAY** A Listening Prayer: Colossians 3:16–27 ▶ **PREVIEW** the With My Family page and the theme of the next chapter.	Bible Grade 2 Music CD **Assessment Tools Booklet:** Assessments 1a and 1b

Assign online Chapter Review and interactive Chapter Test at **BeMyDisciples.com**

CHAPTER **1**

The Bible

❓ What is your favorite story? What is your favorite Bible story?

When we listen to the Bible we listen to God speaking to us. These are words from the Bible. Listen to what God is telling us.

Long ago, God spoke to people who lived before us. He spoke in many different ways. Now God talks to us through his own Son, Jesus. BASED ON HEBREWS 1:1–2

❓ What do you think God is saying to you in these words from the Bible?

⑪

THE TASKS OF CATECHESIS

Teaching to Pray. Before praying, take time to gather the students and provide an opportunity for them to center themselves. Help your second graders to appreciate that when we quiet ourselves, we can hear God speaking to us in prayer, through people, and through the environment. Using the single ring of a bell or a drum beat is a beautiful way to remind the students to prepare themselves for prayer. Urge them to listen to God's Word to them as they pray.

Pray

▶ Welcome the students warmly. Ask them to quiet themselves for prayer.

▶ Pray the Sign of the Cross together.

▶ Extending your hands over the students, say: "Lord, bless all of us gathered here. Help us to open our ears and our hearts to your Word today. Amen."

▶ Ask the first opening questions. *(Affirm all responsible replies.)*

▶ Then ask: What is the Bible? *(The Bible is God's own Word to us.)* The students' responses will help you assess their prior knowledge and understanding.

▶ Then call for responses to the second question.

Reflect

▶ Read the introduction to the Scripture passage. Then ask one of the students to proclaim the passage from Hebrews.

▶ Observe a moment of silence.

▶ Ask the follow-up question. *(Accept all responsible replies.)*

▶ End the prayer time with a brief blessing. Extending your hands over the class, say: *"Lord, bless all of us gathered here. Help us to open our ears and our hearts to your words today. Amen."*

Focus

Tell the students they are about to meet someone who loved the Bible so much he wanted to help other people love it, too.

Introduce

▶ Ask the students to share what it would be like if there were no Bibles to read.

▶ Have the class silently read A Saint Who Loved the Bible. Ask them to underline three things they learned about Saint Jerome.

▶ Read the Disciple Power feature to the class. Point out that paying attention when others are speaking shows respect for them as children of God.

Reinforce

▶ Call for responses to the follow-up question in the text. *(Jerome put the Bible in words people could understand so they could read it and come to love it.)*

▶ Go on to ask: Why is it important to pay attention when you read the Bible? *(Accept all reasonable replies. See whether the students already recognize that God speaks to us through the Bible.)*

Disciple Power

Respect

When we pay attention to what others say to us, we show them respect. Listening is a sign of respect and can help us learn well. Respect for others is a way we show God's love.

The Church Follows **Jesus**

A Saint Who Loved the Bible

Many years ago, some people had trouble reading about God from the Bible. The Bible was not written in a language they could understand. Jerome wanted to help people read and understand God's Word.

Jerome went to good schools. When he grew up, Jerome began to read the Bible. He paid careful attention to what he was reading. Jerome knew he was listening to God.

Jerome loved the Bible. He loved it so much he wanted other people to love it and read it and learn from it. So Jerome decided to help. Jerome put the Bible in words people could read and understand. Today, we know Jerome as Saint Jerome. We honor him as one of the great teachers of the Church.

❓ How did Jerome help other people read and learn from the Bible?

12

DISCIPLE POWER

Respect. Reinforce that Saint Jerome showed respect for God's Word by paying attention when he read the Bible. Invite the students to give examples of showing respect by paying attention to others. List their examples on the board. Possible responses include: only doing one thing at a time; turning off the television or other distractions; listening carefully to our teachers and catechists; being quiet when others are speaking; and thinking about what we are reading and hearing.

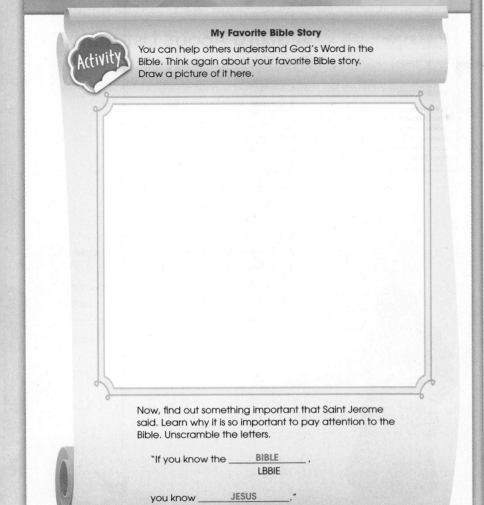

Activity

My Favorite Bible Story

You can help others understand God's Word in the Bible. Think again about your favorite Bible story. Draw a picture of it here.

Now, find out something important that Saint Jerome said. Learn why it is so important to pay attention to the Bible. Unscramble the letters.

"If you know the ___BIBLE___ ,
LBBIE

you know ___JESUS___ ."
EJSSU

(13)

Connect

▶ Invite the students to recall their responses to the question "What is your favorite Bible story?" Then read aloud the introduction to the first part of the activity on page 13.

▶ Allow time for the students to draw a picture of their favorite Bible story. Afterward, have them share their picture with a partner and see if the partner recognizes the story.

▶ Move on to the second part of the activity. Have the students unscramble the words to complete the sentence.

▶ Ask the class to read the quotation from Saint Jerome aloud.

Pray

Gather the class for prayer. Have them echo:

Thank you, God,/
for your Word to us./
Help us always to listen well,/
to your loving Word./
Amen.

TEACHING TIP

Young Children and the Bible. Although children at age seven or eight might have difficulty reading the Bible, they can page through a Bible and become familiar with it. Explain the difference between the Bible and books of Bible stories, often called children's Bibles. Make sure they know that Bible storybooks are great for now, but that they are not Bibles. At the same time, reinforce reverence for the Bible by the way you and the students handle it during your sessions. Always enthrone a Bible in your prayer center and use it during prayer. Keep it open to the Scripture passage being taught or prayed in class.

Key Concept
The Bible is God's own Word
to us.

Pray

Invite the students to quiet themselves
for prayer. Lead them in the Glory Be.

Teach

▶ Ask the students if they have ever
planted seeds. Then ask: What
needed to be done to make sure
the seeds would grow? *(Possible
answers: seeds need good soil, water,
sunshine, weeding, and so on.)*

▶ Tell the class that Jesus used a story
about a farmer planting seeds to
help us see how important it is
to listen carefully to God's Word.
Explain that the seed in Jesus' story
is like God's Word.

▶ Invite volunteers to read A Story
About Listening. Tell the class to
listen carefully and underline the
places where the seeds fall.

Reinforce

Ask the students why it is so important
to listen to God's Word. *(When we
listen to God's Word our faith grows.)*

Faith Focus
What is the Bible?

Faith Words
Bible
The Bible is the written
Word of God.

disciples
Disciples are people who
follow and learn from
someone. Disciples of
Jesus follow and learn
from him.

A Story About Listening

One day Jesus told this story about
listening to the Word of God in the Bible.

"A farmer went to scatter some seeds.
Some fell on a path. The birds ate them.
Some seeds fell on rocks. They dried up and
died. Some seeds fell among thorns. The
thorns grew and choked the seeds. Other
seeds fell on good soil. They grew strong.

People are like the seeds that the farmer
scattered. People who do not listen to God's
Word are like the seeds on the path. People
who listen to God's Word but soon forget it
are like the seeds on the rocks. Some people
hear God's Word, but they let worries about
other things crowd it out. They are like the
seeds among the thorns. Other people hear
God's Word and really pay attention.
They are like the seeds that fall on good
soil. Faith grows in them."

BASED ON MATTHEW 13:3–9, 19–23

14

TEACHING TIP

Creative Movement. Invite the students to add creative movement
to the Bible story, A Story About Listening, by moving about to show
what happens in the story. To do this, have the class stand in a circle.
Then read the Bible story slowly as the students listen and silently act
it out sentence by sentence. Afterward, tell them, "Today you listened
carefully to the Word of God. The seed of God's Word fell on good
soil when it fell on you."

The Written Word of God

The **Bible** is a holy book. It is God's own loving Word to us. When we read or listen to the Word of God in the Bible, we listen to God speak to us. In the Bible, God tells us about his great love for us.

God chose special people to write the Bible. God the Holy Spirit helped people write what God wanted to tell us. The Bible has two main parts. The first main part is the Old Testament. The second main part is the New Testament. The New Testament tells about Jesus and his **disciples**.

We are to live as disciples of Jesus. The Bible tells us to follow Jesus. We are to treat others as God wants us to treat them.

? What does God tell us about in the Bible?

Catholics Believe

The Gospels

The word *gospel* means "good news." The Gospels tell us the Good News of Jesus. They tell us that God loves us very much. We can always count on God's love.

Activity

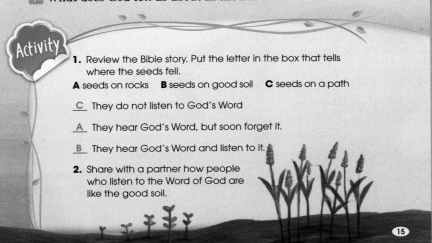

1. Review the Bible story. Put the letter in the box that tells where the seeds fell.

   A seeds on rocks   **B** seeds on good soil   **C** seeds on a path

   _C_ They do not listen to God's Word

   _A_ They hear God's Word, but soon forget it.

   _B_ They hear God's Word and listen to it.

2. Share with a partner how people who listen to the Word of God are like the good soil.

(15)

TEACHING VOCABULARY

Faith Words. Encourage the students to make word cards for each faith word as you teach it this year. Have them print the word in large letters on one side and write its meaning on the back. They can use the cards for word games and review throughout the year. At the end of each unit, you may want to have a "Vocabulary Bee" in which two teams try to best define the faith words presented in the previous four chapters.

Teach

▶ Read aloud the Faith Focus question, and invite responses. Then call attention to the words *Bible* and *disciples* in Faith Words. Have a volunteer read them aloud.

▶ Ask the class to pay attention for these two words as three of their classmates read The Written Word of God to them.

▶ Discuss the reading by calling for responses to the follow-up question in the text.

▶ Then use questions like the following to extend the discussion:

   • What are the two main parts of the Bible? (*Old Testament and New Testament*)

   • What does the Bible help us do? (*The Bible helps us to live as disciples of Jesus and learn how to treat others.*)

Reinforce

▶ Give the students the opportunity to reverently hold a Bible.

▶ Help them find the Bible's two main parts. (*Old Testament and New Testament*)

▶ Point out the Catholics Believe feature about The Gospels. Tell the students that the Gospels are in the New Testament.

Connect

▶ Have the students complete the activity. Review the correct answers.

▶ Review the meaning of the seeds, path, rocks, thorns, and good soil.

Pray

Gather the class for prayer. Have them echo the prayer on page 51 of this guide.

> **Key Concept**
> The Bible contains song prayers called psalms.

Pray

Ask the students to quiet themselves for prayer. Remind them that Jesus is with us as we pray. Pray the Sign of the Cross together.

Teach

▶ Ask the students if they have ever visited a library. Ask, "What do we find in a library?" *(Accept all replies, emphasizing books.)*

▶ Read aloud the first paragraph of Songs in the Bible. Stress that the Bible is God's library of love for us—a collection of books that teach us about God's love and how to love others.

▶ Have the class silently read the second paragraph. Tell them to note the reasons why the Psalms were written.

▶ Call for answers to the follow-up question.

▶ Point out the Faith Focus question and the term in Faith Words. Note how the latter answers the former.

▶ Read aloud the three sentences on the top of page 17. Then have the class read the verses of Psalm 119 aloud together.

▶ Lead a discussion about what the psalmist says about the Word of God. *(Listen for responses such as makes people joyful, helps people know God, and so on.)*

> **Faith Focus**
> What are the Psalms?
>
> **Faith Words**
> ▶ **Psalms**
> Psalms are songs of prayer.

Songs in the Bible

The Bible is like a library. It has many books in it. All of the books tell us of God's love for us. One of those books is called the Book of **Psalms.**

The Book of Psalms is in the Old Testament. The writers of the psalms wrote the psalms for people to pray when they were happy and when they were sad. They wrote psalms to help people tell God that they love him. Psalms also help people ask God for what they need. Other psalms were written to help people remember what God did for them and to thank him.

❓ Why did the writers write the Book of Psalms?

16

LITURGY TIP

Praying the Psalms. Explain to the class that the Psalms are ancient Jewish prayers. Tell the students that Jesus prayed the Psalms often and from memory. These same Psalms are prayed today both by the Jewish people and by Christians.

As part of your lesson, invite one of your parish's leaders of song to class to speak about the Psalms and how the Church prays the Psalms each day. Of course, it would also be a wonderful experience for the class to be led by your guest in singing some of the more familiar Responsorial Psalms used at Sunday liturgy. Above all, invite your guests to make the visit an enjoyable and lively interactive session with the students.

There are 150 psalms in the Book of Psalms. Every psalm is a prayer we can sing.

These words from Psalm 119 praise God and sing about God's Word.

The Word of God makes people joyful.
The Word of God helps people know God.
The Word of God is true and lasts forever.

BASED ON PSALM 119:14, 130, 160

Why do we pray the psalms?

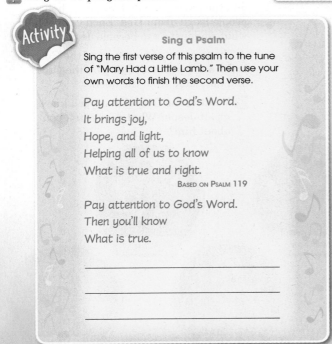

Activity

Sing a Psalm

Sing the first verse of this psalm to the tune of "Mary Had a Little Lamb." Then use your own words to finish the second verse.

Pay attention to God's Word.
It brings joy,
Hope, and light,
Helping all of us to know
What is true and right.

BASED ON PSALM 119

Pay attention to God's Word.
Then you'll know
What is true.

_____

_____

_____

(17)

Faith-Filled People

King David

We read the story of King David in the Old Testament. King David was a musician. He wrote many prayers that were songs. These prayers are called psalms.

FAITH-FILLED PEOPLE

King David. For centuries people believed David wrote the Psalms. However, evidence suggests that many people, including David, may have written them over several centuries. The Book of Psalms is considered by biblical scholars to be a selection from a greater number of psalms written in the first millennium before Christ. The Psalter, a version of the Book of Psalms, has been used and still is used during liturgies. In the Middle Ages, the Psalter was an important book of devotion, often illuminated in rich colors and gold leaf, with intricate illustrations. Regardless of who wrote the psalms, the Book of Psalms is a collection of inspired songs of prayer that help us give glory and praise to God.

Reinforce

▶ Have the students make a faith word card for *Psalms*.

▶ Introduce one of the writers of the Psalms by reading Faith-Filled People to the class.

Connect

▶ Call attention to the activity titled Sing a Psalm. Teach the class about Psalm 119 to the tune of "Mary Had a Little Lamb." Allow the students to sing it two or three times.

▶ Explain the directions for completing the activity and do so as a class. Write the new words of the verse on the board large enough for all to see and copy in their books.

Pray

Conclude the session by leading the students in sung prayer. Have them sing together both verses of the song in the "Sing a Psalm" activity. Sing through the song two or three time. Try it as a round. If you wish, add gestures. Consider using it as a sort of processional by having the students follow a leader, who reverently holds a Bible high enough for all to see.

> **Key Concept**
> The Gospels announce the Good News of Jesus.

Pray

Gather the class for prayer. Lead them in the following echo prayer:

Praise to you, O Lord, / for the gift of this day, / for the smiles on our faces, / for the love that we share. / Blessed be God forever./
Amen.

Teach

▶ Call attention to the Faith Focus question and read it aloud.

▶ Ask the students what they remember about the Gospels (hint: they can turn to page 15 and read the Catholics Believe feature to refresh their memories).

▶ Ask the students when they regularly listen to God's Word from the Gospels. *(We listen to God's Word at Sunday Mass.)*

▶ Read aloud the section titled The Bible Tells Good News. Pause after each paragraph to answer questions and make sure the students are grasping the faith concepts.

Reinforce

Ask and discuss: What do all four Gospels do? *(They tell us what Jesus said and did; they tell us what we must do to become Jesus' disciples; they spread the Good News that God loves us very much.)*

Connect

Read the follow-up questions aloud and have the students share with a partner their "good news" Gospel story and what it tells them about Jesus.

> **Faith Focus**
> What are the Gospels?
>
> **Faith Words**
> ▶ **Gospels**
> The Gospels are the first four books in the New Testament.

The Bible Tells Good News

The **Gospels** are the most important books in the Bible. The Bible has four Gospels. They are in the New Testament.

The Gospels were written by Saint Matthew, Saint Mark, Saint Luke, and Saint John. All four Gospels spread the Good News. The Good News is that God loves us very much.

Each Gospel tells what Jesus said and did. Each Gospel tells how Jesus helped people learn about God. Each Gospel tells what we must do to become Jesus' disciples.

The most important part of the Gospels is the story of Jesus' dying on the Cross and his rising from the dead.

[?] What is one Gospel story you know about Jesus? What does it tell you about him?

Matthew Mark Luke John

(18)

HUMAN METHODOLOGIES

Learning Through the Witness of the Teacher/Catechist. The *National Directory for Catechesis* teaches that catechists (religion teachers) "powerfully influence those being catechized by their faithful proclamation of the Gospel of Jesus Christ" *(NDC 29E).* Your sincere love for Sacred Scripture will be apparent to your second graders if you treat the Bible with reverence and proclaim the readings you share with them with joy and conviction. They are eager to follow your lead. Help the students to see in your attitude and behavior that you believe with all your heart that God speaks to us in the Bible.

Disciples of Jesus respect others. You are a disciple of Jesus. You can pay attention to God's Word. You can tell others about Jesus. You can help people come to know more about God's great love for them.

I Follow Jesus

Activity

✦ Sharing the Good News ✦

Write or draw a picture of one way you can tell people about Jesus. Show how you can show respect to a friend or someone in your family.

My Faith Choice

This week, I will read from the Bible. I will share with others what I read. I will

_____

_____

Pray, "Thank you, Holy Spirit, for helping me to pay attention and learn from the Bible. Amen."

(19)

TEACHING TIP

I Follow Jesus. This is an important page. Be sure to give the students the time they need to process it. Processing this page is an integral part of helping the students to discover the connection between the teachings of the Catholic Church and their personal lives. It allows the students to move from what they have learned to how they can live their faith in their daily lives. Allow time for the students to share faith stories with one another.

Reinforce

Remind the class that listening to God's Word from the Bible can help us learn, change, and follow Jesus as his disciples.

Respond

▶ Ask the students what they do when they want to show respect to someone or something.

▶ Explain and encourage the students to show respect for and pay attention to God's Word. This will help them come to know more about God and his love for them.

▶ Read the introductory paragraph and explain the directions to the activity Sharing the Good News. Allow time for the students to complete it. Ask volunteers to share their pictures

Choose

▶ Call attention to My Faith Choice.

▶ Challenge the students to commit themselves to a specific, daily span of time for Bible reading. If necessary, suggest five minutes.

▶ Encourage the students to follow through on their decisions.

Pray

Lead the class in praying the prayer at the bottom of the page, thanking the Holy Spirit for helping them to pay attention to and learn from the Bible, God's Word to us.

Pray

Begin by leading the class in praying the Glory Be.

Recall

▶ Help the class recall the main faith concepts presented in the chapter by reviewing the To Help You Remember sentences with them.

▶ Turn statements into riddles by leaving out a word or phrase. Invite the students to solve each riddle by guessing who or what is being described.

▶ Explain the directions and allow the students time to complete the five review sentences. Consider reading aloud the first part of each sentence, followed by the choices for the second part.

▶ Check responses and go over any concepts the students misunderstood or forgot.

Reflect

Ask one of the students to read aloud the sentence, *"How do the Gospels spread the Good News?"* Have the students think a moment before writing their responses.

Share

▶ Have the students share responses with a partner.

▶ Challenge partners to agree on one way to share what they have learned with someone in their families.

TO HELP YOU REMEMBER

1. The Bible is the written Word of God.
2. In the Bible, God tells us of his love for us.
3. The Bible helps us learn about Jesus and how to live as his disciples.

Chapter Review

Recall

Read each sentence. Draw a line through each ending that does not belong.

1. The Bible is the written
   - history of the world.
   - Word of God.

2. The two main parts of the Bible are the
   - Psalms and the Gospels.
   - The Old Testament and the New Testament.

3. The Gospels tell us about
   - the creation of the world.
   - what Jesus said and did.

4. The Book of Psalms is in the
   - Old Testament.
   - New Testament.

5. The most important part of the Gospels is the story of
   - Jesus' dying on the Cross and his rising from the dead.
   - Jesus and his disciples.

Reflect

How do the Gospels spread the Good News?

_____

_____

Share Share with a friend one way you are a disciple of Jesus.

(20)

TEACHING TIP

Liturgy Connection. Remind the class that every Sunday we hear readings from the Bible. The first reading is usually from the Old Testament. Our response to hearing that reading is a Psalm. The second reading is from the New Testament, generally from one of the Epistles (a word that means *letter*) or from the Acts of the Apostles. Finally, a passage from one of the four Gospels is proclaimed. Tell the students that the whole first half of the Mass is dedicated to proclaiming and listening to the Word of God in the Bible.

A Listening Prayer

Pray together. Ask God to help you listen to his Word.

Leader O God, open our ears to hear you.
Open our hearts to love you.

All **Help us pay attention to your Word.**

Leader Let us lift our voices in song.
Sing the song on page 17.
Now let us listen to God's Word.

Reader *Let the word of Christ dwell in you
richly, as in all wisdom you teach . . .
one another, singing psalms, hymns,
and spiritual songs with gratitude in
your hearts to God. And whatever
you do, in word or in deed, do
everything in the name of the Lord Jesus.*
COLOSSIANS 3:16–17

The word of the Lord.

All **Thanks be to God.**

Leader Let us think about what we heard
God saying to us in this reading.
(Pause).
We thank you, O God,
for your Word to us in the Bible,
for the Good News of the Gospels,
and for making us disciples of
Jesus, your Son.

All **O God, we are happy to hear
your Word and keep it. Amen.**

(21)

LITURGY CONNECTION

Blessings. Tell the class that a blessing is a prayer that asks God to be with us and to love and care for us. Before you pray A Listening Prayer with the class, tell the students that you are going to bless their ears, and ask God to help them listen well to his Word. Call them forward by name, one at a time. Gently trace the Sign of the Cross on both the right and left ear, while praying, *"Loving God, help us to listen to your Word."* Ask each student to respond "Amen." Then pray *A Listening Prayer* together.

Pray

▶ Prepare the class for prayer by reading the introductory paragraph aloud and explaining the importance of paying attention and listening to God as we pray. Explain that prayer is more than talking. It is also listening.

▶ Explain that you will play the part of leader. Choose a volunteer to be the reader and allow him or her to practice the reading.

▶ Point out the responses to the class. Tell them to be ready to make the responses boldly.

▶ Teach the student at the end of the reading, how he or she should say, "The Word of the Lord."

▶ Ask the students to remember that God is with them. *(Pause.)* Lead the students in praying A Listening Prayer.

▶ If time allows, discuss ways the students can live out the biblical message.

▶ Conclude by praying the Sign of the Cross.

Preview

▶ Have the students carefully tear out pages 21 and 22 along the perforation.

▶ Encourage the students to share these pages with their families, and to complete the activities together.

▶ If they did not complete the review activity on page 20 by the end of the session, emphasize that they can complete it with their families at home.

▶ Point out the title and theme of the next lesson to the students.

Visit BeMyDisciples.com

▶ Take time with the students to explore the many activities and resources available at the *Be My Disciples* Web site.

▶ Encourage them to join with their families to discover the many resources available at the Web site.

Before Moving On ...

As you finish today's lesson, reflect on the following question before moving on to the next chapter.

What can I do to help the students improve their listening skills?

With My Family

This Week . . .

In Chapter 1, "The Bible," your child learned:

▶ The Bible is the written Word of God. The Old Testament and the New Testament are the two main parts of the Bible.

▶ The Holy Spirit inspired the human writers of the Bible. This means that they wrote what God wished to communicate.

▶ The four accounts of the Gospel are the most important books in the Bible.

▶ Paying attention shows respect.

For more about related teachings of the Church, *see Catechism of the Catholic Church*, 101–114, and the *United States Catechism for Adults* pages 11–32.

■ Sharing God's Word

Choose a favorite story or passage from the Gospels. Invite your child to really listen and pay attention as you read the story to him or her. Afterward, invite your child to tell what she or he heard.

■ Living as Disciples

The Christian home and family is a school of discipleship. Choose one or more of the following activities to do as a family, or design a similar activity of your own.

▶ Display your family Bible in a place of prominence in your home. Gather around the Bible to read the Bible and for family prayer. Read one brief passage each night. Your church bulletin may have the passages that are used at Mass for that day.

▶ Teach your child the good habit of paying attention. Paying attention is a sign of respect. Paying attention enables us to hear God speaking to us. Paying attention makes us aware of people in need and opens us up to reach out to them. That awareness leads us to respond—to act with charity and justice.

■ Our Spiritual Journey

Daily prayer is a vital element in the life of the Catholic family. It is one of the foundational spiritual disciplines of a disciple of Christ. In this chapter, your child prayed and listened to Scripture. This type of prayer is called *lectio divina*. Learn the rhythm of lectio divina and pray this form of prayer often as a family. Read and pray together the prayer on page 21. Then pray the following response from Luke 11:28: "*Blessed are those who hear the word of God and observe it.*"

For more ideas on ways your family can live as disciples of Jesus, visit **BeMyDisciples.com**

22

ENRICHING THE LESSON

Optional Activities. At the conclusion of every chapter in your Teacher Edition, you will find strategies for engaging the students in different ways. These activities have been designed to accommodate the different ways children learn. For example, although all the students will enjoy identifying classroom sounds, as suggested on the following page, those youngsters who learn best when several of their senses are actively engaged will truly profit from the experience. As you plan your weekly lessons, be sure to consider incorporating one or more of the activities on the Enriching the Lesson page.

Enriching the Lesson

The Listener Game

Purpose

To reinforce the importance and practice of paying careful attention when listening (taught on page 15)

Directions

▶ Choose numerous items that make different sounds, e.g., a pencil, a book, a handkerchief, and so on.

▶ Have the students sit in a circle and play a game.

▶ Designate one student as the Listener, and have him or her sit in a chair at the center of the circle with eyes closed.

▶ Have the other students chant: *"Listen, listen, do you hear? / Someone's coming very near!"*

▶ Designate another student to choose one of the collected items and then to drop it on the floor.

▶ After hearing the sound, the Listener tries to guess which item was dropped.

Materials

common classroom items

Proclaiming God's Word

Purpose

To reinforce the understanding of the importance of reading the Bible and the practice of paying attention as we are reading (taught on page 18)

Directions

▶ Prepare several short Gospel readings. Provide each student with a paper on which you have printed in large type the words of one of the readings. Underline words that should be emphasized.

▶ Ask the students to read the reading on their paper silently and rehearse it quietly.

▶ Invite volunteers to stand one at a time at the prayer center and proclaim their reading. At the conclusion, have them say, "The Gospel of the Lord."

▶ Be sure to have the class stand for the reading and to respond afterwards, "Praise to you, Lord Jesus Christ."

Materials

sheets of paper printed with Gospel readings

Literature Connection

Purpose

To connect the practice of paying attention to the Bible with the importance of paying attention during daily activities

Directions

▶ Read *The Listening Walk* by Paul Showers (Harper Collins, San Francisco, 1993), in which a young girl likes to go on walks with her father. They walk around the neighborhood together, but do not talk, only listen. She describes the sounds she hears on her walk, and then challenges the reader to sit still in the quiet and notice the sounds around them.

▶ Then take the students on a "listening walk" around your school, both inside and out. What sounds are in the office? Do you hear different sounds in the church? What sounds are outside?

Materials

The Listening Walk by Paul Showers

BACKGROUND

Living Signs of God's Love

Signs of God's love surround us. All of creation, living and non-living, points to the existence of the living God and his love for us. Joined at Baptism to Christ, the Incarnate Son of God, we are called and given the grace to be the clearest of those signs. We are the Body of Christ in the world.

Baptism

With Baptism comes the responsibility to share the gift of our life in Christ with others. By our lives we are to be living signs, inviting others to know and believe in God, the Holy Trinity—One God who is Father, Son, and Holy Spirit.

Jesus is the Incarnate Son of God, who came that all people might live in communion with God the Holy Trinity. Our Christian vocation is to extend the same invitation to all. How do we fulfill such a vocation? How do we share our faith in Christ?

We respond to the grace of the Holy Spirit and live as Jesus taught by loving God and neighbor. We join with the Church, the Sacrament and instrument of Salvation in the world, and proclaim the Good News of Salvation by our words and deeds—by our whole life.

Lights in the World

Christ described the work of his followers to be lights in the world.

"[Y]our light must shine before others, that they may see your good deeds and glorify your heavenly Father."

Matthew 5:16

In the Sermon on the Mount, Matthew summarizes for all Christians the way of discipleship in Christ. He teaches how we are to be to such lights in the world. Central to the Sermon on the Mount is Jesus' teaching on the Beatitudes.

The Beatitudes

Living the Beatitudes will transform our lives and deepen our identity with Christ. We are to keep the Beatitudes before our eyes and invite the Holy Spirit to teach and strengthen us to live the Beatitudes.

We are to strive to be poor in spirit, meek, merciful, clean of heart, and peacemakers. We are to mourn for the oppressed, the suffering, and those treated unjustly. We are to hunger and thirst for righteousness. We are to be ready to be persecuted for the sake of righteousness.

As the Beatitudes transform who we are, we will become living signs of God, in whose image we have been created, among those we live and work with each day. We will be the lights that Christ calls us to be and will enable others to more clearly see and come to know the presence and love of the living God.

For Reflection

Who were some of the "lights," my early teachers in the ways of faith, who helped me come to know God?

How am I serving as a light for the students whom I teach?

Teacher to Teacher

As You Begin

As you begin this second chapter, you and the students have already begun the process of getting to know one another. It may be important to remind yourself that seven-and eight-year-olds will just be themselves. Be patient with them and with yourself.

Begin with Prayer

Remember to begin each session with prayer. It will not only remind the students of God's presence in their lives, but will also have a calming effect on both you and them. During this session take the opportunity to re-teach the Sign of the Cross. Tell the students that they are now old enough to understand this beautiful prayer and its importance to us as Christians. Then begin and end this session by praying the Sign of the Cross slowly and reverently.

The Church Teaches ...

"Catechesis links human experience to the revealed word of God, helping people ascribe Christian meaning to their own existence. It enables people to explore interpret, and judge their basic experiences in light of the Gospel" (*National Directory for Catechesis*, 29A).

That is why every chapter begins by helping the students to situate the chapter concepts in their own life experience. As the students learn to reflect on their life experiences, they can begin to see the hand of the almighty Creator at work. Through continued catechesis, the students can grow to recognize God's Revelation in their daily lives.

Further Reading and Reflection

For more related teachings of the Church, see the *Catechism of the Catholic Church*, 27–43, 50–67, and 142–197; and the *United States Catholic Catechism for Adults*, pages 1–9, 11–19, and 35–47.

Teacher Prayer

Lord, I place my trust in you.
Strengthen me in faith and love.
Guide me to be a clear light
for the students to come
to know and believe in you.
Amen.

Lesson Planner

Chapter 2 We Know and Love God

Focus To learn ways we come to know and love God

LESSON PART	PROCESS	MATERIALS and RESOURCES
DAY 1 EXPLORE **Focus** To explore how we have come to know God **Pages** 23–25	▶ Proclaim and discuss Psalm 25:4. (Teach me your ways, God.) ▶ Reflect on the story of a family being hospitable at its parish. **Disciple Power:** Hospitality **Activity:** Write ways to show respect and color to discover what hospitality means	Bible Pencils or pens Crayons or colored markers
DAY 2 DISCOVER **Focus** To discover ways God invites us to know and believe in him **Pages** 26–27	▶ Learn that creation tells us about God. ▶ Discover that people, made in God's image and likeness, are God's most important creation. **Faith Words:** Believe **Catholics Believe:** The Parish Church **Scripture:** Creation gives God glory and praise. Psalm 69:35 **Activity:** Finish a prayer about Creation.	Bible Pencils or pens **Enriching the Lesson:** Teacher Guide, page 77, Making Creation Posters **Additional Activities Booklet:** Activities 2a and 2b, or see *BeMyDisciples*.com.
DAY 3 DISCOVER **Focus** To discover that Jesus reveals the most about God **Pages** 28–29	▶ Learn that Jesus invites us to have faith in God. **Faith Words:** faith **Scripture:** Matthew 6:26–34 **Faith-Filled People:** Saint Philip the Apostle **Activity:** Draw a picture showing trust in God's love.	Pencils or pens Crayons or markers **Enriching the Lesson:** Teacher Guide, page 77 Taking the Scriptures Outdoors
DAY 4 DECIDE **Focus** To discover that the Church helps us to know God, and to decide on a way to show God's love to others **Pages** 30–31	▶ Discover how the Church helps us know God better and grow in faith. **Activity:** Create an invitation to come to know more about God. **My Faith Choice:** Choose a way to show you know and love God. **Pray:** "Thank you, Holy Spirit."	Pencils or pens Crayons or markers **Literature Connection:** *What Is God Like?* **Additional Activities Booklet:** Activities 2a and 2b or see *BeMyDisciples*.com
DAY 5 CONCLUDE **Focus** To pray an Act of Faith **Pages** 32–34	▶ **REVIEW** Review concepts: Recall, Reflect, and Share. ▶ **PRAY** An Act of Faith ▶ **PREVIEW** the With My Family page and the theme of the next chapter.	Bible Grade 2 Music CD **Assessment Tools Booklet:** Assessments 2a and 2b

Assign online Chapter Review and interactive Chapter Test at **BeMyDisciples.com**

CHAPTER **2**

We Know and Love God

? Who helps you read a story, play a game, or pray?

Listen to these words from the Bible. They ask God to help us come to know him better.

Make known to me your ways, Lord; teach me your paths. PSALM 25:4

? Who else has helped you come to know and love God?

23

Pray

▶ Welcome the students warmly. Help them quiet themselves for prayer.

▶ Pray the Sign of the Cross together.

▶ Offer a short prayer that the students can repeat after you. Thank God for the people who help us to know God's love.

▶ Ask the two opening questions. *(Affirm all responsible replies.)*

Reflect

▶ Read the introduction to the Scripture passage. Call on a volunteer to read the passage from the Book of Psalms.

▶ Observe a moment of silence.

▶ Ask the follow-up question. *(Accept all responsible replies.)*

▶ Conclude the prayer by thanking God for the people who help us to know God's love.

▶ Conclude with the Sign of the Cross.

Focus

Invite the students to turn the page to discover what a family does to help people in its parish come to know and love God.

HUMAN METHODOLOGIES

Learning Through Human Experience. The *National Directory for Catechesis* explains that "(h)uman experiences provide the sensible signs that lead the person, by the grace of the Holy Spirit, to a better understanding of the truths of the faith" **(NDC, 29A)**. As you ask your second graders to share their experiences of being taught by others, try to draw even the shyest student into the discussion. Emphasize that every member of your class has something important to contribute to the learning process. Your patience and affirmation will help all the students feel comfortable about sharing their personal stories.

Introduce

▶ Write the name of your parishes on the board and make sure all the students know it. Share with them that the name of your parish church reminds the parish members of their Catholic faith. If possible, share some facts about the name of your parish. This will help the students identify with the parish and the Catholic Church.

▶ Write the name of the pastor on the board and ask volunteers what they may know about him and his work for their parish.

▶ Read Disciple Power with the class. Point out that hospitality is important for a parish. Share with the students that they will hear about a family who shared the virtue of hospitality with its parish.

▶ Call on different volunteers to read the section titled Welcome!

Reinforce

Divide the class into partners. Call attention to the follow-up questions on the page. Have partners share their answers with each other. Review the answers as a class.

Disciple Power

Hospitality

Jesus tells us to treat all people with hospitality. Hospitality helps us welcome others as God's children. It helps us treat others with dignity and respect.

The Church Follows Jesus

Welcome!

It is a great Sunday. The sun is shining. Mr. and Mrs. Chen are standing at the door of Holy Trinity Catholic Church. They are smiling as they greet everyone, one by one, "Welcome! Glad to see you!"

Mr. and Mrs. Chen are ushers who greet the people as they arrive for Mass each Sunday. The Chen family is proud to be a member of Holy Trinity parish.

The Chen family do more than join with other members of Holy Trinity for Mass on Sunday. The Chen children attend Holy Trinity Catholic School. Mrs. Chen is a second grade teacher. Mr. Chen runs the Holy Trinity Community Care Center.

They share food and clothing, books and toys, and other things with families who do not have enough money. Best of all, they treat everyone with respect. They are proud to live as joyful disciples of Jesus.

? In what ways are the Chens good disciples of Jesus?

24

TEACHING TIP

Church Tour. The *National Directory for Catechesis* reminds us that "Human experiences provide the sensible signs that lead the person, by the grace of the Holy Spirit, to a better understanding of the truths of the faith" (*NDC*, 29A). Plan a class tour of the parish church to have the students look for signs of our faith. Point out statues, stained-glass windows, the crucifix, and other objects that help us grow in faith. Call special attention to any sacred representations of your parish patron saint. Check page 514 of this guide for a lesson plan to help make the tour a hospitable and rewarding experience for the class.

The Chens are good disciples of Jesus. They show hospitality and invite others to know God better. They treat everyone with respect. They welcome others as God's children.

? In what ways are you a good disciple?

Activity

Color each space that has an X to discover what hospitality means.
(ALL ARE WELCOME)

Show Respect

Like the Chens, you can help others to know and love God. Tell how you can show hospitality and respect.

To your family

_____

_____

To your friends

_____

_____

(25)

DISCIPLE POWER

Hospitality. Talk with the students about the different ways your parish promotes hospitality. For example, many parishes have greeters who welcome worshipers on Sunday mornings at church. Other parishes invite families to sign up to be greeters at Mass on a designated Sunday. New parishioners are visited by welcome ministers in many parishes. These volunteers tell newcomers about the parish and often invite them to parish events. In other parishes, members of the welcome ministry serve coffee, juice, and snacks after Sunday Mass. Ask the students to suggest ways they might welcome a new member to your class. Reinforce that Jesus' disciples offer hospitality to others.

Connect

▶ Read aloud the paragraph on the top of page 25. Help the students experience the virtue of hospitality by engaging them in a role play using welcoming and non-welcoming words and gestures. Help the students understand that using welcoming words and gestures means that they are acting as good disciples.

▶ Afterward, direct attention to the first part of the activity. Give the students time to color and discover the meaning of hospitality.

▶ When the students finish coloring, ask them to read the discovered words aloud. (*All are welcome.*)

▶ Write the word *Catholic* on the board. Tell the class that "catholic" means *all are welcome*. Say: We are members of the Catholic Church, a Church of hospitality, a Church that welcomes all.

▶ Go on to read the directions to the writing activity and have the students complete it.

▶ Invite sharing.

Pray

▶ Gather the class for prayer. Have the students pray:

God of hospitality,
help us welcome you
and come to know you
more and more each day.
Amen.

▶ Conclude with the Sign of the Cross.

Key Concept
Creation helps us come to know and believe in God.

Pray

Invite the students to quiet themselves for prayer. Lead them in reverently praying the Sign of the Cross.

Teach

▶ Have the class reflect on the picture of the children playing on page 27. Ask: What can you tell about these children by looking at them? *(We can tell what they look like and that they are happy or having fun.)*

▶ Ask the class: What are some of the ways people tell us about themselves? *(They tell us about themselves by how they speak, by the things they do and say.)*

▶ Read the Faith Focus question aloud. Tell the class that one of the ways God invites us to know and believe in him is through his creation.

▶ Call on volunteers to read the paragraphs of Creation Tells Us About God on page 26.

▶ Call attention to Faith Words. Have the students read *believe* and its meaning aloud. Invite them to make a word card for *believe*.

Faith Focus
What are some ways God invites us to know and believe in him?

Faith Words
believe
To believe in God means to know God and to give ourselves to him with all our heart.

Creation Tells Us About God

The Chens helped people learn about God. God's creation also helps us to come to know and **believe** in him. Creation is everything that God has made. All creation helps us come to know and give glory to God. The Bible tells us:

> Let the heavens and the earth sing praise,
> the seas and whatever moves in them!
>
> Psalm 69:35

The moon, the stars, and the sun help us come to know God. The snow-covered mountains and the deep blue oceans tell us something about God.

The birds, the fish, and the animals help us come to know God. Fields of crops and beautiful flowers are gifts that remind us of God's goodness. All the good things in the world help us come to know God.

❓ What and who help us to know and believe in God?

TEACHING VOCABULARY

Faith and Believe. *Faith* and *believe* are similar words in some ways, and second graders may tend to confuse them or use them synonymously. You might tell them that *faith* is a "naming" word. It tells about our whole relationship with God. *Believe* is an "action" word. It tells what we do because we have faith in God. Encourage the students to demonstrate that they understand the difference between the two words by asking volunteers to use *faith* and *believe* in simple sentences.

People are the most important part of God's creation. All people are created in the image of God. People are signs of God's love.

Our families and people in our Church help us to know God, to love him, and to serve him. But God is the one who best invites us to believe in him. God invites us to know him better and to love and serve him. God invites us to give ourselves to him with all our heart.

? How are you a sign of God's love?

Catholics Believe

The Parish Church

Every Catholic parish has a special name. These names, such as Holy Trinity, tell us about our faith in God. Other names, such as Divine Savior, tell us about our faith in Jesus. Other parishes are named after Mary and the other Saints.

Activity

Thank You, God

Finish the prayer.

Thank you, God, for

_____ .

Thank you, God, for

_____ .

(27)

Reinforce

▶ Have a volunteer read the two paragraphs on page 27 to find out the most important part of God's creation.

▶ Ask: What or who is the most important part of God's creation? *(People are the most important part of God's creation.)*

▶ Point out the follow-up questions on pages 26 and 27 and call for responses. *(Look for responses from the first question, such as: all creation, our families, catechists, pastors, and others in our Church.)*

Connect

▶ Have the students complete the prayer-writing activity.

▶ Invite a volunteer to read Catholics Believe about The Parish Church. Discuss with the students how the names of Churches, or creation, helps us come to know and believe in God.

Pray

▶ Gather the class for prayer.

▶ Give every student the opportunity to share what he or she wrote as the closing prayer for today's lesson.

▶ Conclude by praying the Sign of the Cross.

TEACHING TIP

Extending the Activity. After the students have written their "Thank You, God" prayers, have them create a collage. Distribute magazines, scissors, glue, and paper. If necessary, have the students work with partners so that there are enough supplies. Ask the students to cut out images of God's creation that they find in the magazines. It may be helpful to go through some pictures together to help them distinguish between something that is man-made and something of God's creation. Have the students then create a collage with the title "God's Creation." Give each student the opportunity to share his or her work with the class.

> **Key Concept**
> Jesus tells us the most about God.

Pray

Ask the students to quiet themselves for prayer. Pray the Sign of the Cross together. Then have them echo this or a similar prayer after you:

> Lord God, / open our hearts and minds / to learning more about our faith. / Amen.

Teach

▶ Have the students read the Faith Focus question and ask them for possible answers. Point out that these two pages will help them learn what Jesus told us about his Father.

▶ Read aloud the first paragraph of Jesus Helps Us Know God. Emphasize that Jesus told us the most about God.

▶ Ask the group to listen to find out what Jesus said to the people about having faith in God. Invite a volunteer to read the passage from Matthew's Gospel.

▶ Ask: What did Jesus want to teach the people about God by telling this story? (*Jesus wanted the people to believe in and trust God with all their hearts.*)

▶ Ask the class to pay attention and listen for the word *faith* as you read aloud the paragraph at the top of page 29.

▶ Explain that many people came to believe in Jesus. Read Faith-Filled People to the class.

> **Faith Focus**
> What does Jesus tell us about God?
>
> **Faith Words**
> ▶ **faith**
> Faith is a gift from God that makes us able to believe in him.

Jesus Helps Us Know God

Jesus told us the most about God. One day a crowd of people came to Jesus. They wanted to know about God. Jesus told them that people were more important to God than everything else he created. They should believe in God with all their hearts.

Jesus said, "Look at the birds. They have all the food they need. Your Father in heaven takes care of them.

Your Father in heaven knows you. You are more important to God than the birds and all the animals. Trust God. Have faith in him."

BASED ON MATTHEW 6:26–34

? **What does the Bible story tell you about God?**

28

TEACHING TIP

Storytelling. Children often love a change of scenery. Take them outside to tell the Scripture story on this page from the Bible. Have a volunteer carry a Bible. Share with the students along the way that Jesus' disciples often followed him around and stopped to listen to his stories, just as they are about to do. After finding a quiet place, stop and proclaim Matthew 6:26–34. Use dramatics to enhance the story and keep the students' attention.

In this Bible story, Jesus invites us to have **faith** in God's loving care for us. Faith is God's gift to us. It makes us able to know God and to believe in him. It makes us able to know and believe in what God teaches us. When we say yes to God's invitation to believe in him, we show that we have faith.

? How do you show your faith in God?

Faith-Filled People

Saint Philip the Apostle

Jesus invited Philip to be one of his first followers. Jesus said to Philip, "Follow me." Philip then went to his friend Nathanael and told him about Jesus. Nathanael believed too and became a follower of Jesus.

Activity

Trusting God

Look at the pictures. How are the people in these two pictures showing that they trust in God's love? Draw a picture of yourself that shows how you trust in God's love.

(29)

FAITH-FILLED PEOPLE

Saint Philip and Saint Nathanael. During his life on Earth Jesus called people to follow him. These followers were the Apostles. They were chosen to be the leaders of the Church. Philip and Nathanael, who is also called Bartholomew, were Apostles and Martyrs. Jesus invited Philip to "follow me" (see John 1:43). Then Philip invited Nathanael, "Come and see" (see John 1:46). Both Philip and Nathanael were present at the miracle of the loaves and fishes and in the upper room on Pentecost. We can learn from Saint Philip and Saint Nathanael to love and serve God and people as Jesus taught his followers to do.

Reinforce

▶ Discuss what it means to have faith in God. *(We believe in him and in all he teaches.)*

▶ Share with the class the information about the terms *faith* and *believe* in the Teaching Vocabulary box at the bottom of page 68 in this guide.

▶ Have the students read aloud the faith word *faith* on page 28 and its meaning and make a **word card** for this term.

Connect

▶ Remind the class that when we trust and love God, we show that we have faith in God.

▶ Ask the follow-up question on page 28, and have the students share with a partner what the Bible story told them about God.

▶ Give the students time to complete the Trusting God activity. Ask volunteers to share their drawings with the class.

Pray

Pray the Our Father together. Conclude with the Sign of the Cross.

Key Concept
The Church helps us grow in faith.

Pray

▶ Lead the following echo prayer:

O God, / all your creation praises you. / We ask you to bless us / and to help us love you. / Amen.

▶ Conclude by praying the Sign of the Cross.

Teach

▶ Remind the children about what they discovered earlier about their parish and its name. Tell them that every Catholic parish has a special name. Some names, such as Holy Trinity, tell us about our faith in God. Other names, such as Divine Savior, tell us about our faith in Jesus. Share that some parishes are named after Mary and the other Saints.

▶ Ask the students to listen for words that tell what *Church* means as you read the first paragraph of The Church Helps Us Know God to them.

▶ Invite the students to read the last two paragraphs silently to find out how the Church helps us.

Reinforce

Invite volunteers to read the sentences from the text that tell us how we grow in and live our faith together.

Connect

Call on volunteers to respond to the follow-up question. (*Look for responses such as being kind, praying with others, celebrating the Eucharist.*)

Faith Focus
Who are the People of God?

The Church Helps Us Know God

Jesus gave us the Church. The Church is a sign of God's love in the world. The Church is the People of God who believe in Jesus Christ.

We belong to the Catholic Church. The Catholic Church goes all the way back to the time of Jesus and the Apostles. The Church helps us to know God and his love for us. The Church helps us grow in faith.

We grow in faith with the people of our Church in many ways. We grow in faith when we pray together. We grow in faith when we are kind to family, friends, and other people. We grow in faith when we care for God's creation.

We grow in faith when we live our faith with our Church family. When we live our faith, we are signs of God's love for others to see.

? What are the ways that you share your faith with others?

TEACHING TIP

Learning Styles and Behavior. Be aware that some students are uncomfortable reading aloud. Give them opportunities to participate in other ways. Many of the students may need visual aids to assist them in learning. You might want to start a picture file and add to it as the year goes on. In addition to having varied learning styles, second graders also have varied personalities and behaviors. Encourage the students who are shy, while giving positive attention to those who will demand it. Do not accept behaviors that are rude, unkind, or potentially dangerous.

You are a sign of God's love. You can help other people to know and believe in God by what you say and what you do.

One way we live as disciples of Jesus is to practice hospitality. You can invite and welcome others to know and believe in God.

 I Follow **Jesus**

 Activity

Signs of God's Love

Who can you invite to learn more about God? Write that person's name on the invitation.

You Are Invited to Believe in God

God Invites

_____

friend's name

to know and believe in him.

 My Faith Choice

This week, I will show someone that I have faith and know and love God. I will

_____

_____

Pray, "Thank you, Holy Spirit, for the gift of faith. Help me share with others how much you love them. Amen."

(31)

Reinforce

Recall with the class that the gift of faith helps us come to know God and believe in him and to live our faith as disciples of Jesus. God invites each of us to live as a disciple of Jesus by showing his love to others.

Respond

▶ Read aloud the first and second paragraphs to the class.

▶ Explain the directions for Signs of God's Love and guide the students in completing the activity.

Choose

Ask the students to complete My Faith Choice. Have the students write their decisions and encourage them to put them into practice this week.

Pray

Lead the class in the prayer to the Holy Spirit at the bottom of the page. Conclude with the Sign of the Cross.

THE TASKS OF CATECHESIS

Education for Community Life. Your classroom can provide a weekly experience of hospitality for each of your second graders. Greet the students by name as they arrive for class. When doing group work, rotate the participants in each group regularly to encourage the students to get to know one another. Reach out to students who seem isolated or lonely. Remind the students that we can best show our love for God by showing love for others.

Pray

Lead the class in praying the Glory Be.

Recall

▶ Scramble the letters to the words *believe, Jesus,* and *Church* and write the scrambled letters for the words on the board.

▶ Ask the students to help you unscramble the letters to create the correct words. As each word is unscrambled, invite a volunteer to find the word in one of the To Help You Remember statements and read it aloud.

▶ Give directions and invite the students to complete the fill-in-the-missing-letters activity. Assist the students with word recognition difficulties by giving them a word list to refer to.

Reflect

Read aloud the unfinished sentence, *"What are the ways you can grow in faith?"* Have the students think a moment before writing their response.

Share

Have the students write their responses. Remind them to share their responses with a family member.

▶ **TO HELP YOU REMEMBER**

1. God invites us to know and believe in him.
2. Jesus, the Son of God, tells us the most about God.
3. God gave us the Church to help us grow in faith.

Chapter Review

Recall

Complete the missing letters in the sentences.

1. Faith is to k _n_ o _w_ God and to b _e_ l _i_ e _v_ e in him with all our h _e_ a _r_ ts.

2. _J_ e _s_ u _s_ told us the most about God.

3. The C _h_ u _r_ c _h_ helps us grow in faith.

4. Hospitality helps us treat others with re _s_ p _e_ c _t_ .

Reflect

What are ways you can grow in faith?

_____

_____

_____

_____

_____

Share | Write a sentence that tells what faith means to you. Share it with a family member.

(32)

SPECIAL NEEDS

Pairing Up Students. Students with reading and writing difficulties need special consideration when it comes to creating pairs. Write the names of students who display adequate reading and writing ability skills on index cards with a green marker. Write the names of students with reading or writing difficulties on index cards with a red marker. When you create partners for activities choose one student from each group to ensure that you have a student with adequate reading and writing ability in each pair.

Need: Students with reading and writing difficulties

We Believe in God!

Vocal prayers are said aloud with others. An act of faith is a vocal prayer. Pray this act of faith as a class.

Leader   Let us tell God we believe in him with all our hearts. Let us pray.

All   **God, we believe in you with all our hearts.**

Group 1   God our loving Father, all creation reminds us of your love.

All   **God, we believe in you with all our hearts.**

Group 2   Jesus, Son of God, you showed us how much God loves us.

All   **God, we believe in you with all our hearts.**

Group 3   God the Holy Spirit, you help us to know and believe in God.

All   **God, we believe in you with all our hearts.**

Leader   God, thank you for your gift of creation and sending your Son to live among us. Jesus helps us to live as your faithful children.

All   **Amen.**

33

Pray

▶ Tell the class that today's prayer is an act of faith. Point out that it is an expression of faith in the Holy Trinity—God the Father, God the Son, God the Holy Spirit. It is a response to God's invitation to know and believe in him. Tell the students that they will discover more about the Holy Trinity in Chapter 3.

▶ Divide the class into three groups. Assign each group a part in the prayer. Invite each group to practice its reading aloud.

▶ Gather the students in the prayer center with their books.

▶ Call the class to prayer with a brief moment of silence.

▶ Lead the students in praying the "We Believe in God!" prayer. Begin and end by praying the Sign of the Cross.

LITURGY TIP

Prepare and Gather. Over the course of the year, the longer prayers that end the chapters expose the students to different types of prayers and rituals. Like the prayer on this page, these experiences require more preparation than the opening and closing prayers for each day. To help avoid any disruption in the flow of the prayer experience, take as much time as possible to prepare for prayer by choosing leaders and readers ahead of time, rehearsing readings or parts, and so forth. To help the class ready themselves for prayer, pay special attention to the gathering rite. This ritual of gathering may be a simple procession to the prayer center. Include a short moment of reflection or silence and your own call to prayer.

Preview

▶ Have the students carefully tear out pages 33 and 34 along the perforation.

▶ Encourage the students to share these pages with their families, and to complete the activities together.

▶ If they did not complete the review activity on page 32 by the end of the session, emphasize that they can complete it with their families at home.

▶ Point out the title and theme of the next lesson to the students.

Visit BeMyDisciples.com

▶ Take time with the students to explore the many activities and resources available at the *Be My Disciples* Web site.

▶ Encourage them to join with their families to discover the many resources available at the Web site.

Before Moving On ...

As you finish today's lesson, reflect on the following question before moving on to the next chapter.

What more can I do to make sure everyone is involved in class activities?

With My Family

This Week . . .

In Chapter 2, "We Know and Love God," your child learned:

▶ Faith is God's gift that makes us able to believe in him. God invites us to believe in him.

▶ All creation, especially our families and people in our Church, help us come to know and believe in God.

▶ Jesus revealed to us the most about God. He is the greatest sign of God's love and invites us to have faith in God.

▶ The virtue of hospitality guides us to share our faith in God with others.

For more about related teachings of the Church, see the *Catechism of the Catholic Church* 50–67, 84–95, and 142–175, and the *United States Catholic Catechism for Adults,* pages 50–53.

■ Sharing God's Word

Read together Matthew 6:26–34, where Jesus invites the people to have faith in God. Or read the adaptation of the story on page 28. Talk about how your family blessings strengthen your faith in God.

■ Living as Disciples

The Christian home and family is a school of discipleship. Choose one of the following activities to do as a family, or design a similar activity of your own.

▶ List some people who help your family come to know and believe in God. Write a note of thanks to each person on the list over the next few weeks.

▶ Identify the ways that your family lives the virtue of hospitality. Help your child grow as someone who is open and welcoming. Do this by the example of your own words and actions.

■ Our Spiritual Journey

Prayer is vital to the Christian life. Conversing with God in prayer can help us find and receive direction for living as a Catholic family. Help your child develop the habit of praying regularly. In this chapter, your child learned to pray an act of faith. Read and pray together the prayer on page 33. Then pray, *"God of hospitality, we have faith in you. Welcome us day by day to an even deeper faith."*

For more ideas on ways your family can live as disciples of Jesus, visit **BeMyDisciples.com**

34

PARTNERING WITH PARENTS

Building Relationships. You and the parents and adult family members of your second graders have one goal in common: to help the children grow in faith. Demonstrate that commitment by greeting the parents and adult family members at the door as they drop their children off. Learn the parents' names and make it a priority to speak directly to as many as possible before or after class. Collect e-mail addresses and communicate with the parents about class events. If a student is absent, e-mail the family and let them know the chapter you covered during the missed session. Assuring parents that you want to help them in their role as their child's primary catechist will go far in making this a successful year for the students, their parents and families, and you.

Enriching the Lesson

Making Creation Posters

Purpose

To reinforce the practice of reflecting on creation and coming to grow in our faith in God (taught on page 26)

Directions

▶ Talk with the students about their favorite parts of creation, such as their favorite animals or flowers.

▶ Have the students find pictures in magazines of things in creation that they particularly like.

▶ Invite the students to make a poster using the pictures they found in the magazines and ones they would like to draw.

▶ At the top of each completed poster print: "All Creation Tells Me About God."

Materials

large sheets of poster board

magazines

scissors and glue sticks

crayons and markers

Taking the Scriptures Outdoors

Purpose

To reinforce the Gospel story that Jesus told to invite us to have faith in God (taught on page 28)

Directions

▶ Take the students outdoors for a dramatic telling of *Matthew* 6:26–34.

▶ Have the students sit comfortably. Tell the Scripture story. Use gestures, facial expressions, and voice inflection as you speak.

▶ Emphasize that God's love for the students is far greater even than his love for the birds, whom he watches over faithfully.

Materials

Bible

Literature Connection

Purpose

To reinforce coming to know God better (taught on page 30)

Directions

▶ Share with the class that some books we read can also help us come to know God. One of these books is *What Is God Like?* By Kathleen Bostrom (Tyndale House Publishers 1998)

▶ Show the book to the students and read it aloud to them. After reading the book, ask open-ended questions that will enhance their thinking about what they heard. Elicit from the students how they imagine God.

▶ Invite them to ask their questions.

Materials

What Is God Like? by Kathleen Bostrom

BACKGROUND

The Mystery of God

God has come to us and comes to us now. He has unveiled, or revealed, himself and his loving plan of goodness (of creation and Salvation) to us.

The Mystery of the Holy Trinity

When we make the Sign of the Cross, we profess in prayer, "In the name of the Father, and of the Son, and of the Holy Spirit." We do not pray, "In the names of . . ." By using the singular, we confess there is One God in Three distinct Divine Persons: "the almighty Father, his only Son, and the Holy Spirit: the Most Holy Trinity" (*Catechism of the Catholic Church, 233*).

The Holy Trinity is the central mystery of Christian life and faith. This truth about God is something that we would never be able to know about him unless he revealed it to us. Before his Passover, Jesus told the disciples that they would not be alone in their ministry. The Holy Spirit would come to them and remain with them. The Father would send the Holy Spirit to them in Jesus' name. Just as the Holy Spirit spoke through the prophets, he will now accompany, teach, and guide Jesus' disciples. That means us!

The Mystery of God with Us

As disciples of Jesus Christ we are never alone. At Baptism, we were joined to Jesus, received the gift of the Holy Spirit, and became adopted children of God the Father. By virtue of our Baptism in Christ, the Holy Trinity dwells with us and within us for the entirety of our lives on Earth. We hope to see face to face and be with the Trinity forever in Heaven after we die.

The Holy Trinity is our constant source of enlightenment and blessing. The grace of our Lord Jesus Christ and the love of God the Father and the fellowship of the Holy Spirit are always with us. We live in the presence of the Holy Trinity. We live in communion and covenant with God.

As we live as followers of Christ, we believe and trust that the Father draws us near to him, and that the Holy Spirit moves us near to him to live our new lives in Christ, the Incarnate Son of God. Joined to Christ in Baptism, we have been sanctified by the grace of God. We are temples of the living Triune God. As Jesus promised,

"Whoever loves me will keep my word, and my Father will love him, and we will come to him and make our dwelling with him." John 14:23

In our journey toward a life of everlasting communion with God, we pray with Blessed Elizabeth of the Trinity:

"O my God, Trinity, whom I adore, help me to forget myself entirely that I may be established in You. . . . may each minute carry me further into the depth of your mystery!"

For Reflection

How do I relate and pray to each Person of the Holy Trinity?

How has my faith in and awareness of the Holy Trinity dwelling within me shaped my life?

Teacher to Teacher

The Mystery of Who God Is

We spend a lifetime getting to know ourselves and those we love. Slowly and often cautiously we reveal our true selves to others. Such revelation is done with trust and from the desire to grow in friendship and intimacy with someone. God has revealed his true identity to us—an identity we could never have known without his revealing it. He is One God in Three Divine Persons—God the Father, God the Son, and God the Holy Spirit. God has revealed his true identity out of his desire that we come to know and love him, and live in communion and intimacy with him not for a few years but forever.

Expressing Faith in the Trinity

Seven- and eight-year-olds are concrete thinkers. Keep this in mind during this session on the Holy Trinity. For example, include prayers to the Father, to his Son, Jesus, and to the Holy Spirit as you meet throughout the year. When presenting the Scripture passages, especially the Gospel account of the Annunciation and Jesus' promise to send the Holy Spirit, make reference to the Father, Son, and Holy Spirit. Use concrete images such as a triangle, shamrock, or other objects with three equal parts to help them grasp the concept of three-in-one.

The Church Teaches ...

"The Christian message is inherently Trinitarian because its source is the incarnate Word of the Father, Jesus Christ, who speaks to the world through his Holy Spirit" (*National Directory for Catechesis,* 25B).

This is why the mystery of the Trinity is introduced early, helping the students to center themselves in a Trinitarian faith.

Further Reading and Reflection

For more related teachings of the Church, see the *Catechism of the Catholic Church,* 232–260; and the *United States Catholic Catechism for Adults,* pages 50–53.

Teacher Prayer

Father, help me share your love for the students with them. Jesus, be my guide as I use your example to teach about our Father. Holy Spirit, be my inspiration as I help these little ones know and live their faith. Amen.

Lesson Planner

Chapter 3   The Holy Trinity

Focus To learn that God is one in Three Divine Persons

LESSON PART	PROCESS	MATERIALS and RESOURCES
DAY 1 EXPLORE **Focus** To explore the Church's universal faith in the Holy Trinity **Pages 35–37**	▶ Proclaim and discuss John 14:25–26 (Jesus' promise to send the Holy Spirit). ▶ Review the Sign of the Cross. **Disciple Power:** Wonder **Activity:** Draw self making Sign of the Cross and learn the prayer in a new language.	Bible Pencils or pens Crayons or markers **Additional Activities Booklet:** Activity 3a or see *BeMyDisciples*.com
DAY 2 DISCOVER **Focus** To discover what Jesus told us about who God is **Pages 38–39**	▶ Explore the Church belief in the Holy Trinity, ▶ Discover that human beings have a body and a soul. ▶ Recognize that Jesus invites us to call God Father/Abba/Daddy. **Faith Vocabulary:** Holy Trinity, soul **Catholics Believe:** Sign of the Cross **Activity:** Discover a prayer to God the Father.	Pencils or pens Crayons or markers **Enriching the Lesson:** Teacher Guide, page 93 Illustrating the Holy Trinity Celebrating the Trinity with Music **Additional Activities Booklet:** Activity 3b or see *BeMyDisciples*.com
DAY 3 DISCOVER **Focus** To discover that Jesus is the Second Person of the Holy Trinity, true God and true man. **Pages 40–41**	▶ Discover that Jesus is the Son of God who became one of us. ▶ Learn Jesus' Great Commandment of love. **Faith Vocabulary:** Son of God **Faith-Filled People:** Saint Patrick **Activity:** Sign Jesus' message of love. **Scripture Story:** The Great Commandment (Matthew 22:37, 39).	Bible Pencils or pens **Enriching the Lesson:** Teacher Guide, page 93 Role-playing Living as Children of God
DAY 4 DECIDE **Focus** To discover what the Holy Spirit teaches us about God and to decide a way to tell others about the Holy Trinity **Page 42–43**	▶ Learn that God the Holy Spirit, given at Baptism, is with us always. ▶ Discover how Holy Spirit helps us live as God's children and Jesus' disciples. **Scripture:** The promise of the Holy Spirit (Luke 11:13). **Activity:** Write on each shamrock leaf how you can tell others about the Holy Trinity. **My Faith Choice:** Choose how to tell others about the Holy Trinity. **Pray:** "Thank you, Holy Spirit."	Bible Pencils or pens Crayons or markers
DAY 5 CONCLUDE **Focus** To join in a ritual prayer– the Sign of the Cross **Pages 44–46**	▶ **REVIEW** Review concepts: Recall, Review, and Share. ▶ **PRAY** The Sign of the Cross ▶ **PREVIEW** the With My Family page and the theme of the next chapter.	Bible Bowl of water Grade 2 Music CD **Assessment Tools Booklet:** Assessments 3a and 3b

Assign online Chapter Review and interactive Chapter Test at **BeMyDisciples.com**

80 Grade 2

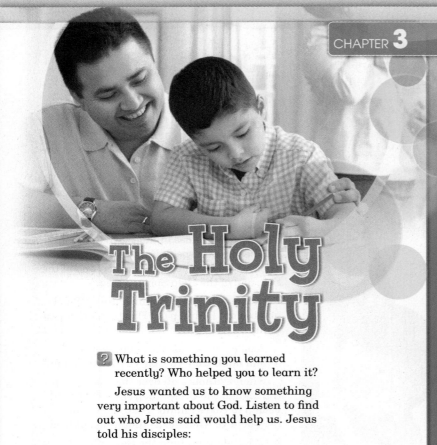

CHAPTER **3**

The Holy Trinity

? What is something you learned recently? Who helped you to learn it?

Jesus wanted us to know something very important about God. Listen to find out who Jesus said would help us. Jesus told his disciples:

"I will ask the Father to send you the Holy Spirit. He will always be with you as your helper and teacher."   BASED ON JOHN 14:25–26

? What did Jesus tell us about God?

35

Pray

▶ Welcome the students warmly. Help them quiet themselves for prayer.

▶ Reverently pray the Sign of the Cross together.

▶ Then pray, "Lord, help us to learn more about you from this lesson. Amen."

▶ Read aloud the two opening questions. Ask for responses. *(Accept all replies.)*

Reflect

▶ Ask one of the students to read aloud the introduction to the Scripture passage. Afterward, call on another student to read the passage.

▶ Observe a moment of reverent silence.

▶ Ask the follow-up question. Remind the students that Jesus told us that God is Father, Son, and Holy Spirit.

▶ Conclude by leading the class in the Sign of the Cross.

Focus

Invite the students to turn the page to discover a prayer that helps us know more about who God is.

HUMAN METHODOLOGIES

Learning by Discipleship. The *National Directory for Catechesis* states, "Discipleship is . . . centered on the person of Jesus Christ and the kingdom he proclaims" **(NDC, 29B)**. Reinforce learning about the Holy Trinity in this chapter by giving the students shamrock stickers to wear on their shirts or blouses. Encourage them to be disciples by telling one other person why they are wearing the shamrock and how it is a symbol of the Holy Trinity.

Introduce

▶ Present the text of Many Languages on page 36. If there are students in the class who speak Spanish or Vietnamese, have them pray the words of the Sign of the Cross aloud when you come to those parts of the text.

▶ Read aloud the paragraph at the top of page 37. Briefly review with the students the correct way to pray the Sign of the Cross.

▶ Ask the follow-up question on page 36. *(It shows that we believe what Jesus taught about God—that God is Father, Son, and Holy Spirit.)*

▶ Talk with the students about the times when they and their families pray the Sign of the Cross. Encourage them to pray the Sign of the Cross every day. Then follow-up with the question on page 37.

Disciple Power

Wonder

Wonder is a Gift of the Holy Spirit. It helps us see God's greatness. Wonder helps us to discover more about God. It then moves us to praise him.

The Church Follows Jesus

Many Languages!

People all around the world belong to the Catholic Church. People read the Bible and listen to the words of Jesus in their own languages. They talk with God in prayer in their own languages.

Catholics all over the world pray the prayers of the Mass in their own languages, too. People who speak English begin the Mass, "In the name of the Father, and of the Son, and of the Holy Spirit. Amen."

People who speak Spanish pray, "En el nombre del Padre, y del Hijo, y del Espíritu Santo. Amen."

People who speak Vietnamese pray, "Nhan danh Cha Va Con Va Thanh. Than."

When Catholics all over the world pray the Sign of the Cross, they show that they belong to God's family. They show that they believe what Jesus taught about God.

? What does praying the Sign of the Cross show us?

36

DISCIPLE POWER

Wonder. Wonder is one of the seven Gifts of the Holy Spirit. Traditionally, this gift is called Fear of the Lord. It is also described as "awe." Explain that God sees and hears all that we see and do. Emphasize that we can use all our words and actions to tell God we love him. Tell the class that sharing a toy, helping a classmate, or obeying our parents are just a few of the ways we can show our wonder at God's love. Reinforce that these actions give praise to God, Jesus, and the Holy Spirit. Ask your second graders to offer other examples.

As we say the words of the prayer, we bless ourselves. We touch our forehead, our shoulders, and our chest over our heart. We remember that we are baptized. We show that we belong to God's family.

? When do you pray the Sign of the Cross?

Activity

Praying the Sign of the Cross

Draw yourself making the Sign of the Cross. Then learn to pray the Sign of the Cross in a different language. Repeat the words below with your class. Share the prayer with your family.

In the name of the Father,	and of the Son,	and of the Holy Spirit. Amen.
En el nombre del Padre,	y del Hijo,	y del Espíritu Santo. Amen.
Nhan danh Cha	Va Con,	Va Thanh. Than.

(37)

Reinforce

▶ Share how wonderful it is that Jesus told us that God is Father, Son, and Spirit.

▶ Present Disciple Power on page 36 to the class. Then, reinforce by leading them in song, using the melody of "If You're Happy and You Know It." Simply change the words to "If you feel wonder and you know it,
. . . clap your hands!
. . . shout hooray!
. . . give God praise!" and so on.

Connect

▶ Read aloud the activity directions. Give the students time to complete their drawings. Check to see that they have illustrated the correct procedure for praying the Sign of the Cross.

▶ Offer help to students learning to pray the Sign of the Cross in a new language. Encourage them to practice and pray it every day.

Pray

Conclude the lesson by reverently praying the Sign of the Cross.

TEACHING TIP

Presenting Mystery. When talking about the Holy Trinity, keep in mind that the Triune God is not a problem to be solved—*How can God be Three-in-One?*—but rather a mystery to be entered into. It is nigh to impossible to wrap our minds around the notion of the Trinity, but then a God small enough to fit the mind is not large enough to fit the heart. As you present the mystery of the Trinity to the class, realize that the goal is not so much to produce understanding as it is to engender wonder, that delightful virtue that leads us to awe and praise. Saint Augustine put it this way: "Seek not to understand that you may believe, but believe that you may understand." Put another way, we adore what we cannot quite contain, and that is just fine.

Pray

Invite the students to quiet themselves for prayer. Lead them in reverently praying the Sign of the Cross in one or more of the languages presented in the previous lesson.

Teach

▶ Have a volunteer read aloud the meaning of the Faith Words term *Holy Trinity*.

▶ Ask the students how they showed their belief in the Holy Trinity at the beginning of class. (*We showed our belief by praying the Sign of the Cross*)

▶ Tell them to listen for this term as you read aloud the introductory paragraph of One God.

▶ Remind the class that the Holy Trinity is a wonderful mystery of faith that we cannot fully understand. We believe it because God has revealed it.

▶ Ask volunteers to read the next two paragraphs. Ask the Faith Focus question. (*Jesus told us who God is.*)

▶ Go on to read aloud the two paragraphs at the top of page 39.

▶ Invite the students to tell what name they call their fathers. Briefly discuss the good things fathers do for us.

Faith Focus
Who is the Third Person of the Holy Trinity?

Faith Words
Holy Trinity
The Holy Trinity is One God in Three Divine Persons—God the Father, God the Son, and God the Holy Spirit.

soul
Our soul is that part of us that lives forever.

One God

Jesus told us who God is. There is only one God who is God the Father, God the Son, and God the Holy Spirit. We call the One God in Three Persons the **Holy Trinity.** The word *trinity* means "three in one."

God the Father

In the Apostles' Creed, Christians around the world pray, "I believe in God, the Father almighty, Creator of heaven and earth." God the Father is the First Person of the Holy Trinity.

God the Father created everyone and everything out of love. He created all people in his image and likeness. He created each person with a body and a **soul.** The soul is that part of each person that lives forever.

? Who is the Holy Trinity?

38

THE TASKS OF CATECHESIS

Promoting Knowledge of the Faith. As humans, we cannot fathom the mystery of the Holy Trinity. Instead, the Church tells us to revere this great mystery. Explain to your second graders that even though we can never understand how it is possible for the One God to be Three Persons, we have faith in this Revelation. Review the definition for faith that you taught in Chapter 2. As you talk to the students about the mystery of the Holy Trinity, relate it to the gift of wonder and encourage the students to praise God the Father, God the Son, and God the Holy Spirit.

Jesus used the word "Abba" when he prayed to God the Father. The word *Abba* is the word for "father" in the language Jesus spoke. "Abba" means "daddy" in English, "papi" in Spanish, and "ba" in Vietnamese.

Jesus wanted us to know that God the Father loves us and cares for us. He created us to be happy with him now and forever in Heaven.

? What is one way that you can thank God for loving you?

Catholics Believe

Sign of the Cross

We can pray the Sign of the Cross in different ways. Before we listen to the Gospel, we make a small Sign of the Cross on our foreheads, on our lips, and over our hearts.

Activity

Thanking God the Father

We listen to God and thank him. Circle the second letter. Then circle every other letter to find a prayer to God the Father.

L A V B K B W A Q F J A F T L H X E S R
H T L H U A S N L K R Y C O D U G F K
O G R L Y Q O A U T R Z L F O H V K E

ABBA, FATHER, THANK YOU

FOR YOUR LOVE.

TEACHING TIP

Trinity Bracelets. Have the students make a tangible reminder of the Mystery of the Holy Trinity.

▶ Give each student three pieces of different-colored string or yarn, equal in length (about 8″ long). Note: Having three *different* colors of string/yarn illustrates how each strand complements the other two and is part of the whole.

▶ Show the students how to braid the strings.

▶ As the students work, help them see that the *three* strings must be intertwined to produce *one* bracelet. Similarly, the *One* God is made up of *Three* Divine Persons.

▶ Once the students finish braiding, help them tie off the ends to complete their bracelets, and allow them to wear their creations in class.

Reinforce

▶ Ask the follow-up question on page 38.

▶ Point out the term *soul* in Faith Words. Invite volunteers to share what they learned about the term from the text.

▶ Have the students make word cards for *Holy Trinity* and *soul*.

Connect

▶ Call attention to Catholics Believe. Have the class read the section silently. Tell the students we pray the Sign of the Cross this way at Mass before we listen to the Gospel reading. Remind the students that we pray in the name of the Father, Son, and the Holy Spirit, the Third Person of the Trinity.

▶ Ask the students the follow-up question on page 39 and then lead them into the activity.

▶ Read the directions to the activity Thanking God the Father. Give the students time to uncover the hidden prayer.

▶ When the students finish, write the prayer on the board. *(Abba, Father, thank you for your love.)*

Pray

▶ Invite the students to quiet themselves for prayer.

▶ Remind them that the First Person of the Holy Trinity is their loving Father.

▶ Have the students stand and pray the prayer which they uncovered in the activity and which you wrote on the board.

▶ Conclude by praying the Sign of the Cross.

Key Concept

Jesus, the Son of God, is the Second Person of the Holy Trinity.

Pray

Invite the students to quiet themselves for prayer. Lead them in the Glory Be.

Teach

▶ Read the Faith Focus question aloud and ask for possible answers. Tell the students that today they will learn about the Second Person of the Holy Trinity.

▶ Tell the students some things about a friend of yours. Explain that they now know these things because you told them.

▶ Explain that Jesus does the very same thing. He tells us about God, the Holy Trinity.

▶ Ask the students to listen for who Jesus is and what he told us as you read God the Son aloud to them.

▶ Ask the students to respond to the reading's follow-up question on page 40. *(Jesus is the only Son of God, was born of the Virgin Mary, and became man.)*

▶ Call attention to the term *Son of God* in Faith Words. Have the students read the term aloud as a class and then make a word card for it.

▶ Point out Faith-Filled People. Tell the class about Saint Patrick, who also taught about the Holy Trinity.

Faith Focus
Who is the Second Person of the Holy Trinity?

Faith Words
Son of God
Jesus Christ is the Son of God who became one of us. He is the Second Divine Person of the Holy Trinity.

God the Son

In the Apostles' Creed, we pray that we "believe in Jesus Christ, his only Son, our Lord." The word *Lord* means "God." Jesus is the **Son of God** who became one of us. God the Son is the Second Person of the Holy Trinity.

God the Father loves us very much. He wanted us to know more about him. So he sent his Son to become one of us and to live with us.

In the Apostles' Creed, we also pray that we believe Jesus was "born of the Virgin Mary." We believe that Jesus is both true God and true man. Jesus is the only Son of God the Father. Jesus is also the Son of the Virgin Mary.

 What do we pray about Jesus in the Apostles' Creed?

40

FAITH-FILLED PEOPLE

Saint Patrick (389–461). As a young boy Patrick was taken from his father's farm in Britain and made a slave in Ireland. There he tended sheep and was terribly isolated and lonely. His loneliness led him to a deep experience of prayer. Patrick finally escaped from slavery and returned to Britain. He became a priest and returned to Ireland as a missionary. He traveled throughout Ireland and introduced thousands of Irish people to Christianity. For more information on Saint Patrick, go to the Saints Resource at www.BeMyDisciples.com.

Jesus told us to call God our Father. The Bible tells us we are children of God. We are to live as children of God. Jesus taught us how to do this. He said,

"You shall love the Lord your God, with all your heart, . . .
You shall love your neighbor as yourself."

MATTHEW 22:37, 39

❓ How do you show that you love God and others?

Faith-Filled People

Saint Patrick

Patrick was a bishop. He taught people about the Holy Trinity. Patrick showed people a shamrock as a symbol of the Holy Trinity. A shamrock is a plant that has three leaves connected to one stem.

Activity

Sign Jesus' Message

Sign this message for your family and friends!

Love   God   with

all   your   heart.

(41)

PRAYING TIP

"Trinity Candle." Consider using a three-wicked candle when you pray with the class. Point out how all three wicks are separate, each giving off its own light and heat. At the same time, note that all three wicks constitute but one candle. The students should quickly be able to see how the three wicks signify the Father, Son, and Holy Spirit, all the while being just one candle. Likewise, point out how each wick contributes to the candle's overall goal—to give off light and heat.

Reinforce

▶ Review learning with these or similar questions:

— Who is the Second Person of the Holy Trinity? *(Jesus, God the Son)*

— What do we believe about Jesus, Second Person of the Holy Trinity? *(He is true God and true man.)*

— What did Jesus tell us to do to live as children of God? *("Love God with all your heart. Love other people as much as you love yourself.")*

▶ Read the first paragraph at the top of page 41. Then have the class read the Scripture from Matthew with you.

▶ Discuss the follow-up question on page 41.

Connect

▶ Introduce the activity. Tell the class that the pictures across the bottom of the page show a child communicating in American Sign Language (ASL).

▶ Teach the students to sign Jesus' message. Have them sign it to a partner at least twice.

▶ Encourage them to share and sign Jesus' message for their families.

Pray

Have the students quiet themselves for prayer. Invite them to echo the following after you:

God the Holy Trinity,/
we love you with all our hearts,/
our minds,/ and bodies,/
Help us to tell others about you/
and about the wonder of your
    love for us./
Amen.

> **Key Concept**
> The Holy Spirit is the Third Person of the Holy Trinity.

Pray

Gather the students for prayer. Pray the following as an echo prayer:

> Holy Spirit, / strengthen us / so we may come to know you, / God the Father, and God the Son better. / Amen.

Teach

▶ Remind the class that God the Father sent his only Son, the Second Person of the Holy Trinity, to be one of us. Jesus is the Son of God who became one of us.

▶ Read aloud the Faith Focus question and ask the students to silently think about how they might answer it.

▶ Ask the students to underline the words *Holy Spirit* every place they see it on the page as you read aloud the section titled God the Holy Spirit.

Reinforce

Have the students join with a partner and compare their underlining.

Connect

▶ Ask volunteers to read the sentences in which they have underlined the words *Holy Spirit*.

▶ Read the follow-up question aloud. List the students' responses on the board. (*The Holy Spirit helps us [1] know, love, and serve God better; [2] live as children of God; and [3] live as disciples of Jesus.*)

Faith Focus
Who is the Third Person of the Holy Trinity?

God the Holy Spirit

In the Apostles' Creed we pray, "I believe in the Holy Spirit." God the Holy Spirit is the Third Person of the Holy Trinity.

Jesus told us about the Holy Spirit. He said to his disciples,

> "The Father in heaven will send you the Holy Spirit."
>
> BASED ON LUKE 11:13

At Baptism the priest or deacon baptizes in the name of the Father, and of the Son, and of the Holy Spirit. This shows that we share in the life of the Holy Trinity.

We first receive the gift of the Holy Spirit at Baptism. The Holy Spirit is always with us. He helps us to know and to love and to serve God better. The Holy Spirit helps us to live as children of God and disciples of Jesus.

❓ What are three things the Holy Spirit helps us do?

42

TEACHING TIP

Get Moving. It is difficult for the average second grade student to sit more than 15 to 20 minutes for one activity. As you lead the class in a lesson, incorporate movement in simple ways. When you read a story or read from the Scriptures, have the students gather near you. When you go to pray, move to the classroom prayer center or to a devotional or other area set aside for prayer in the school. Have the students move when they pair up or form small groups. Or simply have them stand and stretch. Moving around may take a little time, but it is worth the effort. The students will often work better because of it.

I Follow Jesus

God the Holy Spirit gives you the gift of wonder. The gift of wonder helps you want to know God more. The more you know about God, the more you can tell others about God.

Activity

Telling Others About the Holy Trinity

On each leaf of the shamrock, draw or write one thing you can tell others about the Holy Trinity.

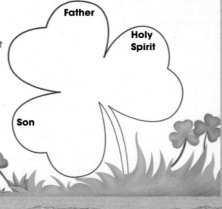

Father

Holy Spirit

Son

My Faith Choice

I will tell other people about the Holy Trinity this week. I will

_____

_____

 Pray, "Thank you, Holy Spirit, for the gift of wonder. Thank you for helping me to learn about you. Amen."

43

Reinforce

▶ Remind the class that God wants everyone to know who he is. Jesus, the Son of God, told us that there is One God in Three Divine Persons—God the Father, God the Son, and God the Holy Spirit. God is the Holy Trinity.

▶ Read aloud the introductory paragraph.

▶ Remind the class about Saint Patrick and the shamrock.

Respond

Explain the activity and have the students complete it. Invite volunteers to share what they have drawn or written.

Choose

▶ Present My Faith Choice. Help the students brainstorm ideas to complete their faith choices.

▶ Encourage the students to follow up on what they have decided in the week ahead.

Pray

Gather the students in the prayer center. Lead them in praying the prayer to the Holy Spirit at the bottom of the page. Conclude by praying the Sign of the Cross.

TEACHING TIP

Providing Visuals. Many students have never seen an actual shamrock. Shamrock plants are readily available in supermarkets or you or a friend may have one at home. If possible, bring one in for the class to see. Place it on your prayer table during today's lesson.

Pray

Lead the class in reverently praying the Sign of the Cross.

Recall

▶ Create three overlapping images on the board, such as triangles. Write the words *Holy Trinity* above the images. Write *Father, Son,* and *Holy Spirit* in each of the three spaces.

▶ Ask the students to help you label the images properly as the First, Second, and Third Persons of the Holy Trinity.

▶ Call on volunteers to read aloud each point in the To Help You Remember section.

▶ Explain the directions for the sentence completion activity. When the students finish, check responses.

▶ Introduce the true/not true activity. Have the students work in pairs, and then share their responses with another pair of students.

Reflect

Have the students complete the sentence, *"How do you show your love for God?"*

Share

▶ Invite the students to share responses with a partner and with their families.

▶ Ask representatives from each group to share what was discussed with the entire class.

▶ **TO HELP YOU REMEMBER**

1. God is the Holy Trinity. God the Father is the First Person of the Holy Trinity.
2. God the Son is the Second Person of the Holy Trinity.
3. God the Holy Spirit is the Third Person of the Holy Trinity.

Chapter Review

Recall

Complete the sentences. Use the words in the word box.

Lord	One	Three	Trinity

1. We believe in the Holy ____Trinity____.

2. There is ____One____ God in ____Three____ Divine Persons.

3. The word ____Lord____ means God.

Color the 😊 if the sentence is true.
Color the ☹ if the sentence is not true.

4. God creates each person with a body and a soul.
5. God creates us to be happy with him now and in Heaven.
6. Jesus is the Son of God. He is the Third Person of the Holy Trinity.
7. The Holy Spirit helps us know and love God better.

Reflect

How do you show your love for God?

_____

Share Explain to a classmate how the Holy Spirit helps us.

(44)

TEACHING TIP

Partners Students' feelings can be easily hurt when it comes to choosing partners. Instead of allowing them to choose a partner, place the students' names on index cards and shuffle them. At the beginning of each month have the students discover the partners whom they will work with that month by selecting cards. At the beginning of each of the following months, reshuffle the cards and have the students select new partners. This will give students the opportunity to have many different partners throughout the year.

The Sign of the Cross

A ritual uses words, gestures, or actions to help us pray.
Pray now using a ritual action.

Leader Come forward one at a time. Bow before the Bible. Trace a cross on your forehead, your lips, and over your heart.

All *(Come forward and sign yourself.)*

Leader Loving God, you are Father.

All **Thank you for creating us.**

Leader You are Son.

All **Thank you for coming among us.**

Leader You are Holy Spirit.

All **Thank you for being always with us.**

Leader Loving God, you are Father, Son, and Holy Spirit.

All **Three in one!**

Leader We praise you, God, and mark ourselves as your children.

All *(Pray the Sign of the Cross in the language you choose.)*

45

LITURGY TIP

Demonstrate Some students may be frightened or uncomfortable with the idea that you are going to sign them. It may be helpful to ask for a volunteer and demonstrate for the class exactly what is going to happen when they are blessed. If students are still uncomfortable, show them how to sign themselves. Always respect your students' wishes.

Pray

▶ Prepare the class for prayer by reading aloud the introductory paragraph. Demonstrate several prayer-gestures for the students, for example, genuflecting, kneeling, folding one's hands, and so on.

▶ Explain the order of prayer and draw attention to the responses. Pay particular attention to the directive calling the students to conclude the prayer by praying the Sign of the Cross in a language of their choosing. Explain that it is all right to have different languages spoken at the same time.

▶ See to it that you have a bowl of water available.

▶ Gather the students in the prayer center and lead them in the prayer The Sign of the Cross.

Preview

▶ Have the students carefully tear out pages 45 and 46 along the perforation.

▶ Encourage the students to share these pages with their families, and to complete the activities together.

▶ If they did not complete the review activity on page 44 by the end of the session, emphasize that they can complete it with their families at home.

▶ Point out the title and theme of the next lesson to the students.

Visit BeMyDisciples.com

▶ Take time with the students to explore the many activities and resources available at the *Be My Disciples* Web site.

▶ Encourage them to join with their families to discover the many resources available at the Web site.

Before Moving On ...

As you finish today's lesson, reflect on the following question before moving on to the next chapter.

Which students seem to work especially well together?

With My Family

This Week . . .

In Chapter 3, "The Holy Trinity," your child learned:

▶ God is the Holy Trinity. The mystery of the Holy Trinity is the mystery of One God in Three Divine Persons: Father, Son, and Holy Spirit.

▶ We could never have come to know this wonderful truth about the identity of God on our own. We only know this about God because he has revealed this about himself in Jesus Christ.

▶ The Church's belief in the mystery of the Holy Trinity is at the heart of the Church's living faith.

▶ Wonder, one of the seven Gifts of the Holy Spirit, urges us to come to know and praise God for who he is.

For more about related teachings of the Church, see the *Catechism of the Catholic Church*, 232–260, and the *United States Catholic Catechism for Adults*, pages 51–53.

■ Sharing God's Word

Read together John 14:26, the promise of Jesus that the Holy Spirit would come to his disciples. Talk about how wonderful it is that Jesus revealed that there is one God who is Father, Son, and Holy Spirit.

■ Living as Disciples

The Christian home and family is a school of discipleship. Choose one of the following activities to do as a family, or design a similar activity of your own.

▶ Awaken your child's awareness of the gift of wonder. Share both your curiosity and your delight in the mystery of God manifested in the world around you. Point out the many elements of God's creation that help you come to know more about him.

▶ Create a Holy Trinity banner. Display it at the entrance to your home. Use it as a reminder that God the Holy Trinity dwells in your home with your family.

■ Our Spiritual Journey

Praying a doxology is an ancient tradition of the Church. A doxology is a prayer giving praise and honor to God. Remind one another that all you say and do is to give glory to God. Pray the Glory Be regularly together with your child.

Glory be to the Father
and to the Son
and to the Holy Spirit,
as it was in the beginning
is now, and ever shall be
world without end. Amen.

For more ideas on ways your family can live as disciples of Jesus, visit **BeMyDisciples.com**

46

PARTNERING WITH PARENTS

Blessings. E-mail a note to parents or significant adult family members to explain that by virtue of their own Baptism, they have the right and privilege of imparting blessings. Explain that the blessings they give might include such ritual actions as sprinkling with water or tracing the cross on the person(s) being blessed. Let the parents know that this is a very special ritual for their children. Encourage the parents to bless their children when they put them to bed at night, send them off to school in the morning, or share in an activity outside the home during the day. As they bless their child, urge them to use their own words. For example, "May God be with you today." Model this ritual by blessing the students individually as they leave your classroom.

Enriching the Lesson

Illustrating the Holy Trinity

Purpose

To reinforce learning the Three Persons of the Holy Trinity as they are named in the Sign of the Cross (taught on pages 36 and 37)

Directions

▶ Provide the students with heavy paper that you have folded into three sections.

▶ Then have them write *Father* at the top of the first section, *Son* at the top of the middle section, and *Holy Spirit* at the top of the third section.

▶ Challenge the students to write as many things as they can remember about each of the Three Persons of the Trinity.

▶ Have the students decorate their lists with crayons or markers.

▶ Invite the students to take their lists home and share them with their families.

Materials

construction paper

crayons or markers

Role-playing Living As Children of God

Purpose

To reinforce making choices to live as children of God (taught on page 41)

Directions

▶ Brainstorm with the students ways we show we are living as children of God.

▶ In small groups, have the students create a scenario showing second graders living as children of God.

▶ Have the groups present their role plays and have the other students give them a silent cheer for their good work, which is another way of living as children of God.

Materials

Celebrating the Trinity with Music

Purpose

To reinforce expressing faith in the Holy Trinity using music

Directions

▶ Distribute copies of the song, or write the lyrics on the board.
▶ Practice saying the lyrics with the students and singing them to the tune of "Row, Row, Row Your Boat" to help the students recall some of the things they have learned about the Holy Trinity and to celebrate their faith in song.

> One, two, three Persons,
> In the Trinity.
> Father, Son, and Spirit
> God is one-in-three.
> God is our Father,
> Jesus is his Son,
> God the Holy Spirit,
> God is three-in-one.

▶ Sing the song several times.

▶ Invite the students to sing the song for their family.

Materials

copies of the song—one for each student to bring home to their families

God, Our Father

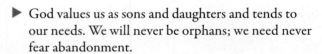

BACKGROUND

Love God with Your Whole Heart

Belief in God is the starting point of faith. Everything in our lives as Christians, as disciples of the Incarnate Son of God, refers back to the simple words of faith, "I believe in God." All the articles in the Apostles' Creed, all the works and wonders of Jesus Christ, the creation, and the progress of humanity speak of God.

God Who Is Abba, Father

The Old Testament reads like a record book of God's involvement with his people. Jesus most fully reveals God, inviting us to place our faith, hope, and love for God above all else. We are not invited to believe and love a God who is unfeeling, capricious, or distant. We are invited to believe in God, who is Abba, our loving, caring, ever-present, unconditionally merciful Father.

The Bible is a moving testimony to God the Father, who lavishes upon us his kindness, grace, goodness, and unending love. The works of God in Sacred Scripture reveal that he is always faithful and true, reliable and loyal. If we turn to him, we will not be disappointed. His love will never leave us (see Isaiah 54:10).

Living in Communion with God

Our faith in a living God, in whose presence we live and who never abandons us even when we turn our back on his love, is the source of deep blessing. It the source of blessing that shares with us the divine gift of peace.

There are many dimensions to this blessing. Here are a few:

▶ In a rapidly changing world, constantly defying us to adapt, there is one constant: God, "with whom there is no alteration or shadow caused by change" (James 1:17). When everything else is taken from us, God will always remain.

▶ God values us as sons and daughters and tends to our needs. We will never be orphans; we need never fear abandonment.

▶ God always guides everything back to his will. "God cares for all, from the least things to the great events of the world and its history" (CCC 303).

▶ The greatness and goodness of God are inexhaustible. Our quest for God can be a source of endless discovery and delight.

▶ Since everything we are and have comes from God, we can transform our lives into an act of thanksgiving.

▶ God created all people in his image and likeness. Thus, we can look upon our neighbors and see their true dignity and worth.

We live in sacred space. We learn in sacred space. Jesus reminds and promises, "For wherever two or three are gathered in my name, I am there among them" (Matthew 18:20).

For Reflection

How is God working in my life?

When do I give my whole heart to God? What are the consequences?

Teacher to Teacher

Awe and Wonder

Seven- and eight-year-olds are still very much in awe of God's creation. The beauty of creation stimulates the religious imagination for children. Be sure to nurture the wonderful curiosity of these young people. Encourage them to observe their world more clearly, see the beauty of creation, and give thanks and praise to God.

Images for God

Another thing to remember is that children this age often find images a wonderful aid in learning. The following is one way to help convey the message of God the Father's unconditional love for them. Have the students imagine all of the people in their lives who love and care for them. Have them imagine all these people rolled up into one. Tell them that all these people are a small sign of God the Father's love for them.

The Church Teaches...

"(Catechesis) seeks to bring about a conversion to Christ that leads to a profession of faith in the Triune God and to a genuine personal surrender to him" (*National Directory for Catechesis*, 28B).

As you interact with the students during your sessions with them, be aware that they come to know Jesus through the experience of being loved and loving others. The source of this love comes from God the Father.

Further Reading and Reflection

For more related teachings of the Church, see the *Catechism of the Catholic Church*, 268–274, 279–314, 325–327, and 337–349; and the *United States Catholic Catechism for Adults*, pages 53–56.

Teacher Prayer

Father,
sometimes in the hurrying of
* my days,*
I forget to notice the wonders
with which you have surrounded me.
Awaken once again in me
that sense of wonder and awe
that I possessed as a child.
Amen.

Lesson Planner

Chapter 4   God, Our Father

Focus To learn that God is Creator of all

LESSON PART	PROCESS	MATERIALS and RESOURCES
DAY 1 EXPLORE Focus **To explore how we respond to God's love by honoring his creation** **Pages** 47–49	▶ Proclaim and discuss 1 John 3:1. (We are God's children.) ▶ Share the story about students honoring God through serving others. **Disciple Power:** Honor **Activity:** Write words about creation and draw yourself caring for creation.	Bible Pencils or pens Crayons or markers
DAY 2 DISCOVER Focus **To discover that God is our Father and Creator** **Pages** 50–51	▶ Learn what it means to call God Father and Creator. **Scripture Story:** Creation (Genesis 1) **Faith Words:** Creator **Catholics Believe:** The Lord's Prayer **Activity:** Create a creation rebus.	Pencils or pens **Enriching the Lesson:** Teacher Guide, page 109 Using Gestures in Storytelling Choosing a Nature Project **Literature Connection:** *Old Turtle* **Additional Activities Booklet:** Activity 4a or see *BeMyDisciples*.com
DAY 3 DISCOVER Focus **To discover that God has the power to do everything** **Pages** 52–53	▶ Discover why God is almighty. **Scripture:** God is good, loving, and caring (Psalm 145:9) and God is almighty (Psalm 89:9). **Faith Words:** almighty **Faith-Filled People:** Saint Bonaventure **Activity:** Word search of words that tell about God.	Bible Pencils or pens **Additional Activities Booklet:** Activity 4b or see *BeMyDisciples*.com
DAY 4 DECIDE Focus **To discover why we call God our Father and to decide on a way to honor God by caring for creation** **Pages** 54–55	▶ Learn that Jesus taught us that God his Father is our Father, too. ▶ Discover that Jesus taught us to pray the Our Father. **Activity:** Show that you are proud to be children of God. **My Faith Choice:** Tell how I will honor God this week. **Pray:** Ask the Holy Spirit for help in honoring God.	Bible Pencils or pens Crayons or markers **Enriching the Lesson:** Teacher Edition, page 109 Choosing a Nature Project
DAY 5 CONCLUDE Focus **To pray the prayer that Jesus taught us** **Pages** 56–58	▶ **REVIEW** Review concepts: Recall, Reflect, and Share. ▶ **PRAY** The Lord's Prayer ▶ **PREVIEW** the With My Family page and the theme of the next chapter.	Bible Grade 2 Music CD **Assessment Tools Booklet:** Assessments 4a and 4b

Assign online Chapter Review and interactive Chapter Test at **BeMyDisciples.com**

CHAPTER **4**

God, Our Father

[?] What are some of the things parents do to show their love for their children?

Listen to what Saint John wrote about God the Father.

God our Father loves us with a wonderful love! We are so glad to be his children.

BASED ON 1 JOHN 3:1

[?] What are some ways God the Father shows his wonderful love for you?

(47)

Pray

▶ Welcome the students warmly.

▶ Invite them to quiet themselves for prayer.

▶ Pray the Sign of the Cross together.

▶ Have the students take turns thanking God for showing love to them.

▶ Call for responses to the opening question. *(Accept all replies.)*

Reflect

▶ Introduce the passage from 1 John, then read it aloud.

▶ Observe a moment of silence.

▶ Call for responses to the follow-up question. *(Affirm all replies.)*

▶ Have the students end the opening prayer by taking turns thanking God for showing love to them.

Focus

Share with the class that they are going to learn how some children their age honored God the Father for his wonderful love.

LITURGY CONNECTION

Signing Prayer. The more students repeat something, the more it becomes a part of them. Last week they learned American Sign Language signs for "Love God with all your heart." Take a moment before you pray the opening prayer to go over these signs. Then you can make the signing part of your prayer. The more movement and gestures you are able to incorporate into their prayers, the more meaningful they will be to the students.

A good resource is *Religious Signing: A Comprehensive Guide for All Faiths* (Elaine Castello, Ph.D., New York: Bantam Books, 2009).

Introduce

▶ Tell the class that we show our love for God the Father when we take care of creation and share its fruits with other people.

▶ Either tell the class the story of Saint Augustine's school garden in your own words or call on different students to read it to the class.

▶ Afterward, read Disciple Power with the students. Ask them to name other ways they honor God and people.

Reinforce

▶ Ask: How are the children in this story caring for creation and sharing it with others? *(They are helping plants to grow; they are helping to feed hungry people.)*

▶ Ask the students if they have ever worked in a garden. Then divide the class into pairs and let them answer the follow-up question and share the ways that they care for creation.

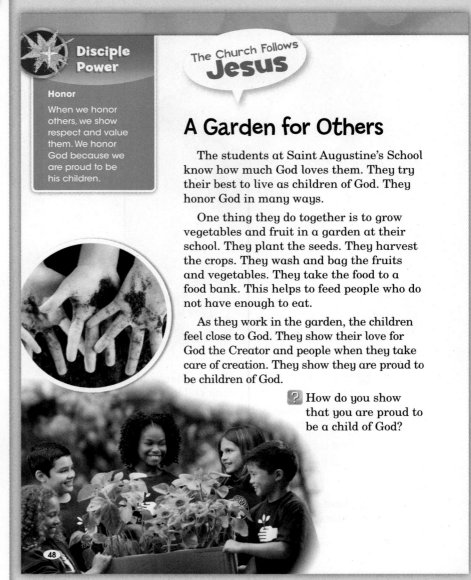

Disciple Power

Honor

When we honor others, we show respect and value them. We honor God because we are proud to be his children.

The Church Follows **Jesus**

A Garden for Others

The students at Saint Augustine's School know how much God loves them. They try their best to live as children of God. They honor God in many ways.

One thing they do together is to grow vegetables and fruit in a garden at their school. They plant the seeds. They harvest the crops. They wash and bag the fruits and vegetables. They take the food to a food bank. This helps to feed people who do not have enough to eat.

As they work in the garden, the children feel close to God. They show their love for God the Creator and people when they take care of creation. They show they are proud to be children of God.

? How do you show that you are proud to be a child of God?

48

DISCIPLE POWER

Honor. Help the students understand how the Saint Augustine Garden Project honored God by drawing a visual summary for them. Draw a timeline on the board. Invite the students to help you mark the key events: planting seeds, harvesting crops, washing the fruits and vegetables, and so forth. This will give your second graders a good image to help recognize the big effect that can come from many small actions that show respect for God's creation. Conclude by inviting the students to name ways they honor and show respect for their parents and siblings.

Activity

Caring for Creation

When the students of St. Augustine's School tend the garden, they are taking care of creation. See the word *CREATION* below. Think of something in creation that begins with each letter. Write the words on the lines. The first one is done for you.

C   clouds

R _____

E _____

A _____

T _____

I _____

O _____

N _____

Draw yourself in this photo caring for creation.

49

TEACHING TIP

Providing Options. If time allows, you may wish to give the class other options as well. For example, you can suggest that they mime how they care for God's creation and invite the class to guess what they are miming. Another option would be to have the students draw the tiniest and biggest things of God's creation they have ever seen. Help them brainstorm their ideas. If time permits, they can mime what they are thinking of for the class to guess. This can be a lot of fun if they choose a gift of creation such as a grain of sand or an amoeba (for "tiniest") or a mountain or a skyscraper (for "biggest").

Connect

▶ Call attention to the activity, Caring for Creation. Invite a volunteer to read the directions aloud.

▶ Work on the activity as a group. Brainstorm things God has made. Point out the first letter *C*, which has been done. Have the class suggest other words beginning with the letter *C*, for example, *cow, cat, corn*. Write the words on the board. Move on to the letter *R*; examples, *robin, rose, raindrop*.

▶ For vowels, consider the following: *A—acorn, ant, alligator, apple; E—elephant, eel, earth, egg; I—ice, insect, ivy, island; O—ocean, ox, orange, owl.* Continue to brainstorm for each letter in the word *creation*.

▶ Tell the students they can choose any of the words on the board to write in the spaces.

▶ Go on to have the students draw themselves in the photo caring for creation. As an alternative, you may have the students write rather than draw about how they care for creation.

Pray

Gather the class for prayer. Have them echo the following:

Loving God, / Creator and Father, / we give you thanks for all your works. / They are wonderful, / wonderful indeed! / Amen.

Key Concept
God alone is the Creator of all things.

Pray

Invite the students to quiet themselves for prayer. Lead them in reverently praying the Sign of the Cross.

Teach

▶ Have a volunteer read Faith Focus aloud. Then go on to read the first paragraph of page 50.

▶ Point out the definition for *Creator* in Faith Words. Then ask the students to reread the first paragraph silently and look for something new that they have learned about the Creator.

▶ Proclaim the Scripture story of creation, based on Genesis 1:1–31.

▶ Ask the students to recall some of the wonderful things God created.

▶ Discuss what creation tells us about God the Creator. *(God made everything out of love. God loves us.)*

▶ Call attention to the follow-up question in the text. Have the students tell what the story of creation says about God. *(He alone is the Creator; he saw that his creation was very good.)*

Faith Focus
Why do we call God, our Father?

Faith Words
Creator
God alone is the Creator. God made everyone and everything out of love and without any help.

God, the Creator

You are getting to know more and more about God. God is the Father and the **Creator.** He made everyone and everything out of love and without any help. He made the creatures we can see and the angels we cannot see.

God tells us that he alone is the Creator. He tells us this in the first story in the Bible.

In the beginning, God created the heavens and the earth. He made the sun, the other stars, and the moon. He made the sky, the earth, and the sea.

God made plants, trees, and flowers. He made all the fish and the birds. He made all the animals and other creatures that live on the land. Then God created people in his image and likeness. God looked at all that he had created. He saw that it was very good.

BASED ON GENESIS 1:1, 7–12, 16, 20–21, 24–25, 27, 31

? Which part of God's creation was made in his image and likeness?

50

CATHOLIC SOCIAL TEACHING

Care for God's Creation. We show our respect for God the Creator by caring for all that he created. Caring for creation is, in fact, a requirement of Christian faith. First of all, we are called by God to show respect for all people, since we are all created in his image. This is the foundation of our human dignity. We are to be stewards of the Earth as well. Christians must measure every choice by the impact it has on human life and on the environment.

Activity

God's Creation

God made everything. Draw pictures for this rebus to retell the creation story.

God made _____. This is good!
(Earth)

God made _____. This is good!
(stars and moon)

God made _____. This is good!
(animals)

God made _____. This is good!
(people)

God looked at everything he had made, and he found it very good.

GENESIS 1:31

Catholics Believe

The Lord's Prayer

The Our Father is the prayer of all Christians. It is called the Our Father because the first words of the prayer are "Our Father." Jesus our Lord gave this prayer to the Church. This is why the Our Father is also called the Lord's Prayer.

51

Reinforce

Ask a volunteer to reread the definition for *Creator* in Faith Words. Have the students create a word card for *Creator*.

Connect

▶ Ask the students which part of God's creation named in the Bible story they are most thankful for.

▶ Have the students examine the photos on pages 50 and 51. Ask volunteers to describe other parts of creation that show that God's creation is good. (*Affirm all appropriate responses.*)

▶ Have the students complete the God's Creation activity by drawing pictures for the rebus. Afterward, call on different students to share what they wrote.

Pray

Point out the Catholics Believe feature about the Lord's Prayer. Tell the students that God is our Father and the Creator. God created everything and everyone because he loves us. We believe in and love God the Father with all our hearts. Then together pray the Our Father. Conclude the prayer with the Sign of the Cross.

TEACHING TIP

Helpful hints A rebus story is told with little pictures as additional elements to the words. These objects or symbols represent syllables or words needed to complete the sentences. Provide clear instructions for the students; emphasize that they are retelling the creation story by drawing pictures. It may be helpful with second graders to go through each line of the Scripture together and point out line by line what types of symbols or drawings they will make for the missing words of the rebus.

> **Key Concept**
> God alone is all-powerful in doing good.

Pray

Gather the students for prayer. Have them echo the following:

> God the Creator, / your love surrounds us / in the beauty of the heavens and Earth. / Help us to rejoice / in your love and care for us. / Amen.

Teach

▶ Invite volunteers to name someone they know who can do many things well.

▶ Read the Faith Focus question and ask volunteers to give possible answers.

▶ Write the words *God the Almighty* on the board. Then have the students look at Faith Words. Read the definition of *almighty* out loud as a class. Have the students make a word card for the term.

▶ Ask the students to follow along as you read the section titled God the Almighty on page 52 to them.

▶ Summarize your reading by telling the students that only God can do everything good because he alone is almighty.

> **Faith Focus**
> What does it mean that God has the power to do everything?
>
> **Faith Words**
> **almighty**
> God alone is almighty. This means that only God has the power to do everything good.

God the Almighty

We can learn a lot about God when we look at creation. We can come to know that God is good. We can see how much God loves us. The Bible tells us:

Our God is good to all. God loves and cares for every creature.

BASED ON PSALM 145:9

We can also learn that God is **almighty.** The Bible says:

O Lord God Almighty, there is no one and nothing like you!

BASED ON PSALM 89:9

This means that only God has the power to do everything. And everything God does is very good.

God tells us that he does everything out of love. He is always good and loving. We believe in and love God the Father with all our hearts.

We show God and others our trust and love for him by what we say and do. When we do and say things that show we love God, we are signs of God's love for others to see.

[?] Why did God create us?

52

TEACHING TIP

Extending the Activity. Instead of having the students tell you what each word in the Find Words About God activity on page 53 says to them about God, have them write sentences for each of the words in the word bank. If the students are good writers, have them create a paragraph or story using the words to describe God. Ask volunteers to share their work with the class. This activity can also serve as a great review at the end of the chapter.

Activity

Find Words About God

Find and circle the words in the puzzle that tell about God. What does each word tell you about God?

Creator Father Almighty Love Good

```
C  B (G  O  O  D) R  D  G  O  D
A  Z  D  X  U  H  S  G  B  E  Q
K  X  E  L  M  K  B  D  C  X  W
L  F  J (A  L  M  I  G  H  T  Y)
(C  R  E  A  T  O  R) V  G  N  K
I  K  Y  Z (L  O  V  E) F  B  R
X  B (F  A  T  H  E  R) Y  Q  F
```

(53)

Faith-Filled People

Saint Bonaventure

Bonaventure looked at creation and came to know and love God. He said that creation was like a mirror. Whenever he looked at creation, Bonaventure saw and believed that God was good and loving. The Church celebrates the feast day of Saint Bonaventure on July 15.

FAITH-FILLED PEOPLE

Saint Bonaventure (1221–1274). Bonaventure was a great theologian, preacher, and leader. He was a person of compassion, virtue, and deep prayer. The words and actions of Saint Bonaventure are based on loving God with one's whole mind, heart, and soul. The Church honors him as a Doctor of the Church, which means he is an accomplished teacher. Legend tells us that Saint Bonaventure received his name when, in response to the pleading of his mother, Saint Francis of Assisi prayed for his recovery from a dangerous illness and, foreseeing the future greatness of the boy, cried, "O Buona ventura!"—O good fortune! For more information on Saint Bonaventure, go to the Saints Resource at www.BeMyDisciples.com.

Reinforce

▶ Have the students respond to the follow-up question. Help the students recognize that God created us and everything else out of love.

▶ Direct the students to read Faith-Filled People silently to learn about a Saint who came to know and love God through creation.

Connect

▶ Introduce the activity by asking the students to respond to the question: What does your favorite part of creation tell you about God?

▶ Explain the activity and allow the students time to complete it. Note: While the students are working, write the prayer below on the board.

▶ When the students finish, invite volunteers to share what each word tells them about God.

Pray

Gather the class for prayer. Pray together:

Almighty God, when we look at your creation, as Saint Bonaventure did, we see your goodness and love. Help us to see that same goodness and love in all those we meet. Amen.

Key Concept
God is our Father.

Pray

Invite the students to quiet themselves for prayer. Lead them in praying the Glory Be.

Teach

▶ Read the Faith Focus question aloud. Then tell the students to raise their hands if they know who taught us to call God, "Our Father." *(Elicit the response "Jesus.")*

▶ Invite a volunteer to read the first two paragraphs of God Our Father.

▶ Direct the students to read the last paragraph silently to discover what Jesus taught us about God our Father. Ask them to share what they discover. *(Accept all appropriate responses that reflect the concepts presented in the text.)*

Reinforce

▶ Recall the Catholics Believe on student page 51 and ask the students to recall why we also call the Our Father the Lord's Prayer.

▶ Ask, "What is the name of the prayer Jesus taught us to pray?" *(Our Father, Lord's Prayer)* What does the word *hallowed* mean? *(Hallowed means very holy.)*

Connect

Point out the picture on the page. Invite volunteers to share when they could pray the Our Father with their families. *(They can pray the Our Father home, in church, at bedtime, and so on.)* Encourage them to pray the Our Father every day.

Faith Focus
Who is God the Father?

God Our Father

Jesus told us the most about God. One day, Jesus' friends asked him to teach them to pray. He taught them to pray:

Our Father in heaven,
  hallowed be your name.

MATTHEW 6:9

The word *hallowed* means "very holy." We give great honor to God when we say, "hallowed be your name."

Jesus taught that God his Father is our Father. God the Father loves and cares for us. He knows what we need before we ask for it. God always does what is best for us. We are to believe in him and trust him. We are to honor God as Jesus did.

? What did Jesus teach us about God the Father?

54

BACKGROUND: OUR CATHOLIC FAITH

The Our Father. We invoke the name of God and call him "Father" because through Baptism we were reborn as his adopted children. Jesus taught us to call God "Father" because he wanted us to trust God the Father as he did. The Lord's Prayer invites us to call upon our Father with a sense of humility and trust.

God created everyone and everything out of love. God shares the gift of his love with you every day. You can give honor to God the Father by caring for creation.

I Follow Jesus

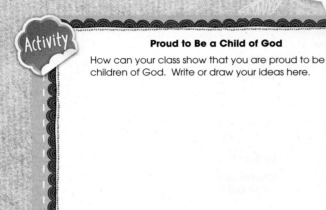

Activity

Proud to Be a Child of God

How can your class show that you are proud to be children of God. Write or draw your ideas here.

My Faith Choice

This week, I will honor God by showing my love for creation. I will

_____

_____

 Pray, "Thank you, God the Holy Spirit, for helping me to honor God the Father by caring for creation. Amen."

55

HUMAN METHODOLOGIES

Learning Through the Witness of the Teacher/Catechist. The *National Directory for Catechesis* teaches, "catechists powerfully influence those being catechized by the . . . transparent example of their Christian lives" (*NDC*, 29E). As you help the students consider what they will do this week to show their love for creation, share with them the different ways creation helps you to be aware of God's goodness, power, and love. Invite the students to see all of creation as a gift from God.

Reinforce

▶ Help the class recall that God created everyone and everything out of love and that his love for us will last forever.

▶ Emphasize that we honor God when we care for and share creation with others.

Respond

Explain the directions to the activity. Give the students sufficient time to complete it. Invite volunteers to share their work with the class.

Choose

▶ Present My Faith Choice. Help the students brainstorm ideas to complete their faith choices.

▶ Encourage the students to follow up on what they have decided in the week ahead.

Pray

Lead the class in praying the prayer to the Holy Spirit at the bottom of the page. Conclude with the Sign of the Cross.

Pray

Begin by reminding the students that God is present with them and by leading the class in the Lord's Prayer.

Recall

▶ Write the words *Creator, almighty,* and *Father* on the board. Invite the students to use each word in a sentence. Invite the students to share their sentences.

▶ Compare the students' sentences to the To Help You Remember sentences.

▶ Introduce the crossword activity and allow time for the students to complete it. Afterward, check responses

Reflect

Point out the Reflect and Share questions. Have the students write their responses. If you wish, refer the students to pages in their text for responses. *(To answer the first question, see pages 51 and 55; for the second question, see page 54.)*

Share

Canvass the group for responses to the two reflection questions. Then have the students turn back to page 55 and reread their Faith Choice. Challenge them to put that choice into action this week.

▶ **TO HELP YOU REMEMBER**

1. God is the Creator. He made everyone and everything because of his love.

2. God is almighty. He alone can do everything good.

3. Jesus taught us that God the Father is our Father.

Chapter Review

Recall
Complete the crossword puzzle.

Across

2. Creation is a sign of God the ____.

4. The word *hallowed* means very ____.

Down

1. God the ____ made everyone and everything out of love.

3. Jesus taught us to ____ the Our Father.

Crossword answers: 2 Across — F a t h e r; 4 Across — h o l y; 1 Down — C r e a t o r; 3 Down — p r a y

Reflect
What does it mean that God does everything out of love?

_____

_____

_____

_____

_____

_____

Share Why does Jesus want us to call God, "Father?" Tell your class.

56

TEACHING TIP

Involving Parents. Always remember that parents are the child's first educators, especially with regard to faith. Send a note home to parents urging them to get involved in the religious education of their child. Encourage them to review the material with their child at the end of each chapter. Encourage them to seek the answers to their own faith questions.

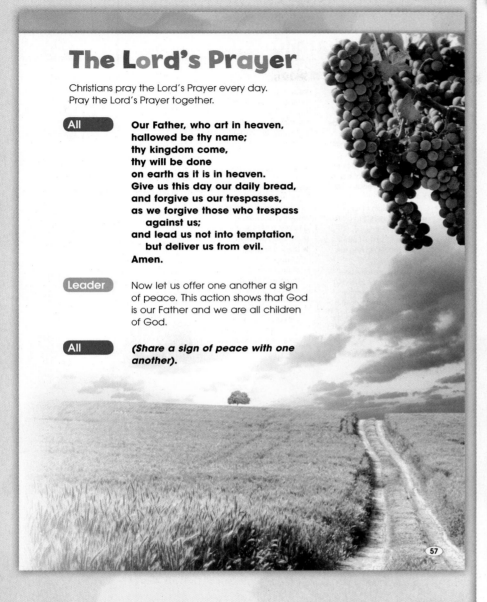

The Lord's Prayer

Christians pray the Lord's Prayer every day.
Pray the Lord's Prayer together.

All

**Our Father, who art in heaven,
hallowed be thy name;
thy kingdom come,
thy will be done
on earth as it is in heaven.
Give us this day our daily bread,
and forgive us our trespasses,
as we forgive those who trespass
   against us;
and lead us not into temptation,
   but deliver us from evil.
Amen.**

Leader

Now let us offer one another a sign
of peace. This action shows that God
is our Father and we are all children
of God.

All

*(Share a sign of peace with one
another).*

57

Pray

▶ Practice the orans prayer position
with the students—hands raised,
palms up. Invite the students to
use this prayer posture when you
pray together.

▶ Prepare the students for prayer by
reading aloud the introductory
paragraph.

▶ Gather the students in the prayer
center.

▶ Call the class to prayer by lowering
the lights and taking a moment of
silence.

▶ Pray The Lord's Prayer together.

▶ Invite students who know how to
pray the Lord's Prayer in languages
other than English to lead the class
in prayer in those languages.

▶ Conclude the prayer by sharing a
sign of peace.

THE TASKS OF CATECHESIS

Promoting Knowledge of the Faith. The Our Father has been
called the summary of the whole Gospel. Saint Augustine said that
if you were to read all the prayers of the Scriptures, you would not
find anything in them that is not included in the Our Father, or Lord's
Prayer. Saint Thomas Aquinas pointed out that the Lord's Prayer is
the perfect prayer because it teaches us not only what things to
pray for, but also the order in which we should ask for them. The
early Church prayed the Our Father three times a day. The prayer
has been a part of the liturgy of the Church from her beginning.
Today it is also included in the celebration of the Sacraments of
Baptism, Confirmation, and the Eucharist. Review the meaning
of each phrase in the Lord's Prayer to ensure that the students
understand it.

Preview

▶ Have the students carefully tear out pages 57 and 58 along the perforation.

▶ Encourage the students to share these pages with their families, and to complete the activities together.

▶ If they did not complete the review activity on page 56 by the end of the session, emphasize that they can complete it with their families at home.

▶ Point out the title and theme of the next lesson to the students.

Visit BeMyDisciples.com

▶ Take time with the students to explore the many activities and resources available at the *Be My Disciples* Web site.

▶ Encourage them to join with their families to discover the many resources available at the Web site.

Before Moving On ...

As you finish today's lesson, reflect on the following question before moving on to the next chapter.

What students could use more praise from me?

With My Family

This Week . . .

In Chapter 4, "God, Our Father," your child learned:

▶ God is the Creator of all that exists. God alone made everyone and everything out of love without any help.

▶ We call God almighty because he has the power to do everything that is good. His power is universal, loving, and merciful.

▶ God is the origin of all that exists. God loves and cares for us.

▶ We honor God the Father when we join in caring for his creation.

▶ When we honor someone, we show them the love and respect that they deserve.

For more about related teachings of the Church, see the *Catechism of the Catholic Church*, 268–274, 279–314, and 325–349, and the *United States Catholic Catechism for Adults*, pages 50–54.

■ Sharing God's Word

Read together the Bible story in Matthew 6:9–13 where Jesus teaches his friends how to pray. Emphasize that Jesus taught us to pray the Our Father, also called the Lord's Prayer.

■ Living as Disciples

The Christian home and family is a school of discipleship. Choose one or more of the following activities to do as a family, or design a similar activity of your own.

▶ Draw a creation mural. Write "God the Creator" at the top of the mural. Decorate the mural with pictures of God's creation. If you have photos from family trips to a park, a zoo or camping, use them with your child to talk about the beauty of creation and add them to the mural.

▶ By your example, help your child honor God's creation. Demonstrate how you use water, energy, food, and your treatment of living creatures. Model respect for all people. Decide as a family what you can do together.

■ Our Spiritual Journey

In the Sermon on the Mount, Jesus gave his disciples guidelines for living as his disciples. He taught them to pray the Lord's Prayer. In this chapter, your child prayed the Lord's Prayer. Pray the Lord's Prayer together as a family this week at bedtime. If you know the prayer in another language besides English, help your child learn it and pray it with you.

For more ideas on ways your family can live as disciples of Jesus, visit **BeMyDisciples.com**

THE LAST WORD

Celebrate Learning. As you conclude Unit 1, affirm the students for all they have learned in the first four chapters of the text. For example, you may want to invite volunteers to name some of the new words they learned (e.g., *disciples, soul, hospitality*), or encourage your second graders to recall a favorite Scripture story or activity from the unit. Remind the students that Jesus taught us about our almighty Father and that we also learn about God the Father from the Bible and the Church. Have the students recall what the words *Holy Trinity* mean. Reinforce that we praise God the Father, God the Son, and God the Holy Spirit.

Enriching the Lesson

Using Gestures in Storytelling

Purpose	Directions	Materials
To reinforce the story of creation (taught on pages 50–51)	Retell the biblical account of creation by reading aloud Genesis 1:1–31. ▶ Add gestures for the various works of creation to reinforce concepts. Invite the students to echo each gesture after you. For example: In the beginning God created the heavens and the Earth. *[Raise arms slowly, cross wrists overhead, and bring arms down slowly.]* Then he said, "Let there be plants and trees." *[Move hands down to floor and then raise hands overhead.]* ▶ Invite the children to retell the story using the gestures.	Bible

Choosing a Nature Project

Purpose	Directions	Materials
To reinforce the teaching about our responsibility to care for creation (taught on pages 50–51 and page 55)	Children love to be outdoors and have a natural love for nature and all that it holds. ▶ Brainstorm with the students several projects they can do to take care of creation. ▶ Have the students agree on a project that they can do as a group. ▶ Have the students write a note to themselves to remind them to work on their project.	paper pencils

Literature Connection

Purpose	Directions	Materials
To reinforce that we can learn about God when we look at creation (taught on pages 50–51)	A wonderful book that will reinforce the students' sense of the depth and breadth of God's love is *Old Turtle* by Douglas Wood (Pfiefer-Hamilton, 1992). ▶ Tell the students that in the book each part of creation is insisting that God is most like the qualities that it possesses. ▶ Have them predict what the wind might say and ask them to listen to see if they were correct. ▶ When you have finished reading the story you might invite the students to make small movements with each part of creation, such as blow like the breeze, move their hands like fish, and so on, and retell the story. ▶ An open-ended question might be, "Why did the people finally listen?"	*Old Turtle*, by Douglas Wood

Catholic Social Teaching Unit 1

Pray

Invite the students to quiet themselves for prayer. Pray the Lord's Prayer together.

Introduce

▶ Invite the students to share some of the ways they learn about God. Then ask a volunteer to read aloud the Catholic Social Teaching principle in the sidebar.

▶ Tell the class that being caretakers of God's creation is an important duty that every person has.

▶ Take your class on a quick tour of the school campus. Tell them that they are going to find out how well the students are taking care of God's creation. As they tour, ask them each to silently count the number of pieces of trash they see lying around.

▶ Back in class, go from student to student, asking how many pieces of trash they counted.

▶ Ask and discuss: What do you think? How well do we take care of God's creation?

Teach

▶ Introduce the story Pick Up and Clean Up by asking the students to look at the picture on the page. Ask volunteers to describe what they see.

▶ Invite volunteers to read the story aloud.

Pick Up and Clean Up

The whistle blew loudly. It was Mr. Gomez, the school principal. He wanted the children's attention at the end of the lunch period on Field Day. "Look around you," he said. "How many pieces of trash do you see?"

The children looked. There was trash everywhere, even in the bushes.

"We have a problem," Mr. Gomez announced. "First, I want you to pick up all this trash, please. Then I want you to go back to your classroom and come up with a plan. Our school yard can be beautiful, but everyone needs to take care of it."

> **WE ARE CARETAKERS OF GOD'S CREATION**
>
> When we look at God's creation, we learn about God. We have a special duty to care for God's creation. It is one way we can honor and show our love for God.

59

BACKGROUND: CATHOLIC SOCIAL TEACHING

Responsibility for the Environment Chapter 10 of the *Compendium of the Social Doctrine of the Church* (CSDC) speaks to the Church's teaching on safeguarding the environment. It teaches: "The Magisterium underscores human responsibility for the preservation of a sound and healthy environment for all." We have the responsibility "to promote the environment as a home and a resource for (all) . . . and to guarantee adequate conditions of hygiene and health . . ." (*CSDC*, 465).

Making Connections

We can do our part to take care of God's creation. The school yard is a good place to start. Develop a plan.

with Math and Science

Pretend you are in a helicopter looking down at your school. Draw a map of what you see with the buildings and the outside areas. Divide the map into sections. Chart the sections. Assign each grade one section to care for. Make a color key to color each grade's section on your map. Find out if there are trash cans in each section. How many more trash cans are needed?

with Language Arts

Talk about how each grade can keep its area clean. Make a list of three ideas. People need reminders that being caretakers of God's creation is our responsibility. Create slogans for a "Keep Our School Clean" campaign.

with Creative Arts

Design "Caretakers of God's Creation" posters to display in each classroom and on school bulletin boards. Use the slogans and simple tips for keeping the school clean. Take before and after pictures. Then with your teacher's help, upload them to your school's Web site. Show how taking care of God's creation makes a difference at your school.

Faith Action

I am God's creation caretaker. Here is one way that I am going to take care of God's creation in my neighborhood.

_____

_____

TEACHING TIP

Activity Centers. You can organize the cross-curricular projects into activity centers. Most of the activities can be done cooperatively with small groups of students. The students can rotate to each center. For the activities in this unit, however, everyone must complete the math and science diagram and charting activity before they can move on to the other activities. Explain the math and science activity to the class and allow them to work in groups to complete it. Be flexible and creative when choosing how to process the activities. Take into account your personal teaching style, your lesson plans, and the learning styles of the students.

Catholic Social Teaching

Reinforce

Have the students look again at the picture on page 59. Ask them to describe what happened to the schoolyard.

Connect

Tell the students that they will explore ways to keep the school clean and encourage other students to do so also. Introduce the three cross-curricular activities under Making Connections and carefully explain all three to the students. Invite and answer any questions that the students might have. Ask the students to choose the activity or activities that they wish to work on.

▶ **Math and Science:** Have the students work in small groups to create their chart and map. Afterward, discuss what they discovered.

▶ **Language Arts:** Assign this activity to small groups within the class or to several classes or grades throughout the school.

▶ **Creative Arts:** Provide the supplies the students need to complete the activity. Decide where to display the posters.

Choose

Read the Faith Action on page 60 aloud. Give the students time to make their choices.

Pray

Once again, lead the class in the Lord's Prayer.

Unit 1 Review

The Unit Review provides the opportunity to assess the students' understanding of the concepts presented in the unit and to affirm them in their growing knowledge and love of God. Here are a few suggestions for using these pages.

▶ Share with the students that the next two pages are an opportunity to stop and review what they have learned.

▶ Provide time for the students to ask questions.

▶ Have the students complete the review alone or with a partner.

▶ Encourage the students to share the Unit Review pages with their families.

A. Choose the Best Word

This section reviews the main concepts of the unit.

▶ Read the directions for section A. By working together on the first sentence, you are teaching the students a strategy for completing these types of sentences.

▶ When the students have finished this section, invite volunteers to share their answers. Review any sentence that the students seem to have difficulty completing.

B. Show What You Know

This section reinforces what the students have learned about Jesus.

▶ Read the directions to the students. Have the students complete the section.

▶ Invite volunteers to share their answers.

Unit 1 Review

Name _____

A. Choose the Best Word

Complete the sentences. Color the circle next to the best choice for each sentence.

1. The _____ is One God in Three Divine Persons.
   - ● Holy Trinity   ○ Holy Spirit   ○ Holy Family

2. God the Father is the _____ who made everyone and everything out of love.
   - ○ Apostle   ● Creator   ○ Holy Spirit

3. Jesus is the _____ Person of the Holy Trinity.
   - ○ First   ● Second   ○ Third

4. The part of us that lives forever is called the _____.
   - ○ heart   ○ mind   ● soul

5. We honor the Holy Trinity when we pray the _____.
   - ○ Hail Mary   ● Sign of the Cross   ○ Lord's Prayer

B. Show What You Know

There is One God in Three Divine Persons. Match the numbers in Column A with the letters in Column B.

Column A	Column B
b 1. God the Father	a. Savior
a 2. God the Son	b. Creator
c 3. God the Holy Spirit	c. Helper

TEACHING TIP

Assessing Learning. Throughout the year, use multiple forms of assessment at the end of each unit. Students learn and communicate their understanding in multiple ways. Some forms of communication, for example, writing paragraphs, work better for some students. Other forms of communication, for example, artwork and verbal responses, work better for others. Asking questions, observing small group interactions, and using different activities throughout the chapter will provide you with multiple ways of identifying the students' understanding of the truths of the faith.

C. Connect with Scripture

What was your favorite story about Jesus in this unit?
Draw something that happened in the story.
Tell your class about it.

D. Be a Disciple

1. *What Saint or holy person did you enjoy hearing about in this unit? Write the name here. Tell your class what this person did to follow Jesus.*

_____

_____

2. *What can you do to be a good disciple of Jesus?*

_____

_____

62

C. Connect with Scripture

This section reinforces the students' experience and knowledge of Scripture and the teachings of Jesus.

▶ Help the students review the Scripture stories in the unit, beginning with the Unit Opener story. You may wish to write the names of these stories on the board to assist them.

▶ Ask volunteers to share their favorite stories with the class.

▶ In the space, invite the students to draw something that happened in the story. Invite volunteers to share their drawings now, or at the completion of the Unit Review.

D. Be a Disciple

This section provides the students with the opportunity to recall how the Church, Saints, and holy people followed Jesus. It reinforces the ways students can choose to live as disciples of Jesus.

▶ Ask the students to remember their favorite stories of Saints or holy people that they learned about in this unit. Refresh their memories as needed, and write their responses on the board.

▶ Give each student time to write the name of their favorite Saint or holy person on the line. Ask volunteers to share the reason for their choices.

▶ Lead a discussion about the actions that make us good disciples of Jesus. Give the students time to write on the lines their idea of what they could do.

We Believe

Part Two

Objectives

In this unit, the students will learn:

▶ The birth of Jesus Christ, the Son of God, is a sign of God's love and mercy.

▶ Jesus sacrificed his life on the Cross to save all people from their sins.

▶ The Holy Spirit is our helper and teacher.

▶ The Church is the People of God who follow Jesus Christ.

Spiritual Insights

When we speak of the Paschal Mystery, we refer to Christ's death and Resurrection as one inseparable event. It is a mystery because it is a visible sign of an invisible act of God. It is paschal because it is Christ's passing through death into new life. For us it means that we can now die to sin and its domination of our lives, and we pass over into divine life already here on earth and more completely in heaven.

United States Catholic Catechism for Adults, page 93

"Remain in me, as I remain in you. . . . I am the vine, you are the branches."   *John 15:4–5*

Living the Six Tasks of Catechesis

Liturgical Education: Saint Elizabeth Ann Seton (1774–1821)

Elizabeth was raised in a wealthy Episcopalian family in New York. The family read the Scriptures and prayed together often. Her parents also encouraged Elizabeth to participate in charitable activities.

Elizabeth fell in love with and married Will Seton when she was nineteen. They had five children together. Then Will contracted tuberculosis. He was unable to work and his successful business failed. Family friends in Italy invited the Seton family to stay with

them while William recovered. They also wanted to help Elizabeth with the responsibility of caring for her children.

Elizabeth was deeply moved by her friends' Catholic faith. She began to visit Catholic churches to pray before the Blessed Sacrament. She had no doubt that Jesus was truly present in the consecrated bread and wine at Mass. Elizabeth also felt drawn to our Blessed Mother, especially after Will died. She knew that Mary had suffered the loss of her beloved son, Jesus. As she knelt before the tabernacle, praying to Jesus and his mother, Elizabeth felt the Lord calling her to join the Catholic Church.

A year later, back in America, she professed her faith as a Catholic although many friends and family turned their backs on her. She decided that the best way she could support herself and her children was to open a Catholic boarding school for girls. In this way, she could provide both faith and education for the girls.

In time, Elizabeth formed a religious order for women called the American Sisters of Charity. With Elizabeth's leadership, the nuns opened orphanages and schools for the poor. Mother Seton, as she became known, was one of the first to reach out to developmentally challenged children. The American Sisters of Charity also worked in hospitals and homes for the elderly.

We honor Elizabeth Ann Seton as the first American-born Saint. As catechists, we respond to the gift of Jesus' Body and Blood in the Eucharist through our service to others, as Saint Elizabeth did.

Sharing Your Faith

Find a partner to work with: a spouse, a friend, a fellow teacher. Come together at the beginning or end of each unit for shared prayer and discussion. Use the questions below as a starting point. As an alternative, record your thoughts in a personal journal.

▶ Why are the Cross and the Resurrection inseparable for us as Jesus' disciples?

▶ Describe an experience of the Holy Spirit inspiring or encouraging you.

▶ How do you build up the Body of Christ, the Church?

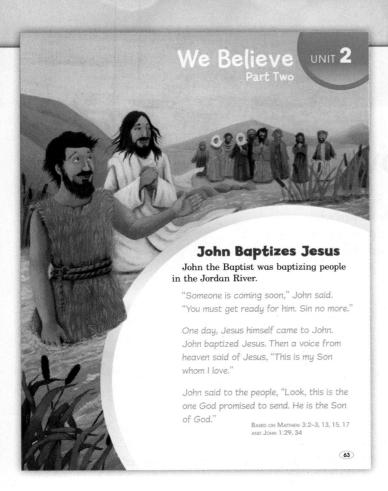

We Believe UNIT 2
Part Two

John Baptizes Jesus

John the Baptist was baptizing people in the Jordan River.

"Someone is coming soon," John said. "You must get ready for him. Sin no more."

One day, Jesus himself came to John. John baptized Jesus. Then a voice from heaven said of Jesus, "This is my Son whom I love."

John said to the people, "Look, this is the one God promised to send. He is the Son of God."

BASED ON MATTHEW 3:2–3, 13, 15, 17 AND JOHN 1:29, 34

(63)

What I Know

What is something you already know about these faith concepts?

Jesus Christ

_____

_____

The Holy Spirit

_____

_____

The Mother of the Church

_____

_____

Put an X next to the faith words you know. Put a ? next to the faith words you need to learn more about.

____ Resurrection ____ Pentecost ____ Body of Christ

____ Covenant ____ Ascension ____ Communion of Saints

What do you know about God's promises to his people in the Bible?

_____

A Question I Have

What question would you like to ask about living as a member of the Church?

_____

_____

(64)

Unit 2 Opener

The Unit 2 opener pages help to assess the students' prior knowledge about the key faith concepts in the unit. Processing these pages should take no more than fifteen minutes.

Opening Page

Invite the children to tell you what they see in the images on the page. Proclaim the Scripture story. Ask: What did John ask the people to do to get ready for Jesus? What can you do to show Jesus that you believe in him? Accept their answers, but do not respond further at this time.

▶ Reverently proclaim the Bible passage.

▶ Since the reading is from a Gospel, say, *"The Gospel of the Lord."* The students reply, *"Praise to you, Lord Jesus Christ."*

▶ Point out to the class that in this unit they will learn much more about the God's own Son, Jesus.

Getting Ready

This page continues the activation of prior knowledge. Do not correct the children's responses. You will invite them to return and correct themselves at the end of the unit.

▶ Have the students write their responses under What I Know and Questions I Have. You may also do the exercises orally.

▶ Record the students' questions on a chart. Refer back to the chart as you progress through the unit and ask volunteers to respond when they can answer the questions. You may also wish to use these questions during a unit assessment.

▶ Ask the students to turn to the next page and begin Chapter 5.

Jesus, the Son of God

BACKGROUND

The Mystery of Love

The mystery of the Incarnation—the Son of God, the Second Person of the Holy Trinity, taking on flesh and becoming fully human while remaining divine—is a mystery of divine love beyond the comprehension of the human mind and heart. What kind of life on Earth did the Incarnate Son of God, Jesus, live?

Ordinary Life

Jesus could have been a monarch so splendid that he would make the greatest kings the world has ever known blush with envy. He could have been whoever and whatever he wanted to be. And who did this Incarnate Son of God, the Holy One of God, choose to become? Instead of ruling by regal pomp or power, the Son of God chose to identify himself by humility, servanthood, and suffering. God's own Word to us could not have more clearly revealed this:

> Who, . . . though he was in the form of God, . . .
> he emptied himself, . . .
> becoming obedient to death,
>   even death on a cross.
>
> Philippians 2:6–8

Jesus of Nazareth, the only Son of God, took on the life most common to humans, that of powerlessness, obedience, and poverty. By doing so he showed us how the human condition could be transformed into the Kingdom of God.

The Christ

Jesus, the Incarnate Son of God, is the Christ. The English word *Christ* is from the Greek word *Kristos,* which is the Greek translation of the Hebrew *masch* (Messiah), a word meaning "anointed." Jesus Christ, anointed by the Holy Spirit to be Priest, Prophet, and King, established a kingdom that would last forever.

The true meaning of Christ's kingship was revealed only after his Crucifixion, Death, Resurrection, and glorious Ascension. By his Paschal Mystery, Christ effectively destroyed death's power and gave people the promise of eternal life. He freed people from the tragic death-bearing consequences of sin and opened the way to new and everlasting life.

In Jesus we have the promise of life in the Kingdom of God. He invites us to a life of holiness—to a life of everlasting communion with God the Father, Son, and Holy Spirit.

The Way of Jesus

Jesus is the truth, the life, and the way (see John 14:6). Like Jesus, we are to trust in the Father, whom we address and know as Abba. In childlike surrender, we trust in the providential care of our heavenly Father, who knows our needs.

> We seek first the kingdom, and then all we need will be ours as well (see Matthew 6:33). To those who think that wealth, power, and fame are the paths, or way, to happiness, Jesus proclaims that happiness resides in the poor in spirit and in those struggling to achieve peace (see Matthew 5:3, 9). By his poverty, the Incarnate Son of God shows us how to transform the hardships and sufferings that may come our way.

For Reflection

Who is Jesus for me?

How willing am I to give all for love of God and neighbor?

Teacher to Teacher

The Heart of Christmas

This chapter tells the Christmas story. Get out those bathrobes, pillowcases, and towels. Nothing makes a story come alive more quickly for seven- and eight-year-olds than acting out the Gospel accounts of the Nativity. Enlist the help of parents and set up a video camera. The script in this chapter is short so you could even have two or three casts. Save the video and show it during the Christmas season. The actors and actresses will be delighted!

Jesus' Presence with Us

As we celebrate the birth of Christ, we need to remind ourselves that Jesus is present with us whenever we gather in his name. Remind the students that he is uniquely present in every celebration of the Eucharist during which the bread and wine, through the words of the priest and power of the Holy Spirit, become the Body and Blood of Christ. Celebrate with the class that Jesus' presence with us is the real and true reason for our happiness. It gives us the hope that we live out and keep in our hearts. Through this lesson help the students realize that the gift of Jesus' presence is with us, and this is cause for joy.

The Church Teaches...

"The incarnation of the only Son of God is the original inculturation of God's word. The mystery of the incarnation is also the model of all evangelization by the Church" (*National Directory for Catechesis,* 21A).

It is important that teachers introduce their students to the person of Jesus so that they may develop a personal relationship with him.

Further Reading and Reflection

For more related teachings of the Church, see the *Catechism of the Catholic Church,* 51–67 and 456–560; and the *United States Catholic Catechism for Adults,* pages 77–87.

Teacher Prayer

Jesus, you are my Savior—willing to give all so that I may live. Help me to be willing to give myself for others. Amen.

Lesson Planner

Chapter 5 Jesus, the Son of God

Goal To learn that God sent his Son, Jesus, to restore our friendship with him

LESSON PART	PROCESS	MATERIALS and RESOURCES
DAY 1 EXPLORE **Focus** To explore how the virtue of mercy leads followers of Jesus to treat others with kindness **Pages 65–67**	▶ Proclaim and discuss Isaiah 7:14; 9:5–6 (Promise of Jesus' Birth). ▶ Learn and discuss the story of Saint Martin de Porres and how he showed others Jesus loved them. **Disciple Power:** Mercy **Activity:** Identify ways to build a merciful world.	Bible Pencils or pens Crayons or markers Globe or world map **Enriching the Lesson** Teacher Guide, page 131 Literature Connection: *Mrs. Katz and Tush*
DAY 2 DISCOVER **Focus** To discover the Covenant—God's special promise and commitment of loving kindness to his people **Pages 68–69**	▶ Learn how the Covenant shows God loves people. ▶ Discover that God promised a Savior, Jesus, who is the fulfillment of God's promise. **Faith Words:** Covenant, Jesus Christ **Catholics Believe:** Works of Mercy **Activity:** Use a code to discover an important message about Jesus.	Pencils or pens
DAY 3 DISCOVER **Focus** To discover how Jesus was born **Pages 70–71**	▶ Discover that Mary, the Mother of Jesus, is the Mother of God. **Scripture Story:** The Birth of Jesus (Luke 2:4-7) **Faith-Filled People:** The Blessed Virgin Mary **Activity:** Create a Nativity rebus.	Bible Pencils or pens **Additional Activities Booklet:** Activity 5b or see *BeMyDisciples*.com.
DAY 4 DECIDE **Focus** To discover how Jesus showed that God always loves people and to decide on a way to be a sign of God's mercy and love **Pages 72–73**	▶ Learn how Jesus showed that God cares deeply for all people. **Scripture:** The Feeding of the Five Thousand (Matthew 14:13, 15–20) **Activity:** Identify how people care for others. **My Faith Choice:** Choose how you will live as a sign of God's love. **Pray:** "Thank you, Holy Spirit."	Bible Pencils or pens **Enriching the Lesson:** Teacher Guide, page 131 • Pantomiming a Scripture Story • Making Headlines **Additional Activities Booklet:** Activity 5a or see *BeMyDisciples*.com.
DAY 5 CONCLUDE **Focus** To praise God for the birth of Jesus **Pages 74–76**	▶ **REVIEW** Review concepts: Recall, Reflect, and Share. ▶ **PRAY** The Angelus ▶ **PREVIEW** With My Family page and the theme of the next chapter.	Grade 2 Music CD **Assessment Tools Booklet:** Assessments 1a and 1b

Assign online Chapter Review and interactive Chapter Test at **BeMyDisciples.com**

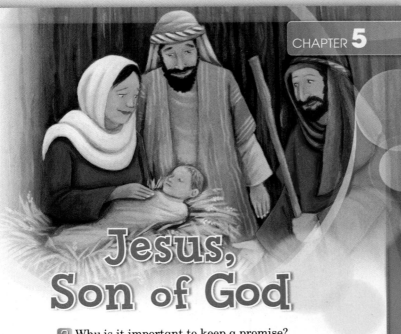

CHAPTER **5**

Jesus, Son of God

? Why is it important to keep a promise?

God made this promise to his people.
He said a child would be born to them.

*A virgin will have a baby. They will name him
Wonder-Counselor, God-Hero, Father-Forever,
and Prince of Peace. The child will grow up and
begin rebuilding a world of kindness and love.*

BASED ON ISAIAH 7:14; 9:5-6

? Who is the child God promised?

65

Pray

▶ Invite the students to quiet themselves for prayer. Remind them that God hears us when we pray.

▶ Pray the Sign of the Cross together.

▶ Ask the children to echo this prayer:

> Dear Jesus,
> help us to follow you
> each and every day.
> Amen.

▶ Call on different students to offer their responses to the opening question. Stress the importance of fulfilling one's promises.

Reflect

▶ Have the students look at the picture and describe what they see.

▶ Introduce the Scripture passage, and then have a volunteer read the Word of God from Isaiah.

▶ Afterward, observe a moment of prayerful silence.

▶ Ask the class to respond to the Scripture question. *(Answer: Jesus)*

▶ Conclude by praying the Sign of the Cross.

Focus

Tell the class that they will read about someone whose merciful deeds helped build a world of kindness and love.

HUMAN METHODOLOGIES

Learning Within the Christian Community. The *National Directory for Catechesis* tells us that the parish is the place "where the Christian faith deepens and where the Christian community is formed" (*NDC, 29C*). On Day 5, explain to the students that the Angelus was prayed three times a day in ancient times—at 6:00 a.m., at 12:00 noon, and at 6:00 p.m. The church bells rang to call people to prayer wherever they were—at work, at school, or at home—and everyone stopped to pray the Angelus. If your parish rings bells listen to them and pray the Hail Mary. Remind the students that people pray this prayer all over the world. Participating in this tradition can help the students appreciate that we are a universal Church, joined together by our love for Jesus.

Introduce

▶ Read Disciple Power with the students. Tell them that when they treat others with care and kindness, they are acting with mercy.

▶ Show the students a globe or map on which they can identify the United States and South America. Point out the country of Peru. Explain that most people there live in the high Andes Mountains.

▶ Ask the students to listen as volunteers read the story about Brother Martin. Ask them to listen to find out why Martin was so kind.

▶ Invite volunteers to read the story one paragraph at a time.

Reinforce

▶ Call for responses to the follow-up question.

▶ Afterward, share with the students ways they might show mercy. For example, we act with mercy:

— when someone says something bad about us, and we choose to say something good.

— when we give someone more than his or her fair share.

▶ Invite volunteers to share a work of mercy they have done.

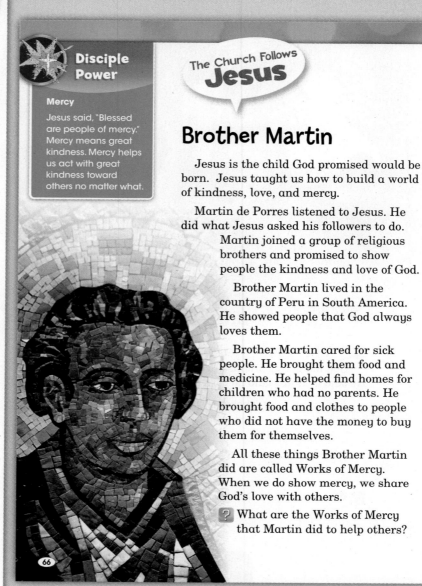

Disciple Power

Mercy

Jesus said, "Blessed are people of mercy." Mercy means great kindness. Mercy helps us act with great kindness toward others no matter what.

The Church Follows **Jesus**

Brother Martin

Jesus is the child God promised would be born. Jesus taught us how to build a world of kindness, love, and mercy.

Martin de Porres listened to Jesus. He did what Jesus asked his followers to do. Martin joined a group of religious brothers and promised to show people the kindness and love of God.

Brother Martin lived in the country of Peru in South America. He showed people that God always loves them.

Brother Martin cared for sick people. He brought them food and medicine. He helped find homes for children who had no parents. He brought food and clothes to people who did not have the money to buy them for themselves.

All these things Brother Martin did are called Works of Mercy. When we do show mercy, we share God's love with others.

❓ What are the Works of Mercy that Martin did to help others?

DISCIPLE POWER

Mercy or Kindness. The Hebrew word in the Bible that we translate into English as mercy is *hesed*. This Hebrew word is often connected to the Covenant that God entered into with his people. It is used to describe the unconditional kindness with which God reaches out to his people. Such is the mercy or kindness that we acknowledge when we pray, "Lord, have mercy." Such is the kindness and mercy that we are to offer to one another, especially those who "trespass against us." Help the students appreciate that Jesus asks us to continue his work in the world. We can do this by acting with mercy or kindness toward others. Brainstorm with the class situations in which second graders can act with mercy toward family members, classmates, and neighbors.

Acting with Mercy

When we act with mercy, we are working to build a world of kindness and love. We are doing what Jesus taught us to do. We are following in the footsteps of Brother Martin.

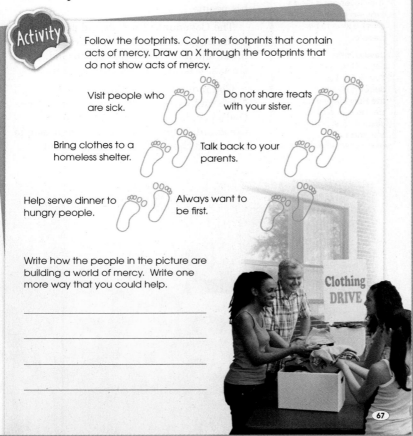

Activity

Follow the footprints. Color the footprints that contain acts of mercy. Draw an X through the footprints that do not show acts of mercy.

Visit people who are sick.

Do not share treats with your sister.

Bring clothes to a homeless shelter.

Talk back to your parents.

Help serve dinner to hungry people.

Always want to be first.

Write how the people in the picture are building a world of mercy. Write one more way that you could help.

_____

_____

_____

_____

Clothing DRIVE

67

Connect

▶ Read aloud the section titled Acting with Mercy.

▶ Explain the directions for the activity.

▶ Provide crayons or markers and allow time for the students to work individually.

▶ Afterward, call on different students to read aloud each footprint one at a time and discuss answers as a class.

▶ Remind the students that God calls us to act with mercy and help build a world of kindness and love.

Pray

Invite the children to quiet themselves for prayer. Have them echo the following after you.

God our Father, /
teach us to be like Brother Martin /
and follow the way of Jesus. /
Help us show mercy to all we meet. /
Amen.

TEACHING TIP

Extend the Activity. Enhance and extend the activity by having the students make sets of their footprints. Provide heavy construction paper, markers and scissors. Have the students work in pairs to help trace one another's footprints. Direct the students to cut out the footprints and then to write on each one way they can act with mercy. Either place the completed footprints around the room and "walk a mercy path" with the class, or create a bulletin board on which to post the footprints. Point out how each footprint offers a way to act with kindness and love.

> **Key Concept**
> God fulfills his promise in Jesus.

Pray

Invite the students to quiet themselves for prayer. Lead the class in praying the Glory Be.

Teach

▶ Ask a volunteer to read aloud the Faith Focus question. Tell the students they are going to learn more about a special promise God made.

▶ Review the students' earlier discussion about keeping promises. Point out that some promises are easy to keep, while others are very difficult.

▶ Together read the Faith Words *Covenant* and *Jesus Christ* and their meanings. Then have the students follow along as you read the section titled God's Special Promise to discover God's promise and how he kept it.

▶ Have the students make word cards for both Faith Words on this page.

Faith Focus
How did Jesus show that God always loves people?

Faith Words
Covenant
The Covenant is God's promise always to love and be kind to his people.

Jesus Christ
Jesus Christ is the Son of God. He is the Second Person of the Holy Trinity who became one of us. Jesus is true God and true man.

God's Special Promise

The Bible tells us about a very special promise God made with his people. This promise is the **Covenant**. In the Covenant God promised to always love and be kind to his people.

The Covenant that God and people made began at creation. Our first parents broke the promise they made to God. They sinned. We call this sin Original Sin.

God made the Covenant again with Noah and with Abraham and with Moses. God's people still sometimes broke the Covenant. When they did, God sent people to remind them to keep the Covenant.

68

TEACHING VOCABULARY

Covenant. The word *covenant* refers to a promise entered into by two people or groups. Each person or group pledges to be loyal to their promise by holding up their end of the bargain. Remind the students that while God's people often broke the Covenant they made with God, he always kept his part of the Covenant. Tell them that God's promise to love us will never be broken.

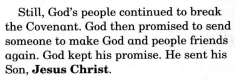

Still, God's people continued to break the Covenant. God then promised to send someone to make God and people friends again. God kept his promise. He sent his Son, **Jesus Christ**.

Jesus is the Second Person of the Holy Trinity who became one of us. Jesus is true God and true man.

❓ Why did God send his Son, Jesus?

Catholics Believe

Works of Mercy

The Church teaches us the Works of Mercy. They are ways to be as kind and loving to people as Jesus.

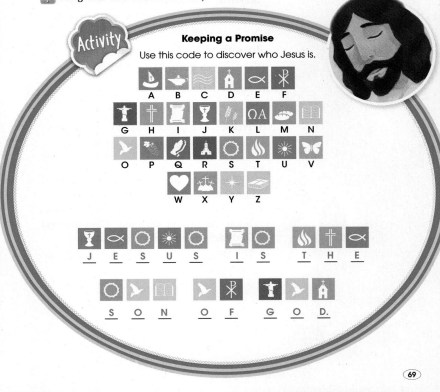

Activity

Keeping a Promise

Use this code to discover who Jesus is.

A	B	C	D	E	F
G	H	I	J	K	L	M	N
O	P	Q	R	S	T	U	V
W	X	Y	Z		

J E S U S   I S   T H E

S O N   O F   G O D.

(69)

Reinforce

▶ Ask the follow-up question. *(Answer: to make God and people friends again)*

▶ Write on the board:
_____ is the Son of God.
_____ is the Second Person of the Holy Trinity.
_____ is true God and true man.

▶ Invite volunteers to fill in the blank in each sentence.

▶ Emphasize that God kept his covenantal promise by sending his Son, Jesus to become one of us.

▶ Invite volunteers to name one or two acts of mercy that they identified in the previous lesson. Then, read aloud Catholics Believe about Works of Mercy as a reminder that we are called to love people as Jesus did.

Connect

▶ Make sure the students understand the directions to the activity Keeping a Promise. Give them time to discover the hidden message.

▶ When the students finish, have them read aloud the decoded message.

▶ Stress again that Jesus Christ is true God and true man, the Second Person of the Holy Trinity.

Pray

Gather the students for prayer. Lead them in praying the Lord's Prayer.

TEACHING TIP

The Nativity Story—Setting the Scene. Prepare the class to better understand the Scripture story of fulfillment of the Covenant in the birth of Jesus. Help the students gain some sense of the land in which Jesus lived. Explain that Jesus lived in Palestine, a land that today includes Israel and the West Bank. In the time of Jesus, the land was ruled by the Roman Empire. The people who lived in Palestine had to do what the Romans told them to do. Once, when the Romans wanted to count all the people living in Palestine, Mary and Joseph had to make a trip to Bethlehem, the hometown of Joseph's family. When Mary and Joseph arrived in Bethlehem, there was no place for them to stay. An innkeeper let them stay in his stable, or barn. It was there, among the animals, that Jesus was born.

> **Key Concept**
> The birth of Jesus is called the Nativity.

Pray

Gather the students for prayer. Pray together as an echo prayer:

Lord Jesus, / you are a precious gift! / We honor and praise you. / We thank you for becoming one of us. / Amen.

Teach

▶ Remind the students that God kept his promise to send someone to make him and his people friends again.

▶ Ask the class what special promise God made that we celebrate at Christmas. (*God promised to send the Savior.*)

▶ Write the word *Nativity* on the board and tell the students that *Nativity* is the name we give the Bible story of the birth of Jesus.

▶ Choose volunteers to take the parts of the narrator, Joseph, and the innkeeper. The rest of the group can be the people of the village.

▶ Allow the volunteers a few minutes to practice reading and acting out their parts.

▶ When the volunteers are ready, have them perform the play.

▶ Read the Faith Focus question aloud and ask the students for possible answers.

> **Faith Focus**
> What does Saint Luke tell us about the birth of Jesus?

The Birth of Jesus

The Bible tells about the birth of Jesus. We call this story the Nativity.

Narrator   *Just before Jesus' birth, Joseph and Mary traveled to Bethlehem. Mary and Joseph stopped to find a room in an inn.*

Action   *Joseph knocks on the door of the inn. The innkeeper opens the door.*

Joseph   *My wife and I need a room. She is going to have a baby.*

Innkeeper   *There are no rooms left. You may stay in the stable.*

Narrator   *Mary and Joseph went to the stable. Jesus was born there.*
BASED ON LUKE 2:4–7

The Bible tells us that angels told shepherds about the birth of Jesus. The shepherds went to see Baby Jesus. They were filled with joy. They praised God for what they heard and saw.

❓ What do we call the story of Jesus' birth?

70

TEACHING TIP

Greater Participation. If there are enough students in your class, divide the class into several acting groups. This way all children have the opportunity to participate and feel special. Let each group choose a narrator, innkeeper and someone to play Joseph. Take time to work with each group to be sure they can read the words and understand the directions. Each group may also take some time to create backgrounds and choose props and costumes. Have plenty of newsprint and markers available to work with. If possible, provide costume materials such as cloth, rope, robes, and pillowcases.

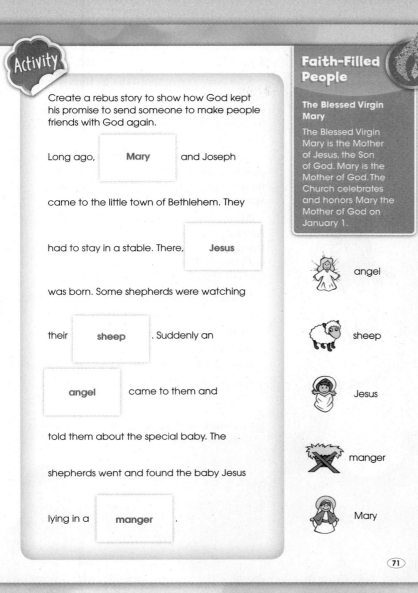

Activity

Create a rebus story to show how God kept his promise to send someone to make people friends with God again.

Long ago, | Mary | and Joseph

came to the little town of Bethlehem. They

had to stay in a stable. There, | Jesus |

was born. Some shepherds were watching

their | sheep |. Suddenly an

| angel | came to them and

told them about the special baby. The

shepherds went and found the baby Jesus

lying in a | manger |.

Faith-Filled People

The Blessed Virgin Mary

The Blessed Virgin Mary is the Mother of Jesus, the Son of God. Mary is the Mother of God. The Church celebrates and honors Mary the Mother of God on January 1.

- angel
- sheep
- Jesus
- manger
- Mary

(71)

Reinforce

▶ Have the students recall when we celebrate the Nativity of Jesus. *(Christmas)* Discuss other ways they may be reminded of God's promise to us. *(e.g., the Nativity scenes set up at church or at home)*

▶ Call attention back to page 65. Have the students reread the passage from Isaiah. Ask: Who do you think is the virgin the Bible talks about? *(Mary)*

▶ Have a volunteer read Faith-Filled People. Share that Mary is so important because she agreed to be the Mother of God.

Connect

▶ Read aloud the activity directions.

▶ Explain that the students can look at the illustrations on the right side of the page to help them complete the rebus. Make sure they understand that these illustrations are only a guide for their own drawings.

▶ When the students finish drawing, have different volunteers read the rebus story, one sentence at a time.

▶ Encourage the students to share their finished rebuses with their families.

Pray

Invite the students to quiet themselves for prayer. Pray together the Hail Mary.

FAITH-FILLED PEOPLE

The Blessed Virgin Mary. Mary is honored with many titles that express the Church's faith in her. Many of these titles are named in the Litany of the Blessed Virgin Mary. The Gospel of John refers to Mary as the "Mother of Jesus." Luke's Gospel honors Mary as God's favored one who was full of grace from the very beginning of her existence *(Luke 1:28)*. The Gospel accounts name Mary as the mother of the Son of God. Mary is truly the Mother of God because she is the Mother of Jesus, the eternal Son of God. For more information on the Blessed Virgin Mary, go to the Saints Resource at *BeMyDisciples*.com.

> **Key Concept**
> Jesus taught about God's mercy and love.

Pray

Lead the class in praying the Lord's Prayer.

Teach

▶ Have a volunteer read the Faith Focus question aloud and invite the students to think silently about how they might answer it.

▶ Read aloud the two opening paragraphs of God Cares for All People. Then ask the students to listen for why Jesus fed the crowd as you proclaim the Scripture story.

Reinforce

Have the students respond to the first follow-up question. (*Jesus showed the people God's kindness and mercy by caring about their hunger and feeding them.*)

Connect

▶ Ask volunteers to respond to the second follow-up question.

▶ Discuss how the students can be signs of God's love when they are kind to others.

Faith Focus
How does Jesus help us come to know God's love?

God Cares for All People

The New Testament tells us that when Jesus grew up, he traveled from place to place. Sometimes he walked. Sometimes he rode a donkey. Sometimes he rode in a boat.

All the things Jesus said and did taught people about God's mercy and love. Mercy means "great kindness." Read this Bible story about God's mercy.

Many people had followed Jesus all day. As nighttime came, Jesus saw that the people were hungry. But there were only two fish and five loaves of bread to feed all the people. This is what Jesus did:

Taking the five loaves and the two fish, and looking up to heaven, he said the blessing, broke the loaves, and gave them to the disciples, who in turn gave them to the crowds. They all ate and were satisfied, and they picked up the fragments left over.

MATTHEW 14:19–20

❓ In what way did Jesus show that God is kind to people?

72

TASKS OF CATECHESIS

Moral Formation. The *Catechism* teaches that "the works of mercy are charitable actions by which we come to the aid of our neighbor in his spiritual and bodily needs" (*CCC*, 2447). The origin of the Works of Mercy is found in *Matthew* 25:31-46. (See Catholics Believe on student page 69.) Reinforce that Jesus tells us that when we do these works we are following him. Recall the kindness Jesus showed in feeding the crowd in the Scripture story. Explain that Jesus shows his love for us and feeds us in the Eucharist. Emphasize that receiving Holy Communion helps us to grow closer to Jesus and to live as his followers.

Jesus is the greatest sign of God's love and mercy. You can be a follower of Jesus. You can be a sign of God's love and mercy, too.

Signs of God's Love and Mercy

Look at the pictures. How are the people caring for others? Write in each bubble what the helping person might be saying.

 My Faith Choice

This week, I promise to live as a sign of God's love and mercy. I will

_____

_____

 Pray, "Thank you, Holy Spirit, for helping me to live as a sign of God's love and kindness. Amen."

(73)

DAY 4 — DECIDE

Reinforce

Remind the students that Jesus is the fulfillment of God's promise and the greatest sign of God's love and mercy.

Respond

▶ Share a story you have heard or read about recently in which people cared for others as Jesus did.

▶ Point out the illustrations on page 73. With partners have the students describe what is happening in each.

▶ Introduce the writing activity and give clear directions. Invite the students to fill in the bubbles.

▶ Ask several volunteers to share their completed work with the class.

Choose

▶ Invite the students to read silently My Faith Choice.

▶ Encourage them to write their decisions and to put them into practice this week.

Pray

Invite the class to offer a silent prayer of thanks to the Holy Spirit.

TEACHING TIP

Writing Stories. The outline in the activity above can be a starting point that enables you to meet the students' individual needs as time allows. The students can use these outlines to tell a fuller story in a way that they best express their learning. For example, students who express themselves best through drawing might create a storyboard showing a beginning, middle, and end for their stories. Students who prefer writing can create a narrative for their stories. Students who express themselves well through movement can work with others to create skits. Try to offer students opportunities for more than one kind of activity in each week's lesson.

Pray

Begin class by leading the class in the Hail Mary.

Recall

▶ Write the words *love* and *mercy* on the board. Ask the class to brainstorm three things they have learned about God's love and mercy for his people. List ideas on the board.

▶ Read the To Help You Remember statements aloud, and ask the students to compare them with their ideas.

▶ Give instructions for the matching and sentence completion parts of the review activity and allow time for the students to complete them. Ask all to share their work with partners.

Reflect

Give the students a few moments to silently read and think about how they would answer the question, *"How do you show God's love and mercy to others?"* Then have them write their answers.

Share

Canvas the room for responses. Then have the students turn to page 73 and reread their faith choices. Ask them to think carefully how they will put their choices into action.

TO HELP YOU REMEMBER

1. The Covenant is a promise of God's love and mercy.
2. The birth of Jesus Christ, the Son of God, is called the Nativity.
3. Everything Jesus said and did shows us God's love and mercy.

Chapter Review

Recall

Match the words to their meanings.

 b **1.** Mary   **a.** This Person is the Son of God.

 d **2.** Nativity   **b.** She is the Mother of the Son of God.

 c **3.** Joseph   **c.** He is the foster father of Jesus.

 a **4.** Jesus   **d.** This is the name we give to the Bible story of Jesus' birth.

Add letters to complete the words in the sentences.

6. God's promise to always love and be kind to his people is called the

C _o_ _v_ _e_ _n_ _a_ _n_ t.

7. J _e_ s _u_ _s_ is the Son of God.

8. Jesus showed us God's love and

m _e_ _r_ _c_ y.

Reflect

What are the ways that you show God's love and mercy to others?

_____

_____

 Share   Share with your class how you know God loves you.

(74)

The Angelus

The Angelus is a prayer that praises God for the birth of Jesus.

Group 1 The angel spoke God's message to Mary,

Group 2 and she conceived of the Holy Spirit.

All **Hail, Mary, full of grace,**
the Lord is with thee.
Blessed art thou among women,
and blessed is the fruit of thy
**   womb, Jesus.**
Holy Mary, Mother of God,
pray for us sinners,
now and at the hour of our death.
Amen.

Group 1 "I am the lowly servant of the Lord:

Group 2 let it be done to me according to your word."

All **Hail, Mary . . .**

Group 1 And the Word became flesh

Group 2 and lived among us.

All **Hail, Mary . . .**

75

We Pray

▶ Tell the students that today they are going to pray the Angelus, a very old prayer of the Church.

▶ Point out that the name *Angelus* comes from the word "Angel" in the prayer's first line.

▶ Divide the class into two groups. Have each group practice its responses to the prayer. Point out that each one is different.

▶ Tell the students that after each response they will pray the Hail Mary together. Explain that you will recite the first part, and they will finish the prayer.

▶ Encourage the students to memorize the Hail Mary if they do not know it.

▶ Gather the students in the prayer area with their books and call the students to prayer with a brief moment of silence.

▶ Pray the Sign of the Cross, and then lead the students in the Angelus.

LITURGY CONNECTION

Praying Antiphonally. The Angelus is often prayed as an antiphon—the prayers are said or sung with one person or group starting a line and another completing it. As you divide the class for the praying of the Angelus, it would be helpful to choose a volunteer to be a prayer leader for each group. Ask the leaders to stand facing the groups and gesture when it is time for their peers to recite the response.

Preview

▶ Have the students carefully tear out pages 75 and 76 along the perforation.

▶ Encourage the students to share these pages with their families, and to complete the activities together.

▶ If they did not complete the review activity on page 74 by the end of the session, emphasize that they can complete it with their families at home.

▶ Point out the title and theme of the next lesson to the students.

Visit BeMyDisciples.com

▶ Take time with the students to explore the many activities and resources available at the *Be My Disciples* Web site.

▶ Encourage them to join with their families to discover the many resources available at the Web site.

Before Moving On ...

As you finish today's lesson, reflect on the following question before moving on to the next chapter.

How much quiet time do I allow the students to think about the concepts I am presenting?

With My Family

This Week . . .

In Chapter 5, "Jesus, the Son of God," your child learned that:

▶ God and his people made the Covenant with one another.

▶ The Covenant is the promise of God's love and mercy, and the promise of his people to love and serve God above all else.

▶ When Adam and Eve sinned and broke the Covenant, God promised to send someone to renew the Covenant.

▶ God fulfilled his promise by sending his Son, Jesus Christ, who became man and lived among us. Jesus Christ is true God and true man. He is the new and everlasting Covenant.

▶ The virtue of mercy helps us act with kindness toward others.

For more about related teachings of the Church, see the *Catechism of the Catholic Church*, 51–67 and 456–560, and the *United States Catholic Catechism for Adults*, pages 77–87.

■ Sharing God's Word

Read together Luke 2:1–14, about Jesus' birth. Or read the play about the Nativity on page 70. Emphasize that Jesus Christ is the Son of God. Jesus' birth is one of the most important signs that God always keeps his promise to love us.

■ Live as Disciples

The Christian home and family is a school of discipleship. Choose one of the following activities to do as a family, or design a similar activity of your own:

▶ Share ways that your family is already a living sign of God's love and kindness.

▶ Jesus told people repeatedly about God's love for them. Look around your home for something that reminds you of God's love. Talk about what it tells you about God's love.

■ Our Spiritual Journey

Devotion to Mary is a hallmark of Catholic living. Mary is an exemplar of holiness and hope and a witness to faith. She is the Mother of Jesus and our mother, too. Include a devotion to Mary, the Mother of God, in the spiritual journey of your family. In this chapter, your child prayed part of the Angelus. This prayer was traditionally prayed three times a day. Read and pray together the prayer on page 75. Pray the Hail Mary as a family each day.

For more ideas on ways your family can live as disciples of Jesus, visit **BeMyDisciples.com**

76

PARTNERING WITH PARENTS

Works of Mercy. Write a note to the parents of your second graders, encouraging them to look at BeMyDisciples.com and find the list of the Corporal and Spiritual Works of Mercy. After discussing the lists, invite families to choose one practical way they can put one of the Works of Mercy into action. For example, each family can donate non-perishable foods to your parish pantry or, with your help in networking, several families can work together to prepare food baskets for parish families in need. Both of these activities are in response to Jesus' command to feed the hungry.

Enriching the Lesson

Literature Connection

Purpose

To reinforce the teaching about kindness (taught on pages 66–67)

Directions

Mrs. Katz and Tush by Patricia Polacco (Dragonfly Books, 1994) illustrates how kindness leads to friendship. This book describes the relationship between a young African-American and Mrs. Katz, a Jewish widow.

▶ Brainstorm with the students ways they could make someone who is lonely feel happy.

▶ Have the students listen for how Lionel makes Mrs. Katz happy as you read the story.

▶ In pairs, have the students retell all the acts of kindness they heard in the story.

Materials

Mrs. Katz and Tush, by Patricia Polacco

Pantomiming a Scripture Story

Purpose

To reinforce the students' understanding of Matthew 14:13–20 (taught on page 72)

Directions

▶ Involve the students in a Scripture pantomime of Matthew 14:13–20. The following will help you begin:

People followed Jesus from the towns.
(Walk in place; put hand over eyes and point to someone up ahead.)

As nighttime came, Jesus saw that people were hungry.
(Raise arms above head and pull down the darkness; then hold stomach as if hungry.)

The disciples had only two fish and five loaves of bread to feed all the people.
(Raise two fingers, then five fingers on the other hand; point to people all around you.)

▶ Divide the class into several groups and teach each group gestures for one part of the story. When the students are ready, place the groups in the correct sequence and have them pantomime the Scripture story as you read it aloud.

Materials

Bible

Making Headlines

Purpose

To reinforce the students' living of Jesus' teaching about God's mercy (taught on page 72)

Directions

▶ Brainstorm with the students ways that they show kindness to one another in the classroom. Tell them you will be observing the ways they care for others.

▶ As you observe the students showing care for one another, affirm those behaviors immediately and make a note of them.

▶ Start a mini-newspaper. Elicit the help of an aide or parent to type up the short descriptions of kindness you see in the students each week.

▶ Include the stories of kindness in the "newspaper" and send copies of the newspaper home with the students.

Materials

copies of children's newspaper for parents

BACKGROUND

Public Ministry

As soon as Jesus' public ministry began, he attracted the distrust and enmity of some religious and political leaders. Jesus expelled demons, forgave sins by his own powers, healed on the Sabbath, and interpreted the Law of Moses in a new way.

Some people interpreted these actions of Jesus to be the works of a false prophet and a man possessed by an evil spirit. A few judged Jesus to be guilty of blasphemy, a man who falsely claimed to be God (*see John* 10:33). Such a claim, under the Jewish law, was worthy of death. Many came to understand that Jesus is truly the Son of God (*see John* 1:14).

Jesus the Savior

The suffering and Death of Jesus are at the heart of God's plan of Salvation in Christ that had been prefigured in Isaiah's prophecy about the Suffering Servant (*see Isaiah* 52:13–53:12; *Acts* 8:32–35). Jesus gave "his life as a ransom for many" (*Matthew* 20:28). Jesus died for everyone without exception. The Church states clearly: "There is not, never has been, and never will be a single human being for whom Christ did not suffer" (*Council of Quiercy*, 853).

Death into Life

If the Death of Jesus on the Cross had been the end of the story of his life and work, he might have become just an inspirational footnote in history. But the life and work of Jesus did not did end on the Cross. Jesus was raised from the dead to a new and glorified life. The Resurrection was, in a sense, the Father's seal of approval on his Son, Jesus, and the work he was sent to do.

Christ's Resurrection both fulfills the promises of the Old Testament and is our promise of a new and glorified life. It is the divine assurance that Christ has conquered death and sin, and that they no longer have power over human life. Christ's Resurrection is the divine promise that we, like Christ, shall live forever. Death has lost its sting!

The Hope of Resurrection and New Life for All

The Resurrection is the source of our own future resurrection, which we profess in the Apostles' Creed: "I believe in . . . the resurrection of the body." By Adam's sin, we all die. By the Death and Resurrection of Christ, we are given the gift of new life in Christ. The Risen Christ lives in us. We no longer live for ourselves but for him who has died for our sake (*see 2 Corinthians* 5:15).

For Reflection

What does being baptized into Christ's Death and Resurrection mean for me?

How do I live no longer for myself but for him who has died for me—and for all people?

Teacher to Teacher

Jesus' Death and Resurrection

Catholic students are familiar with the crucifix, candles, and other symbols of Christianity. Asked where they would see a crucifix and candles, they would readily reply, "In church!" They are now at an age where they can begin to comprehend the basic tenets of our faith that the crucifix and candles symbolize.

True God and True Man

Since most of the students you are teaching this year will soon receive for the first time the Sacraments of Penance and Reconciliation and the Eucharist, it is important for them to understand that Jesus is true God and true man. Jesus is the Son of God who became a man and died for each one of us. Jesus suffered and died for all people of all time. Three days later Jesus was raised from the dead. Because of Jesus' Resurrection, we too will live forever. The Easter candle reminds us of Jesus' Resurrection. Remind the children that we are to love one another—all people—as Jesus commanded us to do.

The Church Teaches...

"The *Catechism of the Catholic Church* is intended to complement Sacred Scripture. Together with Sacred Tradition, Sacred Scripture constitutes the supreme rule of faith" (*National Directory for Catechesis,* **24C**).

As the students prepare for Jesus, the "Lamb of God who takes away the sin of the world," they must learn the importance of listening to Jesus and living as he taught.

Further Reading and Reflection

For more related teachings of the Church, see the *Catechism of the Catholic Church,* 422–451, 456–478, and 599–655; and the *United States Catholic Catechism for Adults,* pages 91–98.

Teacher Prayer

Lord Jesus, help me to prepare my mind, heart, and soul to be ready to receive your message in whatever way you choose to bring it to me. Amen.

Lesson Planner

Chapter 6 Jesus, the Savior

Goal To understand that Jesus Christ is the Savior of the world

LESSON PART	PROCESS	MATERIALS and RESOURCES
DAY 1 EXPLORE **Focus** To explore how we show God's love to others by sacrificing out of love **Pages** 77–79	▶ Proclaim and discuss John 13:34; 15:13 (The greatest love is to give up your life for your friends.) ▶ Learn and discuss the story of Saint Elizabeth of Hungary. **Disciple Power:** Sacrifice **Activity:** Decide who is making sacrifices and write a sacrifice you are willing to make.	Bible Pencils or pens
DAY 2 DISCOVER **Focus** To discover how God fulfilled his promise by sending his Son Jesus as our Savior **Pages** 80–81	▶ Learn that God fulfilled his promise to send a Savior. ▶ Discover that Jesus is the fulfillment of God's promise. **Scripture Story:** The Birth of Jesus (Matthew 1:20-23) **Catholics Believe:** The Crucifix **Activity:** Discover the name of Jesus.	Bible Pencils or pens Crayons or markers
DAY 3 DISCOVER **Focus** To discover why we call Jesus Christ the Savior of all people **Pages** 82–83	▶ Learn how the Crucifixion showed Jesus' love for all people. ▶ Discover that Jesus' sacrifice on the cross brought us forgiveness and opened the way to heaven for all people. **Scripture Story:** The Crucifixion and Death of Jesus (Luke 23:33-34, 44, 46) **Faith Words:** Crucifixion	Bible Pencils or pens **Enriching the Lesson:** Teacher Guide, page 147 • Making Story Cards • Parish Bulletin Board • Literature Connection: *The Legend of the Three Trees* **Additional Activities Booklet:** Activity 6a or see *BeMyDisciples*.com
DAY 4 DECIDE **Focus** To discover that God raised Jesus to new life and to choose a way to share the Good News of Jesus' saving love **Pages** 84–85	▶ Learn that Jesus is raised to new life. **Scripture Story:** The Resurrection of Jesus (Luke 24:4, 6, 9, 11–12) **Faith Words:** Resurrection **Activity:** Design a bookmark. **My Faith Choice:** Share a story of Jesus with others this week.	Bible Pencils or pens Crayons or markers **Additional Activities Booklet:** Activity 6b or see *BeMyDisciples*.com
DAY 5 CONCLUDE **Focus** To praise God with prayer acclamations **Pages** 86–88	▶ **REVIEW** Review concepts: Recall, Reflect, and Share. ▶ **PRAY** Praise God ▶ **PREVIEW** the With My Family page and the theme of the next chapter.	Bible, candle, cross for prayer space Grade 2 Music CD **Assessment Tools Booklet:** Assessments 1a and 1b

Assign online Chapter Review and interactive Chapter Test at **BeMyDisciples.com**

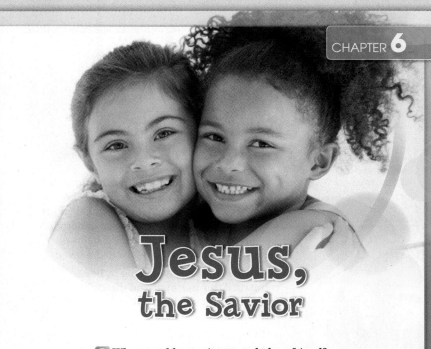

CHAPTER **6**

Jesus, the Savior

? What would you give up to help a friend? Jesus told his friends,

"Love one another. You know how I have loved you. Love one another the same way. Remember, the greatest love you can show is to give up your life for your friends."

BASED ON JOHN 13:34; 15:13

? What are some ways that Jesus showed love for others?

77

TASKS OF CATECHESIS

Promoting Knowledge of the Faith. In the proclamation of the New Commandment from John's Gospel, Jesus emphasizes the importance of the loving relationship that his disciples must share with one another. Jesus also foretells his coming sacrificial Death. Christ's Death is both an example and a model for his disciples. In this chapter and throughout the year, the students will grow in their understanding of how and why Jesus gave his life for us. For now, it is enough for them to begin to recognize that Jesus' friends live with love, as he did. As a sign of that love, you may want to invite the students to exchange a sign of peace with one another at the beginning or end of each class session.

Pray

▶ Ask the students to quiet themselves for prayer. Remind them that Jesus is with us when we pray.

▶ Pray the Sign of the Cross together.

▶ Call on different students to respond to the opening question. *(Affirm all reasonable replies.)*

▶ Invite the students to tell what they would give up for a friend. Assure them that while giving up things is not easy, it is a powerful way to show our love for another.

Reflect

▶ Choose a volunteer to read the Scripture passage. Afterward, observe a moment of prayerful silence.

▶ Invite the students to respond to the Scripture question. *(Accept all reasonable answers.)*

▶ Have the students conclude prayer time with a moment of thanksgiving for Jesus' gift of love.

Focus

Have the students turn the page to see what a princess gave up to show her love for her people.

Introduce

▶ Introduce the word *sacrifice* in Disciple Power. Point out that most of the sacrifices we make will be small in comparison to Jesus' sacrifice.

▶ Ask volunteers to read aloud the story of Saint Elizabeth of Hungary. As they do so, ask the students to underline what Elizabeth did to love and help others.

Reinforce

▶ Ask for responses to the follow-up question. *(Accept all reasonable replies.)* List responses on the board.

▶ Go on to invite the students to recall what they said they would be willing to give up in order to help another.

▶ Call attention to the list of things on the board that Saint Elizabeth did to show her love for Jesus and her people. Invite the students to tell how they can show their love for Jesus and for their families.

▶ Point out that showing such love sometimes requires sacrifice.

▶ Before moving on, draw attention once again to the meaning of *sacrifice* in Disciple Power.

Disciple Power

Sacrifice

You sacrifice when you give up something because you love someone. Jesus sacrificed his life for all people. Followers of Jesus make sacrifices out of love for God and for people.

The Church Follows Jesus

Saint Elizabeth of Hungary

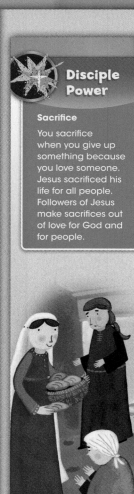

Elizabeth was born many years ago. Her parents were the king and queen of the country called Hungary. Princess Elizabeth was very rich. She was also very generous. She loved Jesus very much. She followed Jesus' Commandment to love as he loved.

Elizabeth loved the people in her country. After her husband died, she gave up everything she had, out of her love for God and others.

Princess Elizabeth gave away her fancy clothes and jewels and money to help people. She shared her money with people who were poor. She gave food to people who were hungry. She cared for people who were sick and even had a hospital built to care for them.

Today we remember Princess Elizabeth as Saint Elizabeth of Hungary. We celebrate her feast on November 17.

 How did Saint Elizabeth show her love for Jesus and for the people of Hungary?

78

DISCIPLE POWER

Sacrifice. Emphasize that like Saint Elizabeth, we can show our love for Jesus and others by making sacrifices. Point out that some sacrifices are small. Ask volunteers for examples (letting a classmate in greater need go ahead of us in line, sharing a bag of treats with a friend, and so forth). Explain that we can also make big sacrifices out of love. Recall that Jesus sacrificed his life and that Saint Elizabeth gave up everything she had to help others. Invite the students to name a "big" sacrifice that second graders might make (choosing to play with a younger sibling rather than watching a favorite television show or using allowance money to buy a Christmas gift for children from families in need instead of a toy for themselves). Affirm the students' ideas and help them to see that their sacrifices are signs of love.

Saint Elizabeth shows us that loving God and loving people is not always easy. Sometimes we have to put the needs of others first. Sometimes we have to give up what we want and make a sacrifice.

Activity

Loving Sacrifices

To sacrifice is to give up something out of love. Read the sentences below. Decide which children are putting the needs of others first and choosing to sacrifice. Circle their names.

Manuel

My brother wants to change the TV station from my favorite channel to his favorite channel. I let him.

Doreen

My little sister wants to wear my bracelet. No way!

Linh

My mom is sick. Instead of playing after school, I'll come right home to help take care of my baby brother.

Write something you could sacrifice or give up out of love for someone else.

_____

_____

_____

(79)

TEACHING TIP

Brainstorming. Brainstorm things second graders can give up to help others. Suggest they use some examples from the activity on page 79. Then brainstorm time they can give things up. Write their ideas on the board. Have the class vote on the most difficulty things to give up and on the times they are most difficult. Discuss the results of the voting.

Connect

▶ Call on a volunteer to read aloud the opening paragraph on page 79.

▶ Invite the students to tell of a time they sacrificed for another.

▶ Read aloud the first sentence under Loving Sacrifices. *(To sacrifice is to give up something out of love.)* Have the students underline the word *sacrifice*. Then explain the directions for the activity.

▶ Give the students time to read each situation and to circle the names of the children who are putting the needs of others first and choosing to sacrifice.

▶ Check responses. Ask what each "sacrificing" child sacrificed. *(Manuel—his desire to watch his TV program; Linh—her after-school play time)*

▶ Finally, give the students a moment to write what they would be willing to sacrifice or give up out of love.

▶ Have the students share their responses with partners.

Pray

▶ Gather the class for prayer. Have them echo the following prayer.

> Help me, Lord Jesus, / be willing to love others / as you love me. / Amen.

▶ Conclude by praying the Sign of the Cross.

Key Concept
Jesus is the Savior sent by God the Father.

Pray

Invite the students to quiet themselves for prayer. Invite the class to echo the following:

Thank you, Jesus, / for the people who make sacrifices for me. / Help me be willing to do the same. / Show me how to love / more and more each day. / Amen.

Teach

▶ Ask a student to read aloud the Faith Focus question. Share with the students that they will learn why God said his Son should be called "Jesus."

▶ Read aloud the opening paragraph of God Sends the Savior.

▶ Remind the students of the words from Isaiah they heard in their last lesson (Isaiah 9:5). If you wish, have the children turn back to page 65 and read the passage again.

▶ Go on to tell the class that now they are going to hear how God kept his promise to send the Savior to his people. Ask the students to close their books and listen as you proclaim the Scripture based on Matthew 1:20–23.

▶ Present the last paragraph in your own words.

Faith Focus
Why was Mary and Joseph's baby named Jesus?

God Sends the Savior

God promised to send his people a savior. A savior is a person who sets people free. God the Father sent his Son Jesus to be the Savior of the world. God sent Jesus to save people from their sins.

Read this Bible story. Saint Matthew tells us about the announcement that God would send the Savior.

One night when Joseph was sleeping, an angel brought him a message from God. The angel said to Joseph, "Mary, your wife, will give birth to a son. You are to name him, Jesus. He will save his people from their sins. All this will happen to fulfill God's promises."

BASED ON MATTHEW 1:20–23

When the child was born, Joseph named him Jesus. When Jesus grew up, he loved God and us so much he made a great sacrifice for us. Jesus died on the Cross to free us from our sins.

? How was Jesus our Savior?

80

TEACHING TIP

Sharing God's Love. Words help us to show our love for others. Provide a collection of markers, drawing paper, scissors, and glue. Divide the class into groups to share the supplies. In their groups, have each student create a greeting card for someone. Using their own words on the cards, invite them to share God's love with someone in need.

The Name of Jesus

Look at this name:

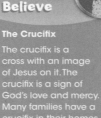

It is the name *Jesus*. It is written in the language Jesus spoke.

Do you know what the name *Jesus* means? Find out. Color the spaces marked with an X blue. Color spaces marked with a Y with other bright colors.

GOD SAVES

(81)

Catholics Believe

The Crucifix

The crucifix is a cross with an image of Jesus on it. The crucifix is a sign of God's love and mercy. Many families have a crucifix in their homes. Some Christians wear a crucifix on a chain around the neck to show their love for Jesus. There is a crucifix always placed near the altar in church.

CATHOLICS BELIEVE

The Crucifix. From the Latin words, *crux fixus*, crucifix means "fastened to a cross." A cross bearing an image of our Lord's body has been venerated among Christians since the sixth century. When blessed, it is an important sacramental. A crucifix should always be placed over the altar on which the Sacrifice of the Mass is to be offered. It may also serve as a processional cross at the beginning of Mass. The faithful are also urged to have a crucifix in their homes as a reminder of Jesus' sacrifice and our faith and belief in him.

Reinforce

▶ Ask the students to underline the angel's message to Joseph in the Scripture passage.

▶ Ask the children to respond to the follow-up question. (*A savior is a person who sets people free.*)

▶ Invite a volunteer to read Catholics Believe. Remind the students that Jesus died on the cross to free us from our sins.

Connect

▶ Tell the students that many names have meanings. Use the names of the students in the activity on page 79 as examples and write on the board:

—*Manuel*—"God with us"

—*Doreen*—"gift"

—*Linh*—"spring"

If possible offer the meanings of some of the students' names.

▶ Call attention to the section titled The Name of Jesus on page 81. Ask the students if they know what the name Jesus means. Then have them do the activity to find out.

▶ When the students finish, have the class read the meaning aloud. (*God saves.*)

▶ Ask: Why is Jesus such a good name for God's Son?

Pray

Gather the class for prayer. Lead them in the following.

Loving God, thank you for sending us Jesus. Thank you for being the God who saves. Amen.

> **Key Concept**
> Jesus died on the Cross to save us.

Pray

Gather the children for prayer. Lead them in the Glory Be.

Teach

▶ Read the Faith Focus question aloud and ask for possible answers. Tell the students that these two pages will help them discover why Jesus is the Savior of all people.

▶ Ask a volunteer to read the first paragraph of Jesus Died on the Cross.

▶ Guide the students in an imaginative exercise. Have them picture being there when Jesus was crucified. Ask the class to listen carefully as you proclaim the Scripture based on Luke 23:33–34, 44, 46.

▶ Have the students underline the name of the hill where Jesus died. (*Calvary*) Then discuss their thoughts and feelings about what it must have been like at Jesus' Crucifixion.

▶ Have the students read the last paragraph on page 82 silently to find out why Jesus died on the Cross.

▶ Ask the follow-up question. (*Jesus showed his love for the Father and for us by freely dying on the Cross. Accept all other appropriate responses.*)

> **Faith Focus**
> Why do we call Jesus Christ the Savior of all people?
>
> **Faith Words**
> ▶ **Crucifixion**
> The Crucifixion is the Death of Jesus on a cross.

Jesus Died on the Cross

Jesus showed his love for his Father and for all people by freely dying on the Cross. Jesus' death on a cross is called the **Crucifixion**.

This is part of the story of what happened at the Crucifixion. Saint Luke tells us,

On a hill near the city of Jerusalem, soldiers put Jesus to death on a cross. The name of the hill is Calvary. The sky became very dark. Jesus said, "Father, forgive them." Then Jesus died.

BASED ON LUKE 23:33–34, 44, 46

Jesus' Death on the Cross is also called the Sacrifice of the Cross. Jesus sacrificed his life to save and free us from sin and death. Through Jesus' Death on the Cross, God forgives us our sins.

? What does the Crucifixion mean?

82

TEACHING TIP

Church Visit. For this lesson about the Crucifixion, it may be a good idea to make a visit to the church to see the Stations of the Cross. Have the students study each station carefully to determine what is happening. Then have the class gather in the pews for the proclamation of the Scripture based on Luke 23:33–34, 44, 46. Lead a discussion about what the students saw and heard.

Jesus' loving sacrifice has made us friends with God again. Because of Jesus' love, we can live forever with God in Heaven. The Bible says:

> By his cross, Jesus forgave our sins. Now we can live forever with God.
>
> BASED ON 1 PETER 2:24

Jesus is our Savior. Jesus is the Savior of the world!

? Why do we make sacrifices?

Faith-Filled People

Saint Mary Magdalene

Mary Magdalene stood by the Cross of Jesus with Mary, the Mother of Jesus, and with several other disciples of Jesus. She was one of the first disciples to whom the Risen Jesus appeared. The Church celebrates her feast day on July 22.

Activity

Praying to Jesus

Match the numbers with the letters. Fill in the missing letters. Discover a prayer to our Savior.

E = 1	U = 5	S = 9
H = 2	A = 6	F = 10
R = 3	K = 7	K = 11
O = 4	N = 8	G = 12

T H A N K   Y O U ,   J E S U S .
2 6 8 7   4 5   1 9 5 9

F O R   S A v i N G   U S !
10 4 3   9 6   8 12   5 9

83

FAITH-FILLED PEOPLE

Saint Mary Magdalene. There are many stories about Saint Mary Magdalene, yet the Bible tells us one thing for sure. Scripture tells us that Jesus cured her from the possession of no less than seven demons. Saint Mary Magdalene, from the town of Magdala, became one of a group of women who followed Jesus from Galilee and ministered to him. Having been saved from her own torment, Mary was a devoted follower of Jesus. She witnessed the Crucifixion and was among the first who witnessed the empty tomb on Easter and saw the Risen Christ. For this reason, she is often referred to as the Apostle to the Apostles. For more information on Saint Mary Magdalene, go to the Saints Resource at *BeMyDisciples*.com.

Reinforce

▶ Read aloud the definition of *Crucifixion* in Faith Words and have the students make a word card for the term.

▶ Ask the students to name three facts they know about the Crucifixion.

▶ Present Faith-Filled People about Mary Magdalene. Note especially that while almost all the other disciples of Jesus fled as he hung upon the Cross, Saint Mary Magdalene remained by him until the end.

Connect

▶ Read aloud the text of Jesus, Savior of the World, including the Scripture verse from 1 Peter.

▶ Then present the activity directions, making sure the students understand them. If you wish, help the students along with a letter or two. Likewise, consider allowing the students to work with partners.

Pray

▶ Gather the students with their books for prayer. Lead them in offering the words of the prayer revealed in the activity. *(Thank you, Jesus, for saving us.)*

▶ Conclude with the Sign of the Cross.

Key Concept
God raised Jesus from death to new life.

Pray

Lead the students in praying the Sign of the Cross.

Teach

▶ Have a volunteer read the Faith Focus question aloud and invite the students to think silently about how they might answer it.

▶ Go on to read aloud the first paragraph on page 84.

▶ Invite volunteers to mime the parts of the different characters in the Resurrection story based on Luke 24 as you read it.

▶ Have the class read the last paragraph aloud together.

Reinforce

▶ Ask the follow-up question. Make sure the children recognize that because of Jesus' Resurrection, we too, will live forever with God. Explain that we celebrate the Resurrection of Jesus at Easter.

▶ Point out *Resurrection* in Faith Words. Have the students make a card for the term.

Connect

▶ Have the students read Catholics Believe to discover why the crucifix is a sign of God's love.

▶ If you wish, lead the class in singing a familiar Easter hymn.

Faith Focus
What happened three days after Jesus died on the Cross and was buried?

Faith Words
Resurrection
The Resurrection is God the Father raising Jesus from the dead to new life.

Jesus Is Raised to New Life

Something amazing happened three days after Jesus died and was buried in the tomb. Mary Magdalene and two other women disciples of Jesus went to the place where Jesus was buried. When they arrived there, the women saw that the body of Jesus was not there.

Two men dressed in bright white robes appeared to the women and said, "Jesus is not here. He has been raised." The women left the tomb and told the Apostles and others what happened. Peter and the others did not believe them. Peter rushed to the tomb to see for himself if what the women disciples said was true.

BASED ON LUKE 24:4, 6, 9, 11–12

Jesus rose from the dead to new life. We call this the **Resurrection**.

We too shall live after we die. All the faithful friends of Jesus will live in happiness with God forever in Heaven.

❓ Why is the Resurrection so important?

84

TEACHING TIP

Symbols of Jesus. Ask the students if they know any signs or symbols the Catholic Church uses to represent Jesus. Most will think of a cross or crucifix. Remind them of the fish symbol that is used often today. Tell the class that in the early Church Christians often had to meet secretly. When they did, they sometimes drew a fish to identify themselves as followers of Jesus. Remind the students that a loaf of bread and cup of wine are symbols for Jesus, too. These remind us that the Eucharist is the Body and Blood of Christ.

Jesus is the Savior of all people. He sacrificed his life out of love for his Father and for all people. The Holy Spirit invites you to share this Good News with everyone.

 Activity

Alleluia! Praise God!

Design this bookmark with colors and pictures that help you remember Jesus is the Savior of the world.

Save us, Savior of the world,
for by your Cross and Resurrection
you have set us free.

Alleluia!

MEMORIAL ACCLAMATION C, ROMAN MISSAL

 My Faith Choice

Think of how you can tell others about the Good News of Jesus' saving love for all people. I will

_____

_____

Pray, "Thank you, Jesus, for your sacrifice. Thank you for giving up your life to free us from sin. Amen."

85

Reinforce

Remind the class that the Holy Spirit is always with us, inviting and helping us to tell everyone about Jesus, the Savior of the world.

Respond

▶ Present the introductory paragraph in your own words.

▶ Divide the class into small groups and have each group name ways it can share with others the Good News that Jesus is the Savior of the world. Walk around and give encouragement as needed.

▶ Direct the students' attention to the activity and invite them to decorate the bookmark.

Choose

▶ Have the students read My Faith Choice and write their responses.

▶ Encourage the students to put their decisions into practice this week.

Pray

Have the students quiet themselves for prayer. Lead them in praying the prayer to Jesus at the bottom of page 85.

LITURGY TIP

Music Experience. Play a recording of a song written for the Easter season. This will help the students learn about the meaning of the Resurrection in a different way. Try to find one that might be familiar to them or written especially for young students.

Pray

Begin by leading the class in the Glory Be.

Recall

▶ Introduce the fill-in-the blank and yes-or-no sentence activities and allow time for the students to complete them. Invite the students to check their answers with partners.

▶ Ask the students to look at the acclamation they just prayed. Ask volunteers to tell you how they would explain part of the acclamation to someone. Invite the students to use the To Help You Remember statements to explain the acclamation.

Reflect

Give the students a few moments to silently read and think about how they might answer the Reflect question. Then give them time to write their responses.

Share

▶ Have the students share what they wrote with partners.

▶ Have the students turn back to page 85 and reread their faith choice. Ask them to think about how they will put that choice into action. Then have them share one way people will see them putting their faith choices into action this week.

▶ **TO HELP YOU REMEMBER**

1. Jesus Christ is the Savior of the world.
2. Jesus sacrificed his life on the Cross to save all people from their sins.
3. God the Father raised his Son, Jesus, from death to new life.

Chapter Review

Recall

Use the words in the box to complete the sentences.

Savior	Resurrection	Crucifixion

1. God the Father raising Jesus to new life is called the ___Resurrection___.

2. God the Father sent Jesus to be the ___Savior___.

3. Jesus' Death on a Cross is called the ___Crucifixion___.

Circle yes or no for each sentence.

4. Jesus died on the Cross because he loves us. **(Yes)** No

5. The Crucifixion means that Jesus was raised from the dead. Yes **(No)**

6. The Resurrection is God's promise that we will live forever with him in Heaven. **(Yes)** No

Reflect

Why is Jesus' Resurrection so important to us?

_____

_____

Share Share with a friend or classmate something that you sacrificed.

86

HUMAN METHODOLOGIES

Learning within the Christian Family. The family is the "place in which the word of God is received and from which it is extended" (*NDC*, 29D). Prepare a worksheet on which families can explore their homes for signs of faith. In your note to the parents encourage them to purchase a crucifix for the family if they do not already have one. Remind parents that one of the ways we express our faith is through signs and symbols in our homes. Other signs of faith the family can look for include: a Bible, a rosary, icons, and a picture of the Pope. On the worksheet, invite parents to explain the meaning of these signs to their children. When the students return their completed assignments, allow time for them to share the lists with the class.

Praise God

Acclamations are prayers of praise. We pray acclamations to praise God for all the wonderful things he has done.

Leader Saint John was with Jesus as he died on the Cross. Listen to this reading from John's Gospel.

Reader 1 *On the first day of the week, Mary Magdala came to the tomb early in the morning, while it was still dark, and saw the stone removed from the tomb.*

Reader 2 *So she ran and went to Simon Peter and to the other disciple whom Jesus loved, and told them,*

Reader 3 *"They have taken the Lord from the tomb, and we don't know where they put him."*

JOHN 20:1–2

The Gospel of the Lord.

All **Praise to you, Lord Jesus Christ.**

Leader Now let us proclaim the mystery of faith.

All **Save us, Savior of the world, for by your Cross and Resurrection you have set us free.**
MEMORIAL ACCLAMATION C, ROMAN MISSAL

87

We Pray

▶ Tell the students that today they are going to close their prayer with a special prayer called an acclamation. Use the prayer introduction to explain about acclamations.

▶ Point out the acclamation in the prayer. Remind the students that this acclamation is the one on the bookmark they decorated in their last session.

▶ Practice the acclamation together.

▶ Ask for three volunteers to act as readers. Give them some time to practice their readings.

▶ Gather the class in the prayer center.

▶ Remind the students that when they gather together in Jesus' name, Jesus is with them.

▶ Lead the class in the prayer, beginning and ending with the Sign of the Cross. If the students are familiar with a sung version of the acclamation, consider singing it with them.

LITURGY CONNECTION

The Memorial Acclamation. The acclamation that follows the Consecration at Mass is called the Memorial Acclamation. In addition to the acclamation that is used for the prayer on this page, there are two other forms of the Memorial Acclamation:

We proclaim your Death, O Lord,
and profess your Resurrection
until you come again.

When we eat this Bread and drink this Cup,
we proclaim your Death, O Lord,
until you come again.

MEMORIAL ACCLAMATIONS A AND B, *ROMAN MISSAL*

Preview

▶ Have the students carefully tear out pages 87 and 88 along the perforation.

▶ Encourage the students to share these pages with their families, and to complete the activities together.

▶ If they did not complete the review activity on page 86 by the end of the session, emphasize that they can complete it with their families at home.

▶ Point out the title and theme of the next lesson to the students.

Visit BeMyDisciples.com

▶ Take time with the students to explore the many activities and resources available at the *Be My Disciples* Web site.

▶ Encourage them to join with their families to discover the many resources available at the Web site.

Before Moving On ...

As you finish today's lesson, reflect on the following question before moving on to the next chapter.

How well am I allowing the students to use their talents in the various class activities?

With My Family

This Week . . .

In Chapter 6, "Jesus, the Savior," your child learned:

▶ Salvation flows from God's initiative of love and mercy. God the Father sent his Son, Jesus, who freely chose to sacrifice his life on the Cross to free all people from sin.

▶ Three days after his Death and burial, Jesus rose from the dead to a new and glorified life. We call this event the Resurrection.

▶ We too shall live after we die. God invites us to live an eternal life of happiness.

▶ Jesus sacrificed his life for all people. Followers of Jesus make sacrifices out of love for God and for people.

For more about related teachings of the Church, see the *Catechism of the Catholic Church*, 422–451, 456–478, and 599–655, and the *United States Catholic Catechism for Adults*, pages 91–98.

■ Sharing God's Word

Read together the Bible story about Jesus' dying on the Cross and his rising from the dead. Emphasize that the Death and Resurrection of Jesus are the greatest signs of God's love for people.

■ Living as Disciples

The Christian home and family is a school of discipleship. Choose one of the following activities to do as a family, or design a similar activity of your own:

▶ The crucifix reminds us of God's love for us. Display a crucifix in your home. Gather around it and talk about God's love for your family.

▶ Help your child practice making sacrifices. Offer him or her opportunities to choose others over him- or herself. For example, if your child receives an allowance, suggest ways he or she can give a portion to help the hungry.

■ Our Spiritual Journey

The Sacrifice of the Cross is the greatest expression of God's love for people. Christians are people of sacrifice. In this chapter, your child learned to pray a Memorial Acclamation used at Mass. Read and pray together the prayer on page 86. Pray the acclamation: *Save us, Savior of the world, for by your Cross and Resurrection you have set us free* (Memorial Acclamation C, Roman Missal).

For more ideas on ways your family can live as disciples of Jesus, visit **BeMyDisciples.com**

88

ENRICHING THE LESSON

Alternative Bulletin Board In addition to, or as an alternative to, working with the students to design a parish bulletin board as suggested on page 147, consider working with your second graders to write an article, accompanied by digital photographs, about what they have learned about Jesus in Chapters 5 and 6. The article can be published in the weekly parish bulletin, your religious education program newsletter, or a special "take home" page for the students' families that you duplicate for each class member.

Enriching the Lesson

Making Story Cards

Purpose

To reinforce the story of the Crucifixion and the Resurrection (taught on pages 82–84)

Directions

▶ Provide the students with heavy tag board folded in half so that it stands up.

▶ Have the students draw images and write words about the Crucifixion on one side and images and words about the Resurrection on the other.

▶ Invite the students to use their pictures to tell their families about Jesus. Suggest that they display them at home.

Materials

tag board
crayons or markers

Designing a Parish Bulletin Board

Purpose

To reinforce the children's knowledge about Jesus, the Savior (taught on pages 82–83)

Directions

One way to strengthen the students' participation in parish life is to create a parish bulletin board. The bulletin board will show the entire parish what the children are learning.

▶ Discuss with the students the kinds of things they might want to tell the parish about what they have learned about Jesus, the Savior of the world.

▶ Have the students work in pairs to draw what they have learned. Their drawings might illustrate the crucifix, the Risen Jesus, or other topics.

▶ Have the students decide on a title for the bulletin board and display their pictures on the board. Place the bulletin board where parishioners can enjoy it.

Materials

corkboard for the bulletin board

crayons

push pins

construction paper

Literature Connection

Purpose

To reinforce the story of the birth and Death of Jesus (taught on pages 82–84)

Directions

The students will enjoy hearing *The Legend of the Three Trees* by Catherine McCafferty (Thomas Nelson Publishers, 2008). In this lovely picture book, three trees are cut down, but each is remade into an object that plays a part in the life of Jesus.

▶ The story reinforces themes of sacrifice and how death leads to new life. (This story is told by a second grade catechist in the *Echoes of Faith* module "Methods for Grades 1 and 2.")

▶ Tell the story and invite the students to share which tree they think had the biggest job of all.

▶ Ask what it must have felt like to play the role that each tree played.

Materials

The Legend of the Three Trees, by Catherine McCafferty

BACKGROUND

The Gift of the Holy Spirit

The Holy Spirit is the Third Divine Person of the Holy Trinity, distinct from the Father and the Son. Of the same substance with the Father and the Son, the Holy Spirit is inseparable from them. The Holy Spirit always works with the Father and the Son. He was there at creation. He was there at the beginning of God's plan of Salvation. He will be at its completion.

Fifty Days

On the day of Pentecost, the work of the Church began with the outpouring of the Holy Spirit upon the disciples.

> To fulfill this divine plan, Jesus Christ founded the Church, built on the Apostles. He gave them the Holy Spirit from the Father and sent them to preach the Gospel to the whole world. . . .
>
> As the Church lives the Gospel she is continually made fruitful by the Holy Spirit. The Spirit causes her to grow constantly in her understanding of the Gospel, prompts her and sustains the task of proclaiming the Gospel in every corner of the world..
> *General Directory for Catechesis,* 43

The outpouring of the Holy Spirit never ceases to guide the Church and make present the mission of Christ in the world until the end of time.

Water and Sacred Chrism

When we were baptized, we received the Holy Spirit, the Sanctifier. The sign of water in Baptism signifies the new birth given to us by the Holy Spirit *(see John* 3:4-5). The sign of anointing symbolizes our union with Christ, Priest, Prophet, and King. The sign of fire signifies the transforming power given to the Church by the Holy Spirit to keep the flame of faith in Christ alive in the world until the end of time.

Fruits of the Spirit

In a world that often seems to prize greed and selfishness, the Holy Spirit is at work in the life of the Church and in the lives of all the baptized, bringing "love, joy, peace, patience, kindness, generosity, faithfulness, gentleness, self-control" *(Galatians* 5:22-23) to the world.

For Reflection

When do I converse in prayer with the Holy Spirit who dwells within me?

How has the Holy Spirit been my Advocate and Guide in living the gift of new life in Christ?

Teacher to Teacher

Come, Holy Spirit

Seven- and eight-year-olds are trying to understand the world around them. As they do so, they soon discover that there are some things they cannot understand. In the Church they have learned about God the Father and Creator, Jesus the Incarnate Son of God and the Savior, and the Holy Spirit the Sanctifier. They have done this by their participation in the celebrations of the Church and by listening to stories of our faith.

The Holy Spirit's Work

This session provides the students with an opportunity to learn more about the Holy Spirit. Their faith in the Holy Spirit will be deepened as they discover more about the Spirit's work in helping them learn to live as Christians. The prayer life of children this age is just beginning to be personal. Share with them that the Holy Spirit will help them as they, more and more, pray in their own words.

The Church Teaches...

"The Holy Spirit inspired the sacred authors to preserve the message of salvation in writing and to ensure the authentic interpretation of the word of God contained in Sacred Scripture through the Magisterium" (*National Directory for Catechesis*, 16A).

For this reason, each chapter opens up with prayer focusing on a passage from Sacred Scripture.

Further Reading and Reflection

For more related teachings of the Church, see the *Catechism of the Catholic Church*, 687–741; and the *United States Catholic Catechism for Adults*, pages 102–108.

Teacher Prayer

Jesus,
the depth of your love
for me is overpowering.
You gave your life for me.
May the gift of the Holy
Spirit promised by you bear
fruit in me day by day.
Amen.

Lesson Planner

Chapter 7   The Holy Spirit

Goal To learn more about the work of the Holy Spirit

LESSON PART	PROCESS	MATERIALS and RESOURCES
DAY 1 EXPLORE **Focus** To explore how followers of Jesus use their gifts from the Holy Spirit **Pages 89–91**	▶ Proclaim and discuss 1 Corinthians 12:4–11 (The Holy Spirit gives spiritual gifts for us to help others). ▶ Share and discuss the story of Kids' Kitchen. **Disciple Power:** Generosity **Activity:** Determine gifts to meet needs.	Bible Pencils or pens
DAY 2 DISCOVER **Focus** To discover the promise Jesus made before his Ascension **Pages 92–93**	**Scripture Story:** Jesus promised to send the Holy Spirit to his disciples (Luke 24:49). ▶ Discover that the Ascension is when the Risen Jesus returned to his Father in heaven. **Faith Words:** Ascension **Catholics Believe:** Gifts of the Holy Spirit **Activity:** Solve a crossword puzzle about Jesus' promise of love.	Bible Pencils or pens **Additional Activities Booklet:** Activity 7a or see *BeMyDisciples*.com
DAY 3 DISCOVER **Focus** To discover what took place on Pentecost **Pages 94–95**	▶ Discover the story of Pentecost. **Scripture Story:** The Coming of the Holy Spirit (Acts of the Apostles 2:6) ▶ Learn about the work of the Holy Spirit. **Faith Words:** Pentecost **Faith-Filled People:** Saint Luke **Activity:** Complete a maze about the Holy Spirit.	Bible Pencils or pens **Literature Connection:** *Gilberto and the Wind*
DAY 4 DECIDE **Focus** To discover that the Holy Spirit gives us gifts to use to help others and to decide on a way to use our gifts **Pages 96–97**	▶ Discover that the Holy Spirit is always with us as Teacher, Helper, and Guide. **Scripture:** When we do not know what to pray for, the Spirit prays for us (Romans 8:26). **Activity:** Write a talent you have. **My Faith Choice:** Choose how to use my talents this week to share God's love.	Bible Pencils or pens Crayons or markers **Enriching the Lesson:** Teacher Guide, page 163 • Making Holy Spirit Prayer Cards • Making a Holy Spirit Collage **Additional Activities Booklet:** Activity 7b or see *BeMyDisciples*.com
DAY 5 CONCLUDE **Focus** To pray to the Holy Spirit **Pages 98–100**	▶ **REVIEW** Review concepts: Recall, Reflect, Share. ▶ **PRAY** Come, Holy Spirit ▶ **PREVIEW** the With My Family page and the theme of the next chapter.	Bible, candle, cross for prayer space Grade 2 Music CD **Assessment Tools Booklet:** Assessments 1a and 1b

Assign online Chapter Review and interactive Chapter Test at **BeMyDisciples.com** ⟩

CHAPTER **7**

The Holy Spirit

? **What is the best gift someone ever gave you?**

Saint Paul tells us,

God loves you very much. God sends you the Holy Spirit. The Holy Spirit gives special spiritual gifts to each person. The Holy Spirit wants us to use our gifts to help and serve others. BASED ON 1 CORINTHIANS 12:4–11

? **What special gifts do you have that help and serve others?**

89

HUMAN METHODOLOGIES

Learning through Human Experience. The *National Directory for Catechesis observes* that human experience "enables people to explore, interpret, and judge their basic experiences in light of the Gospel" **(NDC 29A)**. As you teach about Pentecost, help the students to imagine the Apostles receiving the Holy Spirit. Distribute red construction paper and instruct the students to cut out a flame-shaped piece. Once the students have heard the Pentecost story (on page 94), work with them to prepare a skit based on the story, holding their paper flames over their heads to indicate the descent of the Holy Spirit. Ask them to set the flame shapes aside until they complete the activity on page 97.

Pray

▶ Welcome the students and quiet them for prayer.

▶ Pray the Sign of the Cross together.

▶ Ask the children to echo each line of this prayer:

> Come Holy Spirit,
> be with us today
> as we learn
> about your works.
> Amen.

▶ Ask the students to respond to the opening question. *(Accept and affirm all reasonable replies.)*

Reflect

▶ Choose a volunteer to read aloud the Scripture passage.

▶ Afterward, observe a moment of prayerful silence.

▶ Ask: How does the Holy Spirit help us? *(by giving us special gifts)* What do these gifts help us do? *(help and serve others)*

▶ Invite the children to respond to the Scripture question. *(Accept all reasonable replies.)*

▶ End with a moment of reflection. Call upon the Holy Spirit to be with the students and inspire them to use their gifts for the good of others.

Focus

▶ Read aloud the Looking Ahead feature.

▶ Tell the students that people in a parish share the Spirit's gifts. Then have the students turn the page to see what sort of people the Spirit's gifts inspire us to become.

Introduce

▶ Read Disciple Power with the students. Share some examples of people in the community who generously share their gifts with others.

▶ Have the students examine the picture on the page. Then point out and read aloud the title of the story, Kids' Kitchen. Have the children tell what they think the story may be about.

▶ Ask the students to listen carefully to discover why Sagen started Kids' Kitchen.

▶ Call on different students to read the various paragraphs.

Reinforce

▶ Point out the follow-up question in the text. Have volunteers tell why Sagen started Kids' Kitchen.

▶ Discuss the gifts she shared with the community.

▶ Have the students brainstorm all of the ways they have seen people in the parish being generous. List the ways on the board.

Disciple Power

Generosity
You show generosity when you use the gifts you receive from God to help others.

The Church Follows Jesus

Kids' Kitchen

We all receive blessings and gifts from the Holy Spirit. Even second graders get these gifts! One of these gifts is the gift of generosity.

Sagen was in second grade when she saw that some children ate free lunches at school. She wondered, "What do they do during the summer? Do they get to eat lunch every day? How can I help?"

Sagen went to Sam, who was in charge of the soup kitchen in her parish. Sam helped Sagen organize her own kitchen for kids. She called it Kids' Kitchen.

The word spread about Kids' Kitchen. Soon, ten parishes were donating food. Sagen and her friends were serving lunch to over 600 children. Those children also took food home to their families.

Someone asked Sagen why she started Kids' Kitchen. "To help people," she said. "That's what I hear in church on Sunday."

❓ Why did Sagen start Kids' Kitchen?

DISCIPLE POWER

Generosity. Ask volunteers to name a generous person they know and to provide an example of the individual's generosity. Pair the students up with partners and have each twosome decide on one way they can be more generous at home, school, or with their friends. After a brief discussion period, invite the children to share their ideas with the class. Affirm the students' suggestions and encourage them to put them into practice, emphasizing that Jesus' followers try always to be generous. In the coming weeks, praise the students for the generosity you notice in their behavior.

Sagen saw what was needed. Hungry children needed lunch in the summertime. So Sagen generously used her gifts to meet the need.

Activity

Gifts Help the Need

Look at each picture below. Write what you think is needed in each. Then think of your gifts. Write how you could be generous with your gifts to meet the need.

1. What is needed?

_____

Here is how I can use my gifts to meet the need.

_____

_____

2. What is needed?

_____

Here is how I can use my gifts to meet the need.

_____

_____

3. What is needed?

_____

Here is how I can use my gifts to meet the need.

_____

_____

(91)

Connect

▶ Call on a volunteer to read aloud the opening paragraph of Gifts Help the Need on page 91.

▶ Invite the students to discuss what gifts Sagen used to meet the hungry kids' need.

▶ Point out the activity directions and read them aloud.

▶ It is probably best to go through each example one at a time with the students.

▶ Help them identify the need pictured.

▶ Discuss possible gifts the students could draw on to meet the need.

▶ Have the students write what they would do to act with generosity.

Pray

Gather the students for prayer. Have them echo the following:

Gifting God, /
thank you for /
the gifts you give me. /
Help me always /
to be as generous as you. /
Amen.

TEACHING TIP

Special Needs—Students with ADHD. It is important to help children who have Attention Deficit Hyperactivity Disorder (ADHD) stay focused. After looking at the pictures about discovering needs, have the students role-play the situations. You may wish to discuss the role playing possibilities beforehand. The students will be excited about "acting" and more inclined to stay focused and on-task.

Key Concept
Jesus promised to send the Holy Spirit.

Pray

Invite the students to quiet themselves for prayer. Pray the Glory Be.

Teach

▶ Invite the students to think about times they have made a promise to help someone and times someone has made a promise to help them. Ask why it is important to keep the promises we make to help people. *(Accept all reasonable replies.)*

▶ Read aloud the Faith Focus question and invite the children to think silently about how they might answer it. Tell the students that today they will learn about the special promise Jesus made.

▶ Read aloud the section titled The Gift of the Holy Spirit. Tell the students to listen carefully to what Jesus promised, *(Jesus promised the gift of the Holy Spirit.)* and when he made the promise. *(He made the promise before he returned to his Father in heaven.)*

▶ Read aloud or paraphrase Catholics Believe to tell about how the Gifts of the Holy Spirit help us to follow Jesus.

Faith Focus
What does the New Testament tell us about the Holy Spirit?

Faith Words
▶ **Ascension**
The Ascension is the return of the Risen Jesus to his Father in Heaven after the Resurrection.

The Gift of the Holy Spirit

After the Resurrection, Jesus made a special promise to his disciples. He said,

I am sending the promise of my Father to you. It is the gift of the Holy Spirit.

BASED ON LUKE 24:49

The Holy Spirit is the Third Person of the Holy Trinity.

Jesus made this promise after the Resurrection, just before he returned to his Father in Heaven. We call the return of the Risen Jesus to his Father in Heaven the **Ascension**.

❓ What did Jesus promise his disciples?

92

TEACHING TIP

Filled with the Holy Spirit. Students that are full of energy are often referred to as "spirited." Sometimes this is also what is said about a challenging student. It is important to recognize that these students are indeed filled with the Holy Spirit. As a religion teacher, God calls you to recognize the Gifts of the Holy Spirit in each student. Affirm these gifts by giving the challenging student tasks that utilize his or her unique qualities. Put the outgoing student in charge of making a new student feel welcome or the "helpful" student in charge of cleaning the board and so on.

Activity

A Promise of Love

Jesus' promise filled the disciples with great joy. Use the words in the box. Fill in the crossword puzzle about the promise of love.

Ascension	Jesus	Spirit
Gift	Heaven	Resurrection

```
                    ⁴S
            ¹R      P
    ²A  S  C  E  N  S  I  O  N
            S      R
        ³J  E  S  U  S
            R      I
            R      T
            E
            C
            T
        ⁵G  I  F  T
            O
        ⁶H  E  A  V  E  N
```

Down

1. Jesus made his promise after the _____.

4. The Holy _____ is the Third Person of the Holy Trinity.

Across

2. The return of the Risen Jesus to the Father is called the _____.

3. _____ made a special promise to his disciples.

5. Jesus promised a special _____.

6. Jesus returned to his Father in _____.

(93)

Catholics Believe

Gifts of the Holy Spirit

The Holy Spirit blesses us with spiritual gifts. These gifts help us to follow Jesus and to live as children of God.

TEACHING TIP

Doing Our Best. Remember that students need varying lengths of time for given tasks. Students with disabilities may need more time to do certain things. Some students may rush through activities, wanting and needing to be the first child finished. Explain that doing our best work should always be our goal, no matter how much time that might take.

On the other hand, students who are easily distracted may need to be reminded that doing our best also involves working steadily toward the goal. They may need to be reminded of the time remaining to complete an activity.

Reinforce

▶ Ask the follow-up question.

▶ Point out the Faith Words feature to the children. Print the word *Ascension* on the board.

▶ Ask a volunteer to read the meaning of *Ascension* aloud.

▶ Have the students make word cards for the term.

Connect

▶ Call attention to the section titled A Promise of Love on page 93. Ask one of the children to read aloud the opening sentence.

▶ Go over the directions to the crossword activity with the students. If they are unfamiliar with crosswords, you may need to go through each clue with them to help them see how to write responses "Up" and "Down."

▶ Allow ample time for the students to complete the activity.

▶ Call on different students to share a solution to one of the six puzzle clues.

Pray

Help the students quiet themselves for prayer. Have them echo the following:

Come, Holy Spirit. / Come, promise of Jesus. / Come, gift of the Father. / Come, Holy Spirit, come. / Amen.

> **Key Concept**
> Jesus sent the Holy Spirit promised by God the Father to help us live as children of God and as followers of Jesus.

Pray

Gather the students for prayer. Lead them in the prayer with which they concluded the previous lesson.

Teach

▶ Call attention to Faith Focus. Read the question aloud. Tell the students that they will learn when the Holy Spirit came to fulfill Jesus' promise.

▶ Have a volunteer read aloud the opening paragraph of the section titled Pentecost.

▶ Point out the illustration. Have the students close their eyes and imagine they are with Mary and the disciples.

▶ Proclaim the Pentecost story based on Acts of the Apostles 2:1–6.

▶ Invite the students to open their eyes and share the thoughts and feelings they had as they listened.

▶ Have volunteers read the final two text paragraphs. Draw attention to *when* we celebrate Pentecost. *(We celebrate Pentecost fifty days after Easter.)* Emphasize that the Holy Spirit helps us tell others about Jesus.

▶ Ask volunteers to share one thing they want to tell others about Jesus.

Faith Focus
How is the Holy Spirit always with us?

Pentecost

The promise of the Holy Spirit came true fifty days after the Ascension. The day that the Holy Spirit came to the Apostles is called **Pentecost**. Saint Luke tells us that after Jesus returned to his Father, the disciples and Mary, the mother of Jesus, were praying together in a room.

And suddenly there came from the sky a noise like a strong driving wind, and it filled the entire house in which they were. Then there appeared to them tongues as of fire, which parted and came to rest on each one of them. And they were all filled with the holy Spirit . . . .

ACTS OF THE APOSTLES 2:1–4

Peter and the disciples then left the house. They went to tell others about Jesus.

Each year, fifty days after Easter, we remember and celebrate Pentecost. We celebrate the wonderful gift of the Holy Spirit.

We first receive the gift of the Holy Spirit at Baptism. He gives us special gifts to live as followers of Jesus. The Holy Spirit helps us tell others about Jesus as Peter did.

❓ What is one thing you want to tell someone about Jesus?

94

CATHOLIC TRADITION

Pentecost. Pentecost celebrates the descent of the Holy Spirit on the Apostles in tongues resembling fire. The Solemnity of Pentecost has been a Christian feast since the first century. The name *Pentecost* is derived from the Greek word meaning "fifty," and the feast of Pentecost occurs fifty days after Easter, much as the Jewish harvest feast of Pentecost occurs fifty days after Passover. Originally, Pentecost simply marked the end of the Easter season. Traditions surrounding Pentecost vary around the world. In Italy, many churches release rose petals from the ceiling to resemble tongues of fire. In France, trumpets blow to recall the roar of the wind as the Holy Spirit descended upon the disciples in the upper room in Jerusalem.

Activity

The Holy Spirit

The circle maze has five paths that form five sentences about the Holy Spirit. The name *Holy Spirit* in the center is the first word of each sentence. Find a path from the center to the outside row. The words will be in order forming a sentence. Write each sentence on a line.

THE HOLY SPIRIT . . .

1. is the Third Person of the Holy Trinity.

2. is with us day in and day out.

3. comes to help us spread the Good News about Jesus.

4. comes to live in us at Baptism.

5. gives us gifts to live as followers of Jesus.

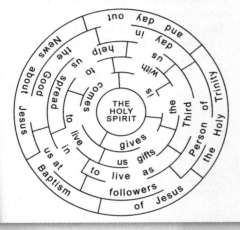

Faith-Filled People

Saint Luke

Luke sometimes traveled from place to place with Saint Paul. Together they preached the Gospel. They told people all about Jesus. Saint Luke is one of the four Evangelists, or "tellers of the Gospel."

95

FAITH-FILLED PEOPLE

Saint Luke the Evangelist. The word *evangelist* means "one who announces the Good News." Saint Luke the Evangelist wrote one of the four Gospels as well as the Acts of the Apostles. His account of the Gospel takes us from the announcement of the birth of John the Baptist to the Ascension of Jesus. The Acts of the Apostles tells us what happened in the early Church after the Ascension. Saint Luke traveled with Saint Paul when he preached the Gospel and stayed with him when he was in prison. Throughout his life, Saint Luke showed great concern for the poor and needy. He is the patron Saint of physicians and painters. The Feast of Saint Luke is celebrated on October 18. For more information on Saint Luke, go to the Saints Resource at *BeMyDisciples*.com.

Reinforce

▶ Use the follow-up question to review the Scripture passage.

▶ Ask one of the students to read the definition of *Pentecost* in Faith Words on page 94. Have each student make a word card for *Pentecost*.

▶ Ask a volunteer to read Faith-Filled People about Saint Luke the Evangelist. Tell the students that in the Acts of the Apostles, Saint Luke wrote how the Holy Spirit helped the Church grow.

▶ Ask the students to name one thing they could tell someone about the Holy Spirit.

Connect

▶ Go over the instructions to the activity with the students.

▶ Perhaps the best way to facilitate the experience is to take one sentence at a time.

▶ Have the students start each sentence in the center. Show them with your finger on the center space.

▶ Then invite the students to follow you with their finger as you move your finger along the path of each of the five sentences, one at a time.

▶ As you finish a sentence, write it on the board, and have the students copy it in their books.

▶ Conclude by having the students read all five sentences aloud.

Pray

Lead the class in praying the Glory Be.

Key Concept
The Holy Spirit helps us believe and trust in God the Father and in Jesus Christ.

Pray

Gather the students for prayer. Lead them in praying the Sign of the Cross.

Teach

▶ Read aloud the Faith Focus question. Then help the students recall that the Holy Spirit, the Third Person of the Holy Trinity, helps us believe and trust in God our Father and in Jesus Christ, who is the Son of God.

▶ Invite the students to work with partners. Tell them to take turns reading the section titled The Holy Spirit Is Always with Us, check the follow-up question, and then find two other things the Holy Spirit helps us to do. *(The Holy Spirit teaches us how to follow Jesus and how to pray; he helps us believe and trust in God the Father and in Jesus Christ.)*

Reinforce

Remind the students that prayer is talking and listening to God. Stress that the Holy Spirit helps us to pray, and that when we don't know what to say, the Spirit will help us.

Connect

Invite the students to observe a moment of silent prayer where they let the Holy Spirit to do the talking for them.

Faith Focus
How is the Holy Spirit always with us?

The Holy Spirit Is Always with Us

The Holy Spirit is the Helper and Teacher Jesus sent to us. The Holy Spirit helps us to believe and trust in God the Father and in Jesus Christ.

The Holy Spirit helps and teaches us to pray. He helps us to pray the way Jesus taught us. We pray to God our Father. We tell God the Father what is in our thoughts and in our hearts.

The Holy Spirit helps us to pray even when we do not know what to say. The Bible tells us,

> When we do not have the right words to pray, the Holy Spirit prays for us in ways more powerful than words.
>
> BASED ON ROMANS 8:26

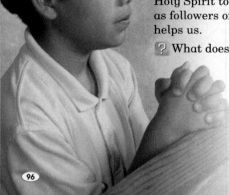

So, we ask the Holy Spirit to help us pray. We ask the Holy Spirit to teach us and help us to live as children of God. We ask the Holy Spirit to teach us and help us to live as followers of Jesus. The Holy Spirit always helps us.

? What does the Holy Spirit help us to do?

96

TASKS OF CATECHESIS

Missionary Initiation. We are all called to be missionaries, giving witness to our faith in Jesus by our words and actions. Although second graders are too young to understand the meaning of all of the Gifts of the Holy Spirit, they are able to practice the gift of right judgment. Tell the students that through this gift, the Holy Spirit helps us to make good choices and to be a good example of our faith. Invite volunteers to share a story about a good choice they made and how it showed that they were a follower of Jesus.

The Holy Spirit gives you gifts. These gifts are sometimes called talents. Talents help us to do good things. These gifts help you to know God's love. Generosity helps you use those gifts to help others.

I Follow **Jesus**

 Activity

Sharing the Gift of God's Love

A flame of fire is one symbol the Church uses for the Holy Spirit. Think of your talents. In the flame, show how you use one talent to help others.

 My Faith Choice

This week, I will be generous. I will use my talents. I will share the gift of God's love with other people. I will

_____

_____

 Pray, "Thank the Holy Spirit for helping you to use your talents to help others. Amen."

97

TEACHING TIP

Catholic Social Teaching. Help the students make the connection between the Holy Spirit's help and guidance in our lives and the good works we do for others. As Christians, we are called to respect all people and to share what we have with those in need. Without the help of the Holy Spirit, we could soon forget that Jesus asks us to care for others, or we may grow weary in our caring efforts and give up. The Holy Spirit helps us recall all that Jesus has taught us, invigorates us, inspires us, and gives us the courage and strength to keep helping others.

Reinforce

Remind the students that the Holy Spirit, the Third Person of the Holy Trinity, gives us special gifts to help us share God's love with other people.

Respond

▶ Talk with the students about how the talents given them by the Holy Spirit help them to live as Jesus, the Son of God, taught.

▶ Have the students complete the Sharing the Gift of God's Love activity.

▶ When they are finished, let them share what their gifts/talents are and how they will use them.

▶ If the students made paper flames earlier, have them retrieve the flames.

▶ Invite the students to write their gifts/talents and their names on the cut-out flames.

▶ Display the flames in the prayer center on a bulletin board or as a mobile.

Choose

Invite the students to read My Faith Choice and to record their decisions. Encourage them to act on their choices this week.

Pray

Gather the students for prayer. Invite them to silently offer a prayer of thanks to the Holy Spirit for the talents/gifts they have been given.

Pray

Begin by leading the class in the following:

Come, Holy Spirit.
Fill the hearts of your faithful.
Kindle in us the fire of your love.
Amen.

Recall

▶ Allow time for the students to complete the matching activity. Afterward, check answers.

▶ Write a word bank on the board with the words *Holy Spirit, Pentecost,* and *Father.* Turn each of the To Help You Remember statements into a question for which one of these words provides the answer. Ask volunteers to guess the right word; invite them to come up and erase or cross out the word they used.

Reflect

Give the students a few moments to silently read, reflect, and then write their responses to the two statements.

Share

▶ Canvass the room for responses to the first two statements.

▶ Invite the students to share with partners the most important lesson they learned this week.

▶ **TO HELP YOU REMEMBER**

1. Before he returned to his Father in Heaven, Jesus promised that the Father would send the Holy Spirit.
2. The Holy Spirit came to the disciples on Pentecost.
3. The Holy Spirit is our Helper and Teacher.

Chapter Review

Recall

Match each word with its correct meaning.

	Words	Meanings
b	1. Pentecost	a. One who asked the Father to send the Holy Spirit
d	2. Ascension	b. the day the work of the Church began
a	3. Jesus	c. Third Person of the Holy Trinity
c	4. Holy Spirit	d. the return of the Risen Jesus to his Father in Heaven

Reflect

Reflect and then complete each of the following statements.

△ I think a good title for the Holy Spirit would be

_____

_____.

△ I believe the Holy Spirit can help me

_____

_____.

Share Share your responses with the class to make a prayer list for the ways the Holy Spirit can help you and your classmates.

98

TEACHING TIP

The Power of the Holy Spirit. Unfortunately, too many young children live in situations that cause them fear. Events in the daily news can also create anxiety for them. Remind them that the Holy Spirit helped Saint Peter and the other Apostles and disciples to follow Jesus and to be courageous enough to preach and live the Gospel. Knowing this may encourage the students to turn to the Holy Spirit when they too need the courage to make good decisions and do the things they know God wants them to do. When they experience fear or anxiety before a test, for example, the Holy Spirit will help them. Encourage them to memorize the simple beginning of today's prayer: "Come, Holy Spirit, fill the hearts of your faithful," and to pray it at the beginning of each day.

Come, Holy Spirit

Pray this prayer to the Holy Spirit.

Leader Let us pray to the Holy Spirit.

All **Come, Holy Spirit.**

Group 1 Fill the hearts of your faithful.

All **Come, Holy Spirit.**

Group 2 Kindle in us the fire of your love.

All **Come, Holy Spirit.**

Group 3 Send forth your Spirit and we shall be created.

All **Come, Holy Spirit.**

Group 1 Enter our hearts that we may love.

All **Come, Holy Spirit.**

Group 2 Guide our minds that we may understand your teaching.

All **Come, Holy Spirit.**

Group 3 Inspire our imaginations that we may know your presence.

All **Come, Holy Spirit, renew the face of the Earth. Amen.**

99

We Pray

▶ Tell the students that they are going to pray a prayer that is based on one of the Church's best-known prayers to the Holy Spirit.

▶ To prepare for the prayer, divide the class into two groups. Point out the parts. Note that the word *kindle* might be unfamiliar to the students. Explain that *kindle* means to prepare a fire in such a way that it will burn quickly and easily.

▶ Allow the groups a few moments to practice their parts.

▶ Lead the class in procession with their books to the prayer center. If you wish, sing a favorite Spirit song as the students process.

▶ If possible, light a candle. Note how the flame reminds us of the flame of the Spirit at Pentecost.

▶ Lead Come, Holy Spirit, beginning with the Sign of the Cross.

▶ Conclude with the Glory Be.

LITURGY TIP

Symbols of the Holy Spirit. For the closing prayer, include as many symbols of the Holy Spirit as possible. The color red symbolizes the tongues of fire that descended upon the Apostles at Pentecost; a lit candle is also a telling symbol of God's love burning within the Apostles. The dove is a symbol of the Holy Spirit, as is the wind. A trumpet is sometimes used to signify the blowing of the wind and is a wonderful instrument to call the students to prayer. Place these and other symbols on the prayer table or around the prayer area before prayer today. Use symbols to create a focal point for prayer. Dimming the lights and placing a lit candle, if allowed, in a central location can be a very effective centering prayer device as well.

Preview

▶ Have the students carefully tear out pages 99 and 100 along the perforation.

▶ Encourage the students to share these pages with their families, and to complete the activities together.

▶ If they did not complete the review activity on page 98 by the end of the session, emphasize that they can complete it with their families at home.

▶ Point out the title and theme of the next lesson to the students.

Visit BeMyDisciples.com

▶ Take time with the students to explore the many activities and resources available at the *Be My Disciples* Web site.

▶ Encourage them to join with their families to discover the many resources available at the Web site.

Before Moving On ...

As you finish today's lesson, reflect on the following question before moving on to the next chapter.

What opportunities have I provided for the students to tell personal faith stories?

With My Family

This Week . . .

In Chapter 7, "The Holy Spirit," your child learned:

▶ The Holy Spirit is the Third Person of the Holy Trinity.

▶ The Father and the Son sent the Holy Spirit to be our helper and teacher.

▶ The Holy Spirit is the source of all the Church does.

▶ The Holy Spirit helps the whole Church to learn and to live what Jesus taught.

▶ The Holy Spirit helps all the baptized to pray and to live as children of God and followers of Christ.

▶ When we practice the virtue of generosity, we show that we are thankful for the gifts we receive from God.

For more about related teachings of the Church, see the *Catechism of the Catholic Church,* 687–741, and the *United States Catholic Catechism for Adults,* pages 102–108.

■ Sharing God's Word

Read together Acts of the Apostles 2:1–6 about the coming of the Holy Spirit on Pentecost. Or read the adaptation of the story on page 94. Emphasize that the Holy Spirit came to the disciples on Pentecost to help them do the work that Jesus gave them, namely, to tell the world about Jesus and make disciples of people. Share that the Holy Spirit is always with your family to teach and help you to do the same.

■ Living as Disciples

The Christian home and family is a school of discipleship. Choose one of the following activities to do as a family, or design a similar activity of your own:

▶ Pray to the Holy Spirit before meals or bedtime this week. Use the prayer on page 98. Talk about how your family can tell others about Jesus.

▶ Help your child grow in generosity. Before they will receive gifts, such as birthday gifts, have him or her give something else away. After giving, remind your child that disciples are generous with others.

■ Our Spiritual Journey

Almsgiving is sharing our material and spiritual blessings because of our love for God and for people. Almsgiving is an expression of generosity which flows from one's gratitude to God. Pray the refrain, "Come, Holy Spirit, come." Praise and thank God, both in words and deeds, for his blessings.

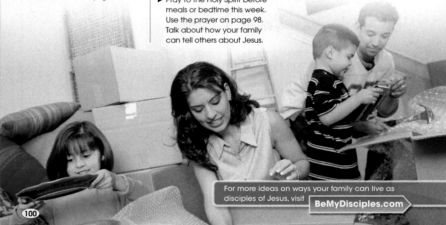

For more ideas on ways your family can live as disciples of Jesus, visit **BeMyDisciples.com**

100

PARTNERING WITH PARENTS

The Story of Pentecost. Through a note or an e-mail, suggest an alternative to having parents read the story of Pentecost to their children. Instead, encourage them to ask their children to retell it for them. If you had your second graders do the activity in the Human Methodologies box on page 151, invite them to take home their flame shapes to assist in the telling of the story of Pentecost. Ask the students to share with their parents the talent they identified and ask their parents to name a talent they possess.

Enriching the Lesson

Making Holy Spirit Prayer Cards

Purpose	Directions	Materials
To reinforce that the Holy Spirit helps us to pray (taught on page 96)	▶ Tell the students that they will be making Holy Spirit prayer cards. ▶ Provide each student a large index card. ▶ Write the words "Holy Spirit, help me when . . ." on the board. ▶ Have the students copy the words on their index cards as the beginning of a prayer to the Holy Spirit. Then tell them to complete the prayer by describing a time when they might need the help of the Holy Spirit, for example, ". . . when I get angry and want to hurt someone." ▶ Invite the students to share their prayers with partners. ▶ Encourage the students to take their prayer cards home and post them near their beds as a reminder to pray to the Holy Spirit for help. ▶ Finally, remind the students that if they do not know exactly what to pray for, they can simply be quiet and let the Holy Spirit do the talking for them.	Index cards pens or pencils

Making a Holy Spirit Collage

Purpose	Directions	Materials
To reinforce that the Holy Spirit gives us gifts/talents to help others (taught on page 97)	Remind the students that we can see the Holy Spirit through the actions of other people. Have the students make collages that show people using their talents to help others. ▶ Divide the students into groups of three. Have them look through magazines and newspapers for appropriate pictures. ▶ Have the students glue their pictures to a piece of art paper that you have labeled with the title "Holy Spirit People." ▶ Ask each group to describe its collage for the class.	art paper magazines and newspapers glue sticks or glue

Literature Connection

Purpose	Directions	Materials
To reinforce the concept of the coming of the Holy Spirit on Pentecost (taught on page 94)	Use the picture book *Gilberto and the Wind* by Marie Hall (Puffin Books, 1978) to help the students grasp the concept of the Holy Spirit. In this perennial favorite, a young Brazilian boy learns about the wind by seeing its effects. ▶ Tell the story to the children, giving the group time to see all the pictures. ▶ Discuss the story by asking the students to name all the things the wind does. Point out that the wind moves, that it has power, and that it changes things. ▶ Point out that the Holy Spirit is like that. The Holy Spirit is with us, even though we cannot see the Spirit with our eyes. We can, however, see the Holy Spirit through our good actions and those of others.	*Gilberto and the Wind* by Marie Hall

BACKGROUND

The People of God

Have you ever yearned for a community that transcends national boundaries, ethnic groupings, religious affiliation, or cultural background? Have you ever wished for a community that is dedicated to charity and caring, family-like support and loving kindness? God has called such a community together in the name of Jesus, his Incarnate Son. As God first called the Israelites to be his people, he gathers a new People of God in Jesus, the new and everlasting Covenant.

Salt of the Earth

The Church is the new People of God. The vocation of all members of the Church is to be salt of the Earth and light of the world (*see Matthew 5:13–16*). In our families and workplaces and communities, our mission is to live Jesus' message of hope and love.

> The Church is both the means and the goal of God's plan: prefigured in creation, prepared for in the Old Covenant, founded by the words and actions of Jesus Christ, fulfilled by his redeeming cross and his Resurrection, the Church has been manifested as the mystery of salvation by the outpouring of the Holy Spirit.
>
> *Catechism of the Catholic Church, 778*

The Body of Christ

The new People of God, or the Church, is the Body of Christ. Not only have we been gathered in his name, but we are one in him. When Saint Joan of Arc was put on trial, her judges asked about her beliefs in the Church. She replied: "About Jesus Christ and the Church, I simply know they're just one thing, and we shouldn't complicate the matter."

Christ and the Church make up the "whole Christ." Christ is the Head of the Church, his Body, and we are her members. We are one with Christ himself. Christ is present in us, uniting our sorrows with his Passion, helping us grow strong in him.

Mary and the Church

Mary shows us best what it means to be a member of the Body of Christ. She had steadfast faith in God the Father and in her Son and opened her heart to the working of the Holy Spirit. When the darkness of Jesus' Death clouded the disciples' vision, Mary gave them hope. Just as Mary stood at the foot of her son's Cross, she stands by us in our trials and suffering. She is our Mother. She is the Mother of the Church. United with Christ, the Head of the Church, her heart beats with our hearts. Her prayers join our prayers.

For Reflection

How does my being a member of the People of God affect my relationships with other people?

In what concrete and practical ways am I, a member of the Body of Christ, the Church, a sign of Christ present in the world?

Teacher to Teacher

Belonging

This is the age when the students will begin to feel more a part of the Church. In addition to the fact that most of them will be receiving the Eucharist for the first time this year, they are now able to read more and thus participate more fully in the Mass. They have grown to better understand the concept of being part of the Church and helping one another.

Living Reminders of Jesus

Seven- and eight-year-olds are ready spiritually to become more active members of the Church. They have grown in their belief that God is working in their lives. They see God as someone whom they can love and with whom they can communicate. Their prayers are simple and beautifully honest and heartfelt. They bring an enthusiasm to the community and to its celebrations that reminds us that we are all members of the Body of Christ with unique and special gifts and talents to share.

The Church Teaches...

"While the content of the faith cannot be reduced to formulas that are repeated without being properly understood, learning by heart has had a special place in catechesis and should continue to have that place in catechesis today" (*National Directory for Catechesis*, 29F).

Therefore, the stories, sayings, and prayers of Jesus are good subjects for students to begin to memorize.

Further Reading and Reflection

For more related teachings of the Church, see the *Catechism of the Catholic Church*, 751–776, 781–801, and 874–972; and the *United States Catholic Catechism for Adults*, pages 143–147.

Teacher Prayer

Lord, help me set my priorities
by what is important in your sight.
Let me always use the talents
you have given me
to join with the whole Church
in doing your work.
Amen.

Lesson Planner

Chapter 8   The Church

Goal To understand that the Church is the People of God who follow Jesus Christ

LESSON PART	PROCESS	MATERIALS and RESOURCES
DAY 1 EXPLORE **Focus** To explore how we live as members of the Church family Pages 101–103	▶ Proclaim and discuss Acts 2:41–47 (Communal Life) ▶ Learn and discuss the story of Fr. Augustus Tolton. **Disciple Power:** Goodness **Activity:** Write about ways to be together with our parish community.	Bible Pencils or pens
DAY 2 DISCOVER **Focus** To discover how the Church is the new People of God Pages 104–105	▶ Identify the Church as the People of God. **Scripture Story:** The Commissioning of the Disciples (Matthew 28:19–20) **Faith Words:** Catholic **Catholics Believe:** Patron Saints **Activity:** Write a prayer for your bishop.	Bible Pencils or pens **Enriching the Lesson:** Teacher Guide, page 179 • Acting Out Scripture Stories • Catholic Social Teaching: Creating a Mural
DAY 3 DISCOVER **Focus** To discover that the Church is the Body of Christ Pages 106–107	▶ Discover the meaning of the Church as the Body of Christ. **Faith Words:** Body of Christ **Faith-Filled People:** The Faithful **Scripture:** We are the Body of Christ (1 Corinthians 12:12-13). **Activity:** Write how people live as followers of Jesus.	Bible Crayons or markers **Enriching the Lesson:** Literature Connection: *The Patchwork Quilt* **Additional Activities Booklet** Activities 8a–8b or see *BeMyDisciples*.com.
DAY 4 DECIDE **Focus** To discover that the Church is the Communion of Saints and to decide on a way to live as a member of the Church Pages 108–109	▶ Learn about the Communion of Saints. **Faith Words:** Communion of Saints **Activity:** Write or draw things to do together with the Church. **My Faith Choice:** Choose how to work with one's Church to help others.	Pencils or pens Crayons or markers
DAY 5 CONCLUDE **Focus** To lift our hearts in prayer to the saints Pages 110–112	▶ **REVIEW** Review concepts: Recall, Reflect, and Share. ▶ **PRAY** A Litany of Saints. ▶ **PREVIEW** the With My Family page and the theme of the next chapter.	Bible, candle, cross for prayer space Grade 2 Music CD **Assessment Tools Booklet:** Assessments 1a and 1b

Assign online Chapter Review and interactive Chapter Test at **BeMyDisciples.com**

CHAPTER **8**

The Church

? To which communities do you belong?

The Church is a community. Saint Luke tells us,

The followers of Jesus shared everything with one another. They prayed and broke bread together. They praised God together. They learned more about what Jesus taught. Other people saw how the followers of Jesus loved one another. Every day God helped more and more people join the Church.

BASED ON ACTS OF THE APOSTLES 2:42–47

? What can you can do with other members of the Church?

101

CATHOLIC DOCTRINE

The People of God. The Vatican II document on the Church described the Church as the new People of God. The Church teaches that grace is given to all the baptized and forms us into the new People of God. All people are called to belong to the People of God. As the People of God we are called to lives of love, and failure to put love into practice is a rejection of salvation itself (*see Dogmatic Constitution on the Church [Lumen Gentium], chapter 2*).

Pray

▶ Invite the students to quiet themselves for prayer.

▶ Pray the Sign of the Cross together.

▶ Ask the opening question.

▶ Point out that communities make us feel welcome and that people in a community share and care for one another.

Reflect

▶ Invite the class to listen carefully to God's Word about the first Church community and what the people shared.

▶ Proclaim the Word of God from the Acts of the Apostles.

▶ Afterward, invite the students to look at the picture on the page and tell what they see.

▶ Have the students respond to the two Scripture questions. *(Accept all reasonable replies.)*

▶ End with a blessing.

"Lord, help our words and actions build up our Church." Amen.

Focus

Have the students turn the page to learn about the first black priest in the United States and the work he did to build up the Church community.

Introduce

▶ Show the students a map on which they can identify the United States and Africa. Explain that African Americans are black people whose ancestors came originally from Africa.

▶ Invite volunteers to read each paragraph of the story of Father Augustus Tolton. Ask the class to listen carefully to find out why Father Tolton became a priest.

▶ Read the Disciple Power section with the students. Invite them to tell how they are good to other people in their community and the Church.

Reinforce

▶ Ask the students to respond to the follow-up question by reviewing the fourth paragraph and to name two things that priests do for the Church.

▶ Ask the students to tell you three things they learned about Father Tolton.

▶ Ask how Father Tolton showed goodness to the people he served. *(Accept all reasonable replies.)*

▶ Assure the students that later in the lesson they will learn how all members of the Church are called to act with goodness and love to all people, especially those in need.

Disciple Power

Goodness

Goodness is a sign that we are living our Baptism. When we are good to people, we show that we know they are children of God. When we are good to people, we honor God.

The Church Follows Jesus

Father Augustus Tolton

Augustus' family was very poor. He and his family came from Africa. They were brought to America to be slaves. But the family escaped from slavery.

They lived at a time when black children were not allowed to go to the same school as other children. Augustus' mother did not give up and found a school he could attend. He grew up knowing God wanted him to become a priest.

Augustus became the first black priest in the United States of America. Father Augustus became the pastor of a parish and school.

Priests do special work in the Church. They lead the members of the Church in worship. Priests help people understand the Word of God.

? What kinds of work does the pastor do with the people of your parish?

DISCIPLE POWER

Goodness. Goodness is one of the twelve Fruits of the Holy Spirit, cited in Galatians 5:22. The Fruits are signs that the Holy Spirit is alive within us and helping us to live the Catholic faith every day. Help the children to recall that we received the Holy Spirit at Baptism. When we are good to others, it is a sign that we are cooperating with the Holy Spirit's presence in our lives. The Holy Spirit helps us to live out our Baptism by showing that we are God's children through our words and actions. Invite the children to give examples of being good to others. Encourage them to be specific. How can we be good to our parents, friends, brothers and sisters, and our neighbors?

Father Tolton was the pastor of a special community called a parish. A pastor is a priest who helps and leads the people of a parish community.

Activity

The Parish Community

Write the name of your pastor.

The pastor of my parish is

_____

Parish is a very old word. It comes from a word that means "being close together." Write the name of your parish community.

The name of my parish is

_____

Today, people in a parish are close together in many ways. They worship, pray, and celebrate together. They also share in giving service to help others.

Write about a favorite way you like to be together with your parish community.

_____

_____

_____

103

TEACHING TIP

Church Leaders and Helpers. Take the time to talk with the students about the work of priests, religious brothers and sisters, missionaries, and other parish ministers. Consider inviting one of these ministers to speak to the students about the kind of work he or she does for God and the Church. Encourage the students to ask any questions they may have.

Connect

▶ Read aloud the first sentence at the top of the page. Then write the word *pastor* on the board. Ask the students if they know what it means.

▶ Read the second sentence aloud. Ask the students if they know the name of their pastor. Print his name on the board for the students to copy in their books.

▶ Read aloud the meaning of *parish* on page 103.

▶ Ask the children to name their parish. Write it on the board, and have the students copy it in their books.

▶ Emphasize that a parish is a community of people who are "close together."

▶ Have the students look at the pictures on the page as you explain how people in a parish are close together in worship and prayer, in celebration and joy, and in service and sharing.

▶ Direct the students to write how they like to be together with their parish community.

▶ Invite the students to find partners and share what they wrote.

Pray

Lead the class in the following:

Gracious God, / keep us one in prayer, celebration, and service. / Keep us one in your love. / Amen.

Key Concept
The Church is the new People of God.

Pray

Gather the students for prayer. Repeat the prayer you prayed to conclude the previous lesson.

Teach

▶ Ask a volunteer to read the Faith Focus question. Explain that we belong to the Catholic Church. Invite the students to talk about some of the best things about belonging to the Catholic Church.

▶ Have the students follow along as you read aloud Names for the Church on pages 104–105. Ask them to listen for the name of the Church we belong to. *(Catholic Church)*

▶ Ask a volunteer to read aloud a sentence that tells about the new People of God.

▶ Draw attention to the final text paragraph. Explain that the Pope and bishops are the leaders of the Church. They take the place of the Apostles, who were the first leaders of the Church chosen by Jesus.

▶ Point out the photo of the Pope. See if the students know his name. Write it on the board.

▶ Likewise, ask if the students know who their local bishop is. Write his name on the board.

▶ Suggest the students write the names of the pope and bishop in their texts.

Faith Focus
Who is the Church?

Faith Words
▶ **Catholics**
Catholics are followers of Jesus who belong to the Catholic Church.

Names for the Church

God sent Jesus to all people. Jesus told the Apostles to invite all people to become his followers. Jesus said,

"[M]ake disciples of all nations, baptizing them . . . teaching them to observe all that I have commanded you."

MATTHEW 28:19–20

The Holy Spirit invites all people from every race and nation to become disciples of Jesus. The Church is the new People of God.

We are **Catholics**. We belong to the Catholic Church. We become members of the Church at Baptism. God's people in the Catholic Church share the same faith and Sacraments.

❓ What do members of the Catholic Church share?

(104)

TEACHING TIP

Teaching Difficult Concepts. Help the students distinguish between the whole Catholic Church (the Church led by the Pope), their diocese (led by their bishop), and their parish (led by their pastor). To help make it clearer, draw a big circle on the board. Label it "The Catholic Church." Then draw a smaller circle within the larger circle. Label this "Our Diocese." Draw an even smaller circle within the diocese circle and label it "Our Parish." Take a few moments to review the circles and what they stand for. Help the students recognize the differences among the three communities of the Church.

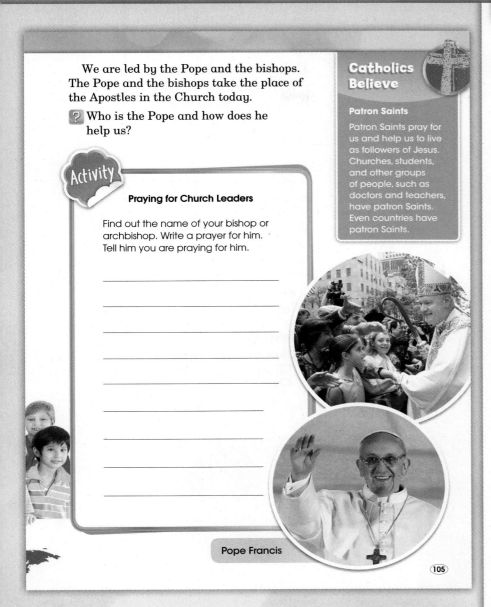

We are led by the Pope and the bishops. The Pope and the bishops take the place of the Apostles in the Church today.

? Who is the Pope and how does he help us?

Activity

Praying for Church Leaders

Find out the name of your bishop or archbishop. Write a prayer for him. Tell him you are praying for him.

_____

_____

_____

_____

_____

_____

_____

_____

Catholics Believe

Patron Saints

Patron Saints pray for us and help us to live as followers of Jesus. Churches, students, and other groups of people, such as doctors and teachers, have patron Saints. Even countries have patron Saints.

Pope Francis

(105)

Reinforce

▶ Point out the Faith Word *Catholics* and have each child create a word card for it.

▶ Ask the follow-up question. *(Accept all reasonable responses.)*

▶ Remind the students that the Holy Spirit invites all people to become disciples of Jesus.

▶ Point out Catholics Believe about Patron Saints. Tell the students that they will learn more about Saints later in the chapter.

Connect

▶ Read the activity directions aloud.

▶ Have the children do the activity on their own.

▶ When the students finish writing or drawing, have them share their work with partners. Then call on volunteers to share with the entire class.

Pray

Write this prayer on the board. Invite the students to pray it with you.

> Holy Spirit, we are your people. We are your Church. Guide us with your love. Amen.

HUMAN METHODOLOGIES

Learning Within the Christian Community. The *National Directory for Catechesis* tells us: "In the parish the members of the Christian community 'become aware of being the people of God' " (*NDC*, 29C). As you review what it means to be the People of God, display pictures of the Pope and your bishop. Remind the students that just as Jesus is the Head of the Church, the Pope is the pastor of the whole Catholic Church. Explain that the bishop is the leader of all the parishes in your diocese. Have the students repeat the Pope's and bishop's names. Talk with them about your bishop and how he helps your diocese to be a sign of the People of God. Look in your diocesan Web site or newspaper for things your bishop is currently doing to build up the People of God.

Key Concept
The Church is the Body of Christ.

Pray

Invite the students to quiet themselves on the outside and the inside. Observe a moment of silence. Then lead the class in the Glory Be.

Teach

▶ Remind the students that the Church is the new People of God who follow Jesus.

▶ Read the Faith Focus question aloud and ask the students for possible answers. Tell them that these two pages will help them learn a new way of naming the people who belong to the Church.

▶ Talk about how our eyes and ears, our hearts, and our brains are different but each has an important job to do in our bodies.

▶ Have the students listen as you read the section titled The Body of Christ. Ask them to listen for the meaning of the words "the Body of Christ."

▶ Ask the follow-up question. Invite volunteers to explain in their own words that the Church is the Body of Christ. Commend them on their good listening skills.

▶ Present Faith-Filled People about The Faithful (page 107) Remind the students that all members of the Church are called to contribute in Their own way to the work of the Church.

Faith Focus
Who is the Body of Christ?

Faith Words
Body of Christ
The Church is the Body of Christ. Jesus Christ is the Head of the Church. All the baptized are members of the Church.

The Body of Christ

Saint Paul describes the Church as the **Body of Christ.** He wrote,

Our body has many parts, but it is still one body. We have been baptized into one body.

BASED ON 1 CORINTHIANS 12:12–13

The image of the Body of Christ helps us to understand what the Church is like. The Church is the one Body of Christ. Jesus is the Head. All the baptized are the Body.

All the parts of our body make up one body. Our eyes are different from our ears. Our brain is different from our heart.

Every part of our body has something different and important to do. All the members of the Church have something different and important to do.

❓ How does the image of the Body of Christ help us to understand what the Church is like?

106

TEACHING TIP

Reinforce. To the best of your ability draw an outline of a body on the board. Label the eyes, hands, mouth, ears, and so on. Brainstorm with the class how each of the body parts can be used to serve the Lord. For example, one's mouth can be used to share the message of the Gospel with others. One's hands can be used to serve another in need. Write each idea next to the body part. Ask the students to copy the drawing of the body into their notebooks or journals and add any other ideas they might have.

As the Church, we are joined with Jesus, The Holy Spirit gives all members of the Church the grace to live as followers of Jesus.

? What is one way you live as a follower of Jesus?

Activity

Followers of Jesus

Look at each picture. Next to the number for each picture, write how the people are living as followers of Jesus. Next to the number 3, write how you live as a follower of Jesus.

1._____.

2._____.

3._____

_____

_____.

(107)

FAITH-FILLED PEOPLE

The Faithful. The vocation of bishops, priests, and deacons is to preach the Gospel, shepherd the Faithful in unity, and celebrate divine worship. The vocation of laymen and laywomen is to give the light of Christ to the world wherever they live by the example of their lifestyle, prayer, and work. The vocation of religious men and religious women is to consecrate their entire lives to God by serving his people. All the People of God are called to live holy lives.

Reinforce

▶ Ask a volunteer to read aloud the definition of *Body of Christ* in Faith Words.

▶ Have the students make word cards for this term.

Connect

▶ Call attention to the pictures on page 106. Call on different students to suggest how the people in the illustrations activity are living as followers of Jesus.

▶ Point out the activity, Followers of Jesus, on page 107 and read aloud the directions.

▶ Have the students complete the activity. Ask them to write one thing they can do to follow Jesus.

Pray

Invite the students to pray by placing one of their hands over their hearts. Have them echo you:

Loving Lord, / I am your follower. / I give you my heart. / Keep me always close to your heart. / Amen.

Key Concept
The Church is the Communion of Saints.

Pray

Have the students quiet themselves. Then pray the Sign of the Cross.

Teach

▶ Read the Faith Focus question aloud and ask for answers.

▶ List the following names of the Church on the board: *the People of God, the Body of Christ.* Then tell the students they are going to learn yet another name for the Church. Add *Communion of Saints.*

▶ Have a volunteer read the first paragraph of The Communion of Saints to discover whom the Communion of Saints includes.

▶ Have the students turn to page 105 and read Catholics Believe. Explain that we all have a patron saint for whom we were named at Baptism.

▶ Tell the students that Mary is the greatest Saint in Heaven. Then read aloud the rest of the text.

Reinforce

▶ Have the students read the definition of *Communion of Saints* in Faith Words and then make word cards for the term.

▶ Invite the students to name their favorite Saints and to tell why.

Connect

Ask the students who they know who belongs to the Communion of Saints. Remind them to include the names of family members who have died.

Faith Focus
Who are the Saints?

Faith Words
Communion of Saints
The Church is the Communion of Saints. The Church is the unity of all the faithful followers of Jesus on Earth and those in Heaven.

The Communion of Saints

The Church is called the People of God and the Body of Christ. Another name for the Church is the **Communion of Saints,** all the faithful People of God. The Church, the Communion of Saints, includes all the faithful followers of Jesus who live on Earth and those in Heaven.

The Church names some people who have died "saints." These Saints live in Heaven. They join with Mary and the angels and praise God with their whole hearts.

Mary is the greatest Saint. She is the Mother of God. Jesus told us that Mary is our mother. Mary is the Mother of the Church.

The Church honors Mary and the other Saints in many ways. We pray to Mary and the Saints. We have images of Mary and the other Saints to help us love God and other people with our whole heart.

❓ Who is your favorite Saint? Why?

ELIZABETH ANN SETON   ELIZABETH OF PORTUGAL   ANDRE BESSETTE

108

CATHOLIC DOCTRINE

Mary, Our Mother. Mary is the greatest Saint. Millions of girls are given her name at birth. Thousands of churches are dedicated to her. Popular devotions to Mary span the centuries. Her exceptional faith inspires us. When we pray the Hail Mary, we honor Mary because she is "full of grace." Mary shared in God's life and love in a unique way. God the Father chose her to be the mother of his Son, Jesus. Mary is the Mother of God. Have the children slowly recite the Hail Mary, pausing on the phrase "full of grace." Ask the children: What is grace? Emphasize that grace is both sharing in God's life and love and the help he gives us to live holy lives.

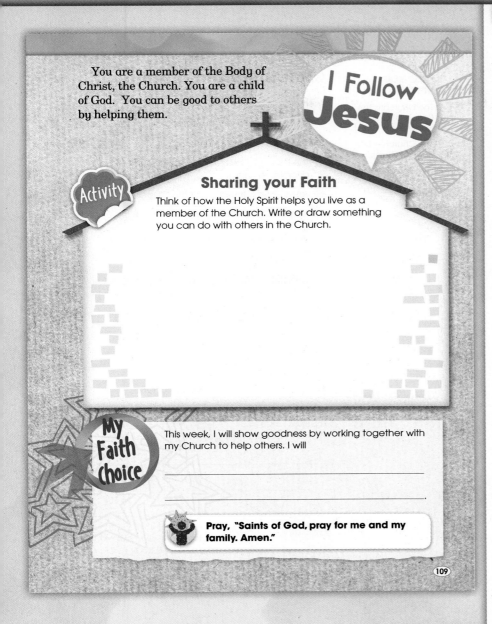

You are a member of the Body of Christ, the Church. You are a child of God. You can be good to others by helping them.

I Follow Jesus

Activity

Sharing your Faith

Think of how the Holy Spirit helps you live as a member of the Church. Write or draw something you can do with others in the Church.

My Faith Choice

This week, I will show goodness by working together with my Church to help others. I will

_____

_____

Pray, "Saints of God, pray for me and my family. Amen."

109

Reinforce

Remind the students that each member of the Church is important.

Respond

▶ Explain the directions for the activity to the students.

▶ Give them time to complete the activity and let them share their work with partners.

▶ Remind the students that they can call on the saints to pray for them to help them live their faith in God by following Jesus.

Choose

▶ Have the students read My Faith Choice and record their decisions.

▶ Encourage them to follow through on their choices this week.

Pray

Then have them offer the silent prayer on the page. Have the students echo this prayer.

Thank you, God, / for making us your new People. / Thank you for calling us / to act as the Body of Christ. / Thank you for including us / in the great Communion of Saints. / Amen.

TASKS OF CATECHESIS

Education for Community Life. Invite volunteers to share experiences of participating in parish community activities. Help them to appreciate that events like the parish picnic or the annual blessing of pets on the Feast of Saint Francis of Assisi help us to feel united. Remind them that we gather each week to join in the celebration of the Mass. Encourage the students to identify how we show our care for others at Mass. Help them to recall that we pray for the Church and our Church leaders, we pray for the members of our parish, the sick, and those who have died. Help the students appreciate that the Mass is our most important community celebration. Through the Eucharist, we are strengthened in our desire to love and care for others. We celebrate our solidarity at Mass.

Pray

Begin by inviting the students to silently pray to their patron Saint or to the patron of their parish. Allow the class a few moments of silent prayer. Tell the students that the Virgin Mary is the patron of all the Americas. Then lead the class in praying the Hail Mary.

Recall

▶ Draw a circle on the board and write the word *Church* inside it.

▶ Using the To Help You Remember statements, help the students recall three names/phrases that describe the people who belong to the Church. List them on the board. *(People of God, Body of Christ, Catholic)*

▶ Go on to have the students color in the boxes next to the statements that are true. *(All four are true.)*

▶ Direct the students to continue the review by completing the fill-ins with the correct word from the word bank. Allow the students to share their answers with partners. Be sure to check responses.

Reflect

Give the children a few moments to reflect on what they think is the most important lesson they learned this week. Then invite them to write it in the space.

Share

▶ Invite the students to share their responses in small groups.

▶ Ask representatives from each group to share what was discussed with the entire class.

▶ **TO HELP YOU REMEMBER**

1. The Church is the People of God who follow Jesus Christ.
2. The Church is the Body of Christ.
3. The Church is the Communion of Saints.

Chapter Review

Recall

Color the box next to the sentences that are true.

■ Jesus gave us the Church.

■ The Holy Spirit invites all people to become disciples of Jesus.

■ Jesus Christ is the Head of the Church.

☐ Augustus Tolton is the greatest Saint of the Church.

Use the best word in the box to complete each sentence.

Catholic	Mary	Church	Body of Christ

1. The ___Church___ is the People of God.

2. Saint Paul tells us that the Church is the ___Body___ ___of___ ___Christ___.

3. ___Mary___ is the Mother of God.

Reflect

Why is the Church the Communion of Saints?

_____

_____

_____

Share Share with a classmate how you are an important part of the Body of Christ.

(110)

TASKS OF CATECHESIS

Using Manipulatives. Write the four fill-in-the-blank sentences in the review on the board. Cut word strips of appropriate length from construction paper. Write one of the four words/phrase from the word bank on each strip. Attach tape to each strip. Invite different students to place the words in the correct sentences. When they have arranged them, they can copy the correct words into their texts.

Need: All young learners; students with visual difficulties

A Litany of Saints

A litany is one kind of prayer the Church prays. When we pray a litany, we repeat one part over and over again. Pray the litany with your class.

Leader   Holy Mary, Mother of God

All   **pray for us.**

Leader   Saint Joseph

All   **pray for us.**

Leader   Saint Martin de Porres

All   **pray for us.**

Leader   Saint Elizabeth of Hungary

All   **pray for us.**

Leader   Saint Patrick

All   **pray for us.**

Leader   All holy men and women

All   **pray for us.**

Leader   Now, as one body, let us join in prayer to the Saints.

All   **Holy Saints, please pray for me in your gentle way. Help me learn how I should be. Watch over me each day. Amen.**

(111)

LITURGY CONNECTION

Litany of the Saints. The Litany of the Saints is a prayer that most people can easily sing. The melody line is repeated, only the name of the Saint changes. Ask your parish director of religious education or music minister if they have a recording of the litany on CD. Play this prayer for the students, encouraging them to join in. Have them conclude with the final prayer marked "All."

We Pray

▶ Point out the title of the prayer, "A Litany of the Saints."

▶ Remind the students of the structure of a litany.

▶ Tell the students that the litany they are about to pray calls upon some of the saints of the Church and invites them to pray for us.

▶ If you wish, have the students add names of Saints—canonized or otherwise—to the list of Saints. Write their names on the board and include them in the litany

▶ Practice the response.

▶ Gather the class in the prayer center. Begin with the Sign of the Cross and lead the class in praying the Litany of the Saints.

▶ Afterward, lead the students in singing "When the Saints Go Marching In." Have the students march and process around the room as they sing.

▶ Conclude by praying the Sign of the Cross.

Preview

▶ Have the students carefully tear out pages 111 and 112 along the perforation.

▶ Encourage the students to share these pages with their families, and to complete the activities together.

▶ If they did not complete the review activity on page 110 by the end of the session, emphasize that they can complete it with their families at home.

▶ Point out the title and theme of the next lesson to the students.

Visit BeMyDisciples.com

▶ Take time with the students to explore the many activities and resources available at the *Be My Disciples* Web site.

▶ Encourage them to join with their families to discover the many resources available at the Web site.

Before Moving On ...

As you finish today's lesson, reflect on the following question before moving on to the next chapter.

How well have I modeled affirming comments and behaviors that I would like the students to use with one another?

With My Family

This Week . . .

In Chapter 8, "The Church," your child learned:

▶ The Church is the community of the faithful followers of Jesus.

▶ The Church is the People of God, the Body of Christ, and the Communion of Saints. Mary is the greatest Saint and Mother of the Church.

▶ All of the baptized have important roles in the work of the Church.

▶ As members of the Church, we are one in Christ. With the Holy Spirit, we can show goodness to one another. We support and care for and show respect for one another as Jesus taught.

For more about related teachings of the Church, see the *Catechism of the Catholic Church*, 751–776, 781–801, and 874–993, and the *United States Catholic Catechism for Adults*, pages 143–147.

■ Sharing God's Word

Read together Matthew 28:19–20, about Jesus giving the Apostles the mission to make disciples of all people. Or read the adaptation of the passage on page 104. This mission is called evangelization. It is the primary work of the Church. Emphasize that the Church today continues the work Jesus gave to the first disciples.

■ Living as Disciples

The Christian home and family is a school of discipleship. Choose one of the following activities to do as a family, or design a similar activity of your own:

▶ Talk about the many ways your family is already taking part in the work of the Church.

▶ Goodness is one of the twelve Fruits of the Holy Spirit. When we cooperate with the Holy Spirit, we are good to others. As a family, become more involved in your parish's outreach ministries to show the goodness of God to others. Look to your family's special gifts and then decide on ways you can be good to others.

■ Our Spiritual Journey

Joined to Christ and all the members of Church at Baptism, we are strengthened and made stronger with Christ and with all the Saints in the celebration and reception of the Eucharist. Take part in the Eucharist frequently. Your child prayed part of the Litany of the Saints. Read and pray together the prayer on page 111. Add the names of your favorite and/or patron Saints. After each name, have all respond, "Pray for us."

For more ideas on ways your family can live as disciples of Jesus, visit **BeMyDisciples.com**

(112)

THE LAST WORD

Reviewing Faith Choices. As you complete this unit, have the students think about the faith choices they made in the chapters. Ask them to identify those choices they have successfully implemented. Invite volunteers to share success stories. Include everyone who wants to share his or her story. Affirm everyone for striving to put their choices into practice.

Enriching the Lesson

Acting Out Scripture Stories

Purpose

To review the Scripture passages from the chapters taught in Units 1 and 2

Directions

The end of Unit 2 is a good time to help second graders recall Scripture stories they have heard the past few weeks in your class.

▶ Divide the students into groups of three. Tell the groups to decide on a favorite story they would like to retell to the class. They may look through their books to refresh their memories if necessary.

▶ Invite each group to prepare and perform a role play of the story.

▶ Ask the class to guess the name of the story the group is acting out.

Materials

Literature Connection

Purpose

To reinforce the meaning of living as a member of the Body of Christ (taught on page 106)

Directions

The picture book *The Patchwork Quilt* by Valerie Flournoy (Dial Books, 1985) tells the story of a young girl who works with her family to finish a patchwork quilt for her grandmother, who has become ill. The story can help the students understand what it means to do the work of Jesus within a community of love, as we do in the Church.

▶ Read the story to the class, giving them time to examine all of the illustrations.

▶ Discuss the story. Ask the students who in the story is showing love. Ask what they like best about the story. Ask if they have ever worked together with family members on a project

▶ Point out that members of the Body of Christ work together in solidarity to live as followers of Jesus. We do this at home, at school, in our parishes, and in our communities.

Materials

The Patchwork Quilt, by Valerie Flournoy

Catholic Social Teaching: Creating a Mural

Purpose

To reinforce the concept of the Church as the worldwide People of God (taught on page 104)

Directions

▶ Take a large piece of mural paper and draw a large globe on it. Draw a cross at the top of the circle. Label the mural "We Are the People of God."

▶ Give each student a piece of light colored construction paper. Ask the students to trace the shape of one of their hands on their sheets and cut it out.

▶ Have each student write or draw on the hand shape something he or she has done as a member of the Church. Give the students ideas, such as celebrating a Sacrament, praying as a family, or making a good choice.

▶ Invite the students to glue their hand shapes inside the globe on the mural paper.

▶ Display the finished mural in the classroom, and affirm the students' good work.

Materials

mural paper

pencils and markers or crayons

scissors

glue

construction paper

Catholic Social Teaching Unit 2

Pray

Lead the students in the Hail Mary.

Focus

▶ Invite them to talk about who they think is their neighbor.

▶ Emphasize that every person, no matter how different they might seem to be from us, is our neighbor—actually, our brother and sister—because each is a child of God.

Introduce

▶ Write the word *solidarity* on the board. Explain that solidarity means that we are united with each other. It helps us remember that we are *all* children of God. Solidarity also helps us care for and respect one another. Then read aloud the principle of Catholic Social Teaching in the sidebar.

▶ Write the words *refugee, Hmong,* and *Karen* on the board. On a map or globe, point out that the Hmong are people from Vietnam and Laos, and other mountainous regions of Southeast Asia and that Karen people are from an area near Tibet. Likewise, explain that *refugee* means someone who has been forced to leave his or her country.

Teach

Invite volunteers to read the story Caring for All aloud.

Catholic Social Teaching

Caring for All

Mr. Moody was the head of a school for one hundred and twenty Hmong and Karen refugee children. He was proud of his students. They were learning new things, especially, how to speak and read English.

Soon, the school year would end. Mr. Moody wanted his students to keep reading and learning English over the summer. But he knew they did not have the money to buy books. Mr. Moody started to worry.

Sally Curran lived next door to Mr. Moody. When she heard about his worry, she decided to talk to her teacher and friends about it at her school, St. Cecilia's. Sally told her class about Mr. Moody's problem. She said that she wished they could help.

The class thought and thought and then decided. They asked every student in St. Cecilia's school to donate new or gently used books for Mr. Moody's students. They collected lots of books. On the last day of school, the students from St. Cecilia's delivered them to the Hmong and Karen refugee children. Each child received six books. Mr. Moody smiled!

> **WE ARE UNITED WITH OTHERS**
>
> We are all God's children. We are one human family. We must care for people of all nations just as we care for those closest to us.

(113)

BACKGROUND: CATHOLIC SOCIAL TEACHING

Solidarity. In his encyclical *Solicitudo Rei Socialis (On Social Concern),* Blessed Pope John Paul II wrote, "Solidarity . . . is not a feeling of vague compassion or shallow distress at the misfortunes of so many people, both near and far. On the contrary, it is a firm and persevering determination to commit oneself to the common good; that is to say to the good of all and each individual, because we are all really responsible for all . . ." #38.

Making Connections

Blessed Pope John Paul II said, "We are all really responsible for all." That means we are to care about all people, not just those close to us. No matter our differences, we are one human family called to care for one another.

with Language Arts

Imagine you are a student at St. Cecilia's school. Write a letter to one of the Hmong or Karen students at Mr. Moody's school. Invite the student to be your pen pal. Then tell your pen pal about your favorite book. Be sure to include the title and author of the book. Also, tell why you like it so much.

with Math and Science

The children at St. Cecilia's collected enough books for each child at Mr. Moody's school to have six books. There are 120 Hmong and Karen students. How many books did the St. Cecilia students collect? Each student at St. Cecilia's gave three books. How many St. Cecilia students are there?

with Creative Arts

A quilt is made of many different parts. All the parts make a quilt. A quilt is a way to show how people are different but all part of God's family. Create a paper solidarity quilt. Decide on a theme. Everyone creates a drawing on an 8" x 8" square paper "patch." Put the "patches" together to form a "quilt."

> **Faith Action**
>
> Decide to be more welcoming to classmates who may be left out by others. I will show that we are all one as part of God's family by _____
> _____
> _____

(114)

TEACHING TIP

Solidarity—Whenever & Wherever. Although Catholic Social Teaching's main call is to practice solidarity with people in different countries, as the story Caring for All demonstrates, it also summons us practice it "at home" with our families and local communities. Help the students recognize that whenever and wherever they reach out to help others, donate to charity, refuse to talk about others in hurtful ways, or stand up for someone who being is left out or bullied, they are showing solidarity.

Catholic Social Teaching

Reinforce

Ask the students to describe what is happening in the picture on page 113 and why it is happening.

Connect

▶ Call attention to the three cross-curricular activities and carefully explain each one to the students. Ask them to choose the activity or activities that they wish to work on.

▶ **Language Arts:** Have the children work independently on this writing project. If you wish, get the students started by reviewing the parts of a letter. Have writing materials available.

▶ **Math and Science:** Work with the students to determine the number of books the Saint Cecilia students collected (720 books) and then how many students attend Saint Cecilia's School (240 students).

▶ **Creative Arts:** Invite the class to decide on a solidarity theme for their "quilt." Tell the students they can draw pictures or symbols or use words on their quilt patches.

Pray

Once again, lead the class in the Hail Mary.

Unit 2 Review

The Unit Review provides the opportunity to assess the students' understanding of the concepts presented in the unit and to affirm them in their growing knowledge and love of God. Here are a few suggestions for using these pages.

▶ Share with the students that the next two pages are an opportunity to stop and review what they have learned.

▶ Provide time for the students to ask questions.

▶ Have the students complete the review alone or with a partner.

A. Choose the Best Word

This section reviews the main concepts of the unit.

▶ Read the directions for section A. By working together on the first sentence, you are teaching the students a strategy for completing these types of sentences.

▶ When the students have finished this section, invite volunteers to share their answers. Review any sentence that the students seem to have difficulty completing.

B. Show What You Know

This section reinforces what the students have learned about Jesus.

▶ Read the directions to the students. Have the students complete the section.

▶ Invite volunteers to share their answers.

Unit 2 Review

Name _____

A. Choose the Best Word

Fill in the blanks to complete each of the sentences. Use the words from the word bank.

Pentecost	Covenant	People of God
Baptism	crucifixion	

1. God made a solemn __Covenant__ with his people.

2. We call Jesus' dying on the Cross the __crucifixion__.

3. God sent the Holy Spirit on the day of __Pentecost__.

4. We first receive the Holy Spirit in the Sacrament of __Baptism__.

5. The Church is also called the __People of God__

B. Show What You Know

Match the items in Column A with those in Column B.

Column A

_C_ 1. Communion of Saints

_D_ 2. the faithful

_B_ 3. Resurrection

_E_ 4. Ascension

_A_ 5. mercy

Column B

A. The virtue that helps us to act with kindness toward others no matter what

B. God the Father raising Jesus from the dead to new life

C. The unity of all the faithful followers of Jesus on Earth and those who have died

D. What members of the Church are called

E. What we call the return of the Risen Jesus to his Father in Heaven

(115)

TEACHING TIP

Assessment as Affirmation. Assessment is a time of affirmation more than correction. Take the time to affirm the students in all that they have learned. Be sure to acknowledge their many efforts at living the faith that they have been learning about. Do not use this time to overemphasize the ways the ways they have fallen short. If you discover areas that they have not learned well, take time to re-teach key concepts at the appropriate time, or perhaps encourage the parents to review the material with their children at home. Remember that throughout the program, many key concepts are reinforced to help students retain them. They will also have opportunities in succeeding years to extend their knowledge of all key faith concepts.

C. Connect with Scripture

What was your favorite story about Jesus in this unit?
Draw something that happened in the story.
Tell your class about it.

D. Be a Disciple

1. *What Saint or holy person did you enjoy hearing about in this unit? Write the name here. Tell your class what this person did to follow Jesus.*

_____

_____

2. *What can you do to be a good disciple of Jesus?*

_____

_____

116

TEACHING TIP

Recall Faith Choices. As you complete this unit, remember to take the time to reinforce the importance of the faith choices that the students have made in each chapter. Invite volunteers to share more success stories about putting their faith choices into action. Perhaps you might also invite a discussion of some challenges the students faced in their efforts to implement their faith choices. Summarize by affirming their good choices, and encouraging them to continue their journey in faith.

C. Connect with Scripture

This section reinforces the students' experience and knowledge of Scripture and the teachings of Jesus.

▶ Help the students review the Scripture stories in the unit, beginning with the Unit Opener story. You may wish to write the names of these stories on the board to assist them.

▶ Ask volunteers to share their favorite stories with the class.

▶ In the space, invite the students to draw something that happened in the story. Invite volunteers to share their drawings now, or at the completion of the Unit Review.

D. Be a Disciple

This section provides the students with the opportunity to recall how the Saints and holy people followed Jesus. It reinforces the ways students can choose to live as disciples of Jesus.

▶ Ask the students to remember their favorite stories of Saints or holy people that they learned about in this unit. Refresh their memories as needed, and write their responses on the board.

▶ Give each student time to write the name of their favorite Saint or holy person on the line. Ask volunteers to share the reason for their choices.

▶ Lead a discussion about the actions that make us good disciples of Jesus. Give the students time to write on the lines their idea of what they could do.

UNIT 3 We Worship
Part One

Objectives

In Unit 3, you will help the children learn that:

▶ The Sacraments are the seven signs of God's love for us that Jesus gave the Church.

▶ The Sacrament of Baptism joins us to Christ and makes us members of the Church.

▶ Confirmation is the Sacrament in which the gift of the Holy Spirit strengthens us to live our Baptism.

▶ In the Sacrament of Reconciliation, we ask for and receive forgiveness for our sins.

Spiritual Insights

"Liturgy is centered on the Holy Trinity. At every liturgy the action of worship is directed to the Father, from whom all blessings come, through the Son in the unity of the Holy Spirit. We praise the Father who first called us to be his people by sending us his Son as our Redeemer and giving us the Holy Spirit so that we can continue to gather, to remember what God has done for us, and to share in the blessings of salvation" *(United States Catholic Catechism for Adults, page 167).*

"For where two or three are gathered together in my name, there am I in the midst of them" *(Matthew 18:20).*

Living the Six Tasks of Catechesis

Moral Formation: Saint Martin De Porres (1579–1639)

Martin grew up in poverty in the slums of Lima, Peru. His father was a Spanish nobleman, and his mother was a Black former slave. She was left to raise Martin after his father abandoned them. As poor as the family was, Martin saw that other people were in greater need. Even as a young boy, he gave his food and clothing away to the poor.

When he was twelve, Martin took a job as an apprentice to a barber. In those days in Peru, many barbers also served as surgeons for their villages, and so in addition to learning how to cut hair, Martin learned how to treat wounds and injuries.

A few years later, Martin volunteered to work as a lay helper at the local Dominican monastery. He was given menial jobs, which he did cheerfully. He also spent many hours in prayer—in the chapel, in the kitchen while he was cleaning up after serving meals, or in the fields while he tended crops. Martin managed to find God in everything he did. The Dominicans noticed his great faith and invited him to become a brother. Martin knew that being a member of the Dominican order would help him do more good in the world, so he eagerly accepted. He took his vows when he was twenty-four.

Martin began to reach out to Lima's poor through his ministry at the monastery. He served leftover food to the hungry each day and brought the sick into the monastery for treatment until every available space was taken. When the Dominicans complained, Martin found lodging for people in abandoned buildings. He also opened a home for homeless children. He arranged for the children to be cared for by a paid staff of teachers, doctors, nurses, cooks, and even counselors. Martin and his helpers raised the money to pay the workers so that they would receive a just wage. It is believed that Martin's children's home was the first of its kind in both North and South America.

Martin de Porres was canonized a Saint in 1962 by Blessed Pope John XXIII. The Pope named Martin the patron of interracial justice. Saint Martin was a living example of the Corporal and Spiritual Works of Mercy. As we share the moral teachings of the Catholic Church with our students, we can ask God to help us emulate Martin's example. Like Martin, we can teach them what it means to follow Jesus' command: "Love one another" *(John 13:34).*

Sharing Your Faith

Find a partner to work with: a spouse, a friend, or a fellow teacher. Come together at the beginning or end of each unit for shared prayer and discussion. Use the questions below as a starting point. As an alternative, record your thoughts in a personal journal.

▶ How do you follow Jesus' command to "love one another"?

▶ How do the moral teachings of the Catholic faith inspire you to live your Baptism?

▶ When and where do you most feel Christ's presence?

We Worship UNIT 3
Part One

Zacchaeus and Jesus

A tiny man named Zacchaeus lived in the town of Jericho. He collected money from the town's people to give to the rulers.

One day Jesus came to Jericho. Tiny Zacchaeus could not see him, so he quickly climbed a tree. Just then, Jesus walked by. "Zacchaeus," Jesus shouted, "come down! I want to stay with you."

Zacchaeus hopped down and welcomed Jesus. Jesus taught him to treat people fairly. Zacchaeus said, "I will give half of all I own to the poor."

Jesus smiled and said, "You are part of God's family."

BASED ON LUKE 19:1–10

(117)

What I Know

What is something you already know about these faith concepts?

Baptism

_____

_____

Sin

_____

_____

Reconciliation

_____

_____

*Put an **X** next to the faith words you know. Put a **?** next to the faith words you need to learn more about.*

____ worship ____ grace ____ Confirmation

____ Sacraments ____ penance ____ Spiritual Gifts

What do you know about God's promises to his people in the Bible?

_____

A Question I Have

What question would you like to ask about forgiveness?

_____

_____

(118)

Unit 3 Opener

The Unit 3 Opener pages assess the students' prior knowledge about the key faith concepts in the unit. Processing these pages should take no more than fifteen minutes.

Opening Page

Invite the students to tell you what they see in the image on the page. Proclaim the Scripture story. Ask: What would you say to Jesus if he asked to come and visit you and your family? Accept their answers, but do not respond further at this time.

Getting Ready

This page continues the activation of prior knowledge. Do not correct the children's responses. You will invite them to return and self-correct at the end of the unit.

▶ Have the students write their responses under What I Know and Questions I Have. You may also do the exercises orally.

▶ Record the students' questions on a chart. Refer back to the chart as you progress through the unit and ask volunteers to respond when they can answer the questions.

▶ Ask the students to turn to the next page and begin Chapter 9.

We Celebrate God's Love

The Work of God

The meaning of the Greek word from which the English word *liturgy* derives means "a public work" or "a service on behalf of the people." The Church has adopted the word *liturgy* to name its participation in the work of God the Holy Trinity—One God who is Father, Son, and Holy Spirit—among us in the Sacraments (*see John* 17:4).

For the liturgy, "making the work of our redemption a present actuality," most of all in the divine sacrifice of the eucharist, is the outstanding means whereby the faithful may express in their lives and manifest to others the mystery of Christ and the real nature of the true Church.

Constitution on the Sacred Liturgy (Sacrosanctum concilium), 2

Joined with Christ

In every liturgical act of the Church, especially the celebration of the Eucharist and the other Sacraments, we join with Jesus Christ in giving praise to the Father in unity with the Holy Spirit. In the liturgy, we not only remember the saving work of Christ, but we are made sharers in the Paschal Mystery of Christ's Passion, Death, Resurrection, and glorious Ascension.

Mary and the Saints

In our work and worship as the Body of Christ, we join with Mary and all the Saints and angels. We sing hymns and give praise to God the Father who makes all things new in Christ, sends us the gift of the Holy Spirit, and unites us as the People of God. We are given a taste of the heavenly banquet that awaits us at the end of this life's pilgrimage.

Emmanuel, God with Us

Jesus said, "For where two or three are gathered together in my name, there am I in the midst of them" (*Matthew* 18:20). When the Church prays and celebrates, Christ is present. When we are baptized or forgiven or healed, it is Christ who is truly acting. When we hear the Scriptures read during the liturgy, Jesus himself is present and speaking. Jesus is in our midst and, with the grace of the Holy Spirit, we are transformed into the adopted sons and daughters of God the Father.

For Reflection

When I take part in the celebration of the Eucharistic liturgy, what helps me to be aware of Christ's presence?

When have I experienced the transforming power of the liturgy in my life?

Teacher to Teacher

Our Church Home

When taking part in Mass and other Church celebrations, we should feel at home and able to participate easily and comfortably. To do this we need to understand what is happening and what is expected of us. Teaching students the basic words and actions of Catholic worship will allow them to celebrate with joy rather than watch with anxiety.

The Language of the People

One of the characteristics of Catholic worship is the constancy of the words and actions from day to day and from place to place. As we attend different Catholic churches to worship, we need to accept and appreciate the small differences, legitimately recognized by the Church, that "manifest the catholicity of the Church, because they signify and communicate the same mystery of Christ" (*Catechism of the Catholic Church* 1208).

The Church Teaches...

"Catechesis both precedes the Liturgy and springs from it. It prepares people for a full, conscious, and active participation in the Liturgy by helping them understand its nature, rites, and symbols. It stems from the Liturgy insofar as it helps people to worship God and to reflect on their experience of the words, signs, rituals, and symbols expressed in the Liturgy; to discern the implications of their participation in the Liturgy; and to respond to its missionary summons to bear witness and offer service" (*National Directory for Catechesis*, 33).

That is why throughout every chapter, prayer from the liturgical traditions and prayerful experiences of the Church are included as a regular part of this curriculum.

Further Reading and Reflection

For more related teachings of the Church, see the *Catechism of the Catholic Church*, 1066–1186; and the *United States Catholic Catechism for Adults*, pages 168–170 and 295–298.

Teacher Prayer

Spirit of God,
as an adult I have experienced
your assistance in my life.
May I continue to be aware of
your ever-present love and guidance.
Help these young children to understand
that you will always surround them
with that same love.
Amen.

Lesson Planner

Chapter 9   We Celebrate God's Love

Goal To learn that we worship God when we celebrate the Sacraments

LESSON PART	PROCESS	MATERIALS and RESOURCES
DAY 1 EXPLORE **Focus** To explore what it means to worship Pages 119–121	▶ Proclaim and discuss Psalm 100:1–2 (Shout with joy to God). ▶ Learn and discuss the story of Blessed Pope John XXIII. **Disciple Power:** Piety **Activity:** Find the right helping words.	Bible Pencils or pens **Additional Activities Booklet** Activity 9a or see *BeMyDisciples*.com
DAY 2 DISCOVER **Focus** To discover that Jesus used words and actions to help people come to faith in God Pages 122–123	▶ Discover how Jesus' words and actions led people to believe in God. **Faith-Filled People:** Saint Mark **Scripture Story:** Jesus heals Jarius' daughter (Mark 5:22-24, 38, 41-42). **Activity:** Create a skit that shows Jesus' words and actions in the story of Jarius.	Bible Pencils or pens **Enriching the Lesson:** Teacher Guide, page 201 Retelling Scripture Stories
DAY 3 DISCOVER **Focus** To discover how our Church worships God Pages 124–125	▶ Learn how the Church worships God. ▶ Discover how the Sacraments use words and actions to help us worship. **Faith Words:** worship, Sacraments **Catholics Believe:** sacramentals **Activity:** Identify from pictures sacramental celebrations of the Church.	Crayons or markers **Enriching the Lesson:** Teacher Edition, page 201 Making a Sacrament Booklet **Additional Activities Booklet** Activity 9b or see *BeMyDisciples*.com
DAY 4 DECIDE **Focus** To discover that the sacraments are signs of God's love and to decide when in the week to pray with words and actions Pages 126–127	▶ Discover that the Seven Sacraments help us share in God's love. ▶ Learn how the Sacraments are divided into three groups: initiation, healing, and service. **Activity:** Pray with words and actions **My Faith Choice:** Choose when to pray with words and actions this week	Pencils Sample sacramentals: e.g., rosaries, crucifixes, holy water, etc. **Enriching the Lesson:** Teacher Edition, page 201 Preparing Skits About Love for God
DAY 5 CONCLUDE **Focus** To pray a prayer blessing the Lord Pages 128–130	▶ **REVIEW** Review concepts: Recall, Reflect, and Share. ▶ **PRAY** We Bless the Lord ▶ **PREVIEW** the With My Family page and the theme of the next chapter.	Bible, candle, cross for prayer space Grade 2 Music CD **Assessment Tools Booklet:** Assessments 1a and 1b

Assign online Chapter Review and interactive Chapter Test at **BeMyDisciples.com**

CHAPTER **9**

We Celebrate God's Love

❓ What is your favorite celebration?

The Holy Family celebrated God's love together. Listen to one of their prayers.

Shout joyfully to the Lord,
all you lands;
worship the Lord with cries
of gladness;
come before him with joyful song.

Psalm 100:1–2

❓ What are some things you say or do when you celebrate God's love with your school or parish family?

(119)

HUMAN METHODOLOGIES

Learning by Heart. The *National Directory for Catechesis* teaches that memorizing important elements of our faith "not only deepens the common understanding of the faith but also forms an indispensable condition for living that faith" **(NDC 29F)**. As you begin chapter 9, challenge the students to memorize the names of the Seven Sacraments, as well as a brief description of each of them. A list of the Seven Sacraments can be found on page 126 of this chapter. Create a poster listing each of the students' names so they can chart their progress.

Pray

▶ Welcome the students warmly. Have them quiet themselves for prayer.

▶ Begin and end the prayer by praying the Sign of the Cross together. Ask the children to echo the following prayer:

Dear God,
Through your holy Sacraments, we celebrate your love for us. Amen.

Reflect

▶ Ask the students to tell what they see happening in the image on the page. *(Accept all reasonable replies.)*

▶ Have the students respond to the opening question. List responses on the board.

▶ Introduce the Scripture passage.

▶ Ask one of the students to read Psalm 100:1–2 with enthusiasm.

▶ Afterward, observe a moment of prayerful silence.

▶ Invite the students to respond to the Scripture question. *(Accept all reasonable replies.)*

▶ Conclude by praying the Sign of the Cross.

Focus

Have the students turn the page to discover how the Pope and bishops have helped and continue to help us better celebrate God's love.

Introduce

▶ Remind the students that we use special words and actions when we gather to worship and celebrate God's love with our parish.

▶ Call attention to the photos of Blessed Pope John XXIII and the gathering of bishops. Tell about the Pope in your own words. Emphasize that Blessed Pope John and the other bishops worked to make sure the words and actions we use at Mass help us to better understand what is happening, and so to better worship God.

▶ Ask the students to read silently to themselves to learn something new about Blessed John XXIII.

▶ Read Disciple Power with the students. Explain that piety is a gift from the Holy Spirit and that we can ask the Spirit's help to love God and worship him better.

Reinforce

▶ Invite volunteers to respond to the follow-up question.

▶ Note the students' responses and list their responses on the board.

Disciple Power

Piety

Piety is a Gift of the Holy Spirit. Piety is the love we have for God. That love makes us want to worship and give God thanks and praise.

The Church Follows Jesus

Blessed John XXIII

Pope John XXIII wanted all Catholics to celebrate God's love in the Mass. He wanted everyone to love and take part in the Mass.

Many years ago, Pope John XXIII called a meeting of all the bishops in the world. They worked together to make changes to some of the ways we celebrate the Mass.

The bishops worked together to make sure everyone could understand the words. They wanted to make sure that everyone could worship God at Mass in their own language.

Today we continue to celebrate Mass with a greater love for God. The words and actions we say and do at Mass help us worship God with thanks and praise.

❓ Which words and actions at Mass do you enjoy?

DISCIPLE POWER

Piety. This gift of the Holy Spirit encompasses all forms of worship: participating in the Sacraments, especially the celebration of the Eucharist; demonstrating reverence for sacramentals, such as crosses, medals, blessings, and statues of Jesus, Mary, and the Saints; and praying popular devotions, such as the Stations of the Cross. Piety is also related to both the First and Third Commandments. We are called to love the Lord with all our heart, mind and soul and to set aside one day each week to honor God through worship and rest. Encourage the students to praise and thank God each day. Help them to appreciate that they have a special opportunity to worship God with their families and the members of your parish at Mass.

Using words and actions at Mass help us worship God. The words and actions that we say and do with each other is important too. They help us to honor God and others.

? What are some words and actions that you say or do to honor God and others?

Activity

The Right Words

For each picture below decide which words in the word bubbles will help. Draw a line from the word bubble to the picture.

I will help.

I am sorry.

Let's say grace.

Do it yourself.

(121)

Connect

▶ Call on a volunteer to read the directions to the activity The Right Words. If necessary, help the students identify what they think is happening in each picture.

▶ Allow time for the students to connect the helping word bubbles to the pictures.

▶ Afterward, call on different students to share what words they chose for each picture.

▶ Conclude by stressing how important the right words are in helping us live as followers of Jesus.

Pray

▶ Invite the children to call on the Holy Spirit in prayer, reminding them that when we do not have the right words to pray, the Holy Spirit will help us (see Chapter 7).

▶ Have the students echo the following prayer to the Spirit:

Holy Spirit, guide our words. / Help us say and help us do / what is always right and good. / Amen.

TEACHING TIP

Finding the Right Words—Cross-Curricular. Put a story filled with homonyms like the following on the board. Have the students circle/ pick the right words. Discuss how the right words make a difference.

WON ONE day Madeline's mom decided to bake a PI PIE. SO SEW, she CENT SENT Madeline to BY BUY SUM SOME FLOUR FLOWER. It was a CHILI CHILLY day, so Mom MAID MADE Madeline WHERE WEAR her READ RED hat and her BLEW BLUE mittens.

On her WEIGH WAY, Madeline walked PASSED PAST a fancy SHOE SHOO shop. Madeline stopped to look and forgot all about the getting the FLOUR FLOWER. That KNIGHT NIGHT, THERE THEIR was no DESSERT DESERT at Madeline's house for SUPPER SUPER.

Key Concept
Jesus used words and actions to reveal God's saving love.

Pray

Gather the students for prayer. Lead them in the same prayer to the Holy Spirit that you used to conclude the previous lesson.

Teach

▶ Ask a volunteer to read the Faith Focus question aloud. Tell the class they are going to learn about words and actions Jesus used.

▶ Explain that the Scripture story of Jesus and Jairus' daughter is one example of how Jesus used words and actions to do his saving work.

▶ Tell the students to listen carefully for the action and the words Jesus used to make the little girl better. *(He took her by the hand and said, "Little girl, I say to you, arise!")*

▶ Read the story of Jairus's daughter aloud, including the text on the top of page 123.

Faith Focus
What do the words and actions of Jesus teach us?

We Worship God

Jesus used words and actions to show God's love for us. One time, a man named Jairus came to Jesus.

Jairus was a religious leader who had great faith in God. Jairus asked Jesus to help his daughter who was very sick. Read what happened next:

Jesus and his disciples followed Jairus to his house. When they arrived there, Jesus saw the family and neighbors weeping. He then took Jairus, his wife and the disciples and entered the house and went over to the daughter of Jairus. Jesus took her by the hand and said, "Little girl, I say to you, arise!" The girl got up immediately and walked around. And Jesus told her parents to give her something to eat.

BASED ON Mark 5:22–24, 38, 41–42

(122)

FAITH-FILLED PEOPLE

Saint Mark. Around the year a.d. 60, Mark wrote a vivid account of the life and Death of Jesus. He wrote in Greek for the Gentiles who converted to Christianity. During that time the Church was enduring great persecution. The key points of Mark's Gospel are an attempt to understand the humanity of Jesus and his suffering and Death. Tradition says that Mark died as a martyr in Alexandria, Egypt. The symbol of Mark's Gospel is a winged lion. The lion is a desert animal that symbolizes the regal power of Christ. The Feast of Saint Mark is celebrated on April 25. For more information on Saint Mark, go to the Saints Resource at *BeMyDisciples*.com.

People listened carefully to what Jesus said. They watched carefully everything Jesus did. After this, more people came to believe in Jesus and to place their trust in him.

The words and actions of Jesus helped the people believe that Jesus is the Son of God. The words and actions of Jesus helped them understand how much God loves us.

? What do Jesus' words and actions show us?

Faith-Filled People

Saint Mark

Mark is one of the four Evangelists. He wrote one of the four Gospels in the New Testament. In Mark's Gospel, we read about the words and actions of Jesus. The Church celebrates the feast day of Saint Mark the Evangelist on April 25.

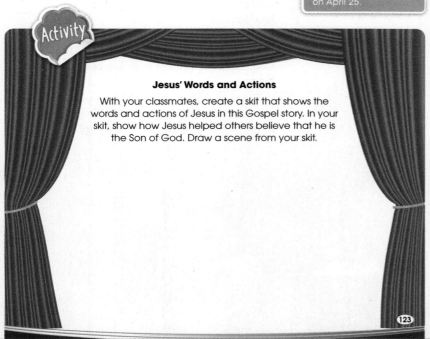

Activity

Jesus' Words and Actions

With your classmates, create a skit that shows the words and actions of Jesus in this Gospel story. In your skit, show how Jesus helped others believe that he is the Son of God. Draw a scene from your skit.

123

Reinforce

▶ Write three sentences on the board that tell the beginning, the middle, and the end of the story, but do not put them in order. Ask volunteers to put the sentences in order by numbering them 1, 2, and 3.

▶ Call for responses to the follow-up question on page 123. (*They show how much God loves us.*)

▶ Have a volunteer reread the two text paragraphs at the top of page 123 aloud. Emphasize that the words and actions of Jesus were signs of God's love.

▶ Read Faith-Filled People about Saint Mark to the students. Tell them that Saint Mark wrote the first Gospel. He wanted us to know all about the words and actions of Jesus, so that we could offer God worship and praise.

Connect

▶ Invite the students to read the directions for the Jesus' Words and Actions activity and then complete the activity on their own.

▶ Have the students share their work with a partner.

Pray

Gather the students for prayer. Lead them in praying the Our Father.

You, O Lord, / are worthy of

our respect and honor. /

Blessed is your name. /

Amen.

TEACHING TIP

Helpful Hints. The activity for this lesson is quite open-ended. Second graders may need some help brainstorming. Discuss some of the stories the students know about Jesus' ministry. Write on the board the things Jesus said or did in each story the students suggest. Narrow their brainstorm responses to a handful of ideas before having students complete the activity. They may refer to the ideas on the board when they share how Jesus' actions helped them to believe and trust in God. They can discuss their ideas with a partner.

Key Concept
We use words and actions to worship God.

Pray

Invite the students to quiet themselves inside and out for prayer. Have them echo the following:

Jesus, you are God's living Word. /
Help us listen to your Word. /
Teach us how to act like you. /Amen.

Teach

▶ Remind the students that Jesus used words and actions to show God's love.

▶ Have them read the Faith Focus question aloud. Ask the students for possible answers. Tell them that they will be learning about some of the words and actions the Church uses to worship God.

▶ Write the word *worship* on the board. Point out its definition in Faith Words. Have the students make a word card for the term.

▶ Have the students read the section titled We Praise God and underline the words that define worship.

Faith Focus
How does the Church worship God?

Faith Words
worship
Worship means to honor and love God above all else.

Sacraments
The Sacraments are the seven signs of God's love for us that Jesus gave the Church. We share in God's love when we celebrate the Sacraments.

We Praise God

God loves us very much. One way we show our love for God is to **worship** him. To worship God means to honor and love God above all else.

The Church uses words and actions to worship God. They tell God we believe in him, hope in him, and love him.

All the words and actions we use in worship show that God is sharing his love with us. We use them to celebrate the **Sacraments**. The Sacraments help us to give thanks and praise to God for all he has done for us.

Jesus gave the Church the Seven Sacraments as a special way to worship God. Each Sacrament is a sign of God's love for us.

Jesus is present with us when we celebrate the Sacraments. The Holy Spirit helps us to celebrate the Sacraments.

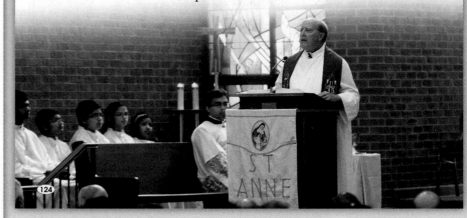

124

FAITH WORDS

Worship. From the Middle English *worshipe* or *worthiness,* the term *worship* is used to denote being worthy of respect and honor. Hence, when we show honor and respect for the divinity of Jesus or the greatness of God, we take part in the act of expressing reverence in the form of worship. Worship can take many forms and usually includes devotion and ritual. The Catholic liturgy is the work of the people. The Mass includes the ritual of proclaiming God's Word and the celebration of the Eucharist.

We worship God in the Sacraments. We listen to God. We honor and praise God. We pray aloud and we sing. We stand and sit and walk in procession.

Sometimes water is poured over us. Sometimes we are marked with oil. We offer and share bread and wine. We bless and receive blessings. We make promises.

? Why do we worship God? How do we worship him?

Catholics Believe

sacramentals

The Church uses objects and blessings, words and actions to help us worship God. These are called sacramentals. Holy water is one of the objects.

Activity

We Worship

Which of these pictures do you recognize as celebrations of the Church? Write what you see happening in each picture.

(125)

TEACHING TIP

Using Sacramentals. The use of sacramentals at home is not as widespread as it was in the past. For example, holy water fonts at the doorways of rooms, crucifixes on display, and the rosary prayed together every evening or once a week were once more common. Display and use the sacramentals the Church has given us in your classroom prayer. Especially use the sacramentals that are part of the liturgical celebrations of the Church.

Reinforce

▶ Invite the students to name some of the ways we worship. Jot the students' answers on the board. Then have them read the last two paragraphs silently to check their answers.

▶ Call for responses to the first follow-up question. *(Answers may vary but should show an understanding that we worship in order to show our love for God. We worship God in the Sacraments.)*

▶ Challenge the students to show with their bodies some of the actions we use when we worship God. If you wish, offer suggestions such as: stand to listen attentively; bow heads to show honor; genuflect; process; kneel; shake hands to share peace, etc.

▶ Read Catholics Believe about sacramentals. If possible, display some sacramentals for the students to identify. Rosaries, crucifixes, and holy water are examples of sacramentals.

Connect

Invite the students to do the activity on the page. Ask several volunteers to share their ideas.

Pray

Gather the students for prayer. Have them echo the following:

You, O Lord, / are worthy of our respect and honor. / Blessed is your name. / Amen.

Key Concept
The Sacraments are signs of God's love.

Pray

Lead the students in praying the Sign of the Cross.

Teach

▶ Read aloud the Faith Focus question. Invite volunteers to share their understanding of what the Sacraments are.

▶ Remind the students that Jesus' words and actions show us God's love. Then explain that the Church uses words and actions to celebrate seven special signs of God's love called the Sacraments. Explain that Jesus is present with us when we celebrate the Sacraments.

▶ Go through the text titled The Seven Sacraments to list the Sacraments with the students.

▶ Point out the symbol for each of the Sacraments and explain its connection to its corresponding Sacrament.

Reinforce

▶ Call for responses to the follow-up question on page 126. To help the students respond, have them turn to page 124 and read the definition of *Sacraments* in Faith Words.

▶ Ask the students to make a word card for this term.

Connect

Invite the students to tell which Sacraments they have celebrated or have seen celebrated.

Faith Focus
What are the Seven Sacraments?

The Seven Sacraments

The Sacraments are seven signs of God's love for us. When we celebrate the Sacraments, we share in God's love. The Sacraments are divided into three groups.

Sacraments of Christian Initiation

Baptism
We are joined to Jesus and become a part of his Church.

Confirmation
The Holy Spirit helps us to live as children of God.

Eucharist
We receive the Body and Blood of Jesus.

Sacraments of Healing

Penance and Reconciliation
We receive God's gift of forgiveness and mercy.

Anointing of the Sick
We receive God's healing strength when we are sick or dying.

Sacraments at the Service of Communion

Holy Orders
A baptized man is called by God to serve the Church as a bishop, priest, or deacon.

Matrimony
A baptized man and a baptized woman make a lifelong promise to love and respect each other.

❓ Why do we celebrate the Sacraments?

126

TEACHING TIP

Sacraments Game. Play a matching game with the students to help them learn the Seven Sacraments. Write the name of each Sacrament on seven different note cards. On seven other cards, write the description of each of the Sacraments that appears on student page 126. (You can make several sets of cards.) Working with a partner or in small groups, have the students match the correct Sacrament card with its corresponding correct description. (Also see Additional Activities Booklet: 9b.)

The words and actions of the Sacraments are signs of God's love. Your words and actions can help people believe and trust in God's love. The Holy Spirit's gift of piety helps you want to be a sign of God's love.

I Follow **Jesus**

 Activity

Praying with Actions

You can use many different actions when you pray. Finish each line of the prayer. Pray your prayer with the actions.

With hands outstretched, I ask you, God, for

_____.

With hands folded, I praise you, God, for

_____.

With head bowed, I thank you, God, for

_____.

With hands raised high, I show my love for you, O God! Amen.

 My Faith Choice

This week, I will pray using both words and actions.

I will say my prayer

☐ in the morning.   ☐ after school.

☐ at dinnertime.   ☐ at bedtime.

 Pray, "O Holy Spirit, let all my words and actions give praise and glory to God. Amen."

(127)

LITURGY CONNECTION

Gestures in Prayer. When we pray, we use gestures that express our reverence toward God. Such gestures include folded hands, bowing, and genuflecting. Have the children name gestures they use when they pray. List them on the board and add some of your own. Then have the students tell when or with what prayers they use gestures. Write their responses next to the gestures listed on the board.

Reinforce

Remind the students that our words and actions can be signs that help others come to know God's love.

Respond

▶ Present the opening text paragraph in your own words.

▶ Discuss Praying with Actions and invite the students to finish each line of the prayer.

▶ When everyone is finished, have the students practice the actions and use them as you pray together.

Choose

▶ Have the students read My Faith Choice and check off their decisions.

▶ Encourage the students to put their choices into practice this week.

Pray

Conclude by leading the class in the prayer to the Holy Spirit at the bottom of the page.

Pray

Begin class by leading the class in praying the Glory Be.

Recall

▶ On separate paper strips, write the words *worship, Sacraments,* and *Holy Spirit.* Prepare enough strips so that there is one for every student. Hand one of the strips to each student.

▶ Write the three To Help You Remember statements on the board, leaving out the key words on the strips.

▶ Read each statement aloud, leaving out the key words.

▶ Invite each student who has the missing word to stand up and hold the strip for all to see.

▶ Have the rest of the class say the word and then read the complete sentence together.

▶ Go on to have the students do the sentence completions.

▶ Call on volunteers to share their responses

Reflect

Give the students a few moments to complete the statement under Reflect.

Share

▶ Canvass the room for responses to the statement.

▶ Encourage the students to share their reflection with their family.

▶ **TO HELP YOU REMEMBER**

1. We worship God by using words and actions.

2. We worship God when we celebrate the Sacraments.

3. The Holy Spirit helps us to celebrate the Sacraments and worship God.

Chapter Review

Recall

Complete the sentences, using the words below.

Sacraments	love	actions	Seven

1. The words and actions of Jesus helped people to know God's _____love_____.

2. We share in God's love when we celebrate the _____Sacraments_____.

3. The Church uses words and _____actions_____ to worship God.

4. Jesus gave the Church _____Seven_____ Sacraments.

Reflect

What are the ways that you can share in God's love?

_____

_____

_____

_____

Share — Share with your class how the Sacraments you have received have helped you.

(128)

TEACHING TIP

Words and Actions Review. To help students review the material from this chapter, ask them about the different Sacraments their family members have received. Discuss the words and actions they remember from the celebrations of the Sacraments. Write their responses on the board.

We Bless the Lord

*God has blessed us in many ways. We can offer God
our thanks and bless his name in word and action.*

Leader The Bible tells us to call upon
the Lord with blessing.

*Bless the Lord at all times.
Praise God forever.*

BASED ON PSALM 34:2

Group 1 We bless your name and praise you,
God, with this our grateful prayer.

Group 2 We bless you for the gifts of joy
and laughter that we share.

Group 1 We bless you for Lord Jesus,
his piety and care,

Group 2 And for his life and Cross that saved
all people everywhere.

Group 1 We bless you for the words he spoke
and all his actions, too.

Group 2 We bless you for the Sacraments,
that help us love like you.

Group 1 We bless you for your constant love
that's with us all our days.

Group 2 We bless you, God, and offer you
our worship, thanks, and praise.

All **Amen.**

129

We Pray

▶ Have the students help you choose
a favorite hymn of praise to use in
their prayer service today.

▶ Divide the class into two groups
and assign parts. Tell each group
that every time it prays its part,
group members should lift their
right arm, palm up, in prayerful
blessing.

▶ Allow time for the groups
to practice their parts and
accompanying gesture.

▶ Gather the students with their
books in the prayer center. Remind
them that we are a community of
faith when we pray together.

▶ Tell them that as a sign that they
are a community of faith they will
stand and form a circle as they pray.

▶ Call the students to prayer with a
brief moment of silence.

▶ Begin the prayer by proclaiming the
passage from Psalm 34.

▶ Conclude with the hymn the
students chose.

THE TASKS OF CATECHESIS

Liturgical Education. Help the students to recognize that they can
take on various roles in prayer. For example, they can serve as prayer
leaders from time to time. Be sure to prepare them for their role. Let
them know a week ahead of time, or at least at the beginning of
class, so they have time to rehearse their lines. Teach them simple
gestures such as raising a hand to indicate to others when to
join in a response. Other students can take the part of Scripture
readers. The students can also be divided into two groups to recite
antiphonal (or alternating) prayer responses, as in today's prayer.

Preview

▶ Have the students carefully tear out pages 129 and 130 along the perforation.

▶ Encourage the students to share these pages with their families, and to complete the activities together.

▶ If they did not complete the review activity on page 128 by the end of the session, emphasize that they can complete it with their families at home.

▶ Point out the title and theme of the next lesson to the students.

Visit BeMyDisciples.com

▶ Take time with the students to explore the many activities and resources available at the *Be My Disciples* Web site.

▶ Encourage them to join with their families to discover the many resources available at the Web site.

Before Moving On …

As you finish today's lesson, reflect on the following question before moving on to the next chapter.

What do I do to encourage and affirm the sense of humor I see in some of the students?

With My Family

This Week . . .

In Chapter 9, "We Celebrate God's Love," your child learned:

▶ The Church comes together to worship God.

▶ The words and actions of Jesus helped people come to believe in God and in his love for us.

▶ Through the celebration of the Sacraments, we worship God, and we are made sharers in the life and love of God.

▶ The Church uses special words and actions to celebrate the Sacraments.

▶ The virtue of piety, a special gift of the Holy Spirit, strengthens our desire to worship God.

For more about related teachings of the Church, see the *Catechism of the Catholic Church* 1066–1186, and the *United States Catholic Catechism for Adults,* pages 168–169 and 295–298.

■ Sharing God's Word

Read together Mark 5:41–42, Jesus healing the daughter of Jairus. Or read the adaptation of the story on page 122. Emphasize that Jesus healed people to show them God's love. Name and talk about some of the words and actions of your family that are signs of God's love.

■ Living as Disciples

The Christian home and family is a school of discipleship. Choose one of the following activities to do as a family, or design a similar activity of your own:

▶ Talk about the Sacraments that each family member has received. What words and actions do you remember from the celebration of each Sacrament? Discuss the meanings of those words and actions.

▶ Body language and gestures help us pray. This week hold hands when you pray as a family. Remember that you all belong to God's family as well as your family.

■ Our Spiritual Journey

Our spiritual journey is marked by signposts. The celebration of and participation in the Sacraments is vital and essential to the Christian life, in particular, participation in Mass and frequent reception of Holy Communion. Help your children learn to pray silently after Holy Communion, thanking God for his blessings in their own words. As a family say the prayer on page 129.

For more ideas on ways your family can live as disciples of Jesus, visit **BeMyDisciples.com**

130

PLAN AHEAD

Baptism Photographs. Notify parents through email or a note sent home from class that the students will need to bring a photograph of their Baptism to your next session. Explain to the parents that since you will be using the photograph in a class project, you will not be able to return it. Suggest to the parents that they may want to send a photocopy of a picture from their child's baptismal day if they have pictures that cannot be replaced.

Note: The photographs will be used in the activity in the box at the bottom on page 213.

Enriching the Lesson

Retelling Scripture Stories

Purpose

To reinforce the story of Jairus's daughter (taught on page 122)

Directions

Students enjoy a variety of ways to retell Scripture stories.

▶ Divide the class into groups of three. Ask one student to be Jairus, another Jesus, and the third Jairus's daughter.

▶ Allow each group to practice retelling the story using their person.

▶ Have the groups present their retellings. After each presentation have the students give a silent cheer for each group.

Materials

Making Sacrament Booklets

Purpose

To reinforce the words and actions of the sacraments (taught on pages 124–126)

Directions

▶ To prepare for this activity take four pieces of construction paper and staple them together on the short side. Make one booklet for each student.

▶ Pass out the booklets and have the students write *My Sacrament Booklet* in the center of the top cover sheet. Have them print their names in the corner.

▶ Have the students write the names of the Seven Sacraments on the back of the cover sheet. Tell them they can turn to page 126 to recall the names of the Sacraments.

▶ Invite the students to look on page 126 in their books and draw something they know about one of the Sacraments.

▶ Remind the students that as they work through the chapters in this unit they will write and draw many more words and actions in their booklets.

▶ Collect the My Sacrament booklets and store them for the students.

Materials

booklets for each student pencils

crayons or markers

Preparing Skits About Love for God

Purpose

To reinforce that through our words and actions we show our love for God (taught on page 127)

Directions

▶ Remind the students that our words and actions in everything we do show our love for God.

▶ Brainstorm with the students all the different activities they do during the week. Make a list of these on the board.

▶ Working with a partner, have the students prepare a skit demonstrating how through the words and actions of one of these activities they show their love for God.

▶ Have the students present their skits and discuss other ways they can show their love for God.

Materials

BACKGROUND

Sacrament of Baptism

The Sacraments are rich in importance and inspiration for Catholics. They accompany us through all the stages and transitions in our lives. Baptism is the gateway to all the other Sacraments. Baptism joins us to Christ and incorporates us into the Church. We receive the gift of the Holy Spirit, new life in Christ, and become adopted sons and daughters of God the Father. Through Baptism we are made sharers in the divine plan of Salvation. Original Sin and all personal sins are forgiven. An indelible sign, or character, is marked on the soul of the newly baptized, identifying us as belonging to Christ forever.

Triple Immersion

The most expressive way to be baptized is by triple immersion into the sacred water. Three times we enter into the water and rise from it to new life. This signifies our baptism into the Death and Resurrection of Christ. However, from its earliest days, the Church has also used the rite of a triple pouring of water over the head as an expression of a person's being baptized. In both Baptism by immersion and by the pouring of water, the celebrant baptizes as Christ commanded, "In the name of the Father, and of the Son, and of the Holy Spirit" (see *Matthew* 28:19).

Baptism by Desire

You might ask, "Is Baptism by water the only form of Baptism? Does a person have to be baptized in water to be saved?" The answer is no. A person who truly Desires to be baptized and does not have the opportunity to receive the Sacrament can be saved through the Baptism of Desire. The Church also teaches that those who have not come to know and believe in Christ and who sincerely seek God and strive to lead a virtuous life can be saved even though they have not been baptized. God loves all people and desires all to live in communion with him forever.

Images of Baptism

Baptism constitutes the foundation for the whole Christian life. As a Sacrament of Christian Initiation, it accomplishes what it implies—it initiates a person into the life of Christ and into the life of the Church, the Body of Christ.

The word *baptism* comes from a Greek word that means "to plunge" or "immerse" into water. This description of Baptism points to the reality that when we are baptized, we are immersed into Christ's Death and Resurrection. In Baptism we die to sin and rise to new life in Christ.

Baptism has also been described as a "washing." The reality captured by this image is one of purification. By Baptism all sins, both Original Sin and personal sins, are washed away. We are washed clean of all that separates us from God.

The words *renewal* and *enlightenment* have also been applied to Baptism. These words point to the activity of the Holy Spirit, who gives us the power of hope and love to embrace life. Baptism is also called a "gift." In other words, it is something we neither earn nor deserve.

For Reflection

When I reflect on my initiation into Christ and the Church, what is my most vivid memory?

What does this memory say to me about my identity?

Belonging to God's Family

Most of the students in your class probably were baptized as infants and have no recollection of their Baptism. Some may have experienced the Baptism of family members or have been present at a parish baptismal celebration. It is important to help the students understand just how they became Catholics.

Sacraments of Christian Initiation

To belong, to be a part of something, to be welcomed, are all human cravings that last a lifetime. In the Sacraments of Baptism and Confirmation and the Eucharist we are joined to Christ and are initiated into the Church. As the students come to better understand the Sacraments of Christian Initiation, they will be able to respond in a more complete way to the graces of these Sacraments.

The Church Teaches...

"Catechesis has a distinctly ecclesial character because the Christian community transmits the Gospel essentially as it has received it, understands it, celebrates it, lives it, and communicates it. . . . Although the community of the disciples of Jesus Christ is spread throughout the world, the Gospel message that binds them together is one; it is the same faith that is transmitted in many different languages and through many cultures" (*National Directory for Catechesis*, 25D).

This chapter helps the students deepen their knowledge of and faith in the Holy Spirit, who is ever present to them, guiding them to live their Baptism. This knowledge or awareness in faith has a spirit of being invited and welcomed into the Church.

Further Reading and Reflection

For more related teachings of the Church, see the *Catechism of the Catholic Church*, 1213–1274; and the *United States Catholic Catechism for Adults*, pages 183–197.

Teacher Prayer

Lord, I am so blessed to have been welcomed into the Catholic Church. I have the Sacraments to celebrate your presence in my life. May my life itself be a daily thank-you for these blessings. Amen.

Lesson Planner

Chapter 10 Our Church Welcomes Us

Goal To learn that the Sacrament of Baptism joins us to Christ as members of the Church

LESSON PART	PROCESS	MATERIALS and RESOURCES
DAY 1 EXPLORE **Focus** To explore how followers of Jesus show they love and follow him **Pages** 131–133	▶ Proclaim and discuss Galatians 3:26–28 (Your Baptism makes you friends of Jesus.) ▶ Learn and discuss the story of Saint Kateri Tekakwitha. **Disciple Power:** Faith **Activity:** Draw a picture of faith and learn a Mohawk peace greeting.	Bible Crayons or markers
DAY 2 DISCOVER **Focus** To discover that we become followers of Jesus in the Sacraments of Initiation **Pages** 134–135	▶ Learn about the Sacraments of Initiation. ▶ Discover the effects of Baptism. **Faith Words:** Baptism, deacon, grace **Catholics Believe:** Baptismal candle **Activity:** Write captions of people showing love for God and neighbor.	Pencils Crayons or markers
DAY 3 DISCOVER **Focus** To discover the importance of Baptism **Pages** 136–137	▶ Read about the Baptism of Cornelius and his family. **Scripture Story:** Baptism of Cornelius and his family (Acts of the Apostles 10:30-48). **Faith-Filled People:** Saint Paul the Apostle **Activity:** Discover a prayer of thanks for Baptism.	Bible Pencils **Enriching the Lesson:** Teacher Guide, page 217 Continuing Sacrament Booklets
DAY 4 DECIDE **Focus** To discover what happens at Baptism and to decide on a way to act as a light in the world **Pages** 138–139	▶ Learn about the Rite of Baptism **Activity:** Write about ways to live your faith. **My Faith Choice:** Choose how to live as a light of Jesus in the world.	Pencils **Enriching the Lesson:** Teacher Edition, page 217 • Stage a Baptism Role-Play • Literature Connection: *The Legend of the Indian Paintbrush*
DAY 5 CONCLUDE **Focus** To pray a prayer of adoration **Pages** 140–142	▶ **REVIEW** Review concepts: Recall, Reflect, and Share. ▶ **PRAY** Glory to God ▶ **PREVIEW** the With My Family page and the theme of the next chapter.	Bible, bowl of holy water, candle, cross for prayer space Grade 2 Music CD **Assessment Tools Booklet:** Assessments 10a and 10b

Assign online Chapter Review and interactive Chapter Test at **BeMyDisciples.com**

CHAPTER **10**

Our Church Welcomes Us

❓ Who are your friends? How did you become friends?

Saint Paul wrote many letters to Jesus' followers. Listen to what he wrote in this letter,

*You have been baptized in Christ.
It does not matter where you come from.
It does not matter whether you are a
boy or a girl, or a man or a woman. By
Baptism you are all friends of Jesus.*

BASED ON GALATIANS 3:26–28

❓ How do you show others that you are a friend and follower of Jesus?

(131)

THE TASKS OF CATECHESIS

Missionary Initiative. After the students have learned about the Rite of Baptism (see student page 138) show them a parish bulletin and read aloud the names of the newly baptized. Distribute construction paper and demonstrate how to fold the paper into a card. Invite the students to make "Welcome to the Church" cards for newly baptized parish infants. Encourage them to decorate the card with the signs and symbols of Baptism that they have learned about. Give the completed cards to a member of the Baptismal Preparation Team to distribute. Help the students recognize that Jesus' followers welcome others to the Church. Emphasize that through our words and actions, we can show new members, especially younger children, what it means to be a follower of Jesus.

Pray

▶ Welcome the students warmly and by name.

▶ Have them quiet themselves for prayer, then pray the Sign of the Cross together.

▶ Ask the children to repeat after you:

Loving God, / you have welcomed us to your family, the Church. / Help us to welcome others. / Amen.

▶ Close with the Sign of the Cross.

Reflect

▶ Use the opening questions and invite responses.

▶ Read the introductory sentences aloud. Then give the students a moment to quiet themselves to hear God's Word.

▶ Have a volunteer proclaim the passage from Galatians.

▶ Observe a moment of prayerful silence.

▶ Ask the Scripture question. (*Affirm all reasonable replies.*)

▶ End the prayer with the Sign of the Cross.

Focus

Tell the students that they will learn about a Native American girl who became a friend and follower of Jesus through Baptism, and then helped others become Jesus' friends, too.

Introduce

▶ Remind the students that the Church uses special words and actions to celebrate seven special signs of God's love. Baptism is one of these signs.

▶ Read the story about Saint Kateri Tekakwitha. Afterward, discuss with the students why they think Kateri wanted to be friends with Jesus so badly. *(Accept all reasonable answers.)*

▶ Share Disciple Power with the children. Point out how faith is a gift from God that enables us to believe in him. Ask: "How did Kateri show she had faith and was a true friend of Jesus?" *(Kateri showed her faith by her prayer, thankfulness, and helping others.)*

▶ Invite the students to share one way they show they have faith.

Reinforce

▶ Ask the students why Kateri wanted so much to be baptized. *(She wanted to become a friend and follower of Jesus.)*

▶ Discuss some of the ways Kateri helped others have faith. *(She helped those in need, she helped others become baptized.)*

Disciple Power

Faith

The virtue of faith is a gift from God. It gives us the power to come to know God and believe in him.

The Church Follows **Jesus**

Saint Kateri

Kateri Tekakwitha was the daughter of a Native American Mohawk warrior chief. When Kateri was only four years old, her parents died from a terrible sickness. The same sickness left Kateri almost blind and with marks on her face.

One day, a priest visited her village. He told everyone that they could become followers of Jesus.

Kateri learned more and more about Jesus. Then she said she wanted to be baptized. She became a follower of Jesus. She became a member of the Church.

Kateri prayed to God every day. She thanked God for her faith. She helped people in need. Even when others treated her badly, she was always thankful for her Baptism and her faith.

❓ How did Kateri show her faith in God?

(132)

 DISCIPLE POWER

Faith. The *Catechism of the Catholic Church* teaches us that " 'the invisible God, from the fullness of his love, addresses men as his friends, and moves among them, in order to invite and receive them into his own company.' The adequate response to this invitation is faith" (CCC 142). Help the students to understand that, like Kateri, we must accept God's gift, or invitation to faith. Point out that many of the villagers heard the priest talk about Jesus, but they did not open their hearts to Jesus' love as Kateri did. They turned away from the gift of faith. Encourage the students to open their hearts to Jesus and to thank God for the gift of faith. For more information on Saint Kateri Tekakwitha, go to the Saints Resource at BeMyDisciples.com.

Kateri helped many other Native Americans become part of the Catholic Church. She showed them how to be followers of Jesus.

? What are the ways that you show your faith in God?

Activity

PEACE BE WITH YOU

Learn this Mohawk greeting. Greet others with peace, like Jesus asked his followers to greet people.

She:kon (Say go)

Skennon ko:wa (Sken in go wah).

Hello, great peace be with you!

Now write your own greeting of peace. Share it with your class.

(133)

Connect

▶ Invite the students to think about the ways Kateri showed her baptismal faith. Ask for ideas and list on the board.

▶ Call attention to the activity and allow time for the students to draw. Explain that, if they wish, they can illustrate one of the ways listed on the board.

▶ Afterward, share drawings, inviting the students to explain what they drew to the class.

▶ Point out the Mohawk greeting at the bottom of the page. Explain that it is in the Mohawk language, the language Kateri spoke.

▶ Help the students learn the greeting by having them repeat it after you a few times.

▶ Tell the students that they can use this greeting among themselves to indicate they are peace-filled followers of Jesus.

Pray

Gather the students for prayer. Lead them in the Glory Be. Then invite them to use the Mohawk greeting as they share a sign of peace with one another.

TEACHING TIP

Native American Religious Sites and Customs. Explain that Kateri and her family came from the Mohawk tribe, which was part of the Iroquois Nation. They lived over 300 years ago in what is now upstate New York. Although most Native Americans were not Christians, they did believe in a Great Spirit, whom we call God, the Father and Creator. Native peoples had their own rituals and religious ceremonies, many of which needed to be performed in specific areas of the land where they lived. These sites were sacred to the Native American People, and are still considered sacred today (e.g., the Black Hills in South Dakota, Bear's Lodge/Devils Tower in Wyoming, and Valley of the Shields in Montana).

Key Concept

Baptism joins us to Christ, gives us grace, and makes us God's adoptive daughters and sons.

Pray

Invite the students to pray the Glory Be. Then lead them once again in the Mohawk greeting they learned in the previous lesson.

Teach

▶ Ask a volunteer to read the Faith Focus question aloud. Share with the students that they are going to learn more about the Sacrament of Baptism.

▶ Ask the students to share how a family welcomes a new baby. Establish that the baby's arrival is a time of joy and blessing.

▶ Present the section titled Sacraments of Baptism by asking the students to find the sentences in the text that tell what happens in Baptism.

Faith Focus

Why do we celebrate the Sacrament of Baptism?

Faith Words

Baptism
Baptism is the Sacrament that joins us to Christ and makes us members of the Church. We receive the gift of the Holy Spirit and become adopted sons and daughters of God.

deacon
A deacon is a baptized man blessed in the Sacrament of Holy Orders to serve the Church and to assist bishops and priests.

grace
Grace is the gift of God sharing his life with us and helping us live as his children.

Sacrament of Baptism

You learned about the Sacraments in the last chapter. Three Sacraments make us followers of Jesus. Celebrating the Sacraments of **Baptism**, Confirmation, and Eucharist joins us to Christ and makes us members of the Church. These three Sacraments are called Sacraments of Christian Initiation.

Baptism is the first Sacrament we celebrate. At the beginning of the celebration of Baptism, the priest or **deacon** asks the parents, "What do you ask of God for your child?" The parents answer, "Baptism" or "Faith."

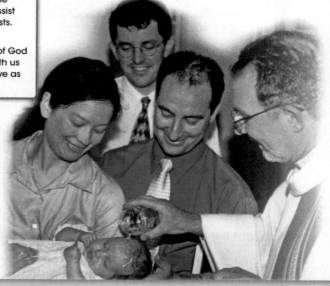

(134)

TEACHING TIP

For Intrapersonal Learners. Write the word *grace* on the board. Review the definition of *grace* in Faith Words. Emphasize that grace is the gift of God's own life to us. Give each of the students a large, blank sticker and colored markers or crayons. Have them write the word *grace* on their stickers and then decorate them any way they please. Invite the students to wear their stickers over their hearts to show that they have the gift of God's own life in them.

This is what happens to us at our Baptism. We are joined to Christ. We celebrate that we are followers of Jesus. We are welcomed into the Church.

We are given the gift of the Holy Spirit. We are given a special gift called sanctifying **grace**. God shares his life with us. We are called to live a holy life.

We become adopted sons and daughters of God. We are called to love God and our neighbor as Jesus taught.

? What does Baptism call us to do?

Catholics Believe

Baptismal Candle

At Baptism, we receive a lighted candle. The baptismal candle is lighted from the Easter candle. Each of us is given the lighted baptismal candle to remind us that we are to live our faith every day.

Activity

Living Our Baptism

Look at the pictures. The children are showing love for God and neighbor. Write a title for each picture. Talk with a partner about what you write.

_____   _____

_____   _____

(135)

LITURGY CONNECTION

Learning Through the Senses. In order to understand a concept, students at this age often need to use their five senses. The lesson on Baptism is an opportunity for the students to touch holy water, feel oil on their skin, smell the fragrance of a candle, hear the words and see the actions used in the celebration of this sacrament. Utilize the senses during prayer time. Use water or fragrant oils in a blessing, or light a candle if possible.

Reinforce

▶ Ask the first follow-up question and have the students respond with the sentences they considered important. Fill in any important overlooked concepts.

▶ Have the students read aloud together the Faith Words *Baptism*, *deacon*, and *grace* and their meanings. Give them time to make word cards for these terms. Note: If a deacon serves your parish, be sure to identify him for the students.

▶ Ask for responses to the second follow-up question. *(Baptism calls us to live a holy life.)*

▶ Tell the students that God's grace helps us live holy lives. Emphasize that we always receive God's grace when we celebrate a Sacrament.

▶ Read aloud Catholics Believe about Baptismal candles. Explain that the candle represents the Light of Christ.

Connect

▶ Invite the students to identify what they see happening in each picture.

▶ Read aloud the directions to the activity. Explain that they are to write a caption for each picture.

▶ Explain to the students that their captions should focus on the good actions being done.

▶ Allow time for the students to write their captions and then share them with a partner.

Pray

Have the students quiet themselves for prayer. Ask them to echo the following:

Holy Spirit of God, / fill us with your grace. / Teach us to live lives holy and true. / Amen.

Key Concept
Those who have faith and are baptized will receive forgiveness and salvation.

Pray

Gather the students for prayer. Remind them that Jesus is present when we gather in his name. Have the students echo the prayer:

Lord Jesus, / grace us with your presence. / Deepen our faith in you. / Amen.

Teach

▶ Remind the students that Baptism is the first Sacrament we receive.

▶ Read the Faith Focus question aloud and ask the students for possible answers. Tell them that a story from the Bible will help them understand why Baptism is so crucial a Sacrament.

▶ Have the students describe what they think is happening in the illustration on the page. Explain that it shows the Apostle Peter talking to a Roman soldier whose name was Cornelius.

▶ Ask several students to take turns reading the section titled Welcome to the Church.

▶ Explain that this story took place in the early days of the Church.

Faith Focus
Why is Baptism an important Sacrament?

Welcome to the Church

The Bible tells us about the Baptism of a man named Cornelius and his family.

Cornelius was a soldier in the Roman army. One day he asked Peter the Apostle to tell him about Jesus.

Peter told him all about how Jesus showed his love for God and for us. He told Cornelius about how Jesus died on the cross for all people. Then he told him that Jesus rose from the dead on the third day.

Peter invited Cornelius and his family to believe in Jesus. He said, "All who have faith in Jesus will receive forgiveness of sins." Cornelius and his family felt the Holy Spirit fill them. They believed and had faith. Peter then baptized them all.

BASED ON ACTS OF THE APOSTLES 10:30–48

? Who tells you about Jesus?

136

SCRIPTURE BACKGROUND

Cornelius. Cornelius was a Roman centurion. A centurion commanded one hundred soldiers. Cornelius believed in God, prayed regularly, and tried to live a good life. One day as he was praying, Cornelius had a vision. An angel instructed him to send for Peter. Peter went to Cornelius's house and baptized Cornelius's whole family. The Baptism of Cornelius, a Gentile, shows that God invites all people to faith and salvation in Christ.

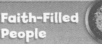

Activity

A Prayer of Thanks

Work with a partner to match the numbers to the letters. Finish this prayer.

A	B	C	D	E	F	G	H	I	J	K	L	M
1	2	3	4	5	6	7	8	9	10	11	12	13

N	O	P	Q	R	S	T	U	V	W	X	Y	Z
14	15	16	17	18	19	20	21	22	23	24	25	26

Dear God our Father,

Thank you for your great L   O   V   E .
                   12 15 22 5

Thank you for sending us J   E   S   U   S .
                   10 5 19 21 19

Thank you for letting me share in your life through

 G   R   A   C   E and the Holy Spirit
7 18 1 3 5

in B   A   P   T   I   S   M .
   2 1 16 20 9 19 13

Thank you for welcoming me to your family

and C   H   U   R   C   H . Help me to be a
     3 8 21 18 3 8

faithful F   O   L   L   O   W   E   R of Jesus.
        6 15 12 12 15 23 5 18

Amen.

(137)

Faith-Filled People

Saint Paul the Apostle

As a young man, Paul hated Christians. One day, the Risen Christ appeared to him and changed his life. Paul was baptized and became a friend of Jesus. Paul traveled everywhere to tell everyone about Jesus. He welcomed many people into the Church.

FAITH-FILLED PEOPLE

Saint Paul the Apostle. Paul was called an Apostle because he experienced the Risen Christ and was called by Christ to preach the Gospel. After his conversion, Paul zealously and tirelessly carried out his mission to proclaim Jesus Christ. Through the power of the Holy Spirit, Paul's teaching, which is summarized in his New Testament letters, helps millions of people live the values of Jesus in today's world. Paul became the Church's foremost example of spreading the Good News far and wide. His missionary travels brought him to many cities throughout the Mediterranean. The Feast of the Conversion of Saint Paul is celebrated on January 25. For more information on Saint Paul, go to the Saints Resource at *BeMyDisciples*.com.

Reinforce

▶ Ask the first follow-up question. *(Accept all reasonable replies.)* Help the students recognize that Peter told Cornelius and his family the Good News (Gospel) about Jesus. Peter instructed them in the faith.

▶ Invite responses to the second follow-up question. *(They were baptized.)* Invite the children to re-read the meaning of *faith* in Disciple Power on page 132.

▶ Call attention to the Faith Focus question again. Highlight for the students that Peter invited Cornelius to have faith. Explain that those who have faith and are baptized receive forgiveness and can go to Heaven.

▶ Read Faith-Filled People about Saint Paul the Apostle to the students. Point out that, like Saint Peter, Saint Paul told many people about Jesus, inviting them to faith and Salvation.

Connect

Have the students work in pairs to complete the activity Discover a Prayer of Thanks. If you wish, get them started by doing the first word with them.

Pray

Gather the children for prayer. Lead them in the Prayer of Thanks they just completed.

> **Key Concept**
> The words and actions are used in the celebration of Baptism.

Pray

Quiet the students for prayer. Lead them in praying the Glory Be.

Teach

▶ Read the Faith Focus question aloud. Remind the students that Jesus and the Church both use words and actions to show God's love. Tell them they are going to learn more about the words and actions the Church uses in the Sacrament of Baptism.

▶ Call on different students to read aloud the text Share in God's Life.

Reinforce

▶ Ask a volunteer to reread the words the priest prays at Baptism.

▶ Ask the follow-up question. *(water, oil, white garment, lighted candle)*

▶ Show the students a bowl of water, a candle, a white baptismal garment, and a small bowl of oil.

Connect

▶ Recall the Catholics Believe feature from page 135 and remind the students how the baptismal candle is a reminder to live our faith.

▶ Call attention to the picture. Point out that besides the child's parents, the godparents are also present. Godparents help us live as Catholics.

▶ Ask: Who helps you live out your faith and be a light for the world as Jesus was? Suggest that the children personally thank the person(s).

> **Faith Focus**
> What happens at Baptism?

Share In God's Life

We celebrate Baptism with words and actions. We are dipped into the water or water is poured over our heads three times. The priest or deacon prays, "I baptize you in the name of the Father, and of the Son, and of the Holy Spirit."

Next, the priest or deacon anoints, or blesses, the top of our heads with special oil. We are then dressed in white garments, and we receive lighted candles.

The words and actions of Baptism show that we share in God's life. They remind us that we are followers of Jesus. We are to live as followers of Jesus, the Light of the world. We are to be lights in the world like Jesus.

? What are the four signs or objects used in the celebration of Baptism?

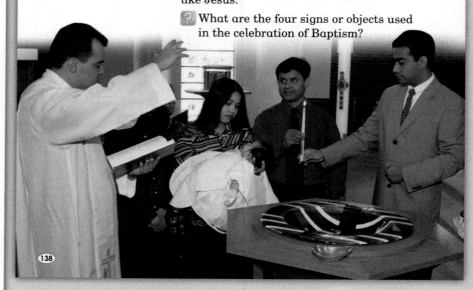

138

LITURGY CONNECTION

Baptismal Candle. The baptismal candle is usually given to a family member or the godparents at the end of the Rite of Baptism. The light is taken from the Paschal candle, which is the candle used during the Easter Vigil and throughout the liturgical year to announce Christ as our light. The candle symbolizes the union of the child with the Passion, Death, and Resurrection of Jesus Christ. The child then becomes a "light in the world." The light is entrusted to the parents and godparents to keep the flame of faith alive in the child's heart.

Every time you live your faith in Jesus, you show your love for God. The Holy Spirit helps you to live as a faithful follower of Jesus. He helps you to be a light in the world.

I Follow Jesus

Activity

Faithful Ways

Think of how the Holy Spirit helps you live out your Baptism and your faith. On the pathway, write three things you can do to live your faith.

My Faith Choice

This week, I will try to live as a faithful follower of Jesus. I will try my best to be a light in the world. I will

_____

_____

_____

Pray, "Help me, O God, to be a faithful follower of your Son Jesus. Amen."

139

Reinforce

Tell the students that when they live faithful lives they show their love for God and can really make a difference—like Saint Kateri—in the lives of others.

Respond

▶ Have the students complete the Faithful Ways activity. Afterward, let them share their ideas with a partner.

▶ Point out that the students are already showing living out their faith in many ways.

Choose

Invite the students to read My Faith Choice and to write their decisions. Encourage them to put their decisions into practice this week.

Pray

Lead the students in the prayer at the bottom of the page.

HUMAN METHODOLOGIES

Making a Commitment to Live the Christian Life. The Social Teachings of the Catholic Church emphasize the solidarity of the human family. That solidarity demands that we serve the common good of all and protect the rights of each person.

Tip: Talk with the students about concrete ways they can share their love for Jesus with others. Have them help you make a "One Family in Jesus" poster. First have the students glue the pictures of their Baptism they brought to class around the outside of the poster. Then help each student trace his or her hands on paper, cut them out, and print his or her name on the palms. Link the hands together on the poster to symbolize that we are joined together as one family in Jesus.

Pray

Begin the session with the Mohawk peace greeting and by leading the students in singing the Welcome Song found in the Teaching Tip box on this page.

Recall

▶ Print the To Help You Remember statements on the board. In each statement write in one wrong word in place of a key word and underline it.

▶ Have the students tell what the correct words should be and allow them to correct the statements on the board.

▶ Introduce the hidden word activity and give the students time to complete it.

▶ Have the students work with a partner and use the found words in a sentence.

Reflect

Give the students a few moments to complete the two reflection statements.

Share

▶ Allow time for the students to share their reflections with a partner.

▶ Encourage the students to share their reflections with their family.

▶ **TO HELP YOU REMEMBER**

1. Baptism is the first Sacrament we receive.

2. The Sacrament of Baptism joins us to Christ and makes us members of the Church.

3. The words and actions of Baptism show that we share in God's life.

Chapter Review

Recall

Find and circle the Sacrament words in the puzzle. Use the words that you circle in sentences on the lines below.

| Baptism | candle | white garment |
| oil | water | Holy Spirit |

H O L Y S P I R I T M C S
W A T E R M D C A N D L E
P W H I T E G A R M E N T
C B A P T I S M Q P O I L

_____

_____

_____

_____

_____

Reflect

Write one way you will live as a follower of Jesus at school.

_____

Share   Share one way you will live as a follower of Jesus with your family.

(140)

TEACHING TIP

Teach a Welcome Song. Teach the song below to the students. It is sung to the tune of "Mary Had a Little Lamb." In the next chapter, the students will add a second verse.

> In Baptism we receive
> God's own grace,
> God's own life.
> In Baptism we become
> part of God's fam-i-ly.

Glory to God

A prayer of adoration gives glory to God.

Leader   Let us give glory to God our Father.

All   **Glory to God, now and forever.**

Leader   Do you believe in God, the Father almighty?

All   **I do.**

Leader   Do you believe in Jesus Christ, his only Son, and our Lord?

All   **I do.**

Leader   Do you believe in the Holy Spirit?

All   **I do.**

Leader   Come forward one at a time. Dip the fingers of your right hand in the bowl of Holy Water. Bless yourself with the Sign of the Cross to remind you of your Baptism.

All   (Dip fingers of your right hand in the Holy Water and make the Sign of the Cross.)
**In the name of the Father,
and of the Son,
and of the Holy Spirit. Amen.**

Give thanks to God!

All   **Glory to God, now and forever.
Amen.**

(141)

TEACHING TIP

At the Font. Ask the parish priest, deacon, or liturgy director to lead a session with your second graders in the church around the baptismal font. Ask that the during the session the students be shown how the Rite of Baptism is celebrated and that they be given an explanation of the words, signs, and symbols employed in the celebration of the sacrament.

We Pray

▶ Have a bowl of water or holy water at the ready for use in the prayer service.

▶ Explain that this prayer includes a prayer of adoration, a prayer that gives glory to God. Tell the students that the prayer also includes part of the promises made in the celebration of Baptism. Explain that their parents and godparents made these promises for them when they were baptized as infants. Now they can make the promises on their own.

▶ Invite a student to be the Leader.

▶ Rehearse the responses for the prayer with the class.

▶ Gather the students in the prayer center.

▶ Begin the prayer by proclaiming the passage from Saint Paul's Letter to the Galatians (Galatians 3:26–28), as found on student page 131.

▶ Direct the Leader to begin the prayer of adoration with the class.

▶ Conclude the prayer by sharing the Mohawk peace greeting learned on Day 1:
She:kon *(Say go)*
Skennon ko:wa
(Sken in go wah).
Hello, great peace be with you!

Preview

▶ Have the students carefully tear out pages 141 and 142 along the perforation.

▶ Encourage the students to share these pages with their families, and to complete the activities together.

▶ If they did not complete the review activity on page 140 by the end of the session, emphasize that they can complete it with their families at home.

▶ Point out the title and theme of the next lesson to the students.

Visit BeMyDisciples.com

▶ Take time with the students to explore the many activities and resources available at the *Be My Disciples* Web site.

▶ Encourage them to join with their families to discover the many resources available at the Web site.

Before Moving On ...

As you finish today's lesson, reflect on the following question before moving on to the next chapter.

Which students could use more attention from me?

With My Family

This Week . . .

In Chapter 10, "Our Church Welcomes Us," your child learned:

▶ Baptism is the first Sacrament we receive.

▶ Baptism joins us to Christ and makes us members of the Church. We receive the gift of the Holy Spirit. We receive the gift of sanctifying grace. We are made adopted sons and daughters of God.

▶ The Church uses water and oil in the celebration of Baptism.

▶ The virtue of faith is a gift from God that gives us the power to come to know God and believe in him. Living as a faithful follower of Jesus means living out our Baptism.

For more about related teachings of the Church, see the *Catechism of the Catholic Church*, 1213–1284, and the *United States Catholic Catechism for Adults*, pages 183–197.

■ Sharing God's Word

Read together Acts of the Apostles 10:1–49, the account of the Baptism of Cornelius and his family or the version found on page 136. Emphasize that at Baptism, we receive the gift of the Holy Spirit and become adopted sons and daughters of God.

■ Living as Disciples

The Christian home and family is a school of discipleship. Choose one of the following activities to do as a family, or design a similar activity of your own:

▶ After Mass this week, visit the baptismal font in your parish church. Talk about why the Church uses water and other baptismal symbols.

▶ Invite all family members to send thank-you notes to their godparents for all they have done to help them grow up in a life of faith.

■ Our Spiritual Journey

Water is a sign of your Baptism, symbolizing dying to sin, rising to new life, and being made a sharer in the very life of God.

How often each day do you drink water? These times are natural moments to reflect on your dignity as a Christian and your spiritual journey. Invite your children to pray each day, "*Glory to God, now and forever. Amen.*"

For more ideas on ways your family can live as disciples of Jesus, visit **BeMyDisciples.com**

(142)

PARTNERING WITH PARENTS

Baptismal Stories. Send home a short note asking the parents to show their child's baptismal garment, candle and photos or videos of the baptism day to their child. Ask families to tell their child about his or her Baptism: Who was there? What was the priest's or deacon's name? Who were/are the godparents? Was there a family celebration afterward? The more the students know about their own Baptisms, the easier it is for them to identify with the Catholic Church's teaching on Baptism. More importantly, it will help the students come to know God's love and their family's love for them.

Enriching the Lesson

Continuing the Sacrament Booklets

Purpose

To reinforce the teaching about Baptism (taught in this chapter)

Directions

This activity will help the students recall some of the important words and actions of the Sacrament of Baptism.

▶ Distribute the Sacrament booklets to the students that they began in chapter 9.

▶ Tell the students to turn to the next page of their booklets and to write Baptism at the top of the page.

▶ Invite them to draw a picture of something that happens in the Sacrament of Baptism on the page. Have them write a title for their picture.

▶ Invite them to share their drawings with one another.

▶ Collect the booklets and store them for the students.

Materials

Sacrament booklets

pencils

crayons or markers

Stage a Baptism Role-Play

Purpose

To reinforce the students' understanding of what happens when we celebrate Baptism (taught in this chapter)

Directions

Baptism will become more real for the students if they can actually role-play the sacrament. Emphasize that this is not a real Baptism.

▶ Take the part of the priest or deacon (or invite your parish priest or deacon to do so).

▶ Invite volunteers to be the parents and the godparents.

▶ Use a doll for the infant to be baptized.

▶ Allow several groups of volunteers to take the parts of parents and godparents as you mime the Rite of Baptism.

Materials

doll

water

oil

candle

white garment

Literature Connection

Purpose

To reinforce the teaching about the role of the baptismal candle to remind us to live our faith for others (taught on page 135)

Directions

Tomie DePaola's colorful book *The Legend of the Indian Paintbrush* (PaperStar Book, 1996) tells the story of a young Plains Indian who uses his talents to paint the stories of his tribe. Later he paints a glorious image that overnight is transformed into a living carpet of flowers—the Indian paintbrush.

▶ Read the story to the students, giving them time to view the illustrations.

▶ Discuss the ways that the young Indian boy used his talents. Ask the students to name their own talents.

▶ Point out that when we use our talents for others, we bring life to them, just as the boy's painting came to life. Remind the class that the baptismal candle reminds us to serve others.

Materials

The Legend of the Indian Paintbrush, by Tomie DePaola

We Celebrate the Holy Spirit

BACKGROUND

Gift of the Holy Spirit

Christ promised the gift of the Holy Spirit. At Pentecost not only was this promise fulfilled, those present also received the ability to give the Holy Spirit to others. "This we read in the Acts of the Apostles. When Saint Paul placed his hands on those who had been baptized, the Holy Spirit came upon them, and they began to speak in other languages and in prophetic words" (*Rite of Confirmation*, bilingual edition, 73).

The Sacrament of Confirmation

Confirmation perfects the graces of Baptism. Sealed with the gift of the Holy Spirit in Confirmation, the baptized are united more firmly to Christ and the Church and strengthened with the Gifts of the Holy Spirit. We are confirmed to be faithful witnesses to the Word planted in us at Baptism (see *Catechism of the Catholic Church*, 1302-1305). Confirmation, like Baptism, seals our souls with a spiritual mark and thus can only be received once.

Ordered to the Eucharist

Baptism and Confirmation are ordered to participation in the Eucharist, which is the third Sacrament of Christian Initiation. The Eucharist unites us most fully with Christ and the members of the Body of Christ, the Church (see *Catechism of the Catholic Church*, 1275).

Images for Confirmation

First, Confirmation has been called an "outpouring of the Holy Spirit." As the Apostles at Pentecost, those who receive this Sacrament are filled and sealed with the gift of the Holy Spirit and receive the power to be witnesses for Christ.

Second, Confirmation has also been describes as "anointing with oil." When we relate this image to the many ways we use oil, such as to cleanse after a bath and to limber up for an athletic event, we get a glimpse of the mystery of God's presence in Confirmation.

In Confirmation we are cleansed, healed, made radiant in Christ, and limbered up for the challenge to be witnesses for Christ to a world that often rejects his message.

Finally, Confirmation is called the "completion of Baptism." The word *confirmation* suggests ratification. In Confirmation our initiation into the new life in Christ is deepened. We are sealed with the gift of the Holy Spirit, and the graces of Baptism are strengthened. Confirmation unites us more firmly to Christ, increases the gifts of the Holy Spirit in us, renders our bond with the Church more perfect, and gives us a special strength of the Holy Spirit to spread and defend the faith (see *Catechism of the Catholic Church*, 1303).

For Reflection

What does it mean for me that I am joined to Christ and marked as belonging to him forever?

How do Baptism and Confirmation empower me to be a witness for Christ?

The Sacraments

The life of the Church revolves around the Sacraments. The Sacraments enable us to encounter Christ and empower us to live the life of faith more deeply and more courageously. The Sacraments of Christian Initiation provide the building blocks for Christian living. They welcome us into the Church, the People of God, and they call us to a life of conversion and service.

The Sacrament of Confirmation

At Confirmation, the Spirit of God, who inspired and enlivened God's people throughout history, was fully manifest in Jesus, and was poured out on the Church at Pentecost, comes to empower us. The Gifts of the Holy Spirit bestowed in Confirmation dispose us to a life of service and witness. The Spirit's gifts strengthen and challenge us to help the world understand that all people are created in God's image and to make sure that the work Jesus began on Earth goes on in the lives of those who are his disciples. (See *Catechism of the Catholic Church* 1302.)

The Church Teaches...

"God draws every human being toward himself, and every human being desires communion with God. Prayer is the basis and expression of the vital and personal relationship of a human person with the living and true God . . . His (God's) initiative comes first; the human response to his initiative is itself prompted by the grace of the Holy Spirit. That human response is the free self-surrender to the incomprehensible mystery of God. In prayer, the Holy Spirit not only reveals the identity of the Triune God to human person, but also reveals the identity of human persons to themselves" (*National Directory for Catechesis*, 34).

In teaching about the Sacrament of Confirmation, focus on the role of the Holy Spirit in the lives of the children. The Holy Spirit guides each of us on our faith journey, prompting us to follow Jesus.

Further Reading and Reflection

For more related teachings of the Church, see the *Catechism of the Catholic Church*, 1285–1314 and 1830–1832; and the *United States Catholic Catechism for Adults*, pages 203–209.

Teacher Prayer

Spirit of God, power in our lives,
come and be present. O Great
  Inspiration,
electrify me with your gifts that
I may share them with your children,
and so kindle in them the fire of love—
a spark that will light the way
to their following your dynamic
direction now and forever.
Amen.

Lesson Planner

Chapter 11   We Celebrate the Holy Spirit

Goal To understand that the spiritual gifts of the Sacrament of Confirmation come from the Holy Spirit

LESSON PART	PROCESS	MATERIALS and RESOURCES
DAY 1 EXPLORE **Focus** To explore how we are to use the gifts given to us by the Holy Spiri **Pages** 143–145	▶ Proclaim and discuss 1 Corinthians 14:1, 12 (Use your spiritual gifts). ▶ Learn and discuss the story of St. Catherine of Siena and St. Thomas Aquinas. **Disciple Power:** Knowledge **Activity:** Draw a gift you have.	Bible Wrapped gift box with lid
DAY 2 DISCOVER **Focus** To discover what the Sacrament of Confirmation does for us. **Pages** 146–147	▶ Discover the relationship of the seven spiritual Gifts of the Holy Spirit to Confirmation. **Activity:** Find the words that tell about the Holy Spirit. **Faith Words:** Confirmation, spiritual gifts **Catholics Believe:** Sacred Chrism	Pencils Crayons or markers **Additional Activities Booklet** Activities 11a and 11b, or see BeMyDisciples.com.
DAY 3 DISCOVER **Focus** To discover the importance of using your spiritual gifts **Pages** 148–149	**Scripture:** Using the Holy Spirit's gifts (Romans 12:5–6, 9–12, 18, 21) **Activity:** Complete a checklist about using the Holy Spirit's gifts. **Scripture:** The Holy Spirit gives us different gifts (Romans 12:5–6, 9–12, 18).	**Enriching the Lesson:** Teacher Guide, page 183 **Literature Connection:** The Friendly Beasts: an Old English Christmas Carol
DAY 4 DECIDE **Focus** To discover what happens at Confirmation and to decide how God wants you to use spiritual gifts of the Holy Spirit **Pages** 150–151	▶ Learn about the Rite of Confirmation. **Activity:** Draw yourself using the gift of wisdom, courage, or knowledge **My Faith Choice:** Choose a way to use a gift the Holy Spirit.	**Enriching the Lesson Activities:** Teacher Guide, page 183 • Continuing Sacrament Booklets • Creating a Collage of Gifts
DAY 5 CONCLUDE **Focus** To remember that every time we pray, the Holy Spirit is with us **Pages** 152–154	▶ **REVIEW** Review concepts: Recall, Reflect, and Share. ▶ **PRAY** A Prayer to the Holy Spirit ▶ **PREVIEW** the With My Family page and next week's lesson theme.	Bible, candle, cross for prayer space Grade 2 Music CD **Assessment Tools Booklet:** Assessments 11a and 11b

Assign online Chapter Review and interactive Chapter Test at **BeMyDisciples.com**

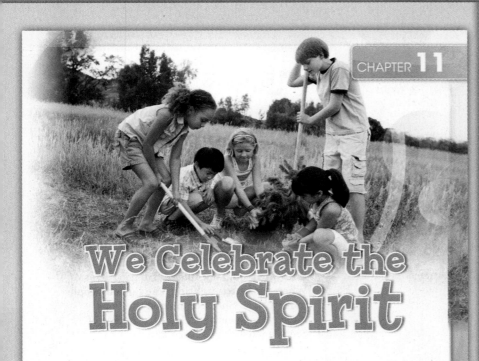

CHAPTER 11

We Celebrate the Holy Spirit

❓ What special gifts or talents do you have?

Saint Paul reminds us we all have special gifts.

There are different gifts, but one Spirit. The Spirit gives all these gifts so that we can use them to do good things.

BASED ON 1 CORINTHIANS 12:4–11

❓ How can you use your gifts to help others?

143

Pray

▶ Welcome the students warmly. Begin and end with the Sign of the Cross.

▶ Ask them to echo these words after you:

Spirit of God, we thank you / for the gifts you give us / to help us live / as disciples of Jesus. / Amen.

Reflect

▶ Show the class a wrapped gift box with a removable lid.

▶ Read aloud the opening question. Have the students write their responses to the question on a blank note card.

▶ Have the students place their cards in the "gift" box.

▶ Read the passage from 1 Corinthians.

▶ Point out the photos on the page. Ask: In each picture, what gifts do you see being shared? *(Accept all replies.)*

▶ Point out the Scripture question. Randomly draw from the gift box some of the gifts the students named. Invite them to tell how the gifts they wrote about could be used to help others and build up the Church.

▶ Conclude by returning the cards to the box and telling the students that, as a class, they have wonderful gifts to share.

Focus

Tell the students that they will be learning about two Saints of the Church who used their gifts to help the Church be a light in the world.

HUMAN METHODOLOGIES

Learning by Apprenticeship. The *National Directory for Catechesis* states that apprenticeship "links an experienced Christian believer, or mentor, with one who seeks a deeper relationship with Christ and the Church" (*NCD*, 29H). Invite a newly confirmed teen to visit the class to speak to your students in very simple terms about the process of preparing for Confirmation in your parish. For example, the teen might talk about the Confirmation retreat, services experiences, and how he or she felt on the day of Confirmation. Encourage your guest to explain what it means to him or her to be a confirmed member of the Catholic Church.

Introduce

▶ Remind the students that the gifts the Holy Spirit gives us are gifts that are meant to be shared.

▶ Invite the students to listen to how two Saints shared their spiritual gifts to help others. Read aloud the introductory paragraph.

▶ Then have volunteers read about Saint Catherine of Siena and Saint Thomas Aquinas.

Reinforce

▶ Ask the follow-up question. *(Accept all replies.)*

▶ Write the Gift of the Holy Spirit, *knowledge,* on the board. Have the students tell what they think it means.

▶ Read Disciple Power. Ask: Do you think it took courage for Saint Catherine to tell the Pope how to make wise decisions? *(Accept all reasonable replies.)* Ask the students what gift Saint Thomas shared with others. *(The gift of knowledge.)* Then ask the students how he used this gift. *(He wrote books about the Catholic faith.)*

▶ Invite volunteers to tell how they could share the gift they placed in the "gift" box. Ask if it would take courage to do so.

Disciple Power

Knowledge
The virtue of knowledge is one of the Gifts of the Holy Spirit. Knowledge helps us better hear and understand the meaning of the Word of God.

The Church Follows **Jesus**

Gifted Saints

The Holy Spirit gives us many gifts to share. The Saints of the Church show us many ways to use those gifts. Saint Catherine of Siena and Saint Thomas Aquinas are two of these Saints.

The Holy Spirit gave Saint Catherine of Siena the gift of wisdom. Catherine used this gift to guide people to live good lives. When there was fighting, she helped people make peace. She even helped the Pope make wise decisions. Saint Catherine of Siena's feast day is April 29.

The Holy Spirit gave Saint Thomas Aquinas the gift of knowledge. Thomas was a great teacher. He wrote many books about the Catholic faith. Thomas helped people learn about their faith. We celebrate his feast on January 28.

❓ How did these two Saints use their gifts?

(144)

DISCIPLE POWER

Knowledge. Invite volunteers to name things they know how to do, such as using a computer, playing video games, searching for information on the Internet, and so forth. Emphasize that the Holy Spirit's gift of knowledge helps us to know how to follow Jesus. It helps us know which things are important to live our faith. The more we know about God, the more we want to show our love for God and our neighbor. Explain that the Catholic Church teaches that we are all a part of a single human family, and we are responsible for one another. Point out that we can show love for our neighbors in practical ways.

The gift of wisdom helps us to see how God wants us to live. The gift of knowledge helps us to understand what the Church teaches. You have gifts to share too. These gifts come from God.

 What are the ways that you use your gifts?

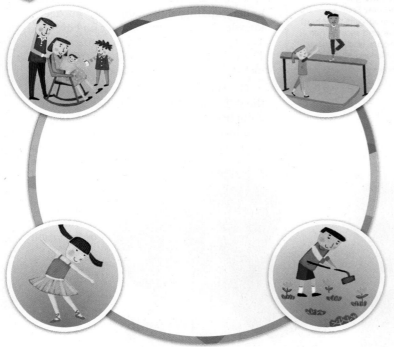

Your Gifts

Look at the gifts pictured on this page. In the center of the circle, draw one of the gifts you can share.

(145)

Connect

▶ Read aloud the directions to the activity, Your Gifts.

▶ Invite volunteers to identify the gifts they see illustrated on the page. Note: while responses may differ, the students should be able to recognize the following gifts:

— Mom in rocker holding baby, dad and female child helping: gift of caring/nurture.

— two girls playing: gift of joy or athletic ability.

— girl dancing; gift of dancing.

— boy hoeing a garden: gift of caring for nature.

▶ Give the students time to draw one of the gifts they have to share in the space provided on the page. Suggest they draw one of the gifts they named and placed in the gift box.

▶ Invite the students to stand and hold up the pictures of their gifts.

▶ Again, remark that, as a class, the students have wonderful gifts to share.

Pray

Lead the class in the Glory Be.

TEACHING TIPS

Discovering Gifts. Help the students discover both what their gifts are and how to use the gifts they have. Write each of the following sentences on the board or newsprint. Have the students copy them and fill in the blanks.

I think my best gift is _____.

The best gift I have to share with others is _____

_____.

Invite the students to share gifts and ideas. Note how they help one another discover and utilize their gifts.

Key Concept
In the Sacrament of Confirmation the Holy Spirit bestows spiritual gifts.

Pray

Have the students quiet themselves for prayer. Invite them to echo the following after you.

Come, Holy Spirit. /
Come and be with us. / Fill us with your gifts. / Help us to love. /
Amen.

Teach

▶ Read the Faith Focus question aloud. Tell the students that they are going to learn about the Sacrament of Confirmation.

▶ Explain that in the Sacrament of Confirmation we receive the Holy Spirit who comes to us bringing spiritual gifts.

▶ Call on different students to read the three paragraphs of text as the class follows along. Tell the class to listen for the names of the spiritual gifts.

Reinforce

▶ Point out the Faith Words *Confirmation* and *spiritual gifts* and their meanings. Direct the students to make word cards for each.

▶ Ask the follow-up question. *(Accept all replies.)*

▶ Point to the picture on the page. Ask the students which of the Holy Spirit's gifts they think this family is sharing. *(knowledge or understanding)*

▶ Ask a volunteer to read Catholics Believe about Sacred Chrism. Emphasize that we are marked with Sacred Chrism as a sign that we receive the gift of the Holy Spirit.

Faith Focus
What happens at Confirmation?

Faith Words
Confirmation
Confirmation is the Sacrament in which the gift of the Holy Spirit strengthens us to live our Baptism.

spiritual gifts
The Holy Spirit gives us spiritual gifts to help us love and serve other people, and so show our love for God.

Confirmation

We receive the Sacrament of **Confirmation** after Baptism. In Confirmation, we celebrate and receive the gift of the Holy Spirit.

The Holy Spirit is our teacher, helper, and guide. In Baptism the Holy Spirit gives us seven **spiritual gifts**. These seven special Gifts of the Holy Spirit are wisdom, understanding, right judgment, courage, knowledge, piety, and wonder and awe. These gifts are increased in Confirmation. They help us live our Baptism. They help us better love God and others.

The Holy Spirit teaches us how to share the gifts with others. He guides us in our daily lives. He helps us show our love for God by using our gifts to help others. He helps us to be lights in the world that help other people come to know Jesus.

❓ How does the Holy Spirit help us through the Sacrament of Confirmation?

146

THE TASKS OF CATECHESIS

Promoting Knowledge of the Faith. Your role as a second-grade teacher, is to provide what the *Nationals Directory for Catechesis* calls the "initial proclamation of the Gospel" (*NCD*, 20) and an introduction to Jesus. It is often tempting to over teach, to give the students too much information and overwhelm them with concepts that are beyond their understanding. Always strive to provide age-appropriate catechesis, keeping in mind that what you teach at this level will be developed and presented again at a deeper level as the students progress in age and in grade.

Activity

The Holy Spirit

Fill in the words that tell you about the Holy Spirit. One has been done for you. Use words from the list below.

SHARE	FAITH	GUIDE	WISDOM
COURAGE	HELPER	TEACHER	PIETY
KNOWLEDGE		SPIRITUAL GIFTS	

T E A C H E R

      C O U R A G E

K N O W L E D G E

P I E T Y

   W I S D O M

  H E L P E R

S P I R I T U A L   G I F T S

S H A R E

G U I D E

F A I T H

Tell a partner about how you can use the gift of knowledge.

(147)

Catholics Believe

Sacred Chrism

Sacred Chrism is special oil that the Church uses in the celebration of some of the Sacraments. It is made from olive oil and balsam. At Confirmation, the bishop marks us with Sacred Chrism in the form of the cross. This is a sign we receive the gift of the Holy Spirit.

Connect

▶ Go over the activity directions with the students. Answer any questions they may have.

▶ Work through the puzzle with the students. Have them count the number of spaces and compare that number to the number of letters in the clue words. Point out how letters in the clue words must contain vertical matches to the letters of *HOLY SPIRIT.*

▶ Take plenty of time with this activity. Help, but allow the students to work at the puzzle on their own.

▶ Afterward, ask the students to tell what gifts they drew on to help complete the puzzle.

▶ Be sure to commend the students on their cooperation and work.

Pray

Gather the class for prayer. Invite them to echo the following after you.

Come, Holy Spirit. /
Come and be with us. /
Help us love. / the many
   gifts you give. /
Amen.

BACKGROUND: SPIRITUAL GIFTS

Gifts of the Holy Spirit. The Gifts of the Holy Spirit given in Confirmation are more than useful talents. Rather, they are gifts that make sure the work Jesus began on Earth goes on in the lives of those who follow him. The Gifts of the Holy Spirit empower the confirmed with the wisdom, understanding, judgment, courage, and knowledge needed to be people who live for others. They also move the confirmed to reverence (piety) and to seek communion in wonder and awe with the God who is Father, Son, and Holy Spirit.

Key Concept
The Gifts of the Holy Spirit are meant to be used to share God's love with others.

Pray

Help the students to quiet themselves for prayer. Invite them to echo the following after you.

> Come, Holy Spirit. / Come and be with us. / Show us how we should best use / the wonderful gifts you give. / Amen.

Teach

▶ Have a volunteer read the Faith Focus question. Invite the class to think silently how they might answer it. Tell the students that today they will learn why the Holy Spirit gives us gifts in Confirmation.

▶ Invite the students to recall who Saint Paul was. Explain that the letter on page 148 is one of the many Saint Paul wrote.

▶ Call on volunteers to read aloud the passage from Saint Paul's letter.

▶ Afterward, point out how Saint Paul says that we are part of the Body of Christ, which is the Church.

▶ Call attention to the Scripture follow-up question. Ask: What does Saint Paul say God wants us to do with the gifts the Spirit gives? *(God wants us to share them in order to share his love with others.)*

Faith Focus
How does the Holy Spirit help us?

Using Our Spiritual Gifts

You have learned that Paul wrote many letters to the first Christians. In these letters, he reminded them to use the gifts the Holy Spirit gave them. Here is what he wrote to Christians living in Rome:

> You are all part of the Body of Christ. The Holy Spirit gives you different gifts. You must use your gifts to share God's love with others.
>
> Show that you love one another. Turn away from what is wrong. Be brave. Do what is right and good. Care for one another. Respect one another. Serve God. Trust in God's promises and be full of hope. Pray and live together in peace.
>
> BASED ON ROMANS 12:5–6, 9–12, 18

❓ How do you use your spiritual gifts?

148

CATHOLIC SOCIAL TEACHING

Solidarity of the Human Family. The students learned in Chapter 8 and in the Catholic Social Teaching lesson at the end of Unit 2 that the Church teaches that we are all a part of a single human family and that we are responsible for the material and spiritual well-being of one another. This is true regardless of our national, racial, ethnic, and ideological differences. Solidarity is the virtue that promotes the material and spiritual well-being of all people. Solidarity demands that we serve the common good of all and protect the rights of each person. Solidarity challenges us to use our gifts to secure justice for all.

God wants us to open our hearts to the Holy Spirit. God wants us to use the spiritual gifts the Spirit gives.

? Choose one of the spiritual gifts. What is one way you use this gift?

Activity

Check ✔ Yes, if the person is using gifts to share God's love. Check ✔ No, if the person is not. Then share how you are using your gifts to share God's love.

	Yes	No
Cameron is a good reader. He does not want to help his little brother learn to read.	☐	☐
Yelina sings well. She sings with the children's choir at Mass.	☐	☐
Diego prays with his sick grandfather.	☐	☐
Ali can draw beautiful pictures. She draws one for Grandma Sue.	☐	☐
Linh is funny, so she makes fun of other children at school.	☐	☐

My gift is _____
I share this gift by

_____

_____

_____.

(149)

Faith-Filled People

Saint Stephen

Stephen helped the Apostles as a deacon. Stephen used the gift of courage to bravely tell everyone about Jesus. Some people, who were not followers of Christ, did not like what Stephen was doing. They killed him because he was telling everyone about Jesus. The Church celebrates the Feast of Saint Stephen on December 26.

FAITH-FILLED PEOPLE

Saint Stephen, Deacon and First Martyr. Acts 6:1–5 describes Stephen the Deacon as a man of courage and unshakable faith. In the speeches attributed to him that are recorded in Acts 7, Stephen boldly speaks out, proclaiming Jesus and the importance of believing in Jesus. Infuriated, his listeners stoned Stephen to death. Stephen is honored as Christianity's first martyr. The Feast of Saint Stephen is celebrated on December 26. For more information on Saint Stephen, go to the Saints Resource at BeMyDisciples.com.

Reinforce

▶ Read about Saint Stephen in Faith-Filled People. Ask what gift Stephen used to tell about Jesus. *(courage)*

▶ Explain that deacons in the early Church were called to serve the physical needs of the poor in the Church. Today, deacons continue to serve the Church in many ways, especially in helping people to share their gifts with others.

▶ Also explain that a Christian martyr is a person who is faithful to Jesus and has the courage to face death in order to remain faithful.

▶ Ask: How did Saint Stephen show he had the gift of courage? *(He shared the Good News of Jesus and faced death.)*

Connect

▶ Read the activity directions and have the students complete the activity on their own.

▶ Go over responses. For each "No" checked, ask volunteers to explain what the person could do to use his or her gift to share God's love.

Pray

Gather the students for prayer. Invite them to echo the following:

Come, Holy Spirit. /
Come and be with us. /
Come guide us. / as we use
our gifts. /to share God's love. /
Amen.

Key Concept
The Sacrament of Confirmation strengthens us to live our Baptism.

Pray

Have the students quiet themselves for prayer. Pray:

Come, Holy Spirit. / Help us to live out our Baptism. / Amen.

Teach

▶ Read aloud the Faith Focus question to introduce the session's topic, the Sacrament of Confirmation.

▶ Tell the students that we can only receive this sacrament after we have been baptized. Ask the students to share if they have been to a celebration of Confirmation.

▶ Explain the first paragraph of Celebrating Confirmation to the students in your own words.

▶ Ask the students to read the remainder of the text to continue to discover what happens next in the celebration of Confirmation.

Reinforce

Ask the follow-up question. *(Accept all reasonable replies.)*

Connect

As time allows, invite volunteers to come to the front of the room and mime a celebration of Confirmation. Remind them not to use any words. Ask the rest of the class to tell what words would be spoken.

Faith Focus
What happens during the celebration of the Sacrament of Confirmation?

Celebrating Confirmation

In Confirmation, the Holy Spirit strengthens us to live our Baptism. The Holy Spirit helps us to remember and share God's love with others.

We celebrate the Sacrament of Confirmation after we are baptized. If we are baptized as infants, we receive this Sacrament when we are older. Grown-ups who are baptized receive Confirmation right after their Baptism.

The bishop usually leads the celebration of Confirmation. During the celebration, he holds hands in the air and prays, "Send your Holy Spirit upon them to be their Helper and Guide." Next, he prays that we will receive Gifts of the Holy Spirit.

Then the bishop places his right hand on top of our heads. He signs our foreheads with Sacred Chrism as he prays, "Be sealed with the Gift of the Holy Spirit." We respond, "Amen."

The bishop then shares a sign of peace with us, saying, "Peace be with you." We answer, "And with your spirit."

? How will you be a follower of Jesus?

150

TEACHING TIP

Bishops. Many of the students may have never met a bishop and may not know who their bishop is. Borrow a picture of your bishop from the religious education office or the rectory for the students to look at. Tell the students a little about him and have the students learn their bishop's name.

God invites you to open your heart to the Holy Spirit. God wants you to use the spiritual gifts you have been given by the Holy Spirit. Three of these gifts are wisdom, courage, and knowledge.

I Follow Jesus

Activity

A Gift from the Heart

Remember that the Holy Spirit has given you spiritual gifts to share. In the heart shape, draw yourself caring for the needs of others.

My Faith Choice

This week, I will use the gift of

_____

I will

_____

Pray, "Thank you, Holy Spirit, for your gifts to me. Help me use the gift of courage to use my gifts to help others. Amen."

(151)

Reinforce

Point out to the students that they are already using their gifts in many ways to share God's love and help others.

Respond

Call attention to the A Gift from the Heart activity. Read the directions. Allow time for the students to draw. Afterward, encourage sharing.

Choose

Invite the students to read My Faith Choice and then to write their decisions. Encourage them to do their best to use and share their gift this week.

Pray

Gather the students for prayer. Lead them in the prayer to the Holy Spirit at the bottom of the page.

LITURGY CONNECTION

Committed to Prayer. The Sacrament of Confirmation commits the confirmed to prayer and welcomes them to full participation in the liturgy. Those who are confirmed are more permanently enrolled in the reconciling mission of Jesus. Christians share in that reconciling work when we pray. In the early Church, catechumens were not allowed to participate in the Prayer of the Faithful at Mass, because they were not yet prepared for the serious work which it entailed. After Baptism and Confirmation, reciting the Prayer of the Faithful was the first act of the newly initiated members of the Church. At last, they were ready to respond to God's Word in the Prayer of the Faithful and join with Christ in strengthening the bond of love between and among people and God.

Pray

▶ To begin class, lead the students in a prayer of thanks. Invite each student to name a gift for which he or she is thankful. After each student mentions a gift, have everyone respond, *"Thank you, Holy Spirit."*

▶ Conclude by praying the Glory Be and, if the students have learned the "Welcome Song," by singing together.

Recall

▶ Print the To Help You Remember statements on the board. In each statement write in one wrong word in place of a key word and underline it.

▶ Have the students tell what the correct words should be and allow them to correct the statements on the board.

▶ Invite any questions the students may have.

▶ Read directions to the circling activity and give the students time to complete it.

▶ Check responses.

Reflect

Ask the students to work with a partner and to agree on responses to the reflection question.

Share

▶ Have partners share what they decided.

▶ Then help the class decide on one way they will share what they learned with their families.

▶ **TO HELP YOU REMEMBER**

1. Confirmation is received after the Sacrament of Baptism.

2. In Confirmation, the Holy Spirit gives us spiritual gifts to help us love and serve God and one another.

3. The Sacrament of Confirmation strengthens us to live our Baptism.

Chapter Review

Recall

Circle the word that best completes each sentence.

1. The Church needs the _____ of each person.

   books   (gifts)   pictures

2. The Holy Spirit is our _____, helper, and guide.

   priest   parent   (teacher)

3. The gift of _____ helps us choose what is good and do what is good.

   (courage)   wisdom   wonder

4. In Confirmation, the Church uses _____.

   water   ashes   (Sacred Chrism)

5. The _____ usually leads the celebration of Confirmation.

   deacon   priest   (bishop)

Reflect

How does using your spiritual gifts help your family?

_____

_____

_____

Share | Write one way the Holy Spirit wants us to use our spiritual gifts with others. Share this with a classmate.

(152)

SPECIAL NEEDS

Working with a Partner. Students with reading difficulties may be more successful with the multiple choice questions in the review if they are able to work with a classmate. Pair the students up and have each pair complete the activity after discussing the questions together. When they agree on the correct response, have the children then circle that choice in their texts.

Need: Students with reading deficits

Send Your Spirit

Leader The Holy Spirit teaches us and helps us to pray. God sent the Holy Spirit to help us know that we are God's children. Listen to what the Bible tells us.

Reader *God sent the spirit of his Son into our hearts, crying out, "Abba, Father!"*

Galatians 4:6

The word of the Lord.

All **Thanks be to God.**

Leader Let us pray that we may open our hearts to the Spirit and use the gifts he gives us to help others and to build up the Church. O God, send your Spirit

Group 1 into our hearts that we may love.

All **Holy Spirit be our teacher.**

Leader O God, send your Spirit

Group 2 into our minds that we may understand.

All **Holy Spirit be our helper.**

Leader O God, send your Spirit

Group 3 into our lives that we may serve.

All **Holy Spirit be our teacher.**

Leader Come, Holy Spirit, fill us and guide us. Give us the courage to live as disciples of Jesus. Amen.

(153)

We Pray

▶ Read aloud the introductory paragraph with the students.

▶ Go on to tell them that this prayer of petition to the Holy Spirit is based on a prayer written by Saint Anthony of Padua (1195–1231), a talented speaker and theologian, whose very first public speech dealt with the role of the Holy Spirit in our lives.

▶ Ask one of the students to act as Reader and allow him or her time to look over the passage from Galatians.

▶ Have the students form three groups. Have each group practice its lines.

▶ Gather the students with their books in the prayer center.

▶ Take the role of the leader and lead the students in this prayer to the Holy Spirit.

TEACHING TIP

Add to a Welcoming Song. Teach the students a second verse to the song they learned in Chapter 10. Remind the students that in the first verse, they sang about Baptism. In this new verse, they will sing about Confirmation. Recall that the song is sung to the tune of "Mary Had a Little Lamb."

Holy Spirit gives us gifts,
Gives us gifts,
Gives us gifts.
Holy Spirit gives us gifts,
to share God's love with all.

Preview

▶ Have the students carefully tear out pages 153 and 154 along the perforation.

▶ Encourage the students to share these pages with their families, and to complete the activities together.

▶ If they did not complete the review activity on page 152 by the end of the session, emphasize that they can complete it with their families at home.

▶ Point out the title and theme of the next lesson to the students.

Visit BeMyDisciples.com

▶ Take time with the students to explore the many activities and resources available at the *Be My Disciples* Web site.

▶ Encourage them to join with their families to discover the many resources available at the Web site.

Before Moving On ...

As you finish today's lesson, reflect on the following question before moving on to the next chapter.

Which students need more help from me in order to exercise and share their gifts?

With My Family

This Week . . .

In Chapter 11, "We Celebrate the Holy Spirit," your child learned:

▶ We receive the Sacrament of Confirmation after we receive the Sacrament of Baptism.

▶ The Church uses the actions of the laying on of hands and the anointing with Sacred Chrism in the celebration of Confirmation.

▶ In the Sacrament of Confirmation we receive and celebrate the Holy Spirit and his seven spiritual gifts.

▶ The gift of knowledge is one of the seven Gifts of the Holy Spirit. It enables us to discern the meaning of God's Word.

For more about related teachings of the Church, see the *Catechism of the Catholic Church*, 1285–1314 and 1830–1845, and the *United States Catholic Catechism for Adults*, pages 203–209.

■ Sharing God's Word

Read together 1 Corinthians 14:1, 12. Share the gifts your family has to help others and to build up the Church. Talk about how you use them to be lights in the world.

■ Living as Disciples

The Christian home and family is a school of discipleship. Choose one of the following activities to do as a family, or design a similar activity of your own:

▶ After Mass this week visit the place where the sacred oils are kept. Explain that this place is called the ambry. Point out the three containers holding the holy oils; OI stands for Oil of the Sick, OC stands for Oil of Catechumens, and SC stands for Sacred Chrism.

▶ Name some of the times you have seen one another using the gift of knowledge at home. Talk about these, as they are moments you are living your Baptism and are "lights" to one another.

■ Our Spiritual Journey

Almsgiving, or sharing our blessings with others, is one of the three major spiritual disciplines of the Church. While we are used to sharing our material blessings, such as money and food, with those in need, we are also to share our spiritual blessings. Encourage your children to give a portion of any money they receive for the good of others and the Church. This week, pray with your family: *Holy Spirit, be our teacher and helper.*

For more ideas on ways your family can live as disciples of Jesus, visit **BeMyDisciples.com**

154

ENRICHING THE LESSON

Conducting Interviews. If you are having the students work on Sacrament booklets as an ongoing project, invite them to add one or more pages about Confirmation. Encourage them to interview a parent, an older sibling, or another relative about the experience of preparing for and celebrating the Sacrament of Confirmation. Have them record what they learn on their booklet pages. Suggest that they ask the person they interview to supply a picture from their Confirmation day that they can include in the booklets.

Enriching the Lesson

Continuing Sacrament Booklets

Purpose

To reinforce the teaching about Confirmation (taught in chapter 11)

Directions

This activity will help the students recall some of the important words and actions of the Sacrament of Confirmation.

▶ Distribute the Sacrament booklets to the students that they began in chapter 9 and worked on in chapter 10.

▶ Tell the students to turn to the next page of their booklets and to write Confirmation at the top of the page.

▶ Invite them to draw a picture of something that happens in the Sacrament of Confirmation on the page. Have them write a title for their picture.

▶ Invite them to share their drawings with one another.

▶ Collect the booklets and store them for the students.

Materials

Sacrament booklets

pencils

crayons or markers

Creating a Collage of Gifts

Purpose

To reinforce the students' understanding that gifts are given to be shared (taught on page 148)

Directions

▶ Post on a bulletin board the note cards/slips of paper from the "gift box" the students wrote at the beginning of this lesson. Then refer the students to the pictures they drew of spiritual gifts on page 145. Note the many gifts the class has to share.

▶ Have copies of old magazines and newspapers available. Direct the students to find and cut out pictures or words they feel show a spiritual gift.

▶ Help the students attach the words and photos to a large sheet of art paper. If you wish, include the students' cards/slips of paper from the "gift box."

▶ Post the collage in the classroom. Allow the students to choose a title for their collage. Post the title above it.

Materials

copies of old magazines and newspapers

scissors

glue sticks

markers or crayons

art paper

Literature Connection

Purpose

To reinforce understanding of the importance of sharing gifts (taught on pages 148–149)

Directions

The Friendly Beasts: an old English Christmas Carol, by Tomie dePaola (Penguin Putnam Books for Young Readers, 1998), is a beautiful rendering of a lovely old English Christmas carol that speaks to the sharing of gifts—no matter how simple.

▶ Read the story aloud to the class. Even better, sing or play a recording of the carol as you display dePaola's charming illustrations.

▶ Afterward, discuss the story with the students. Ask, "Who gives gifts?" "What gift does each animal give?" "What do you think the carol says about sharing gifts?" and finally, "What special gift did God give?"

Materials

The Friendly Beasts: an old English Christmas Carol, by Tomie dePaola

a recording of the Christmas Carol, "The Friendly Beasts" and player (optional)

We Celebrate Forgiveness

BACKGROUND

Asking and Receiving Forgiveness

The parable of the Two Sons in Matthew 21:28-32 is a story that gives us a glimpse of the Kingdom of God: who may enter, how to gain entry, and the necessity of deeds as well as words of faith.

The parable has three characters: the father, a wayward son, and a righteous brother. The "father" is the loving and caring God the Father. It is his will to bring everyone into his kingdom. He wants everyone, including sinners who have turned away from his love, to share in the divine life. God the Father announces his kingdom and gathers us into it through his Son, Jesus. This gathering is the Church which is "on earth, the initial budding forth of that kingdom" (*Dogmatic Constitution on the Church* [Lumen gentium], 5).

Dishonoring God, Others, and Ourselves

When we sin, we deeply offend God's love for us. We dishonor and sever our communion with God. Quite often, one sin leads to another, and eventually we find ourselves, like the prodigal son, far away from our true home, far from our own souls.

When sin has finally made us ashamed, we gain an intimate understanding of the magnitude of Christ's gift of reconciliation. When our sorrow and regret humble us, we get a personal insight into Christ's call for conversion. It is a hand reaching through our darkness to rescue us.

Instituted by Christ

But where do we go to disclose our wrongs, to obtain a tangible and effective sign of forgiveness, to begin making amends, and to undertake the healing journey back into the welcoming arms of God the Father? Before Jesus returned to his Father, he appeared to his disciples: "[H]e breathed on them and said to them, 'Receive the holy Spirit. Whose sins you forgive are forgiven them, and whose sins you retain are retained'" (*John 20:22–23*). Thus, Christ gave to the Church a way to welcome sinners back home.

The Sacrament of Penance and Reconciliation

The Sacrament of Penance and Reconciliation, accomplishes what its name implies. It heals the divisions sin creates between the sinner and God, and between the sinner and others. This Sacrament brings God's forgiveness into the life of sinners. It reconciles sinners with God and with the Church.

Sin is before all else an offense against God, a rupture of communion with him. At the same time it damages communion with the Church. For this reason conversion entails both God's forgiveness and reconciliation with the Church, which are expressed and accomplished liturgically by the sacrament of Penance and Reconciliation (*Catechism of the Catholic Church*, 1440).

The Sacrament of Penance and Reconciliation also brings inner healing. It brings the gift of grace into the inner life of the sinner and effects an inner reconciliation as well.

For Reflection

How do I relate to God's constantly calling me to heal what keeps me from his love?

How has the Sacrament of Penance and Reconciliation helped me get my life on the right track?

Teacher to Teacher

First Reconciliation

The better prepared the students are for their first celebration of the Sacrament of Penance and Reconciliation, the more positive and comfortable they will be. Give the students in your class time to understand the process and the opportunity to ask questions or share any concerns they may have about receiving this Sacrament. This is time well spent and will ensure that the students are well prepared for their first celebration of this Sacrament.

Overcoming Obstacles

Even at the age of seven or eight, some students are very shy. Some students may be more nervous than others and may have a more difficult time adjusting to confessing their sins to the priest and sharing with him the things they have done wrong. Help these students and all the students by pointing out that many people feel this way. Assure them that the priest will help them too.

The Church Teaches...

"The Good News of the Kingdom of God, which proclaims salvation, includes a message of liberation for all, but especially for the poor … Liberation from sin is the fundamental form of freedom from which all liberation emerges" *(National Directory for Catechesis, 25C)*.

The Church has the task to be witnesses for Christ, to proclaim the Gospel, and to invite all people to faith in Christ. An old adage says, "Practice what you preach." Jesus set such an example by his own life. As teachers, our ministry is a spirit of service. If you intend to teach about forgiveness, make sure that your manner in the classroom reflects a forgiving spirit. Such an atmosphere can help establish a sense of freedom to choose to follow Jesus.

Further Reading and Reflection

For more related teachings of the Church, see the *Catechism of the Catholic Church*, 976–983, 1420–1484, and 1846–1851; and the *United States Catholic Catechism for Adults*, pages 234–243.

Teacher Prayer

God of mercy and forgiveness, let the students recognize in me some of your warmth and compassion. Help them forgive when others hurt them and ask for forgiveness when they hurt others. Let them be comfortable with the Sacrament of Penance and Reconciliation so that they may feel the healing peace of your welcoming embrace.
Amen.

Lesson Planner

Chapter 12   We Celebrate Forgiveness

Goal To learn that in the Sacrament of Penance and Reconciliation, we ask for and receive forgiveness for our sins

LESSON PART	PROCESS	MATERIALS and RESOURCES
DAY 1 EXPLORE **Focus** To explore how followers of Jesus are signs of God's forgiving love Pages 155–157	▶ Proclaim and discuss Luke 15:7 (There is joy in heaven when we ask for forgiveness). ▶ Learn and discuss the story of St. John Vianney and how he was a sign of God's forgiving love. **Disciple Power:** Forgiveness **Activity:** Practice forgiving and asking forgiveness.	Bible
DAY 2 DISCOVER **Focus** To discover the meaning of sin and our need for forgiveness Pages 158–159	▶ Discover what sin is. ▶ Learn how the Holy Spirit helps us seek forgiveness. **Faith Words:** sin **Catholics Believe:** Act of Contrition **Activity:** Write or draw about forgiving and asking forgiveness.	Pencil or pens Crayons or markers **Enriching the Lesson:** Teacher Guide, page 249 • Using Puppets to Learn Forgiveness Literature Connection: "Ol' Meany McCrank," in *A Child's First Book of Virtues*
DAY 3 DISCOVER **Focus** To discover that God is merciful and forgiving Pages 160–161	▶ Learn about the story of the two sons and forgiving father. ▶ Discover that God forgives us. **Scripture Story:** The Parable of the Forgiving Father (Luke 15:11–24) **Faith-Filled People:** Zacchaeus **Activity:** Find the way to forgiveness through a maze.	Bible Crayons or markers Optional: ice cream sticks and paper plates **Enriching the Lesson:** Teacher Guide, page 249 Continuing the Sacrament Booklets **Additional Activities Booklet:** Activities 12a and 12b, or see *BeMyDisciples*.com
DAY 4 DECIDE **Focus** To discover what happens in the Sacrament of Penance and Reconciliation and to decide how to be a peace maker Pages 162–163	▶ Learn about the celebration of the Sacrament of Penance and Reconciliation. **Faith Words:** reconciliation, penance **Activity:** Describe how to be a peacemaker. **My Faith Choice:** Choose how to forgive others this week.	Pencil or pens
DAY 5 CONCLUDE **Focus** To believe and trust that God will hear our prayers and help us Pages 164–166	▶ **REVIEW** Review concepts: Recall, Reflect, and Share. ▶ **PRAY** Prayer of Petition ▶ **PREVIEW** the With My Family page and the theme of the next chapter.	Bible, candle, cross for prayer space Grade 2 Music CD **Assessment Tools Booklet:** Assessments 12a and 12b

Assign online Chapter Review and interactive Chapter Test at **BeMyDisciples.com**

CHAPTER **12**

We Celebrate Forgiveness

What do you say when you need forgiveness?

Listen carefully to what happens in Heaven when someone asks forgiveness for doing wrong.

There is great joy in heaven for one who asks for forgiveness.   BASED ON LUKE 15:7

Why do you think this causes great joy in Heaven?

155

Pray

▶ Welcome the students warmly. Begin and end with the Sign of the Cross.

▶ Ask the children to echo tis prayer after you:

Dear Jesus, / Help us to forgive others / and to ask forgiveness / when we hurt others / by our actions. / Amen.

Reflect

▶ Have the children respond to the opening question. *(I'm sorry. I forgive you.)*

▶ Tell the students that the words from the Bible they are about to hear are words Jesus spoke.

▶ Call on a volunteer to read the passage from the Gospel of Luke.

▶ Afterward, observe a moment of prayerful silence.

▶ Invite the students to describe what they see happening in the picture. *(Accept all reasonable replies.)*

▶ Have the students respond to the Scripture questions. Point out that just as Heaven rejoices when we are sorry and ask for forgiveness, so does the Church.

▶ End by praying the Sign of the Cross.

Focus

Invite the students to turn the page to learn about a kindly saint who was a special sign of God's forgiveness.

HUMAN METHODOLOGIES

Learning Through the Witness of the Teacher/Catechist. The *National Directory for Catechesis* explains, "(c)atechists must hand on the teachings of Christ to those being catechized (and) they must prepare them for the sacraments instituted by Christ" (*NDC,* 29E). Working with your class on a weekly basis, you have many opportunities to model God's love and forgiveness for them. Be genuine in forgiving students who apologize for breaking a class rule. Like Saint John Vianney, whom they will learn about in this chapter, be a sign to your second graders of God's mercy and love.

Introduce

▶ Remind the students that a Saint is a person who tries to make good choices, following Jesus' example.

▶ Ask the students to listen for how Saint John Vianney followed Jesus' example and helped the people of France.

▶ Call on volunteers to read the story of Saint John Vianney.

Reinforce

▶ Ask volunteers to respond to the question on the page and describe how Saint John Vianney was a sign of God's forgiving love. *(Accept responses that indicate an understanding that the Saint was welcoming, kindly, and forgiving. He helped people celebrate the Sacrament of Penance and Reconciliation.)*

▶ Present the information in Disciple Power on the virtue of forgiveness.

▶ Invite the students to think about how they ask for and extend forgiveness. Encourage volunteers to share responses with the class.

Disciple Power

Forgiveness
Forgiveness is a sign of love. We ask for forgiveness because we love God. We want everything to be right again. We share God's forgiving love with others when we forgive people who hurt us.

The Church Follows **Jesus**

Saint John Vianney

Jesus taught his followers about forgiveness. He taught them that they are to forgive over and over again.

Saint John Vianney was a priest. He was honored and respected because of his kindness to people who were sorry for their sins. Through forgiveness, he showed people God's mercy and love. Saint John Vianney was a special sign of God's forgiveness.

There is a story that a special railroad track was built to the village where Father John Vianney lived. The railroad track was built because so many people from all over France wanted to come to John Vianney to confess their sins.

John Vianney was named a Saint in 1925. He is the patron Saint of parish priests.

[?] How was Saint John Vianney a sign of God's forgiving love?

DISCIPLE POWER

Forgiveness. Forgiveness is a Spiritual Work of Mercy. Help the students to recognize that forgiveness does not come easily for most of us. It is our natural instinct to protect ourselves when we have been wronged. Explain that forgiveness is a choice we make. When we act with forgiveness, we are cooperating with the Holy Spirit's presence and activity in our lives. Encourage the students to pray for forgiveness for the wrongs they have committed and to pray for those who have wronged them. Point out that because we are human, it can be difficult at times to overcome hurt feelings, but if we want to live as disciples of Jesus, we will do our best to live the virtue of forgiveness.

Sometimes we need to forgive others. And sometimes we need to ask others to forgive us.

? How can we be a sign of God's forgiving love?

Activity — Forgiving Ways

Read the short stories. Decide what each person might say or do.

Shawna's dad gave her a special balloon for her birthday. Malik teases her and pops the balloon.

- To make things okay again, what can Malik say or do?

- What can Shawna say or do?

Randy is on the computer doing homework. His older sister Becca sends him a hurtful message that makes fun of him.

- To make things right again, what might Randy say or do?

- What might Becca say or do?

FORGIVENESS

157

Connect

▶ Present the opening on page 157 in your own words. Invite the students to share why forgiving and asking for forgiveness are sometimes difficult.

▶ Divide the class into two groups. Read the directions to the activity.

▶ Have Group 1 read the problem of Shawna and Bobby, decide what each can do to make things right again, and then act out their solution.

▶ Have Group 2 do the same with the problem of Randy and Rebecca.

▶ After each group has presented its skit to the class, call attention to the word *forGIVEness* on the bottom of the page. Ask the students what they notice about it.

▶ Help the students recognize that inside the word *forgiveness* is the word *GIVE*.

▶ Call attention to the first sentence in the definition of forgiveness in Disciple Power on page 156: "Forgiveness is a sign of love."

▶ Emphasize that forgiveness is always about giving love.

Pray

Invite the students to echo the following:

> Loving God, /
> help me be forgiven /
> and forgiving. /
> Help me be / a sign of your love. /
> Amen.

Pray

Lead the students in the Lord's Prayer.

Teach

▶ Read aloud the Faith Focus question. Tell them that these two pages will help them learn why we need forgiveness.

▶ Have the students think about some of the choices they have made today.

▶ Ask them if they think these were good or bad choices. Explain that many choices we make every day are neither right nor wrong. Other choices do make a difference.

▶ Read aloud Sacraments of Penance and Reconciliation. Ask the students to listen carefully to learn the meaning of the word *sin*.

▶ Have them underline the words that define sin in the text.

Reinforce

▶ Ask the follow-up question. Call for responses. *(Ask for forgiveness.)*

▶ Point out the Catholic Believe about the Act of Contrition which is a part of the celebration of the Sacrament of Penance and Reconciliation. Impress upon the students that we need to seek forgiveness and express sorrow for our sins because sin hurts our friendship with God, others, and ourselves.

Faith Focus
Why do we need forgiveness?

Faith Words
sin
Sin is to freely choose to do or say something we know God does not want us to do or to say.

Penance and Reconciliation

Each day we make many choices. Most of the time, we make good choices. Sometimes we choose to do or say something that we know God does not want us to do or say. This is called a **sin**.

Sometimes we may choose not to do or say something we know God wants us to do or say. This also is a sin. Sin always harms our friendship with God and with other people.

When we sin, we need to turn to God and other people and ask for forgiveness. We also need to make things better when we sin.

The Holy Spirit helps us to ask for forgiveness. We need to say, "I am sorry. Please forgive me." This shows we are truly sorry for our sins. God hears and forgives us when we say we are sorry for our sins.

❓ What do we need to do when we sin?

158

TEACHING TIP

Prejudice. This would be an excellent time to speak to the students about the sin of prejudice. Point out that prejudice happens when we judge a person or a whole group of people without really knowing them. Prejudice often happens when people from different cultures come together. Neither group knows much about the other, but they judge the other group by the color of their skin, the language they speak, or the religion they practice. Point out to the students how prejudice can affect our lives and the lives of others in serious ways. Work with the students to brainstorm a list of practical things they could do to avoid prejudice, such as getting to know a child in their neighborhood who has a different cultural background than they do.

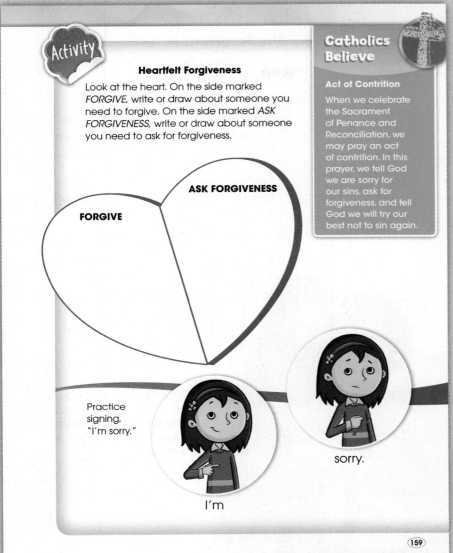

Activity

Heartfelt Forgiveness

Look at the heart. On the side marked *FORGIVE*, write or draw about someone you need to forgive. On the side marked *ASK FORGIVENESS*, write or draw about someone you need to ask for forgiveness.

ASK FORGIVENESS

FORGIVE

Practice signing, "I'm sorry."

I'm

sorry.

Catholics Believe

Act of Contrition

When we celebrate the Sacrament of Penance and Reconciliation, we may pray an act of contrition. In this prayer, we tell God we are sorry for our sins, ask for forgiveness, and tell God we will try our best not to sin again.

159

Connect

▶ Read the directions for the activity Heartfelt Forgiveness. Make sure the students understand what they are to draw or write.

▶ Allow ample time for the students to complete the activity.

▶ Have the students share their work with a partner.

▶ Challenge the students to act on what they drew or wrote: Forgive whoever needs forgiveness; seek forgiveness from whomever they have hurt.

Pray

Gather the students for prayer. Lead them in the following:

Dear Jesus, / sometimes I need to forgive. / Sometimes I need forgiveness. / Help me open my heart to say, / "I forgive you." / Help me open my heart to say, / "Please forgive me." / Amen.

TEACHING TIP

Holding a Grudge. There is a wonderful little book titled *The Hurt* by Teddi Doleski (Paulist Press, 1983). It is about a little boy who just cannot let go of a hurt. It follows him everywhere he goes, and it gets bigger and bigger and bigger. Of course, in the end, the boy learns how to get rid of the monster he created. This story teaches the students that forgiveness is a choice. Consider reading it to the students or suggesting it to their families.

Key Concept
God is ready to forgive when we are sorry for sin.

Pray

Have the students quiet themselves for prayer. Together pray the Sign of the Cross.

Teach

▶ Read the Faith Focus question. Tell the students they are going to discover a story Jesus told about a father and his son that can help us understand what it means to be sorry and the power of God's love to forgive us.

▶ Set the scene for the story of The Forgiving Father.

▶ Then have volunteers proclaim the parable.

▶ Discuss the feelings of the father after the return of his son.

Reinforce

▶ Divide the class into two groups and have each group role-play the story or use stick puppets. *(ice cream sticks fastened to paper plates)*

▶ Have the students imagine that they are the younger son in the story. Discuss: What was it like when your father held you in his arms and told you that he was happy to have you home? *(Affirm all appropriate responses.)*

▶ Ask the Scripture follow-up question and invite responses. *(God's love and forgiveness are always given to us when we say we are truly sorry. Accept all other appropriate responses.)*

Faith Focus
What does the Bible teach us about forgiveness?

The Forgiving Father

Jesus told a story about forgiveness.

A father had two sons. The younger son told his father, "I want my share of the family's money now." The father gave the son his share of the family money. The son left home and quickly wasted his money.

The son thought about his home and his father. He was very sorry for what he had done and decided to return home.

The father saw his son walking toward the family home. The father ran down the road to welcome his son back home. The father hugged his son and kissed him. The son said, "Father, I am very sorry." The father was so happy that he gave a big party to celebrate.

BASED ON LUKE 15:11–24

❓ What do you think Jesus was teaching about God in this story?

BACKGROUND: SCRIPTURE

Scripture Stories. We all know the value of a good story and how a well-told story captures our imaginations and interest, draws us into the world of the story, and helps us gain insight into the message of the story. "In Sacred Scripture, God speaks to man in a human way" (*Catechism of the Catholic Church,* 109). By using parables, Jesus spoke to his listeners in a truly human way, getting his point across in a way only a good story can. The parable of the Forgiving Father, or the Lost Son, as it is also called, is one of the three parables that Saint Luke gathers together in the fifteenth chapter of his Gospel. The other two are the parable of the Lost Sheep (*Luke* 15:1–7) and the parable of the Lost Coin (*Luke* 15:8–10).

Jesus wants us to know that God loves and forgives us. When we are sorry and ask God for forgiveness for our sins, God forgives us. God rejoices and welcomes us back home.

 What are ways you can show forgiveness?

Activity

God's Forgiveness

Find your way to God's forgiveness. Draw a line to find your way to forgiveness.

I'm sorry.

I did something wrong.

I promise to do better.

I ask for forgiveness.

I want to come back home to God.

You are forgiven. Let's celebrate!

(161)

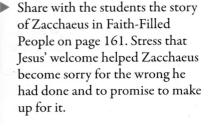

FAITH-FILLED PEOPLE

Zacchaeus. The students have already encountered Zacchaeus in the story Zacchaeus and Jesus, which begins this unit (see student page 117). The story of Zacchaeus is only told in the Gospel according to Luke (*see Luke* 19:1-10). Zacchaeus was the chief tax collector in Jericho on behalf of the Roman authorities. He was extremely unpopular since he acquired wealth by being dishonest. Zacchaeus was probably aware of Jesus' pastoral outreach to all people, even unpopular people like himself. He climbed a sycamore tree to avoid a large crowd. Jesus saw Zacchaeus and invited himself to Zacchaeus' house. Joyful Zacchaeus was a changed man. He gave half of his possessions to the poor and gave back to people from whom he had dishonestly taken money four times the amount he had taken. Zacchaeus' new life reflects the joy of being accepted by Jesus.

▶ Share with the students the story of Zacchaeus in Faith-Filled People on page 161. Stress that Jesus' welcome helped Zacchaeus become sorry for the wrong he had done and to promise to make up for it.

▶ Emphasize that like the forgiving father and like Jesus, God will forgive us if we are sorry for our sins.

Connect

▶ Point out the activity titled The Forgiveness of Our Father. Read the introductory paragraph aloud.

▶ Give the students time to trace their way through the maze from admitting having done wrong to forgiveness and celebration. Invite volunteers to share their responses.

▶ Tell the students that in their next lesson they will discover how the Church celebrates forgiveness.

Pray

Gather the students for prayer. Lead them in the following:

Loving Father, / watch over us. / Call us back to you when we sin. / Help us become sorry for our wrongdoing. / Welcome us home. Amen.

> **Key Concept**
> In the Sacrament of Penance and Reconciliation we celebrate the forgiveness of sin.

Pray

Quiet the students for prayer. Lead them in praying the Glory Be.

Teach

▶ Read the Faith Focus question aloud. Tell the students that today they will learn that they can receive and celebrate forgiveness and reconciliation in a very special Sacrament.

▶ Tell the students that when we sin, we need to ask for forgiveness and try to make things better. Present the first two paragraphs of the text.

▶ Tell the students that we can celebrate the sacrament by ourselves, or we can gather with other members of our parish, and then meet with the priest. Stress that confessing our sins to the priest is always done in private.

▶ Have volunteers read aloud the four parts of the Sacrament.

Reinforce

Read the definitions of *reconciliation* and *penance* in Faith Words. Have the students make word cards for the terms.

Connect

▶ Ask the follow-up question.

▶ Write the four parts of the Sacrament on poster board. Mix up the order and invite volunteers to place them in the correct order.

Faith Focus
What happens in the Sacrament of Penance and Reconciliation?

Faith Words
reconciliation
Reconciliation means to become friends again.

penance
Penance is something we do or say to show we are truly sorry for the choices we made to hurt someone.

We Celebrate Reconciliation

We too need to ask for forgiveness when we sin. Jesus gave us a Sacrament to help us do this. It is called the Sacrament of **Penance** and **Reconciliation**.

In this Sacrament, we share in God's mercy and forgiving love. God is always ready to forgive us if we are sorry for our sins. Our sins are forgiven. We receive God's grace. God's grace helps us to make good choices to live as children of God. We receive the gift of peace.

Every celebration of this Sacrament always has four parts. The four parts are:

1. **Confession.** We meet with the priest by ourselves and tell him our sins.

2. **Contrition.** We tell God we are truly sorry for our sins. We pray an act of contrition.

3. **Penance.** We are given a penance. Doing our penance helps repair, or heal, the harm we have caused by our sins.

4. **Absolution.** The priest lays his hands on or over our heads while he says a special prayer. The words and actions of the priest tell us we have received God's forgiveness.

? How does the Sacrament of Penance and Reconciliation help us?

(162)

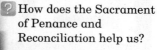

LITURGY CONNECTION

Listening to One's Conscience. Take just a few extra minutes at the end of each session to help the students develop a habit of listening to their consciences. First, have the students think about the things they might have done that were unkind or disobedient. Then have them silently pray an act of sorrow. Next, have the children think about the good choices they made. Then have the students pray aloud together, *"Thank you, God, for helping me make good choices."*

In the Sacrament of Penance and Reconciliation, God forgives you. You need to forgive others as God forgives you. When you forgive others, you are acting with kindness. You are a peacemaker.

Activity

Sharing God's Gift of Forgiveness

Fill in the empty spaces. Describe how you can be a peacemaker.

I can ask the Holy Spirit to help me live as a peacemaker.

I will forgive _____ .

I will show my forgiveness by saying _____ .

I will show my forgiveness by doing _____ .

My Faith Choice

This week, I will forgive others. I will do what I have written on the lines above.

 Pray, "Thank you, Father, for your mercy and kindness. Holy Spirit, teach and help me to be forgiving as Jesus taught. Amen."

(163)

THE TASKS OF CATECHESIS

Moral Formation. We can thank God each and every day that because of his mercy and forgiveness, we are gifted with a lifetime of new beginnings. Saying "I am sorry" helps to reconcile us with those we have hurt. When a person finds the courage and takes the time to apologize, we should accept the apology graciously. Many people have a tendency to answer "It's all right" when someone apologizes or asks to be forgiven. Have the students repeat this phrase after you, "I forgive you." Encourage them to use these or similar words to accept an apology when someone asks their forgiveness.

Reinforce

Remind the students that God forgives us our sins in the Sacrament of Penance and Reconciliation.

Respond

▶ Invite the students to read the introductory paragraph.

▶ Ask: "When are you a peacemaker?" (*Accept appropriate responses; for example, "When I forgive others, I can be a peacemaker."*)

▶ Explain to the students that the Sharing God's Gift of Peace activity will give them an opportunity to be peacemakers.

▶ Allow the students sufficient time to complete the activity.

Choose

▶ Invite the students to read My Faith Choice.

▶ Encourage them to follow through on their decisions about forgiveness in the week ahead.

Pray

Lead the students in the prayer to the Father and Holy Spirit at the bottom of the page.

Pray

Invite the students to remember that God is present. Pray the Sign of the Cross together to begin class.

Recall

▶ Scramble the letters of the words sin, forgiveness, Reconciliation, and absolution on the board.

▶ Ask volunteers to come up and write the words correctly underneath each of the scrambled words.

▶ Ask other volunteers to find each of the words in the To Help You Remember statements and read the statements aloud to the class.

▶ Give directions for the fill-in-the-blank activity, and allow time for the students to complete it.

▶ Check responses.

Reflect

Give the students a few moments to write out their response to the reflection statement.

Share

▶ Ask volunteers to share their reflections with the class.

▶ Challenge the students to share their new learning and reflections with their families.

▶ **TO HELP YOU REMEMBER**

1. Sin is choosing to do or say something against God.

2. In the Sacrament of Penance and Reconciliation, we ask for and receive forgiveness for our sins.

3. Contrition, confession, penance, and absolution are always part of the Sacrament of Penance and Reconciliation.

Chapter Review

Recall

Complete the sentences. Use the words in the word bank.

Absolution	Confession
Contrition	Penance

1. _Confession_ is the telling of our sins to the priest.

2. _Contrition_ is true sorrow for our sins.

3. _Penance_ is making up for our sins.

4. _Absolution_ is receiving God's forgiveness for our sins.

Reflect

Why is forgiveness important in your life to be a follower of Jesus?

_____

_____

_____

_____

_____

Share Write and then share with a classmate how you have forgiven someone.

(164)

TEACHING TIP

Peacemakers. As students are sent forth from the Sacrament of Penance and Reconciliation, they are asked to be peacemakers. Give them the opportunity to reflect on how they can be peacemakers. Some ideas may include being generous with a sibling, merciful with a friend, and kind to a neighbor. Ask students to brainstorm concrete examples. Challenge them to be peacemakers this week.

Prayer of Petition

In a prayer of petition, we believe and trust that God will hear our prayers and help us.

Leader   God is always ready to forgive us and to welcome us home. Let us listen to the Word of God.

Reader   A reading from the holy Gospel according to John.

All   **Glory to you, O Lord.**

Reader   *John 20:19–23.*
The Gospel of the Lord.

All   **Praise to you, Lord Jesus Christ.**

Leader   Lord, our God, you always forgive us because of your great love.

All   **Fill our hearts with joy.**

Leader   For the times we did what was wrong, we pray,

All   **Forgive us and welcome us home.**

Leader   For the times we did not forgive others, we pray,

All   **Forgive us and welcome us home.**

Leader   Lord, our God, you always forgive us.

All   **Fill our hearts with peace.**
Amen.

165

We Pray

▶ Tell the students that the prayer today is a prayer of petition. Then practice the responses.

▶ Provide a Bible, and invite a volunteer to read John 20:19–23, the Risen Jesus' appearance to his disciples, giving them the power to forgive sins.

▶ Gather the students with their books in the prayer center.

▶ Invite the students to take a few deep breaths to quiet and center themselves.

▶ Lead the prayer.

LITURGY CONNECTION

Mass Responses. Point out to the students that the responses just before and after the Gospel reading in this chapter's closing prayer are the responses the assembly makes before and after the Gospel is proclaimed at Mass. Help the students to learn these responses by heart as they prepare for their First Communion. Continue to use these responses whenever a Gospel passage is read as part of your classroom prayer services.

Preview

▶ Have the students carefully tear out pages 165 and 166 along the perforation.

▶ Encourage the students to share these pages with their families, and to complete the activities together.

▶ If they did not complete the review activity on page 164 by the end of the session, emphasize that they can complete it with their families at home.

▶ Point out the title and theme of the next lesson to the students.

Visit BeMyDisciples.com

▶ Take time with the students to explore the many activities and resources available at the *Be My Disciples* Web site.

▶ Encourage them to join with their families to discover the many resources available at the Web site.

Before Moving On ...

As you finish today's lesson, reflect on the following question before moving on to the next chapter.

How flexible am I in adjusting timeframes if the students are working well on an activity?

With My Family

This Week . . .

In Chapter 12, "We Celebrate Forgiveness," your child learned:

▶ Jesus gave the Church the Sacrament of Penance and Reconciliation.

▶ Sin harms our relationship with God and others. When we sin, we need to seek forgiveness.

▶ In the Sacrament of Penance and Reconciliation, we ask for and receive God's forgiveness for the sins we have committed after Baptism. This Sacrament reconciles us with God and with the Church.

▶ When we practice the virtue of forgiveness we offer God's forgiving love to others.

For more about related teachings of the Church, see the *Catechism of the Catholic Church*, 545–546, 587–590, 976–983, 1846–1848, and 1420–1484, and the *United States Catholic Catechism for Adults*, pages 234–243.

■ Sharing God's Word

Read together Luke 15:11–24, the parable of the Forgiving Father (Prodigal Son). Or read the adaptation of the parable on page 160. Emphasize the joy of the forgiving father when his prodigal son returned home. Talk about the joy and peace the members of your family experience when you forgive one another.

■ Living as Disciples

The Christian home and family is a school of discipleship. Choose one of the following activities to do as a family, or design a similar activity of your own:

▶ Discuss ways your family members ask for forgiveness and forgive one another. Discuss why it is important to forgive one another. Emphasize that when we forgive someone it does not mean that what the person did to hurt us is all right.

▶ Ask each family member to name some of the ways they have been a peacemaker at home. Promise to help one another live as a family of peacemakers. At dinnertime this week, pray to the Holy Spirit to help you live as peacemakers.

■ Our Spiritual Journey

At the heart of Jesus' work is forgiveness and reconciliation. The Hebrew word *mercy* cannot be easily translated into English. It points to the infinite mercy of God and the undeserved and limitless nature of divine forgiveness. This is the forgiveness we are to show others. Pray the Prayer of Petition for forgiveness with your family this week.

For more ideas on ways your family can live as disciples of Jesus, visit **BeMyDisciples.com**

166

THE LAST WORD

Celebrating Learning. As you conclude Unit 3, affirm the students for all they have learned in the last four chapters. For example, you may want to invite volunteers to name some of the new words they learned or you can encourage the students to recall a favorite Scripture story or activity from the unit. Remind the students that they have learned that we celebrate God's love in the Sacraments and through the seasons of the Church year.

Enriching the Lesson

Using Puppets to Learn Forgiveness

Purpose

To reinforce the importance of asking forgiveness and forgiving others (taught on page 158)

Directions

Students can use puppets to help them learn the techniques of showing and asking forgiveness.

▶ In small groups, have the students make simple puppets using small paper plates and craft sticks. Invite them to draw faces on the plates and then glue a craft stick to the back of each one to provide handles for the puppets. Have each student in the group make a puppet—a girl, a boy, an adult, and perhaps a younger child.

▶ When the groups are ready, have the students give their puppet performances for the whole class.

Materials

glue

paper plates

craft sticks

crayons or markers

Continuing the Sacrament Booklets

Purpose

To reinforce the words and actions used in the Sacrament of Penance and Reconciliation (taught on page 162)

Directions

Have the students continue to work in their Sacrament booklets by adding a page for the Sacrament of Penance and Reconciliation.

▶ Distribute the booklets to the students.

▶ Help them recall some key actions of the Sacrament of Penance and Reconciliation.

▶ Invite them to write the words *Penance* and *Reconciliation* at the top of the next blank page of their booklets. Direct them to draw a picture of an action of the sacrament and to label their picture. Invite them to share their pictures with one another.

▶ Collect the booklets and store them for the students.

Materials

Sacrament booklets

crayons or markers

pencils

Literature Connection

Purpose

To reinforce the need to ask for forgiveness when we sin (taught on page 158–159)

Directions

Read the story called "Ol' Meany McCrank," found in *A Child's First Book of Virtues* by Emily Hunter, Harvest House Publishers, 1995. It is a wonderful story of how repeated forgiveness can actually change a person.

Materials

A Child's First Book of Virtues by Emily Hunter

Catholic Social Teaching Unit 3

Pray

Gather the students for prayer. Lead them in echoing the following section of the Prayer of Saint Francis of Assisi:

Lord, make me an instrument of your peace; / where there is hatred, let me sow love, / where there is injury, pardon, / . . . where there is darkness, light, / and where there is sadness, joy. / Amen.

Focus

Write the word *peace* on the board. Invite the students to brainstorm its meaning. List ideas on the board.

Introduce

▶ Invite a volunteer to read aloud the principle of Catholic Social Teaching in the sidebar, We Make Peace.

▶ Contrast and compare the principle to the list on the board. Emphasize how peace is not merely the absence of conflict, but the efforts we make to build a just world.

Teach

▶ Invite volunteers to read aloud Kids for Peace.

▶ Ask the students what the children in Kids for Peace do to work for peace.

▶ Point out how serving others, being kind, showing respect, caring for creation, and loving one's neighbor are all acts of justice that make peace.

Catholic Social Teaching

Kids for Peace

Kids for Peace is a world-wide group made up of kids who want to be peacemakers. Young persons who are part of Kids for Peace work to serve others. They act with kindness. They respect others. They care for the Earth, and they believe that they are neighbors with people all over the world.

Members of Kids for Peace make a peace pledge. A pledge is a special promise. This is the promise they make:

> **WE MAKE PEACE**
> Everyone who wants peace must work for justice. When we care for others, act with kindness, and respect all people, we are being peacemakers.

heiwa Pokój salam

Paix Achukma Pax Peace shalom

I pledge to use my words
to speak in a kind way.

I pledge to help others
as I go throughout my day.

I pledge to care for our earth
with my healing heart and hands.

I pledge to respect people
in each and every land.

I pledge to join together
as we unite the big and small.

I pledge to do my part
to create PEACE for one and all.

paz Hòa Bình

(167)

BACKGROUND: CATHOLIC SOCIAL TEACHING

Promoting Peace. There is a close relationship in Catholic Social teaching between peace and justice. That is why the Church promotes peace as a positive, action-oriented concept. *The Pastoral Constitution on the Church in the Modern World* (Gaudium et Spes) #78, states: "Peace is not merely the absence of war; nor can it be reduced solely to the maintenance of a balance of power between enemies.; nor is it brought about by dictatorship. Instead, it is rightly and appropriately called an enterprise of justice. Peace results from that order structured into human society by its divine Founder, and actualized by men as they thirst after ever greater justice." Peace, then, is the fruit of justice and is dependent upon right order among human beings.

Making Connections

Peace is Jesus' promise, gift, and command. Jesus calls us to make peace, and he calls peacemakers, "children of God" (Matthew 5:9). When we work for peace, we are acting as God's own children.

with Creative Arts

Make a handprint peace wreath. Everyone trace their hands, color them, cut them out, and then, on tag board, paste them together to form a wreath. Make a dove shape for the center of the wreath. Post the wreath in the classroom.

with Language Arts

Make a list of the Disciple Power words you have discovered. Each one is a virtue or gift that can help you act as a peacemaker. Choose two of the Disciple Power words. Write each one on an index card. Then write how the two virtues you chose will help you be a peacemaker. Choose to do what you write.

with Social Studies

Look at the words found on page 167. Each word is in a different language, but each means, *Peace*. Find the country of the language you chose on a map. Write a prayer for peace and use the peace word in the language you chose. Pray for peace in that country and in the world.

Faith Action

Decide on one way you can be a peacemaker in your family or at your school. One way I will choose to be a peacemaker is _____

_____

_____

(168)

TEACHING TIP

Affirm the Students. Each time you observe the students acting as peacemakers or offering forgiveness, make a point of affirming them. When the students are praised for making good choices, they will be encouraged to make more good choices. It is important to affirm the students for living as Jesus calls them to live.

Catholic Social Teaching

Reinforce

▶ Invite the students to make the peace pledge. Have them stand, place their hands over their hearts, and recite the pledge with you.

▶ If possible, make copies of the pledge for the students to share at home.

Connect

▶ Explain the three cross-curricular activities. Ask the students to choose the one or ones they wish to work on.

▶ **Creative Arts:** Have plenty of stiff construction paper. Students can help each others trace their hands. Tell the students to color their handprints any color they wish. You may have to help the students cut them out and arrange into a wreath shape.

▶ **Social Studies:** Briefly review the Disciple Power terms from Chapters 1–12 with the class and talk about ways they can help us make peace. Distribute large index cards and allow the students to choose two terms and to write about them.

▶ **Language Arts:** Make sure the students understand they are to choose a "peace" word (from page 167) not in their own language for their poem. Show them how to write it vertically on a sheet of paper. Then allow them to work on their own. Post completed poems in the classroom.

Unit 3 Review

The Unit Review provides the opportunity to assess the students' understanding of the concepts presented in the unit and to affirm them in their growing knowledge and love of God. Here are a few suggestions for using these pages.

▶ Share with the students that the next two pages are an opportunity to stop and review what they have learned.

▶ Provide time for the students to ask questions.

▶ Have the students complete the review alone or with a partner.

▶ Encourage the students to share the Unit Review pages with their families.

A. Choose the Best Word

This section reviews the main concepts of the unit.

▶ Read the directions for section A. Illustrate what you expect the students to do by completing the first question together. By working together on the first sentence, you are teaching the students a strategy for answering these types of sentences.

▶ When the students have finished this section, invite volunteers to share their answers. Review any sentence that the students seem to have difficulty answering.

B. Show What You Know

This section reinforces what the students have learned about Jesus.

▶ Read the directions to the students. Have the students complete the section.

▶ Invite volunteers to share their answers.

Unit 3 Review   Name _____

A. Choose the Best Word

Complete the sentences. Color the circle next to the best choice for each sentence.

1. The Seven _____ are signs of God's love for us.

○ Bibles   ● Sacraments   ○ Prayers

2. Water and oil are used in the Sacrament of _____.

● Baptism   ○ Penance and Reconciliation   ○ Matrimony

3. Jesus told the story of the Forgiving _____ to teach us about God's forgiveness.

○ Son   ○ Brother   ● Father

4. In the Sacrament of Confirmation, we receive _____.

○ Jesus   ● spiritual gifts   ○ forgiveness

5. _____ is freely choosing to do or say something we know God does not want us to do or to say.

○ Penance   ○ Reconciliation   ● Sin

B. Show What You Know

Draw a line to connect the clues to the correct Sacrament.

Sacrament	Clue
1. Baptism	**a.** strengthens us by the Holy Spirit
2. Confirmation	**b.** forgiveness of sins committed after Baptism
3. Penance and Reconciliation	**c.** first Sacrament we receive

(169)

TEACHING TIP

Student-directed Assessment. Part of varying the type of assessment might include inviting students to develop, implement and facilitate the unit reviews. Placing them in the forefront of the learning process is a way not just to empower them in their learning, but a vital way of learning retention. When students teach what they have learned, the knowledge is retained and appreciated at a deeper level of understanding. Rotate through the year, volunteer students to lead the class in the unit reviews. Be sure to guide the students along the way.

C. Connect with Scripture

What was your favorite story about Jesus in this unit?
Draw something that happened in the story.
Tell your class about it.

D. Be a Disciple

1. *What Saint or holy person did you enjoy hearing about in this unit? Write the name here. Tell your class what this person did to follow Jesus.*

_____

_____

2. *What can you do to be a good disciple of Jesus?*

_____

_____

(170)

TEACHING TIP

Memorization. Throughout the year, encourage the students to learn key concepts and teachings through the use of memorization. Expressing the faith is not something to be reduced to mere statements robotically mimicked. Memorizing important Scripture verses and traditional faith formulas are important as an essential learning strategy to help activate the mind in keeping to heart the key teachings of the faith.

C. Connect with Scripture

This section reinforces the students' experience and knowledge of Scripture and the teachings of Jesus.

▶ Help the students review the Scripture stories in the unit, beginning with the Unit Opener story. You may wish to write the names of these stories on the board to assist them.

▶ Ask volunteers to share their favorite stories with the class.

▶ In the space, invite the students to draw something that happened in the story. Invite volunteers to share their drawings now, or at the completion of the Unit Review.

D. Be a Disciple

This section provides the students with the opportunity to recall how the Saints and holy people followed Jesus. It reinforces the ways students can choose to live as disciples of Jesus.

▶ Ask the students to remember their favorite stories of Saints or holy people that they learned about in this unit. Refresh their memories as needed, and write their responses on the board.

▶ Give each student time to write the name of their favorite Saint or holy person on the line. Ask volunteers to share the reason for their choices.

▶ Lead a discussion about the actions that make us good disciples of Jesus. Give the students time to write on the lines their idea of what they could do.

Objectives

In Unit 4, the students will study the Mass. You will help the children learn that:

▶ The Mass is the most important celebration of the Church.

▶ The Liturgy of the Word is the first main part of the Mass.

▶ At the celebration of the Eucharist, the bread and wine become the Body and Blood of Jesus.

▶ At the end of the Mass we receive God's blessing to live as Jesus' disciples.

Spiritual Insights

Jesus gave us the Sacraments to call us to worship God, to build up the Church, to deepen our faith, to show us how to pray, to connect us with the living Tradition of the Church, and to sanctify us. While God works primarily through the Sacraments, he also touches us through the community of the Church, through the lives of holy people, through prayer, spirituality, and acts of love. But, "for believers, the sacraments of the New Covenant are necessary for salvation".

Catechism of the Catholic Church 1129

Through these, he has bestowed on us the precious and very great promises, so that through them, you may come to share in the divine nature.   2 Peter 1:4

Living the Six Tasks of Catechesis

Teaching to Pray: Saint Thérèse of the Child Jesus (1873–1897)

Marie Martin was raised in France. She was the youngest of five daughters. Marie was somewhat spoiled and used to getting her own way.

When the family was granted an audience with Pope Leo XIII during a visit to Rome, Marie boldly asked the Holy Father for special permission to enter the Carmelite order. The Pope granted her request. She eagerly gave her life to God by entering the Carmelite cloister, shutting herself away from the distractions of the world. Marie was given the name Sister Thérèse.

Sister Thérèse was given dull work—washing floors, scrubbing pots, and cleaning the chapel. She tried to do every task with love. She called it her "little way" of serving God. Her daily work became a prayer to God. Thérèse called herself Jesus' little flower.

Sister Thérèse Marie was asked to write about her "Little Way". Today, her autobiography is still read today by people who want to lead a more spiritual life. Thérèse was canonized in 1925.

In 1997, Blessed Pope John Paul II declared Saint Thérèse a Doctor of the Church, a title given to the greatest teachers of our faith.

Sharing Your Faith

Find a partner to work with: a spouse, a friend, a fellow teacher. Come together at the beginning or end of each unit for shared prayer and discussion. Use the questions below as a starting point. As an alternative, record your thoughts in a personal journal.

▶ What can be done to increase participation in weekly Sunday liturgy among Catholics in our nation? Is this important to you? Why or why not?

▶ How have you experienced the transforming power of prayer in your life?

▶ Name two ways that teaching about the Sacraments has deepened your faith.

"Thank You, Jesus"

One day, Jesus met ten sick people by the side of the road. They had an awful sickness called leprosy.

When the ten saw Jesus, they called out to him. "Jesus, help us!" they shouted. "Jesus, have mercy on us!" they cried.

Jesus healed all ten people. As they were leaving, one of the ten turned right around to thank Jesus. "Praise God!" he shouted. "Thank you, Jesus!"

Jesus smiled and said, "Stand up and go; your faith has saved you."

BASED ON LUKE 17:11–19

(171)

What I Know

What is something you already know about these faith concepts?

The Liturgy of the Word

_____

_____

The Liturgy of the Eucharist

_____

_____

Mission

_____

_____

*Put an **X** next to the faith words you know. Put a **?** next to the faith words you need to learn more about.*

_____ Mass   _____ Gospel   _____ Eucharist
                        Acclamation
_____ assembly   _____ procession

What do you know about God's promises to his people in the Bible?

_____

A Question I Have

What question would you like to ask about the Mass?

_____

_____

(172)

Unit 4 Opener

The Unit 4 opener pages assess the students' prior knowledge about the key faith concepts in the unit. Processing these pages should take no more than fifteen minutes.

Opening Page

Invite the students to tell you what they see in the image on the page. Proclaim the Scripture story about the ten lepers. Ask: When have you remembered to thank others when they do something for you? Why is it important to thank others when they do something for us? Accept their answers, but do not respond further at this time.

Getting Ready

This page continues the activation of prior knowledge. Do not correct the children's responses. You will invite them to return and self-correct themselves at the end of the unit.

▶ Have the students write their responses under What I Know, and A Question I Have. You may also do the exercises orally.

▶ Record the students' questions on a chart. Refer back to the chart as you progress through the unit and ask volunteers to respond when they can answer the questions. You may also wish to use these questions during a unit assessment.

▶ Ask the students to turn to the next page and begin Chapter 13.

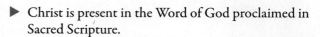

BACKGROUND

Christ with Us

The Eucharist is the source and summit of the Christian life. Sharing in the Eucharist deepens our communion with Christ and with the other members of the Church. Nourished at the table of the Lord, we receive both the grace to live as disciples of Christ in our own time and the pledge, or promise, of life everlasting with God, and with Mary and all the Saints.

Life-giving Bread

All of the Sacraments, ecclesial ministries, and works of the apostolate lead to and are bound up with the Eucharist. There is no moment in which the Church is not directed toward the Eucharist because ". . . in the most blessed Eucharist is contained the whole spiritual good of the Church, namely Christ himself, our Pasch and Living Bread, which gives life to men through his flesh–that flesh which is given life and gives life through the Holy Spirit" *(Decree on the Ministry and Life of Priests, 5)*.

Instituted by Christ

Jesus instituted the Sacrament of the Eucharist at the Last Supper. At the Eucharist, the passover of Christ from his Death to his Resurrection is made present, and we are made sharers in it. When the Church gathers to celebrate the Eucharist, it is the whole Body of Christ, Head and members, that gathers. Christ is present, joined with us in praising and thanking the Father.

Christ's Presence at the Mass

To accomplish the great work of our Salvation, Christ is always present in the Church, especially in the liturgical celebrations. Christ's presence in the Church is uncountable. However, at Mass, the Church speaks of his presence in these four ways:

▶ Christ is present in the priest who presides over the gathering in the name of Christ.

▶ Most especially, Christ is present under the consecrated species of bread and wine, which have become his Body and Blood.

▶ Christ is present in the Word of God proclaimed in Sacred Scripture.

▶ Christ is present in the believers who are gathered to celebrate.

Invited to the Table of the Lord

The Lord addresses an invitation to us, inviting us to receive him, his Body and Blood, in the Sacrament of the Eucharist:

> "Amen, amen, I say to you, unless you eat the flesh of the Son of Man and drink his blood, you do not have life within you."
>
> John 6:53

We dare to approach the table of the Lord and partake of this great gift, the Bread of Life, only after appropriate personal preparation. Our ritual words prior to receiving the Eucharist express both our unworthiness and our being made whole, healed in Christ. Having shared in the Eucharist, we go forth to share Christ within our families and among our neighbors, coworkers, and all people.

For Reflection

How aware am I of the presence of Christ throughout the day?

In my daily life how do I participate in the mission of Christ? When I do, how am I living bread for others?

We Celebrate the Mass

Each student you teach comes with his or her own unique set of experiences of Mass. Some take part in Mass every Sunday with their families. Others may only attend on special occasions. Some may have been in Sunday school programs while parents and older siblings attended Mass. No matter what the student's previous experience, your role is to help all the students appreciate their rightful place in the worshiping assembly of the Church.

Prayer Gestures

When introducing the Mass to the students, there are many prayers, postures, responses, and songs to teach, but those are secondary to what must first take place. A sense of love and sharing, celebration and reverence is most important. Through the efforts of the parish staff and caring parents, you can help the students realize that Jesus is present with us when we listen to his word and celebrate the Eucharist.

The Church Teaches...

"Christ's methodology was multi-dimensional. It included his words, his signs, and the wonders he worked. He reached out to the poor, to sinners, and to those on the margins of society. He proclaimed insistently the coming of the Kingdom of God, the forgiveness of sins, and reconciliation with the Father . . . Christ invited his listeners to a whole new manner of life sustained by faith in God, encouraged by hope in the kingdom, and animated by love for God and neighbor" (*National Directory for Catechesis*, 28A.2).

As a teacher and an evangelist, it is your responsibility in partnership with the parents to share the Gospel message and guide the children in the footsteps of Christ. That is why this program puts much emphasis on the actions and mission of the Body of Christ, the Church.

Further Reading and Reflection

For more related teachings of the Church, see the *Catechism of the Catholic Church*, 1322–1332 and 1346 and 1348; and the *United States Catholic Catechism for Adults*, pages 215–218.

Teacher Prayer

Gracious giving God, you call your people together to celebrate and to pray. Be with your children as they gather to learn of your love. Keep them diligent in the faith and thankful for the great freedom to worship that we enjoy. Amen.

Lesson Planner

Chapter 13   We Gather for Mass

Goal To learn about the Introductory Rites of the Mass

LESSON PART	PROCESS	MATERIALS and RESOURCES
DAY 1 EXPLORE **Focus** To explore why followers of Jesus gather to worship God **Pages** 173–175	▶ Proclaim and discuss Joel 2:15–16, 23 (Worship the Lord). ▶ Learn and discuss two stories about gathering to celebrate Mass. **Disciple Power:** Love **Activity:** Write a prayer giving praise to God.	Bible Pencils or pens
DAY 2 DISCOVER **Focus** To discover that God calls us to assemble for worship **Pages** 176–177	▶ Discover how Jesus shared the good news of God's love. ▶ Discover that Sunday is the day Catholics gather together to worship God at Mass. **Faith Words:** Mass, assembly **Scripture:** Matthew 18:20; Acts of the Apostles 2:42 **Catholics Believe:** The Lord's Day **Activity:** Draw and act out something we do at Mass.	Bible Pencil or pens
DAY 3 DISCOVER **Focus** To discover what happens when we gather for Mass **Pages** 178–179	▶ Learn about the Introductory Rites of the Mass. **Faith-Filled People:** Saint Justin **Activity:** Write names of those who gathered with you at Mass.	Crayons or markers Newsprint **Enriching the Lesson:** Teacher Guide, page 271 Role Playing the Entrance Procession
DAY 4 DECIDE **Focus** To decide on a way to take part in the Mass **Pages** 180–181	▶ Learn about the Penitential Act, the Gloria, and the Opening Prayer. **Activity:** Draw yourself gathered with your Church family. **My Faith Choice:** Choose how I will take part in Mass.	Pencil or pens Crayons or markers **Enriching the Lesson:** Teacher Guide, page 271 • Continuing Sacrament Booklets • Learning an Entrance Hymn **Additional Activities Booklet** Activities 13a and 13b or see *BeMyDisciples*.com
DAY 5 CONCLUDE **Focus** To offer God thanks and praise **Pages** 182–184	▶ **REVIEW** Review concepts: Recall, Reflect, and Share. ▶ **PRAY** Praise God ▶ **Preview** the With My Family page and the theme of the next chapter.	Bible, candle, cross for prayer space Grade 2 Music CD **Assessment Tools Booklet:** Assessments 13a and 13b

Assign online Chapter Review and interactive Chapter Test at **BeMyDisciples.com**

CHAPTER **13**

We Gather for Mass

❓ **When do families gather to celebrate?**

God invites us to gather to celebrate.
Listen to what God says to his people.

*Call my people together. Gather all the
people. Gather the old, the young, even the
babies. Rejoice and celebrate. Worship the
Lord, your God!* BASED ON JOEL 2:15–16, 23

❓ **When do Catholics gather to worship
God?**

(173)

HUMAN METHODOLOGIES

Learning by Human Experience. The *National Directory for
Catechesis* teaches that experiences are "the means through
which human beings come to know themselves, one another, and
God" (*NDC* 29A). Borrow the following books from the church sacristy:
the Roman Missal, which contains the prayers used at Mass; the
Lectionary, which contains the Scriptures read at Mass; and the
Book of the Gospels, which the priest or deacon uses to proclaim
the Gospel. As you teach the students about the Mass in Unit 4,
allow them to look carefully through these books, which are used
during the Eucharistic celebration. Point out that all three are used
throughout the world whenever the Mass is celebrated.

Pray

▶ Welcome the students warmly.
Invite them to quiet themselves
for prayer.

▶ Pray the Sign of the Cross
together. Ask the children to echo
each line after you:

> Jesus, be with us
> as we gather today
> to learn about
> the Holy Mass.
> Amen.

Reflect

▶ Ask the opening question. Invite
the students to share ways in
which they celebrate birthdays,
holidays, and other special days
with their families. (*Accept
all responses.*)

▶ Invite the children to listen to a
Bible passage that invites God's
people to gather to celebrate. Ask
them to listen for who is invited
to gather.

▶ Give the students a moment to
center themselves to pay attention
to God's Word. Call on a volunteer
to read Joel 2:15–16, 23.

▶ After the reading, observe a
moment of silence.

▶ Invite responses to the follow-up
question.

▶ Ask the students to tell what they
see in the photograph on page 173.
Explain that Catholics all over
the world gather to celebrate the
Mass. Conclude with the Sign of
the Cross.

Focus

Direct the students to turn the
page to find out more about how
the Church has always gathered to
celebrate to keep their faith alive.

Introduce

▶ Call attention to Disciple Power and present the information on the virtue of love.

▶ Invite the students to share when they were loving and loved even when it was hard to do so. (*Affirm all appropriate responses.*)

▶ Point out the title of the story. Ask the students to listen for how Christians have gathered to keep faith in God alive.

▶ Call on different students to read the two parts of the story.

Reinforce

▶ Invite responses to the story by asking the follow-up question.

▶ Continue the discussion by asking how the people in the story showed love. (*They continued to worship because of their great love for God*) Then ask: Why do you think Catholic Christians have always gathered to worship together no matter what? (*Accept all appropriate responses.*)

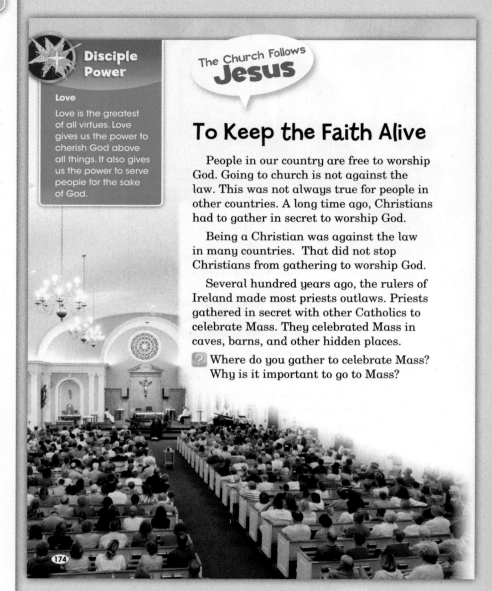

Disciple Power

Love

Love is the greatest of all virtues. Love gives us the power to cherish God above all things. It also gives us the power to serve people for the sake of God.

The Church Follows **Jesus**

To Keep the Faith Alive

People in our country are free to worship God. Going to church is not against the law. This was not always true for people in other countries. A long time ago, Christians had to gather in secret to worship God.

Being a Christian was against the law in many countries. That did not stop Christians from gathering to worship God.

Several hundred years ago, the rulers of Ireland made most priests outlaws. Priests gathered in secret with other Catholics to celebrate Mass. They celebrated Mass in caves, barns, and other hidden places.

? Where do you gather to celebrate Mass? Why is it important to go to Mass?

174

DISCIPLE POWER

Love. Love of God and love of neighbor summarizes the Ten Commandments. God's relationship with us is a story of love. God continually offers love through the wonders of creation. God's love is revealed to us in the person of Jesus. Jesus is both the messenger and the message of love. Jesus is God's promise of his abiding love. Jesus' ultimate act of love was freely accepting his Death on the Cross. Discuss with the children how they are aware of God's love in their lives. Encourage volunteers to name specific things that they can do to be messengers of God's love for others.

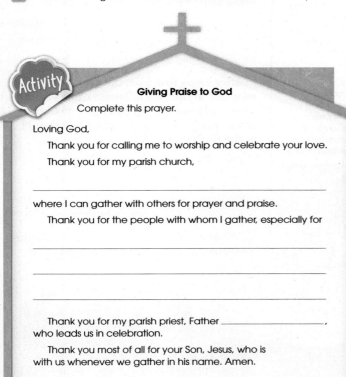

Not long ago, the government of the Czech Republic did not want people to be Catholic. But Father Petr Pit'ha and many other priests continued to gather people for Mass and other Sacraments. Today, Catholics in that country can celebrate their faith without fear.

❓ What are ways that we celebrate our faith?

Activity

Giving Praise to God

Complete this prayer.

Loving God,

Thank you for calling me to worship and celebrate your love.

Thank you for my parish church,

_____

where I can gather with others for prayer and praise.

Thank you for the people with whom I gather, especially for

_____

_____

_____

Thank you for my parish priest, Father _____, who leads us in celebration.

Thank you most of all for your Son, Jesus, who is with us whenever we gather in his name. Amen.

175

Connect

▶ Have the students write their responses to the following questions on a separate sheet of paper:

- What is the name of our parish?

- Who do I regularly gather with for Mass on Sunday? (Note: Invite the students to list people in addition to family members.)

- What is the name of our pastor?

▶ Call attention to the activity on page 175. Have the students draw on their answers to the three questions above to complete the prayer. If you think it will be beneficial, go through each section of the prayer one at a time with the class.

Pray

▶ Invite the students to quiet themselves inside and outside for prayer.

▶ Lead them in the prayer of thanks they just composed, allowing each student to mention the names of the people he or she listed in the second part of the prayers.

▶ Conclude with the Sign of the Cross.

Key Concept
Catholics gather as an assembly to worship God.

Pray

Gather the students for prayer. Lead them in the Glory Be.

Teach

▶ Read aloud the Faith Focus question. Explain that these next two pages will help them appreciate why Catholics gather for worship.

▶ Present the text titled We Gather at Mass on page 176.

Reinforce

Invite the students to respond to the question:

• What did Jesus promise whenever and wherever people gathered in his name? *(He promised his presence.)*

• Point out Catholics Believe about the Lord's Day. We gather as an assembly on the Lord's Day to worship God at Mass.

Faith Focus
Why do we gather for worship?

Faith Words
Mass
The Mass is the most important celebration of the Church. At Mass, we gather to worship God. We listen to God's Word. We celebrate and share in the Eucharist.

assembly
The assembly is the People of God gathered to celebrate Mass. All members of the assembly share in the celebration of Mass.

We Gather at Mass

Jesus gathered people. He invited people to come together on mountainsides, near lakes, and around tables in homes. He gathered people to share the good news of God's love. Jesus promised,

For where two or three are gathered together in my name, there am I in the midst of them.

MATTHEW 18:20

After Jesus rose from the dead and returned to God, his followers came together. They gathered to pray and listen to God's Word. They remembered Jesus and shared in the Eucharist.

The followers gathered to listen to the teaching of the Apostles, to break bread, and to pray together.

BASED ON ACTS OF THE APOSTLES 2:42

 What do you do when you gather together with your Church family at Mass?

176

TEACHING TIP

Keep Connected. Students sometimes do not feel connected to unfamiliar adult language—*assembly, Introductory Rites, Penitential Act,* etc.—and symbolic actions of the Mass. Throughout this unit, keep emphasizing that everyone is important to the celebration. At Mass, no one is simply a spectator. Each and every one present is to take an active part in the liturgical experience. Make sure the students feel the deep meaning of the words and gestures they are learning.

Today we gather too. Every Sunday, we come together to worship God in the celebration of the **Mass**.

At Mass, Catholics gather as an **assembly**. We come to Mass. We pray aloud and sing. We stand and sit and kneel. We show we are disciples of Jesus. Together we worship God the Holy Trinity.

? Why do we gather as an assembly at Mass?

Catholics Believe

The Lord's Day

Sunday is the Lord's Day for Christians. Jesus rose from the dead on Sunday. Catholics remember Jesus by gathering as an assembly on the Lord's Day to celebrate Mass.

Activity

With a partner, talk about all of the things you do at Mass. Choose one thing and draw it in the space. Then together, act it out for the class.

177

THE TASKS OF CATECHESIS

Liturgical Education. At the beginning of Mass, we gather together and form a worshiping community. We call this praying community "the assembly." Every member of the assembly has an active role in the Mass. In the Liturgy of the Word, the assembly listens and responds to the Word of God. In the Liturgy of the Eucharist, we join with the priest in preparing our gifts of bread and wine. We join with him in giving thanks to God the Father, and we remember and take part in the Death and Resurrection of Jesus. We prepare our minds and hearts to receive the Body and Blood of Christ. We receive the Eucharist and then are dismissed to go forth and bring peace to the world.

Teach

▶ Ask the question at the bottom of page 176. *(We gather to thank God for the gift of his Son.)* Encourage the students to name some of the words and actions that take place when they gather together with the Church family at Mass.

▶ Write the word "assembly" on the board. Ask the students if they have ever received a gift that came in pieces that said "assembly required." *(Accept all replies.)*

▶ Point out that *assembly* means "a joining together." Go on to tell the students that the Church requires assembly, too.

▶ Present the text on page 177. Emphasize how the Church gathers as an *assembly,* not an audience. Everyone plays an important part in celebrating the Mass. At Mass, we are not watchers; we are active members.

▶ Have the students go back over the text and underline ways in which the assembly takes an active part.

Reinforce

▶ Read aloud the meanings of the Faith Words *Mass* and *assembly.*

▶ Have the students make word cards for the terms.

Connect

▶ Have the students work with partners to choose something they do at Mass to act out.

▶ Allow time for partners to act out their choices for the class.

Pray

Gather the students for prayer. Lead them in the Lord's Prayer.

Key Concept
The Introductory Rites of the Mass gather us as disciples of Jesus.

Pray

Gather the students for prayer. Lead them in the Lord's Prayer.

Teach

▶ Ask a volunteer to read aloud the Faith Question and have the students think silently about how they may answer it.

▶ Remind the students that our most important gathering is the Mass. Tell them that the Mass begins with the Introductory Rites. This is a time when we gather, enter, and are greeted.

▶ Invite a volunteer to read the paragraph The Mass Begins. Afterward, have the students say what they do to get ready to gather for Mass.

▶ Ask another volunteer to read the paragraph titled The Entrance. Have the students follow along to discover who leads us in the celebration of Mass.
(A priest or bishop leads us in the celebration of the Mass.)

▶ Before moving on, sing a song of unity. Invite the students to stand and sing a familiar hymn they sing at Mass or a simple unity song such as "He's Got the Whole World in His Hands."

▶ Afterward, go on to summarize the text that is titled The Sign of the Cross and the Greeting for the students. Write the priest's greeting and the assembly's response on the board. Invite the students to role-play it.

Faith Focus
What happens when we gather for Mass?

The Mass Begins

The Mass is the most important celebration of the Church. We gather together in church with our Catholic community. We take our place as part of the assembly.

When we gather for Mass, we show that we are disciples of Jesus. We gather to praise God the Father for the great gift of Jesus. We give thanks to God for all our blessings.

The Entrance

The Introductory Rites begin the celebration of Mass. The priest or bishop and other ministers enter in procession. Only a priest or bishop can lead us in the celebration of Mass. He wears special clothes called vestments.

We stand and sing. The cantor, or song leader, leads us in the entrance hymn. Singing helps to join us together. We sing our praise and thanks to God.

❓ How does gathering for Mass show that we are disciples of Jesus?

(178)

TEACHING TIP

Highlighting Liturgy. Take the students through a role-play of the Introductory Rites. By engaging the senses of the children, you can help them learn the parts of the liturgy and remember them. Choose volunteers to be the priest, altar servers, lectors, and so forth. Gather sacramentals, such as candles (unlit), the Book of the Gospels, and the processional cross. Walk through the Introductory Rites with the students. Have the rest of the class form the assembly and follow along using a printed handout of the liturgy you can create. Take time following the role-play to answer students' questions and to reflect on the experience.

Sign of the Cross and the Greeting

The priest welcomes or greets us. He leads the assembly in praying the Sign of the Cross. This reminds us how Jesus gave himself for us on the Cross. We also remember our Baptism.

Then the priest greets us with open arms, saying, "The Lord be with you." We respond, "And with your spirit." These words remind us that God is with us in our gathering.

? How does the celebration of the Mass begin?

Faith-Filled People

Saint Justin

Justin lived about 100 years after Jesus rose from the dead and returned to his Father in Heaven. Justin wrote about the ways Christians gathered to worship God. We celebrate Saint Justin's feast on June 1.

Activity

Gathering at Mass

Write the names of those who helped you participate in Mass last Sunday.

• With whom did you assemble?

_____

• Who led the assembly in song?

_____

• Who led the assembly in prayer?

_____

(179)

FAITH-FILLED PEOPLE

Saint Justin (103–165). Justin was a professor of philosophy. He was a pagan who was searching for the true meaning of life. A wise man told him that he would find answers to his questions only by studying the Old Testament. Then Justin heard people talking about Jesus. They called him the Messiah who was promised in the Old Testament. Justin began to talk to Christians about their belief in Jesus. He was baptized and became a disciple of Christ. Justin shared his faith by opening a school of Christian studies in Rome. He became the first person to write about how and why the Christian community worshipped. Even today, his writings are treasured by the Church. Justin was martyred for his diligent teaching and defense of the Christian faith. To learn more about Saint Justin, go to the Saints Resource at *BeMyDisciples*.com.

Reinforce

▶ Ask the follow-up question. Have the students list in order the beginning elements of the Mass: *(1) entrance procession; (2) hymn; (3) Sign of the Cross; (4) greeting.* Write these elements on newsprint. Label it *Introductory Rites.* Preserve the list, so as to add to it later.

▶ Read Faith-Filled People with the class. Point out how Saint Justin tells us that Catholics have always gathered as an assembly to worship and celebrate.

Connect

▶ Read the activity directions aloud.

▶ Allow time for the students to draw and share their pictures of the Mass.

Pray

Pray the Sign of the Cross together.

Key Concept
The Introductory Rites ready us to offer thanks and praise to God.

Pray
Lead the class in praying the Sign of the Cross.

Teach

▶ Read aloud the Faith Focus question. Continue the presentation of the Introductory Rites by calling on a volunteer to read the paragraph, Penitential Act.

▶ Go on to the paragraph, The Gloria. Read it aloud and have the students underline the words *thanks* and *praise*. Explain that in the Gloria, we give praise and thanks to God.

▶ Summarize the paragraph, The Collect (Opening Prayer). Note that after the priest's call to prayer, we pause to "collect" our thoughts and prayers in order to bring them to God.

Reinforce
Ask for responses to the follow-up question. *(In the Penitential Act, we remember God's forgiving love.)*

Connect
Add *Penitential Act, Gloria,* and *Collect* to the list of elements of the Introductory Rites.

Faith Focus
What are the other parts of the Introductory Rites of the Mass?

The Assembly Prays
The Introductory Rites of the Mass continue after the Sign of the Cross and the greeting. Together we pray special prayers.

Penitential Act
After the greeting, the priest invites us to remember God's forgiving love. We pray aloud, asking for the Lord's mercy.

The Gloria
On most Sundays, we sing or pray aloud a special hymn called the "Gloria." It is a beautiful hymn of thanks and praise. This is how it begins.

Glory to God in the highest,
and on earth peace to people of good will.

The Collect
The priest then says, "Let us pray." We spend a moment in silent prayer. Then the priest leads us in the Collect. This prayer collects all our prayers and brings them to God the Father in the name of Jesus. We respond to the prayer by saying, "Amen."

? What do we do in the Introductory Rites of the Mass?

A song leader at Mass

(180)

TEACHING TIP

The Lord's Day. Remind the students that Sunday is a special day for Christians. This is the day that we call the Lord's Day. It is the day that the Lord Jesus was raised from the dead. Catholics keep the Lord's Day holy by taking part in Mass, not doing unnecessary work, and spending time with their families. Tell the students that Sunday is not the Lord's Day for non-Christians. Explain that the Jewish people celebrate Saturday as their Sabbath and holy day. The Jewish Sabbath begins at sundown on Friday night. Jewish families gather in their homes to praise and thank God for all his gifts and gather at their synagogues to worship God together as a people of faith. Then explain that our Muslim friends celebrate Friday as their holy day.

On Sunday, you and your family gather with your Church family to worship God. You offer God thanks and praise together.

I Follow Jesus

The Church Family Gathers

Activity Draw yourself gathered with your Church family for worship. In your picture, show how you are worshiping God at Mass.

My Faith choice I will pay attention at Mass. I will help my family take part in Mass on Sunday. I will

_____

_____

Pray, "Gather me in your love, O God, so I can offer you praise. Amen."

(181)

LITURGY CONNECTION

Praying with Gestures. Have the students look at the opening line of the Gloria or write the words on the board: *Glory to God in the highest, and on Earth peace to people of good will.* Remind the children that these are the words of the angels who told the shepherds of Jesus' birth. Go on to invite the students to suggest gestures that they can use to accompany this phrase. Practice the gestures with the class until all the students are able to perform them easily. Then use a missal to pray the Gloria aloud. Have the students pray the opening phrase with the gestures as a refrain, pausing after reading each of the three major stanzas of the Gloria.

Reinforce

Remind the students that the Introductory Rites of the Mass gather us as an assembly to give God praise and thanks.

Respond

▶ Call attention to the activity, The Church Family Gathers. Direct the students to draw themselves gathered with their Church family for worship.

▶ Have the students share their work with a partner.

Choose

▶ Spend a moment or two with the students discussing how they might help their families get ready to celebrate Mass on Sunday.

▶ Have the students decide what to do, and then to record their decisions on the page. Point out that their choices can help keep faith alive.

▶ When the students finish writing, tell them to be sure to share their faith choices with their families.

Pray

Invite the students to quiet themselves for prayer. Lead them in the prayer at the bottom of the page.

Pray

Begin by by leading the class in praying the Glory Be.

Recall

▶ Summarize today's teaching on the Introductory Rites of the Mass by sharing the To Help You Remember statements with the students. Read each statement, leaving out a key word. Ask volunteers to respond with the missing word.

▶ Introduce the numbering activity, and give the students time to complete it.

▶ Afterward, display the poster you made listing the elements of The Introductory Rites and check responses.

Reflect

Give the students a few moments to complete the statement under Reflect.

Share

Encourage the students to share their reflections with their families.

▶ **TO HELP YOU REMEMBER**

1. The Mass is the most important celebration of the Church.
2. Everyone at Mass has a part to play in the celebration of the Mass.
3. The Introductory Rites of the Mass gather us and prepare us to worship God.

Chapter Review

Recall

Number the sentences in the order in which these actions happen at Mass.

  2   **A.** The priest greets us, and we pray the Sign of the Cross.

  4   **B.** We sing or pray aloud the "Gloria."

  5   **C.** The priest leads us in the Collect.

  3   **D.** We pray for the Lord's mercy.

  1   **E.** The priest enters in procession.

Reflect

In what ways do you prepare to worship God?

_____

_____

_____

_____

_____

_____

Share   Share with a classmate your favorite part of the Mass and why.

182

TEACHING TIP

Sequencing. Here are two additional strategies for the students to use in sequencing activities like the chapter review.

1. Write the statements on sentence strips. Display the five sentence strips in incorrect order. Invite volunteers to come to the front of the room and place the sentence strips in the correct order.

2. Assemble the students in small groups of five. Ask each group to role-play one of the parts of the Introductory Rites. Have the groups perform their demonstrations in the proper order.

Praise God

At Mass, we offer God thanks and praise. We pray aloud or sing with joy. Pray this psalm of joy with your class.

Leader Loving God, we gather in your name to give you thanks and praise.

Group 1 Shout with joy to God, all the Earth. Worship the Lord with gladness. Come before him singing for joy.

All **Shout with joy to God, all the Earth.**

Group 2 Enter God's gates with thanksgiving. Go into God's presence with praise. Indeed, let us give thanks and bless God's name.

All **Shout with joy to God, all the Earth.**

Group 3 The Lord our God is good; He is kind and merciful. His faithful love lasts forever.

All **Shout with joy to God, all the Earth.**

BASED ON PSALM 100

(183)

We Pray

▶ Tell the students that today's prayer is from the Book of Psalms in the Bible. It speaks about gathering to offer God praise and thanks for his faithful love.

▶ Divide the class into three small groups. Assign a part of the prayer to each group, and allow groups time to practice reading together.

▶ Point out the refrain *Shout with joy to God, all the earth*. Practice it with the class.

▶ Gather the students in the prayer center.

▶ Lead the prayer, beginning with the Sign of the Cross.

TEACHING TIP

Helpful Hint. Much of what your second-graders are learning appeals to their emotional side. Therefore, students tend to remember what they need to know about prayer through the experience of prayer. In addition to the prayers and prayer experiences found in the lesson plans, pray often with the students. Pray spontaneously aloud so that they can hear you. Pray the learned prayers of the Church as well as using words from your heart. This way the students will get to know that God is always ready and willing to listen to our needs, that we can pray anytime and any place, and that we can tell God anything.

Preview

► Have the students carefully tear out pages 183 and 184 along the perforation.

► Encourage the students to share these pages with their families, and to complete the activities together.

► If they did not complete the review activity on page 182 by the end of the session, emphasize that they can complete it with their families at home.

► Point out the title and theme of the next lesson to the students.

Visit BeMyDisciples.com

► Take time with the students to explore the many activities and resources available at the *Be My Disciples* Web site.

► Encourage them to join with their families to discover the many resources available at the Web site.

Before Moving On ...

As you finish today's lesson, reflect on the following question before moving on to the next chapter.

What more can I do to gather my students effectively as a community that is eager to grow in the faith?

With My Family

This Week . . .

In Chapter 13, "We Gather for Mass," your child learned:

► The Mass is the Church's most important celebration.

► At Mass, we gather as an assembly—the Church, the People of God. Together we take part in the Eucharistic celebration.

► The celebration of Mass begins with the Introductory Rites. We prepare ourselves for the celebration of God's Word and of the Eucharist.

► The virtue of love empowers us to love God and love others because of our love for God.

For more about related teachings of the Church, see the *Catechism of the Catholic Church,* 1322–1332 and 1346 and 1348, and the *United States Catholic Catechism for Adults,* pages 215–227.

■ Sharing God's Word

Read together Acts of the Apostles 2:42–47, an account of the gathering of the early Church. Emphasize that from the beginning of the Church, Christians gathered to listen to the teachings and writings of the Apostles and to celebrate the Eucharist.

■ Living as Disciples

The Christian home and family is a school of discipleship. Choose one of the following activities to do as a family, or design a similar activity of your own.

► Form the habit of reading the upcoming Sunday readings before Mass. You can find them at the *Be My Disciples* Web site, or in special books for this purpose. On the way home, discuss the readings and the homily.

► Talk about the different ways your family gets ready to gather for Mass. Point out that these activities are all part of preparing to celebrate the Eucharist. These moments, too, can be a form of prayer.

■ Our Spiritual Journey

The Theological Virtues of faith, hope, and love invite and empower us to glorify God in all we say and do. Deepen your understanding of these virtues. They are the driving power that enables you to respond and give direction to your response, "Here I am, Lord. Send me." Teach this prayer to your child.

For more ideas on ways your family can live as disciples of Jesus, visit **BeMyDisciples.com**

184

ENRICHING THE LESSON

Choosing Songs. Before class, gather several recordings of songs appropriate for an entrance hymn at Mass. You might use the songs suggested in the Music Connection or consult either your parish music minister or catechetical leader for ideas. Play selections from the songs for the students, and have them vote on their favorites. Ask them to tell you the reasons for their choices. Help the students understand that on Sundays, the entrance hymn tells us what we will be hearing and praying about during the Mass.

Enriching the Lesson

Role Playing the Entrance Procession

Purpose

To reinforce the elements of the Introductory Rites of the Mass (taught on pages 178–180)

Directions

▶ Teach the students the refrain to a familiar entrance hymn sung at your parish's Sunday liturgy.

▶ Invite students to take the parts of members of a Sunday entrance procession.

▶ Place signs around the students' necks that identify them as the priest, the deacon, extraordinary ministers of Holy Communion, lector, altar servers, and crossbearer. Role-play the entrance procession. Have the rest of the class be the assembly.

▶ Have everyone sing the entrance hymn as the students process to the prayer center.

▶ Repeat the activity so that other students can be a part of the procession.

Materials

small pieces of poster board

pieces of yarn or sturdy string

a processional cross and a Bible

Continuing Sacrament Booklets

Purpose

To reinforce the words and actions used in the Introductory Rites of the Mass (taught in Chapter 13)

Directions

▶ Have the students continue to work on their Sacrament booklets. Have them label the next page in their booklet, Eucharist: Introductory Rites.

▶ Invite the students to draw a picture that shows something that happens during the Introductory Rites at Mass. Tell them to label their pictures.

▶ Invite the students to share their drawings with one another.

Materials

Sacrament booklets

pencils, crayons, or mark

Learning an Entrance Hymn

Purpose

To reinforce teaching about the Introductory Rites of the Mass (taught on page 122)

Directions

One goal of the *Be My Disciples* Music Program is to invite greater participation in the Mass. Take this time to teach the children an entrance hymn from the Grade 2 Music CD. Choose the hymn "We Are Marching" or another hymn commonly sung at your parish.

▶ Distribute lyric songbooks to the children or write the words of the hymn on the board or a sheet of poster paper for the children to follow.

▶ Play the song several times to acquaint the children with the melody.

▶ Invite them to sing along with you as you play the song again.

▶ When the children are comfortable with singing the hymn, invite them to join you in a procession to the prayer center and lead them in the Praise God prayer on page 125 of their texts.

Materials

Grade 2 Music CD

Lyric songbooks (optional)

rhythm instruments (optional)

BACKGROUND

Source and Summit

The Eucharist, "the source and summit of the Christian life," holds a preeminent place among the Seven Sacraments. In the Mass the whole of the Paschal Mystery—Jesus' Passion, Death and Resurrection, and Ascension—is celebrated and remembered.

Two Parts

In the Mass we celebrate one liturgy consisting of two parts, the Liturgy of the Word and the Liturgy of the Eucharist. They are so closely connected that they form one act of worship. In the Liturgy of the Word we listen and respond to the Word of God proclaimed and preached. In the Liturgy of the Eucharist we give thanks for all that God has done for us, especially for the gift of Salvation.

Two Tables

In the Christian community the disciples of Jesus Christ are nourished at a twofold table: "that of the word of God and that of the Body of Christ." The Gospel and the Eucharist are the constant food for the journey to the Father's House. The action of the Holy Spirit operates so that the gift of "communion" and the task of "mission" are deepened and lived in an increasingly intense way.

General Directory for Catechesis, 70

Give Thanks and Praise

In the Eucharist the sacrifice of Jesus Christ on the Cross is made present again, and we are made sharers in it.

We join with Jesus, who offers this sacrifice of his very self on our behalf to save us from sin and death, and offer ourselves to God the Father.

> In the Eucharist the sacrifice of Christ becomes also the sacrifice of the members of his Body.
>
> *Catechism of the Catholic Church,* 1368

At the Eucharist, the gifts of bread and wine become the Body and Blood of Jesus. Feeding on the Body and Blood of Christ, we are nourished for our own spiritual growth as well as for the work of participating in the mission of the Church.

Each and every time that we celebrate the Eucharist, we are remembering that Jesus restores us to our rightful place as adopted children of the Father through the Salvation he won for us. This free and generous gift of God's love causes us to give thanks to him and to rejoice.

This Sacrament of the mystery of our Salvation in Christ concludes with the sending forth of the assembly to live and proclaim the Gospel. We are to be the leaven of the Good News in the world.

For Reflection

Why is my regular participation in Mass vital to my life?

How does my regular sharing in the Eucharist strengthen me to be leaven of the Good News in the world?

The Liturgy, the Work of the Faithful

The liturgy is the work, or activity, of the whole Church. This is an important concept for young people to appreciate since the Church clearly teaches that "all the faithful should be led to that fully conscious and active participation in liturgical celebrations which is demanded by the very nature of the liturgy" (*Constitution on the Sacred Liturgy* 14). The word *all* means "all" and includes young people as well as adults. The students need to understand this and not see the liturgy solely as the work of the priest and other ministers.

Encouraging Participation

Help the students see that the liturgy is a community activity, or the work of the whole Church. Perhaps list the names of all the participants in the celebration of the Mass, including the worshiping assembly, priest and deacon, ministers of the Word, extraordinary ministers of Holy Communion, cantor, organist, choir, altar servers, and greeters. Point out the importance of the role of each of the people on the list. Detail all the ways the assembly participates and relate those roles to the students' participation. Emphasize their membership in the Church.

The Church Teaches...

"Christ calls all the faithful to proclaim the Good News everywhere in the world and to hand his message on to successive generations by professing, living, and celebrating the faith in Liturgy and prayer. . . . Catechesis is an indispensable stage in the rich, complex, and dynamic reality of evangelization" (*National Directory for Catechesis*, 15).

Catechesis is the echoing of God's Word. By communicating the Word of God, you reveal his gentle love to the students who are invited by the Word to keep it in their hearts.

Further Reading and Reflection

For more related teachings of the Church, see the *Catechism of the Catholic Church*, 1322–1332 and 1346 and 1349; and the *United States Catholic Catechism for Adults*, page 218.

Teacher Prayer

Generous God, plant the seed of your Word deep within me. For the sake of your children, gift me with a newer syntax, a mightier metaphor, a more than active verb. Rain down your Spirit that your Word may grow and thrive in me. May I prove to be good ground for the blossoming of your Word. Amen.

Lesson Planner

Chapter 14   We Listen to God's Word

Goal To learn about the Liturgy of the Word as the first main part of the Mass

LESSON PART	PROCESS	MATERIALS and RESOURCES
DAY 1 EXPLORE **Focus** To explore how followers of Jesus hear and keep God's Word **Pages 185–187**	▶ Proclaim and discuss Luke 11:27–28 (Blessed are those who hear God's Word and keep it). ▶ Learn about signing the words of the Mass for those who cannot hear. **Disciple Power:** Compassion **Activity:** Learn to sign Luke 11:28.	Bible Pencils or pens **Enriching the Lesson:** Teacher Guide, page 287 Literature Connection: *Marianthe's Story*
DAY 2 DISCOVER **Focus** To discover what happens when we celebrate the Liturgy of the Word **Pages 188–189**	▶ Learn that the Liturgy of the Word is the first main part of the Mass. ▶ Discover that Sunday is the day Catholics gather together to worship God at Mass. **Faith Words:** Liturgy of the Word **Catholics Believe:** The Sanctuary **Activity:** Learn to sign the word "Alleluia".	Bible Pencil or pens
DAY 3 DISCOVER **Focus** To discover the most important part of the Liturgy of the Word **Pages 190–191**	▶ Discover that the Gospel is the most important part of the Liturgy of the Word. **Scripture Story:** Parable of the Mustard Seed (Matthew 13:31–32) **Faith-Filled People:** Saint Paul Chong Ha-sang **Activity:** Learn to sign the Gospel response.	Crayons or markers Newsprint **Additional Activities Booklet:** Activities 14a and 14b or see *BeMyDisciples*.com
DAY 4 DECIDE **Focus** To discover how we respond to the Good News and to decide on a way to take part in the Mass **Pages 192–193**	▶ Learn about the homily, profession of faith, and Prayer of the Faithful. **Activity:** Draw or write about a Bible story you heard at Mass. **My Faith Choice:** Choose a new way to take part in Mass.	Pencil or pens Crayons or markers **Enriching the Lesson:** Teacher Guide, page 287 • Role Playing the Liturgy of the Word • Continuing Sacrament Booklets **Additional Activities Booklet:** Activities 14a or 14b or see *BeMyDisciples*.com
DAY 5 CONCLUDE **Focus** To ask the Lord to hear our prayers **Pages 194–196**	▶ **REVIEW** Review concepts: Recall, Reflect, and Share. ▶ **PRAY** Lord, Hear Our Prayer ▶ **Preview** the With My Family page and the theme of the next chapter.	Bible, candle, cross for prayer space Grade 2 Music CD **Assessment Tools Booklet:** Assessments 14a and 14b

Assign online Chapter Review and interactive Chapter Test at **BeMyDisciples.com**

CHAPTER **14**

We Listen to God's Word

❓ What stories or words do you like to hear over and over?

Here is a story we hear at Mass. Jesus was helping people in a village. He was teaching them about God's love. Then something surprising happened.

A woman said in a loud voice, "Blessed is your mother to have such a wonderful son." Jesus said to the woman, "Blessed are those who hear the Word of God and keep it." BASED ON LUKE 11:27–28

❓ What does it mean to keep the Word of God?

(185)

THE TASKS OF CATECHESIS

Education for Community Life. As the students learn about the Liturgy of the Word in this chapter, help them understand that during this part of the Mass, we gather together to hear and reflect on God's Word. The readings and the homily nourish us to live as disciples of Christ. They challenge us, as individuals and as a community called together by the Lord, to put into practice what has been proclaimed. The Liturgy of the Word forms us and enables us to continue Christ's work in the world. It is our weekly opportunity to form a community of faith.

Pray

▶ Have the students quiet themselves for prayer on the outside and the inside.

▶ Begin and end with the Sign of the Cross.

▶ Ask the children to repeat after you:

Dear God, / open my heart / to receive your Word to me. / Amen.

Reflect

▶ Have the students tell what they see happening in the photograph on the page, and then ask the opening question. *(Accept all responses.)*

▶ Invite the students to listen to what Jesus said about people who hear and keep God's Word.

▶ Call on a volunteer to read the passage from Luke 11:27–28.

▶ After the reading, observe a moment of silence.

▶ Invite responses to the Scripture question.

▶ Conclude with the Sign of the Cross.

Focus

Tell the students to turn the page to learn how the Church works to help everyone hear and respond to God's Word—even people who can't hear.

Introduce

▶ Call attention to Disciple Power. Ask a volunteer to read it aloud.

▶ Emphasize that the virtue of compassion helps us to hear and understand God's Word.

▶ Read aloud the first three paragraphs of Announcing God's Word and see whether the students know how if people who are deaf and hard-of-hearing can "hear" and respond to God's Word. *(Accept all reasonable replies.)*

▶ Go on and read aloud the remainder of the article (pages 186–187). Make sure that the students understand that ASL is a true language—not a translation of English or any other language, but a language of signs.

Disciple Power

Compassion

Compassion means to care about others when they are hurt or feeling sad. Having compassion makes us want to help them feel better.

The Church Follows **Jesus**

Announcing God's Word

Jesus told us that he is the Word of God. When we listen to Jesus and do what he says, we are blessed. We are friends of God.

Jesus had Good News from his Father to share with everyone. But what if you could not hear God's Word?

The Catholic Church helps everyone come to know Jesus. They show compassion to all who need help. Pope Benedict XVI said that deaf people are not only hearers of the Word of God, but also "its announcers."

Deaf people can learn to hear and share God's Word. They use a language of hand gestures called American Sign Language, or ASL.

Many priests, deacons, brothers, sisters, and laypeople work with people who cannot hear at all and with people who are hard-of-hearing. They teach the Catholic faith. They share the Word of God using ASL.

❓ How can people who are deaf and hard-of-hearing be hearers and announcers of God's Word?

186

✦ **DISCIPLE POWER**

Compassion. The word *compassion* means to bear with the sufferings of another. It is related to sympathy, which implies an affinity for other's thoughts and feelings. But compassion also involves a desire to alleviate or relieve the other person's situation. Compassion also is much more than pity, which can involve a condescending attitude toward the suffering person. A compassionate person is one who, like Jesus, offers love and hope to a person who is sorrowful or in pain. Seven- and eight- year-old children are just developing an ability to see things from the perspective of others. Research is showing that asking children questions about how they think the other person is feeling or thinking can be very useful in helping them to develop this human virtue of a Christian.

In many parishes, someone signs the words that the priest and others say aloud at Mass. The deaf and hard-of-hearing people sign their responses.

Activity

Signing the Word of God

What do you think the person in the pictures below is saying in ASL? Hint: It is the Word of God from Luke 11:28. Write the words on the lines.

BLESSED   PEOPLE   HEAR

WORD   GOD   FOLLOW

187

Reinforce

Point out the follow-up question. Ask the students how the deaf or hard-of-hearing can be hearers and announcers of God's Word.

Connect

▶ Direct attention to the activity and the pictures of the person using ASL to announce God's Word. Note: If you have a deaf or hard-of-hearing student or a student who knows ASL, ask him or her to make the signs for all to see.

▶ Read the activity directions aloud. Then, to see if the students can "hear" God's Words through the ASL signs, have them complete the activity.

▶ Check to see whether or not the students have figured out what the ASL signs mean. *(Blessed are those who hear the Word of God and keep it.)*

▶ Invite the students to name people whom they know who help them hear and better understand the meaning of God's Word.

Pray

Have the students echo this prayer.

Loving God, Help us come to know and love your Word to us. Amen.

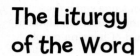

Key Concept
Catholics listen to the Word of God at Mass.

Pray

Invite the students to quiet themselves for prayer. Pray the Sign of the Cross together.

Teach

▶ Remind the students that the Mass begins with the Introductory Rites.

▶ Read the Faith Focus question aloud and ask the students for possible answers. Tell them that these two pages will help them begin learning about the first main part of the Mass, which is called the Liturgy of the Word.

▶ Call on a volunteer to read the opening paragraph of The Liturgy of the Word.

▶ Ask the students to read the meaning of *Liturgy of the Word* found in Faith Words.

▶ Present the text The Readings from the Bible (pages 188–189) in your own words, and have the students listen for how many readings we listen to during the Liturgy of the Word.

Faith Focus
What happens when we celebrate the Liturgy of the Word?

Faith Words
▶ **Liturgy of the Word**
The Liturgy of the Word is the first main part of the Mass. God speaks to us through the readings from the Bible.

The Liturgy of the Word

After the Introductory Rites, we celebrate the **Liturgy of the Word.** The Liturgy of the Word is the first main part of the Mass. We listen and respond to God's Word.

The Readings from the Bible

At Mass on Sundays and on Saturday evenings, we listen to three readings. We sit for the first two readings.

The First Reading is usually from the Old Testament. We hear stories about God's people who lived many years before Jesus.

After the first reading, we sing or pray the Responsorial Psalm. Then we listen to the Second Reading. It is from the New Testament. We hear stories about the first Christian communities.

At the end of both the first and the second readings, the reader says, "The word of the Lord." We respond, "Thanks be to God."

? Why do you think we say, "Thanks be to God" after we listen to the readings?

188

LITURGY CONNECTION

Christ's Presence in the Word. The Liturgy of the Word is not simply a prelude to the "important" part of the Mass—the Liturgy of the Eucharist. On the contrary, the Liturgy of the Word is the first main part of the Mass. During the Liturgy of the Word, Christ is present among us through the Scriptures in a unique and powerful way. Stress to the students that listening and responding carefully to the Scripture readings can put us in touch with God and his plan for our lives.

A reading from one of the four Gospels comes next. We get ready to listen to the Gospel by standing and singing or praying aloud the Gospel Acclamation. This is a short hymn of praise. On most days, we stand and sing, "Alleluia." This word means "Praise the Lord!"

❓ Why do you think we sing or say "Alleluia," before we listen to the Gospel?

Catholics Believe

The Sanctuary

The sanctuary is the place in the church where you see the altar and the ambo. The word sanctuary means "holy place." The ambo is the stand where the readers, the deacon, and the priest proclaim the Word of God.

Activity

Praying Alleluia

Learn to sign this word that we say or sing at Mass.

Alleluia!

Write the meaning of the word, Alleluia, below.

_____

_____

(189)

Reinforce

▶ Ask the follow-up question. *(Accept all reasonable responses.)*

▶ Have the students make a word card for the term *Liturgy of the Word.*

▶ Write the assembly's responses to the First and Second Readings at Mass (priest's and assembly's parts) on the board. Invite volunteers to come forward and take the part of the priest. Practice the responses with the students.

▶ Invite a volunteer to read Catholics Believe about the sanctuary.

Connect

▶ Help the students learn the responses in American Sign Language.

▶ Again, If you have a student who is deaf or hard-of-hearing in class or a student who knows ASL, ask him or her to lead the class in the ASL signs.

▶ Help the students learn the responses by heart in both spoken word and ASL. (Note: If you have students in class who speak a language other than English, invite them to share the responses in their language, if they know them. Recognize, however, that the signs in the text are *American* Sign Language signs. The sign language of people in other countries does differ.

Pray

Gather the students for prayer. Lead them in the Glory Be.

SPECIAL NEEDS

Providing Visual Cues. After reading The Readings from the Bible in the text, write the assembly's response to the readings and the Gospel Acclamation on the board or a poster: *Thanks be to God. Alleluia.* Practice the response with the class by proclaiming, "The word of the Lord." Practice the Alleluia by singing a familiar one and using the ASL sign.

Have the students recite the responses clearly, with conviction. Encourage the students to respond in the same enthusiastic way at Sunday Mass. Later in the lesson, after reading We Listen to God's Word (pages 190–191), add the response to the Gospel reading to the poster: *Praise to you, Lord Jesus Christ.* Display the poster in the classroom for use as you proceed through the chapter and for use whenever you celebrate Mass with the students.

Need: Students with reading difficulties

Key Concept
The Gospel is the Good News of Jesus Christ.

Pray

Have the students quiet themselves for prayer. Ask them to echo the following:

Wonderful Father, / fill us with your Word. / Help us rejoice in the Good News of Jesus / today and for always. Amen.

Teach

▶ Read the Faith Focus question aloud and ask the students for possible answers. Then immediately present the material in the first paragraph of We Listen to God's Word.

▶ Ask the Faith Focus question again. Emphasize that everything in the Liturgy of the Word that comes before the Gospel prepares us to hear it. Everything that comes after it in the Liturgy of the Word is a response to the Good News.

▶ Say that in today's Gospel story which is the Parable of the Mustard Seed, Jesus teaches us about what faith.

▶ Invite volunteers to read aloud the passage from Matthew 13:31–32 *(all reasonable responses.)*

Faith Focus
What happens at the Communion Rite?

We Listen to God's Word

The deacon or priest proclaims the Gospel. The Gospel is the Good News of Jesus Christ. We stand to show our respect.

Listen to this Gospel reading about the Kingdom of God. Jesus said,

"What is the kingdom of God like? It is like a tiny mustard seed. A person takes the mustard seed and plants it in the garden. The tiny seed grows and when it becomes fully grown, it becomes a large tree. Birds in the sky build nests in the branches of the tree." BASED ON LUKE 13:18–19

The Kingdom of God will grow with all the people who will love God. This is the Good News of Jesus Christ.

❓ How is a tiny mustard seed like the Kingdom of God?

190

TEACHING TIP

Creating Movement for Gospel Stories. Tell the students that in the Gospel of Matthew in the passages that appear before the Parable of the Mustard Seed, Jesus tells us that people who listen to God's Word are like "good soil." Gather the students in a circle and invite them to listen to the Gospel story in Matthew 13:1–9, 18–23. Tell them to listen for people in the story who were blessed because they knew and accepted Jesus. After you read the Gospel story invite the students to name those people (the blind, the crippled, lepers, the deaf, the dead, and the poor). Ask the students to think of a way to prayerfully, quietly act out what happened to the people in the story (for example, have them cover and then uncover their eyes for the phrase *the blind see*). Invite the students to act out the phrases you just practiced together as you once again proclaim the Gospel story. Afterward, praise the students for their attention and for their active participation.

When the priest or deacon finishes the reading, he holds up the Book of the Gospels for all to see and says, "The Gospel of the Lord." The assembly responds, "Praise to you, Lord Jesus Christ." With these words, we thank Jesus for showing us God's love.

❓ Why is the Gospel reading important?

Faith-Filled People

Saint Paul Chong Ha-sang

Catholic laypeople, not priests or nuns, first brought the Word of God to the people of Korea. One of those laypeople was Paul Chong Ha-sang. Korea's leaders did not want Christians there. Paul worked all his life to share God's Word. The feast day of Saint Paul Chong Ha-sang is September 20.

Activity

Learn to sign the response to the Gospel reading at Mass.

Praise   you

Lord   Jesus   Christ

"Praise to you, Lord Jesus Christ."

(191)

FAITH-FILLED PEOPLE

Saint Paul Chong Ha-sang. Paul was baptized in secret at a time when being Catholic was forbidden by the Korean government. Soon after his Baptism, the priest who baptized him was caught and put to death, along with many other believers. The Catholics in Korea did not abandon their faith. Paul became a catechist, sharing the truths of our faith with others. Paul risked his life many times by traveling to China to bring missionaries back to his homeland. During one of these missions, a brave bishop came with Paul. He helped Paul see that God was calling him to become a priest. Before Paul could begin his studies, he was arrested and put to death. Today the Church is strong in Korea because of Catholic heroes like Paul, who kept the faith alive during dangerous times. To learn more about Saint Paul Chong Ha-sang, go to the Resource Center at BeMyDisciples.com.

Reinforce

▶ Invite responses to the follow-up question.

▶ Point out to the students that this Gospel story invites us to consider what faith is.

▶ Call attention to Faith-Filled People. Read it aloud with the children. Point out how much Saint Paul Chong Ha-sang and the Korean Catholics valued God's Word.

Connect

▶ Have the students find the response to the Gospel in the text *(Praise to you, Lord Jesus Christ.)* and underline it.

▶ Help the students learn the response in both English and American Sign Language.

Pray

▶ Have the students use the ASL signs for the responses they have learned so far in this lesson in their prayer.

▶ Pray a line of the following prayer, then lead the students in response—in both English words and ASL:

O God, for your wonderful Word to us, we say: Thanks be to God. O God, for bringing us such Good News, we shout: Alleluia! For your many blessings to us, we rejoice and say: Praise to you, Lord Jesus Christ.

Key Concept
We respond to God's Word at Mass with the Profession of Faith and the Prayer of the Faithful.

Pray
Lead the students in the Sign of the Cross.

Teach
▶ Write *Liturgy of the Word* on the board. Discuss with the students what they have already learned.

▶ Read aloud the Faith Focus question. Remind the students that every part of the Liturgy of the Word that comes after the Gospel is a way for us to respond to the Good News of Jesus.

▶ Ask a volunteer to read the section titled The Homily. Then tell the students that the homily helps us respond to the Gospel by helping us better understand what God's Word means for us.

▶ Invite other volunteers to read The Profession of Faith and The Prayer of the Faithful.

Reinforce
▶ Ask the follow-up question. Explain that in the Profession of Faith we respond to the Gospel by stating what we believe. The Prayer of the Faithful is our response to the call of the Gospel to act as followers of Jesus.

Connect
Invite the students to share the part or parts of the Liturgy of the Word that they enjoy the most. Tell them your favorite part.

Faith Focus
What happens during the Liturgy of the Word after the Gospel?

We Respond to God's Word

The Homily
After the Gospel is proclaimed, we sit. The priest or deacon talks to us. He helps us to understand the readings. This is called the Homily.

The Profession of Faith
After the Homily, we stand. Together we respond to God's Word. We pray aloud a profession of faith, or a creed of the Church. We say we believe in God the Father, God the Son, and God the Holy Spirit.

The Prayer of the Faithful
The last part of the Liturgy of the Word is the Prayer of the Faithful. We ask God to help the Church and our country. We pray for other people and for ourselves. We ask God's help for everyone.

How do we respond to the Word of God?

(192)

HUMAN METHODOLOGIES

Learning within the Christian Community. The *National Directory for Catechesis* states that the parish is "where the Christian faith deepens and where the Christian community is formed" *(NDC, 29C)*. The sanctuary is the focal point for worship in the Christian community. For Catholics, it is a holy place. The sanctuary makes us aware that we are in the presence of God and away from the distractions of the outside world. Take your second graders into the sanctuary of the church during your session. Ask them why we call this space "sacred." Discuss with them why it is a holy place for the entire Christian community. Have them name some of the things they have learned about that take place in the sanctuary during Mass.

At Mass, you are part of the assembly. You take part in the celebration of Mass in many ways. During the Liturgy of the Word, you listen and respond to the Word of God.

I Follow **Jesus**

Activity

I Listen and Respond

Draw or write about a Bible story you heard at Mass. Write the title of your story on the line. Share what the story tells you about God's love.

_____

My Faith Choice

The next time I take part in Mass, I will

☐ say the responses   ☐ sing the hymns
☐ listen carefully   ☐ pray the profession
   to the readings   of faith
☐ _____ "

Pray, "Open my ears to hear your Word, O God. Open my heart to live it every day. Amen."

(193)

Reinforce

Remind the students that during Mass we listen and respond to the Word of God.

Respond

▶ Have the students work with a partner to complete the activity. Remind the students that they can either draw or write their responses.

▶ Invite volunteers to share what their Bible story tells them about God's love.

Choose

▶ Invite the students children to read silently My Faith Choice and put a check next to their faith choices.

▶ Encourage everyone to put their faith choices into practice this week.

Pray

Ask students to silently pray the prayer on the page.

Cultural Diversity. Explain to the students that in some parishes on Sunday, the Scripture readings are proclaimed in more than one language. This is done because there are many parishioners who come to Mass whose first language is not English. They may or may not understand English and so the priest, deacon, or lector reads the Scriptures in the people's first language. That language may be Spanish, Korean, Polish, Chinese, one of the Native-American dialects, ASL, or another language. Tell the students that this is another way in which the Church helps all people to he ar and understand God's Word.

Pray

Ask the students to quiet themselves and remember God's presence. Begin class by reverently praying the Sign of the Cross together.

Recall

▶ Write the phrase *Liturgy of the Word* on the board. As the students recall for you what happens at Mass, write key words from their responses around the word *Mass*.

▶ Invite volunteers to read the To Help You Remember statements and ask the students which key words written on the board are also in the statements.

▶ Give directions for both parts of the Chapter Review activity, and allow time for the partners to complete it.

▶ Ask volunteers to share their answers.

Reflect

Ask the students to work on their own to complete the reflection question.

Share

▶ Canvass the room for responses.

▶ Encourage the students to share their reflections at home with their families.

TO HELP YOU REMEMBER

1. The Liturgy of the Word is the first main part of the Mass.
2. The Gospel is the main part of the Liturgy of the Word.
3. At Mass, we listen and respond to the Word of God.

Chapter Review

Recall

Match each word with its correct description.

Words	Descriptions
c 1. readings	a. The priest or deacon helps us to understand God's Word.
a 2. Homily	b. We profess our faith in God the Father, God the Son, and God the Holy Spirit.
b 3. creed	c. We listen to God's Word.
d 4. Prayer of the Faithful	d. We ask God to help us and other people.

Number the parts of the Liturgy of the Word in the correct order that they happen during Mass.

6	Profession of Faith	2	Responsorial Psalm
7	Prayer of the Faithful	3	New Testament Reading
5	Homily	1	Old Testament Reading
		4	Gospel

Reflect

What is one way the Liturgy of the Word can help you?

_____

_____

Share After Mass this week, share what you learned from the Homily with your family.

(194)

LITURGY CONNECTION

Gospel Preparation. Try to make time during your class session to prepare the students for the upcoming Sunday's Gospel reading. Hearing the Gospel reading ahead of time and discussing it with one another will prepare them to be more receptive to the Gospel when they listen to it on Sunday. It will also give them something familiar to look forward to hearing. In addition, those students who might not take part in Mass this weekend will have the chance to hear God's Word. You can find resources at BeMyDisciples.com to help you in presenting the Gospel reading.

Lord, Hear Our Prayer

At Mass we sometimes pray "Lord, hear our prayer" during the Prayer of the Faithful. This shows that we believe God is with us.

All **(Pray the Sign of the Cross.)**

Leader Let us pray.
God our Father, we ask for your help. We pray for the Church, for our country, for our family, and for our friends. We pray for people who are sick. We pray for all people.

All **Lord, hear our prayer.**

Leader We pray for people who are sick.

All **Lord, hear our prayer.**

Student For _____, we pray to the Lord.

All **Lord, hear our prayer.**

Leader God our Father, send the Holy Spirit upon all who need your help. We ask this in the name of Jesus.

All **Amen.**

(195)

We Pray

▶ Tell the students that today's prayer is a prayer of intercession that is similar to the Prayer of the Faithful at Sunday Mass.

▶ Teach the ASL response to the students. Practice it until they are comfortable.

▶ Point out the section of the prayer where the students can add their own petitions. Invite them to think carefully about someone or something they would like the class to pray for.

▶ Gather the students in a circle in the prayer center.

▶ Lead the prayer, beginning with the Sign of the Cross.

▶ At the appropriate place in the prayer, go around the circle inviting each student to offer a prayer if he or she wishes.

▶ Conclude by sharing a sign of peace and acclaiming, in word and ASL, "Alleluia!"

PARTNERING WITH PARENTS

Organize a Teaching Mass. Obtain permission from your pastor and catechetical leader for a qualified parishioner to videotape one of your parish's Sunday liturgies to use as an instructional tool. Schedule a special session for parents and students to view the video together as preparation for the students' First Communion. Put the video on pause several times during the viewing so that the parents and students can discuss what is happening and the meaning of the different parts of the Mass. Prepare questions for the family members to discuss each time you pause the video.

Preview

▶ Have the students carefully tear out pages 195 and 196 along the perforation.

▶ Encourage the students to share these pages with their families, and to complete the activities together.

▶ If they did not complete the review activity on page 194 by the end of the session, emphasize that they can complete it with their families at home.

▶ Point out the title and theme of the next lesson to the students.

Visit BeMyDisciples.com

▶ Take time with the students to explore the many activities and resources available at the *Be My Disciples* Web site.

▶ Encourage them to join with their families to discover the many resources available at the Web site.

Before Moving On ...

As you finish today's lesson, reflect on the following question before moving on to the next chapter.

What am I doing to involve students who seldom volunteer for activities?

With My Family

This Week . . .

In Chapter 14, "We Listen to God's Word," your child learned:

▶ The Liturgy of the Word is the first main part of the Mass.

▶ The Gospel is the center of the Liturgy of the Word.

▶ During the Liturgy of the Word, we listen to God's Word and make it part of our lives.

▶ We profess our faith and pray for the living and the dead.

▶ The quality of compassion helps us to respond to the needs of others.

For more about related teachings of the Church, see the *Catechism of the Catholic Church,* 1322–1332, and 1346 and 1349, and the *United States Catholic Catechism for Adults,* page 218.

■ Sharing God's Word

Read together 1 Timothy 3:16. Discuss how Scripture can help your family find ways to offer compassion to others like Jesus. Talk about ways you can make reading the Scripture something you do each day.

■ Living as Disciples

The Christian home and family is a school of discipleship. Choose one of the following activities to do as a family, or design a similar activity of your own.

▶ Read to your child every day—stories, the Bible, even the daily paper. Listening to a reading is not only pleasing but helps prepare us to listen to the proclamation of God's Word in the liturgy.

▶ Review the responses for the Liturgy of the Word with your child. These can be found on pages 188–191 in your child's book. Knowing the responses helps us better participate in the Mass.

■ Our Spiritual Journey

At Mass, the Prayer of the Faithful allows us to pray to God for the needs of others. Helping your child to form the habit of praying for the needs of others helps him or her to see the world through a wider perspective and to remember that God brings all blessings. Pray the prayer on page 195 together at home.

For more ideas on ways your family can live as disciples of Jesus, visit **BeMyDisciples.com**

196

TEACHING TIP

Evaluate. Take a few moments to evaluate this week's lesson. I feel about this week's lesson (circle one):

a. very pleased
b. OK
c. disappointed

The activity the students enjoyed most was . . .
The concept that was most difficult to teach was . . .
It was difficult because . . .
Something I would like to do differently is . . .

Enriching the Lesson

Role-playing the Liturgy of the Word

Purpose

To reinforce the elements of the Liturgy of the Word (taught in chapter 14)

Directions

▶ Assign volunteers to role-play the Liturgy of the Word: two readers, a psalm leader/cantor, a priest or deacon, and members of the assembly.

▶ Prepare a simple retelling of Isaiah 55:10–13 and Romans 8:18–23. Print these retellings on two sheets of paper for the two readers. For the Gospel, use the text retelling of Luke 7:18–23 on page 190.

▶ For the cantor, prepare a simple, familiar setting of a psalm with a refrain that the students can sing.

▶ Prepare a brief homily for the priest or deacon.

▶ Encourage members of the assembly to respond after each reading.

▶ If possible, pray together a profession of faith (Nicene Creed) and prepare Prayers of the Faithful for one of the readers to offer.

Materials

Bible

paper

pens

student books

music for psalm (optional)

Continuing Sacrament Booklets

Purpose

To reinforce the words and actions used in the Liturgy of the Word (taught in chapter 14)

Directions

▶ Have the students continue to work on their Sacrament booklets. Have them label the next page in their booklet *Eucharist: Liturgy of the Word.*

▶ Invite the students to draw a picture that shows something that happens during the Liturgy of the Word at Mass. Tell them to label their pictures.

▶ Invite them to share their drawings with one another.

Materials

Sacrament booklets

pencils, crayons, or markers

Literature Connection

Purpose

To reinforce the teaching about the Liturgy of the Word (taught in chapter 14)

Directions

The beautifully illustrated children's storybook *Marianthe's Story: Painted Words and Spoken Memories* by Aliki tells the story of a young immigrant girl who struggles to tell the story of her people to her class. Because she does not speak English, she decides to tell her story in pictures, or "painted words."

▶ You then turn the book over and a second book appears. Marianthe has now learned English and tells her family's history in what are now "spoken memories."

▶ Ask the students which stories they know about their grandparents or other ancestors. Ask them to share why they enjoy telling or listening to others tell these stories.

Materials

Marianthe's Story, by Aliki (Greenwillow Books, 1998)

BACKGROUND

The Breaking of Bread

The Mass has several other names that help us come to know the meaning of the mystery of the Eucharist. One such name is the Breaking of Bread. Just as Christ broke and distributed bread at the Passover meal of the Last Supper, the Mass repeats these actions. Jesus told his disciples that by doing this they will recognize him in times to come. Thus, the celebrating of the Eucharist in the first Christian assemblies was known as the Breaking of Bread.

Mass During Apostolic Times

The Acts of the Apostles tells us that the early Church in Jerusalem devoted itself to the "teaching of the apostles and to the communal life, to the breaking of the bread and to the prayers" (Acts of the Apostles 2:42).

The early Christians met together on Sunday, the day on which they celebrated the Lord's Resurrection, for the breaking of the bread, and the celebration of the Eucharist has continued since this time. Today we encounter it everywhere in the Church with the same fundamental structure. It remains the center of the Church's life.

See Catechism of the Catholic Church 1343

Then and Now

The rites of the Mass as they are celebrated today bear a close resemblance to the breaking of bread, or the celebration of the Eucharist, in the early Church. Around the year 155, Saint Justin Martyr wrote a description of the Eucharistic celebration. Here is a summary of what he had to say:

▶ "On the day we call the day of the sun, all who dwell in the city or country gather in the same place." (Gathering)

▶ We read from the "memoirs of the apostles and the writings of the prophets." (Liturgy of the Word)

▶ The presider challenges the faithful "to imitate these beautiful things." (Homily)

▶ Then we all stand and "offer prayers for ourselves . . . and for all others." (Prayer of the Faithful)

▶ "When the prayers are concluded, we exchange the kiss." (Sign of Peace)

▶ Then bread and a mixture of water and wine are brought to the presider. (Presentation of the Gifts)

▶ The presider offers praise and glory to God: Father, Son, and Holy Spirit. "He gives thanks that we have been judged worthy of these gifts." (Eucharistic Prayer)

▶ The "eucharisted bread" is then given to those present and sent to those absent. (Communion)

From St. Justin, Apologiae 1, 65–67: PG 6 428–429, in CCC 1345

For Reflection

What does the term "breaking of bread" evoke in me about my participation in the Eucharist?

How does my participation in the Eucharist strengthen my participation in the communal life of the Church?

Teacher to Teacher

The Gift of the Eucharist

The celebration of special meals is a part of most students' experience. Use these experiences to help students understand the story of the Last Supper. Capitalize on their vivid imaginations and memories of celebrations that are special to them.

A Special Meal

Help the students understand what a special meal the Last Supper was for Jesus and his disciples. Help them see that the gift of his Body and Blood Jesus first gave to the disciples at the Last Supper he also gives to us at every celebration of the Mass. Every week, every day if we wish, we can approach the Lord's table to be fed with Jesus' own Body and Blood. We too hear the same request, "Do this in memory of me." We are now entrusted to retell and do what Jesus did at the Last Supper.

The Church Teaches. . .

"(T)he Eucharist constitutes the principal liturgical celebration of the Paschal Mystery of Christ and the ritual memorial of our communion in that mystery. . . . Since the Eucharist is the 'source and summit of the Christian life,' catechesis for the Eucharist recognizes it as the heart of Christian life for the whole Church" (*National Directory for Catechesis*, 36A.3).

Sharing experiences of participating in the celebration of Mass is rudimentary to catechesis. Therefore, we gather as the People of God for the celebration of Mass and, putting aside private prayer, participate in the Holy Sacrifice of the Mass.

Further Reading and Reflection

For more related teachings of the Church, see the *Catechism of the Catholic Church*, 1345–1405; and the *United States Catholic Catechism for Adults,* pages 218–220.

Teacher Prayer

Gracious Lord,
I am full of thanks for the gift of your Body and Blood in the Eucharist.
May I always approach our table conscious of the gift I am blessed to receive.
Help me to lead your children to know your love.
Amen.

Lesson Planner

Chapter 15 We Give Thanks

Goal To learn what happens in the Liturgy of the Eucharist

LESSON PART	PROCESS	MATERIALS and RESOURCES
DAY 1 EXPLORE **Focus** To explore how followers of Jesus show they are thankful to God Pages 197–199	▶ Proclaim and discuss Psalm 35:18 (I will thank God in the assembly). ▶ Learn and discuss how some Franciscans share Christ's love with the poor. **Disciple Power:** Thankfulness **Activity:** Write and draw about what you are thankful for.	Bible Pencils or pens Crayons or markers **Enriching the Lesson:** Teacher Guide, page 303 A Blessing to Thank God
DAY 2 DISCOVER **Focus** To discover what happens when we celebrate the Liturgy of the Eucharist Pages 200–201	▶ Discover what happens at the Preparation of the Gifts. **Faith Words:** Liturgy of the Eucharist, Eucharist **Catholics Believe:** The Holy Sacrifice **Activity:** Fill the Blessings Bucket with blessings you have received.	Bible Pencil or pens **Enriching the Lesson:** Teacher Guide, page 303 Literature Connection: *Thank You, Grandpa* **Additional Activities Booklet:** Activities 15a and 15b or see *BeMyDisciples*.com
DAY 3 DISCOVER **Focus** To discover that what Jesus did at the Last Supper we also do in the Liturgy of the Eucharist Pages 202–203	▶ Learn about the Eucharistic Prayer and the Consecration. **Scripture Story:** The Last Supper (Luke 22:17–20) **Faith-Filled People:** Saint Pius X **Activity:** Fill in a description of the Consecration.	Bibles Pencils or pens
DAY 4 DECIDE **Focus** To discover how to receive Holy Communion and to decide how to share blessings with others Mass Pages 204–205	▶ Recognize what happens at the Communion Rite. **Activity:** Write a prayer of thanks to God for his blessings. **My Faith Choice:** Choose a way to share God's blessings.	Pencil or pens Crayons or markers **Enriching the Lesson:** Teacher Guide, page 303 Completing Sacrament Booklets
DAY 5 CONCLUDE **Focus** To remember that all of our blessings come from God Pages 206–208	▶ **REVIEW** Review concepts: Recall, Reflect, and Share. ▶ **PRAY** Blessed Be God ▶ **Preview** the With My Family page and the theme of the next chapter.	Bible, candle, cross for prayer space, pencils Grade 2 Music CD **Assessment Tools Booklet:** Assessments 15a and 15b

Assign online Chapter Review and interactive Chapter Test at **BeMyDisciples.com**

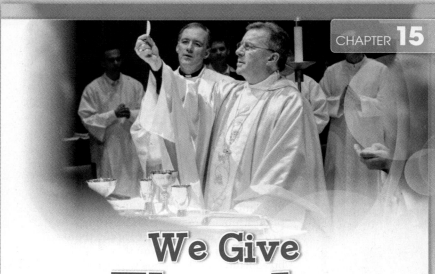

CHAPTER 15

We Give Thanks

❓ What is a gift you have received?

All good things come from God. Think of your many blessings. Join with all God's people and pray,

> I will join with your people, Lord God.
> I will thank you in the great assembly.
>
> BASED ON PSALM 35:18

❓ What do you want to thank God for?

197

DAY 1 · EXPLORE

Pray

▶ Welcome the students warmly. Then have them quiet themselves for prayer.

▶ Begin and end with the Sign of the Cross.

▶ Pray aloud: "Dear Jesus, we offer you praise and thanks. Amen."

Reflect

▶ Ask the opening question. *(Accept all replies.)*

▶ Invite the students to listen to what the Bible says about giving thanks.

▶ Ask one of the students to read the passage from Psalm 35:18.

▶ After the reading, observe a moment of silence.

▶ Have the students tell what they see happening in the picture on the page. Then invite responses to the Scripture question.

▶ Conclude with the Sign of the Cross.

Focus

Tell the students to turn the page to learn how the Church shares its gifts.

HUMAN METHODOLOGIES

Learning by Discipleship. The *National Directory for Catechesis* states, "By following the example of (Jesus') self-giving love, we learn to be Christian disciples in our own time, place, and circumstances" **(NDC 29B)**. Help the students understand that as they prepare for First Eucharist, they are like the disciples at the Last Supper, learning from Jesus and getting ready to share a special meal with him. Bring to class a large white sheet on which you have drawn a seven-inch circle for each student. Place the sheet on the floor or a large table. Invite the students to choose an empty circle and use fabric markers to draw a sign of the Mass or their love for Jesus. Request permission to use the decorated sheet as a banner or altar cover at the First Communion celebration.

Introduce

▶ Have the students examine the pictures on the page and tell what they see happening.

▶ Explain to the students that they are going to explore a special way some members of the Church help others.

▶ Tell the students about the Franciscans in New York who every day feed people who are hungry.

▶ Call on volunteers to read aloud the article titled Thank You, Lord.

▶ Invite the students to read about the virtue of thankfulness in Disciple Power. Remind them that we show our thankfulness when we serve one another and help people in need.

Reinforce

Ask the follow-up question. Discuss ways the students and their families might show their thankfulness by serving others.

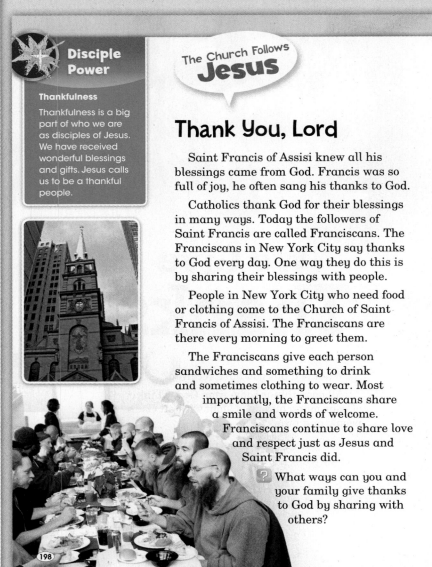

Disciple Power

Thankfulness

Thankfulness is a big part of who we are as disciples of Jesus. We have received wonderful blessings and gifts. Jesus calls us to be a thankful people.

The Church Follows **Jesus**

Thank You, Lord

Saint Francis of Assisi knew all his blessings came from God. Francis was so full of joy, he often sang his thanks to God.

Catholics thank God for their blessings in many ways. Today the followers of Saint Francis are called Franciscans. The Franciscans in New York City say thanks to God every day. One way they do this is by sharing their blessings with people.

People in New York City who need food or clothing come to the Church of Saint Francis of Assisi. The Franciscans are there every morning to greet them.

The Franciscans give each person sandwiches and something to drink and sometimes clothing to wear. Most importantly, the Franciscans share a smile and words of welcome. Franciscans continue to share love and respect just as Jesus and Saint Francis did.

❓ What ways can you and your family give thanks to God by sharing with others?

198

DISCIPLE POWER

Thankfulness. Help the students understand that we have done nothing on our own to deserve all the blessings God has given us. Like the Franciscans, we can show our thankfulness to God by helping others. Invite the students to work with you to plan a future class service project as a sign that they are thankful disciples of Jesus. Possible ideas include: visiting a nursing home to dramatize Scripture stories and serve snacks; making and decorating placemats for the tables at a soup kitchen or shelter; making food baskets for needy families; and saving money and using it to purchase items to fill Easter baskets for poor children. Enlist the assistance of parent volunteers to help in planning and completing the project. As much as possible, tie the project to concepts that the students are learning as they prepare for First Communion: sharing a special meal; giving thanks; and showing our love for Jesus.

Listen to what God's people said in the Bible.

Give thanks to the LORD, for he is good,
for his kindness endures forever.

1 CHRONICLES 16:34

Just like God's people and Saint Francis, we give thanks and praise to God today.

? What is one way you praise God?

Activity

Giving Thanks

Write four things for which you are especially thankful.

_____ _____

_____ _____

Draw a picture that shows how you can show your thankfulness by sharing love and respect just as Jesus did.

(199)

Connect

▶ Point out the Scripture quote on the top of the page. Make sure the students understand it is from the Bible.

▶ Call on one of the students to proclaim the passage from 1 Chronicles. If necessary, explain that the word *endures* means "lasts."

▶ Invite the students to think about the things for which they are especially thankful. Help them along by offering to name some things—people, places, ideas, and so on—for which they are grateful.

▶ Have the students write four things in the space provided. Then have them share with a partner.

▶ Call attention to the drawing activity. Tell the students to choose one of the things they just listed and to draw how they can show they are thankful for that choice by sharing love and respect like the Franciscans.

▶ Afterward, invite the students to share and explain their drawings.

Pray

Gather the students for prayer. Have them echo the following after you:

Generous God, /
you bless us in so many ways. /
Keep us always as your thankful
　children. /
Amen.

TEACHING TIP

Teaching Justice. This is an ideal time to reinforce our baptismal call to justice. For second graders, this means that, as a baptized follower of Jesus, they are called to help those in need by showing love and respect. Remind the students that all persons are gifts from God and are a part of God's family. God calls each of them to be kind and courteous to everyone, even those who are most difficult to love. Be sure to differentiate between showing respect and befriending a stranger who could present potential danger.

Key Concept

Catholics are a thankful people—a "eucharistic" people.

Pray

Invite the students to pray the Glory Be together.

Teach

▶ Remind the students that the first main part of the Mass is called the Liturgy of the Word.

▶ Ask a volunteer to read the Faith Focus question aloud. Tell the students that in this chapter they will learn about the Liturgy of the Eucharist, the second main part of the Mass.

▶ Read aloud the opening paragraph of The Liturgy of the Eucharist.

▶ Point out the Faith Words and their meanings.

▶ With regard to the definition of Liturgy of the Eucharist, ask the students to tell what they know—if anything—about the Last Supper. Explain that they will learn more about the Last Supper in their next lesson.

▶ Write the words *Eucharist* and *Eucharistic* on the board. Have the students say each word aloud. Then refer the students back to Disciple Power on page 198. Explain that Catholics are a *eucharistic* people, a people who "give thanks."

▶ Move on and have the students read about what the priest does and says when he accepts the gifts of bread and wine from us in the section titled The Preparation of the Gifts.

Faith Focus
What happens when the Church celebrates the Liturgy of the Eucharist?

Faith Words
▶ **Liturgy of the Eucharist**
The Liturgy of the Eucharist is the second main part of the Mass. The Church does what Jesus did at the Last Supper.

▶ **Eucharist**
The Eucharist is the Sacrament of the Body and Blood of Jesus Christ.

The Liturgy of the Eucharist

The Church celebrates the **Liturgy of the Eucharist** as the second main part of the Mass. The word *eucharist* means "thanksgiving."

The **Eucharist** is the Sacrament of the Body and Blood of Jesus Christ. During the Liturgy of the Eucharist at Mass, we give thanks to God for all he has done for us. At Mass, we give thanks to God for the gift of Jesus.

The Preparation of the Gifts

The Liturgy of the Eucharist begins with the Preparation of the Gifts. Members of the assembly bring the gifts of bread and wine to the altar.

This procession is important. It shows that we are bringing our love for God and others to the altar with the bread and wine.

❓ What are the ways the Church gives thanks at Mass?

200

The priest accepts our gifts and places them on the altar. Then he tells God all our blessings come from him. We respond, "Blessed be God for ever." We call these blessing prayers. When we pray a blessing prayer, we are telling God that he is the maker of everything good.

After he washes his hands, the priest invites us to pray. He then leads us in the Prayer Over the Offerings. We respond, "Amen."

? What are the ways you and your family give thanks to God?

Catholics Believe

The Holy Sacrifice

The Mass is also called the Holy Sacrifice. Jesus' sacrifice on the Cross is the greatest act of love for God the Father and for all people. At Mass, we are made sharers in the sacrifice of Jesus. We join with Jesus and show our love for God. We receive God's grace to love one another as Jesus commanded us to do.

Activity

Think of the blessings God has given you and your family. Fill the Blessings Bucket with words and images that tell of blessings you have received. Share what is in it with your classmates. Show that you are thankful. Pray with your class, "Blessed be God for ever."

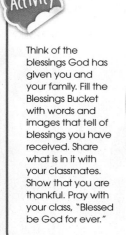
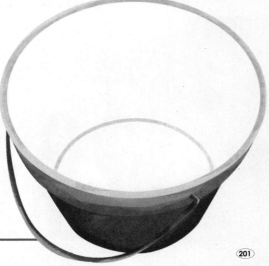

(201)

CATHOLIC TRADITION

Preparation of the Gifts. In the early Church, members gathered to celebrate the Eucharist at someone's home. It was the custom that each family bring something from home to share with those gathered to break bread. From the items gathered, unleavened bread and the best wine were chosen and prepared for the celebration of the Eucharist. The food that was not eaten was divided and shared among needy and hungry people in the community. Today, we continue this tradition when a member of the assembly brings the gifts of bread and wine to the altar at Mass. At this time, they might also bring the offering that has been collected from those assembled to be used for the needs of the community.

Connect

▶ Call for responses to the follow-up question. *(Accept all reasonable replies.)*

▶ Have the students highlight the responses "Blessed be God for ever" in the text.

▶ Remind the students that this is a blessing prayer. Ask: What are we telling God when pray these blessing prayers? *(God is the maker of all good things.)*

▶ Briefly review the Faith Words and have the students make word cards for both terms.

▶ Read and explain Catholics Believe.

Connect

Invite the students to complete the activity. If possible, bring a plastic bucket to the class and label it as Our Bucket of Blessings. Place it in the prayer center. Invite the students to write their blessings on strips of paper and place them in the bucket at prayer time.

Pray

▶ Gather the students for prayer, but tell them to keep their books open to page 201.

▶ Have the children lift their open books over their heads. Then have the children echo you:

Generous God, /
look at the many gifts / you have
    given us. /
We are a gifted people. /
We give you thanks and say: /
Blessed be God for ever. /
Amen.

Key Concept
At the Last Supper, Jesus gave us the gift of himself in bread and wine.

Pray

Have the students quiet themselves. Pray the following prayer as an echo prayer:

Lord God, / we thank and praise you / for your many gifts to us. / Amen.

Teach

▶ Remind the students that the Liturgy of the Eucharist is the second main part of the Mass.

▶ Read the Faith Focus question aloud and ask for possible answers. Tell the students that these two pages will help them learn about a special prayer that is a crucial part of the Liturgy of the Eucharist.

▶ Have the students look at the illustration on the page. Draw on the first paragraph of the text, the Eucharistic Prayer, to set the scene for the account of the Last Supper. Explain that Jesus shared a special meal with his disciples. At that meal, Jesus gave them a special gift.

▶ Proclaim the Gospel of the Last Supper based on Luke 22:17–20.

Reinforce

▶ Ask the students to underline the words that Jesus said at the Last Supper.

▶ Use the follow-up question as starting points to discuss with the Last Supper is so important for Christians.

Faith Focus
What happens during the Eucharistic Prayer?

The Eucharistic Prayer

The Eucharistic Prayer is the Church's great prayer of thanksgiving. It is during this prayer that we do what Jesus did at the Last Supper the night before he died.

During the meal, Jesus took bread into his hands and said a blessing prayer. He broke the bread. Giving the bread to his disciples, Jesus said, "Take and eat. This is my body. Do this in memory of me."

Jesus took a cup of wine and gave thanks to God. Giving the cup of wine to his disciples, he said, "Drink it." They all drank from the cup. Jesus said, "This is my blood, which is poured out for many." BASED ON LUKE 22:17–20

❓ Who says the words of Jesus at Mass?

202

TEACHING TIP

Acting Out the Last Supper. Many second graders remember a story best if they are actively involved with the telling of it. Invite the students to gather around a table or sit in a circle on the floor. Place a pitcher of grape juice (white grape juice will be best), some small paper cups, and a platter of unleavened bread, such as pita bread, in the center of the space. Pass cups of grape juice to each student. Pass around the platter of bread and ask each student to tear off a piece. Emphasize that they are simply acting out the Last Supper and that this is not in any way the celebration of the Eucharist. Take the part of Jesus yourself and act out the story as told in Luke 22:17–20.

The Consecration

The priest takes bread and says, "**T**AKE THIS, ALL OF YOU, AND EAT OF IT, FOR THIS IS MY **B**ODY, WHICH WILL BE GIVEN UP FOR YOU."

Then he takes the cup of wine and says, "**T**AKE THIS, ALL OF YOU, AND DRINK FROM IT, FOR THIS IS THE CHALICE OF MY **B**LOOD, THE **B**LOOD OF THE NEW AND ETERNAL COVENANT, WHICH WILL BE POURED OUT FOR YOU AND FOR MANY FOR THE FORGIVENESS OF SINS. **D**O THIS IN MEMORY OF ME"

These are called the words of consecration. Through the words of the priest and the power of the Holy Spirit, the bread and wine become the Body and Blood of Christ.

At the end of the Eucharistic Prayer, the assembly stands. We sing or say aloud, "Amen."

❓ How are the Eucharistic Prayer and the Last Supper alike?

Faith-Filled People

Saint Pius X

Pope Pius X made a rule that Catholics who are seven years old or older could receive Holy Communion. He also told Catholics that it was important that they receive Holy Communion often. The Church celebrates the feast day of Saint Pius X on August 21.

Activity

Complete this sentence:
The bread and wine are changed to the _____ and _____ of Jesus Christ.

(203)

FAITH-FILLED PEOPLE

Saint Pius X (1835–1914). Pius X was elected Pope on August 4, 1903. The motto for his papacy was "To restore all things in Christ." The new Pope was determined to make his papacy truly pastoral. In addition to lowering the age for receiving Holy Communion to the age of discretion, approximately seven years of age, he reorganized the Roman Curia, updated Canon Law and seminary curricula, and encouraged the laity to advance the Kingdom of God. He fully realized that the Eucharist unites us more closely with Christ and one another. For more information on Saint Pius X, go to the Saints Resource at *BeMyDisciples*.com.

Teach

▶ Introduce the Eucharistic Prayer by explaining that at Mass the priest does what Jesus did at the Last Supper.

▶ Read aloud the text, The Consecration.

Reinforce

▶ Have the students respond to the follow-up question. Note that the words of Consecration are the same words that Jesus said at the Last Supper.

▶ Stress that at Mass, through the power of the Holy Spirit and the words of the priest, the bread and wine become Jesus' Body and Blood.

Connect

▶ Have children work with a partner to complete the activity.

▶ Check answers.

▶ Ask the students when they will receive their First Holy Communion (or when they received it). Then read Faith-Filled People aloud to help the students learn what rule Saint Pius X made about children their age receiving the Body and Blood of Jesus in Holy Communion.

Pray

Have the students quiet themselves for prayer. Invite them to thank and bless God in silence for the gift of the Body and Blood of Jesus in Holy Communion. Conclude by praying the Sign of the Cross.

Key Concept
In the Liturgy of the Eucharist, we share the gift of Jesus—his Body and Blood.

Pray

Gather the students and lead them in praying the words of 1 Chronicles on page 199.

Teach

▶ Read Faith Focus aloud. Tell the students that today they will learn about receiving Holy Communion.

▶ Write the word *communion* on the board. Explain that being in communion with someone means being very close to him or her.

▶ Tell the students that like the Last Supper, the Eucharist is a sacred meal, the meal Jesus told us to celebrate in memory of him.

▶ Read aloud The Communion Rite.

Reinforce

Ask for responses to the follow-up question (same as the Faith Focus question). Make sure the children realize that we receive the Body and Blood of Christ in Holy Communion.

Connect

Write the word *Amen* on the board. Explain that it means "It is true." Practice the responses with the children. Encourage them to say a bold "Amen."

Faith Focus
What happens at the Communion Rite?

The Communion Rite

After we pray the Our Father and share a sign of peace, the priest invites us to come forward to receive Holy Communion. We receive the gift of Jesus himself. We receive strength to live as his disciples.

We walk in procession to receive Holy Communion. The consecrated bread is offered to us with the words, "The Body of Christ." We respond, "Amen."

The cup of consecrated wine is then offered to us. We hear the words, "The Blood of Christ." We respond, "Amen." We take the cup and drink from it.

In the Communion Rite we receive the Body and Blood of Christ. We become closer to Jesus, Mary and the other Saints, and all the members of the Church. The Communion Rite ends with the Prayer after Communion.

? What do we receive in Holy Communion?

204

LITURGY CONNECTION

Bread and Wine. At Mass we use unleavened bread made from wheat and wine made from grapes as Jesus did at the Last Supper. Unleavened bread is made without yeast. At Mass the bread and wine become the Body and Blood of Jesus through the words of the priest and the power of the Holy Spirit.

At Mass, you receive the gift of the Body and Blood of Christ. One way you can give thanks for the blessings God gives you is by sharing your blessings with other people.

I Follow Jesus

Activity

Sharing My Blessings

Think of how the Holy Spirit helps you share the many blessings you have been given. Write a prayer of thanks to God for all his blessings. Ask the Holy Spirit to help you share your blessings with others.

_____

_____

_____

_____

_____

My Faith Choice

This week, I will share the blessings God has given me. I will

_____

_____

Pray, "You have blessed me, O Lord. Teach me and help me to share my blessings. Amen."

205

Reinforce

Remind the students that Catholics are a eucharistic people, a thankful people. We thank God for his blessings by sharing them with others.

Respond

▶ Have the students read the introductory paragraph.

▶ Emphasize that we give thanks to God for his blessings by sharing our blessings with others.

▶ Explain the Sharing My Blessings activity and give the students time to write their prayers of thanks. You can choose to have the students do this on their own, with a partner, or as a group.

Choose

Invite the students to read My Faith Choice and write their faith decisions. Encourage everyone to put their choices into practice this week.

Pray

Lead the students in the prayer of thanks on the bottom of page 205.

THE TASKS OF CATECHESIS

Moral Formation. The *National Directory for Catechesis* teaches that moral catechesis "aims to . . . bring about personal transformation and conversion" (NDC 20). Saint Thomas Aquinas called the Eucharist our "spiritual food." He said that receiving the Eucharist turns the person who receives Communion into Jesus himself and leads us to becoming more Christ-like. In other words, through the Eucharist, if we receive the Body and Blood with reverence, thankfulness, and a willingness to allow Jesus to work through us, the mystery of the Eucharist continues in us: we are able to become what we have received—Jesus himself—and to continue his mission of love in the world. Tell the students that we must make room in our hearts so that Jesus can live in us.

Pray

Lead the students in praying the Lord's Prayer to begin class.

Recall

▶ Write the terms *Eucharist, Liturgy of the Eucharist, Mass,* and *Communion* on the board. Ask different students to explain what each term means.

▶ Call on volunteers to read aloud each To Help You Remember statement one at a time.

▶ Introduce the sentence completion activity. Allow the students time to complete it. Afterward, check responses.

▶ Go on to the circling activity. Have the students work with a partner to complete it. Then ask volunteers to read the solutions.

Reflect

Point out the important lesson question. Have the students think about what they feel was the most important lesson they learned this week and write it in the space provided.

Share

▶ Go around the classroom, inviting the students to share their reflections.

▶ Encourage the students to share their reflections with their families at home.

▶ **TO HELP YOU REMEMBER**

1. At the Last Supper, Jesus gave the Church the Sacrament of the Eucharist.

2. At the celebration of the Eucharist, the bread and wine become the Body and Blood of Jesus.

3. We receive the Body and Blood of Jesus in Holy Communion.

Chapter Review

Recall

Draw a line from each of the words in the left column to the sentence it completes in the right column.

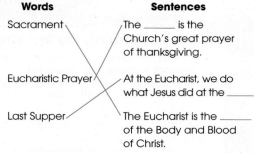

Words	Sentences
Sacrament	The _____ is the Church's great prayer of thanksgiving.
Eucharistic Prayer	At the Eucharist, we do what Jesus did at the _____.
Last Supper	The Eucharist is the _____ of the Body and Blood of Christ.

Circle Yes or No after each sentence about the Liturgy of the Eucharist

The gifts of bread and wine remind us of all God's people.   Yes   **No**

At Mass the bread and wine become the Body and Blood of Jesus.   **Yes**   No

Reflect

Why is receiving Holy Communion important?

_____

_____

Share | Share with your class how you will give thanks to God.

206

TEACHING TIP

Making Altar Bread and Wine. Tell the students that many orders of religious sisters support themselves by making altar bread (hosts). The hosts are bought by parishes and other Catholic groups for use as sacred bread at Mass. Contact your diocesan office to locate a monastery in your area that is involved in this special ministry. Contact the monastery and ask the sisters if they could loan you photographs of what is involved in each step of the host-making process.

Blessed Be God

Blessing prayers tell God we believe that all our blessings come from him. Learn the Mass response, "Blessed be God for ever."

Leader God our Father, we thank you for all your blessings.

All **Blessed be God for ever.**

Leader For family and friends, we thank you, God, and say,

All **Blessed be God for ever.**

Leader For the gifts you give us to share, _____, we thank you, God, and say,

All **Blessed be God for ever.**

Leader And most especially, for the gift of Jesus in the Eucharist, we thank you, God, and say,

All **Blessed be God for ever.**

(207)

LITURGY CONNECTION

Blessings. When we say, "Blessed be God for ever" we are saying, "Praise the Lord." A blessing prayer is a prayer of praise that gives God the glory for all that he has given us. Before the students offer this blessing prayer today, give them plenty of time to reflect on those things they are thankful for and would like to praise God for. Give students the opportunity to write down their thoughts on a separate sheet of paper.

Pray

▶ Tell the students that today's prayer is a blessing prayer that is similar to the one we pray at Mass. Practice the response, and invite the students to raise their hands in praise as they say it aloud.

▶ Call attention to the section of the prayer that states, "For the gifts you give us to share." Explain that at this point in the prayer, everyone—one at a time—will have the opportunity to offer a prayer blessing God for one of their gifts. Tell the students to be ready to name their gift when you point to them. Suggest the students look at the gifts they wrote about and/or drew on pages 199 and 201.

▶ Gather the class in the prayer center.

▶ Lead the prayer, beginning with the Sign of the Cross.

Preview

▶ Have the students carefully tear out pages 207 and 208 along the perforation.

▶ Encourage the students to share these pages with their families, and to complete the activities together.

▶ If they did not complete the review activity on page 206 by the end of the session, emphasize that they can complete it with their families at home.

▶ Point out the title and theme of the next lesson to the students.

Visit BeMyDisciples.com

▶ Take time with the students to explore the many activities and resources available at the *Be My Disciples* Web site.

▶ Encourage them to join with their families to discover the many resources available at the Web site.

Before Moving On ...

As you finish today's lesson, reflect on the following question before moving on to the next chapter.

How well do I communicate to the students that I enjoy and am thankful for being their teacher?

With My Family

This Week . . .

In Chapter 15, "We Give Thanks," your child learned:

▶ Jesus gave the Church the Sacrament of the Eucharist at the Last Supper.

▶ During the Eucharistic Prayer at Mass, the Church remembers and does what Jesus did at the Last Supper.

▶ At Mass, the bread and wine become the Body and Blood of Jesus through the power of the Holy Spirit and the words of the priest. Jesus is really and truly present under the appearances of bread and wine.

▶ In Holy Communion, we receive the Body and Blood of Jesus.

▶ We thank God for this wonderful gift by the way we live our lives.

For more about related teachings of the Church, see the *Catechism of the Catholic Church*, 1345–1405, and the *United States Catholic Catechism for Adults*, pages 218–220.

■ Sharing God's Word

Read together Luke 22:11–20, part of the account of what happened at the Last Supper. Or read the adaptation of the story on page 202. Emphasize that at the Last Supper, Jesus gave the Church the Sacrament of the Eucharist.

■ Living as Disciples

The Christian home and family is a school of discipleship. Choose one of the following activities to do as a family, or design a similar activity of your own.

▶ This week at Mass, remind your child that what Jesus did at the Last Supper is part of the Eucharistic Prayer. After Mass, talk with your child about the Last Supper and its connection with the Mass. Discuss the importance of receiving Holy Communion.

▶ Sharing family meals together is a practical way to help your child appreciate and understand the meaning of the Eucharist. When your family shares meals together, you are sharing the gift of yourselves. Be sure to give thanks to God by praying Grace Before Meals.

■ Our Spiritual Journey

One of the effects of receiving the gift of the Eucharist in Holy Communion is living out a commitment to the poor. Practicing the spiritual discipline of almsgiving enables us to live out that grace and also to thank God for all his blessings, not only in words but also in our actions. This week, pray *"Blessed be God for ever"* at the end of each family meal prayer.

For more ideas on ways your family can live as disciples of Jesus, visit **BeMyDisciples.com**

PLAN AHEAD

Practicing the Communion Rite. Plan to ask the parish sacristan, your catechetical leader, or pastor for enough unconsecrated hosts for everyone in your class if you plan to do the Human Methodologies Learning by Apprenticeship activity during your next session. You will also need grape juice, a plate, and a cup.

Enriching the Lesson

Completing Sacrament Booklets

Purpose

To reinforce the teaching about the Liturgy of the Eucharist (taught in chapter 15)

Directions

Today the students will complete the Sacrament booklets they have been making over the past seven chapters.

▶ Invite the students to turn to the next page in their booklets and write the words *Eucharist: Liturgy of the Eucharist* at the top of the page.

▶ Help the students recall some of the actions of this part of the Mass. Have them draw a picture of one of these actions beneath the page title. Invite them to share their drawings with one another.

▶ Praise the students for all their work on the Sacrament booklets. Encourage the students to take their booklets home and share them with their families.

Materials

Sacrament booklets

pencils

crayons or markers

A Blessing to Thank God

Purpose

To reinforce the importance of thanking God for everything that he has done (taught on pages 197–198)

Directions

▶ Discuss with the students the importance of thanking God before their meals.

▶ Practice the Grace Before Meals found on page 369.

▶ Using an easy recipe for bread, have the students work with you to prepare the ingredients and place them in plastic bags.

▶ Send the ingredients for making bread home with the students. Include both a card with baking instructions and a card with the Grace Before Meals.

▶ Remind the students to pray the Grace Before Meals before they serve and eat the bread.

Materials

ingredients for bread

plastic bags

cards with the Grace Before Meals

Literature Connection

Purpose

To reinforce the theme of thanksgiving in the Eucharist (taught in Chapter 15)

Directions

The picture book *Thank You, Grandpa* by Lynn Plourde (Dutton, 2003) explores the theme of thanksgiving for the fleeting gifts of life. In this touching story, a young girl and her grandpa take walks together. In their encounters with nature, the old man shows the little girl how to say "thank you and good-bye" to the gifts of nature that come and go. Finally, as her grandfather dies, the girl, now older, is able to look back with gratitude on the many gifts he gave to her.

▶ Read the story aloud to the students. Share the illustrations with them and help them notice the differences in the two characters as they grow older.

▶ Ask the students to share the things for which they are most grateful in their lives.

▶ Remind them that the Eucharistic Prayer at Mass is the Church's great prayer of thanksgiving for the gift of Jesus.

Materials

Thank You, Grandpa, by Lynn Plourde

BACKGROUND

Sharing Our Gifts

The celebration of the Eucharist calls us to transformation. The proclaiming of God's Word challenges us to die to self so that we can take up our baptismal commitment to live a life of dying and rising in the mystery of Christ. The Eucharistic Prayer pulls us into the story of our Salvation. We are encouraged, invited, and enabled to participate ritually in our very own redemption. We are thus in communion with God and one another.

The Works of Mercy

The four accounts of the Gospel are filled with Jesus' concern for the poor, the hungry, the outcast, and the sick. In his action of feeding the hungry crowd (see Matthew 14:13–21, Mark 6:30–44, Luke 9:10–17, and John 6:1–15), Jesus instructed the disciples, saying, "You feed them." This command, which was originally given to the first disciples, has been passed on to all disciples of all time through the living Word of God, Sacred Scripture.

Solidarity with the Poor

Joined to Christ and to all of humanity in Baptism, we continue Christ's work in our time. No need can be left unmet—no child can go hungry, no person left homeless, no one abandoned. Loving our neighbor is inseparable from living as a disciple of Christ. This standard for measuring our fidelity to the Lord has been clearly stated:

> Then the righteous will answer him and say, "Lord, when did we see you hungry and feed you, or thirsty and give you drink? When did we see you a stranger and welcome you, or naked and clothe you? When did we see you ill or in prison, and visit you?" And the king will say to them in reply, "Amen, I say to you, whatever you did for one of these least brothers of mine, you did for me."
>
> Matthew 25:37–40

Stewards of Creation

Our love and service to our neighbor includes our faithful stewardship of creation. A false attitude of our dominion over creation has led us to waste and deplete creation's abundant resources. The union we share with the entire cosmos challenges the Christian to pause and reflect on new ways to respect and honor and share the goods of the created world.

The Gospel admonishes us to be wise stewards of the Earth and her bounty and warns us of the dangers of hoarding our rich and varied resources. With love tempered by justice, all the baptized, especially those who have much, are responsible to share and to create just structures aimed at distributing the goods of the Earth.

In the simple action of "taking, blessing, and sharing," Christ fed the multitudes. As we receive God's gifts, we are to give him thanks and bless him by sharing those gifts, especially with people in need. We are to be in solidarity with them.

> And the crowds asked [Jesus], "What then should we do?" He said to them in reply, "Whoever has two cloaks should share with the person who has none. And whoever has food should do likewise."
>
> Luke 3:10–11

For Reflection

What experiences of the interconnectedness of humanity have I had?

How can I become more focused on living the Works of Mercy?

Teacher to Teacher

What We Give

Children love to receive and give gifts. However, because they are children, there is often much more excitement over receiving gifts than over giving gifts. Many times children and adults alike will say they get nothing out of going to Mass. We need to teach the students that they need to give at Mass. They need to offer the gift of themselves along with the gifts of bread and wine—their attention, their voices, their desire to go out and make a difference by living as Jesus did.

Participating in Mass

While it is important to teach students reverence and respect, sometimes we place more emphasis on how well they behave during Mass than on how well they participate. It is important for the students, who have come to join with the parish community, to celebrate, to be nourished, and to praise and thank God the Father with their whole beings.

The Church Teaches...

"The Christian faith, is above all, conversion to Jesus Christ, full adherence to his person and the decision to walk in his footsteps . . . Catechesis nourishes a living, explicit, and fruitful faith lived in discipleship to Jesus Christ" (*National Directory for Catechesis*, 29B).

The stories about the miracles of Jesus taught in this chapter help the students become nourished by the love of Jesus Christ, who cares for all peoples. Jesus becomes our model of providing for those in need.

Further Reading and Reflection

For more related teachings of the Church, see the *Catechism of the Catholic Church*, 1333–1405 and 1822–1823; and the *United States Catholic Catechism for Adults*, pages 220–227.

Teacher Prayer

Lord, you lovingly washed the feet of your disciples. Bless me with a loving servant heart like yours. Provide me with all I need to answer your call to serve. And when I grow weary in that service, strengthen me again and again.
Amen.

Lesson Planner

Goal To learn about the purpose of the Concluding Rites of the Mass

LESSON PART	PROCESS	MATERIALS and RESOURCES
DAY 1 **EXPLORE** **Focus** To explore how followers of Jesus share the message of God with others Pages 209–211	▶ Proclaim and discuss Isaiah 6:8 (Here I am, Lord). ▶ Learn and discuss the story of two Catholic **Disciple Power:** Courage **Activity:** Write about being a missionary.	Bible Pencils or pens Crayons or markers Large map of the Americas
DAY 2 **DISCOVER** **Focus** To discover what happens during the Concluding Rites at Mass Pages 212–213	▶ Discover what happens at the Concluding Rites **Faith-Filled People:** Saint Damien de Vuester **Activity:** Write what you can say or do to live as a follower of Jesus.	Bible Pencil or pens **Additional Activities Booklet:** Activities 16a and 16b or see *BeMyDisciples*.com
DAY 3 **DISCOVER** **Focus** To discover what we must do to glorify God by our lives Pages 214–215	▶ Learn about the mission Jesus gives each of us. **Scripture Story:** Jesus washes his disciples feet (John 13:4–5, 13–14, 34–35). **Catholics Believe:** Washing of Feet **Activity:** Break the code to discover your mission.	Bibles Pencils or pens
DAY 4 **DECIDE** **Focus** To discover the importance of the concluding procession and to decide on a way to live, love, and serve others Pages 216–217	▶ Recognize what happens at the Concluding Procession. **Faith Words:** procession **Activity:** Decide how you can love and serve others; act it out for your class. **My Faith Choice:** Choose a way to glorify God this week.	Pencil or pens Crayons or markers **Enriching the Lesson:** Teacher Guide, page 319 • Making Streamers for Processions • Reinforcing Faith Words • Catholic Social Teaching: Bread for the Poor
DAY 5 **CONCLUDE** **Focus** To realize that prayer can help us tell other's about God's love Pages 218–220	▶ **REVIEW** Review concepts: Recall, Reflect, and Share. ▶ **PRAY** Here I am Lord ▶ **Preview** the With My Family page and the theme of the next chapter.	Bible, candle, cross for prayer space Grade 2 Music CD **Assessment Tools Booklet:** Assessments 16a and 16b

Assign online Chapter Review and interactive Chapter Test at **BeMyDisciples.com**

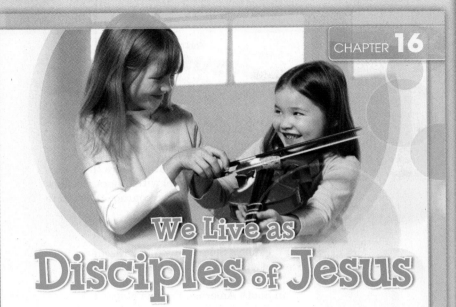

CHAPTER **16**

We Live as Disciples of Jesus

❓ When did someone call on you to do something important?

Each day God calls on us to help him. Close your eyes and imagine you lived many years before Jesus was born. Listen to God calling on you to help him.

I heard the voice of the Lord saying, "Whom shall I send? . . . "Here I am;" I said; "send me!"

ISAIAH 6:8

❓ What message would you share about Jesus with another?

(209)

HUMAN METHODOLOGIES

Learning by Apprenticeship. The *National Directory for Catechesis* explains that apprenticeship "includes . . . celebration of the mysteries of the faith" (*NDC*, 29H). As continued preparation for First Eucharist, practice the Communion Rite with the students, using unconsecrated hosts and a cup, similar in shape to a chalice, filled with juice. Explain that the hosts are ordinary bread because they have not yet been blessed during Mass. Review the proper way to receive Holy Communion on page 204 of the students' text. Call each student forward one at a time to receive the unconsecrated host and to drink from the cup. Emphasize the importance of reverence as we receive the Body and Blood of Jesus.

Pray

▶ Welcome the students warmly. Then have them quiet themselves for prayer.

▶ Pray the Sign of the Cross together.

Pray with the children, "Dear Jesus, help us to be your disciples. Amen."

Reflect

▶ Ask the opening question. (*Accept all replies.*)

▶ Invite the students to listen to God's call to be his messenger.

▶ Read the opening paragraph aloud. Then have one of the students proclaim the passage from Isaiah 6:8.

▶ Afterward, observe a moment of silence.

▶ Invite the students to tell which sort of call they think the children in the photograph are answering.

▶ Point out the Scripture question. Have the students respond by sharing the message with a partner.

▶ Conclude with the Sign of the Cross.

Focus

Invite the students to move on to the next page, where they will hear about some people who answered God's call to be his messengers.

Introduce

▶ Write the word *missionaries* on the board, and ask the students if they know what missionaries are.

▶ Call attention to the first paragraph of Spreading the Gospel. Emphasize that missionaries listen to God's call.

▶ Divide the class into four groups. Assign each group to one of the missionaries listed on pages 210–211. Have each group read about one missionary and then report about him or her to the rest of the class.

▶ Invite the students to read about the virtue of courage in Disciple Power. Ask them to tell how each of the missionaries showed courage.

Reinforce

▶ Have each group create a character map of their favorite Saint. This is a graphic organizer with the name of the Saint in the middle circle and characteristics of the Saint in the branches of the organizer. Share organizers by posting them in the classroom.

▶ Use the follow-up questions to help the students consider what it takes to be a missionary, to respond, "Here I am. Send me" to God's call.

Disciple Power

Courage

We receive the gift of courage from the Holy Spirit at Baptism. This gift helps us choose to do what is good.

The Church Follows **Jesus**

Spreading the Gospel

God continues to call on people to be missionaries. Missionaries share the message of the Gospel with others. See how these missionaries used courage to listen to God's call.

Saint Francis Solano

Francis Solano was a Franciscan missionary priest. He brought the Good News of Jesus to the people of Argentina in South America. Francis played the violin. People would come to listen to him play. Then Francis would teach them about Jesus.

Jean Donovan

Jean Donovan left her home in Ohio to go to the country of El Salvador in Central America. Jean shared God's love and showed her love especially to people who were poor. Jean ran a home for the hungry and the sick. Jean Donovan was killed by people who did not want her to be a missionary in their country.

❓ How did these missionaries share the Gospel message?

210

DISCIPLE POWER

Courage. Courage is both a Cardinal Virtue and a Gift of the Holy Spirit. It is also called fortitude. Tell the students a story from your own life when the Holy spirit gave you the courage to make a good choice. An example that they may appreciate is your decision to become their religion teacher. Then invite volunteers to share an experience of choosing to do good. Affirm the students for the examples they cite. Encourage them to pray to the Holy Spirit for courage whenever they are faced with a difficult choice.

Saint Frances Cabrini

Frances Cabrini brought her missionary sisters from Italy to New York. They helped the sick and cared for orphans. They built schools and orphanages in the United States and South America. She became so loved by the people they called her "Mother Cabrini."

[?] If you were a missionary, where would you go? How would you help?

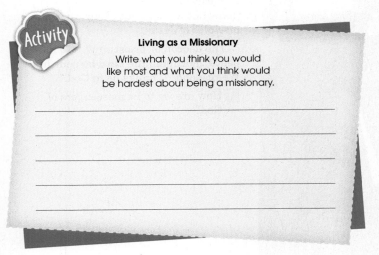

Saint Francis Solano, Saint Frances Cabrini, Jean Donovan

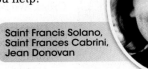

Activity

Living as a Missionary

Write what you think you would like most and what you think would be hardest about being a missionary.

_____

_____

_____

_____

_____

(211)

Connect

▶ Read aloud the activity's first set of directions. You will probably have to point out places on the map. Consider using a larger map of the area that you can post in the classroom.

▶ Go through each missionary, one at a time, to help the students draw a line linking him or her to the country in which he or she served.

▶ Point out the second set of activity directions. Give the students time to write their thoughts.

▶ Invite sharing. Discuss what is exciting and what is hard about being a missionary.

Pray

Gather the students for prayer. Lead them in praying the Lord's Prayer.

TEACHING TIP

Extending Activity. Extend the second part of today's activity. Gather information about a current mission, perhaps one that your local diocese supports. Locate the mission on a map. Invite the students to imagine themselves as missionaries there. Write two columns on the board. Print "Good Stuff" and "Hard Stuff" at the head of the columns. Have the students think of five or six items under each heading. Offer an idea for each such as: "You are doing God's work" and "It is hard to learn a new language."

> **Key Concept**
> The Concluding Rites send us forth to love and serve.

Pray

Invite the students to quiet themselves inside and out for prayer. Pray the Glory Be together.

Teach

▶ Point out the Faith Focus question on the page and then read it aloud. Tell the students that in this chapter they will learn what the Concluding Rites of the Mass send us to do. *(go forth to be messengers of God by our words and actions.)*

▶ Read aloud the text Final Blessing. Ask the students to listen for the words of the priest and for our response. Ask: What is our response? *(Amen.)* Who can remember what "Amen" means? *(It is true.)*

▶ Go on to read the section titled Dismissal aloud. When you get to the words "Go in peace . . ." read them prayerfully and ask the group to read the response.

▶ Invite the students to follow along as you finish reading the rest of the page.

> **Faith Focus**
> What does the Mass send us to do?

The Concluding Rites

The Concluding Rites end the celebration of the Mass. We receive God's blessing and go forth to tell others about Jesus.

Final Blessing

The priest asks for God's blessing on us. He says, "May almighty God bless you, the Father, and the Son, and the Holy Spirit."

We end Mass the same way we began. We bless ourselves with the Sign of the Cross. We respond, "Amen."

Dismissal

The word *mass* means "sending forth." What we have done at Mass, we must now do in the world. We are to be messengers of God by what we say and what we do. That is our work as disciples of Jesus.

The deacon or priest says, "Go in peace, glorifying the Lord by your life." We respond, "Thanks be to God."

❓ How are we to be messengers of God?

212

TEACHING TIP

A "Fishin' " Mission. Tell or retell the Scripture account of Jesus' calling of four of the Apostles away from their fishing for fish (Luke 5:1–11) to a brand new mission of fishing for people to follow Jesus. Ask how missionaries are "fishers" today. Point out that the dismissal of the Mass calls all the faithful to the mission of "fishing for" and serving others.

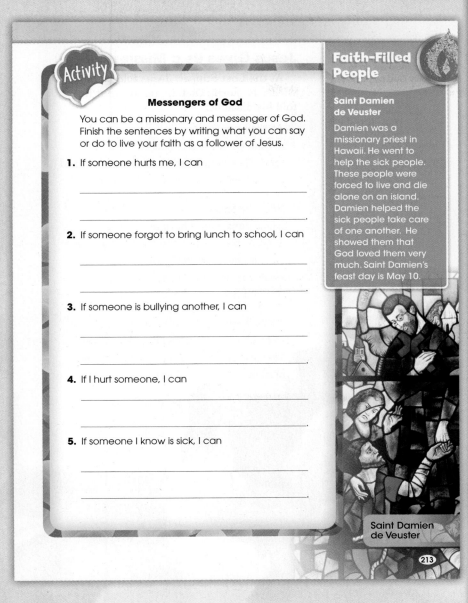

Activity

Messengers of God

You can be a missionary and messenger of God. Finish the sentences by writing what you can say or do to live your faith as a follower of Jesus.

1. If someone hurts me, I can

_____

_____

2. If someone forgot to bring lunch to school, I can

_____

_____

3. If someone is bullying another, I can

_____

_____

4. If I hurt someone, I can

_____

_____

5. If someone I know is sick, I can

_____

_____

Faith-Filled People

Saint Damien de Veuster

Damien was a missionary priest in Hawaii. He went to help the sick people. These people were forced to live and die alone on an island. Damien helped the sick people take care of one another. He showed them that God loved them very much. Saint Damien's feast day is May 10.

Saint Damien de Veuster

213

FAITH-FILLED PEOPLE

Saint Damien de Veuster (1840–1889). Before Damien began his ministry, few people knew anything about leprosy (Hansen's disease), an infection that can destroy the skin and tissues. By the time he died of leprosy at the age of 49, people all over the world knew about this disease. Damien, forced to quit school to work on his family farm in Belgium, entered the Congregation of the Sacred Heart of Jesus and Mary. In May 1864, he was ordained a priest in Honolulu and assigned to the island of Hawaii. In 1873, he went to the Hawaiian government's leper colony on the island of Molokai. After several months there, Fr. Damien volunteered to live on Molokai permanently, caring for the people's physical, medical, and spiritual needs. Damien was canonized in 2009. To learn more about Saint Damien de Veuster, go to the Saints Resource at *BeMyDisciples*.com.

Reinforce

▶ Have the students underline the meaning of the word *Mass* in the text. *(sending forth)*

▶ Ask the follow-up question. *(Help the students recognize that we act as God's messengers by what we say and do, especially by how we share our many God-given gifts and blessings.)*

▶ Invite a volunteer to read aloud Faith-Filled People about Saint Damien de Veuster, a missionary priest in Hawaii. Ask: How did Saint Damien live out the mission Jesus gave us?

Connect

▶ Point out the activity Messengers of God. Read the directions aloud.

▶ Allow ample time for the students to write what they would say or do to act as Jesus' follower.

▶ When they finish writing, call on different students to share their responses.

Pray

Gather the class for prayer. Have them echo the following after you.

> Gracious God of all, / fill me with your love. / Help me be your messenger. / Send me forth to glorify your name. / Amen.

Key Concept
Jesus gives a new command—
to love and serve God and others.

Pray

Quiet the students for prayer. Lead
them in the Glory Be.

Teach

▶ Call on one of the students to read
aloud the Faith Focus question
and have the rest of the class think
silently about how they might
answer it. Tell the students that
these two pages will help them
learn how following Jesus' new
command allows us to glorify God
by our lives.

▶ Ask the students to tell what they
recall about the Last Supper. Have
them tell what great gift Jesus gave
us. *(his Body and Blood)*

▶ Have the students settle themselves to
hear a Bible story. Tell them that the
story took place at the Last Supper.

▶ Present the biblical account of the
washing of the feet. You can read it
yourself, have an individual student
read, or call on various students to
share in the reading.

▶ After the Scripture reading, have
the students read Catholics Believe
to learn more about the rite of the
washing of the feet.

▶ Go on to present the final text
paragraphs on the top of page 215.

Faith Focus
What must we do to
glorify God by our lives?

Jesus Gives Us a Mission

At the Last Supper, Jesus told us how
we are to glorify God. Listen to what he
told his disciples.

*At the Last Supper, Jesus tied a towel
around his waist and poured water into a
bowl. Then he washed his disciples' feet and
dried them with the towel.*

*When he finished, Jesus said, "Do you
understand what I have done for you?
You call me teacher and Lord. That is who
I am. If I have washed your feet, you must
wash one another's feet. You must serve
one another.*

*"Here is what you are to do. You are
to love one another as I have loved you.
Then everyone will know that you are my
disciples."* BASED ON JOHN 13:4–5, 13–14, 34–35

? What is the work
that Jesus gave us
to do?

LITURGY CONNECTION

Washing of the Feet: Helping Hands. Emphasize that the rite of
washing of the feet is a call to serve others, as Jesus did. To help the
students understand the meaning of this rite, have them trace and
cut out outlines of both of their hands on art paper. On the outline of
one hand, have the students write their names. In the outline of the
other hand, have them write or draw one way they can serve or help
people at home. Encourage the students to post their handprints in a
place at home where they will see them every day and be reminded
to carry out the service that they decided to perform. Explain to the
class that Jesus wants us to serve others out of love.

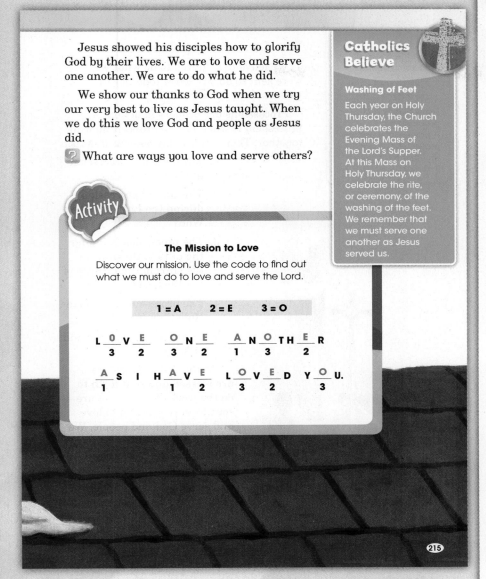

Jesus showed his disciples how to glorify God by their lives. We are to love and serve one another. We are to do what he did.

We show our thanks to God when we try our very best to live as Jesus taught. When we do this we love God and people as Jesus did.

? What are ways you love and serve others?

Catholics Believe

Washing of Feet

Each year on Holy Thursday, the Church celebrates the Evening Mass of the Lord's Supper. At this Mass on Holy Thursday, we celebrate the rite, or ceremony, of the washing of the feet. We remember that we must serve one another as Jesus served us.

Activity

The Mission to Love

Discover our mission. Use the code to find out what we must do to love and serve the Lord.

1 = A	2 = E	3 = O

L O V E   O N E   A N O T H E R
  3 2   3 2   1   3   2

A S   I   H A V E   L O V E D   Y O U.
1   1 2   3   2   3

215

Reinforce

Ask the follow-up question. *(Accept all replies that evidence an understanding that the work Jesus gives us is to love and serve one another.)*

Connect

▶ Direct attention to the activity Love Power. Read the directions aloud.

▶ Give the students time to complete the activity by using the key letters to discover the mission that Jesus left us.

▶ Once the students have decoded the message, share it. Then invite the students to share ways that they can live out their missions. If you wish, offer some specific examples to get the students thinking.

Pray

Gather the students for prayer. Lead them in the Lord's Prayer.

Pray

Quiet the students for prayer. Lead them in the Sign of the Cross.

Teach

▶ Read aloud the Faith Focus question. Then write the word *procession* on the board, and ask the students if they know what a procession is.

▶ Invite the students to tell whether they have ever been part of a procession.

▶ Summarize the first two paragraphs of The Concluding Procession. Point out the difference between simply walking and processing.

▶ Invite volunteers to read about the Mass' five processions.

▶ Finally, have the students follow along as you read the closing paragraphs of text.

Reinforce

Ask the follow-up question. Help the students see that the concluding procession reminds us of our mission to join together to love and serve God and others.

Connect

Point out *procession* in Faith Words. Have the students make a word card for the term.

Faith Focus
Why is the concluding procession at Mass important?

Faith Words
procession
A procession is people prayerfully walking together. It is a prayer in action.

The Concluding Procession

We leave the Church to do what we were sent to do. We leave together in **procession**.

Processions are prayers in action. A procession is when people prayerfully walk together. There are five processions at Mass.

1. The entrance procession at the start of Mass
2. The Gospel procession during the Liturgy of the Word
3. The procession bringing the gifts to the altar at the start of the Liturgy of the Eucharist
4. The procession to receive Holy Communion
5. The procession at the end of Mass

At the end of Mass, we are blessed and sent forth to do the work of Jesus. We are sent from the church to love and serve God and people. We know that the Eucharist gives us the strength to be disciples of Jesus.

 What is the work that Jesus gave us to do?

216

TEACHING TIP

Lead a Procession. Lead the students in a joyful procession. Choose a favorite hymn or song to sing or a favorite prayer to pray—litanies work great—as the students process. Have the students carry the class banner, cross, or Bible in procession. Consider having the students wave streamers or simply lengths of brightly colored ribbons as they walk. If possible, process to, through, and from the parish church, or simply process around the classroom. Make this a joyful and prayerful event.

You can give glory to God when you live as Jesus taught. You show love to others. You can show courage and do things that are difficult because of your love for God. When you do this, you love God and serve people as Jesus did.

To Love and Serve

 Activity

The Holy Spirit helps you give glory to God. Think of how you will live, love, and serve others with courage. Put a ✔ next to ways you can do this. Act out one of these ways for your class.

_____ I can help out at home.

_____ I can pray for people around the world who suffer from poverty.

_____ I can say no to fighting and arguing with my family.

_____ I can donate some of my toys to children who have less than I do.

_____ I can be a respectful listener at school.

 My Faith Choice

I will glorify the Lord this week. I will

_____

_____

_____

Pray, "Help me show my love for you, Lord God, in all I do for others. Amen."

(217)

THE TASKS OF CATECHESIS

Missionary Initiative. Remind the children of the actions that precede and follow the Dismissal. The priest first prays that we will take the graces that we have received at the Eucharist and carry them into our everyday lives. He then invokes God's blessing upon us and dismisses us to continue the work of the Eucharist. The words remind us that it is only in a spirit of peace that we can do the fruitful work of loving and serving the Lord and one another. Our response is a prayer of thanksgiving for all the gifts that we have received and the opportunity we now have to share them with others. We pray "Thanks be to God" and join in singing a final hymn as the priest, deacon, and servers process from the Church. Like Francis Solano, Frances Cabrini, Damien de Veuster and Jean Donovan, we are sent forth to be messengers of God's love to everyone we meet.

Reinforce

Remind the students that in the Eucharist we receive a mission. God calls us to love and serve him and others.

Respond

▶ Explain the activity directions to the students clearly.

▶ Have them complete the activity on their own or with a partner.

Choose

▶ Invite the students to read My Faith Choice and to write their decisions.

▶ Encourage the students to put their choices into practice this week.

Pray

Lead the students in the prayer at the bottom of the page.

Pray

Lead the students in praying the response that they will use in today's prayer: "Here I am Lord. Send me."

Recall

▶ Summarize the teaching on the Concluding Rites of the Mass by sharing the To Help You Remember statements with the children. Read each statement, leaving out a key word. Ask volunteers to respond with the missing word.

▶ Point out the missing word activity. Read the directions. Then have the students work on their own to complete the sentences. Afterward check responses.

▶ Introduce the numbering activity and allow the class time to complete it. Check for correct numbering. Ask different students to describe each element of the Concluding Rites.

Reflect

Invite the students to consider what they think was the most important thing they learned this week. And then go on to write it in the space provided.

Share

▶ Have the students share their reflection with a partner.

▶ Call on partners to share with the class what their partner wrote.

▶ Tell the students that they can share their reflections at home.

▶ **TO HELP YOU REMEMBER**

1. At the end of Mass we receive God's blessing to live as Jesus' disciples.
2. The dismissal sends us forth from Mass to glorify God.
3. The concluding procession reminds us that we are people sent on a mission.

Chapter Review

Recall

Write the missing words in the sentences. Use the words below to help you.

| mass | procession | love | missionaries |

1. _____Missionaries_____ teach and help poor people all over the world.

2. The word _____mass_____ means "sending forth."

3. A _____procession_____ is a prayer in action.

Number the parts of the Concluding Rites in the correct order.

 3 The Concluding Procession

 2 The Dismissal

 1 The Final Blessing

Reflect

In what ways will you go forth to love and serve others?

_____

_____

_____

Share | Share with your class the ways that you will give glory to God this week.

(218)

TEACHING TIP

Reviewing. In the last four chapters, the students have learned a great deal about the celebration of the Mass. Make four columns on the board: The Introductory Rites, The Liturgy of the Word, The Liturgy of the Eucharist, and the Concluding Rites. Have volunteers name the parts of the Mass that make up each of these four categories. Allow the students to use their books so that the listing on the board is complete. You might want to have the students copy the completed chart onto paper to use as a study tool.

Here I Am, Lord

*Prayer can help us tell others about God's love.
Say this prayer with your class.*

Leader   Prayer can help us say, "Here I am. Send me." Therefore, let us pray.

Group 1   Loving Lord, you ask us to be your messengers.

All   **"Here I am, Lord. Send me."**

Group 2   You bless and call us to love one another.

All   **"Here I am, Lord. Send me."**

Group 1   You bless us and call us to serve others.

All   **"Here I am, Lord. Send me."**

Group 2   Lord, whenever you call us to love and to serve, help us say,

All   **"Here I am, Lord. Send me. Amen"**

219

We Pray

▶ Tell the students that today they will join in a call-and-answer prayer. Practice the response. If you wish, suggest that the students point to themselves as they make their responses.

▶ Divide the class into two groups and assign parts. Give the groups time to practice their lines.

▶ Gather the class in the prayer center.

▶ Lead the students in prayer, beginning with the Sign of the Cross.

▶ Conclude by inviting all to share a sign of peace.

TEACHING TIP

Deepening Prayer. After making preparations for today's prayer, but before leading it, guide the students through a brief meditation. First, ask the students to straighten their backs so that they can breathe evenly and deeply. Invite them to close their eyes. Pause until they seem to be quiet outside and inside. Describe Jesus coming to the classroom. He smiles at everyone. Then he asks, "Who will be my messenger? Who will I send?" Suddenly, Jesus is gone. Have the students open their eyes. Invite them to respond to Jesus by joining in the prayer. *Here I am, Lord. Send me.*

Preview

► Have the students carefully tear out pages 219 and 220 along the perforation.

► Encourage the students to share these pages with their families, and to complete the activities together.

► If they did not complete the review activity on page 218 by the end of the session, emphasize that they can complete it with their families at home.

► Point out the title and theme of the next lesson to the students.

Visit BeMyDisciples.com

► Take time with the students to explore the many activities and resources available at the *Be My Disciples* Web site.

► Encourage them to join with their families to discover the many resources available at the Web site.

Before Moving On ...

As you finish today's lesson, reflect on the following question before moving on to the next chapter.

What more could I do to incorporate movement and music into our sessions?

With My Family

This Week . . .

In Chapter 16, "We Live as Disciples of Jesus," your child learned:

► The Concluding Rites end the celebration of Mass.

► In the Concluding Rites of the Mass, we are blessed and sent forth as messengers of the Gospel.

► The concluding procession alerts us to the fact that we are sent forth together and are to work together as messengers of the Gospel.

► Exercising courage in living as Jesus taught is an important characteristic of Jesus' disciples.

For more about related teachings of the Church, see the *Catechism of the Catholic Church*, 1333–1405 and 1822–1823; and the *United States Catholic Catechism for Adults*, pages 220–227.

■ Sharing God's Word

Read together John 13:1–15 and 33–34, the account of Jesus giving the disciples his New Commandment. Or read the adaptation of the story on page 214. Point out how Jesus calls us to love and serve others as he did.

■ Livings as Disciples

The Christian home and family is a school of discipleship. Choose one of the following activities to do as a family, or design a similar activity of your own.

► Review the assembly's responses to the Blessing and Dismissal of the Concluding Rites. Make sure your child knows them by heart. This will help them participate more fully and actively in the celebration of Mass.

► Discuss and decide how your family can glorify God by your lives; for example, by taking part in a service project of your parish or school that serves your neighborhood or local community.

■ Our Spiritual Journey

Developing the virtues can occur through human effort - dilligence, consistent practice, and courage - assisted by God's grace. In this chapter, your child was introduced to the virtue of courage. Model this virtue: help your child learn and practice it through your example. Pray this simple prayer each day with your family, "Here I am, Lord. Send me."

For more ideas on ways your family can live as disciples of Jesus, visit **BeMyDisciples.com**

(220)

THE LAST WORD

Reviewing Faith Choices. As you complete this unit, have the children think about the faith choices they made in the last four chapters. Ask them to identify those choices that they have successfully implemented. Invite volunteers to share success stories. Include everyone who wants to share his or her story. Affirm their striving to put their choices into practice.

Enriching the Lesson

Making Streamers for Processions

Purpose

To reinforce the teaching about processions at Mass (taught on page 147)

Directions

▶ Review with the children the five kinds of processions they experience at Mass, discussing what happens in each one, what objects may be carried in the procession and by whom.

▶ Divide the children into groups and assign a procession to each group. Tell the children that they are going to make wands with streamers attached that can be used in prayerful processions.

▶ Distribute dowels, six lengths of ribbon in particular liturgical colors, and masking tape to the groups. Demonstrate how to affix the streamers to the dowel with tape.

▶ Use the wands with streamers in classroom processions for your prayer services.

Materials

thin 24-inch wooden dowels for each group

two-foot lengths of ribbon in purple, green, white or gold, and red

masking or transparent tape

Reinforcing Faith Words

Purpose

To reinforce the new vocabulary—"Faith Words" (taught in chapters 13 to 16)

Directions

▶ Tell the students to take out the word cards that they have been making during this unit. In partners, have the students play a guessing game.

▶ Model the activity for them by choosing a Faith Word and giving a clue about it. Continue offering clues until someone in the class guesses the word.

▶ Ask the students to take turns quizzing each other on the words in the same way. Have them continue until they have covered all the Faith Words in the unit.

Materials

the children's word cards

Catholic Social Teaching: Bread for the Poor

Purpose

To reinforce the principle option for the poor and vulnerable (taught in chapters 14–16)

Directions

▶ Find an easy quick bread recipe online. Make copies of the directions and assemble enough ingredients for each child to make a loaf.

▶ Remind the children that many people are hungry. Tell them they are going to gather dry ingredients and make a loaf of bread at home to give to the poor.

▶ Place the various dry ingredients on a table. Invite each child to measure out the amount of each ingredient they will need and place it in a large plastic zip-lock bag. Have the children affix the directions to the bags.

▶ Tell the children to bring the completed loaves back to class. Arrange for a parish outreach group to distribute the bread.

▶ Re-read the story of the Loaves and Fishes. When we share what we have, others need not be hungry.

Materials

dry ingredients for bread-making, enough for each child

measuring cups and spoons

large plastic zip-lock bags

copy of bread recipe for each child

transparent tape

Catholic Social Teaching Unit 4

Pray

Have the students close their eyes and remember that Jesus is present with them. Remind them that Jesus taught us to help people who are hungry, people who have no place to live, and all people who need our help. Have the students open their eyes and echo after you, *"Lord Jesus, help us live as you taught."*

Focus

Invite a volunteer to read aloud the principle of Catholic Social Teaching in the We Reach Out to People sidebar.

Introduce

Write the words *elderly, sick,* and *poor* on the board. Invite volunteers to tell what these words tell about people. Remind them that Christians look for ways to care for these and other people who are in need of our help.

Teach

▶ Invite the students to quietly look at each of the three pictures on the page.

▶ Have them talk with a partner about what they see in each picture.

▶ Suggest that these pictures show us people in need and how we might be able to help them.

▶ Let the students share any experiences they have had that may be similar to what the pictures portray. Share from your own experience as well.

Sharing God's Love

We respect the elders in our community. They may have helped to take care of children, worked to help others, and know a lot about life. Some elderly people live alone. What can you do to show them that you love them and care for them?

It is no fun to be sick. Imagine if you were stuck in bed all day every day because you were too sick to get up. Some children are very sick for a long time. How can you help cheer them up?

Some families do not have the basic things they need. They do not have enough food, clothing, or even a place to live. Places like homeless shelters try to help families who are going through hard times. How can you help?

WE REACH OUT TO PEOPLE

Many people need our love and support. We can share what we have with people who are older, who are sick, and who are poor.

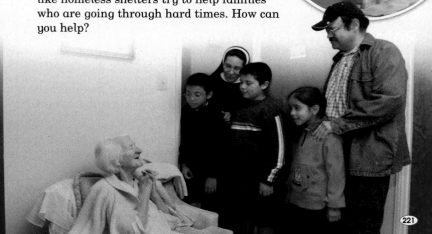

221

BACKGROUND: CATHOLIC SOCIAL TEACHING

Preferential Option for the Poor. Chapter 4 of the *Compendium of the Social Doctrine of the Church* (CSDC) teaches: "The principle of the universal destination of goods requires that the poor, the marginalized and in all cases those whose living conditions interfere with their proper growth should be the focus of particular concern. To this end, the preferential option for the poor should be reaffirmed in all its force. 'This is an option, or a special form of primacy in the exercise of Christian charity, to which the whole tradition of the Church bears witness' " (*CSDC*, 182).

Making Connections

Jesus told us that when we care for people who are elderly, sick, and homeless, we are caring for him. We are to share what we have with those who are in need.

with Math and Science

Your class is going to collect money to donate to the homeless shelter for families in your town. Use a chart to calculate how much your class collected in one week. Then estimate how much you can collect in four weeks.

with Language Arts

Think of someone you know that may be sick or find out the name of someone in your school who is sick. You can show you care by making a get-well card. Think about the picture and words you want on the outside cover. Inside, write a cheery message. Be sure to sign your name.

with Social Studies

Talk with your grandparents or neighbors who are elderly. Ask about what life was like when they were your age. Use a chart to help you find out what is the same between your life and their lives when they were young. Then find out what is different. Thank them for sharing their wisdom with you.

Faith Action

Show Jesus' love to those in need. Choose a project to do on your own to help someone who is elderly, who is sick, or who needs help. The project that I choose is _____
_____
_____.

222

TEACHING TIP

Choosing Activities, Extending Activities. You may wish to let the students choose which of the cross-curricular activities they want to do. Or, over a period of several weeks while you are studying the unit, they can complete all three. Contact the local hospital chaplain for names of children to whom your students can write. Challenge the class to collect money over the course of four weeks to donate to the local homeless shelter.

Catholic Social Teaching

Reinforce

Read aloud the introductory text on page 222 to the class.

Connect

Tell the students that they will explore some ways to show people that they care. Introduce the three cross-curricular activities. Invite and answer any questions the students might have. Ask the students to choose the activity or activities that they want to work on.

▶ **Math and Science:** Have the students make a simple chart listing the days Monday through Friday. Have them total the money collected in one week and then project an amount after four weeks.

▶ **Language Arts:** Distribute stiff paper and have the students fold the paper in half. Have them work with a partner to write and decorate the card.

▶ **Social Studies:** Help make a simple chart listing different categories (e.g., music, family, food, and so on). Show the students how to use the chart in order to compare an older person's experiences with their own. Have all the students work on the activity at home.

Choose

Invite the students to read the concluding paragraph silently. Then have them share with partners ideas on ways that they can show Christ's love to people in need.

Pray

Lead the students in praying the Lord's Prayer.

Unit 4 Review

The Unit Review provides the opportunity to assess the students' understanding of the concepts presented in the unit and to affirm them in their growing knowledge and love of God. Here are a few suggestions for using these pages.

▶ Share with the students that the next two pages are an opportunity to stop and review what they have learned.

▶ Provide time for the students to ask questions.

▶ Have the students complete the review alone or with a partner.

A. Choose the Best Word

This section reviews the main concepts of the unit.

▶ Read the directions for section A. Illustrate what you expect the student to do by completing the first question together. By working together on the first sentence, you are teaching the students a strategy for completing these types of sentences.

▶ When the students have finished this section, invite volunteers to share their answers. Review any sentence that the students seem to have difficulty completing.

B. Show What You Know

This section reinforces what the students have learned about Jesus.

▶ Read the directions to the students. Have the students complete the section.

▶ Invite volunteers to share their answers.

Unit 4 Review

Name _____

A. Choose the Best Word

Fill in the blanks to complete each of the sentences. Use the words from the word bank.

> Word   Mass   Amen   Last Supper   assembly

1. The ____Mass____ is the most important celebration of the Church.

2. We call the people God gathers to celebrate Mass the ____assembly____.

3. The Liturgy of the ____Word____ is the first main part of the Mass.

4. In the Liturgy of the Eucharist, the Church does what Jesus did at the ____Last Supper____.

5. When we receive the consecrated bread and wine in Holy Communion, we say, "____Amen____."

B. Show What You Know

Match the terms in Column A with their meaning in Column B.

Column A

1. The Introductory Rites
2. knowledge
3. Eucharist
4. Eucharistic Prayer
5. love

Column B

__3__ A. Sacrament of the Body and Blood of Christ.

__5__ B. the greatest of all virtues.

__1__ C. rites gather us and prepare us to worship God.

__2__ D. virtue that helps us to better hear and understand the meaning of God's Word.

__4__ E. Church's great prayer of thanksgiving.

223

TEACHING TIP

Selective Review. To use all sections of the unit review during class time may not be necessary and perhaps, depending on your circumstances, may not even be desirable. Choose one of the review sections to be completed at home. Send a note to encourage families to complete this section of the unit review along with the family take-home page. This selective review process can be a means of partnering with the parents to help their children grow and mature in their faith. Furthermore the families can use this unit review also as a faith-sharing tool.

C. Connect with Scripture

What was your favorite story about Jesus in this unit?
Draw something that happened in the story.
Tell your class about it.

D. Be a Disciple

1. *What Saint or holy person did you enjoy hearing about in this unit? Write the name here. Tell your class what this person did to follow Jesus.*

_____

_____

2. *What can you do to be a good disciple of Jesus?*

_____

_____

224

TEACHING TIP

Music Participation. As the time allows, contact your parish music director to find appropriate opportunities throughout the year to help the students learn the music for the upcoming Sunday Liturgy. This could help the students become more comfortable with the music, and encourage them to have a greater active participation in the Mass. This also could be an opportunity for the students to share with the parish music director appropriate songs that they would like to sing during Sunday liturgy.

C. Connect with Scripture

This section reinforces the students' experience and knowledge of Scripture and the teachings of Jesus.

▶ Help the students review the Scripture stories in the unit, beginning with the Unit Opener story. You may wish to write the names of these stories on the board to assist them.

▶ Ask volunteers to share their favorite stories with the class.

▶ In the space, invite the students to draw something that happened in the story. Invite volunteers to share their drawings now, or at the completion of the Unit Review.

D. Be a Disciple

This section provides the students with the opportunity to recall how the Saints and holy people followed Jesus. It reinforces the ways students can choose to live as disciples of Jesus.

▶ Ask the students to remember their favorite stories of Saints or holy people that they learned about in this unit. Refresh their memories as needed, and write their responses on the board.

▶ Give each student time to write the name of their favorite Saint or holy person on the line. Ask volunteers to share the reason for their choices.

▶ Lead a discussion about the actions that make us good disciples of Jesus. Give the students time to write on the lines their idea of what they could do.

We Live

Part One

Objectives

In Unit 5, the students will learn that:

▶ The Holy Spirit helps us to make choices to live as children of God.

▶ The Great Commandment is to love God above all else and to love others as we love ourselves.

▶ God gave us the Ten Commandments to teach us to live happy and holy lives.

▶ The Fourth through the Tenth Commandments teach us to love, honor, and respect other people and ourselves.

Spiritual Insights

"In Christ we have been called to a New Covenant and a New Law that fulfills and perfects the Old Law. We also are invited to experience God's love for us and to return that love to God and to our neighbor" (*United States Catholic Catechism for Adults,* page 325).

"Teacher, what good must I do to gain eternal life?"

Matthew 19:16

Living the Six Tasks of Catechesis

Education for Community Life: Blessed Peter To Rot (1912–1945)

Peter To Rot was born in Rakunai, a village in Papua, New Guinea. Peter's father was the chief of the village. He invited missionaries to preach the Word of God to his people. Soon after, Peter and his whole family were baptized.

When he was 18, Peter was chosen to be a catechist. He was sent to a mission school to learn how to teach the truths of the Catholic faith and lead prayer services.

Three years later, Peter became the chief catechist of his village. He was filled with joy as he helped others to know and love the Lord.

Peter married, and he and his wife had three children. Their lives were filled with love and service to God and their village. Their happiness was shattered in 1942, during World War II, when Japanese soldiers invaded their island. The priests were arrested, as was Peter. However, each time Peter was released he continued to teach, baptize, and lead Communion services with hosts consecrated by the priests in jail.

The Japanese tried to get the Christians to turn away from their faith. They passed a law saying that the people could return to the practice of polygamy, which allowed men to have more than one wife. Peter spoke out against polygamy, reminding people that marriage was a sacred vow between one man and one woman.

Peter was arrested for the last time. The Japanese authorities wanted to make an example of him. Peter knew he was going to be killed in prison. He asked his wife to bring him his best clothes so that he would be dressed properly when he met God face to face in Heaven.

Peter died as a martyr for the Catholic faith. We celebrate his feast day on July 7. Blessed Peter To Rot's life reminds us of our commitment as catechists to share our faith with the students we teach. We are called to build community among them and to prepare them to participate actively in the life and the mission of the Church.

Sharing Your Faith

Find a partner to work with: a spouse, a friend, a fellow teacher. Come together at the beginning or end of each unit for shared prayer and discussion. Use the questions below as a starting point. As an alternative, record your thoughts in a personal journal.

▶ How does your parish community help you to live your faith?

▶ In what ways do you demonstrate love for your neighbor on a regular basis?

▶ How do you put God first in your life?

Blessed by God

Jesus was a wonderful teacher. One day Jesus taught his followers eight special ways to live called the Beatitudes. *Beatitude* means "blessing."

Jesus told the crowds that God will bless, or take care of the people who have the most needs. He will also bless those who help others and care for them.

God's Kingdom will belong to those who do what is right.

Based on Matthew 5:3–10

225

What I Know

What is something you already know about these faith concepts?

Being Holy

_____

_____

Being Happy

_____

_____

Ten Commandments

_____

_____

*Put an **X** next to the faith words you know. Put a **?** next to the faith words you need to learn more about.*

_____ grace _____ courage _____ false witness

_____ honor _____ rabbi _____ justice

_____ Great Commandment

What do you know about the Golden Rule in the Bible?

_____

A Question I Have

What question would you like to ask about living the Ten Commandments?

_____

_____

226

Unit 5 Opener

The Unit 5 opener pages assess the children's prior knowledge about the key faith concepts in the unit. Processing these pages should take no more than fifteen minutes.

Opening Page

Invite the children to tell you what they see in the image on the page. Proclaim the Scripture story. Ask: Whom do you know who is like the people Jesus describes in the Bible? Accept their answers, but do not respond further at this time.

Getting Ready

This page continues the activation of prior knowledge. Do not correct the students' responses. You will invite them to return and correct themselves at the end of the unit.

▶ Have the students write their responses under What I Know and A Question I Have. You may also do the exercises orally.

▶ Record the students' questions on a chart. Refer back to the chart as you progress through the unit and ask volunteers to respond when they can answer the questions. You may also wish to use these questions during a unit assessment.

▶ Ask the students to turn to the next page and begin Chapter 17.

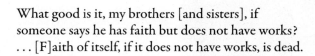

CHAPTER 7

BACKGROUND

Adopted Sons and Daughters of God

When we are baptized into Christ, we become adopted sons and daughters of God the Father. This adoption transforms us. We receive the gift of the Holy Spirit and the grace to live our new life in Christ. In union with Jesus and empowered by the Holy Spirit, we can love one another as Jesus commanded, live heartfelt lives of charity, and experience a peace unlike anything found in this world.

Recommit Daily

While we receive the grace to live our new life in Christ, we also need to accept that grace and respond to it. We have to freely choose to follow Christ. This is not a one- time decision. Choosing to follow Christ is a decision that must be made day in and day out, many times each day.

In which ways can we implement the daily decisions to live our new life in Christ? Saint Augustine of Hippo puts the answer in a nutshell, "Love and do what you like." When the love of God becomes so operative in our lives that all our thoughts and actions are rooted in his will, then we let that love be our guide. Not an easy task, but practice makes for perseverance.

Show Me!

We can utter lovely words about God and charity and our concern for the poor, but as Eliza Doolittle says to Henry Higgins in My Fair Lady, "Show me!" Saint James the Apostle taught the same. Unless our words are translated into practical, concrete actions, they have a hollow ring to them. The Letter to James admonishes,

> What good is it, my brothers [and sisters], if someone says he has faith but does not have works? . . . [F]aith of itself, if it does not have works, is dead.
>
> James 2:14–17

Grace Upon Grace

Our life in Christ must, of necessity, flow outward from us. The Sacraments strengthen us for living Jesus' New Commandment of love. The Holy Spirit lavishes grace upon us so that Christ's life will increase in us. What we do right here, right now, with whatever is in front of us, is the arena of grace. We are to live, as Christ taught, in the present moment (see John 13:34–35).

For Reflection

How convinced am I that when it comes to living the gift of faith in Christ, practice makes for perseverance?

In what situations do I find it most difficult for me to live the New Commandment of Jesus, "Love one another as I love you"?

Teacher to Teacher

Responsibility

Each day seven- and eight-year-olds are learning more and more about responsibility. They have a growing sense of the obligation to be responsible for themselves and for the choices they make. While this is certainly true at home and in school, it is also true in the Church. It is your responsibility to help the students learn that they need to become more aware that belonging to God's family also carries its own set of obligations and responsibilities.

Children of God

As these second graders learn more about how they are expected to live as children of God and followers of Jesus Christ, there is an underlying truth that needs always to be reinforced in their young minds and hearts. The students need to know and trust that God loves them completely, that he will always be there for them. An important place where they can learn this truth is in your classroom. Your encouragement and affirmation can be visible signs of God's love for them.

The Church Teaches...

"Life in Christ is a way of being, a way of loving. It is not a plan of action, even action on behalf of justice. Life in Christ shapes human beings anew and provides a new vital principle for all their activity. It is the radical integration of the person with Christ, the indwelling of Christ in the heart and soul of the Christian, a fusion of the Christian with the Son of God. 'Christ lives in me' is the singular confession of the Christian who has been led by God's grace and who trusts, at the deepest level of being, that true life comes only through the redemptive sacrifice of Jesus Christ" (*National Directory for Catechesis*, 46).

Reflect on this powerful statement from the Church and how it can help inspire you to help the students let Christ live in them.

Further Reading and Reflection

For more related teachings of the Church, see the *Catechism of the Catholic Church*, 1699–1756 and 1996–2016; and the *United States Catholic Catechism for Adults*, pages 307–309, 328–330.

Teacher Prayer

Lord God our loving Father, I am still learning and growing and striving to be the person you created me to be. Give me the strength and the courage to follow the example of Jesus, your Son, and with the help of the Holy Spirit to live my life as his companion. Amen.

Lesson Planner

Chapter 17   In God's Image

Goal   To learn more about what it means to live as children of God

LESSON PART	PROCESS	MATERIALS and RESOURCES
DAY 1 EXPLORE **Focus** To explore how followers of Jesus treat others **Pages** 227–229	▶ Proclaim and discuss 1 John 3:1 (We are children of God). ▶ Learn and discuss the story of Saint Therese of Lisieux (Saint Therese of the Child Jesus). **Disciple Power:** Kindness **Activity:** Choose acts of kindness for the week and draw one of them.	Bible Pencils or pens Drawing paper
DAY 2 DISCOVER **Focus** To discover that we are honored and blessed as children of God **Pages** 230–231	▶ Discover that God created every person in his image and likeness. **Catholics Believe:** Fruits of the Holy Spirit **Scripture:** We are created in God's Image (Genesis 1:27–28); The Lord blesses us with glory and honor (Psalm 8:6); Jesus and the children (Matthew 18:1–4) **Activity:** Act out a scene with Jesus and the children.	Bible Pencil or pens **Enriching the Lesson:** Teacher Guide, page 341 Pantomiming Acts of Kindness
DAY 3 DISCOVER **Focus** To discover what we must do to live as children of God **Pages** 232–233	▶ Discover that Jesus is our Teacher. **Scripture:** I am the way, the truth, and the life (John 14:6). **Faith Words:** honor **Faith-Filled People:** Saint Teresa of Jesus **Activity:** Follow the path to Jesus.	Bibles Pencils or pens **Additional Activities Booklet** Activities 17a and 17b or see *BeMyDisciples*.com
DAY 4 DECIDE **Focus** To discover the importance of the concluding procession and to decide on a way to show an act of kindness **Pages** 234–235	▶ Discover the importance of making good choices. **Faith Words:** grace **Activity:** Write words and acts of kindness. **My Faith Choice:** Choose a way to surprise someone with an act of kindness.	Pencil or pens **Enriching the Lesson:** Teacher Guide, page 341 Creating a Picture Story about Choices Literature Connection: *For the Children: Words of Love and Inspiration from His Holiness Pope John Paul II*
DAY 5 CONCLUDE **Focus** To realize that we can ask God to bless us and help us live as his children **Pages** 236–238	▶ **REVIEW** Review concepts: Recall, Reflect, and Share. ▶ **PRAY** May God Bless Us ▶ **Preview** the With My Family page and the theme of the next chapter.	Bible, candle, cross for prayer space Grade 2 Music CD **Assessment Tools Booklet:** Assessments 17a and 17b

Assign online Chapter Review and interactive Chapter Test at **BeMyDisciples.com**

Chapter **17**

In God's Image

? Who are some of the people who love you? What are some of the ways they show you they love you?

Listen to find out how much God loves you:

See how very much God the Father loves us. He calls us his own children!

BASED ON 1 JOHN 3:1

? What do you think it means that God calls you his child?

(227)

HUMAN METHODOLOGIES

Making a Commitment to Live the Christian Life. The *National Directory for Catechesis* points out that, "(T)he faithful actively respond to God's loving initiative through . . . living the Christian life" (*NDC*, 29G). Encourage the students to share the Good News that they learn about Jesus in this chapter by making "I am the way, the truth, and the life" bookmarks using index card strips and markers. Have them name the person to whom they will give the bookmark. Motivate the students to share with the recipient that the bookmark reminds us that Jesus is our Teacher and that following him leads us to God.

Pray

▶ Welcome the students warmly. Have them quiet themselves for prayer.

▶ Begin and end with the Sign of the Cross.

▶ Ask the students to echo these words:

Father, / thank you /
for creating us in your
image and likeness. / Amen.

Reflect

▶ Ask the opening questions. *(Accept all replies.)*

▶ Invite the students to listen carefully to find out just how much God loves us.

▶ Read aloud the passage from 1 John 3:1.

▶ Afterward, observe a moment of silence.

▶ Invite responses to the Scripture question. *(Accept all replies.)*

▶ Have the children examine the photograph. Ask: Who is the child of God in this photo? *(Both the child and the adult are children of God.)*

Focus

▶ Invite the students to turn the page to discover someone who did her very best to live always as a child of God.

Introduce

▶ Encourage the students to tell what they might know about Saint Thérèse of the Child Jesus.

▶ Invite the students to read about kindness in Disciple Power. Ask the students to share about a time when someone was kind to them.

▶ Share with the students that they will hear about the kindness of Saint Thérèse in the story.

▶ Call on different students to read aloud the story of Saint Thérèse. Invite the students to explain in their own words why they think Saint Thérèse was named a Saint by the Church. *(Her "little" good deeds and her kindness are an important example to us.)*

Reinforce

Read aloud the follow-up question. Discuss the "little" good deeds and kindnesses that people do each day to show respect for God, themselves, and others. Share how each shows honor and respect for God and for people.

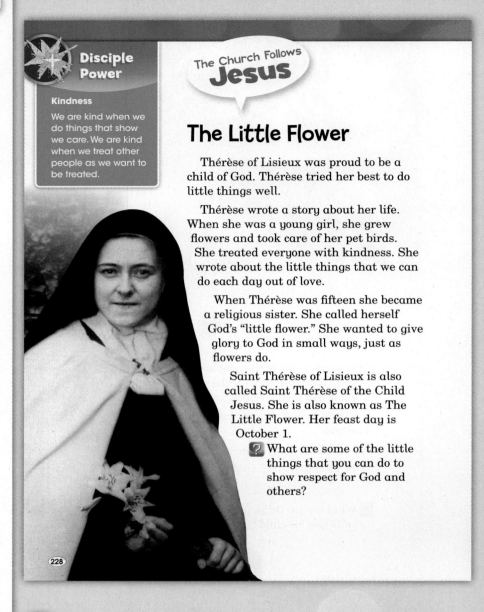

Disciple Power

Kindness

We are kind when we do things that show we care. We are kind when we treat other people as we want to be treated.

The Church Follows **Jesus**

The Little Flower

Thérèse of Lisieux was proud to be a child of God. Thérèse tried her best to do little things well.

Thérèse wrote a story about her life. When she was a young girl, she grew flowers and took care of her pet birds. She treated everyone with kindness. She wrote about the little things that we can do each day out of love.

When Thérèse was fifteen she became a religious sister. She called herself God's "little flower." She wanted to give glory to God in small ways, just as flowers do.

Saint Thérèse of Lisieux is also called Saint Thérèse of the Child Jesus. She is also known as The Little Flower. Her feast day is October 1.

❓ What are some of the little things that you can do to show respect for God and others?

228

DISCIPLE POWER

Kindness. Kindness is a Fruit of the Holy Spirit, a sign that the Spirit is helping us live our Catholic faith. Before the session, write descriptions on slips of paper of everyday situations to which the students can respond with kindness. If you wish, simply draw on the list of "little kindnesses" on page 229. Place the slips in a small box and invite a volunteer to draw a slip of paper from a box. Read the situation aloud. Encourage the students to act out how they can respond to the situation with kindness. Your second graders will enjoy taking turns dramatizing the situations in different ways. Recall that Saint Thérèse did her best to show her love for God by being kind to everyone. Conclude the activity by reminding the students that Jesus' friends act with kindness.

Activity

Little Kindnesses

Saint Thérèse of the Child Jesus knew that the little kindnesses we do matter. Look at the many little kindnesses. Choose a different one to do each day this week. Check the ones you choose.

- ❏ Tell your parents you love them.
- ❏ Smile at everyone today.
- ❏ Bring one of your toys to a homeless shelter.
- ❏ Do a chore without being asked.
- ❏ Let your brother or sister play with your toys.
- ❏ Make and send a card to a friend.
- ❏ Sing someone a song.
- ❏ Pick up litter.
- ❏ Forgive someone who has hurt you.
- ❏ Tell a joke.
- ❏ Give a hug.
- ❏ Surprise someone with a little gift.
- ❏ Be polite.
- ❏ Make someone laugh.
- ❏ Offer to help at home or at school.
- ❏ Tell someone, "You're doing great!"

(229)

Connect

▶ Read the activity directions. Then read through each of the suggestions.

▶ Give the students time to check their choices.

▶ Distribute drawing paper. Tell the students they will draw themselves doing one of the acts of kindnesses they checked.

▶ Canvass the room to discover which act each student wants to illustrate. If you have sixteen or more students in your class, see if you can have all of the acts illustrated.

▶ Give the students time to complete their drawings.

▶ Collect and post the art work around the classroom.

▶ Tell the students that their class is now surrounded by kindness.

Pray

Gather the students for prayer. Have them echo the following after you.

> Father, / we are your children. /
> Teach us how much /
> all the little things matter. /
> Show us the way / of
> kindness and love. /
> Amen.

TEACHING TIP

Good Manners. While you are discussing acts of kindness, remind the students that good manners are ways of being kind. Encourage the students to remember the value of using such words as "please" and "thank you." Ask the students if they have noticed that teachers and parents listen more carefully when they speak politely. Extend this teaching by further reminding the students that good manners can also be shown in church when they take part in Mass. By acting respectfully while at Mass, the students are showing honor and respect to God, who is present among them.

> **Key Concept**
> Jesus teaches us to honor all people as God's children.

Pray

Lead the students in the prayer with which you closed the previous lesson.

Teach

▶ Read the Faith Focus question aloud. Share with the students that in this chapter they will learn that as God's children, created in his image, we are honored and blessed.

▶ Have the students read aloud the Faith Word *honor* and its meaning. Talk about people in their own lives whom they honor and respect.

▶ Ask a volunteer to read the We Are Holy opening paragraph and passage from Genesis. Stress what an honor it is to be made in God's own image.

▶ Have the students stand and read the quote from the Book of Psalms aloud.

▶ Have the class remain standing. Ask the girls to read aloud the next paragraph about our being holy.

▶ Ask the boys to read the final paragraph on the page, which speaks to God honoring us by making us his children.

▶ Call attention to the section titled Jesus and the Children on page 231. Have the students sit and listen for how God honors us as you read the paragraph and the passage from the Gospel of Matthew.

Faith Focus
How are we honored and blessed by God?

Faith Words
honor
To honor someone is to treat them with kindness, respect, and love.

We Are Holy

The Bible teaches that God creates us to be holy and gives every person a great **honor**. To honor someone is to treat that person with kindness, respect, and love. The first book of the Bible says:

> God created man in his image;
>   in the divine image he created him;
>   male and female he created them.
> God blessed them, . . .
>
> GENESIS 1:27–28

The Book of Psalms sings of this honor and blessing.

> You have blessed us, O Lord, with glory and honor.
>
> BASED ON PSALM 8:6

We are holy because we are made in God's image. We are called to be like God who is holy.

We are honored because God shares his life with us. We are blessed to be God's own children.

❓ As God's children, how are we to honor God?

230

FAITH WORDS

Honor. From the Latin *honos*, the word *honor* is both a reference to someone of high esteem and deserving of recognition, as well as a way to show respect for someone whose worth is deserving of attention. The Fourth Commandment asks us to honor our mother and father. This means we are called to treat our parents with respect and kindness and to love them. Those who are married are also called to honor their spouse with love, respect, and commitment. The Great Commandment calls us to honor God by loving him with our whole being.

Jesus and the Children

Jesus taught us to honor God, ourselves, and other people. He taught us to treat people with kindness, respect, and love. Jesus taught us to honor all people as children of God.

Jesus' disciples were wondering who would be the greatest in heaven. So Jesus picked up a little child and said to his disciples, "Become like this child and love God as this child loves him. If you do, God will welcome you into heaven."

BASED ON MATTHEW 18:1–4

Catholics Believe

Fruits of the Holy Spirit

The Bible names some signs that show when we are trying to live as children of God. Three of these signs are joy, generosity, and kindness. We call these signs Fruits of the Holy Spirit.

Activity Imagine that you are one of the children in the picture. Act out the scene with a partner. Write what you would say to Jesus.

(231)

CATHOLIC DOCTRINE

We Are All Children of God. It is important that students come to value themselves and all people as children of God. God created every person in his image and likeness. God lives among us and within us. That is the foundation of the dignity of every person. Jesus taught that when we reach out and help our neighbors, we are reaching out and helping him. Help the students brainstorm ways that they can reach out to others.

Reinforce

▶ Ask the follow-up question. *(We honor God by treating others with kindness, respect, and love.)*

▶ Have the students make a word card for *honor* using the definition in Faith Words.

Read aloud Catholics Believe. Explain that the Fruits of the Holy Spirit are signs that show others we are living as children of God.

Connect

▶ Invite the students to draw themselves in the picture of Jesus and the little child and then to add a word bubble where they can write what they would like to say to Jesus.

▶ Invite the students to share their drawing and what they wrote with a partner.

Pray

▶ Gather the students for prayer. Point out the pictures of kindnesses from the last session posted around the room, reminding the children how kindness surrounds them.

▶ Invite the students to echo the following prayer:

Father of all kindness, /
you have made us in your
    holy image. /
You honor us by calling us
    your own. /
Help us follow Jesus your Son. /
Show us the way / to be
blest children of God. /
Amen.

Pray

Gather the students for prayer. Remind them that they are all children of God. Lead them in praying the Lord's Prayer.

Teach

▶ Read the Faith Focus question aloud and ask for possible answers. Remind the students that Jesus teaches us to honor all people as children of God. Tell them they are going to learn more about Jesus the Teacher.

▶ Ask the students to describe what teachers do. (*Affirm appropriate responses.*) Then ask, How do you learn from teachers? (*watching, listening*)

▶ Invite the class to listen as you read aloud Jesus Is Our Teacher on pages 232 and 233.

▶ Have the students find and highlight what Jesus told his disciples about himself.

Faith Focus
How did Jesus teach us to live as children of God?

Jesus Is Our Teacher

The disciples of Jesus honored him in many ways. They honored and respected him as their teacher. In Jesus' time to call someone "Teacher" was a sign of great honor and respect.

Everything Jesus said and did gave honor to his Father. Jesus' disciples listened to him carefully. They did as he said. They believed that Jesus would teach them how to live as children of God.

The disciples learned from Jesus. He taught them about himself:

"I am the way and the truth and the life.

JOHN 14:6

Jesus taught the disciples that he would lead them to God. Jesus will lead us to God.

❓ What does Jesus teach us how to do?

232

TEACHING TIP

Accepting Others. Most students are very accepting of others. We can use this opportunity to point out that differences are to be enjoyed and celebrated. It is important to reinforce that God made all people in his image and likeness, and he loves all people equally. As children of God, we are called to love and respect all others. Organize a class affirmation party. Write the name of each student on a card and place it in a basket. Ask each student to draw a name and then write on the card a gift or talent he or she sees in that student. Place all the cards back in the basket. Once again, ask each student to draw a card, say the name on the card aloud, and then read the words of the affirmation to the class.

Jesus is our Teacher too. He is the way, the truth, and the life. We listen to him. We learn from him. We try our best to live as Jesus taught.

 Why do you think Jesus is our teacher too?

Faith-Filled People

Saint Teresa of Jesus

Teresa of Ávila lived in Spain. The Church honors her as one of the Doctors of the Church. This means that the Church honors her as a great teacher of the faith. The Church celebrates Saint Teresa of Jesus' feast day on October 15.

 Activity

Following Jesus

Follow each path to Jesus. Ask Jesus to teach you to live as a child of God.

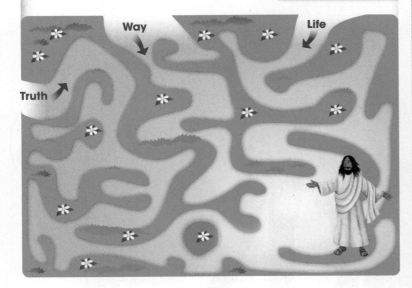

(233)

Reinforce

▶ Ask the follow-up question. Accept replies that evidence an understanding that Jesus teaches us how to live.

▶ Invite the students to memorize the words "I am the way and the truth and the life" (John 14:6).

▶ Read aloud Faith-Filled People. Tell the children about Saint Teresa of Jesus, a great teacher of the Church.

Connect

▶ Have the students look at the maze. Explain that each path leads to Jesus. Tell the students to follow each path to Jesus.

▶ When the students finish, remind them that they are children of God. We follow the *way* of Jesus our Teacher. We who seek to learn his *truth*. And we try to live the life he teaches us to live.

Pray

Invite the students to quiet themselves for prayer. Lead them in praying A Vocation Prayer on page 369 of the student book.

FAITH-FILLED PEOPLE

Saint Teresa of Jesus (1515–1582). Teresa of Jesus' life was marked by great independence and energy. She saw her life as a never-ending spiritual journey to grow in faith and closeness to God. Although ill for long periods, she was an optimist who lived life to the fullest. Saint Teresa was the first woman to be honored as a Doctor of the Church, a person officially acknowledged by the Church as an accomplished teacher because of her tremendous insight and wisdom into the faith. Saint Teresa of Jesus (also known as Saint Teresa of Ávila) is the patron Saint of Spain.

Key Concept
Jesus calls us—and the Holy Spirit helps us—to make good choices.

Pray
Lead the class in praying the Sign of the Cross.

Teach

▶ Read the Faith Focus question aloud. Tell the students that today's lesson will help them learn that we show we are God's children by making good choices.

▶ Invite the students to name some of the choices they make every day. Point out that some choices are more important than others.

▶ Read aloud the first two paragraphs of Making Good Choices. Tell the class to listen to find out what making good choices shows others.

▶ Invite the students to read the third paragraph silently and to underline the sentence that tells what grace means.

Reinforce

▶ Read the follow-up questions to the students. Invite them to share their responses with a partner.

▶ Point out the definition of *grace* in Faith Words. Have the children make a word card for the term.

Faith Focus
How do we show we are children of God?

Faith Words
grace
Grace is the gift of God sharing his life with us. It is also God helping us to make good choices to live as children of God.

Making Good Choices

Jesus taught us how to make good choices. We show that we are proud to be children of God when we make good choices. We show that we are proud and honored to call Jesus "Teacher."

We live as children of God when we make good choices. We show that we are trying our best to live as children of God. We grow in kindness. We love God, ourselves, and other people as Jesus did.

God the Holy Spirit helps us to make good choices. He gives us his **grace**, or help, to make good choices. When we make good choices, we grow as children of God.

❓ Who has helped you make good choices to live as a child of God? Have you helped others?

234

THE TASKS OF CATECHESIS

Promoting Knowledge of the Faith. The *Catechism of the Catholic Church* teaches us that grace is a free gift from God that could never be earned. Through grace we are able to respond to God's call to be his children and to live forever with him. We can talk about God's grace in several ways. Sanctifying grace is what is called a habitual grace, because it disposes us to live in harmony with God and for others. God also intervenes in the course of our lives through what are called actual graces. The Holy Spirit offers us these graces to empower us to make good choices (see *Catechism of the Catholic Church*, 1996–2000).

The Holy Spirit helps you to make choices. He helps you to be kind. He helps you be fair. When you are kind and fair, you show that you are proud to be a child of God.

I Follow Jesus

Activity

Living as a Child of God

Write some words of kindness that you say. Then write acts of kindness that you do to show that you are a child of God.

Words 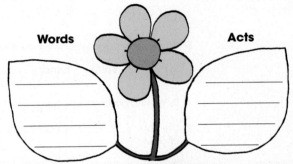 **Acts**

My Faith Choice

This week, I will surprise someone with this act of kindness. I will

_____

_____

 Pray, "Father, thank you for loving me so much. Help me with your grace to make good choices. Help me to grow as your child. Amen."

(235)

Reinforce

Remind the students that the Holy Spirit gives us the grace to make good choices each day. Point out that by making choices to live as Jesus taught, we are living as children of God.

Respond

▶ Brainstorm with the students some of the choices that they can make to show others that they are children of God. List the choices in two separate columns on the board labeled "Words" and "Acts."

▶ Invite the students to write their own choices in their books. Tell them that they may use some of the examples listed on the board.

Choose

▶ Invite the students to read My Faith Choice and write their decisions.

▶ Encourage everyone to put their choices into practice this week.

Pray

Point out the prayer at the bottom of the page. Invite the students to silently pray the prayer.

TEACHING TIP

Models. It is profoundly essential for students to have models of faith and morals as a consistent part of their lives. The media and the secular community often bombard our students with ideas that are contrary to our Christian values. Have the students create a special report about someone who helps them to make good choices as a child of God. Have them create a one-page paper telling why their chosen person is special and how that person helps them to make good choices. Encourage the students to include pictures of this person in their report. If time permits, have the students share their work with the class.

Pray

Gather the children for prayer to begin class. Have them echo the following:

Come, Holy Spirit, /
be with your children. /
Help us choose always /
how best to follow Jesus. /
Amen.

Recall

▶ Write the words *respected, Jesus,* and *choices* on the board. Tell the students that each of these words was an important word in today's lesson.

▶ Read aloud the To Help You Remember statements, leaving out the words *respected, Jesus,* and *choices.* Ask volunteers to guess the missing words.

▶ Introduce the circling activity, and allow the class sufficient time to complete it.

▶ Afterward, check responses.

▶ Introduce the sentence completion activity. Give the class time to complete it.

▶ Afterward, ask volunteers to read the completed sentences aloud.

Reflect

Give the students a few moments to complete the reflection statement.

Share

▶ Canvass the room for responses to the statement.

▶ Encourage the children to share their reflections with their families.

▶ **TO HELP YOU REMEMBER**

1. All people are to be honored and respected. God has created everyone to be a child of God.

2. Jesus taught that we are to live as children of God.

3. The Holy Spirit helps us to make choices to live as children of God.

Chapter Review

Recall

Find and circle the words hidden in the puzzle.

respect	kindness	good	love
follow	choices	honor	faith

R E S P E C T L K I N D N E S S
O F O L L O W P N Z T F A I T H
C H O I C E S T R W L O V E P T
Y H O N O R L I G O O D R W Z A

Finish the sentences below with the following words.

Spirit   honor

1. By making good choices we ___honor___ God.

2. The Holy ___Spirit___ helps us to make wise choices.

Reflect

What are the ways you will choose to live as a child of God? Use the words from the puzzle to help you decide.

_____

_____

Share Write down an act of kindness you will do for a friend or family member this week.

(236)

TEACHING TIP

Review Story. Have the students write a short story about someone who lives his or her life as a child of God. Challenge the students to use the words from the word bank in the We Recall activities. When they have completed their stories, ask volunteers to share their work with the class. Have the students read the To Help You Remember statements to see if the story portrayed the key concepts.

May God Bless Us

Pray this prayer to ask God to bless your class.
Ask him to help you live as children of God.

Leader   Father, we ask your blessing on us.

All   **Father, we are your children.**

Leader   Guide us to choose what is good and to do your will.

All   **Father, we are your children.**

Leader   *(Ask each child to come forward for a blessing. Place a hand on the child's head.)* May God bless you and keep you.

All   **Amen.**

Leader   Together, let us pray that we may live as children of God.

All   **Yes or no?**
Stay or go?
Will or won't?
Do or don't?
Choose what's best
And we'll be blest.
Make good choices.
God rejoices!

(237)

We Pray

▶ Tell the students that they are going to pray a blessing prayer together.

▶ Explain how the students will come forward to you for a blessing. Demonstrate with one of the children.

▶ Practice the responses.

▶ Gather the class in the prayer center. Consider processing there with music and/or song.

▶ Lead the students in the prayer.

LITURGY CONNECTION

Blessings. Asking for God's blessing can be very powerful. This form of prayer strengthens us in times of illness or stress. It unites God's family and sends us forth to do God's work of treating others with respect and dignity. Include prayers asking for God's blessing as a regular part of each lesson. Remember that by virtue of your Baptism, you may bless the students. You can bless them individually by tracing the Sign of the Cross on their foreheads and saying, "May God bless you (name)" at the end of each school day.

Preview

▶ Have the students carefully tear out pages 237 and 238 along the perforation.

▶ Encourage the students to share these pages with their families, and to complete the activities together.

▶ If they did not complete the review activity on page 236 by the end of the session, emphasize that they can complete it with their families at home.

▶ Point out the title and theme of the next lesson to the students.

Visit BeMyDisciples.com

▶ Take time with the students to explore the many activities and resources available at the *Be My Disciples* Web site.

▶ Encourage them to join with their families to discover the many resources available at the Web site.

Before Moving On ...

As you finish today's lesson, reflect on the following question before moving on to the next chapter.

How much effort do I make to reinforce and summarize before moving on to a new concept?

With My Family

This Week . . .

In Chapter 17, "In God's Image," your child learned:

▶ We are to honor and respect all people. Every person has the dignity of being a child of God, because we are created in the image and likeness of God.

▶ Jesus is our Teacher. He showed us how to live as children of God. He said, "I am the way and the truth, and the life. I will lead you to God" (Based on John 14:6).

▶ We honor and respect Jesus as our Teacher when we try our best to live as he taught.

▶ We grow in the virtue of kindness when we try to have all our words and actions show respect for God, for other people, and for ourselves.

For more about related teachings of the Church, see the *Catechism of the Catholic Church*, 1699–1756 and 1996–2016, and the *United States Catholic Catechism for Adults*, pages 307–309, 324–331, 351–354.

■ Sharing God's Word

Read together Mark 10:13–16, "Jesus and the Children." Emphasize that Jesus taught us to love God as children do and to respect all people as children of God.

■ Living as Disciples

The Christian home and family form a school of discipleship. Choose one of the following activities to do as a family, or design a similar activity of your own.

▶ Notice when your child makes good choices. Compliment him or her and point out how the Church helps us make good choices. Praise your child for trying his or her best to live as Jesus taught.

▶ Saint Thérèse of the Child Jesus focused on doing the little things in life out of love. Decide together how your family can live this week as Saint Thérèse did and do the kind things, that are part of daily life, out of love.

■ Our Spiritual Journey

The *Story of a Soul*, the autobiography of Saint Thérèse of the Child Jesus reveals to us the depth of her spirituality. Her childlike simplicity is appealing to young children. Pray these words from a poem of Saint Thérèse this week: "Come reign within my heart, smile tenderly on me, today, dear Lord, today."

For more ideas on ways your family can live as disciples of Jesus, visit **BeMyDisciples.com**

(238)

ENRICHING THE LESSON

Picture Stories. As an alternative to having the students create a picture story about choices, invite them to create flannel board stories, using contemporary flannel figures. Second graders enjoy working with manipulative resources, and this is a wonderful option for students who do not like to draw. Divide the class into several small groups and have them work together to create their "Proud to Be a Child of God" stories. Have them use the format suggested in the directions on the Enrichment page. Ask each group to display and tell its completed flannel board story to the class.

Enriching the Lesson

Pantomiming Acts of Kindness

Purpose

To reinforce that to honor someone is to treat him or her with kindness, respect, and love (taught on pages 230–231)

Directions

▶ In small groups, have the students discuss some of the ways that they show kindness and respect to others.

▶ Have them select one of the ways that they named and pantomime it.

▶ Invite the students to present their pantomimes, and have the other students title each pantomime after it is presented.

Materials

Creating a Picture Story About Choices

Purpose

To reinforce that when we make choices to live as Jesus taught, we are trying our best to live as children of God (taught on pages 234–235)

Directions

▶ Draw three boxes on the board, labeling them "Problem," "Choice," and "Consequences."

▶ Invite the students to create a picture story by drawing three boxes on their papers. Have them include dialogue bubbles that illustrate what the people in each picture are saying.

▶ Tell the students that the first box should depict a problem. The second box should tell the choice being made to solve the problem. The third box relates the consequences of the choice. Have the students title their stories "Proud to Be a Child of God."

▶ Display the students' work.

Materials

construction paper

crayons or markers

pencils or pens

Literature Connection

Purpose

To reinforce the importance of making good choices (taught on page 235)

Directions

You might wish to obtain a copy of *For the Children: Words of Love and Inspiration from His Holiness Pope John Paul II* (Scholastic, 2000) and read a selection to the students from time to time. In this beautifully produced book, the Pope challenges the children of the world to be full participants in their Christian faith and to make the best possible choices. The book is lavishly illustrated with photographs of the Pope with children, many of whom are dressed in their national costumes.

▶ Read a selection to the students and show them the accompanying pictures.

▶ Invite the students to brainstorm various ways to respond to the Pope's challenge. Which faith choice could they make?

Materials

For the Children: Words of Love and Inspiration from His Holiness Pope John Paul II

BACKGROUND

The Great Commandment

The Great Commandment stands at the center of living the gift of faith. It was at the center of the Law of the Old Covenant. It is at the center of living the New Covenant, life in Christ.

"Teacher, which commandment in the law is the greatest?" [Jesus] said to him, "You shall love the Lord, your God, with all your heart, with all your soul, and with all your mind. This is the greatest and the first commandment. The second is like it: You shall love your neighbor as yourself. The whole law and the prophets depend on these two commandments."

Matthew 22:36–40

How Do We Keep It?

Practically speaking, how do we keep the two parts of this Commandment at the center of living our new life in Christ? We can gain an insight into the answer to this question by exploring how we don't keep it.

Caught up in the demands of their busy schedules, many people go about their daily chores with little reference to God. Their hearts, souls, and minds are focused on other more immediate concerns, such as paying bills, raising children, and a seemingly endless round of daily errands.

Should we simply drop these responsibilities and sit in watchful attendance with God? Of course not! The art of Christian living involves integrating our love of God into the activities of the day. It involves placing God at the center of our lives, or allowing God to take center stage.

The Art of Christian Living

Christian living involves working on developing good habits, especially the good habit of setting a deliberate, daily place for God at the tables of our lives. For example, we can regularly include morning prayer and evening prayer in our daily schedule; we can take part in the celebration of Mass not only on Sunday but also on weekdays; we can pray a short prayer upon entering our car or when we make a phone call. In other words, we decide upon and put into action a few appropriate and practical resolutions to allow God some elbow room in our everyday existence. Eventually, all of these actions will become good habits, or virtues.

To live the Great Commandment of love requires attentiveness. It requires a period of concentration which, over time, evolves into a natural rhythm and oneness with God. Over time, expressing our love for God and for others will become as natural as breathing and will become a spontaneous part of living our life in Christ.

For Reflection

How can I integrate attentiveness to God in my daily routine?

What are some of the things I can do to develop a natural rhythm for living the Great Commandment?

Teacher to Teacher

As We Love Ourselves

By age seven or eight, most students can talk about what it means to love God and to love their neighbor. As you help them develop their understanding of the Great Commandment, spend some time helping them better appreciate the concept of love of self. This is a part of the Great Commandment that often goes untreated—God calls us to love and respect ourselves.

The Importance of a Positive Self-Image

Some students and many adults as well have a difficult time really loving themselves. At this young age self-image and feelings of self-worth are continuing to develop. How you treat each student in your care will have a definite influence on how lovable and capable they believe themselves to be.

The Church Teaches...

"Catechesis gives form to the missionary preaching that is intended to arouse the first signs of faith . . . The Church depends on an effective catechesis to be faithful to Christ's command to proclaim the Gospel . . . (The Church also provides) the point of welcome for those who seek to know the Lord" (*National Directory for Catechesis*, 19C).

In this chapter, the students will explore the importance of the Church for their growth in faith. The students will learn that God's law, particularly as expressed in the Great Commandment, is the foundation for living together as his people.

Further Reading and Reflection

For more related teachings of the Church, see the *Catechism of the Catholic Church*, 2052–2055, 2083, and 2196; and the *United States Catholic Catechism for Adults*, pages 307–309.

Teacher Prayer

Lord, I have known the Great Commandment since I was a child. Help me be aware of my actions and reactions as I strive to live by the Law of Love. Amen.

Lesson Planner

Chapter 18   We Live as Children of God

(Goal) To learn more about the Great Commandment as the greatest commandment

LESSON PART	PROCESS	MATERIALS and RESOURCES
DAY 1 **EXPLORE** (Focus) **To explore how followers of Jesus live as children of God** **Pages** 239–241	▶ Proclaim and discuss Psalm 25 (Teach me how to live, Lord). ▶ Learn and discuss the story of Blessed Pedro Calungsod. **Disciple Power:** Fortitude **Activity:** Write the name of someone who teaches you and what that person teaches.	Bible Pencils or pens Drawing paper
DAY 2 **DISCOVER** (Focus) **To discover what sort of teacher Jesus was** **Pages** 242–243	▶ Discover that Jesus was a teacher who taught with the authority of God. **Catholics Believe:** The Cross **Faith Words:** rabbi **Scripture:** Whoever has seen me sees the Father (John 14:9); Love your enemies (Matthew 5:43–44); Jesus taught with authority from God (John 7:16). **Activity:** Solve a puzzle to learn what Jesus teaches	Bible Pencil or pens
DAY 3 **DISCOVER** (Focus) **To discover what the Great Commandment helps us to do** **Pages** 244–245	▶ Learn about the Great Commandment. ▶ Hear the Scripture story about Jesus announcing the Great Commandment **Scripture:** The Greatest Commandment (Matthew 22:36–40) **Faith Words:** Great Commandment **Faith-Filled People:** Saint Peter **Activity:** List ways to live the two parts of the Great Commandment.	Bibles Pencils or pens **Enriching the Lesson:** Teacher Guide, page 357 Literature Connection: *The Paper Dragon*
DAY 4 **DECIDE** (Focus) **To discover the importance of the concluding procession and to decide on a way to show an act of kindness** **Pages** 246–247	▶ Learn that the Great Commandment sums up all of God's laws. **Activity:** Draw two pictures and create role-plays to tell what the Great Commandment means. **My Faith Choice:** Choose a way to show fortitude and live the Great Commandment.	Pencil or pens **Enriching the Lesson:** Teacher Guide, page 357 • Art Activity: The Great Commandment • Making Prayer Stones **Additional Activities Booklet:** Activities 18a–b or see *BeMyDisciples*.com
DAY 5 **CONCLUDE** (Focus) **To realize that God is with us all day long and we can take time each day to be with him** **Pages** 248–250	▶ **REVIEW** Review concepts: Recall, Reflect, and Share. ▶ **PRAY** An Act of Love ▶ **Preview** the With My Family page and the theme of the next chapter.	Bible, candle, cross for prayer space Grade 2 Music CD **Assessment Tools Booklet:** Assessments 18a and 18b

Assign online Chapter Review and interactive Chapter Test at **BeMyDisciples.com**

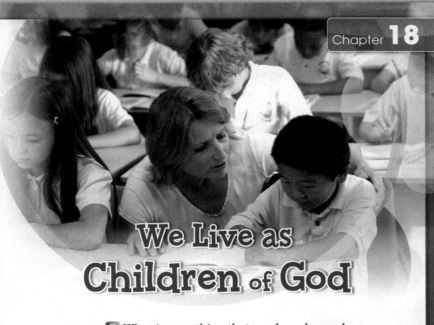

Chapter **18**

We Live as Children of God

? What is something that you have learned from a teacher?

Here is a prayer from the Bible. Listen carefully to what the person is asking God:

Make known to me your ways, LORD;
teach me your paths.
Guide me in your truth and teach me,
for you are God my savior.

PSALM 25:4–5a

? What would you like to ask God to teach you?

(239)

Pray

▶ Welcome the students warmly. Have them quiet themselves for prayer.

▶ Begin and end with the Sign of the Cross.

▶ Pray aloud:
Lord Jesus, teach us to live in your love. Amen.

Reflect

▶ Ask the students to examine the picture on the page and then to respond to the opening question. *(Accept all replies.)*

▶ Ask one of the students to read the passage from Psalm 25.

▶ Afterward, observe a moment of silence. Invite responses to the Scripture question. If you wish, record responses on the board.

▶ Conclude the prayer with the Sign of the Cross.

Focus

▶ Direct the students to turn the page to learn about a young person who taught others how to live as children of God.

HUMAN METHODOLOGIES

Learning Through the Witness of the Catechist. The *National Directory for Catechesis* states that "catechists powerfully influence those being catechized by their faithful proclamation of the Gospel and the transparent example of their Christian lives" (*NDC*, 29E). As you teach your second graders the Great Commandment, bear in mind that they will look to you to see how you show love, honor, and respect for God and others. You are a role model in how faith is meant to be lived for each of the students. Remember that your actions often speak louder than your words.

Introduce

▶ Call attention to Disciple Power and present the information on the virtue of fortitude. Ask the students to tell why someone who wants to teach others about God might need to practice fortitude. *(Accept all appropriate responses.)*

▶ Write the word *missionary* on the board. See if the students can recall what a missionary is. *(A missionary is a messenger for God, someone the Church calls and sends to share the message of Jesus with others—from Chapter 16.)* Tell the students that they are going to be reading a story about a missionary.

▶ Call on different students to read Saint Pedro.

Reinforce

▶ Have the students tell why Pedro was a missionary teacher.

▶ Call attention to the follow-up question and have the students explain how Pedro had fortitude.

▶ Invite the students to tell about a time when they did their best to do what was right and good.

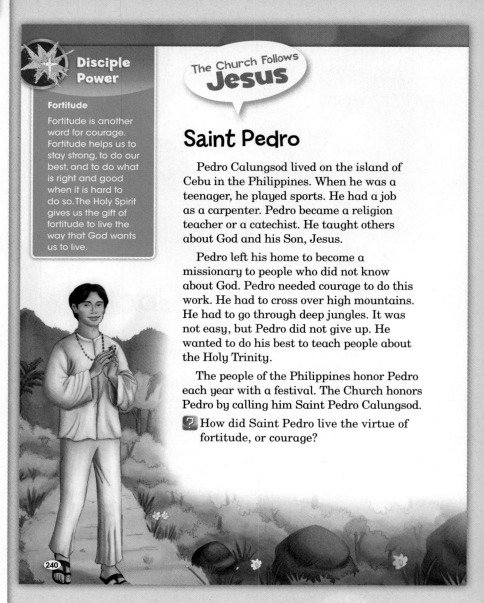

Disciple Power

Fortitude

Fortitude is another word for courage. Fortitude helps us to stay strong, to do our best, and to do what is right and good when it is hard to do so. The Holy Spirit gives us the gift of fortitude to live the way that God wants us to live.

The Church Follows Jesus

Saint Pedro

Pedro Calungsod lived on the island of Cebu in the Philippines. When he was a teenager, he played sports. He had a job as a carpenter. Pedro became a religion teacher or a catechist. He taught others about God and his Son, Jesus.

Pedro left his home to become a missionary to people who did not know about God. Pedro needed courage to do this work. He had to cross over high mountains. He had to go through deep jungles. It was not easy, but Pedro did not give up. He wanted to do his best to teach people about the Holy Trinity.

The people of the Philippines honor Pedro each year with a festival. The Church honors Pedro by calling him Saint Pedro Calungsod.

❓ How did Saint Pedro live the virtue of fortitude, or courage?

240

DISCIPLE POWER

Fortitude. Ask the students if any of their family members are runners. Invite them to name things that runners have to do to stay in shape, such as warm-up exercises or running a specific number of miles each day, in all kinds of weather. Explain that, as Jesus' disciples, there are things that we must do each day to stay in spiritual shape, too. Ask them to brainstorm the things that we do to stay in spiritual shape (i.e., praying, being kind, serving others). Reiterate the many courageous things that Saint Pedro Calungsod did to teach people about God and Jesus. Point out that Jesus calls us to live the virtue of fortitude by always trying to do our best to live according to his teachings.

Pope Benedict XVI and the Church honored Saint Pedro by calling him a Saint in the year 2012. We celebrate the feast day of Saint Pedro on April 2.

Today many teachers live the virtue of fortitude. They share the Good News about Jesus and live as a child of God.

? What are some ways you live the virtue of fortitude, or courage?

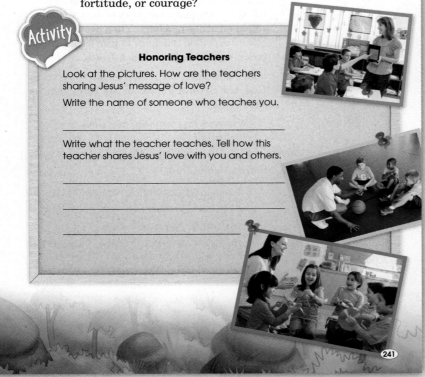

Activity

Honoring Teachers

Look at the pictures. How are the teachers sharing Jesus' message of love?

Write the name of someone who teaches you.

_____

Write what the teacher teaches. Tell how this teacher shares Jesus' love with you and others.

_____

_____

_____

(241)

Connect

▶ Call on different students to identify the teachers in the pictures on page 241. *(classroom teacher, basketball coach, music teacher)*

▶ Brainstorm qualities of a good teacher. *(e.g., patience, knowledge, skill, and so on)* List ideas on the board. Ask the students if they think a teacher needs fortitude— the courage to do what is right and best—to be a good teacher.

▶ Have the students write the name of someone who teaches them and write what the person teaches.

▶ Call on a variety of students to tell who they wrote about and why. Ask why they think the person is a good teacher.

Pray

Gather the class for prayer. Have them echo the following:

Loving God, / come and be with us. / Show us your way. / Teach us your path. / We ask this in the name of Jesus, / the one we call Teacher as well as Lord. / Amen.

TEACHING TIP

Heartfelt Teaching. Albert Einstein said that teaching should be such that what is offered is perceived as a valuable gift not as a hard duty. Jesus taught precisely that way. His teaching was too broad for the head alone. It spoke to and speaks to the heart. As a teacher, make it your enjoyable "duty" to teach from the heart, not just from the book—even this one.

Key Concept
Jesus was a unique teacher who taught on his own authority as the Second Person of the Holy Trinity.

Pray

Lead the students in the prayer with which you closed the previous lesson.

Teach

▶ Ask a student to read the Faith Focus question aloud. *(Accept all answers.)* Tell the children that today they will learn that Jesus was a very special teacher.

▶ Write the word *rabbi* on the board. Remind the students that they saw the word in the previous chapter. Call attention to *rabbi* and its definition in Faith Words.

▶ Then write the words *authority* and *kindness* on the board. Ask the students to listen for these three words and for how Jesus was a special kind of teacher as you present the section titled A Different Kind of Teacher on pages 242–243.
Note: If you wish, call on different students to proclaim the Scripture passages in the text when you come to them in your presentation.

Faith Focus
What kind of teacher was Jesus?

Faith Words
▶ **rabbi**
Rabbi is a Hebrew word that means "teacher."

A Different Teacher

There were many teachers of God's Law in Jesus' time. They were called rabbis. Remember, *rabbi* means "teacher."

Crowds of people followed Jesus everywhere. People wanted to learn about God from him. They said that they had never before heard a teacher like Jesus.

Jesus was different from the other rabbis. All of the religious teachers of Jesus' time relied on other teachers. They needed other respected teachers to prove that their teaching was right, but not Jesus.

Jesus taught about God on his own. He is God, the Second Person of the Holy Trinity Jesus said,

"Whoever has seen me has seen the Father."
JOHN 14:9

Jesus also taught with great kindness and mercy. Jesus said,

"Once you learned that if someone hurts you, you can hurt him back. But now I say, be kind, forgive, and love your enemies."
BASED ON MATTHEW 5:43–44

? What made Jesus' teaching different?

242

TEACHING TIP

Life in Jesus' Time. The students are learning about the life and times of Jesus. Seven- and eight-year-olds still relate most of what they learn through the window of their own experiences. As you talk about Jesus as a great and very special teacher, invite the students to share with you how they picture where Jesus lived, how he was taught, or what people wore. This sharing will make you aware of any prior knowledge and mistaken impressions that they might have about the life and times of Jesus.

The teachings of Jesus came from God. Jesus said,

"My teaching is not my own but it is from the one who sent me."

JOHN 7:16

Jesus' teaching took God's Law and put it into people's hearts. Jesus taught us rules for living and ways to live together. Never before was there a teacher like Jesus.

 Who sent Jesus? What are the ways you live the rules that Jesus taught us?

Catholics Believe

The Cross

The Cross is a sign of how Jesus lived the Great Commandment. Jesus showed his great love for God, his Father, when he died on the Cross. Jesus our Savior also showed his great love for us when he died on the Cross. The Cross reminds us to love God and others as Jesus did.

Activity

The Teachings of Jesus

Learn what Jesus says about following his teaching. Cross out Q, X, and Z in the puzzle.

```
Z W Q X H O Q Z E Q X V Z E X R Z
L X O Q V X E S Z M Z E W Q I X L L
Q F Z X O X L X L X Z O Z W X M Q Y
Z T Q E X Q A Z C Q H Z X I Z N Q G
```

BASED ON JOHN 14:23

Complete the sentence with the words you found in the puzzle.

Jesus said to his disciples,

_____

WHOEVER LOVES ME WILL FOLLOW MY TEACHING.

(243)

CATHOLICS BELIEVE

The Cross. The Cross is a familiar religious symbol for Christians everywhere. It is significant because Jesus was executed by the governor of Judea on a large wooden cross. The Gospels report that the manner of Christ's Death was crucifixion, which involved being tied or nailed to the cross and left to die. This painful method of execution was common for slaves and non-Romans convicted of serious crimes in the Roman Empire at the time. Jesus endured the suffering of the Cross so that he could atone for our sins and become for us the source of eternal life.

Reinforce

▶ Ask the follow-up question. Help the students recognize that Jesus was such a unique teacher because he taught on his own authority as the Second Person of the Holy Trinity.

▶ Point out again the Faith Word *rabbi.* Have the students make a word card for this term.

▶ Before moving on, tell the students that while Jesus was our greatest Teacher, we also learn faith from our family, priest, and special teachers called catechists (religion teachers).

▶ Present Catholics Believe. Explain that Jesus' Death on the Cross was the ultimate way of keeping the Great Commandment—loving God completely and loving others as self.

Connect

▶ Read the directions to the activity. Have the students complete it with a partner.

▶ Afterward, ask one pair to read aloud the message from Jesus the Teacher: *Whoever loves me will follow my teaching.*

▶ Point out the heart-shape. Remind the students that Jesus' teachings are rules for loving—rules for the heart.

Pray

Pray the Glory Be.

Key Concept
Jesus taught us the Great
Commandment.

Pray

Invite the students to quiet themselves
for prayer. Pray together the Sign of
the Cross.

Teach

▶ Have a volunteer read the Faith
Focus question. Ask the students
for possible answers. Tell the
students that today's lesson will
help them discover that Jesus
taught the greatest of God's
commandments.

▶ Invite the students to listen
carefully as you read Jesus' teaching
about the Great Commandment.

▶ Proclaim the Scripture based on
Matthew 22:36–40.

Reinforce

▶ Call for responses to the follow-
up question. *(Answers will vary.)*
Explain that when we keep the
Great Commandment, we keep all
God's other Commandments as well.

▶ Explain that Jesus' Death on the Cross
was the ultimate way of keeping the
Great Commandment — loving
God completely and loving others
as oneself.

▶ Point out Faith-Filled People about
Saint Peter. Remind the students
that all of the Faith-Filled People
they have been learning about are
people who followed Jesus' Great
Commandment in the way they
loved God and others.

Faith Focus
What did Jesus
teach about God's
Commandments?

Faith Words
▶ **Great Commandment**
The Great
Commandment is to
love God above all
else and to love others
as we love ourselves.

Jesus Teaches

One day, a teacher of the Law came to
Jesus and asked,

*"Teacher, which commandment in the law
is the greatest?" He said to him, "You
shall love the Lord, your God, with all your
heart, with all your soul, and with all your
mind. This is the greatest and the first
commandment. The second is like it: You
shall love your neighbor as yourself. The
whole law and the prophets depend on
these two commandments."*

Matthew 22:36–39

Jesus named two
Commandments. We are to
love God above all else. We
are to love our neighbor as
ourselves. Together both
Commandments make up one
Great Commandment.

❓ How do you show love to
God and to others?

244

BACKGROUND: SCRIPTURE

The Scholar of the Law. Matthew 22:37–40 is a response to a
question put to Jesus as part of a longer series of questioning by a
scholar of the Law. Having been asked which commandment was
the greatest, Jesus responded by quoting Deuteronomy 6:5 and
Leviticus 19:18. This was an answer, of course, that a scholar of the
Law already knew. Jesus' summary statement, "'The whole law and
the prophets depend on these two commandments'" (Matthew 22:40)
turned the question back to the scholar of the Law and invited him
to reflect on his own living of the Law.

Activity

Loving God and Others

Read the Scripture verses again. Name the two parts of the Great Commandment.

_____

_____

_____

Write a list of ways you can live the Great Commandment.

Ways I Can Love God

_____

_____

_____

_____

Ways I Can Love Others

_____

_____

_____

_____

_____

Faith-Filled People

Saint Peter

Peter was one of Jesus' twelve Apostles. He was the first one to recognize that Jesus is the Savior. After he rose from the dead, Jesus asked Peter to care for the Church and all its members. Peter was the first Pope. His feast day is June 29.

(245)

FAITH-FILLED PEOPLE

Saint Peter the Apostle. We sometimes see a statue of Saint Peter holding keys in one hand with a rooster siting on his shoulder. The rooster symbolizes Saint Peter's humanity and weakness-he denied that he knew Jesus before the cock crowed three times (Mark 14:66–71). The keys symbolize the "keys to the kingdom" given to Peter by Jesus after Peter confessed his faith in Jesus (Matthew 16:13–20). The keys represent the responsibility of Saint Peter-and his successors, the Popes-as head of the Church. For more information on Saint Peter, go to the Saints Resource at *BeMyDisciples*.com.

Reinforce

(*continued*)

▶ Invite a volunteer to read the definition of *Great Commandment* in Faith Words.

▶ Have the students make a word card for *Great Commandment*. Encourage—and help—the students learn the Great Commandment by heart.

Connect

▶ Have the students do the Loving God and Others activity, then share responses. List ideas on the board.

▶ Divide the class into two groups. Have each group prepare to role-play how they can live the Great Commandment. Tell the groups they can draw on the ideas on the board as they plan their role plays.

▶ Have each group present its role play.

▶ Congratulate the students on their cooperation. Tell them that they are keeping the Great Commandment every time they show their love for God and for others.

Pray

Lead the students in praying the Lord's Prayer.

Pray

Gather the students for prayer. Lead them in the Sign of the Cross.

Teach

▶ Read aloud the Faith Focus question. Tell the students that they will learn more about how we are to live the Great Commandment. Jesus taught the people that the Great Commandment was the greatest Law of God.

▶ Present The Great Commandment in your own words, clearly distinguishing its parts.

Reinforce

Pose the follow-up question. (Accept all responses.)

Connect

Point out the pictures on the page. Ask which shows people living the first part of the Great Commandment and which shows people living the second part.

Faith Focus
How do we follow and keep each part of the Great Commandment?

The Great Commandment

The Great Commandment sums up all of God's Laws. The first part of the Great Commandment teaches that God is the center of our lives. It teaches us to love God above all else.

We live the first part of the Great Commandment in many ways. We show our love for God when we honor and respect God in all we do and say. We show our love for God when we pray.

The second part of the Great Commandment teaches us to treat others as we like to be treated. We live this part of the Great Commandment in many ways. We are to respect and honor all people as ourselves. We respect and honor all people when we help them care for their belongings. We respect and honor people when we treat them fairly.

❓ How are the people in the pictures showing love for God and for one another?

(246)

TEACHING TIP

Jesus: The Unique Teacher. To help the students appreciate the absolute uniqueness and authority of Jesus' teaching, invite them to imagine how they would react if in an arithmetic class a new teacher comes to visit and says, "Boys and girls, forget everything you have heard about adding numbers. You learned that 2 plus 2 equals 4. But here is a new teaching. 2 plus 2 equals 5! Says who? Says *me!* Believe it!"

Because God loves you, you can love others. The Holy Spirit helps you to live the Great Commandment. You can love God above all else. You can love others as you love yourself.

I Follow Jesus

Activity

Teaching Others

Pretend that you are teaching a class about the Great Commandment. Draw two pictures to show what it means.

Love God	Love Others

My Faith Choice

I will show fortitude and live the Great Commandment. This week, I will

_____

_____

 Pray, "Loving God, always be my teacher. Teach me the way to love you and others with all my heart, soul, and mind. Amen."

(247)

Reinforce

Remind the students that when they pray and do acts of kindness, they are already living the Great Commandment. Explain that the Holy Spirit gives them the grace to live the Great Commandment.

Respond

▶ Have the students look at the activity on this page as you read the directions.

▶ Invite the students to complete the activity and then share their ideas with a partner.

Choose

▶ Present My Faith Choice and have the students write their choices.

▶ Encourage the students to put their choices into practice this week.

Pray

Point out the prayer on the bottom of the page. Encourage the students to pray the prayer silently.

TEACHING TIP

Living the Great Commandment. Here is a simple way to help your second graders live the second part of the Great Commandment. Have the students write the names of two family members on a piece of paper. Beside each name have them write three ways in which they can show kindness to this person. Ask the students to take the paper home and put it in a place where they will see it often as a reminder to do what they have written.

Pray

Begin class by having the students place themselves in the presence of God and silently ask the Holy Spirit to help them follow the Great Commandment of love.

Recall

▶ Write the To Help You Remember statements on the board or on poster board in the form of a single paragraph. Leave spaces for the words *greatest, God,* and *ourselves.*

▶ Read the sentences aloud together, pausing for the volunteer to fill in the missing words. At the conclusion, write the correct words in the sentences.

▶ Introduce the Chapter Review and allow time for the students to complete both parts. Have them share their work with a partner.

Reflect

Give the students a few moments to complete the reflection statement.

Share

▶ Canvas the room for responses to the statement.

▶ Encourage the students to share what they wrote with their families.

▶ **TO HELP YOU REMEMBER**

1. Jesus taught that the Great Commandment is the greatest Commandment.

2. The first part of the Great Commandment tells us to love God.

3. The second part of the Great Commandment tells us to love other people as we love ourselves.

Chapter Review

Recall

Write one word that names whom the Great Commandment tells you to love in each heart.

 others   God   self

Match the words to their meanings.

Words		**Meanings**
b	**1.** rabbi	**a.** sums up all of God's Laws
c	**2.** courage	**b.** the word that means teacher
a	**3.** Great Commandment	**c.** another name for fortitude

Reflect

Write about one of Jesus' teachings that has helped you. Tell how it has helped you.

_____

_____

_____

_____

Share Tell a family member about how you live the Great Commandment.

248

TEACHING TIP

We Remember. Create a memory mobile. If time permits, give each student a half sheet of drawing paper or lined writing paper with three holes punched at the top or on the side to write the Great Commandment from memory. Using the We Remember heart activity, have them cut out three hearts from construction paper and write one word on each heart that names the people the Great Commandment tells us to love. Have the students punch holes at the top of each heart, then tie the hearts to the sheet of paper on which the Great Commandment has been written with pieces of thread. Attach the Great Commandment to a hanger and have the students take it home as a reminder to love as God has asked us to.

An Act of Love

God is with us all day long. Take time each day to tell God you love him.

Leader We gather to hear God's Word of love.

Reader *God is love. If we are loving, we are friends with God, and God will be friends with us for ever.*

Based on 1 John 4:16

The word of the Lord.

All **Thanks be to God.**

Leader Let us tell God that we want to live the Great Commandment.

All **O my God,**
I love you above all things.
I love you with my whole
heart and soul.
I love my neighbor as myself
because of my love for you.

Leader O God, give us the fortitude to keep your Great Commandment of love.

All **Amen.**

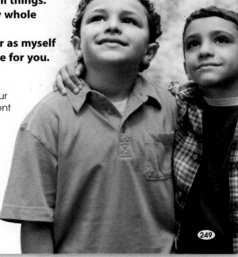

249

We Pray

▶ Tell the students that the closing prayer today is an Act of Love. In the prayer, we tell God that we want to keep the Great Commandment.

▶ Prepare for prayer by having a volunteer get ready to proclaim the Scripture passage from 1 John. 4:16

▶ Gather the students at the prayer center with their books.

▶ Call the students to prayer with the Sign of the Cross.

▶ Take the part of Leader and begin the prayer.

▶ Close your prayer by having all offer one another a sign of peace.

THE TASKS OF CATECHESIS

Teaching to Pray. There are many ways to pray. We can pray verbally or in silence, alone or with the community. We pray with our whole bodies. Standing, sitting, kneeling, and making the Sign of the Cross are just a few examples. Other prayer postures and prayer gestures include bowing in reverence, crossing arms over one's heart to express love, and shaking hands with a partner to express love of neighbor. Include the use of prayer gestures in praying "An Act of Love" and other prayers during your lessons with the students.

Preview

▶ Have the students carefully tear out pages 249 and 250 along the perforation.

▶ Encourage the students to share these pages with their families, and to complete the activities together.

▶ If they did not complete the review activity on page 248 by the end of the session, emphasize that they can complete it with their families at home.

▶ Point out the title and theme of the next lesson to the students.

Visit BeMyDisciples.com

▶ Take time with the students to explore the many activities and resources available at the *Be My Disciples* Web site.

▶ Encourage them to join with their families to discover the many resources available at the Web site.

Before Moving On ...

As you finish today's lesson, reflect on the following question before moving on to the next chapter.

Which activity options am I providing so that all of the students get a chance to express themselves in the way that is best for them?

With My Family

This Week . . .

In Chapter 18, "We Live as Children of God," your child learned:

▶ Jesus taught that the heart of God's Law is the Great Commandment.

▶ The driving spirit of all God's Laws is summarized in two Commandments, namely, to love God and love others as yourself.

▶ The virtue of fortitude or courage helps us live the Great Commandment.

For more about related teachings of the Church, see the *Catechism of the Catholic Church*, 2052–2055, 2083, and 2196, and the *United States Catholic Catechism for Adults*, pages 307–309.

▪ Sharing God's Word

Read together Matthew 22:34–40, Jesus' teaching on the Great Commandment, or read the adaptation of the story on page 244. Emphasize that the Great Commandment has two connected parts: love God, and love your neighbor as yourself. This commandment sums up what is at the heart and purpose of God's Laws.

▪ Living as Disciples

The Christian home and family form a school of discipleship. Choose one of the following activities to do as a family, or design a similar activity of your own.

▶ Create a large heart out of poster paper. Write the Great Commandment within the heart. Display the heart where it will serve as a reminder to the whole family to live the Great Commandment.

▶ The Great Commandment tells us to treat others as we would like to be treated. Talk about some of the practical ways that your family is living this part of the Great Commandment. Encourage your children to ask themselves at bedtime how well they lived the Great Commandment that day.

▪ Our Spiritual Journey

The moral virtues give us strength to live the moral life, but these virtues are acquired through deliberate effort and much practice. The virtue of fortitude helps us keep the Great Commandment—no simple task. Following the Great Commandment means more than embracing a teaching of the faith. It means embracing the Teacher, Jesus himself—or, to be exact, allowing Jesus to embrace us. Help your child pray the Act of Love on page 249. Pray together: *Give us the fortitude to keep your Great Commandment.*

For more ideas on ways your family can live as disciples of Jesus, visit  **BeMyDisciples.com**

250

PLAN AHEAD

Making a Poster Chart. In Chapters 19 and 20, the children will learn the Ten Commandments. To assist your second graders in learning these important laws by heart, make a chart listing each of your student's names. Title the chart, "I Know God's Ten Commandments!" You may want to purchase special stickers or seals for the students to place on the chart when they can recite the Ten Commandments from memory.

Enriching the Lesson

Art Activity: The Great Commandment

Purpose

To reinforce the meaning of the Great Commandment (taught on page 246)

Directions

▶ Print the words of the Great Commandment on a sheet of paper.

▶ Draw a wide decorative border around the words, and duplicate the sheet on white paper so that each student has a copy.

▶ Invite the students to decorate the border, using colors of their choice. Make construction paper frames for the students to use to frame their artwork.

▶ Suggest that they hang their artwork at home to remind them to live as children of God.

Materials

copies of the words of the Great Commandment with a decorative border

construction paper

scissors

glue sticks

crayons or markers

Making Prayer Stones

Purpose

To reinforce that we show our love for God when we pray (taught on page 248)

Directions

Prayer stones are a great tool to remind the students to pray.

▶ Have the students make their own prayer stones by providing them with stones no bigger than three inches long.

▶ Give each child a ribbon to tie a swatch of material around the stone.

▶ Tell the students to keep the prayer stones on their pillows during the day as a reminder to pray their night prayers. At night, the students could place the prayer stones in their shoes as a reminder to pray their morning prayers.

Materials

stones

swatches of material and ribbons

Literature Connection

Purpose

To reinforce the teaching about the Great Commandment (taught on pages 244–247)

Directions

The Paper Dragon, a classic Chinese folk tale, is retold here by Marguerite W. Davol and exquisitely illustrated by Robert Clarke Sabuda (Simon and Schuster, 1997). Mi Fei is a humble, contented painter in a quiet village, but when the dragon Sui Jen awakens one day, it falls to Mi Fei to find a way to return the dragon to his slumber. He chooses a way of love.

▶ Read the story dramatically to the class, making sure to share the dramatic tissue-paper illustrations and fold-out spreads.

▶ Discuss the tactic that Mi Fei uses, and help the students compare his solution to the message of the Great Commandment.

Materials

The Paper Dragon, by Marguerite W. Davol

BACKGROUND

Maxims for Living a Holy Life

The Book of Proverbs is a collection of instructive, or didactic, poetry. It is an example of an early catechism on living a holy life, aimed at the young and the inexperienced among the Israelites. Its title, "Proverbs," is derived from the Hebrew word *Mishle*, which is the first word of the book.

Proverbs

The usefulness and popularity of these proverbs, however, were not limited to the young. These pithy statements were well known and used as guides to wise decision making by those who wished to advance in piety. They frequently seasoned the conversations of God's people in much the same way as maxims color our language today.

The Proverbs Teach

The subject matter of the sayings in Proverbs runs the gamut from secular good sense to lofty inspiration. They can teach us a great deal about God and our relationship with him. For example:

God's power: "Many are the plans in a man's heart, / but it is the decision of the Lord that endures."

Proverbs 19:21

God's providential care: "Say not, 'I will repay evil!' / Trust in the Lord and he will help you."

Proverbs 20:22

God's justice: "The Lord is far from the wicked, / but the prayer of the just he hears."

Proverbs 15:29

It is difficult to say how this wondrous anthology of wisdom came about. Some proverbs were independent collections attributed to authors like King Solomon. Some believe that a religious scholar, probably in the early part of the fifth century before Christ, gathered these disparate collections into the inspired Book of Proverbs.

The First Three Commandments

The first three of the Ten Commandments specifically focus on our relationship with God. The First Commandment is probably the most defining: "I am the Lord your God: you shall not have strange gods before me." God created us for himself. No one and nothing else comes before him. Our whole life is to give honor and glory to him. The Second Commandment, "You shall not take the name of the Lord your God in vain," demands reverence for God and his divine name. The Third Commandment, "Remember to keep holy the Lord's Day," states our obligation to set aside time each week to rest, to worship God, to give him thanks, and to praise him and acknowledge that he is the source of all blessings. Time is such a precious commodity for us that God with this Commandment helps us to keep focus on what is important.

For Reflection

What are some holy maxims that guide my daily decision making to live as a disciple of Christ?

How does the gift of wisdom, one of the seven Gifts of the Holy Spirit, guide and influence my decisions each day?

Teacher to Teacher

Keep the Lord's Day

We live the Third Commandment by keeping the Lord's Day holy. Sunday is the Lord's Day for Christians. Catholics primarily keep Sunday holy by worshiping God by taking part in the celebration of the Mass. We also spend time with our families and friends. In our contemporary society, finding time for families and friends seems to be getting more and more difficult to do. God's command to keep holy the Lord's Day addresses this issue. This commandment includes both taking part in Mass and avoiding all that keeps us away from living as children of God. Keeping the Lord's Day holy calls us to take the time for one another and to keep God at the center of our family life.

Family Time

Family time has become a precious commodity today. Many parents work long hours, and students are involved in numerous extracurricular activities. Life just seems busier than ever. We need to find ways to make Sunday and our time with our families special. Help the students and their families grow in appreciating the wisdom of this commandment. Families whose jobs involve unavoidable Sunday schedules can find another day or time to be together.

The Church Teaches...

"The Ten Commandments (or Decalogue) and the Beatitudes are the primary reference points for the application of Christian moral principles. The Decalogue, the expression of God's covenant with his people, is also a privileged expression of the natural law that sums up love of God and neighbor" (*National Directory for Catechesis*, 44).

To teach as Jesus did means that every catechist/religion teacher is to do more than present information. This is why we both teach about God's Law and also help the students apply his laws, such as the Ten Commandments, to their daily lives.

Further Reading and Reflection

For more related teachings of the Church, see the *Catechism of the Catholic Church*, "First Commandment" (2083–2136), "Second Commandment" (2142–2165), "Third Commandment" (2168–2188 and 2194); and the *United States Catholic Catechism for Adults*, pages 341–369.

Teacher Prayer

Lord, in looking closely at the Ten Commandments, I see how I sometimes casually go about my days without giving them a thought. Help me strive each day to live the spirit of your Laws. Let me grow in age and wisdom and grace. Amen.

Lesson Planner

Chapter 19 We Love God

Goal To explore how the first three Commandments teach us to love and honor God

LESSON PART	PROCESS	MATERIALS and RESOURCES
DAY 1 **EXPLORE** **Focus** To explore why followers of Jesus follow God's rules **Pages** 251–253	▶ Proclaim and discuss Psalm 119:1–3 (Happiness comes from keeping God's laws). ▶ Learn and discuss the story of Saint Benedict and his religious rule. **Disciple Power:** Obedience **Activity:** Write rules you follow at home and at school.	Bible Pencils or pens Drawing paper **Enriching the Lesson:** • Teacher Guide, page 373 Making a Happiness "Mobile" • Literature Connection: *Mrs. Piggle Wiggle*
DAY 2 **DISCOVER** **Focus** To discover why God gave the Ten Commandments **Pages** 254–255	▶ Learn that God gave us the Ten Commandments so we would know how to live as his children. **Catholics Believe:** The Bishop's Motto **Faith Words:** Ten **Activity:** Write how you can show love for God and love for people.	Bible Pencil or pens **Additional Activities Booklet** Activities 19a or see *BeMyDisciples*.com
DAY 3 **DISCOVER** **Focus** To discover how the first three Commandments helps us to love God **Pages** 256–257	▶ Discover that the first three Commandments teach us how to love God. **Faith-Filled People:** Saint Scholastica **Activity:** Find hidden words that relate to the first three Commandments.	Bibles Pencils or pens **Additional Activities Booklet** Activities 19b or see *BeMyDisciples*.com
DAY 4 **DECIDE** **Focus** To discover how proverbs help us keep the Commandments and to decide on a way to show love for God **Pages** 258–259	▶ Learn that the proverbs are wise sayings that help us live as God's children. **Faith Words:** proverbs **Scripture:** Trust in the Lord (Proverb 3:5–6); Honor God (Proverb 3:9–10). **Activity:** Write advice to help you and your family love and honor God. **My Faith Choice:** Choose a way to show my love for God this week.	Pencil or pens **Enriching the Lesson:** Teacher Guide, page 373 Writing Letters of Thanks
DAY 5 **CONCLUDE** **Focus** To realize that the Holy Spirit helps us keep God's Commandments **Pages** 260–262	▶ **REVIEW** Review concepts: Recall, Reflect, and Share. ▶ **PRAY** Come Holy Spirit ▶ **Preview** the With My Family page and the theme of the next chapter.	Bible, candle, cross for prayer space Grade 2 Music CD **Assessment Tools Booklet:** Assessments 19a and 19b

Assign online Chapter Review and interactive Chapter Test at **BeMyDisciples.com**

Chapter 19

We Love God

? What is one rule your family has that everyone has to follow?

In the Bible, God tells why he gives us rules. Listen to what the writer of this psalm discovered.

Happy are those who obey God's rules.
Happy are those who keep God's laws.
They are on their way to God.

BASED ON PSALM 119:1–3

? Why does obeying God's rules make a person happy?

251

HUMAN METHODOLOGIES

Learning by Heart. The *National Directory for Catechesis* states that memorization of certain aspects of the Catholic faith "contribute to the individual's continued growth in understanding and living the faith" (*NDC*, **29F**). As you study the meaning of the Ten Commandments in Chapters 19 and 20, refer to the list in the "Catholic Prayers and Practices" section at the back of the text. Have the students work with a partner to learn the Ten Commandments by heart. Encourage them to continue working on this project at home. Reward those who are able to recite the Ten Commandments from memory with a sticker to place on the Ten Commandments chart you prepared for these chapters.

Pray

▶ Welcome the students warmly. Help them quiet themselves for prayer.

▶ Begin and end with the Sign of the Cross. Ask the students to echo these words after you:

> Dear God, /
> help me to keep your Laws /
> and learn to love you more. /
> Amen.

Reflect

▶ Ask the students to respond to the first opening question. Have volunteers tell who helps them learn family rules.

▶ Point out the illustration on the page, and briefly discuss how it feels when someone does not follow the rules. Stress how following rules can make things safe and fun.

▶ Tell the students that God wants us to be safe and happy, so God has rules, too. Invite a volunteer to read aloud the passage from Psalm 119.

▶ Afterward, observe a moment of silence.

▶ Then invite responses to the Scripture question.

▶ Conclude with the Sign of the Cross.

Focus

Go on to invite the students to turn the page to learn about someone whose rules helped others to love God and to live happy lives.

Introduce

▶ Invite the students to tell what they might know about Saint Benedict.

▶ Call on different students to read aloud the story titled Saint Benedict.

Reinforce

▶ Call attention to the follow-up question and read it aloud.

▶ Have the students explain in their own words how they think Saint Benedict's rules helped the monks.

▶ Invite the students to read about obedience in Disciple Power. Talk about rules that are easy to obey and rules that are hard to obey.

▶ Take this opportunity to have the students turn to page 257 and read about Saint Scholastica, Saint Benedict's twin sister, and her work.

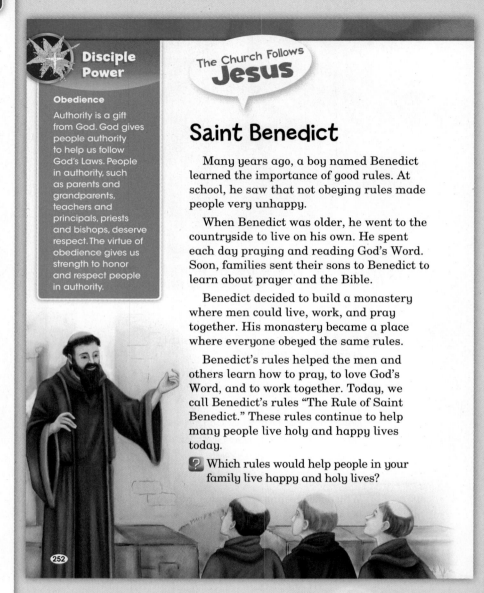

Disciple Power

Obedience

Authority is a gift from God. God gives people authority to help us follow God's Laws. People in authority, such as parents and grandparents, teachers and principals, priests and bishops, deserve respect. The virtue of obedience gives us strength to honor and respect people in authority.

The Church Follows Jesus

Saint Benedict

Many years ago, a boy named Benedict learned the importance of good rules. At school, he saw that not obeying rules made people very unhappy.

When Benedict was older, he went to the countryside to live on his own. He spent each day praying and reading God's Word. Soon, families sent their sons to Benedict to learn about prayer and the Bible.

Benedict decided to build a monastery where men could live, work, and pray together. His monastery became a place where everyone obeyed the same rules.

Benedict's rules helped the men and others learn how to pray, to love God's Word, and to work together. Today, we call Benedict's rules "The Rule of Saint Benedict." These rules continue to help many people live holy and happy lives today.

❓ Which rules would help people in your family live happy and holy lives?

252

DISCIPLE POWER

Obedience. The *Catechism of the Catholic Church* makes clear that all human communities need to be governed by people in authority and that each of us is required to show honor to legitimate authorities by being obedient to them (*CCC*, 1897–1900). Invite the students to name two or three rules that they are expected to obey (e.g., cleaning their rooms, not talking to strangers, doing their homework). Ask for two teams of volunteers, one to role-play a second grader obeying each rule and the other to role-play a second grader disregarding the rule. Discuss with the students the consequences of failing to obey rules. Help your second graders to appreciate that obeying rules help us to live holy, happy, healthy, safe, and respectful lives.

Rules Rule

Rules are important. You can't play a game without rules. Rules let you play fairly and have fun. What rules do you have in your classroom? Why are these rules important for everyone?

Write one rule you have to follow at home. Tell a partner why this rule is helpful.

Write one rule you have to follow at school. Tell a partner why this rule helps the students in your school.

(253)

Connect

▶ Discuss with the students whether they think rules are good or bad things.

▶ Read the section titled Rules Rule. Discuss how obeying good rules can lead to happiness and harmony, for example, as a family, on a sports team, in a classroom.

▶ Call attention to the writing activity. Brainstorm rules that the students think would help everyone in their families and everyone in their classroom live holy and happily "on the way to God."

▶ Give the students time to write their rules. Afterward, share ideas. Note: Perhaps some of the students' ideas can become part of your classroom rules.

Pray

Call the students to prayer. Invite them to echo the following after you.

O God, /
teach us the rules for /
loving living. /
Show us the way to you. /
Amen.

TEACHING TIP

Cooperative Learning. This is an excellent time to review the students' understanding regarding cooperative learning. Have the students share rules about working with others, whether in a small group or with partners. You may wish to post a list of some of the rules in the classroom. Keep it simple and short. Whenever the students are working in small groups, visit each group and affirm its efforts by referring to a rule the group is following, for example, "You are doing a great job of taking turns speaking."

Key Concept
God gave Moses and the people the Ten Commandments to help us live holy lives.

Pray

Lead the students in the prayer with which you closed the previous lesson.

Teach

▶ Ask a volunteer to read the Faith Focus question aloud. Point out the Faith Word, *Ten Commandments*. Explain that the Ten Commandments are special rules that God has given us. Share that we will learn more about why those rules are important.

▶ Write the name *Moses* on the board. Have the students tell what they know about Moses. Point out the illustration on the page and explain that Moses was called by God to be the leader of the Hebrew people.

▶ Invite the students to listen carefully as you read aloud God's Rules on pages 254 and 255; have the students listen for what the first three Commandments teach us. *(The first three Commandments teach us to love and honor God.)*

Faith Focus
What are the Ten Commandments?

Faith Words
▶ **Ten Commandments**
The Ten Commandments are the laws that God gave Moses. They teach us to live as God's people. They help us live happy and holy lives.

God's Rules

Long ago, God chose Moses to lead his people out of slavery in Egypt. God's people were not living as God wanted them to live. God called Moses to the top of a high mountain. God spoke to Moses and gave him the **Ten Commandments**.

God told Moses that he loved the people. The Ten Commandments are God's rules to help all people live happy and holy lives.

The Ten Commandments remind people to honor God above everything else. They tell people to rest and pray on the Lord's Day. They ask people to obey parents and to keep away from telling lies or stealing. The Commandments also say not to hurt other people or be jealous of them.

 How do the Ten Commandments help us live as God wants us to live?

(254)

TEACHING TIP

Considering People of Different Faiths. Students live in a multicultural diverse world. They will notice that Christians gather to worship God on Sunday, Jewish people observe the Sabbath on Saturday, and Muslims come together in prayer assemblies on Friday. All three of the major religions of the world set aside a day each week for their communities to give honor to God. God deserves our honor and respect. Help the students grow in their respect for all people who strive to love God sincerely, with their whole hearts. Discuss ways in which they can show respect for those of all faiths.

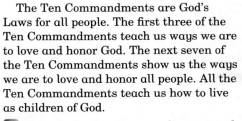

The Ten Commandments are God's Laws for all people. The first three of the Ten Commandments teach us ways we are to love and honor God. The next seven of the Ten Commandments show us the ways we are to love and honor all people. All the Ten Commandments teach us how to live as children of God.

? What do the Ten Commandments teach us?

Catholics Believe

The Bishop's Motto

A motto is a short saying. For example, the motto of the Benedictines is "Work and Pray." Cardinal Donald Wuerl, Archbishop of Washington, DC, uses a motto to describe his work. He chose as his motto, "Thy Kingdom Come."

 Activity

Living as Children of God

Write one way you show your love and honor for God.

Write one way you show your love and honor for people.

255

Reinforce

▶ Call on volunteers to respond to the follow-up question. (*Answers may vary, but the students should be able to respond that the Commandments help us to live well as God's children.*)

▶ Direct attention back to the Faith Word, *Ten Commandments*. Have the students make a word card for this term.

▶ Present the material in Catholics Believe. Emphasize that a bishop's motto is a wise saying that can help the bishop live out his love for God. If possible, learn your bishop's motto and share it with the students. You should be able to find it on your diocese's Web site.

Connect

▶ Remind the students that the Commandments help us show love and honor for God and for people. Then call attention to the writing activity.

▶ Have the students complete the writing on their own. Afterward, encourage sharing with a partner or the entire class.

Pray

Lead the class in praying the Lord's Prayer.

TEACHING TIP

Setting Rules. When you observe a situation that needs fixing, lead the students to create a rule or guideline. Students often respond better to rules that they help create. Give the students practice in making rules. Use situations you have observed (without revealing those involved), or make up scenarios that are common to second-grade students.

Key Concept
The first three Commandments help us honor, appreciate, and love our Creator.

Pray
Have the students quiet themselves for prayer. Lead them in the Glory Be.

Teach
▶ Remind the students that the Ten Commandments guide us to live a happy and holy life.

▶ Ask a volunteer to read aloud the Faith Focus question. Tell the students that they are now going to learn more about the first three Commandments.

▶ Ask different volunteers to read the text sections about the first three Commandments.

▶ After each section is read, invite volunteers to describe the Commandment. Jot their answers on a numbered chart. (You will be adding more to this chart later.)

Faith Focus
How do the First, Second, and Third Commandments help people to love and respect God?

Keeping God First
The First, Second, and Third Commandments name ways that we are to honor and love God.

First Commandment
1. **I am the Lord your God: you shall not have strange gods before me.**

The First Commandment tells us there is only one God. We are to worship God alone. We are to have faith in God, to hope in him, and to love him more than all else.

Second Commandment
2. **You shall not take the name of the Lord your God in vain.**

The Second Commandment teaches us that God's name is holy. We are to honor God's name. We are always to speak it with respect and love. We are also to show respect for holy people, places, and things.

256

TEACHING TIP

Engage the Students. When you read aloud—or have volunteers read aloud—give the students a reason to listen carefully. For example, have them listen for an important word or a specific person in the material being read. Doing this not only engages the students' attention but also enriches their insights.

Third Commandment

3. Remember to keep holy the Lord's Day.

The Third Commandment teaches us that we are to keep Sunday as the Lord's Day. Each Sunday, Catholics have the responsibility to gather to celebrate the Eucharist. We thank and praise God for his goodness to us.

? What are some ways you can keep the first three Commandments?

Activity

Honoring God

Use the words in the word bank to find actions that show how to follow the first three of the Ten Commandments. Find and circle each action in the puzzle.

BELIEVE   OBEY   PRAY   REST   WORSHIP   HONOR

W	N	P	R	A	Y	G	T	U	O
E	P	O	B	E	Y	E	M	J	U
L	L	U	R	E	S	T	V	E	R
O	B	E	L	I	E	V	E	F	G
V	W	O	R	S	H	I	P	U	O
E	D	S	H	O	N	O	R	Z	D

(257)

Reinforce

▶ Go over the first three Commandments with the students, helping them learn them by heart. Have the students make a note card for each.

▶ Call attention to the follow-up question. *(Accept all appropriate responses.)*

Connect

▶ Have the students work as partners to solve the puzzle activity.

▶ Afterward, invite the students to tell which words speak to which Commandment. *(Accept all reasonable replies.)*

▶ Ask the students to think what following the first three Commandments shows. Then tell the students they can find the answer by circling the first and last vertical line of the puzzle: *WE LOVE OUR GOD.*

FAITH-FILLED PEOPLE

Saint Scholastica. Like many twins, Scholastica and Benedict were close. They dedicated their lives to serving God in religious communities that they founded. They strictly obeyed the rules for their communities, which forbid members of the opposite sex from entering either monastery. The twins managed to meet once a year to talk and pray, however. The last time they met, Scholastica was ill and sensed that she would not see her brother again. She begged him to stay with her. Benedict refused because it was against the rule to spend a night away from the monastery. Scholastica prayed that God would intervene. A sudden storm prevented Benedict from leaving. Three days later, back at the monastery, Benedict saw his sister's soul rising toward Heaven. Benedict knew that God was welcoming Scholastica into eternal life. For more information on Saint Scholastica, go to the Saints Resource at *BeMyDisciples*.com.

Key Concept
Proverbs in the Bible can help us make good choices to love God Laws.

Pray

Gather the children for prayer. Lead them in the Sign of the Cross.

Teach

▶ Read aloud the Faith Focus question. Tell the students that they will learn about proverbs today.

▶ Write on the board a saying such as "A stitch in time saves nine." Be sure to explain its meaning. Point out that simple, wise sayings like these can help us to make wise choices.

▶ Read the meaning of *proverbs* in Faith Words. Have the class make a word card for the term.

▶ Invite the students to listen carefully as you read aloud the text, Wise Sayings to Live By.

Reinforce

Ask the follow-up question. Have the students tell how the quoted proverbs help them follow the first three Commandments and live as children of God.

Connect

▶ If time allows, help the students write a class proverb or class motto that can help them love God above all else.

▶ Consider transferring the motto onto a banner or large poster to display.

Faith Focus
What are proverbs?

Faith Words
proverbs
Proverbs are short sayings that help us to make good choices to follow the Ten Commandments.

Wise Sayings to Live By

The writers of the Bible collected many wise sayings to help us follow God's Law. These wise sayings are called **proverbs**. They help us choose to follow the Ten Commandments. You can read them in the Book of Proverbs in the Old Testament.

These proverbs help us show our love for God.

Trust God with all your heart.
Do not think you always have the answers.
In everything you do, keep God in mind.
God will show you the right way.

BASED ON PROVERBS 3:5–6

Honor God with the best you have.
God will take good care of you.

BASED ON PROVERBS 3:9–10

? How do these proverbs help you love God and live as a child of God?

258

THE TASKS OF CATECHESIS

Moral Formation. Emphasize that proverbs help us to make good choices. More than anything else, the proverbs in the Bible tell us ways that we are called to live as children of God. The short sayings in the Book of Proverbs guide us to live the Ten Commandments in practical ways. Like the Commandments, the proverbs give us advice that helps us to know how to show our love for God, other people, and ourselves.

The Holy Spirit will always help you to make wise choices. He will give you the grace to obey the Ten Commandments. He will help you make choices to live a happy and holy life.

I Follow Jesus

Activity

Advice for My Family

What good advice can you give your family to help all of you love and honor God? Write your advice here and share it with them.

My Faith Choice

This week, I will show my love for God. I will

_____

_____

Pray, "Loving God, I am happy to obey your Commandments. Help me grow in love more and more each day. Amen."

(259)

Reinforce

Assure the students that the Holy Spirit gives them the grace to follow good rules and to use wise sayings to follow God's commands and to live as disciples of Jesus.

Respond

▶ Explain the activity and invite the students to complete it.

▶ Let volunteers share how they have followed the rules or guidance of a parent, teacher, or coach.

Choose

▶ Invite the students to read My Faith Choice and write their decisions.

▶ Encourage them to put their choices into practice this week.

Pray

Conclude the session by leading the class in the prayer at the bottom of the page. Encourage the students to silently pray the prayer.

TEACHING TIP

Importance of Brainstorming. Before beginning a writing activity such as the Good Rules and Guidance exercise on this page, take time to brainstorm ideas with the students and write their ideas on the board. This gives the students ideas and vocabulary to use to when using writing activities. It also helps build the students' self-confidence and excitement.

Pray

Begin class by praying the following as an echo prayer:

Lord, / help us
to show / love and respect
for God our loving Creator.
For this, Jesus, /
we pray in your name.
Amen.

Recall

▶ Turn the To Help You Remember statements into questions. Invite volunteers to answer them, and then have the students read the statements aloud together.

▶ Explain the directions to the sentence completion activity and the coloring activity. Allow time for the students to complete both. Afterward, invite them to check their answers with a partner.

Reflect

Point out the reflection statement, and give the students a few moments to complete it.

Share

▶ Canvass the room for responses to the statement.

▶ Encourage the students to share their reflections with their families.

▶ **TO HELP YOU REMEMBER**

1. God gave us the Ten Commandments to teach us to live happy and holy lives.
2. The first three of the Ten Commandments teach us to love and honor God.
3. Proverbs are wise sayings that help us to love God and to live happy and holy lives.

Chapter Review

Recall

Use the words in the box to complete the sentences.

three	Proverbs	Ten

1. God gave us the _____Ten_____ Commandments.

2. The first _____three_____ Commandments tell us ways to love and honor God.

3. _____Proverbs_____ help us show our love for God.

Color the circle next to the best word for each sentence.

4. We love _____ above all else.
   ○ people ● God ○ creation

5. We respect and honor God's _____.
   ○ land ○ face ● name

6. We keep holy the _____ Day.
   ● Lord's ○ Church's ○ family's

Reflect

What can we learn from Saint Benedict?

_____

_____

Share Share with your class some of the rules that you try to follow when playing with others.

(260)

LITURGY CONNECTION

Praying a Mantra. A mantra consists of words that are repeated over and over, helping to clear one's mind and focus on the Lord. "Come, Holy Spirit" comes from a Latin mantra (*Veni, Sancte Spiritus*) that invokes the power of the Holy Spirit. The Holy Spirit can help each of us live the Commandments. Invite the students to pray this mantra. Have them sit quietly, eyes closed, and lead them in saying softly, "Come, Holy Spirit." Repeat this prayer several times, pausing to allow for silence between each repetition. If possible, locate a recording of the music either on the Internet or from you parish library to play for the students.

Come, Holy Spirit

The Holy Spirit helps you keep God's Commandments.
Learn to sign the prayer "Come, Holy Spirit."

Come	Holy Spirit

Group 1   O Holy Spirit, you are our helper and guide. Give us your grace to live the Ten Commandments.

All   *Sign and say: "Come, Holy Spirit."*

Group 2   Holy Spirit, teach and help us to love God above all else.

All   *Sign and say: "Come, Holy Spirit."*

Group 1   Holy Spirit, teach us and help us to use God's name with loving care.

All   *Sign and say: "Come, Holy Spirit."*

Group 2   Holy Spirit, teach us and help us to keep the Lord's Day holy.

All   *Sign and say: "Come, Holy Spirit."*

(261)

We Pray

▶ Prepare for prayer by dividing the class into two groups and assigning parts.

▶ Allow the groups a moment or two to practice their parts.

▶ Call attention to the illustrations of the ASL signs for the prayer's response: "Come, Holy Spirit."

▶ Teach the signs, and practice them with the class.

▶ Gather the students in the prayer center. Remind them that the Holy Spirit is always with us to give us the grace to live the commandments.

▶ Lead the prayer, and then repeat it.

▶ Conclude with the Sign of the Cross.

TEACHING TIP

Helping the Children Understand Concepts. Second graders are just beginning to understand concepts and categories. As you present and review material on the Commandments, help the students realize that Commandments set standards in two ways. They reveal that certain types of behaving are contrary to the love of God and neighbor. At the same time, the Commandments indicate areas of behavior by which human beings express and develop love.

Preview

▶ Have the students carefully tear out pages 261 and 262 along the perforation.

▶ Encourage the students to share these pages with their families, and to complete the activities together.

▶ If they did not complete the review activity on page 260 by the end of the session, emphasize that they can complete it with their families at home.

▶ Point out the title and theme of the next lesson to the students.

Visit BeMyDisciples.com

▶ Take time with the students to explore the many activities and resources available at the *Be My Disciples* Web site.

▶ Encourage them to join with their families to discover the many resources available at the Web site.

Before Moving On ...

As you finish today's lesson, reflect on the following question before moving on to the next chapter.

What have I done to let the students know that they are helping me to grow in faith as I work with them?

With My Family

This Week . . .

In Chapter 19, "We Love God," your child learned:

▶ The Ten Commandments guide us in living happy and holy lives.

▶ The first three of the Ten Commandments name ways that we are to love and honor God.

▶ Proverbs in the Bible are short wise sayings that help us to follow God's Law and to live happy and holy lives.

▶ The virtue of obedience strengthens us to show honor to those who have authority. Authority is a gift from God that he gives people to help us live his Law.

For more about related teachings of the Church, see the *Catechism of the Catholic Church* "First Commandment" (2083–2136), "Second Commandment" (2142–2165), "Third Commandment" (2168–2188 and 2194), and the *United States Catholic Catechism for Adults*, pages 341–369.

■ Sharing God's Word

Read together Exodus 20:1–3, 7–17. Emphasize that the Ten Commandments are God's Laws. Talk about how the Ten Commandments help us to live holy and happy lives.

■ Living as Disciples

The Christian home and family is a school of discipleship. Grow in your love of God together. Choose one of the following activities to do as a family, or design a similar activity of your own.

▶ Make prayer rocks to carry in your pockets. Use them as reminders to set aside time to pray often throughout the day. When you put your hand into your pocket, you will be reminded to pray. You will also be reminded that God is always with you.

▶ Point out and compliment your child when he or she is obedient. Share ways that you, too, are obedient to others. Help your child see that being obedient is showing respect for those in proper authority.

■ Our Spiritual Journey

Remember the Gospel story of Martha and Mary (Luke 10:38–42). It is a story of balancing work and prayer in our daily lives. It is a story about going about our daily lives keeping God at the center of our lives, just as Saint Benedict taught in his Rule. Invite the Holy Spirit to help you rediscover this balance! Pray together as a family, "*Come, Holy Spirit, fill our hearts with your love.*"

For more ideas on ways your family can live as disciples of Jesus, visit **BeMyDisciples.com**

(262)

PARTNERING WITH PARENTS

Connecting with Home. Actively involve the families in this lesson by emailing the parents or sending a note home with the students asking each family to write on a sheet of paper one or more wise sayings that help them make good choices. Collect the families' sayings and create a bulletin board or poster display with them. Be sure that every students' family is represented.

Enriching the Lesson

Making a "Happiness" Mobile

Purpose

To reinforce how following God's Laws can lead to loving and happy lives (taught on pages 251–253)

Directions

▶ Provide each student with a circle shape, a square shape, and a triangle shape—cut from construction paper or poster board. Each student will also need two twist ties and one longer piece of yarn. Beforehand, punch a hole in the top and bottom of each shape so that the students can connect the shapes to one another.

▶ Invite the students to write one phrase of this chapter's opening Scripture passage on each of the three shapes:
Happy are those who obey God's rules.
(circle shape)
Happy are those who keep God's laws.
(square shape)
They are on their way to God.
(triangle shape)

▶ Have the students connect the shapes, threading the twist ties through the punched holes, and threading the piece of yarn through the top shape for hanging. Make a sample for them to follow.

Materials

different shapes made from construction paper or poster board with holes punched in each

twist ties

yarn

pens or pencils

crayons or markers

Writing Letters of Thanks

Purpose

To reinforce the many people who give us guidance (taught on page 259)

Directions

The students can grow in their appreciation of having several people in their lives who guide them.

▶ With the students, make a list of words and phrases they would use in thank you notes expressing their appreciation to someone for giving them good guidance.

▶ Have the students write notes using these words or phrases and thanking a person for his or her guidance.

▶ Provide envelopes for the notes and encourage the students to deliver their thank you notes.

Materials

note cards

envelopes

pencils or pens

Literature Connection

Purpose

To reinforce the concept of rules and how they help us (taught on pages 251–253)

Directions

Children for several generations have enjoyed the hilarious *Mrs. Piggle Wiggle* books by Betty Bard MacDonald. (Harper-Collines paperback, 1976) The first volume, *Mrs. Piggle Wiggle* introduces children to the wonderful grandmotherly lady in the upside-down house who smells like cookies and makes it fun to learn to behave.

▶ You might read the episode to the students about Hubert who never puts anything away or Patsy who hates to take a bath.

▶ Discuss the rules Mrs. Piggle Wiggle imposes and, most important, discuss the happy outcome of each of her strategies.

▶ Remind the students that God's rules, the Ten Commandments, bring us happiness and freedom.

Materials

Mrs. Piggle Wiggle, by Betty Bard MacDonald

BACKGROUND

"I" and "You"

The Ten Commandments as found in Exodus 20 contain a curious diversion from the way God usually addresses the people of the Old Testament. In the Old Testament, he generally addresses the people of Israel collectively, as a community. This is not what happens in the rendering of the Ten Commandments.

"I'm Talking to You"

God, using the first person singular, says, "I am the Lord" (*see Exodus* 20:2), as in "Listen up, what I'm about to say is very important." Then he says, "you," not the plural, collective "you," but "you" as an individual. God is addressing each person individually as he speaks to the whole community. In other words, we need to listen up. These commandments are not "just for others"; they are for me. It is as though he is saying, "Take this personally; I'm talking to you."

In the Revelation of the Ten Commandments, God was not revealing something new. He was not revealing a mystery beyond the comprehension of humans. He was putting in human words what he had already written on every human heart. God was making us aware of what his people, both the community of Israel and each member of it, already should have known and come to understand.

The Fulfillment of the Law

The Ten Commandments do not only belong to the Old Law. Jesus, the Incarnate Son of God, revealed the importance of the commandments. He taught:

> "Do not think that I have come to abolish the law or the prophets. I have come not to abolish but to fulfill . . . . But whoever obeys and teaches these commandments will be called greatest in the kingdom of heaven."
>
> Matthew 5:17, 19

Parable of the Rich Young Man

The story of the rich young man gives us an insight into how Jesus fulfilled the Law. The young man approached Jesus and asked him, "[W]hat good must I do to gain eternal life?" (*Matthew* 19:16). Jesus replied, "If you wish to enter into life, keep the commandments" (19:17). The young man then said, "All of these I have observed. What do I still lack?" (19:20). Jesus confounds the young fellow—and us—with his response, "If you wish to be perfect, go, sell what you have and give to [the] poor, and you will have treasure in heaven. Then come, follow me" (19:21).

Jesus asks his disciples to live the Law of God as it is written on the human heart. Always make love for God and others your motivation in all you say and do. Fulfill Jesus' New Commandment: "love one another as I love you" (*John* 15:12).

For Reflection

When am I most aware of God speaking to me? How attentive and responsive am I?

In what ways do I strive to fulfill the Law of God as Jesus taught?

Teacher to Teacher

The Value of Rules

Sometimes both children and adults see rules as something negative—statements that restrict their freedom. But the contrary is really true. By following the Ten Commandments we are actually freeing ourselves to live our lives to the fullest. We need to help the students appreciate that good and authentic rules and laws protect our rights and privileges. They teach us how to handle freedom and responsibility. They help us grow in love and respect for God, for others, and for ourselves.

Classroom Rules

Be sure the students understand that the rules you have for your time together are meant to give each person the opportunity to be respected and be respectful. Point out that parents too act out of love when they make rules for their children.

This is a good time to review any classroom rules you have established at the beginning of your time together. Ask the students which rules may still need some attention. Ask the students to discuss the positive effects these rules have had on your class.

The Church Teaches...

"In Christ, God reveals how we human beings are to live our lives. God created human beings with the freedom to initiate and direct their own actions and to shape their own lives . . . This human freedom does not, however, entitle the person to say or do just anything. Human beings are not fully self-sufficient. We are capable of sin . . . The more one chooses to do what is good, the more free one becomes . . . Freely choosing to do the good, to obey the universal and unchanging moral norms, in no way diminishes the freedom and dignity of the human person" (*National Directory for Catechesis*, 41A).

Moral formation in Christ calls each and every person to live as Jesus lived—according to the will of the Father. The source of our love for others comes from God loving us first.

Further Reading and Reflection

For more related teachings of the Church, see the *Catechism of the Catholic Church*, "Fourth Commandment" (2196–2246), "Fifth Commandment" (258–2317), "Sixth Commandment" (2331–2391), "Seventh Commandment" (2401–2449), "Eighth Commandment" (2464–2503), "Ninth Commandment" (2514–2527), and "Tenth Commandment" (2534–2550); and the *United States Catholic Catechism for Adults*, pages 375–455.

Teacher Prayer

Gracious God, thank you for your gift of the Commandments. Truly they are golden rules. Help me as I teach my students to follow them that they may grow in goodness and grace. Amen.

Lesson Planner

Chapter 20 We Love Others

Goal To learn that the last seven Commandments teach us to love other people and ourselves

LESSON PART	PROCESS	MATERIALS and RESOURCES
DAY 1 EXPLORE **Focus** To explore why followers of Jesus gather to worship God **Pages** 263–265	▶ Proclaim and discuss Matthew 7:12 (Happiness comes from The Golden Rule). ▶ Learn and discuss the story of Saint Vincent de Paul and the St. Vincent de Paul Society. **Disciple Power:** Justice **Activity:** Decide who is following the Golden Rule.	Bible Pencils or pens Drawing paper **Enriching the Lesson:** Teacher Guide, page 389 A World of Justice
DAY 2 DISCOVER **Focus** To discover how the Fourth, Fifth, Sixth, and Ninth Commandments help us to love other people and ourselves **Pages** 266–267	▶ Learn about the Fourth, Fifth, Sixth, and Ninth Commandments. **Catholics Believe:** Almsgiving **Faith Words:** covet **Activity:** Write how you can follow the Golden Rule.	Bible Pencil or pens **Enriching the Lesson:** Teacher Guide, page 389 Catholic Social Teaching: Respect for our Elders • Discovering a World of Justice
DAY 3 DISCOVER **Focus** To discover how the Seventh, Eighth, and Tenth Commandments teach about treating others with justice **Pages** 268–269	▶ Learn about the Seventh, Eighth, and Tenth Commandments. **Faith-Filled People:** Saint John Bosco **Activity:** Read a story and then write how to help the students make good choices.	Bibles Pencils or pens
DAY 4 DECIDE **Focus** To discover that Jesus teaches us to do more than just obey the Ten Commandments and to decide on a way to keep the Commandments **Pages** 270–271	▶ Discover that Jesus calls us to do more than keep the Ten Commandments. **Scripture:** The Rich Man (Mark 10:17–22) **Activity:** Write or draw a way to live the Ten Commandments. **My Faith Choice:** Choose how to keep the Ten Commandments this week.	Pencil or pens **Enriching the Lesson:** Teacher Guide, page 389 Collecting Food for Those in Need **Additional Activities Booklet:** Activities 20a and 20b or see BeMyDisciples.com
DAY 5 CONCLUDE **Focus** To realize that at Baptism we receive the grace to live God's Commandments. **Pages** 272–274	▶ **REVIEW** Review concepts: Recall, Reflect, and Share. ▶ **PRAY** Trust in the Lord ▶ **Preview** the With My Family page and the theme of the next chapter.	Bible, candle, cross for prayer space Grade 2 Music CD **Assessment Tools Booklet:** Assessments 20a and 20b

Assign online Chapter Review and interactive Chapter Test at **BeMyDisciples.com**

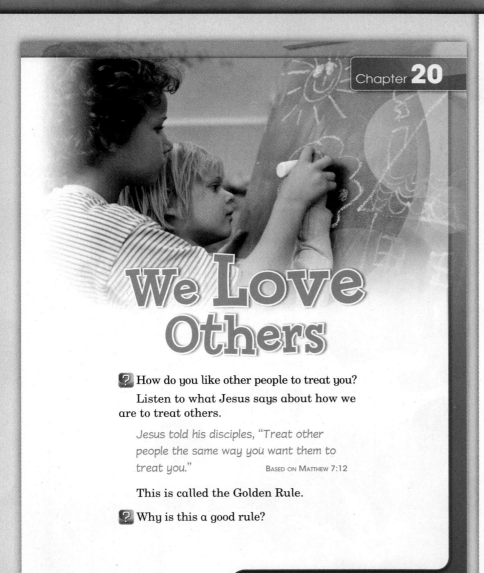

Chapter 20

We Love Others

? How do you like other people to treat you?

Listen to what Jesus says about how we are to treat others.

Jesus told his disciples, "Treat other people the same way you want them to treat you."   BASED ON MATTHEW 7:12

This is called the Golden Rule.

? Why is this a good rule?

263

HUMAN METHODOLOGIES

Learning Within the Christian Family. The *National Directory for Catechesis* reminds us that "(w)ithin the Christian family, parents are the primary educators in the faith" *(NDC 29D)*. Through a written communication with the students' parents, invite them to talk to their children about the importance of living all the commandments. Refer the parents to the complete listing of the Ten Commandments on page 371 of the Catholic Prayers and Practices section of the text and a fuller explanation of each commandment in Chapters 19 and 20. Remind the parents that their example is the greatest witness that their children have in living the Catholic faith.

Pray

▶ Welcome the students warmly. Have them quiet themselves for prayer.

▶ Begin and end with the Sign of the Cross.

▶ Ask the children to echo each line of the prayer:

> Dear Jesus,
> Help me to always treat others as you would treat them. Amen.

Reflect

▶ Ask the students to tell what they see happening in the illustration on the page. *(Accept all reasonable replies.)*

▶ Have the students respond to the opening question.

▶ Invite a volunteer to read aloud the passage from the Gospel of Matthew.

▶ Afterward, observe a moment of silence.

▶ Invite responses to the Scripture question. *(Accept all responses.)*

Focus

Tell the students to turn the page to learn how people in the Church follow the Golden Rule and keep the Commandments by working to build a kind and fair world.

Introduce

▶ Tell the students that one way in which the Church follows the Golden Rule and the Ten Commandments is by following the example of Saint Vincent de Paul.

▶ Explain that the Saint Vincent de Paul Society cares for people in need, in the spirit of Saint Vincent de Paul. Tell about the Saint in your own words.

▶ Underscore what you have shared with the students about Saint Vincent's work by having them read the page silently to themselves.

Reinforce

▶ Ask the follow-up question. *(Accept all appropriate responses.)*

▶ Direct the students' attention to the picture on the page. Ask the students to think about what people of their parish do to show that they are building a kind and fair world. Have them share their thoughts.

▶ Invite the students to read about justice in Disciple Power. Talk about how Saint Vincent de Paul and members of the Saint Vincent de Paul Society treat others with justice by providing them with their basic needs.

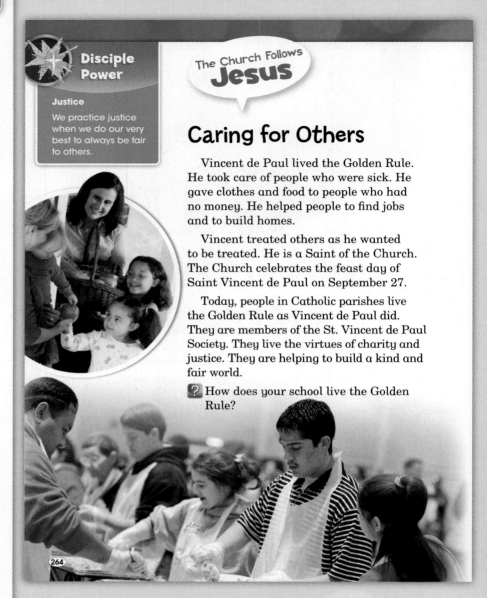

Disciple Power

Justice
We practice justice when we do our very best to always be fair to others.

The Church Follows Jesus

Caring for Others

Vincent de Paul lived the Golden Rule. He took care of people who were sick. He gave clothes and food to people who had no money. He helped people to find jobs and to build homes.

Vincent treated others as he wanted to be treated. He is a Saint of the Church. The Church celebrates the feast day of Saint Vincent de Paul on September 27.

Today, people in Catholic parishes live the Golden Rule as Vincent de Paul did. They are members of the St. Vincent de Paul Society. They live the virtues of charity and justice. They are helping to build a kind and fair world.

❓ How does your school live the Golden Rule?

 264

DISCIPLE POWER

Justice. Justice is one of the four Moral, or Cardinal, Virtues. The Social Teachings of the Catholic Church emphasize that every human being has fundamental human rights—a right to life, to the things required to live a decent and healthy life, to meaningful work, and to freedom—within the limitations required for the common good. Corresponding to these rights, of course, are responsibilities to one another, to our families, and to our community. We are called to be especially responsive to caring for people who are treated unjustly. Reinforce that Saint Vincent de Paul and members of his organization today show respect for others by providing food, clothing, shelter, housing, employment, and medical care to people in need. Through their efforts, God's plan for justice for all grows in the world.

People who live the Ten Commandments live the Golden Rule. They help to build a kind and fair world. They treat people with respect. They know that all people are children of God.

? What is the Golden Rule?

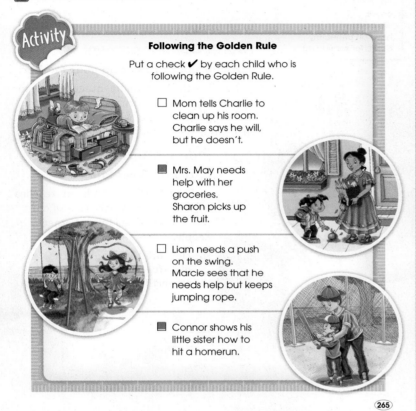

Activity

Following the Golden Rule

Put a check ✔ by each child who is following the Golden Rule.

☐ Mom tells Charlie to clean up his room. Charlie says he will, but he doesn't.

☑ Mrs. May needs help with her groceries. Sharon picks up the fruit.

☐ Liam needs a push on the swing. Marcie sees that he needs help but keeps jumping rope.

☑ Connor shows his little sister how to hit a homerun.

(265)

Connect

▶ Write the Golden Rule (based on Matthew 7:12) on the board: *Treat other people the same way you want them to treat you.*

▶ Briefly discuss how the Golden Rule relates to fairness.

▶ Call attention to the activity, Following the Golden Rule.

▶ Read the directions aloud. Have the students check their choices.

▶ Call on volunteers to share their responses with the class.

▶ Ask the students to tell why they did or did not check a particular scenario.

▶ Congratulate the students on their sense of fairness and justice.

Pray

▶ Invite the students to echo the following prayer:

Loving God, /
guide us along the
way of the Golden Rule. /
Keep us always on the path
to you. /
Amen.

TEACHING TIP

Commandment Examples. As you go through the remaining Commandments with the students, add another column to the chart you have made for the Commandments. In this column, you will write examples of how one would follow the Commandment. After the students read each of the paragraphs about the Commandments, have them come up with concrete examples they can relate to. For example, following the Fourth Commandment to honor and obey your parents includes cleaning your room. Following the Fifth Commandment means avoiding harming one's brother or sister even when they are annoying, and so on.

Pray

Gather the students for prayer. Observe a moment of silence. Then lead them in the prayer with which you closed the previous lesson.

Teach

▶ Ask a volunteer to read the Faith Focus question aloud. Remind the class that the first three Commandments help us love and honor God. Point out that the last seven Commandments teach us to love and respect others and ourselves.

▶ Have the students silently read the opening paragraph. Ask, "Why do all people deserve to be treated with care and respect?" (*All people are children of God.*)

▶ Direct attention to Faith Words. Read the term and its meaning. Have the students make word cards for *covet*.

▶ Call on volunteers to read about the Fourth, Fifth, Sixth, and Ninth Commandments. Ask about their meanings, and jot appropriate answers on the chart you started in the previous chapter. Note: If students ask about the word *adultery,* explain that it pertains mostly to married people who have promised to share their love only with each other. They must keep that promise. The Commandment also reminds us all to treat ourselves and others with respect.

Faith Focus
How do the Fourth through the Tenth Commandments help people to love and respect other people and themselves?

Faith Words
covet
We covet when we have an unhealthy desire for something.

Living the Golden Rule

The first three Commandments teach us how we are to love and honor God. The seven other Commandments help us to follow the Golden Rule. These rules help us to show our love and respect for other people and ourselves. They show us how to act fairly.

Fourth Commandment

4. Honor your father and your mother.

The Fourth Commandment teaches us to honor and obey our parents. We also honor and obey other people whom parents ask to help guide their children.

Fifth Commandment

5. You shall not kill.

The Fifth Commandment teaches us that we are to take care of our own lives and the lives of other people.

❓ How are the people in the pictures showing love and respect for others?

266

CATHOLIC DOCTRINE

Signs of God's Love. All of nature shouts of God's great love for his children. Every good thing is given to us for our happiness. The Law of God handed down through Moses and the Israelites is another example of his loving care for us. To help us live as his children, God gives us the Ten Commandments. In the greatest act of love we know, God the Father sent his only Son into our world to show us how to live his Commandments to perfection.

Sixth and Ninth Commandments

6. You shall not commit adultery.

9. You shall not covet your neighbor's wife.

These two Commandments teach us that we are to respect our own bodies and the bodies of other people. We are not to let people touch us in the wrong way. We are to help families live happy and holy lives.

❓ What are some ways that you can help your family live happy and holy lives?

Catholics Believe

Almsgiving

Jesus teaches that we are to do more than obey the Ten Commandments. We are to share what we have with the poor. Almsgiving is one way we do this. *Almsgiving* is a word that means "sharing something to help the poor." The first Christians did this very well. Their neighbors used to say, "See how much they love one another."

Activity

Respecting Others and Self

Finish the sentences. Tell how you can follow the Golden Rule and show love and respect for others and yourself.

I can show love and respect for my parents and family by

_____

_____

I can show love and respect for my teachers by

_____

_____

I can show love and respect for myself by

_____

_____

267

CATHOLICS BELIEVE

Sharing Material Goods. In Acts 2:44 we read, "All who believed were together and had all things in common; they would sell their property and possessions and divide them among all according to each one's need." These acts of almsgiving by the first Christian communities are the foundation of the great body of Catholic Social Teaching. All members of the Church are called to work to eliminate the sinful inequities that exist between people and to recognize that the needs of poor and vulnerable people have a priority. Help the students to recognize that almsgiving is more than simply giving money or donating toys, clothing, or canned food. We also give alms when we unselfishly give of ourselves—our time and talents—to help others.

Reinforce

▶ Call attention to the follow-up question. Ask the students to respond by working with a partner to describe how the people in the illustrations are showing love and respect.

▶ Read Catholics Believe about almsgiving. Tell the students that almsgiving is a way to practice justice and to do the more Jesus asks of us.

Connect

▶ Point out the activity Respecting Others and Self. Encourage the students to think of ways they can show care and respect for themselves and others. Then have them record their ideas.

▶ Afterward, have the students share ideas.

▶ Challenge the students to keep the Commandments and follow the Golden Rule by putting their ideas into action.

Pray

Pray this as an echo prayer:

Lord, / help us to show love and respect / for other people. / For this we pray / in your name. / Amen.

Key Concept
The Seventh, Eighth, and Tenth Commandments teach us to love and respect others and ourselves.

Pray

Have the students quiet themselves for prayer. Together pray the Lord's Prayer.

Teach

▶ Read the Faith Focus question aloud and have the students think silently about how they might answer it. Tell them that the two pages will help them learn about the Seventh, Eighth, and Tenth Commandments.

▶ Tell the students that loving others also means respecting their property.

▶ Ask volunteers to read aloud the Seventh Commandment, Eighth Commandment, and Tenth Commandment paragraphs on pages 268 and 269.

▶ As others read, ask the rest of the class to notice ways to keep each of the Commandments.

▶ After each paragraph, stop to discuss ways to keep each Commandment. Jot key answers about each Commandment on the chart.

Faith Focus
How do the Seventh, Eighth, and Tenth Commandments help us to live as children of God?

Faith Vocabulary
false witness
Giving false witness means telling lies.

Seventh Commandment

You shall not steal.

The Seventh Commandment teaches us to respect the property of other people. We are not to steal or cheat. When we want to use something that belongs to someone else, we are to ask permission. We are to return the things that we borrow in good condition.

Eighth Commandment

You shall not bear false witness against your neighbor.

The Eighth Commandment teaches that we are to be honest and truthful. We are not to lie. To bear **false witness** means to lie.

Tenth Commandment

You shall not covet your neighbor's goods.

The Tenth Commandment tells us not to be jealous of other people or their things. We are also to use food, water, and other things of creation fairly. We are to share our blessings as gifts from God.

❓ How do the Seventh, Eighth, and Tenth Commandments help you live the Golden Rule?

268

TASKS OF CATECHESIS

Education for Community Life. Present these discussion starters to help the students appreciate the difference it would make if everyone lived the Commandments every day.

▶ A child in your class has cancer. He wears a baseball cap to school because the cancer treatments have made his hair fall out. Everyone feels sorry for him but no one talks to him because they do not know what to say. Is there anything you can say or do for him?

▶ Some children in your neighborhood do not want to play with a new girl who has just moved into the neighborhood because she does not know the rules to the game they are playing. What can you do?

▶ You know one of your friends took candy from the store and is giving it to his friends. What can you do?

Jesus taught his followers that they are to obey and live the Ten Commandments. When we live these Commandments, we are living holy lives. When we live the Ten Commandments, we will find happiness. We are living as children of God.

? What is one way we can choose to live holy lives?

Choosing a Commandment

Read the story below. Then write how the Ten Commandments will help the children make good choices.

Mrs. Andrada has planted beautiful spring flowers. Asad and Chelsea decide it is too far to walk to the playground, so they begin to kick around the ball near Mrs. Andrada's yard. What do the Ten Commandments teach that will help Asad and Chelsea know what to do while they are playing?

_____

_____

_____

_____

Faith-Filled People

Saint John Bosco

John Bosco really had fun going to circuses and learning the tricks magicians performed. After he became a priest, Father John Bosco gathered children around him and did the tricks for them. As they gathered, Father Bosco taught the children about Jesus. The Church celebrates the feast day of Saint John Bosco on January 31.

(269)

Reinforce

▶ Read the follow-up question. Discuss what these three Commandments teach us about treating others fairly. (*Affirm all appropriate responses.*)

▶ Emphasize that the virtue of justice—being fair and generous toward others—will help us live the Seventh, Eighth, and Tenth Commandments.

▶ Ask a volunteer to read aloud Faith-Filled People about Saint John Bosco.

Connect

Read the instructions to the choosing a Commandment activity. Give students the opportunity to respond and then share with a partner what they wrote.

Pray

Ask the students to quiet themselves for prayer. Invite them to silently pray that they may live the Commandments each day. Conclude by praying aloud the Sign of the Cross.

 FAITH-FILLED PEOPLE

Saint John Bosco (1815–1888). John Bosco was ordained a priest in 1841. He worked with homeless boys, teaching them job skills. His theory of education stressed the whole person. He believed that Christ's love and our faith in that love should be a part of every aspect of life—our work, our study, and our play. In 1884, John Bosco founded the Society of Saint Francis de Sales, whose members are called Salesians. He was canonized in 1934. In paying tribute to him, Pope Pius XI praised John Bosco for doing so many positive things in his teaching ministry with young people, especially in changing the ordinary into the extraordinary. He is the patron Saint of young apprentices. For more information on Saint John Bosco go to the Saints Resource at *BeMyDisciples*.com.

Key Concept
Jesus calls us to follow the Commandments and more.

Pray

Lead the students in praying the Glory Be.

Teach

▶ Read the Faith Focus question aloud and have the students think silently about how they might answer it. Tell them that today they will learn what more Jesus asks of his followers beyond keeping the Commandments.

▶ Read the opening paragraph of the text. Then go on to present the story from the Gospel of Mark. As you do so, encourage the students to listen for what more Jesus asks us to do.

Reinforce

After the reading, call attention to the follow-up questions. As the students respond, make sure they are beginning to recognize that Jesus is calling us to a deep solidarity with the poor.

Connect

Recall the information about almsgiving from Catholics Believe on page 267. Create a classroom alms box. Challenge the students to contribute spare change or part of their allowance. Later, they can offer their alms to the parish or to a charitable organization such as the Saint Vincent de Paul Society.

Faith Focus
What more does Jesus call us to do beyond keeping the Ten Commandments?

Share with the Poor

Jesus calls us to love and honor God and to respect one another. In this story, Jesus teaches us to do more than just to obey the Ten Commandments.

One day a man came to Jesus and asked, "Teacher, what must I do to get to heaven?"

Jesus said to the man, "You shall obey the Ten Commandments."

The man told Jesus, "I have always followed all these rules."

Looking at the man Jesus said to him, "There is one more thing you need to do. Give what you have to the poor. Then, come, follow me."

The man was very surprised at Jesus' answer. The man could not do it. He went away sad.

BASED ON MARK 10:17–22

❓ How does your school or parish help the poor? How can you help?

270

TEACHING TIP

Getting to the Point. Revisit the Faith Focus question on occasion and ask volunteers to share their responses. Evaluate whether or not the students have grasped the focus of the lesson. For this lesson, the students should be able to share how the Commandments guide us to live as God wants us to. Give students the opportunity to study the chart you have created for the Commandments and then ask them to answer the Faith Focus question. The students should be able to conclude that when they follow the Commandments they are leading holy lives and living as children of God.

When you live the Ten Commandments, you are living as a child of God. You are building a kind and fair world. When you keep the Golden Rule and share with the poor, you are doing even more. You are living as a disciple of Jesus.

 My Faith Choice

I will keep the Ten Commandments this week. I will do more, as Jesus asked. I will

_____

_____

 Pray, "Holy Spirit, teach me and help me to keep the Commandments. I want to honor you, be fair to others, and do even more. Amen."

(271)

Reinforce

Remind the students that when they live the Ten Commandments they are helping to build a world where God is respected and people are fair and loving toward one another. Read aloud the opening paragraph on the page.

Respond

▶ Have the students suggest ways to follow the Golden Rule by living the Commandments.

▶ Have the students then read the sentences in the activity frame.

▶ Choose a volunteer to read the directions, and invite the students to complete the activity alone or with partners.

Choose

▶ Present My Faith Choice. Have the students write their choices.

▶ Encourage them to put their choices into practice this week.

Pray

Lead the students in the prayer to the Holy Spirit at the bottom of the page.

TEACHING TIP

The Giraffe Project. The Ten Commandments help us live holy lives. Doing the right thing often requires sticking our neck out. Use this opportunity to tell the students about the Giraffe Project. The Giraffe Project, a nonprofit organization, was founded in 1982. Its purpose is to publicize stories of ordinary people, especially children, who have stuck their necks out to do the right thing. The genius of the Giraffe Project is that it tells us about real heroes. Go to BeMyDisciples.com to find links to the Giraffe Project. Share some of the stories with the class, and send home the Web site information so that the students' families can share in this project.

Pray

Begin class by slowly and reverently praying the Sign of the Cross together.

Recall

▶ Turn the To Help You Remember statements into questions. Invite volunteers to answer them. Then have the students read the statements aloud together.

▶ Introduce the activity. Ask the students to stand if they agree and to put their heads down on the table or desk if they do not agree. Then give them time to circle Yes or No.

Reflect

Point out the reflection statement. Encourage the students to think carefully about how they might complete the statement. Then have them write their answers.

Share

▶ Canvass the room for responses to the statement.

▶ Encourage the students to share their reflection with their families.

▶ **TO HELP YOU REMEMBER**

1. People who live the Ten Commandments help to build a kind and fair world.

2. The Fourth through the Tenth Commandments teach us to love, honor, and respect other people and ourselves.

3. Jesus calls us to follow him by keeping the Ten Commandments and the Golden Rule and by doing even more.

Chapter Review

Recall

Circle Yes if a sentence is true. Circle No if a sentence is not true.

1. The Fourth through the Tenth Commandments show us how to honor, respect, and love God.   **Yes** (**No**)

2. The Fourth Commandment is "Treat other people the same way you want them to treat you."   **Yes** (**No**)

3. The Fourth through the Tenth Commandments show us how to follow the Golden Rule and to build a kind and fair world.   (**Yes**) **No**

4. The Sixth and Ninth Commandments teach us that we are to respect our own bodies and the bodies of other people.   (**Yes**) **No**

5. Jesus' followers should do more than just obey the Ten Commandments.   (**Yes**) **No**

Reflect

Reread the Scripture story on page 270. What is Jesus asking us to do in our lives today?

_____

_____

Share | Share with your class how you can live the Golden Rule and do even more.

(272)

TEACHING TIP

Another Review Exercise. Divide the class into groups. Give each student a large sheet of poster paper or newsprint. Display the Commandments chart you created with the students for all to see. Then ask each group to rewrite the Ten Commandments in their own words. They may use some of the examples from the chart to clarify their statements. Restate your instructions as necessary, and be available to help each group as this task may be challenging for some students. Allowing them to title their work by finishing the statement, "God's Ten Commandments according to _____", can make this activity fun.

Trust in the Lord!

At Baptism, we receive the grace to live God's Commandments. Pray this prayer. Tell God you will try your best to live as a follower of his Son, Jesus Christ.

Leader Remember the Lord's teachings. Keep his laws with all your heart.

All **Lord, teach us your laws.**

Leader God, help us to always honor you.

All **Lord, teach us your laws.**

Leader God, help us to always treat others with love and respect.

All **Lord, teach us your laws.**

Leader Help us to love others as ourselves.

All **Lord, teach us your laws.**

Leader Help us to give to the poor and to do even more as Jesus asks.

All **Lord, teach us your laws.**

Leader Trust in the Lord with all your heart. The Lord will lead you on a straight path.

All **Lord, we will always trust in you. Amen.**

273

We Pray

▶ Prepare the students for prayer by reading aloud the opening paragraph of the prayer Trust in the Lord.

▶ Point out the prayer's refrain: *Lord, teach us your laws.* Explain that these words are a prayerful promise to follow the Commandments.

▶ Invite the students to place their hands over their heart in a gesture of promise each time they make the response. Take a moment to practice the response and the prayer gesture.

▶ Gather the students in the prayer center. If possible, process there with musical accompaniment.

▶ Lead the prayer.

▶ Conclude by sharing a sign of peace.

BIBLE BACKGROUND

The Commandments—Not Written in Stone. The image of the Ten Commandments as being written in stone, and therefore absolute and concrete, is hard to shake. Jesus, however, reminded us of a different way—the right way—to look at God's Law. Jesus made it clear that the Ten Commandments, albeit essential, are the very least one can do to bring about God's Kingdom of justice, peace, and love. Jesus says that to seek perfection, it is necessary to do more, to love our neighbor as ourself.

Preview

▶ Have the students carefully tear out pages 273 and 274 along the perforation.

▶ Encourage the students to share these pages with their families, and to complete the activities together.

▶ If they did not complete the review activity on page 272 by the end of the session, emphasize that they can complete it with their families at home.

▶ Point out the title and theme of the next lesson to the students.

Visit BeMyDisciples.com

▶ Take time with the students to explore the many activities and resources available at the *Be My Disciples* Web site.

▶ Encourage them to join with their families to discover the many resources available at the Web site.

Before Moving On ...

As you finish today's lesson, reflect on the following question before moving on to the next chapter.

Do I make a faith choice each week, just as I encourage the students to do? If so, have I ever shared a way that I acted on my choice?

With My Family

This Week . . .

In Chapter 20, "We Love Others," your child learned:

▶ The Fourth through the Tenth Commandments name ways that we are to love, honor, and respect other people, ourselves, and all of God's creation.

▶ The Golden Rule summarizes the Fourth through the Tenth Commandments.

▶ Jesus taught that we are to do more than just obey the Ten Commandments. We are to share our blessings with the poor.

▶ The Ten Commandments help us live as children of God. They guide us to build a kind and fair world. They help us prepare for the coming of the Kingdom of God.

▶ People who live the virtue of justice work to build a kind and fair world.

For more about related teachings of the Church, see the *Catechism of the Catholic Church*, 2196–2246, 2258–2317, 2331–2391, 2401–2449, 2464–2503, 2514–2527, 2534–2550, and the *United States Catholic Catechism for Adults*, pages 375–455.

■ Sharing God's Word

Read together Mark 10:17–22, Jesus' teaching on doing more than just obeying the Ten Commandments. As a family, discuss what more your family can do to act as Jesus' disciples and follow him. Name ways your family can build a just and kind world.

■ Living as Disciples

The Christian home and family is a school of discipleship. Grow in your love for all people as Jesus commanded. Choose one of the following activities to do as a family, or design a similar activity of your own.

▶ Help your children write and illustrate a storybook about how your family shows respect for other people and thus honors God.

▶ Talk about what your school does to build a just and kind world. You might use a copy of your school newsletter or visit your school Web site as a guide for your discussion.

■ Our Spiritual Journey

Every person has a call to holiness. Every person has the inner longing to be the person who they were created to be—the image and likeness of God. Living the Ten Commandments is the minimum we can do to travel the road to happiness and holiness. This week at mealtime, pray the prayer on page 273 at the end of the meal.

For more ideas on ways your family can live as disciples of Jesus, visit **BeMyDisciples.com**

274

THE LAST WORD

Celebrating Learning. As you conclude Unit 5, congratulate the students for all that they have learned in the last four chapters. For example, you may want to invite volunteers to name some of the new words that they have learned, or you can encourage the second graders to recall a favorite Scripture story or activity from the unit. Remind the students that they have learned how Jesus' disciples are called to live in this world.

Enriching the Lesson

Discovering A World of Justice

Purpose

To reinforce and illustrate the virtue of justice (taught on page 264) in action

Directions

▶ Have the students find pictures and headlines from newspapers and magazines that they feel show people working to build a world of justice.

▶ Direct the students to cut out their findings and then glue them to a large inflated ball, for example, a beach ball.

▶ Allow the students to create their own drawings and words to add to the "world."

▶ Arrange to display the finished work for others to admire.

Materials

large inflated ball

magazines

newspapers

scissors

glue sticks

colored markers

crayons

Collecting Food for Those in Need

Purpose

To reinforce how we live the Ten Commandments by sharing our gifts (taught on page 270)

Directions

Students enjoy giving and showing their love for others.

▶ Suggest that the students participate in a monthly food drive.

▶ Together, create a calendar of different food items for each month. A sample calendar of items follows:

September   canned fruit
October   canned soup
November   hot and cold cereals

▶ Remind the students to bring in their food items the week before they are due.

▶ Arrange with your local food bank to receive these donations monthly.

Materials

poster board for calendar

Catholic Social Teaching: Respect for Our Elders

Purpose

To reinforce the Fourth Commandment (taught on page 266)

Directions

▶ Brainstorm with the students words and actions that show respect for their parents and grandparents.

▶ Invite the students to create a collage of words and pictures cut from magazines that indicate respect for elders.

▶ Have the students glue the words and pictures on large pieces of construction paper that you have labeled "We Honor Our Elders."

Materials

magazines

scissors

glue sticks

construction paper with prepared title

Catholic Social Teaching Unit 5

Pray

Gather the students for prayer. Briefly paraphrase the biblical story of creation, emphasizing Genesis 1:27, 31. Conclude by asking the class to echo "Lord God, we are your children" after you.

Focus

Introduce the Catholic Social Teaching principle by reading the text in the sidebar to the class.

Introduce

Ask the students to describe what happens at a talent show. Go around the room and invite volunteers to share what talents they would demonstrate in a talent show. Affirm the gifts and talents of all the students in the class.

Teach

- Invite the students to look at the picture on page 275. Ask volunteers to point out what talents the children in the picture are practicing. Ask why they think some of the children are not involved.

- Read the story aloud to the class.

- Invite volunteers to play the roles of the children in the story and act out the story. You can play the role of Mrs. Chu, the teacher. After the enactment, ask the students to summarize what Mrs. Chu said at the end. *(Each of you is different. Each of you is special. Everyone has good qualities and talents to share.)*

Catholic Social Teaching

A Talent for Everyone

The students in the second grade class wanted to do something special for their families. "Let's put on a talent show!" someone said. Some of the children were very excited.

"I'll play the piano," said Alana. "I can play the drums," John quickly added.

"I can read the poem I wrote," Hector added. "I can jump rope!" said Emily. "And Austin can juggle!"

Some of the children were very quiet. "I don't have a good talent," said Kate.

"But Kate," said Mrs. Chu, their teacher, "you always make us laugh. You are so cheerful and bubbly! What a wonderful quality that is."

"But what will we do for the talent show?" several other students asked.

"Maybe we should stop talking about the talent show," said their teacher. "I think we need to focus on something else first. Each of you is different, and each of you is special. You all have good qualities and talents."

> **WE RESPECT ALL PEOPLE**
>
> God creates every person with good qualities and talents. We have different qualities and talents to share with one another. We value each other's gifts.

(275)

BACKGROUND: CATHOLIC SOCIAL TEACHING

The Equal Dignity of All People. Chapter 3 of the *Compendium of the Social Doctrine of the Church* (*CSDC*) speaks to the Church's teaching on the human person. It teaches "*Since something of the glory of God shines on the face of every person, the dignity of every person before God is the basis of the dignity of man before other men. Moreover, this is the ultimate foundation of the radical equality and brotherhood among all people, regardless of their race, nation, sex, origin, culture, or class*" (*CSDC*, 144).

Making Connections

Each of us has good qualities and gifts that God has given us. We can help each other discover our good qualities. We can share our gifts with others.

with Language Arts

Read the book *Stellaluna* by Janell Cannon. *Stellaluna* is about a bat that has the special qualities of a bat. Her bird friends are different from her, but they still get along with Stellaluna, and she with them. Pretend you are Stellaluna. Write an entry for your diary telling what you think and feel about what happened in the story.

with Social Studies

Stellaluna does not have to be just like her bird friends in order to get along with them. Think about your friends. Describe how you are the same and how you are different. Write one way you are different. Tell how this talent can help your family or your class.

with Creative Arts

All people are special. They are children of God. People differ from one another in many ways. Write a slogan that tells about the importance of each person. Make a banner with your slogan on it. Hang it in your classroom or in the hallway at school.

Faith Action

Think about a person in your class who is different from you. Write how that person can help you. Write how you can help that person. Give friendship a chance.

_____

_____

_____

(276)

Catholic Social Teaching

Reinforce

Paraphrase or read aloud the opening paragraph on page 276. Remind the students that God creates and gives each person good qualities and talents.

Connect

Introduce the cross-curricular activities and carefully explain all three to the students. Invite and answer any questions that the students might have. Ask the students to choose the activity or activities that they want to work on. Tell them they will share their completed activities with the whole class.

▶ **Language Arts:** Distribute the writing paper. Have the students write their diary entries after they have read *Stellaluna*.

▶ **Social Studies:** The students do not necessarily have to read *Stellaluna* to complete this activity, but it would be helpful.

▶ **Creative Arts:** Have the students work in pairs to create and design their slogans. Be sure to invite the students who do this activity to share their slogan with the class.

Choose

▶ Invite the students to read quietly the concluding text.

▶ Challenge them to give friendship with those who are different from them a chance.

Pray

Repeat the opening prayer.

Unit 5 Review

The unit review provides the opportunity to assess the students' understanding of the concepts presented in the unit and to affirm them in their growing knowledge and love of God. Here are a few suggestions for using these pages.

▶ Share with the students that the next two pages are an opportunity to stop and review what they have learned.

▶ Provide time for the students to ask questions.

▶ Have the students complete the review alone or with a partner.

A. Choose the Best Word

This section reviews the main concepts of the unit.

▶ Read the directions for section A. Illustrate what you expect the students to do by completing the first question together. By working together on the first sentence, you are teaching the students a strategy for completing these types of sentences.

▶ When the students have finished this section, invite volunteers to share their answers. Review any question that the students seem to have difficulty completing.

B. Show What You Know

This section reinforces what the students have learned about Jesus.

▶ Read the directions to the students. Have the students complete the section.

▶ Invite volunteers to share their answers.

Unit 5 Review

Name _____

A. Choose the Best Word

Fill in the blanks to complete each sentence. Use the words from the word bank.

| Almsgiving | honor | Golden Rule |
| Ten Commandments | Grace | Great Commandment |

1. The _Great Commandment_ is to love God above all else and to love people as we love ourselves.

2. _Almsgiving_ means sharing something to give to the poor.

3. The _Ten Commandments_ are the laws God gave us to help us live happy and holy lives.

4. To _honor_ a person is to show that person great respect.

5. When we treat others the same way we want them to treat us, we are following the _Golden Rule_.

6. _Grace_ is the gift of God sharing his life with us.

B. Show What You Know

Match the words in Column A with their meanings in Column B.

Column A

1. justice
2. Cross
3. obedience
4. fortitude

Column B

_2_ a. sign of Jesus' great love for his Father and us

_3_ b. strengthens us to respect people in authority

_1_ c. good habit of being fair and kind

_4_ d. strengthens us to do what is right and good when it is difficult

277

TEACHING TIP

Self-assessment. Value the unit reviews as an opportunity for your own assessment. Sharing the faith of the Church with the students and facilitating their growth as persons of faith is not an easy ministry. Listen carefully to the students' responses. Their incorrect responses or their inability to respond will give you insights on ways to improve your presentation of the material, and help you to realize their growth in faith is not your work alone—the Holy Spirit is truly the Teacher during your sessions, and you also support the parents, who are the primary catechists of their children.

C. Connect with Scripture

What was your favorite story about Jesus in this unit?
Draw something that happened in the story.
Tell your class about it.

D. Be a Disciple

1. *What Saint or holy person did you enjoy hearing about in this unit? Write the name here. Tell your class what this person did to follow Jesus.*

_____

_____

2. *What can you do to be a good disciple of Jesus?*

_____

_____

278

C. Connect with Scripture

This section reinforces the students' experience and knowledge of Scripture and the teachings of Jesus.

▶ Help the students review the Scripture stories in the unit, beginning with the Unit Opener story. You may wish to write the names of these stories on the board to assist them.

▶ Ask volunteers to share their favorite stories with the class.

▶ In the space, invite the students to draw something that happened in the story. Invite volunteers to share their drawings now, or at the completion of the Unit Review.

D. Be a Disciple

This section provides the students with the opportunity to recall how the Saints and holy people followed Jesus. It reinforces the ways students can choose to live as disciples of Jesus.

▶ Ask the students to remember their favorite stories of Saints or holy people that they learned about in this unit. Refresh their memories as needed, and write their responses on the board.

▶ Give each student time to write the name of their favorite Saint or holy person on the line. Ask volunteers to share the reason for their choices.

▶ Lead a discussion about the actions that make us good disciples of Jesus. Give the students time to write on the lines their idea of what they could do.

Objectives

In Unit 6, the students will learn that:

▶ Making wise choices now will help us find happiness in Heaven.

▶ Wise choices show that we are forming and following our conscience.

▶ Sanctifying grace is the gift of God's life that he shares with us.

▶ The Our Father helps us to live as children of God.

Spiritual Insights

"The Kingdom is already here because of the redemption of Jesus Christ. But in another sense, it is 'not yet' here, since Christ's final transformation of individuals, society, and culture has yet to happen in its fullness. That is why we need to pray this petition ('thy Kingdom come' in the Lord's Prayer) every day and work for its coming" (*United States Catholic Catechism for Adults*, page 486).

"If a brother or sister has nothing to wear and has no food for the day, and one of you says to them, 'Go in peace, keep warm, and eat well,' but you do not give them the necessities of the body, what good is it?" (*James 2:15–16*).

Living the Six Tasks of Catechesis

Missionary Initiative: Saint Katharine Drexel (1858–1955)

When Katharine Drexel joined the convent, the headlines in the Philadelphia newspapers called her the richest nun in America! Katharine came from a very wealthy family, but was always taught that she had a special responsibility to serve people in need.

Katharine's family frequently traveled throughout the United States and Europe. On one trip, Katharine was saddened to see the poverty of the Native Americans living on reservations. Later, during a family visit to Rome, the family was granted an audience with Pope Leo XIII. Katharine pleaded with the Pope to send missionaries to help the neglected tribes. The Pope asked her, "Why don't you become a missionary yourself?"

Katharine knew that God was calling her to a life of service. When she inherited her father's fortune, she donated money to the neglected Native Americans. The money was used to build schools and to meet the many other physical and spiritual needs of Native peoples.

Yet, it was not enough. Katharine joined the Sisters of Mercy for three years of formation in religious life. With the blessing of the bishop, Sister Katharine left the Mercy order to establish a new religious community, the Sisters of the Blessed Sacrament, dedicated to the education of Native-Americans and Blacks. Over the next six decades, Katharine and her sisters built over 63 schools in 21 states. Mother Katharine, as everyone called her, founded Xavier University in New Orleans, the first Catholic university in the United States for African Americans.

We celebrate Saint Katharine Drexel's feast day on March 3. Saint Katharine never stopped working for justice and equality for all people. Her life reminds all teachers that we are called to continue Christ's work in the world and to do our best to prepare the way for the coming of God's kingdom of perfect peace, love, and justice.

Sharing Your Faith

Find a partner to work with: a spouse, a friend, a fellow teacher. Come together at the beginning or end of each unit for shared prayer and discussion. Use the questions below as a starting point. As an alternative, record your thoughts in a personal journal.

▶ How do you prepare the way for the coming of God's kingdom?

▶ If you inherited a fortune, as Saint Katharine Drexel did, how would you use it to serve others?

▶ What are some of the service activities you have planned to enable your students to reach out to people in need?

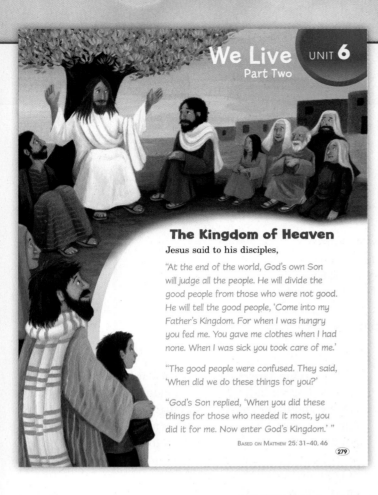

We Live
Part Two
UNIT 6

The Kingdom of Heaven

Jesus said to his disciples,

"At the end of the world, God's own Son will judge all the people. He will divide the good people from those who were not good. He will tell the good people, 'Come into my Father's Kingdom. For when I was hungry you fed me. You gave me clothes when I had none. When I was sick you took care of me.'

"The good people were confused. They said, 'When did we do these things for you?'

"God's Son replied, 'When you did these things for those who needed it most, you did it for me. Now enter God's Kingdom.' "

BASED ON MATTHEW 25: 31–40, 46

279

What I Know

What is something you already know about these faith concepts?

Making Wise Choices

_____

_____

Conscience

_____

_____

The Our Father

_____

_____

Put an X next to the faith words you know. Put a ? next to the faith words you need to learn more about.

____ mortal sin ____ sanctifying grace ____ consequences

____ Heaven ____ Kingdom of God ____ hope

What do you know about the proverbs in the Bible?

_____

A Question I Have

What question would you like to ask about making good choices to live a holy and happy life?

_____

_____

280

Unit 6 Opener

The Unit 6 opener pages help to assess the students' prior knowledge about the key faith concepts in the unit. Processing these pages should take no more than fifteen minutes.

Opening Page

Invite the children to tell you what they see in the image on the page. Proclaim the Scripture story. Ask: When have you kept a promise? Was it easy or hard to do? Why? Accept their answers, but do not respond further at this time.

Getting Ready

This page continues the activation of prior knowledge. Do not correct the children's responses. You will invite them to return and self-correct themselves at the end of the unit.

▶ Have the students write their responses under What I Know and A Question I Have. You may also do the exercises orally.

▶ Record the students' questions on a chart. Refer back to the chart as you progress through the unit and ask volunteers to respond when they can answer the questions. You may also wish to use these questions during a unit assessment.

▶ Ask the students to turn to the next page and begin Chapter 21.

BACKGROUND

Making Moral Choices

Living a holy life involves making moral choices every day. Supported by the Theological Virtues of faith, hope, and love, and the Cardinal Virtues of prudence, justice, fortitude, and temperance, we are asked to make choices to live as children of God and as disciples of Christ. Graced with wisdom, understanding, right judgment, fortitude, knowledge, reverence, and wonder and awe—the Gifts of the Holy Spirit—we are enlightened and strengthened to make those choices.

The Dimensions of Our Moral Choices

Precisely because we are free to choose to do what is good, we are moral subjects. We are responsible for our actions and their consequences. To help us assess the morality of our actions, we need to look at the three dimensions of the moral content of an action that determine whether our choices are morally good or evil: the object, the intention, and the circumstances.

The **object** of an act refers to the action itself. It is the thing that is done. The object may be good in itself or evil by nature. For example, it is good to tell the truth, to give alms to the poor, to save a life; it is evil to cheat, to murder. That is to say that some choices are always evil. They are objectively evil. Nothing can change the fact that they are evil.

The **intention** (or end) of an act refers to the person's goal or purpose in doing the thing that is done. This too may be good or evil. A noteworthy aspect of Catholic teaching is that a good intention cannot make an evil object into something good. In other words, the end does not justify the means. On the other hand, a bad, or evil, intention may corrupt a good action, such as a person giving alms simply because they wish to win the acclaim of their community.

The **circumstances** refer to particular features surrounding the individual situation in which an action is taken and to the consequences that result from it. Circumstances do not in themselves make something good or bad, but they do contribute to the degree of its goodness or evil. For example, one may act out of ignorance or coercion, in which case one's moral culpability is lessened.

Moral Decisions are Complex

Making moral choices is sometimes relatively easy and clear. We decide to tell the truth rather than lie, to be kind rather than cruel, to show mercy rather than seek revenge, to be honest rather than cheat, to be generous rather than selfish.

Sometimes making moral decisions can be complex and difficult, requiring a great deal of reflection and soul searching. We need assistance and guidance to help us arrive at a good moral decision. We need to pray, to read the Scriptures and reflect on the life of Jesus, to listen to Church teaching, and to seek the wise advice from competent individuals.

For Reflection

What do I do when I am faced with making a complex moral decision?

How has another person advised me on evaluating the morality of a particular action?

Teacher to Teacher

Words of Wisdom

The people of the Old Testament used wise sayings collected in the Book of Proverbs to help them live holy lives. These sayings or proverbs can help us think about God and live as his children.

Second graders are familiar with what can be considered wise sayings. They hear them at home and in school, on the radio and TV. They often have to do with safety, such as "Cross at the green, not in-between" and "Buckle up for safety." Families often have their own wise sayings that are passed down from one generation to the next.

Words of Influence

Ask the students to share any sayings their parents or grandparents use frequently. Remind them that words like these, when heard often, will stay with them for a long, long time.

Remember that what you say to the students, even the simplest advice, can influence them and help them live holier lives. You can and do make a difference by sharing your own loving words of wisdom with the students.

The Church Teaches...

"Just as Christ instructed his followers according to their capacity to understand his message, the Church also must take serious account of the circumstances and cultures in which the faithful live in order to present the meaning of the Gospel to them in understandable ways. There is one saving word—Jesus Christ—but that word can be spoken in many different ways" (*National Directory for Catechesis,* **47**).

As you teach this chapter, remember that God invites all people to live in his Kingdom. By respecting and honoring the diverse group of students before you, you will open their minds and hearts to the universal mission to make disciples of all people.

Further Reading and Reflection

For more related teachings of the Church, see the *Catechism of the Catholic Church,* 1720–1724 and 2825; and the *United States Catholic Catechism for Adults,* pages 315–317.

Teacher Prayer

Father, help me grow in love as I share our faith story with the students. Help me use proverbs so that I too may live as a child of God. Amen.

Lesson Planner

Chapter 21 We Make Choices

Goal To discover that making wise choices now will help us find happiness in Heaven

LESSON PART	PROCESS	MATERIALS and RESOURCES
DAY 1 EXPLORE **Focus** To explore how followers of Jesus make wise choices **Pages** 281–283	▶ Proclaim and discuss Joshua 24:15 (My family will serve the Lord). ▶ Learn and discuss the story of Saint Francis of Assisi. **Disciple Power:** Humility **Activity:** Decide whether a Commandment or the Golden Rule helps us make a wise choice.	Bible Pencils or pens Drawing paper
DAY 2 DISCOVER **Focus** To discover that wise choices help us live as children of God **Pages** 284–285	▶ Discover that Jesus shows us how to make wise choices. **Catholics Believe:** Daily Prayer **Faith Words:** wise choices **Activity:** Analyze illustrations and make wise choices.	Bible Pencil or pens **Enriching the Lesson:** Teacher Guide, page 411 • Holding a "Wise Choice" Party • Making Care for Creation Posters
DAY 3 DISCOVER **Focus** To discover that proverbs can help us make wise choices **Pages** 286–287	▶ Learn about the proverbs in the Bible. **Faith-Filled People:** Saint Clare of Assisi **Scripture:** Wise sayings about: becoming a leader (Proverbs 12:24); a cheerful outlook (Proverbs 15:15); following good advice (Proverbs 15:22). **Activity:** Choose proverbs to help make wise choices.	Bibles Pencils or pens
DAY 4 DECIDE **Focus** To discover why it is important to make wise choices and to decide how to be a peacemaker **Pages** 288–289	▶ Discover that making wise choices will help us find happiness in heaven. **Faith Words:** Heaven **Activity:** Finish a proverb. **My Faith Choice:** Choose how to be a peacemaker this week.	Bibles Pencil or pens Crayons or colored markers **Enriching the Lesson:** Teacher Guide, page 411 Drawing Pictures of Peace **Additional Activities Booklet:** Activities 21a and 21b or see *BeMyDisciples*.com
DAY 5 CONCLUDE **Focus** To realize that God will help us to be peacemakers. **Pages** 290–292	▶ **REVIEW** Review concepts: Recall, Reflect, and Share. ▶ **PRAY** Prayer of Saint Francis ▶ **Preview** the With My Family page and the theme of the next chapter.	Bible, candle, cross for prayer space Grade 2 Music CD **Assessment Tools Booklet:** Assessments 21a and 21b

Assign online Chapter Review and interactive Chapter Test at **BeMyDisciples.com**

Chapter **21**

We Make Choices

? What was a good choice you made recently?

Some of God's people were not following God's ways. Listen to what Joshua, the leader of the people, told them they had to do.

Whom will you choose to serve? My family and I choose to serve the Lord our God.

BASED ON JOSHUA 24:15

? How can a family serve the Lord?

281

Pray

▶ Welcome the students warmly. Help them quiet themselves for prayer.

▶ Begin and end with the Sign of the Cross.

▶ Pray together with the children the Glory Be.

Reflect

▶ Have the students describe what they see happening in the picture. *(child making a choice)*

▶ Then direct the students to respond to the opening question. *(Accept all responsible replies.)*

▶ Read the introduction to the Scripture passage from the Book of Joshua. Then call on a volunteer to read the passage aloud.

▶ Afterward, observe a moment of silence.

▶ Invite responses to the Scripture question. *(Accept all responses.)*

▶ Conclude with the Sign of the Cross.

Focus

Invite the students to turn the page to learn about someone who chose to follow the Lord to true happiness.

HUMAN METHODOLOGIES

Learning Through Human Experience. The *National Directory for Catechesis* tells us, "Human experiences provide the sensible signs that lead the person . . . to a better understanding of the truths of the faith" *(NDC 29A)*. As you teach the students about making good choices, keep in mind that second graders sometimes get confused about accidents and mistakes, which are out of their control and not a result of choices they make. Emphasize that no one makes a mistake on purpose. Make clear that mistakes and accidents are not sins by suggesting a pair of situations to the students and have them identify which one is an accident or mistake and which is a sin.

Introduce

▶ Tell the students that making wise choices can make a difference in the way we live our lives.

▶ Invite the students to tell what they may know about Saint Francis of Assisi.

▶ Tell the students to listen to the choice Saint Francis made.

▶ Have volunteers take turns reading about Saint Francis of Assisi.

Reinforce

▶ Have the students respond to the follow-up question.

▶ Invite the students to read about humility in Disciple Power. Talk about how Saint Francis of Assisi lived this virtue.

▶ Ask the students to recall what they have already learned about the followers of Saint Francis of Assisi, the Franciscans. (See Chapter 15, Thank You, Lord on page 198 about the Franciscan bread-line.) Remind the students that the Franciscans serve the Lord by choosing to share with others the same love and respect Saint Francis of Assisi shared with everyone he met.

Disciple Power

Humility

Humility helps us to recognize that all we are and all we have comes from God. We are humble when we choose to follow God's ways and make them our own.

The Church Follows **Jesus**

Saint Francis of Assisi

We have to make choices about the way we want to live. Here is a story about someone who made many important choices.

Francis grew up thinking he would be happy by becoming a rich and famous soldier. So Francis set off to win battles.

But one night, Francis had a dream. In the dream, God asked Francis to return home. Francis chose to do what God asked.

Francis gave away all his riches and began to live a very simple and humble life. Francis chose to serve the Lord.

Today, we know Francis as Saint Francis of Assisi. His followers are called Franciscans. Like Saint Francis, they choose poverty and to humbly serve the Lord. The Church celebrates the feast day of Saint Francis on October 4.

 What was Saint Francis' choice?

282

DISCIPLE POWER

Humility. Recall that the First Commandment teaches us to love God above all else. Help the students recognize that one way we can show our humility is to honor God's greatness with our actions and gestures. Remind them that we bow before receiving the Body and Blood of Jesus in the Eucharist. We genuflect in church before the Blessed Sacrament. We kneel to pray. Sometimes we bow our heads when we say Jesus' name. Take time to practice these humble gestures with the students, including making the Sign of the Cross with reverence.

Saint Francis of Assisi listened to God and chose to do what God asked. Each person has a choice to follow God's Laws. Each person may choose to be a disciple of Jesus.

? What choices have you made when you chose to listen to God?

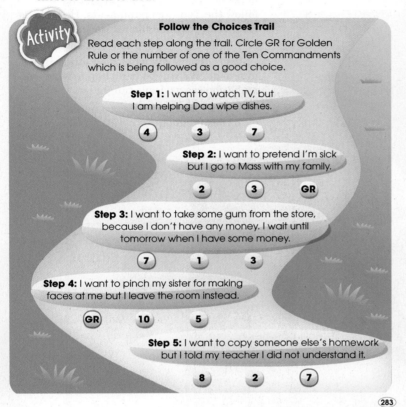

Activity

Follow the Choices Trail

Read each step along the trail. Circle GR for Golden Rule or the number of one of the Ten Commandments which is being followed as a good choice.

Step 1: I want to watch TV, but I am helping Dad wipe dishes.

(4)   (3)   (7)

Step 2: I want to pretend I'm sick but I go to Mass with my family.

(2)   (3)   (GR)

Step 3: I want to take some gum from the store, because I don't have any money. I wait until tomorrow when I have some money.

(7)   (1)   (3)

Step 4: I want to pinch my sister for making faces at me but I leave the room instead.

(GR)   (10)   (5)

Step 5: I want to copy someone else's homework but I told my teacher I did not understand it.

(8)   (2)   (7)

(283)

Connect

▶ Briefly review the Ten Commandments (refer to the chart you made for the commandments in Chapters 19 and 20) and the Golden Rule. If you wish, post the chart and write the Golden Rule on the board.

▶ Direct the students' attention to the activity, Follow the Choices Trail. Explain that they are to read each step and then choose (circle) the number of the commandment or GR for the Golden Rule which they think would guide them in making the best choice.

▶ Give the students time to make their choices.

▶ Canvass the class for responses. *(Step 1: 4; Step 2: 3; Step 3: 7; Step 4: GR or 5; Step 5: 7)*

▶ Emphasize how following the Ten Commandments and the Golden Rule can help us when we are faced with making choices.

Pray

Gather the students for prayer. Lead them in praying the Glory Be.

TEACHING TIP

Connecting with Home. Involve the families in tomorrow's lesson by sending a note home with the students asking each family to write on a sheet of paper one or more wise sayings that help them make good choices. Collect the families' sayings and create a bulletin board with them.

Key Concept
Our wise choices can help us live as God's children.

Pray

Invite the students to quiet themselves for prayer. Invite a volunteer to lead the class in praying the Lord's Prayer.

Teach

▶ Call on a student to read the Faith Focus question aloud. Ask the students for possible answers. Tell them that these two pages will help them learn what our wise choices help us do.

▶ Present Making Wise Choices in your own words.

▶ Afterward, point out the term *wise choice* in Faith Words and have a volunteer read it aloud.

▶ Have the students make a word card for the term.

Reinforce

▶ Ask the follow-up question. *(Answers will vary.)*

▶ Go on to ask: How did Jesus show that he loved God the Father more than anyone or anything else? *(Jesus always chose to do what his Father asked him to do.)*

▶ Remind the students that God the Father sent Jesus to show us how to make wise choices. Jesus taught us to follow the Ten Commandments, the Great Commandment, and the Golden Rule.

▶ Present the material in Catholics Believe. Emphasize that God is with us to help us make good and wise choices.

Faith Focus
Why is it important to make wise choices?

Faith Words
wise choices
A wise choice is a choice that helps us to live as children of God.

Making Wise Choices

God sent Jesus to show us how to make **wise choices**. A wise choice is one that helps us live as God's children.

Jesus gave us many ways to help us make good choices. Jesus taught us to follow the Ten Commandments. He gave us the Great Commandment. He showed us how to live the Golden Rule.

Jesus always did what his Father asked him to do. We will be truly happy when we make choices as Jesus taught us.

❓ What wise choices do you make to live as Jesus taught us?

284

TEACHING TIP

Teaching Discipline. Every once in a while, a serious conduct issue arises as a result of a poor moral choice made by one or more of the students. As the teacher, it is important that you gain or maintain control of the situation while leaving the students' dignity intact. You may begin by pointing out what is wrong with the situation and give the students involved ownership of the problem. "Looks like you two have a problem here, what are you going to do about it?" Working with the students, develop a plan of action that they will carry out. With real world consequences the students will gain a better understanding of what was wrong with the situation and how they might work to prevent it from happening in the future.

God gave us many people to help us make wise decisions. Teachers help us at school, priests help us during the homily at Mass, and parents and families help us at home. God also gave us the Holy Spirit to help us make good choices.

? Who helps you to make wise choices?

Catholics Believe

Daily Prayer

Christians are people of prayer. As Proverbs 16:3 tells us, asking God's help in prayer will help us make good and wise choices. Praying every day helps us grow in humility. It shows that we know we cannot live without God.

Activity

Making Choices

Look and think about what is happening in the pictures. Write what choice you would make next. Share why your choices are wise choices.

_____
_____
_____
_____
_____

285

Connect

▶ Read through the directions for the activity entitled Making Choices.

▶ Direct attention to the two illustrations on the page. Have the students describe what is happening in each.

▶ Give the students time to write what they would do in each situation.

▶ Afterward, call on various students; ask them to share their choices and to tell why they are wise choices.

Pray

Gather the students for prayer. Have them echo the following:

Lord God, / help me each day / in the many choices I have to make. / Teach me to make wise choices / like Jesus. / Amen.

CATHOLIC DOCTRINE

Rewards and Punishment. It is not always an easy thing to admit fault and take responsibility for the harm that results from our choices. It is, of course, easier and more pleasant to take credit for the good that results from our choices. Students this age tend to assess the "goodness" or "badness" of their acts based on the punishment or the reward that result from their choices. While moral growth demands that parents and teachers guide the students to progress beyond this stage of moral development, punishment and reward can be properly and appropriately used as tools to help the students stop and assess their choices—both words and deeds. When punishment is used, its goal should be to lead the student to knowingly and freely make better choices.

Key Concept
Wise sayings and proverbs can help us make wise choices.

Pray

Gather the students for prayer. Lead them in the Sign of the Cross.

Teach

▶ Invite the students to tell what they recall about proverbs from Chapter 19.

▶ Ask a volunteer to read the Faith Focus question aloud. Have the students think silently about how they might answer it. Tell them that these two pages will help them learn how proverbs can help us make wise choices.

▶ Share the opening paragraph of Wise Sayings. Then write on the board a popular saying such as "The early bird gets the worm." Be sure to explain the saying if needed.

▶ Invite the students to offer other wise sayings they know.

▶ Emphasize that simple wise sayings can help us make wise choices.

▶ Present the final two paragraphs of Wise Choices.

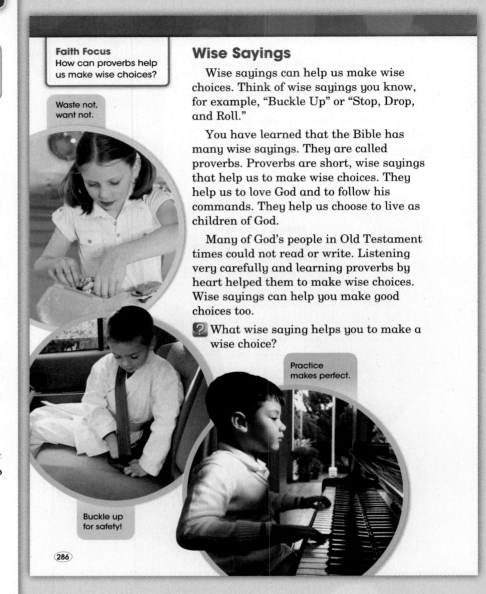

Faith Focus
How can proverbs help us make wise choices?

Waste not, want not.

Buckle up for safety!

Practice makes perfect.

Wise Sayings

Wise sayings can help us make wise choices. Think of wise sayings you know, for example, "Buckle Up" or "Stop, Drop, and Roll."

You have learned that the Bible has many wise sayings. They are called proverbs. Proverbs are short, wise sayings that help us to make wise choices. They help us to love God and to follow his commands. They help us choose to live as children of God.

Many of God's people in Old Testament times could not read or write. Listening very carefully and learning proverbs by heart helped them to make wise choices. Wise sayings can help you make good choices too.

❓ What wise saying helps you to make a wise choice?

286

SCRIPTURE BACKGROUND

Proverbs. The Book of Proverbs is the focal point of wisdom literature in the Old Testament, which also includes Ecclesiastes, Job, Song of Songs, Wisdom, Sirach, and portions of the Psalms. A short saying that usually draws a comparison between two forms of behavior in order to communicate moral or religious wisdom, a proverb concentrates on concrete human experiences rather than on Divine Revelation. Therefore, the purpose of a proverb is to teach rather than to relate a story. The Book of Proverbs contains thirty-one chapters, each consisting of twenty to thirty-five wise sayings.

Remember, the proverbs in the Bible come from God. They helped God's people of long ago make good and wise choices. The proverbs can also help us make good and wise choices today.

Trust in the LORD,
and your plans will succeed.

BASED ON PROVERBS 16:3

? What is one of your favorite wise sayings from the Book of Proverbs?

Activity

Choosing Wisely

Draw lines to connect the children to the proverb from the Bible that will best help them choose wisely.

Maireni wonders if she should listen to her mom. Should she plan the best bus route to her friend's house or just go and hope she finds the right way?

Jake wants to be on the basketball team. He wonders, "Should I practice shooting baskets or just play video games?"

Ichiro wakes up, looks out the window, and wonders, "What will this day be like, happy or sad?"

Work hard and become a leader; be lazy and become a loser.
BASED ON PROVERBS 12:24

For the gloomy person, every day is sad; but for the cheerful person, every day is a delight.
BASED ON PROVERBS 15:15

Say no to good advice, and your plans will fail. Say yes to good advice, and your plans will succeed.
BASED ON PROVERBS 15:22

(287)

Faith-Filled People

Saint Clare of Assisi

Clare was a dear friend of Saint Francis of Assisi. Like Francis, she chose to give up her riches and to serve God. Saint Clare gathered other women around her to live simple lives of service to others. Followers of Saint Clare are called Poor Clares. They live in convents and spend most of their days praying for others. The Church celebrates the Feast of Saint Clare on August 11.

Reinforce

▶ Invite the students to respond to the follow-up question. *(Answers will vary.)*

▶ Present the material on Saint Clare of Assisi in Faith-Filled People.

Connect

▶ Read the directions to the activity titled Choosing Wisely.

▶ Give the students time to connect the choices the children in each situation need to make to the biblical proverb that could help them make that choice.

▶ Call on volunteers to share and explain their connections. *(Maireni, Proverbs 15:22; Jake, Proverbs 12:24; Ichiro, Proverbs 15:15)*

Pray

Have the students echo this prayer.

Holy Spirit, / give us the gift of wisdom /
so that we may always choose wisely. /
Amen.

FAITH-FILLED PEOPLE

Saint Clare of Assisi. Clare grew up rich, but left her privileged life after hearing Francis preach about his love for God. The Franciscan brothers led her to a simple chapel in the woods. Her hair was cut short and she was given a plain garment as a habit. She traded her jeweled belt for a piece of knotted rope to wear around her waist. Francis instructed her in his rule and helped her to begin her religious community, the Poor Clares. The nuns said that when she came from her many hours of prayer each day, her face shined with joy. Clare became so famous for her humility and faithfulness that Popes and bishops came to her convent to seek her advice and ask for her prayers. To learn more about Saint Clare, go to the Saints Resource at *BeMyDisciple*.com.

Key Concept
Our wise choices can lead us to happiness with God forever.

Pray

Lead the students in the prayer with which you concluded the previous lesson.

Teach

▶ Read aloud the first two paragraphs of Choose Happiness Forever, including the passage from 1 Thessalonians 5:16–18.

▶ Then read the Faith Focus question. Call attention to *Heaven* in Faith Words. Emphasize that making wise choices now helps us find happiness forever with God in Heaven.

▶ Read the rest of Choose Happiness Forever. Ask the students to listen for what can help us make the choices that lead to Heaven.

Reinforce

Call for responses to the follow-up question. (*Our wise choices can lead us to happiness with God in Heaven.*)

Connect

Challenge the students to pray before making important decisions.

Faith Focus
Why is prayer so important in making wise choices?

Faith Words
▶ **Heaven**
Heaven is happiness forever with God and all the Saints.

Choose Happiness Forever

God wants us to be happy with him forever. **Heaven** is being happy with God and with all the Saints forever. Making wise choices now will help us find happiness in Heaven.

Praying each day will help us make wise choices. Here is a wise saying about praying from Saint Paul.

Rejoice always. Pray without ceasing. . . . give thanks, for this is the will of God for you in Christ Jesus.

1 THESSALONIANS 5:16–18

Praying every day shows that we are humble and that we know we need God's help to choose wisely. Praying every day shows that we are thankful for all God's gifts to us. Praying every day shows that we want to be happy and that we want to be friends with God today and forever in Heaven.

❓ Why is it so important for us to make wise choices every day?

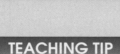

288

TEACHING TIP

Positive Reinforcement. Remember that words of positive reinforcement can help us build our faith. Students need to know that we respect them as faith-filled learners. Use words such as "nice job," "good work," "interesting question," and "great idea" to show that you value their participation and efforts. You will soon hear the students use these expressions themselves to affirm one another.

Remember that Jesus came to show us how to make wise choices. A wise saying in the Book of Proverbs reminds us, "Happy is the person who chooses to make peace" (based on Proverbs 12:20). You choose wisely when you choose to make peace.

I Follow Jesus

Activity

My Proverb

Create a wise saying of your own. Help others to see why they should be humble.

_____

_____

_____

_____

_____

My Faith Choice

This week, I choose to be a peacemaker by speaking kindly. I will remember to

_____

_____

Pray, "Dear Lord, help me grow in humility. Help me choose to serve you in peace. Amen."

289

BACKGROUND: DOCTRINE

The Call to Forgiveness. Many people have discovered that when a deep injury is done to us, we never recover until we forgive. This brings up a basic point about forgiveness: God is the source of forgiveness. We are to forgive as we have been forgiven. Ask yourself, Why is forgiving others a way to inner peace and healing? Discuss with the students the importance of both forgiving others and accepting forgiveness for what they have done. Stress that forgiveness is the hallmark of a peacemaker.

Reinforce

▶ Remind the students that it is important to make wise choices so that we can be happy forever with God.

▶ Go on to read the paragraph at the top of the page.

Respond

▶ Direct attention to the My Proverb activity. Ask a volunteer to read the directions aloud.

▶ Have the students complete the activity on their own.

▶ Afterward, allow the students to share their completed proverbs with the group.

▶ Remind the students how Old Testament people would memorize proverbs to help them make wise choices. Encourage the students to memorize the proverb they just wrote.

Choose

Invite the students to read My Faith Choice and write their decisions. Encourage them to put their kind choices into practice this week.

Pray

Lead the class in the prayer on the bottom of the page.

Pray

Gather the students for prayer. Have them echo the following:

> Come, Holy Spirit, /
> be with your children. /
> Help us choose wisely. /
> Help us to be happy with you /
> forever in heaven. /
> Amen.

Recall

▶ Create word games with the three To Help You Remember statements that will reinforce the students' grasp of the key faith concepts of the lesson. For example, turn the faith statements into false statements by changing a key word. Call on volunteers to supply the correct word for each statement.

▶ Have the students complete the sentences in the review activity. Afterward, invite volunteers to share their answers with the class.

Reflect

Give the students a few moments to complete the reflection statement.

Share

▶ Canvass the room for responses to the statement.

▶ Encourage the students to share their reflections with their families.

▶ **TO HELP YOU REMEMBER**

1. It is important for us to make wise choices.
2. Making wise choices now will help us find happiness in Heaven.
3. The proverbs can help us choose wisely.

Chapter Review

Recall

Two words are missing from each sentence. Use words in the box to complete the sentences.

happy	day	wise	proverbs
praying	sayings	Heaven	choices

1. God wants us to be ____happy____ now and forever in ____Heaven____.

2. Wise ____sayings____ can help us make wise ____choices____.

3. ____Proverbs____ from the Bible can help us make ____wise____ choices today.

4. ____Praying____ every ____day____ can help us make wise choices

Reflect

Write the proverb that will help you the most to make wise choices.

_____

_____

_____

Share | What are some of the reasons you will pray this week? Share your reasons with your class.

THE TASKS OF CATECHESIS

Liturgical Education. Help the students pray often throughout the day for help in making good choices by teaching them short prayers such as the following.

1. "God our Father, help me to do my best." (as they leave for school each day)

2. "Jesus, Son of God, help me to be fair." (every time they go out to play)

3. "Holy Spirit, help me to be a good friend today." (every time they join their friends)

A Peace Prayer

Saint Francis of Assisi prayed that God would help him to be a peacemaker. Let us pray for God's help to live as peacemakers.

| All | **Lord, make us instruments of your peace.** |

| Group 1 | Where there is hatred, |

| Group 2 | let us bring love. |

| All | **Lord, make us instruments of your peace.** |

| Group 1 | Where there is injury, |

| Group 2 | let us bring forgiveness. |

| All | **Lord, make us instruments of your peace.** |

| Group 1 | Where there is darkness, |

| Group 2 | let us bring light. |

| All | **Lord, make us instruments of your peace.** |

| Group 1 | Where there is sadness, |

| Group 2 | let us bring joy. |

| All | **Lord, make us instruments of your peace.** |

BASED ON THE PRAYER OF SAINT FRANCIS

(291)

We Pray

▶ Gather the students in the prayer center with their books.

▶ Tell the students that Saint Francis of Assisi's wise choices led him to work hard to bring peace into the world. Explain that today's prayer is one Saint Francis of Assisi wrote.

▶ Divide the students into Group 1 and Group 2 and point out their parts.

▶ Pray A Peace Prayer together.

TEACHING TIP

Peacemaking. Saint Francis of Assisi's peace prayer gives you the opportunity to commit yourself to learning more about your second graders. For the remainder of this year, as you observe the students' prayer, drawings, writings, and opinions, notice ways to help them choose peaceful ways to follow Jesus. Look for clues: How do the students interpret peace? Where do they need peace in their lives? When do they find peacemaking most difficult? Where do they learn about revenge? Do they willingly forgive others? Do they forgive themselves?

Preview

▶ Have the students carefully tear out pages 291 and 292 along the perforation.

▶ Encourage the students to share these pages with their families, and to complete the activities together.

▶ If they did not complete the review activity on page 290 by the end of the session, emphasize that they can complete it with their families at home.

▶ Point out the title and theme of the next lesson to the students.

Visit BeMyDisciples.com

▶ Take time with the students to explore the many activities and resources available at the *Be My Disciples* Web site.

▶ Encourage them to join with their families to discover the many resources available at the Web site.

Before Moving On ...

As you finish today's lesson, reflect on the following question before moving on to the next chapter.

What can I do to ensure that the students leave the session feeling happy about themselves as faith-filled people?

With My Family

This Week . . .

In Chapter 21, "We Make Choices," your child learned:

▶ God has created us to be happy now and forever with him in Heaven.

▶ The choices we make can lead us to or away from happiness in this world and the next.

▶ Proverbs are wise sayings in the Bible that help us make wise choices today.

▶ Praying each day will help us make wise choices. It shows that we are humble, needing God's help.

▶ The virtue of humility help us recognize that all our blessings and the blessings of others are from God.

For more about related teachings of the Church, *see the Catechism of the Catholic Church*, 1719–1724 and 2825, and the *United States Catholic Catechism for Adults*, pages 315–317.

■ Sharing God's Word

Read together Proverbs 12:24; 15:15; 15:23; and 16:3, or read the adaptation of these verses on page 287. Emphasize that the proverbs in the Bible can help us make wise choices about how to live as God's children.

■ Living as Disciples

The Christian home and family is a school of discipleship. Choose one of the following activities to do as a family, or design a similar activity of your own.

▶ Choose one of the proverbs in this chapter. Tell how the proverb can help your family live and choose what is right and good. Make it a motto for your family this week. Place it on a card on your refrigerator so that the whole family can see it.

▶ When you make family decisions together, join first in humble prayer. Praying together before decision-making not only strengthens family ties but also helps your children grow in humility as they model the humility you show in seeking God's help through prayer.

■ Our Spiritual Journey

Our spiritual journey finds its end in Heaven. Throughout his ministry, Jesus was continually calling us to Heaven. Pray the prayer of Saint Francis on page 291 this week. Your prayer may make all the difference in this world . . . and in the next.

For more ideas on ways your family can live as disciples of Jesus, visit **BeMyDisciples.com**

292

PARTNERING WITH PARENTS

Responding to Wise Choices. In a written communication to the parents, urge them to be lavish in praising their children when they observe them making good and wise choices in their interaction with family members and friends. Help parents recognize that their positive comments and approval will reinforce their child's desire to live as Jesus taught and encourage them to think before they act.

Enriching the Lesson

Holding a "Wise Choice" Party

Purpose

To reinforce the importance of making wise choices (taught on page 284)

Directions

At the completion of the lesson, give the students invitations to a Wise Choice party. Their gifts for the party will be the wise choices they made this past week.

► Have the students write their wise choices on slips of paper and place them in a box.

► Have the students decorate the box with pictures of them making wise choices.

► Provide simple refreshments at the Wise Choice party.

Materials

slips of paper

glue sticks

large box

refreshments

pens, pencils, or crayons

Making Creation Posters

Purpose

To reinforce that the choices we make help us live as followers of Jesus (taught on page 284)

Directions

► Tell the students that Jesus calls his followers to make good choices about the way they use the gift of creation. God calls us to care for his gift of creation.

► Together brainstorm the good choices we make when we treat all of nature, including animals, with respect and care. Some ideas might include not throwing trash in public parks, feeding the backyard birds in winter, and planting flowers and trees. List their choices on the board.

► Invite the students to make creation posters that show (through illustrations or pictures and words cut from magazines) some of the good choices we can make to take care of creation.

► Display their work so everyone can be reminded to make good choices.

Materials

crayons or markers

poster boards

magazines

scissors

glue sticks

Drawing Pictures of Peace

Purpose

To reinforce that one way we can live as a child of God is to be a peacemaker (taught on page 289)

Directions

► Share with the students that many children in the world live in countries that are at war. Give some current examples.

► Invite the students to draw pictures of peace and friendship to send to the children in one of these countries.

► Tell them to place a simple title on their pictures and to sign their first names only, their age, and their country.

► Obtain the address of a local Catholic agency that can send the students' pictures to children in the country(ies) experiencing conflict.

Materials

construction paper

crayons or markers

BACKGROUND

Our Divine Image

Among all of God's creation, the human person is unique. For reasons beyond human comprehension, God decided to create the human person in his divine image and likeness and to enter an everlasting Covenant, making all of humanity sharers in divine life.

The Height of God's Creation

The human person is no ordinary creation, but a creation that is sacred and deserving of the deepest respect, reverence, and loving care. The gift of such a dignity also bears with it a response—a responsibility to strive to become who we have been created to be and have been saved in Christ to be. We are called to respond in faith, hope, and love and to live in covenant and communion with God the Blessed Trinity.

Freedom to Respond to God

Among the many gifts God has given to the human person is the gift of freedom. The gift of freedom that God gives us also comes with responsibility. We are capable of turning toward the good and striving for authentic life in concert with God or of turning toward evil and choosing to reject a life in harmony with him.

The more we live in concert with God and strive to be people of holiness and blessedness, the freer we become. The reverse is also true. The more we choose to turn away from God by sinning, the more we abuse the gift of freedom and the deeper we fall into the slavery of sin.

Each of us has the right to be recognized as a free and responsible person. The ability to exercise one's freedom is an inalienable requirement that flows from the dignity of every human person. As such, true human freedom must be enshrined and protected—even by civil authorities.

Conscience

Freedom, however, does not include license. The formation of our conscience helps us exercise our freedom responsibly. How do we form our conscience? We must attend carefully to the teachings of Christ and the Church, which guides us in interpreting the Gospel, the Ten Commandments, and the Beatitudes. We find strength to form our conscience through our participation in the Sacraments, especially the Eucharist, through prayer, and in our solidarity with other believers in Christ.

A well-formed conscience enables us to responsibly exercise the free will we have been given by God. This authentic exercise of the gift of freedom makes us collaborators in God's work in the Church and in the world. As faithful partners with God and one another, we place our lives at service to his Kingdom.

For Reflection

What do I do that shows that I value my dignity and the dignity of every other person?

How consistent am I in making the effort to form my conscience according to the mind of Christ?

Teacher to Teacher

Making Good Choices

Our lives are filled with choices every day. Many of our choices have nothing to do with the "moral" dimension of our lives, but we would be surprised at how many do. When our conscience is properly formed and we are in the habit of listening carefully to the Holy Spirit, we are better prepared to make sound moral decisions.

Conscience Formation

Conscience formation does not happen automatically. In the very young, it is the guidance of family members and teachers that usually begins the process. Some seven- and eight-year-olds have a difficult time understanding the difference between a mistake, an accident, and a deliberate choice to do something that they know is wrong. Your guidance in this area of conscience formation is very important. Seven- and eight-year-olds can be taught to look at their actions and evaluate them. They can be encouraged to ask themselves, "In what ways was I a true follower of Jesus?"

The Church Teaches...

"Both the private practice and the public witness of knowledgeable and committed Christians are indispensable factors in the sanctification of the world, a responsibility to which all the baptized are called. In such an environment, living an active Christian life becomes a crucial element in effective catechetical methodology" (*National Directory for Catechesis*, 29G).

As a religion teacher, you are a disciple of Jesus, who is your Teacher. The way Jesus taught is the model of how you are to teach the children, the young disciples of Jesus, entrusted to your care. God calls you to teach beyond the classroom—to teach through all aspects of your life.

Further Reading and Reflection

For more related teachings of the Church, see the *Catechism of the Catholic Church*, 1730–1738 and 1776–1794; and the *United States Catholic Catechism for Adults*, pages 314–315.

Teacher Prayer

Help me, Lord,
to strengthen my own conscience
as well as to have the courage
to listen to and follow it.
Guide me to see that it is more
important to please you and follow
your Commandments than it is to
impress others or please myself.
Amen.

Lesson Planner

Chapter 22 We Can Choose Right from Wrong

Goal To discover that we are making wise choices when we live as Jesus taught

LESSON PART	PROCESS	MATERIALS and RESOURCES
DAY 1 EXPLORE **Focus** To explore how followers of Jesus treat others **Pages** 293–295	▶ Proclaim and discuss Deuteronomy 30:19 (Choose life). ▶ Learn and discuss the story of Saint Paula Frassinetti. **Disciple Power:** Joy **Activity:** Decide which choices result in happiness.	Bible Pencils or pens
DAY 2 DISCOVER **Focus** To discover that we are free to choose and that our choices have consequences **Pages** 296–297	▶ Discover that our free choices have consequences. **Scripture:** God gave us free choice (Sirach 15:14–15) **Catholics Believe:** Examination of Conscience **Faith Words:** consequences **Activity:** Draw or write consequences for a story.	Bible Markers or crayons **Enriching the Lesson:** Teacher Guide, page 427 Literature Connection: Fairy tales
DAY 3 DISCOVER **Focus** To discover that God's gift of conscience helps us make wise choices **Pages** 298–299	▶ Discover that our conscience is a gift from God. **Faith Words:** conscience **Faith-Filled People:** Saint Philip Neri **Activity:** Apply the four steps of good decision making to a situation.	Bibles Pencils or pens **Enriching the Lesson:** Teacher Guide, page 427 Do the Right Thing Role-Plays **Additional Activities Booklet:** Activities 22a and 22b, or see *BeMyDisciples*.com
DAY 4 DECIDE **Focus** To discover we must form and examine our consciences and to decide on a wise choice to make this week **Pages** 300–301	▶ Learn how to form a good conscience. **Activity:** Identify wrong and right choices. **My Faith Choice:** Make choices to live as Jesus taught.	Pencil or pens **Enriching the Lesson:** teacher Guide, page 427 Drawing pictures of peace
DAY 5 CONCLUDE **Focus** To learn that Saint Augustine chose to change his life and follow Jesus **Pages** 302–304	▶ **REVIEW** Review concepts: Recall, Reflect, and Share. ▶ **PRAY** Be the Joy of My Heart ▶ **Preview** the With My Family page and the theme of the next chapter.	Bible, candle, cross for prayer space Grade 2 Music CD **Assessment Tools Booklet:** Assessments 22a and 22b

Assign online Chapter Review and interactive Chapter Test at **BeMyDisciples.com**

Chapter **22**

We Can Choose Right from Wrong

? How do we know if a choice is right or wrong?

God wants you to choose for yourself. God also wants you to choose wisely. Listen to what God says in the Bible.

God lets us choose right or wrong, life or death. Choose what is right. Choose life so that you can be happy with God forever. BASED ON DEUTERONOMY 30:19

? Why is it important to do what is right?

293

HUMAN METHODOLOGIES

Learning Through the Witness of the Catechist. The *National Directory for Catechesis* tells us, "For catechesis to be effective, catechists must be fully committed to Jesus Christ" (*NDC* 29E). As you teach the students about the gift of conscience in this chapter, spend some time reflecting on the role of this gift in your own life. Consider how you continue to form your conscience through prayer, reading the Scriptures, and following the example of Jesus, Mary, and the Saints. You may find it helpful to your ongoing faith formation to read the *Catechism of the Catholic Church* 1776–1794 and Chapter 23 of the *United States Catholic Catechism for Adults.* Your own growth in faith will be a great asset in your ministry with the students.

DAY **1** EXPLORE

Pray

▶ Welcome the students warmly. Ask them to quiet themselves for prayer.

▶ Begin and end with the Sign of the Cross.

▶ Tell the children that Catholic Tradition teaches us that we each have a watchful guardian angel who helps us make good choices in our lives. Ask the children to repeat each line of the following prayer after you:

> Angel of God, my guardian dear,
> to whom God's love
> commits me here,
> ever this day be at my side,
> to light and guard,
> to rule and guide.
> Amen.

▶ Ask the opening questions. (*Accept all reasonable replies.*)

Reflect

▶ Read the introduction to the Scripture. Then ask one of the students to proclaim the passage from the Book of Deuteronomy.

▶ Afterward, observe a moment of silence.

▶ Invite responses to the Scripture question. (*The students should be able to recognize that good choices lead to doing God's will and thus to happiness.*)

▶ Invite the students to tell why they think the picture was chosen for this chapter's opening page.

Focus

Invite the students to recall the good choices Saint Francis of Assisi made. Then explain that today they are going to hear about another Saint who made important choices.

Student page 293 **415**

Introduce

▶ Remind the students that making wise choices can make a difference in the way we live.

▶ Explain that today they will learn about another saint who had to make some important choices.

▶ Direct the students to listen for the choices Saint Paula Frassinetti made.

▶ Have different volunteers take turns reading Paula's Choice.

▶ Have the students read about joy in Disciple Power. Point out that Saint Paula used the virtue of joy to make the best of her situation and to bring happiness to others.

Reinforce

▶ Call for responses to the follow-up questions. *(Possible responses: taking care of her brothers, being cheerful, attending Mass, praying while working, opening a school for poor girls, founding a religious order to educate children.)*

▶ Emphasize to the students that making good choices leads to happiness.

▶ Invite the students to think of someone they know who makes good choices, choices that bring happiness and joy to others. Ask: Why do you think the person makes good choices? *(Accept all reasonable replies.)*

Disciple Power

Joy

Joy is one of the Fruits of the Holy Spirit. Joy shows that we are thankful for God's love, and for all that God has made. Joy shows that we enjoy life and delight in making others joyful.

The Church Follows **Jesus**

Paula's Choice

Sometimes, the choices we make are simple ones. But even the simplest choice, if it is a wise choice, can make a big difference. It can bring happiness to us and to others.

When Paula Frassinetti was nine years old, her mother died. Who would take care of her younger brothers? Paula decided that she would.

Paula's choice meant a lot of work for her. She could not go to school. So her brothers shared with her what they learned in school. Paula chose to be cheerful. She went to Mass every day and prayed while she did her chores.

When Paula grew up, she opened a school for poor girls. She later started a religious order to educate children who are poor.

The Church honors her today as Saint Paula. Her feast day is June 11.

 Which choices did Saint Paula make? Did her choices make anyone happy? Who?

294

DISCIPLE POWER

Joy. Help the students express their gratitude for God's love and the many God-given blessings in their lives, by teaching them the lively song, "I've Got the Joy, Joy, Joy, Joy." Add another verse using the words, "I choose to love, love, love, love" to reinforce that God gives us the gift of free will.

I've got the joy, joy, joy, joy
Down in my heart (Where?)
Down in my heart (Where?)
Down in my heart.
I've got the joy, joy, joy, joy
Down in my heart (Where?)
Down in my heart today.

—Credited to George Willis Cooke (1848–1923)

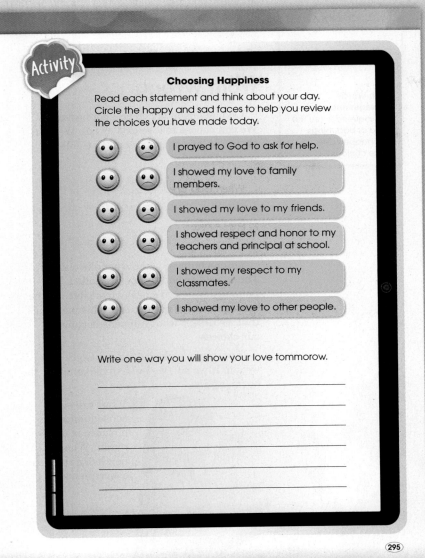

Activity

Choosing Happiness

Read each statement and think about your day. Circle the happy and sad faces to help you review the choices you have made today.

- 😊 😞 I prayed to God to ask for help.
- 😊 😞 I showed my love to family members.
- 😊 😞 I showed my love to my friends.
- 😊 😞 I showed respect and honor to my teachers and principal at school.
- 😊 😞 I showed my respect to my classmates.
- 😊 😞 I showed my love to other people.

Write one way you will show your love tommorow.

_____

_____

_____

_____

_____

(295)

Connect

▶ Remind the students that Jesus showed us how to make wise choices so that we can be happy with God forever.

▶ Call attention to the activity, Choosing Happiness. Read and explain the directions.

▶ Have the students make their choices on their own. Afterward, call on different students to share what they chose.

Pray

Invite the students to quiet themselves for prayer. Have them echo the following after you.

> God of our joy, /
> teach us to choose wisely. /
> Lead us along the path /
> that leads to happiness and to you. /
> Amen.

THE TASKS OF CATECHESIS

Promoting Knowledge of the Faith. Help the students get into the habit of recalling and applying Jesus' teachings to the situations and decisions they face in daily life. Giving them the opportunity to role-play different scenarios will help them to refine their decision-making skills. Have them role-play the following or similar scenarios. After each role-play, ask, "What would Jesus want me to do?"

1. The child in the next desk at school has a new hand-held computer game that you like. You think about sneaking it out of her backpack when no one is looking.

2. Your friends are talking about a boy at school who is not popular. They are saying very mean things about him that you know are not true.

Key Concept
Our free choices all have consequences.

Pray

Gather the students for prayer. Lead them in the prayer with which you concluded the previous lesson.

Teach

▶ Remind the students that happiness and joy are consequences of making choices to do God's will.

▶ Read the Faith Focus question aloud. Explain to the students that in this chapter they will learn to recognize their ability to choose freely and to recognize the consequences of their choices.

▶ Have the students read the meaning of and make a word card for the term *consequences* in Faith Words.

▶ Read the section titled Choose Right and Wrong.

Faith Focus
What is free choice?

Faith Words
consequences
Consequences are the good or bad things that happen after we make choices.

Choosing Right from Wrong

God lets us make choices for ourselves. We can choose to love God or not. We can choose to love others or not. In the Bible we read,

When God created us, he gave us free choice. It is our choice to do or not to do God's will.

BASED ON SIRACH 15:14–15

Things happen when we make choices. These good or bad things are called **consequences**. We are responsible for the consequences of our actions. This means that we accept what happens because of our choices.

If we make a choice against God's Law, we sin. If we sin, we have to make up for the harm we do.

What are some consequences to a choice you have made? What did you learn from the consequences?

296

TEACHING TIP

Establishing Rules and Consequences. Most second graders are at a very elementary level of moral thinking. It is normal for them at this age to be more motivated by the possibilities of reward or punishment than by a lofty ideal. That is why we make rules and establish consequences for breaking them. Experiencing the consequences of their choices will help the students grow in their understanding of the reason for the rules and grow in their love for God and others.

Activity

Choices Have Consequences

Read these stories. Write what you think Sarah or Angel will do. Then draw what will happen next.

Sarah's Choice

Sarah's little sister Katie is sick. Sarah asks her parents, "May I read Katie a story?" But then a friend asks her to come over to play. What will Sarah do?

Angel's Choice

Angel's friend borrows his bike without asking and dents it. Angel thinks he should teach his friend a lesson. He begins to think that he will break his friend's skateboard. What will Angel do?

(297)

Catholics Believe

Examination of Conscience

We examine our consciences to know if the choices we made were wise choices. This helps us to live holy lives. We always examine our consciences to prepare to celebrate the Sacrament of Penance and Reconciliation.

Reinforce

▶ Highlight understanding about consequences by asking the students to share an action that they do every day—tie their shoes, ride their bike, do their chores. Go over the consequences of these actions or inactions. (*They could trip and fall if the shoe isn't tied, and so on.*)

▶ Ask the follow-up questions. Be sure the students understand that we have to accept responsibility for our free choices and for what happens because of our choices. Likewise, help them recognize that choosing to do what God does not want us to do is sin.

▶ Ask a volunteer to read Catholics Believe. Invite the students to highlight the sentence that tells why we examine our conscience.

Connect

▶ Introduce the activity, Choices Have Consequences. Have different students reach each of the scenarios.

▶ After a scenario is read, invite the class to suggest possible consequences of the action or inaction. If you wish, list the students' ideas on the board.

▶ Invite the students to complete the activity on their own.

▶ When the students finish, share responses. Note the variety of consequences. Note, too, the actions whose consequences lead to happiness and those that do not.

Pray

Lead the students in praying the Glory Be.

TEACHING TIP

Extend the Activity. Extend the Choices Have Consequences activity offering additional choices for the students' consideration. The following are suggestions. Add your own, or invite the students to offer their ideas drawn from real-life situations.

Nakayah's Choice—Nakayah's parents are going out for the evening. Her babysitter reminds her to do her homework, but Nakayah plays computer games instead.

Jaeden's Choice—Jaeden sees that someone has thrown trash on his elderly neighbor's front lawn. He gets a garbage bag from home and picks up the trash.

Myra and CJ's Choice—Myra and CJ can tell their mom is tired. The dirty dishes from super are still on the kitchen table. Myra and CJ clear the table and wash the dishes.

Allison's Choice—Allison and her family are at Sunday Mass. The priest is proclaiming the Gospel. Allison is teasing her little brother by stepping on his foot.

> **Key Concept**
> Our conscience helps us make good choices.

Pray

Gather the students for prayer. Invite them to pray the following after you.

Loving God, / choosing to do your will / makes us happy. / Thank you for the choice. / Amen.

Teach

▶ Read the Faith Focus question aloud and invite the students to think silently about how to answer it. Tell them that these two pages will help them understand that God gives us the gift of our conscience.

▶ Read aloud the first two paragraphs of The Gift of Our Conscience. Ask the students to listen for the meaning of conscience.

▶ Read the definition of *conscience* in Faith Words. Have the students make a word card for the term.

▶ Ask the students what happens if we refuse to listen to our conscience. *(We may make choices that are against what God wants us to do or not do.)*

▶ Call on a volunteer to read the third paragraph aloud and to name one way we form our conscience.

▶ Go on to present the final paragraph. Ask the students to listen for where conscience leads us.

Faith Focus
Why is it important to follow your conscience when making choices?

Faith Words
conscience
Conscience is a gift from God that helps us to make wise choices.

The Gift of Our Consciences

A wise choice is a choice to live as Jesus taught. God gives us a gift that helps us to make wise choices. This gift is called a **conscience**. Our consciences tell us whether a choice we are about to make, or have made, is a wise choice.

The gift of conscience helps us know what is right and what is wrong. Conscience is like a compass. It points us in the right direction. It shows us the way to goodness. It leads the way to happiness.

Making wise choices is very important. We make good choices when we know right from wrong. We learn right from wrong from our families. We learn from the good example of others. We learn from God's rules of love. We learn from the teaching and example of Jesus and from the teaching of the Church.

When we learn and remember what is right or wrong, we are forming our consciences. Then our consciences can help us make good choices. Making wise choices makes good things happen. Making wise choices makes us happy.

❓ Where do you learn right from wrong?

298

TEACHING TIP

Accidents, Mistakes, and Sins. Some students this age become very confused about accidents and mistakes, especially if they have serious consequences. We need to make it very clear to them that hurtful accidents and mistakes, which are out of their control, are not a result of choices they made. Accidents and mistakes are not sins. No one makes a mistake on purpose. Sins are always bad choices we make on purpose, knowing that what we say or do is against God's will and hurts our relationship with God, others, or ourselves.

Activity

Let Your Conscience Be Your Guide

These four steps can help you listen to your conscience and make a wise choice.

1. **Think:** What are the possible choices?

2. **Consider:** What might happen next?

3. **Ask:** What does your conscience tell you is the best choice to make?

4. **Act:** Follow your conscience and make your choice.

Read the sentences below. Follow the steps to a decision of good conscience.

Your friend is angry, makes fun of you, and calls you a name. You feel hurt and upset. What do you do?

1. I will **Think** about possible choices.

_____

_____

2. I will **Consider** what might happen next.

_____

3. I will **Ask** what my conscience tells me to do.

_____

4. I will **Act** and follow my conscience.

_____

_____

Faith-Filled People

Saint Philip Neri

Philip Neri made wise choices. He sold all his possessions and gave away his money. He visited banks, shops, and places where people gathered. Every place he visited, he tried to convince people to serve God in all they did. The Church celebrates the feast day of Saint Philip Neri on May 26.

(299)

FAITH-FILLED PEOPLE

Saint Philip Neri (1515–1595). Philip Neri had a lively sense of humor. His own words explained that "the importance of getting through each day is not to fear what might happen tomorrow." Philip had that rare ability to help people probe their hearts while at the same time sharing a joke with them. He is honored as the "Second Apostle of Rome" because of his influence during the Counter-reformation on so many important figures of his day. To learn more about Saint Philip Neri, go to the Saints Resource at *BeMyDisciples*.com.

Reinforce

▶ Call for answers to the two follow-up questions. *(Accept all reasonable replies.)*

▶ Have the students read Faith-Filled People about Saint Philip Neri. Point out that he used his gift of conscience to serve God and that God gives us the gift of our conscience to help us make choices to live as his children.

Connect

▶ Call attention to the section titled Let Conscience Be Your Guide. Present each step of the activity.

▶ Have a volunteer read aloud the scenario about name-calling. Then, before the students begin writing, brainstorm ideas for each step and list the ideas on the board.

▶ Finally, give the students time to complete the activity on their own and to record their responses in their books.

▶ Share decisions and consequences.

▶ As time allows, suggest other situations where students can follow these steps to make conscientious decisions.

Pray

Call the students to prayer. Lead them in the Glory Be.

> **Key Concept**
> We must train our conscience.

Pray

Gather the students for prayer. Lead them in the Sign of the Cross.

Teach

▶ Remind the students that God has given us a conscience to help us make wise choices.

▶ Tell the students that it is *our* job to form our conscience. Then read the Faith Focus question aloud. Explain that this lesson will help them learn how to form and examine their conscience.

▶ Have the students silently read the first two paragraphs of Forming Our Conscience.

▶ Ask the students to underline the ways we form our conscience.

▶ Write some examples on the board.

▶ Present the final paragraph about examining our conscience.

Reinforce

Ask the follow-up questions. Discuss the steps for forming a good conscience.

Connect

Consider sharing with the students the simple examination of conscience in the Liturgy Connection box on this page.

> **Faith Focus**
> How do we form consciences that help us to make wise choices?

Forming Our Conscience

The gift of conscience tells us whether a choice we are about to make or a choice we have made is a good choice. A good conscience helps us to know right from wrong.

To form a good conscience, we need to learn what God wants us to do.

- We pray to the Holy Spirit.
- We read and listen to the Bible.
- We learn what the Church teaches.
- We ask our parents, teachers, and other grown-ups to help us.

We also need to check, or examine, our conscience. We need to ask ourselves, "How have I loved God or how have I turned away from God?" "How have I loved other people or how have I not loved other people as Jesus taught?" We need to answer these questions honestly. This helps us form our conscience.

❓ Why is it important to form a good conscience?

LITURGY CONNECTION

Examination of Conscience. Examining one's conscience is a skill students can develop. For your last few sessions of the year, include this simple examination of conscience in the closing prayer.

▶ How well do I show my love for God? Do I pray? Do I listen to his Word at Mass? Do I use the name of God reverently?

▶ How am I showing love for others and for myself? Do I show respect for my parents? Do I care for my health and follow safety rules? Do I treat others kindly?

Invite the students to silently ask God's forgiveness for any wrong choices they might have made.

A wise choice is a choice to live as Jesus taught. Your conscience helps you to know right from wrong. Your conscience helps you make wise choices.

Activity

Making Choices

Circle the pictures that show children making a good choice to live as Jesus taught. Write an X on the pictures that show a bad choice. Explain your answer.

My Faith Choice

I can choose to make choices to live with joy as Jesus taught. This week, I will

_____

_____

> **Pray, "Holy Spirit, help me listen to my conscience. Let me do what is right and pleasing to you. Amen."**

(301)

TEACHING TIP

A Well-Formed Conscience. Teachers have the responsibility as part of their ministry to support parents in bringing up their children in the practice of the faith. One way teachers meet this responsibility is by helping the students entrusted to them develop the habit of training their conscience. Teach the students about the many things we do to train our conscience: We first pray, then we listen to and learn from Bible stories. We pay attention to our parents, godparents, and other adults who have the responsibility to help us grow in faith. We learn and follow the teachings of the Church. It is important to guide the students, even at this young age, to develop these important habits of conscience formation.

Reinforce

Remind the students that conscience helps us know and choose right from wrong.

Respond

▶ Ask the students if they know anyone who wears a bracelet with the letters WWJD on it.

▶ Explain that the letters stand for the words What Would Jesus Do?, and many Christians wear these bracelets. The words remind them to follow their consciences and make good choices.

▶ Read aloud the introductory paragraph.

▶ Have the students look at the Making Choices activity pictures. Explain the directions. After the students make their choices, call on volunteers to share their work.

Choose

Invite the students to read My Faith Choice and to write their decisions. Encourage them to put their choices into practice this week.

Pray

Gather the students for prayer. Lead them in the prayer to the Holy Spirit at the bottom of the page.

Pray

Gather the students for prayer. Have them echo the following:

Jesus, / open our hearts and minds / so that we may wisely form our conscience /
to make the choice to follow you. / Amen.

Recall

▶ Ask volunteers to share at least one thing they learned in this chapter.

▶ Compare their statements to the To Help You Remember statements.

▶ Remind the students that good choices show we are following our conscience.

▶ Ask the students to name two things that happen when we make good choices. *(We are happy; good things happen.)*

▶ Have the students complete the review activity by unscrambling the words and writing their sentences.

▶ Share answers and sentences.

Reflect

Give the students a few moments to complete the reflection statement.

Share

Invite the students to share their reflections with a partner and at home with their families.

▶ **TO HELP YOU REMEMBER**

1. We are making wise choices when we choose to live as Jesus taught.
2. Wise choices show we are forming and following our consciences.
3. All of our choices have consequences.

Chapter Review

Recall

Unscramble the words.

1. SCICONENCE   CONSCIENCE
2. SEQNOCUENCSE   CONSEQUENCES
3. MINATIONEXA   EXAMINATION
4. SIBLEPONRES   RESPONSIBLE
5. HOCICE   CHOICE

Reflect

Use some of the words above to write a sentence that describes making a wise choice.

_____

_____

_____

_____

_____

_____

Share   Share your sentence that describes making a wise choice with your class.

302

TEACHING TIP

Evaluate. Take a few moments to evaluate the lessons this week. I feel *(circle one)* about the lessons this week:

a. very pleased

b. OK

c. disappointed

The activity the students enjoyed most was . . .

The concept that was most difficult to teach was . . .

because . . .

Something I would like to do differently is . . .

Be the Joy of My Heart

Saint Augustine chose to change his life and to follow Jesus. He became a bishop in the Church. His choice brought him great happiness. This is his prayer. Pray it with joy.

O God,

Be the light of my life.

Be the life of my soul.

Be the strength of my mind.

Help me choose what is right.

Keep me always in your love.

Be the joy of my heart.

Amen.

BASED ON A PRAYER OF SAINT AUGUSTINE

303

We Pray

▶ Gather the students in the prayer center with their books.

▶ Tell the students that Saint Augustine did not live a good life when he was young. He did many wrong things. He was not happy. Then he chose to follow Jesus, and he changed. Explain that today's prayer is one he wrote.

▶ Either pray the prayer as a group, or have the students echo each line after you. Be sure to pray with some enthusiasm and delight.

▶ Consider closing with a bright song of joy, for example, "I've Got the Joy, Joy, Joy, Joy," while leading the students in a procession around the classroom.

TEACHING TIP

Helpful Hint. Much of what the students are learning appeals to their emotional side. Therefore, students tend to remember what they need to know about prayer through the experience of prayer. Pray often with the students. Pray spontaneously aloud so that they can hear you. Pray the learned prayers of the Church as well as using words from your heart. Pray joyfully. This way the students will get to know that God is always ready and willing to listen to our needs, that we can pray anytime and any place, and that we can tell God anything.

Preview

▶ Have the students carefully tear out pages 303 and 304 along the perforation.

▶ Encourage the students to share these pages with their families, and to complete the activities together.

▶ If they did not complete the review activity on page 302 by the end of the session, emphasize that they can complete it with their families at home.

▶ Point out the title and theme of the next lesson to the students.

Visit www.BeMyDisciples.com

Visit BeMyDisciples.com

▶ Take time with the students to explore the many activities and resources available at the *Be My Disciples* Web site.

▶ Encourage them to join with their families to discover the many resources available at the Web site.

Before Moving On ...

As you finish today's lesson, reflect on the following question before moving on to the next chapter.

What can I do to help the students who are more mathematically or scientifically inclined to bring their gifts to our religion activities?

With My Family

This Week . . .

In Chapter 22, "We Can Choose Right from Wrong," your child learned:

▶ We are responsible for the choices we make and their consequences.

▶ God has given us the gift of a conscience to help us discern right from wrong.

▶ We have the responsibility to form a good conscience to help us live according to God's will.

▶ A well-formed conscience leads to decisions that bring happiness both here and in Heaven.

▶ The gift of joy urges us to choose what makes for happiness.

For more about related teachings of the Church, see the *Catechism of the Catholic Church,* 1716–1724, 1730–1738, and 1776–1794, and the *United States Catholic Catechism for Adults,* pages 314–315, and 341–369.

▨ Sharing God's Word

Read together Sirach 15:14–15 or read the adaptation of these verses on page 296. Emphasize that God created us with a free will and the ability to make our own choices.

▨ Living as Disciples

The Christian home and family is a school of discipleship. Choose one of the following activities to do as a family, or design a similar activity of your own.

▶ When you watch a TV show together, point out when characters on the show make good choices and when they make bad choices. If someone makes a bad choice, make suggestions for a good choice.

▶ Talk about the choices family members made during the day and their consequences. Such discussion will get your child started thinking about his or her responsibility for the consequences of his or her choices.

▨ Our Spiritual Journey

We learn to exercise our free will by practicing discernment. We do so by calling on the Holy Spirit to lead or give direction regarding the choices we make. Discernment can open the door to a new way of life—to a life of joy in the Spirit. Pray the prayer, "Be the Joy of My Heart" on page 303, Encourage your child to ask for guidance in making decisions. Pray together, "*Loving God, be the joy of my heart.*"

For more ideas on ways your family can live as disciples of Jesus, visit **BeMyDisciples.com**

304

PLAN AHEAD

Honoring Mary. Gather Marian resources to decorate the prayer area in your classroom for your next session. Both the *Human Methodologies* activity and the closing prayer for Chapter 23 focus on Mary, Jesus' mother and our greatest Saint. Plan to drape the prayer table in blue cloth. Add a statue of Mary, a rosary, flowers, and other appropriate symbols of our Blessed Mother.

Enriching the Lesson

Do the Right Thing Role Plays

Purpose

To reinforce the teaching on free choice/will and making conscientious choices (taught on pages 296 and 298)

Directions

▶ Invite the students to brainstorm ways to tell whether or not something is the right thing to do. List ideas on the board.

▶ Divide the students into small groups. Give each group one of the situations listed below—or similar ones—to role-play. Direct the students to choose what they believe is the right thing to do and then to give reasons for their choice as they do the role-play. Remind them to use the four steps for making a conscientious decision they learned in this lesson:

– **Think:** What are the possible choices?

– **Consider:** What might happen next?

– **Ask:** What does your conscience tell you is the best choice to make?

– **Act:** Follow your conscience and make your choice.

Situations:

– A group of cool kids are picking on another kid. They want you to join them. You want to be part of the cool group, but you think picking on the other kid is unfair. What do you do?

– There is a room at school no students are allowed to enter. One day you notice that the door to the room is open. You really want to go in. No one is around. What do you do?

– You're feeling really hungry as you walk home from school. You pass by a fruit stand. The apples look really tasty. No one is looking. What do you do?

– Your very best friend asks you to help her cheat on a test. She promises, "It'll be just this one time." What do you do?

▶ Discuss the role-plays with the class. If you wish, invite the students to come up with their own situations and to continue the role-plays.

Materials

Literature Connection

Purpose

To reinforce that we are responsible for the consequences of our actions (taught on page 296).

Directions

▶ Brainstorm with the students fairy tales they have heard or read that tell about characters making choices that have consequences. For example: "Pinocchio," "The Three Little Pigs," and "Goldilocks and the Three Bears."

▶ In small groups have the students prepare a retelling of a fairy tale without naming the story and provide the clues about the characters, the choices, and the consequences.

▶ Invite the students to present their fairy tales and have the other students name the story and give the conclusion.

Materials

We Share in God's Life

BACKGROUND

Shalom

Shalom means peace. Hebrew, unlike English, is very efficient and has a relatively small vocabulary. As a result one word can often have many different meaning. When we think of peace, we often think of peace between two entities; for example, between people and God or between two countries. We also may be referencing the well-being, welfare or safety of a person or a group of people.

In the biblical sense, shalom means not only exterior peace but it also means *nothing missing, nothing broken, well-being,* and *completeness.* Shalom is understood in reference to the wholeness of the person in relationship to God and creation.

Biblically

In the Old Testament shalom was used to refer to friendship, well-being (totality of a person) and safety. With friendship, it includes a sense of trust or familiarity *(see Jeremiah 20:10; 38:22).* Probably the most important usage of the word *shalom* is in relation to other synonyms for Salvation.

In the New Testament Jesus told the disciples he would go to the Father and he promised them his *shalom.* He said the Holy Spirit would come and would remind them of all the things He had said to them *(John 14:25–28).* He told the disciple that the peace he was going to give to them was not the peace that the world offers. *(John 14:27).*

The peace of this world is fleeting, temporary and inconsistent. Instead Jesus promised them the shalom of God, which is the essence of Salvation, wholeness, well-being, friendship, safety, prosperity, health, tranquility and contentment. Who could ask for more?

"Blessed are the Peacemakers"

The Beatitudes state the values and actions that lead to the Kingdom of God. They affirm measures of happiness that stand in contrast to the measures promoted and widely accepted by much of the world.

To be a peacemaker in the biblical sense is much more than simply not being at war. To be called to be a peacemaker is to proclaim that there is more than meets the eye. It is to accept that there is a reality at work in this world that calls us beyond power and prestige, money and status. That reality is the *shalom* of God.

For Reflection

What does *shalom* mean for my life?

How has sharing *shalom* with others become a reality within my life?

Teacher to Teacher

God's Gift of Love

Children naturally emulate their parents and other grown-ups. Often even in little children you can hear the same phrases, witness the same behaviors, and encounter the same attitudes you see in their parents. It should be no different for the children of God. We desire to please and thank God. We long to be like him. God responds with an outpouring of grace to allow us to become ever closer to him.

God's Children

This week remind the students of God's love for them. Talk with them about very concrete ways they can show by their words and actions that they are God's children. Also, give yourself a gift. Notice how the students in your class allow you to catch a glimpse of the wonder, innocence, and beauty of our God who created each of us out of pure, unconditional love.

The Church Teaches...

"Catechesis prepares the Christian to live in community and to participate actively in the life and mission of the Church. . . . (Catechesis) should encourage a spirit of simplicity and humility, a special concern for the poor, particular care for the alienated, a sense of fraternal correction, common prayer, mutual forgiveness, and a fraternal love that embraces all of these attitudes" (*National Directory for Catechesis*, **20.5**).

Jesus sets the example of service by his own life. As teachers, our ministry is a work of service to our students and their families.

Further Reading and Reflection

For more related teachings of the Church, see the *Catechism of the Catholic Church*, 1846–1869 and 1996–2016; and the *United States Catholic Catechism for Adults*, pages 193, 328–330.

Teacher Prayer

*Lord, help me let go
of those little annoyances
    and hurts
that come my way.
Help me treat people
with compassion and love.
Amen.*

Lesson Planner

Chapter 23 We Share in God's Life

Goal To learn that sanctifying grace is the gift of God's life that he shares with us

LESSON PART	PROCESS	MATERIALS and RESOURCES
DAY 1 EXPLORE **Focus** To explore how followers of Jesus share God's life with others **Pages 305–307**	▶ Proclaim and discuss John 1:14–16 (Jesus is God's own Son). ▶ Learn and discuss the story prison chaplains and their work. **Scripture:** I was in prison and you visited me (Matthew 25:36). **Disciple Power:** Trust **Activity:** Write captions.	Bible Pencils or pens
DAY 2 DISCOVER **Focus** To discover what the gift of God's grace helps his followers to do **Pages 308–309**	▶ Learn that God gives us the gift of sanctifying grace. ▶ Discover that the Holy Spirit helps us make good choices. **Catholics Believe:** The Gift of Peace **Faith Words:** sanctifying grace **Activity:** Color a coded picture about grace.	Bible Markers or crayons
DAY 3 DISCOVER **Focus** To discover what happens when a person sins **Pages 310–311**	▶ Discover that when we sin, we can celebrate the Sacrament of Penance and Reconciliation. **Faith Words:** mortal sin, venial sin **Faith-Filled People:** Saint Monica **Activity:** Write a "wise choice" story.	Pencils or pens **Enriching the Lesson:** Teacher Guide, page 443 • Creating a Peace Blessing • Literature Connection: Lilly's Purple Plastic Purse **Additional Activities Booklet:** Activities 23a and 23b, or see BeMyDisciples.com
DAY 4 DECIDE **Focus** To discover that Jesus gives us the gift of peace and to decide to be a peacemaker **Pages 312–313**	▶ Learn how Jesus' gift of peace helps us live the Great Commandment. **Activity:** Create an Internet message of peace. **My Faith Choice:** Choose a way to be a person whom others can trust this week.	Bible Pencil or pens **Enriching the Lesson:** Teacher Guide, page 443 Writing Peacemaking Stories
DAY 5 CONCLUDE **Focus** To reflect on how Mary can help us bring peace to others **Pages 314–316**	▶ **REVIEW** Review concepts: Recall, Reflect, and Share. ▶ **PRAY** The Hail Mary ▶ **Preview** the With My Family page and the theme of the next chapter.	Bible, candle, cross for prayer space Grade 2 Music CD **Assessment Tools Booklet:** Assessments 23a and 23b

Assign online Chapter Review and interactive Chapter Test at **BeMyDisciples.com**

Chapter 23

We Share in God's Life

❓ Tell about a special gift that you have received. What made this gift so special?

Grace helps us to live holy lives. Listen to what the Bible tells us about grace.

Jesus is the living Word of God. He is God's own Son, full of grace and truth. From Jesus, we receive grace and more grace.

BASED ON JOHN 1:14, 16

❓ Who helps you to live a holy life?

305

Pray

▶ Welcome the students warmly. Ask them to quiet themselves for prayer, and then pray the Sign of the Cross together.

▶ Ask the students to repeat after you:

Dear God,
thank you for sharing
your life with us.
Amen.

▶ Conclude with the Sign of the Cross.

Reflect

▶ Have the students respond to the opening questions. *(Accept all reasonable replies.)*

▶ Read the introduction to the Scripture passage.

▶ Ask one of the students to proclaim the reading from John's Gospel.

▶ Afterward, observe a moment of quiet reflection.

▶ Take time to discuss the follow-up question to the Scripture reading. Encourage the students to tell how the person they name helps them to live a holy life.

▶ Conclude with the Sign of the Cross.

Focus

Invite the students to turn the page to discover how some people in the Church share God's grace with people in prison.

HUMAN METHODOLOGIES

Learning Within the Christian Community. The *National Directory for Catechesis* teaches that the parish is "the place where the Christian faith is first received, expressed, and nourished" (*NDC* 29C). Decorate your prayer area with signs and symbols of Mary in preparation for the closing prayer, The Hail Mary. Mary is a model of discipleship for the entire Christian community, young and old alike. She shared in God's life in an extraordinary way, as the Mother of Jesus. Take time to talk with the students about the ways your parish honors and celebrates Mary throughout the year. Encourage the second graders to pray often to Mary, our heavenly Mother, to help them grow in living as God's children.

Introduce

▶ Tell the students that Jesus reached out to the outcasts in society. He wanted everyone to know how much God cares for them.

▶ Ask a volunteer to read Disciple Power. Point out that in this lesson they will learn about someone who is a model of trust for those who are in prison.

▶ Invite the students to tell what they think is happening in the picture. Explain that it shows a prison chaplain talking with a person who is in prison.

▶ Direct the students to listen for what prison chaplains do to help people in prison, as you read A Caring Ministry.

Reinforce

Ask the students the follow-up question. Emphasize that we are all called to show others that God still loves them.

Disciple Power

Trust

When we trust people, we know we can rely on them. We can depend on them to help us when we are in need.

The Church Follows **Jesus**

A Caring Ministry

Most people in prison have made decisions that have hurt others and themselves. Still, God gives the gift of grace to them through people who care for them.

Jesus tells us that caring for people like prisoners is the same as caring for him. Jesus said,

[I was] in prison and you visited me.

MATTHEW 25:36

Prison chaplains are trained to care for people in prison. They bring the love of Christ to them. The prisoners know they can trust them.

Sister Natalie Rossi, a Sister of Mercy, works at a women's prison in Pennsylvania. Sister Natalie, and prison chaplains like her, show prisoners that God still loves them. She helps them see that God loves them even though they did wrong.

❓ How do prison chaplains like Sister Natalie help people in prison to be open to God's grace?

306

★ DISCIPLE POWER

Trust. The word *amen* comes from a Hebrew word for faith. From this perspective, faith is understood as "I believe you," a relationship of trust. A total trust in God does not mean we sit back and wait for God to act. Trust in God requires us to use our God-given gifts to help others. Believing that no matter what happens in our life God is always with us reflects total trust in God. It is an act of faith. Invite the students to make a list of the people in their lives. Afterward, ask volunteers to give one reason for trusting a person on their list.

We are grace-filled people. These are people who can be trusted. When we trust someone, we know that we can depend on that person.

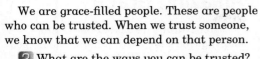 What are the ways you can be trusted?

Activity

Building Trust

The pictures on this page show grace-filled people acting with trust. Write a title for each picture.

_____

_____

_____

_____

_____

_____

307

Connect

▶ Remind the students that visiting people in prison is one of the Church's Works of Mercy. Explain that the Works of Mercy are ways to be compassionate to people, as was Jesus.

▶ Call attention to the activity, Building Trust. Have the students describe what is happening in each of the pictures on the page.

▶ Allow time for the students to write a caption for each picture. Afterward, share captions.

Pray

Invite the students to quiet themselves for prayer. Have them echo the following after you.

God of compassion and love, /
fill me with your grace. /
Teach me to love like Jesus. /
Amen.

CROSS-CURRICULAR

Art. The Church has many titles for Mary, perhaps best expressed in the Litany of the Blessed Virgin Mary (Litany of Loreto). List several examples on the board (see *Catholic Household Blessings and Prayers*, United States Conference of Catholic Bishops, 2007) and invite students to choose and to draw their interpretation of any one of the titles. At the end of class, gather the students and pray a Litany to the Blessed Virgin Mary. Be sure to include the titles the students chose to work with. Invite the students to hold up their drawings when they hear their title being read or sung. At the conclusion of prayer, gather and display the drawings in your classroom.

Materials Needed: drawing paper, crayons or markers

> **Key Concept**
> God shares his life with us through his gift of sanctifying grace.

Pray

Gather the students for prayer. Lead them in the prayer with which you concluded the previous lesson.

Teach

▶ Ask a volunteer to read the Faith Focus question aloud and invite the students to think silently about how they might answer it. Tell the students that in today's lesson they will learn what it means to share in God's life and love.

▶ Invite the students to read the meaning of *sanctifying grace* in Faith Words.

▶ Read aloud the section titled Amazing Grace. Ask the students to listen to find out when we first receive the gift of God's life. *(We first receive the gift of grace in Baptism.)*

> **Faith Focus**
> What does the gift of grace help us to do?
>
> **Faith Words**
> **sanctifying grace**
> Sanctifying grace is the gift of God sharing his life with us.

Amazing Grace

Sister Natalie dedicated her life to sharing God's love with others. She helped others understand that the gift of God's grace is offered to all people.

God also helps us to live as his children. The Holy Spirit always gives us the grace to make wise choices.

God has given us the gift of **sanctifying grace**. The word *sanctifying* means "something that makes us holy." We first receive this gift in Baptism.

The gift of sanctifying grace makes us children of God. The Bible tells us,

For through faith you are all children of God in Christ Jesus.

GALATIANS 3:26

God shares his life with us. God's grace makes us holy.

❓ How does sharing in God's grace help us?

CATHOLIC DOCTRINE

Grace. The word *grace* means "gift." God's grace is both the gift of his sharing his life and love with us (sanctifying grace) and his grace, or help, to live as his friends (actual grace). The more we come to know God, the more we want to spend time with him in prayer and the more we want to show how happy we are to be his friends. Spending time with God in prayer is also a graced moment. We come to him in prayer because he first invites us.

God also helps us to live as his children. The Holy Spirit always gives us the grace to make wise choices. This helps us to live as children of God. Grace helps us live a holy life.

? What is one way you will choose to live a holy life?

Catholics Believe

The Gift of Peace

Peace is a gift from God through Jesus Christ. Peace is also a fruit or result of the Holy Spirit in us that helps us grow closer to God by the way we care for others in our daily lives.

Activity

Discovering God's Gift

Color the X's one color. Color the O's different colors. Thank God for the wonderful gift of grace.

309

Reinforce

▶ Ask: What does God's gift of grace do for us? *(God's gift of grace makes us sharers in God's life and love; it helps us live as his children.)*

▶ Have the students create a word card for *sanctifying grace.* Encourage them to keep it in a place where it can be a reference for them.

▶ Invite the students to read Catholics Believe silently to learn about the gift of peace and how the Holy Spirit helps us grow closer to God. Emphasize that it is only through Jesus that this grace is possible.

Connect

▶ Explain the activity and have the students complete it on their own.

▶ Ask the students what good thing the gift of God's grace could help them do. *(Accept all appropriate answers. Emphasize any that give evidence of reconciliation.)*

Pray

Lead the students in praying the Lord's Prayer.

TEACHING TIP

A Grace-Filled Room. God shares his life with us and makes us holy. He creates us in his image and likeness. As a way of extending the activity, give each student a sheet of drawing paper, crayons or markers, and some scissors. Give students permission to be creative and have them design a picture, symbolic representation, or poem that defines sanctifying grace. It may be necessary to brainstorm some ideas with the students first and then put their responses on the board for students to work with. When they have completed their creations, hang their work around the room.

Key Concept
When we sin, we seek the life of grace by forgiveness in the Sacrament of Penance and Reconciliation.

Pray

Lead the students in praying the Sign of the Cross slowly and reverently.

Teach

▶ Read aloud the Faith Focus question and ask for possible answers. Tell the students that these two pages will help them learn about sin.

▶ Tell the students that while we do try to make good choices to live as children of God, we sometimes freely choose to do what we know is against his will. When we do, we sin.

▶ Present the section titled Living a Holy Life.

▶ Afterward, write *venial sin* and *mortal sin* on the board. Ask volunteers to describe the two kinds of sin in their own words. Write their responses on the board.

▶ Have the students read the definitions of *mortal sin* and *venial sin* in Faith Words and make word cards for both terms.

▶ When the students finish, remind them that we can always ask forgiveness for our sins in the Sacrament of Penance and Reconciliation. Emphasize that we need to confess all serious (mortal) sins in the Sacrament.

Faith Focus
What happens when a person sins?

Faith Words
mortal sin
Mortal sin is a serious sin that causes us to lose the gift of sanctifying grace. We must confess mortal sins in the Sacrament of Penance and Reconciliation.

venial sin
Venial sin is sin less serious than mortal sin. It hurts our relationship with God and other people.

Living a Holy Life

It is not always easy to choose to live a holy life. Sometimes we choose to sin. All sins hurt our relationships with God and other people.

Some sins are very serious. We call this type of sin, **mortal sin**. When we commit serious sins, we lose the gift of sanctifying grace.

We need to confess our mortal sins in the Sacrament of Penance and Reconciliation. When we are sorry for our sins and confess them in the Sacrament, God forgives our sins. We receive the gift of sanctifying grace again. We are filled again with God's life.

❓ What happens when we sin?

310

TEACHING TIP

Living as God's Children. When we love someone, we enjoy their company. Many of the students in your class are friends who enjoy each other's company. God is always present with us, sharing his life and love with us and inviting us to live as his children. Help the students see that we live as God's children when we overcome disagreements peacefully, respect each other's differences and opinions, and make up when we hurt one another.

Other sins are not as serious as mortal sins. This type of sin is **venial sin**. It is good to confess these sins too. In the Sacrament of Penance and Reconciliation we receive God's grace to live a holy life. We are at peace.

? What are some of the ways you can show you are truly sorry for your sins?

Faith-Filled People

Saint Monica

Monica's son was Augustine. When Augustine was young, he often made unwise choices. Monica prayed that her son would make better choices. He did and lived a holy life. Today the Church honors them as Saints. The Church celebrates the feast day of Saint Monica on August 27.

Activity

Writing a Wise Choice Story

Imagine you are an author. You are writing a book to help people to make wise choices to live a holy life. Write the outline of your story here. Tell your story to a partner and to your family.

Character's name: _____

Wise choice: _____

_____

What happened? _____

_____

_____

How did the story end? _____

_____

_____

(311)

FAITH-FILLED PEOPLE

Saint Monica (331–387). Monica is the patron Saint of mothers. Her example of kindness, love, patience, and persistence applies to all Christians. As a young man, her son, Augustine, lived a wild life, and Monica devoted herself to faithfully praying for Augustine's conversion to Christianity. Augustine accepted God's gift of grace and became a Christian. He became one of the greatest teachers of the Church and is honored as a Doctor of the Church. For more information on Saint Monica, go to the Saints Resource at *BeMyDisciples*.com.

Reinforce

▶ Draw attention to the final text paragraph on page 310. Reread the paragraph with the students. Point out how the Sacrament of Penance and Reconciliation helps us. *(God forgives us; we receive the grace to live a holy life.)*

▶ Point out the follow-up question in the text and ask for responses. *(Accept all reasonable replies.)*

▶ Read Faith-Filled People to the students. Point out that Saint Monica prayed for many years that her son would make better choices, seek forgiveness, and be filled with God's grace.

▶ Assure the students that God's gift of grace helps us make the wise choices necessary to avoid sin and live as Jesus did.

Connect

▶ Introduce the Writing a Wise Choice Story activity. Divide class into pairs and have them work on devising a story by answering the questions.

▶ When partners have completed their story, ask volunteers to read their creative work.

Pray

Pray the Lord's Prayer together.

Key Concept
Jesus gives us the gift of peace.

Pray

Have the students turn to page 369. Pray the Act of Contrition as an echo prayer with the students.

Teach

▶ Remind the students that Jesus came to be our Savior and to grant us a share in God's own life.

▶ Then read the Faith Focus question aloud and ask the students to think silently about how they might answer it. Tell them that today they will discover Jesus' final gift to us.

▶ Have volunteers read aloud Jesus Brings Peace to find out how we know when we are at peace.

▶ Ask the children what they learned about the gift of peace in their reading.

Reinforce

Have the students recall the Great Commandment. Then ask the follow-up question in the text. (Accept all reasonable replies.)

Connect

▶ Ask the students what Jesus meant when he said, "Now I send you." Write their responses on the board.

▶ Point out that because we have been given the gift of peace, we must share that gift with others.

Faith Focus
How does the gift of peace help us?

Jesus Brings Peace

After his Resurrection, Jesus' first word and last gift to his disciples was *peace*.

"Peace be with you," Jesus said to his disciples. "The Father sent me. Now I send you." Then Jesus breathed on them, saying, "Receive the Holy Spirit."

BASED ON JOHN 20:21–22

Peace is Jesus' final, grace-filled gift to us. The gift of peace comes from knowing we are living as friends of God and people.

The Holy Spirit brings us God's peace. The Holy Spirit gives us the help we need to remain in God's grace.

When we are at peace, we are loving God above all else and loving others as we love ourselves. We are living the Great Commandment. We are living the life of grace.

❓ How does Jesus' gift of peace help us to live the Great Commandment?

312

LITURGY CONNECTION

The Peace of Christ. When we gather to celebrate Mass, the priest may greet us with the words, "Grace to you and peace from God our Father and the Lord Jesus Christ." When we pray the Gloria, we say, "Glory to God in the highest, and on earth peace to people of good will." Later, just before Communion, we share the sign of peace with one another. When we share the peace of Christ at Mass, it is the same peace Jesus gave his disciples. We are saying that we are Christ for one another.

God shares the gift of his life with us. Jesus gives us the gift of peace. The Holy Spirit helps us to live as children of God. One way you can live as a child of God is to be a peacemaker. When you show that you can be trusted, you bring peace.

Activity

Signs of Peace

Work with your teacher or parent. Create a message that tells how people your age can live as peacemakers.

_____
_____
_____
_____
_____
_____

My Faith Choice

This week, I will be a person whom others can trust. I will

_____
_____

 Pray, **"Thank you, Holy Spirit, for helping me to live as a peacemaker. Amen."**

313

Reinforce

Help the students recall that the Holy Spirit helps us live as children of God. Point out that one way we live as children of God is to live as peacemakers.

Respond

▶ Read the introductory paragraph with the students.

▶ Talk about ways we can be peacemakers.

▶ Help the students with the activity or have them complete it at home with their families.

Choose

▶ Invite the students to read My Faith Choice and write their decisions.

▶ Encourage them to put their choices into practice this week.

Pray

Gather the students for prayer. Lead them in the prayer to the Holy Spirit at the bottom of the page.

THE TASKS OF CATECHESIS

Missionary Initiative. After the students have completed this week's My Faith Choice, point out that they have many opportunities at home and school to use their peacemaking skills. Before your session, make a one-week calendar and give each student a copy. They can write or draw what they do to be peacemakers each day. Offer specific suggestions—sharing a toy with a friend, not bickering with a sibling, being kind to an elderly neighbor. Don't insist that the students complete the calendar during class, but do encourage them to look for opportunities each day to be peacemakers. By extending the My Faith Choice activity in this way, you will help the students see that our faith is meant to be lived every day. Have the students return their calendars after a week and share them with the class.

Pray

Gather the students for prayer. Begin class by praying the Hail Mary.

Recall

▶ Write each To Help You Remember statement on a strip of paper.

▶ Cut each strip into two parts, dividing the term from its meaning.

▶ Mix the sentences up and tape them to a flat surface with double-stick tape.

▶ Have the students complete the review activity.

Reflect

Give the students a few moments to complete the reflection statement.

Share

Invite the students to share their reflection with a partner and at home with their families.

▶ **TO HELP YOU REMEMBER**

1. Grace is a gift from God.

2. Sanctifying grace is the gift of God's life that he shares with us.

3. The gift of peace helps us live holy and happy lives.

Chapter Review

Recall

Match the words to their meanings.

Meanings

a. the gift of God sharing his life with us

b. the choice to say or do what we know is against God's Law

c. the choice that causes us to lose sanctifying grace

Words

c 1. mortal sin

b 2. sin

a 3. sanctifying grace

Reflect

How can we live peaceful and holy lives? Write a sentence to describe one way using words from the chapter.

_____

_____

_____

_____

_____

_____

Share Share ways you can live as a peacemaker with your class.

(314)

TEACHING TIP

Alternative Review. Involve the kinesthetic learners in the review process. Using sidewalk chalk, redraw the pathway outside on the playground or with markers on large sheets of newsprint that has been taped to the floor. Give each student the opportunity to use the chalk and draw or write ways we can live holy lives that will lead us to God and ultimately to Heaven to be with him. After each student writes something, talk about how it can lead us to God.

Hail Mary

Learn the Hail Mary by heart. Pray it every day to show your love for Mary. Ask Mary to help you bring peace to others.

Leader

The Blessed Virgin Mary is full of grace. She was always without sin. She is the greatest and most holy of all the Saints. Let us pray the Hail Mary together and ask Mary to help us to live a holy life.

Group 1

Hail, Mary, full of grace,
the Lord is with thee.

Group 2

Blessed art thou among women
and blessed is the fruit of thy
womb, Jesus.

All

**Holy Mary, Mother of God,
pray for us sinners,
now and at the hour of our
death.
Amen.**

Leader

Now let us raise our voices and ask all the Saints to pray for us.

All

**Blessed Saints, please pray
for me in your gentle way.
Help me learn how I should be.
Watch over me each day.
Amen.**

315

We Pray

▶ Remind the students that Mary, the Mother of Jesus, was always filled with God's grace.

▶ Tell the students that you are going to pray the Hail Mary with them today as the closing prayer.

▶ Point out to the students that in the first line of the prayer, Mary is called "full of grace."

▶ Divide the class into two groups. Have each group find the part of the Hail Mary that they are going to pray aloud.

▶ Gather the students in the prayer center. Remind the students that they prayed the Hail Mary at the beginning of today's class. Tell them that the Hail Mary also will be part of the prayer service today.

▶ Begin with the Sign of the Cross. Then have the students pray the Hail Mary together.

▶ Conclude with a favorite Marian hymn and the Sign of the Cross.

LITURGY TIP

Praying the Hail Mary. The Hail Mary is a traditional Catholic prayer and a beautiful way to honor the Mother of God. Go over the parts of the Hail Mary with the students before beginning the concluding prayer. Help the students understand the language of the prayer so they might be able to better appreciate it as one of the prayers Catholics pray frequently.

Preview

▶ Have the students carefully tear out pages 315 and 316 along the perforation.

▶ Encourage the students to share these pages with their families, and to complete the activities together.

▶ If they did not complete the review activity on page 314 by the end of the session, emphasize that they can complete it with their families at home.

▶ Point out the title and theme of the next lesson to the students.

Visit BeMyDisciples.com

▶ Take time with the students to explore the many activities and resources available at the *Be My Disciples* Web site.

▶ Encourage them to join with their families to discover the many resources available at the Web site.

Before Moving On ...

As you finish today's lesson, reflect on the following question before moving on to the next chapter.

How have I encouraged the students to be peacemakers?

With My Family

This Week . . .

In Chapter 23, "We Share in God's Life," your child learned:

▶ God shares divine life with us in the gift of sanctifying grace.

▶ God calls us to live holy lives.

▶ Sin turns us away from God's love and deters us from living holy lives.

▶ Sharing the gift of peace is crucial for living a holy and happy life

▶ When we trust someone, we kow we can depend on them to help us when we are in need.

For more about related teachings of the Church, see the *Catechism of the Catholic Church*, 1846–1869 and 1996–2016, and the *United States Catholic Catechism for Adults*, pages 193, and 328–330.

■ Sharing God's Word

Read together John 1:14, 16. Emphasize that through Jesus we receive the God-given gift of divine help, or grace, to live as children of God.

■ Living as Disciples

The Christian home and family is a school of discipleship. Choose one of the following activities to do as a family, or design a similar activity of your own.

▶ Help your children create peace place mats. Use the place mats at family meals as reminders to share meals in peace and to be peacemakers for one another. Discuss situations where you can show trust.

▶ Point out to your child the many ways your family is "graced." Show your child how to count blessings and so live a holy, happy, and peace-filled life.

■ Our Spiritual Journey

Catholics look upon Mary as the purest of creatures, not subject to the slavery that sin imposes. Catholics believe that Mary is totally graced, totally responsive to the divine will, and totally faithful. God comes to Mary seeking her consent. Mary's "yes" joins the creature to God in the work of completing the labors of creation. Help your child learn the great prayer to Mary, the Hail Mary on page 315. Use it for your family prayer this week.

For more ideas on ways your family can live as disciples of Jesus, visit **BeMyDisciples.com**

316

ENRICHING THE LESSON

Using Music to Set the Mood. As the students work on their Faith Choice or as a musical interlude during the praying of the Hail Mary, consider playing an instrumental Marian hymn. Also consider teaching the students a simple Marian hymn, such as "Sacred Silence" from the *Be My Disciples* Grade 2 Music CD, which incorporates the words of the Hail Mary into the lyrics. The use of music will contribute to the learning environment and enrich the students' appreciation for Mary as our Mother.

Enriching the Lesson

Creating a Peace Blessing

Purpose

To reinforce the students' appreciation of the gift of peace (taught on page 311)

Directions

▶ Print the following adaptation of a traditional Irish peace blessing on the board. Give the students paper and have them copy it with their best printing. Tell the students that the blessing uses beautiful images of God's creation to ask for peace.

Deep peace of the ocean wave be yours.

Deep peace of the gentle breeze be yours.

Deep peace of the quiet earth be yours.

Deep peace of shining stars be yours.

Deep peace of the Son of Peace be yours.

▶ Ask the students to identify the "Son of Peace."

▶ On the back of their papers, have the students draw a picture to go with the blessing.

▶ Encourage the students to take the blessing home and to bestow it on their families.

Materials

paper

pens or pencils

colored markers or crayons

Writing Peacemaking Stories

Purpose

To reinforce the importance of choosing to be a peacemaker (taught on page 312)

Directions

▶ In partners, have the students write the outlines for a peacemaking story. Have them fill in the characters, the setting (place), and a problem to be solved—a situation involving a choice where peacemaking is needed.

▶ Have each pair pass its outline to another set of partners and have them fill in the peaceful "solution."

Materials

paper and pencils

Literature Connection

Purpose

To reinforce the understanding of the need to be reconciled and to be a peacemaker (taught on pages 310 and 311)

Directions

Kevin Henkes's story *Lilly's Purple Plastic Purse* (William Morrow & Co., 1996) is a humorous tale that makes some very important points about reconciliation and the need to ask forgiveness.

▶ Read the story aloud to the students and discuss it with them. Why does Lilly's teacher Mr. Slinger reprimand Lilly? What is Lilly's initial reaction? What does Mr. Slinger do to make peace with Lilly? Why does Lilly feel remorse by his kindness? In the end, what does Lilly do?

Materials

Lilly's Purple Plastic Purse by Kevin Henke

The Our Father

BACKGROUND

Lord, Teach Us to Pray

The Sermon on the Mount in Matthew's Gospel is a summary of what it means to be a disciple of Christ. The Our Father that is found in the Sermon on the Mount is the model for all Christian prayer and a summary of the entire Gospel (*see General Directory for Catechesis,* 85). If we were so inclined, we could devote a lifetime to meditating on the Our Father and still not have grasped the fullness of its teachings.

Abba Father

The Our Father consists of three petitions directed toward God's glory (hallowed be thy name, thy kingdom come, and thy will be done) and three petitions for human need (food, forgiveness, and freedom from temptation).

Jesus is saying "Keep first things first" by opening his prayer with words of touching intimacy: "Our Father, who art in heaven." God is our Abba, the Father who is above us and watches out for us, in whom we trust unconditionally for our deepest needs.

Ask and You Shall Receive

What are our deepest needs? Again, notice how Jesus lines up the wording of the prayer. He resolutely points us first toward God. Jesus' words carry us toward God's name, his kingdom, and his will. Therein is our deepest need—to merge our earthly priorities and our pursuit of happiness with God's will. Christ is telling us to "seek first the kingdom [of God] and his righteousness, and all these things will be given you besides" (Matthew 6:33).

Lord, Teach Us to Live

In the final set of petitions of the Lord's Prayer, Jesus guides us to place before our Father in Heaven our human needs of daily bread, forgiveness, strength to overcome all that leads us from loving God and from loving one another as Jesus did, and victory over evil, suffering, sin, and death. As we read these petitions, we quickly notice that power, prestige, money, or life's tempting trinkets that assuage our egos do not make it onto Christ's short list.

Jesus, in so many words, advises us to boldly and confidently approach God the Father in prayer, trusting that "all that you ask for in prayer, believe that you will receive it and it shall be yours" (Mark 11:24). As the Roman centurion did (see Matthew 8:10) and as the Canaanite woman did (see Matthew 15:28), we are to express our needs boldly and confidently to the Lord.

For Reflection

When have I used the Our Father as a guide to structure my prayer?

What are some concrete, specific implications of the petitions of the Lord's Prayer for living my life as a disciple of Christ?

The Family of God

Imagine it! You can go into any Christian church anywhere in the world and hear the Our Father being prayed. When Christians all over the world address God, "Our Father," it gives a special meaning to the phrase "family of God."

Stay Focused

We really should focus attentively on the meaning of the words of the Our Father every time we pray them. We need to slow down and let the meaning of this prayer give meaning to our lives. When we do, it changes our day. We respond with love and forgiveness. We understand the meaning of caring for others. We take responsibility for our choices. We see the world as God's gift to us, a sign of his love for us. We see and value others as children of God, created in his image and likeness.

The Church Teaches...

"Catechesis should invite the believer to join Christ in the Our Father. Prayer should be the ordinary environment for all catechesis so that the knowledge and practice of the Christian life may be understood and celebrated in its proper context" (*National Directory for Catechesis*, 20.4).

This year you have begun to develop the students' understanding of and love for God the Father. Jesus is our model and guide in the ways of prayer. This last chapter presents the Our Father as an essential part of the Christian life.

Further Reading and Reflection

For more related teachings of the Church, see the *Catechism of the Catholic Church*, 2777–2856; and the *United States Catholic Catechism for Adults*, pages 481–492.

Teacher Prayer

Jesus, through your words and example you taught us to pray. Help us remember this when we pray the prayer you taught us— and whenever we pray. Amen.

Lesson Planner

Chapter 24 The Our Father

Goal To appreciate that the Our Father helps us live as children of God

LESSON PART	PROCESS	MATERIALS and RESOURCES
DAY 1 EXPLORE **Focus** To explore how followers of Jesus pray **Pages 317–319**	▶ Proclaim and discuss Matthew 6:9 (Jesus teaches the Our Father). ▶ Learn and discuss the story of contemplatives and their lives of prayer. **Disciple Power:** Hope **Activity:** Follow a prayer path and find ways to pray.	Bible Pencils or pens
DAY 2 DISCOVER **Focus** To discover why we pray the Our Father **Pages 320–321**	▶ Learn that the Our Father helps us live as God's children. **Catholics Believe:** Vocation **Faith Words:** Kingdom of God **Activity:** Match parts of the Our Father to their meaning.	Bible Markers or crayons **Enriching the Lesson:** Teacher Guide, page 459 Preparing the Way for the Kingdom of God **Additional Activities Booklet:** Activity 24a, or see *BeMyDisciples*.com
DAY 3 DISCOVER **Focus** To discover what we pray for in the Our Father **Pages 322–323**	▶ Learn what we pray for in the Our Father. **Faith Words:** trespass **Faith-Filled People:** Saint Thomas Aquinas **Activity:** Match more parts of the Our Father to their meaning.	Pencils or pens **Enriching the Lesson:** Teacher Guide, page 459 Catholic Social Teaching: Solidarity with Others
DAY 4 DECIDE **Focus** To discover that the Our Father is the prayer of all Christians and to decide on a way to live the Our Father **Pages 324–325**	▶ Discover that the Our Father is the prayer of all Christians. **Faith Word:** Lord's Prayer **Activity:** Choose ways to live the Our Father as disciples of Jesus. **My Faith Choice:** Choose a way to live the Our Father all summer.	Bible Pencil or pens **Enriching the Lesson:** Teacher Guide, page 459 A Year of Faith Stories **Additional Activities Booklet:** Activity 24a, or see *BeMyDisciples*.com
DAY 5 CONCLUDE **Focus** To reflect on how Jesus calls us to be his disciples **Pages 326–328**	▶ **REVIEW** Review concepts: Recall, Reflect, and Share. ▶ **PRAY** Go Forth! ▶ **Preview** the With My Family page and the theme of the next chapter.	Bible, candle, cross for prayer space Bell or drum Grade 2 Music CD **Assessment Tools Booklet:** Assessments 24a and 24b

Assign online Chapter Review and interactive Chapter Test at

BeMyDisciples.com

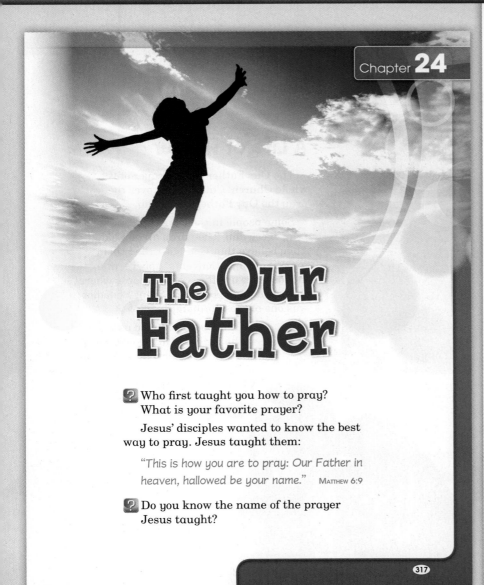

Chapter **24**

The Our Father

? Who first taught you how to pray? What is your favorite prayer?

Jesus' disciples wanted to know the best way to pray. Jesus taught them:

"This is how you are to pray: Our Father in heaven, hallowed be your name." Matthew 6:9

? Do you know the name of the prayer Jesus taught?

317

HUMAN METHODOLOGIES

Learning by Apprenticeship. The *National Directory for Catechesis* points out that apprenticeship "links an experienced Christian believer . . . with one who seeks a deeper relationship with Christ and the Church" (*NDC* 29H). Invite a junior high class to work with your second graders to decide on appropriate gestures to express each phrase of the Our Father. As the older students work with your class, encourage them to explain each phrase to the second graders. Allow time for them to practice incorporating the gestures into the prayer several times until all the students are comfortable praying in this manner. At your year-end celebration, invite the students to pray the Our Father with the gestures they have learned.

Pray

▶ Welcome the students warmly. Ask them to quiet themselves for prayer.

▶ Begin and end with the Sign of the Cross. Pray with the children the first words of the Our Father from Matthew 6:9.

Reflect

▶ Ask the opening questions. *(Affirm all reasonable replies.)*

▶ Read the introduction to the Scripture passage.

▶ Remind the students that they read this passage in Chapter 4 (student text page 54). Then ask one of the students to proclaim the passage from the Gospel of Matthew.

▶ Afterward, observe a moment of silence.

▶ Pose the second question. Afterward, remind the students that the Our Father is sometimes called the Lord's Prayer because it is the prayer the Lord Jesus taught.

▶ Invite the students to tell when they pray the Our Father. *(At Mass; at home; in school. Affirm appropriate responses.)*

Focus

Invite the students to turn the page to learn about people in the Church who dedicate their whole lives to prayer.

Introduce

▶ Introduce the section titled A Life of Prayer by asking the students to share how many times a day they pray. *(Affirm all replies.)*

▶ Go on to explain to the students that the time we spend in prayer makes a difference in the life of the Church.

▶ Have volunteers read A Life of Prayer aloud.

▶ After the reading, tell the students that these praying people are called monks and nuns, or religious brothers and religious sisters. Then talk about the photos with the students.

▶ Have a volunteer read aloud about the virtue of hope in Disciple Power. Stress that hope is not simply wishing for something from God. Rather it is being sure that God will act on our behalf. When we pray, we have hope.

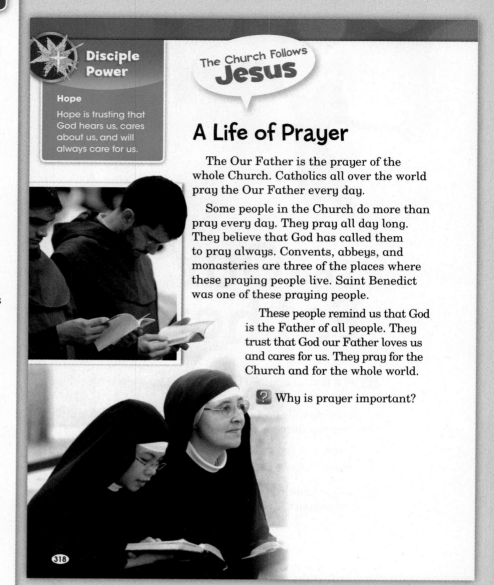

Disciple Power

Hope

Hope is trusting that God hears us, cares about us, and will always care for us.

The Church Follows **Jesus**

A Life of Prayer

The Our Father is the prayer of the whole Church. Catholics all over the world pray the Our Father every day.

Some people in the Church do more than pray every day. They pray all day long. They believe that God has called them to pray always. Convents, abbeys, and monasteries are three of the places where these praying people live. Saint Benedict was one of these praying people.

These people remind us that God is the Father of all people. They trust that God our Father loves us and cares for us. They pray for the Church and for the whole world.

❓ Why is prayer important?

318

DISCIPLE POWER

Hope. Before your session, print the prayer below on a poster. Leave a large space at the bottom of the poster. Before showing the poster to the students, remind them that the Our Father is the prayer that Jesus taught us. After you introduce the virtue of hope, emphasize that the Our Father is a prayer of hope. Show the students the poster and slowly read each phrase aloud together. Then invite the students to express their hope in God our Father by signing their names, one at a time on the poster.

> Dear God,
> We trust in you.
> We believe you hear our prayers.
> We believe you care for us always.
> Amen.

Maybe you cannot pray all day. But you can pray every day. You can pray no matter how you feel. You can make prayer a part of how you live.

When and how do you pray?

Activity

A Prayer Path

Follow the prayer path. At each stop, find a new way to pray and then write your own prayer.

You can share your joy and offer God praise. **I praise you, God, for** ______.

You can tell God you are sorry. You can ask for forgiveness. **Forgiving God, I am sorry for** ______.

You can ask God for what you need. You can ask for help for yourself and for others. **Please, God,** ______.

You can say thanks for the gifts God gives you. **Thank you, God, for** ______.

319

Reinforce

- Ask the follow-up question. *(They feel called by God to do so.)*
- Invite the students to tell why they think the people who pray all day—the religious sisters, brothers, or monks—have hope.

Connect

- Call on a volunteer to read aloud the first paragraph of the activity, A Prayer Path. Tell the students that God loves us so much he wants us to pray whether we are happy or sad, lonely or angry, healthy or sick.
- Read the activity directions aloud. Have the students write their own prayers of joy, sorrow, petition, and thanks, as they progress along the path.

Pray

- Gather the students for prayer. Invite different students to offer their individual prayers of joy, sorrow, petition, and thanks.
- Conclude by praying the Our Father together.

TEACHING TIP

Trust. The virtue of hope enables us to trust that God will act on our behalf. As with any relationship, our relationship with God is about trust. As adults we have learned to trust certain people and situations over others. Yet, most of the time we find it difficult to trust the unknown and prefer to keep things in our control. Teaching your students to trust in God is essential to developing hope and to developing a healthy relationship with God. We are asked throughout our lives to trust in God, especially when it is difficult to understand his will. If the students are to maintain a relationship with God even when things are tough, we have to help them develop a sincere trust in his will for them.

Key Concept
The Our Father is a prayer that helps us live as children of God.

Pray

Gather the students for prayer. Reverently lead them in praying the Our Father.

Teach

▶ Ask a volunteer to read the Faith Focus question aloud. Ask the students to respond to the question. *(Accept all replies.)*

▶ Summarize the students' responses by telling them that praying the Our Father shows God the Father we trust him and we want to live as his children.

▶ Call attention to Faith Words. Have different volunteers read the definitions of *Kingdom of God* and *hallowed*.

▶ Have the class read the text sections "Our Father, who art in heaven," "Hallowed be thy name," and "Thy kingdom come."

Faith Focus
Why do we pray the Our Father?

Faith Words
Kingdom of God
The Kingdom of God is also called the Kingdom of Heaven. It is a people and creation living in friendship with God.

The Our Father

The Our Father helps us to pray to God and understand how to live as his children.

Our Father, who art in heaven
God is the Father of all people. God creates us in his image and likeness. God shares his life and love with us now and forever.

Hallowed be thy name
The word *hallowed* means "very holy." We love God above all else. We adore and worship God. We honor and respect the name of God in all we say and do.

Thy kingdom come
Jesus announced the coming of the **Kingdom of God.** The Kingdom of God is also called the Kingdom of Heaven. When we love God above all else, we live as Jesus taught. We prepare for the coming of the Kingdom of God in its fullness.

❓ What do you do and say that show your love for God the Father?

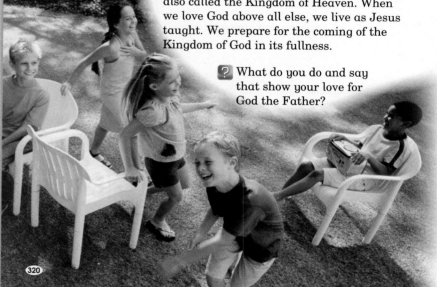

320

TEACHING VOCABULARY

The Kingdom of God. The Kingdom of God is another term for the Kingdom of Heaven. Students this age have many questions about Heaven. Help them grow in their understanding of Heaven as a life of happiness with God forever. It is the very reward Jesus promises to those who love him. Students at this age are concrete thinkers. It is very natural for them to imagine Heaven as a physical place similar to some happy place on Earth that is part of their experience. The students' understanding of Heaven as a state of eternal happiness with God will evolve as they grow in their understanding of the Catholic faith.

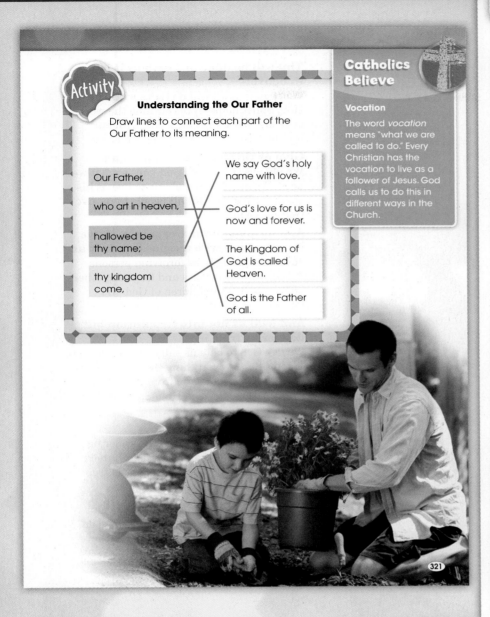

Activity

Understanding the Our Father

Draw lines to connect each part of the Our Father to its meaning.

Our Father,		We say God's holy name with love.
who art in heaven,		God's love for us is now and forever.
hallowed be thy name;		The Kingdom of God is called Heaven.
thy kingdom come,		God is the Father of all.

Catholics Believe

Vocation

The word *vocation* means "what we are called to do." Every Christian has the vocation to live as a follower of Jesus. God calls us to do this in different ways in the Church.

321

Reinforce

▶ Ask the follow-up question. List the students' responses on the board.

▶ Ask what God the Father does to show that he is our loving Father. List the students' responses on the board. *(He shares his life and love with us now and forever.)*

▶ Have the students make word cards for the term *Kingdom of God*.

▶ Read Catholics Believe about the word vocation. Talk with the students about the different ways they can use their gifts and talents to do what they are called to do as followers of Jesus.

Connect

Invite the students to complete the Understanding the Our Father activity. Go over the correct connections with the students.

Pray

▶ Divide the class into two groups.

▶ Have Group One pray the first half of the Our Father—up to "as it is in heaven."

▶ Have Group Two pray the second half.

BACKGROUND: DOCTRINE

Organization of the Catechism. You have obviously noticed that this textbook keeps itself aligned with the *Catechism of the Catholic Church*. This last chapter of the textbook teaches the words of the Lord's Prayer step by step so that students will comprehend the meaning of the prayer. Fittingly, the *Catechism* presents the Our Father as both the conclusion to the section on prayer as well as the conclusion of the Catechism itself. The Our Father is in many ways a summary to the *Catechism of the Catholic Church* in that it is a summary of the Gospel.

> **Key Concept**
> The Our Father is a prayer that teaches us what to pray for.

Pray

Lead the students in the Sign of the Cross.

Teach

▶ Recall with the students what they have learned about the meaning of the Our Father.

▶ Read the Faith Focus question aloud and ask for possible answers. Tell the students that these two pages will help them learn what we pray for in the Our Father.

▶ Have the students read the line *Thy will be done on earth as it is in heaven.* Ask a volunteer to share who helps us continue to do the work of Jesus. *(the Holy Spirit)*

▶ Read aloud the section *Give us this day our daily bread.* Share with the students that bread nourishes our body and fills us just as the Holy Spirit nourishes us.

▶ Point out the definition of *trespass* in Faith Words. Then have a volunteer read aloud the section *And forgive us our trespasses, as we forgive those who trespass against us.* Remind the students that they are to be forgiving and forgiven.

▶ Read the text sections *And lead us not into temptation but deliver us from evil* and *Amen* with the students. Make sure they recognize the meaning of *temptation, evil* and *amen.*

Faith Focus
What do we pray for when we pray the Our Father?

Faith Words
trespass
To trespass means to do or say something that hurts our friendship with God and with other people.

Thy will be done on earth as it is in heaven

We pray that all will do God's will. The Holy Spirit helps us to continue the work of Jesus. We share God's love with our family, friends, and everyone we meet.

Give us this day our daily bread

We always trust God. God knows what we need. We ask God to help us to live as his children. We pray for all people to receive God's blessings.

And forgive us our trespasses, as we forgive those who trespass against us

Jesus taught us to be forgiving persons. Asking for forgiveness and forgiving others help us to live as children of God and followers of Jesus.

And lead us not into temptation but deliver us from evil

We ask God to help us say no to temptation. Temptation is everything that can lead us away from God's love. The Holy Spirit will help us.

Amen

We end our prayer by saying, "Amen." *Amen* means, "Yes, it is true. We believe!"

❓ What does the Our Father ask us to do?

CATHOLIC DOCTRINE

Avoiding Temptation. Telling the truth can be challenging at times for students this age. They want to avoid punishment, but they also really want to do what is right. Tell the students that one of the important signs of a follower of Jesus is a willingness to take responsibility for their choices—good and bad. Tell them to ask God for help if ever they are tempted to lie about their bad choices.

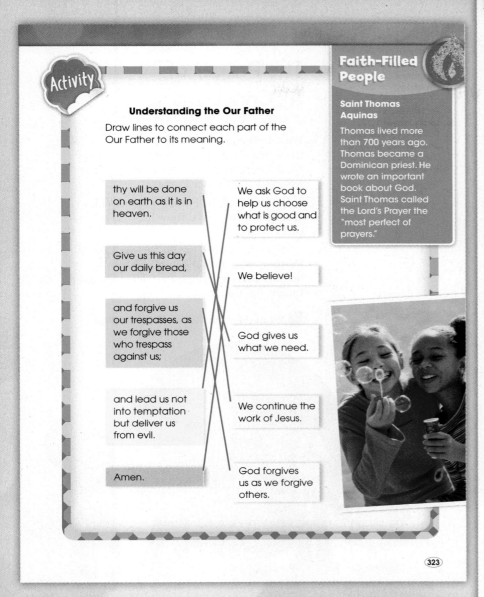

Activity

Understanding the Our Father

Draw lines to connect each part of the Our Father to its meaning.

thy will be done on earth as it is in heaven.	We ask God to help us choose what is good and to protect us.
Give us this day our daily bread,	We believe!
and forgive us our trespasses, as we forgive those who trespass against us;	God gives us what we need.
and lead us not into temptation but deliver us from evil.	We continue the work of Jesus.
Amen.	God forgives us as we forgive others.

Faith-Filled People

Saint Thomas Aquinas

Thomas lived more than 700 years ago. Thomas became a Dominican priest. He wrote an important book about God. Saint Thomas called the Lord's Prayer the "most perfect of prayers."

323

Reinforce

▶ Ask the follow-up question. *(share God's love; pray for the things that we need; forgive and ask forgiveness; avoid evil)*

▶ Have the students make a word card for the term *trespass*.

▶ Ask a volunteer to read aloud Faith-Filled People. Point out that Saint Thomas Aquinas is an important figure in the Church.

Connect

Have the students complete the Understanding the Our Father activity on their own. Check their answers as they work. Have volunteers share their answers.

Pray

Lead the students in praying the Our Father.

FAITH-FILLED PEOPLE

Saint Thomas Aquinas (1225–1274). Thomas was born to a noble family in Italy. He later attended school in Naples and became friends with members of the Dominican order. When he decided to become a Dominican priest, his parents were furious because the order required its members to take a vow of poverty. They forced Thomas to return home and would not let him leave for over a year. Eventually, Thomas convinced them that God was calling him to the Dominican way of life. Thomas was a brilliant theologian and famous for his writing and preaching. He wrote the *Summa Theologica*, a book that is still considered the best summary of Catholic theology. In the *Summa*, he called the Lord's Prayer the "most perfect of prayers" (*CCC* 2763). For more information on Saint Thomas Aquinas, go to the Saints Resource at *BeMyDisciples*.com.

> **Key Concept**
> The Lord's Prayer is the prayer that Jesus our Lord taught the disciples.

Pray

Lead the students in praying the Our Father.

Teach

▶ Read the Faith Focus question aloud. Tell the students that today they will learn that the Our Father is the prayer of all Christians.

▶ Invite the students to consider where and when the Catholic Church prays the Lord's Prayer together. *(At Mass. Affirm all appropriate responses.)*

▶ Read The Prayer of All Christians aloud and have the students raise their hands when they hear why we also call the Our Father the Lord's Prayer.

Reinforce

▶ Call for a response to the follow-up question *(It is the prayer Jesus our Lord taught us.)*

▶ Read the definition of *Lord's Prayer* in Faith Words. Have the students make a word card for the term.

Connect

Point out again that the Lord's Prayer guides us to pray for the things that we need in order to live as children of God. When we pray the Lord's Prayer, we tell God the Father we love him and trust him. Pose the question at the bottom of the page. Invite volunteers to respond.

> **Faith Focus**
> Why is the Our Father the prayer of all Christians?
>
> **Faith Words**
> ▶ **Lord's Prayer**
> The Lord's Prayer is another name for the Our Father.

The Prayer of All Christians

Christians everywhere pray the Our Father. They pray it in all the languages of the world. Jesus taught that his Father is our Father too. No matter what language we speak, God is our Father.

We love God the Father and trust him. God listens to us. We know he loves us and cares for us.

We also call the Our Father the **Lord's Prayer.** We call it the Lord's Prayer because it is the prayer that Jesus our Lord taught the disciples.

❓ What does the Lord's Prayer mean to you?

324

BACKGROUND: CATHOLICS BELIEVE

Daily Prayer. God's people have always been people of prayer. Throughout the Old Testament there are exchanges between God and his people. In the Gospels, we hear accounts of Jesus praying to his Father in Heaven. Jesus also teaches his disciples how to pray. In the early Church, Jesus' followers came together to pray, worship, and sing the Psalms. Later in the history of the Church, praying the Angelus or the Liturgy of the Hours became a prayer tradition. Today, we are called to make room for God in our lives and pray daily. We can still pray the Liturgy of the Hours or the Divine Office. We can pray before meals, in the morning upon waking, and again before we drift off to sleep at night. We can pray anywhere and at any time.

The Holy Spirit is helping you to live the Our Father now. He is helping you to grow in hope. He is helping you to live as a member of the family of God's people.

A Disciple of Jesus

Put a ✔ next to one way that you could try to live the words of the Our Father this summer. Make a plan to put your choice into action.

____ Pray.

____ Make wise choices.

____ Forgive those who hurt me.

____ Say I am sorry when I hurt someone else.

____ Listen to the Holy Spirit, who helps me to make wise choices.

I will live the Our Father. This week, I will do one of the things I checked. I will continue to do the things I checked all summer. I will

_____

 Pray, "Thank you, Holy Spirit, for helping me to live the Our Father. Amen."

(325)

Reinforce

Remind the students that the Holy Spirit teaches us to pray and helps us to live the Our Father.

Respond

▶ Discuss with the students ways they can do the things we pray for in the Our Father.

▶ Give the students sufficient time to complete the activity. You may wish to have them copy this activity onto art paper to make a small poster to hang in their rooms over the summer.

Choose

▶ Invite the students to read My Faith Choice and to write their decisions.

▶ Encourage the students to put their choices into practice throughout the summer.

Pray

Lead the students in the prayer at the bottom of the page.

TEACHING TIP

Share a Story. Explain to the students that God the Father has given all of his children special gifts and talents to use to prepare for his Kingdom to come in fullness. Every person has a vocation, regardless of where they live, which culture they belong to, or which language they speak. Share with the students a story, such as *My Name Is Yoon* by Helen Recorvits (Frances Foster Books, 2003), to help them grow to appreciate that they are gifted and blessed.

Pray

Gather the students for prayer. Begin class by praying the Our Father.

Recall

▶ Ask the students to share some things they have learned this week about the meaning of the Our Father. Read the To Help You Remember statements aloud to the students to summarize what they have learned.

▶ Invite the students to use the clues to solve the crossword puzzle. Then have the students decorate the heart with faith words.

Reflect

Give the students a few moments to complete the reflection statement.

Share

Invite the students to share their reflection with a partner and at home with their families.

▶ TO HELP YOU REMEMBER

1. We pray the Our Father to show our love and adoration of God.

2. The Our Father helps us to live as children of God.

3. The Our Father helps us to prepare for the Kingdom of God.

Chapter Review

Recall

Choose the right word to complete each sentence.

| Temptation | pray | Kingdom |
| Father | Hallowed | |

1. ___Hallowed___ means "very holy."

2. When you ___pray___ you lift up your heart to God.

3. God is our ___Father___.

4. ___Temptation___ is something that leads us away from God.

5. Living as God wants us to live helps us to prepare for the ___Kingdom___ of God.

Reflect

What is one way you will choose to live the Our Father?

_____

_____

_____

_____

Share Decorate a paper heart with faith words you learned this year. Now go forth to share your life of faith.

(326)

TEACHING TIP

Review. Have the students gather all the faith word cards they have created this year and shuffle them. Working with a partner, have them test each other to see how many they know. Have the students separate the cards they are not familiar with into a different pile. Working together, have them drill each other until the deck is cut in half. When each pair has a smaller deck, allow them to write a story together, correctly using the terms from the faith cards that are left

Go Forth!

Jesus taught that we must live our faith in God.
Thank God for all you learned this year. Live your faith
in Jesus and make a difference. Be his disciple!

Leader   We have grown in our faith in many ways
this year. Let us thank God!

All   **Jesus taught us how to pray.**
We can talk to God all day.
Anytime, God always cares.
God always listens,
listens to our prayers.

Reader 1   Lord, each day we will remember
and act like children of God.

All   **Thanks be to God.**

Reader 2   Lord, we will love and serve
you every day.

All   **Thanks be to God.**

Reader 3   Lord, we will treat others with
kindness and bring them hope.

All   **Thanks be to God.**
Jesus taught us how to pray.
We can talk to God all day.
Anytime, God always cares.
God always listens,
listens to our prayers.
Amen.

327

We Pray

▶ Choose three readers and have them practice their parts.

▶ Practice the prayer responses with the entire class.

▶ Share with the students that the closing prayer for the year is a prayer of thanksgiving. Just as we do at the end of Mass, we are going forth to love and serve the Lord and one another until we meet again.

▶ Read the opening paragraph aloud.

▶ Gather the students in the prayer center with their textbooks.

▶ Call the students to prayer with a lively ring of a bell or a drum beat.

▶ Lead the prayer.

▶ Conclude the prayer by going to each student and tracing a cross on his or her forehead, saying, "God bless you, _____, and keep you safe until we meet again."

THE TASKS OF CATECHESIS

Teaching to Pray. The closing prayer for this session is one of praise and thanksgiving. Show the students how to raise their hands high in a gesture of praise and thanks as they say each response. Consider using bells or other rhythm instruments to play during the responses. You might also like to play background music to aid in the prayer celebration.

Preview

▶ Have the students carefully tear out pages 327 and 328 along the perforation.

▶ Encourage the students to share these pages with their families, and to complete the activities together.

▶ If they did not complete the review activity on page 326 by the end of the session, emphasize that they can complete it with their families at home.

▶ Point out the title and theme of next week' chapter to the children.

Visit BeMyDisciples.com

▶ Take time with the students to explore the many activities and resources available at the *Be My Disciples* Web site.

▶ Encourage them to join with their families to discover the many resources available at the Web site.

CONCLUDE

Before Moving On ...

As you finish today's lesson, reflect on the following question before moving on.

What is something I learned from the students that has enriched my own faith life?

With My Family

This Week . . .

In Chapter 24, "The Our Father," your child learned:

▶ Jesus taught his disciples how to pray by teaching them the Our Father.

▶ The Our Father helps us understand how to live as God's children.

▶ When we pray the Our Father, we discover what it means to live as children of God and to prepare for the coming of the Kingdom of God.

▶ The virtue of hope is trusting that God will always act on our behalf.

For more about related teachings of the Church, see the *Catechism of the Catholic Church,* 2777–2856, and the *United States Catholic Catechism for Adults,* pages 481–492.

■ Sharing God's Word

Read together Matthew 6:9–13, where Jesus teaches the Our Father. Emphasize that the Our Father is not only a prayer, it is a "summary of the whole Gospel." Praying the Our Father teaches us how to pray and how to live as children of God.

■ Living as Disciples

The Christian home and family is a school of discipleship. Choose one of the following activities to do as a family, or design a similar activity of your own.

▶ Make an Our Father booklet. As you read each part of the Our Father, write the words of that part in your booklet. Write or draw how you can live each part of the Our Father.

▶ Talk about some of the ways your family lives the Our Father. Pray to the Holy Spirit. Ask the Holy Spirit to help your family live the Our Father each day.

▶ As a family, discuss and list reasons why Christians are a people of hope.

■ Our Spiritual Journey

"**Go in peace**, glorifying the Lord by your life." These words from the Dismissal in the *Roman Missal* send us forth from Mass. They challenge us to live a life worthy of being children of God. Praying the Our Father daily not only reminds us who we are—children of a heavenly Father—but also offers glory to God. Be sure that your children memorize the Our Father. It is part of their Christian identity. Pray it together daily.

For more ideas on ways your family can live as disciples of Jesus, visit **BeMyDisciples.com**

328

THE LAST WORD

Plan a Year-End Celebration. Your second graders have grown as disciples of Jesus during this year. You, too, have grown—as a teacher and in your personal journey of life-long faith formation. Work with a group of parent volunteers to plan a closing party that includes snacks and beverages. Invite all parents to attend. With a little advance planning, the students can sing a favorite song they learned during the year or act out one or more Scripture stories for their parents. Affirm the students for their participation during the year and thank the parents for their support and cooperation. End the celebration by praying together the Lord's Prayer.

Enriching the Lesson

Preparing the Way for the Kingdom of God

Purpose

To reinforce the meaning of the petition "Thy kingdom come" which is prayed in the Our Father (taught on page 320)

Directions

▶ Have the students quietly pray "Thy kingdom come" several times.

▶ Brainstorm with the students ways that they live as Jesus taught. List their responses on the board.

▶ Ask how each of the things on the list prepares the way for the coming of the Kingdom of God.

▶ Encourage the students to continue doing the things on the list. Ask them to identify one thing that they are not doing and to ask their families to help them do it.

Materials

A Year of Faith Stories

Purpose

To reinforce the many stories from the Bible and the faith-filled people taught this year (taught in the chapters in the book)

Directions

▶ In partners, have the students look through their books and name their favorite Bible stories and faith-filled people. List the names on the board.

▶ Using clues, such as "What story am I?" or "Who am I?" ask the students to stand as soon as they know the story or person. Invite volunteers to name the story or person.

▶ After doing several examples, allow the students to present their own clues.

▶ Affirm how much the students have grown in their understanding of Scripture.

Materials

Catholic Social Teaching: Solidarity with Others

Purpose

To reinforce that in the Our Father we ask God to give all people what they need (taught on page 322)

Directions

This closing chapter on the Our Father is an ideal time to retell the classic children's story *Stone Soup*. In the retelling by Marcia Brown (Simon and Schuster, 1986) of the classic French tale, three hungry soldiers enter a village. Through their cleverness they are able to entice the villagers to contribute bit by bit to their "stone" soup—first a carrot, then a bit of beef—until a rich and satisfying soup is prepared and enjoyed by all. Students love the story and will not mind hearing it again.

▶ Read the story aloud to the students with expression and humor.

▶ Ask the students to describe their ideas of what the main point of the story is. Point out that when we all share, all are assured of enough to eat.

▶ Remind the students that all God's children are entitled to their "daily bread." This is what we pray for in the Our Father.

Materials

Stone Soup, by Marcia Brown

Catholic Social Teaching Unit 6

Pray

Gather the students for prayer. Pray the Our Father together. Conclude with the sharing of a sign of peace.

Focus

▶ Point out and read aloud the Catholic Social Teaching principle in the sidebar.

▶ Emphasize that each person has the responsibility to take part in the life of their family and in the other communities to which they belong.

Introduce

▶ Tell the students that you have noticed how well everyone cooperates in the classroom.

▶ Invite them to talk about the ways that students share in the work of the class.

▶ Invite the students to tell about the ways that they contribute to other communities to which they belong, for example, by following bicycle safety rules.

Teach

▶ Read aloud How Can We Help? about the Saint Francis of Assisi parish birthday party.

▶ Ask volunteers to name three tasks that the second graders will do to help prepare for the party.

▶ Emphasize that the class is contributing to their school's celebration by helping.

Catholic Social Teaching

Helping the Community

St. Francis of Assisi parish is having a birthday party! The parish and its school will be twenty-five years old next month.

The second grade class is deciding how it will help plan and celebrate the parish's birthday. The students decide to find out how the parish has helped the community over the last twenty-five years.

The teacher asked the class to interview people in the parish to find ways the parish has helped the community. Each student worked with a partner. Together they decided on who to interview that might remember how the parish has helped others.

The students interviewed family members, older parishioners, the parish priests, and some of the teachers. They discovered that the parish has a lot to celebrate at the birthday party.

The second graders made a big card with a list of all the ways the parish helped the community. Some of the people had given them photographs and they pasted them onto the card. The parish had a very happy birthday party!

> **WE TAKE PART IN OUR COMMUNITY**
>
> We are all important members of the communities where we live. Each of us has a responsibility to contribute to the community.

329

BACKGROUND: CATHOLIC SOCIAL TEACHING

Meaning and Value of Participation in Community Life. Chapter 4 of the *Compendium of the Social Doctrine of the Church* (CSDC) speaks to the Church's teaching on the responsibility of people to participate in the work of the community. It teaches: "(P)articipation . . . contributes to the cultural, economic, political and social life of the civil community to which (one) belongs. Participation is a duty to be fulfilled consciously by all, with responsibility and with a view toward the common good" *(CSDC 189)*.

Making Connections

Every person in a community has a responsibility to take part in the life of that community. This helps others in the community by taking care of one another. St. Francis of Assisi parish helped many people for twenty-five years.

with Social Studies

Saint Francis of Assisi is the patron Saint of St. Francis Parish. The parish wants to remember Saint Francis as part of its celebration by creating a parish Web site about him. Find out something about Saint Francis. Write a paragraph about him and draw a picture with it so it can go on the Web site.

with Language Arts

What do you think were the ways that St. Francis parish helped the community? Find out how your parish or school helps the community. Write a thank you note and send it to the parish pastor or the school principal.

with Creative Arts

Make special Saint Francis of Assisi holy cards. Create a card using a picture of Saint Francis and the Prayer of Saint Francis in this book (Chapter 21, page 290). Share your holy cards with someone special in your life.

Faith Action

Think about one way you can do something for your parish or school. Write it down and pledge that you will do this to help your community. Ask God to help you.

_____

_____

_____

 330

TEACHING TIP

Apprentice Opportunities. Students learn about being Christian by doing Christian things. Help the students put into action the Catholic Social Teaching principle of contributing to their communities. Talk with the leadership at the parish to identify some simple ways your class can contribute to the life of the community. How can the class be involved in parish life? Remind the students that when they share in the responsibilities of the community, they are experiencing what Christian service is all about.

Catholic Social Teaching

Reinforce

Read and explain the opening paragraph on page 330. Affirm the students in all the work they do together to help make your class a community.

Connect

Introduce the cross-curricular activities and have the students silently read them. Ask them to choose the activity or activities that they wish to work on.

▶ **Social Studies:** Share that many parishes and schools are named after Saints. Provide resources from your school's library or the Internet that the students can use to write their paragraphs about Saint Francis of Assisi.

▶ **Language Arts:** Help the students write thank you notes to the principal and pastor of your school and your parish church.

▶ **Creative Arts:** Distribute large blank index cards or pieces of stiff construction paper. Direct the students to Chapter 21 in their texts to find pictures and prayers of Saint Francis of Assisi. Have them draw Saint Francis of Assisi on one side of the card, and write the prayer on the opposite.

Choose

Direct the students to read the closing statement and to follow up on it.

Pray

Repeat the opening prayer.

Unit 6 Review

The Unit Review provides the opportunity to assess the students' understanding of the concepts presented in the unit and to affirm them in their growing knowledge and love of God. Here are a few suggestions for using these pages.

▶ Share with the students that the next two pages are an opportunity to stop and review what they have learned.

▶ Provide time for the students to ask questions.

▶ Have the students complete the review alone or with a partner.

A. Choose the Best Word

This section reviews the main concepts of the unit.

▶ Read the directions for section A. Illustrate what you expect the students to do by completing the first question together. By working together on the first sentence, you are teaching the students a strategy for completing these types of sentences.

▶ When the students have finished this section, invite volunteers to share their answers. Review any sentence that the students seem to have difficulty completing.

B. Show What You Know

This section reinforces what the students have learned about Jesus.

▶ Read the directions to the students. Have the students complete the section.

▶ Invite volunteers to share their answers.

Unit 6 Review

Name _____

A. Choose the Best Word

Complete the sentences. Color the circle next to the best choice for each sentence.

1. Our consciences tell us whether a choice we are going to make is a _____ one.
   - ○ fun
   - ○ sad
   - ● wise or bad

2. God's gift of sanctifying _____ makes us holy and children of God.
   - ○ love
   - ○ help
   - ● grace

3. A very serious sin is called a _____ sin.
   - ● mortal
   - ○ sanctifying
   - ○ venial

4. Jesus taught his disciples the _____.
   - ○ Hail Mary
   - ● Our Father
   - ○ Sign of the Cross

5. The Kingdom of _____ is all people living as God wants them to live.
   - ○ Saints
   - ● God
   - ○ Earth

B. Show What You Know

Color the box to mark the sentences that are true.

- ■ Proverbs can help us make wise choices.
- ☐ We are not free to choose to do what is right or what is wrong.
- ■ Jesus taught us to pray to God the Father.
- ☐ Another name for the Our Father is the Jesus Prayer.

331

TEACHING TIP

Final Review. Use this final unit review to deepen the students' sense of accomplishment this year. Share how much they have learned and what a difference they have made in your life. Take time to remind them that Jesus spent many years in Nazareth with Mary and Joseph, and the people of his synagogue. He spent this time learning the teachings, prayers, and practices of the Jewish religion. Encourage the students to pray each day so that they might come to know, love and serve Christ evermore.

C. Connect with Scripture

What was your favorite story about Jesus in this unit?
Draw something that happened in the story.
Tell your class about it.

D. Be a Disciple

1. *What Saint or holy person did you enjoy hearing about in this unit? Write the name here. Tell your class what this person did to follow Jesus.*

_____

_____

2. *What can you do to be a good disciple of Jesus?*

_____

_____

332

C. Connect with Scripture

This section reinforces the students' experience and knowledge of Scripture and the teachings of Jesus.

▶ Help the students review the Scripture stories in the unit, beginning with the Unit Opener story. You may wish to write the names of these stories on the board to assist them.

▶ Ask volunteers to share their favorite stories with the class.

▶ In the space, invite the students to draw something that happened in the story. Invite volunteers to share their drawings now, or at the completion of the Unit Review.

D. Be a Disciple

This section provides the students with the opportunity to recall how the Saints and holy people followed Jesus. It reinforces the ways students can choose to live as disciples of Jesus.

▶ Ask the students to remember their favorite stories of Saints or holy people that they learned about in this unit. Refresh their memories as needed, and write their responses on the board.

▶ Give each student time to write the name of their favorite Saint or holy person on the line. Ask volunteers to share the reason for their choices.

▶ Lead a discussion about the actions that make us good disciples of Jesus. Give the students time to write on the lines their idea of what they could do.

The Liturgical Year

Seasons and Feasts

Consistency is important to all of our lives, but from time to time we all need a break. Unswerving consistency introduces monotony and can make things pretty dull. Most people like surprises and festive days once in a while, however, like all things, these need to happen in moderation since endless festivities can wear us down. Experience teaches us the value of balancing the routine and the festive, or the ordinary and the extraordinary.

Through the Liturgy, the Church is uniquely positioned to gather us for celebration. Filled with anticipation during Advent, we prepare to celebrate the festive season of Christmas. Our traditional Lenten practices of fasting, praying, and almsgiving prepare us to enter into the Triduum and the Easter season.

Easter is central to the liturgical year. Because Jesus was raised from the dead on Sunday, the Church gathers to celebrate each week on that day. Every Sunday is a memorial of the Paschal Mystery and a commemoration of Easter.

Festive seasons, such as the Easter season, stand in contrast to the long, steady period of Ordinary Time. Generally, of the thirty-four Sundays in Ordinary Time, about ten occur on the Sundays between the seasons of Christmas and Lent. The remainder of the Sundays in Ordinary Time is celebrated after the Solemnity of the Most Holy Body and Blood of Christ (two weeks after Pentecost) and culminates with the celebration of the Solemnity of Our Lord Jesus Christ, King of the Universe. This late autumn feast brings the liturgical year to a close.

The Rhythm of the Liturgical Year

The seasons of the liturgical year help to keep us balanced as nature's seasons pass. Through the seasons of autumn, winter, spring, and summer, significant changes occur. As time passes from season to season, the Church provides a steady rhythm of prayer and celebration throughout the calendar year.

Each Sunday the Church calls us to live out the reality of the abiding presence of the Risen Lord among us. Sunday after Sunday, from the extremes of deep winter to high summer, we remember with gratitude that all time and all ages belong to Christ, who is Yesterday and Today, the Beginning and the End.

The liturgical year is our way to remember with gladness and joy that every day is the day the Lord has made. We celebrate that God calls us to rejoice in Christ.

For Reflection

How does the liturgical year provide a wonderful balance of ordinary and extraordinary time to live our faith?

Which liturgical season is your favorite? Why?

Teacher to Teacher

Colors of the Season

All through the year, the Church gathers to celebrate the liturgy. We join with Christ and the Holy Spirit to bless and give thanks to God the Father. In our celebrations, we incorporate colors to identify the season in which we celebrate. We see these colors in the priest's vestments at Mass. The liturgical colors also decorate the physical environment of the parish church. For example, violet is used during the seasons of Advent and Lent. During Christmas and Easter, the Church uses white or gold. Red signifies specific feast days such as Palm Sunday and Pentecost, while green is the color of celebration during Ordinary Time. Be sure that the classroom reflects the colors of the liturgical season and day to help celebrate what God has done for us.

Signs of the Liturgical Year

Display signs of the liturgical year in your learning space. Surround the children with reminders that will help set the tone of both the seasons and feasts of the liturgical year. For example, consider using a table runner that is the color of each liturgical season in the prayer area. Place a Bible opened to the Sunday Gospel reading on the prayer table.

The Church Teaches...

"Catechesis is enriched when the word of God shines forth in the life of the Church, especially in the lives of the saints and in the Christian witness of the faithful. And it is made more fruitful when the word of God is known from those genuine moral values that, by divine providence, are found in human society" (NDC 18).

During the liturgical year, the feast days of many of the canonized Saints are remembered in the celebration of the liturgy. You may wish to celebrate the feast days of some of the Saints during your sessions, particularly those who may be the patron Saints of the parish and community.

Further Reading and Reflection

For more on the teachings of the Catholic Church on the liturgical year, see *Catechism of the Catholic Church* 1168–1171 and 1172–1173; *United States Catholic Catechism for Adults* 166–179.

Teacher Prayer

God, Father and Creator, through the prayer of Jesus, your Son, may your blessings be poured out on us and keep us safe in your care. Amen.

Based on the Collect for the Fifth Sunday in Ordinary Time

Liturgical Year Unit Opener

The unit opener pages are designed to assess, through a variety of questioning techniques, the students' prior knowledge about key faith concepts presented in the unit. Processing these pages should not take more than ten or fifteen minutes.

Background

The Greeks had two words for time that we still use today: *chronos* and *kairos*. *Chronos* refers to chronological time and has to do with quantity. *Kairos* refers to sacred time. It has to do with quality, and it cannot be measured.

The liturgical year is shaped from both *chronos* and *kairos*. Chronologically, the Church's year begins on the First Sunday of Advent and ends on the last Sunday of Ordinary Time, the Solemnity of Our Lord Jesus Christ, Christ King of the Universe.

The Church's year is built on *kairos* because it focuses on the celebration of various aspects of the two greatest mysteries of our faith, the Incarnation and the Redemption. It is the Christian faithful's active celebration of and conscious participation in those mysteries in chronological time that leads communities and individual to *kairos* and ongoing conversation. Because of this, we call each year of the liturgical cycle a year of grace.

The sixteen two-page lessons in this section give you many opportunities to celebrate the Church's year with your students. The lessons follow the liturgical cycle of major feasts and seasons. The lessons are designed so that you can complete theme in approximately twenty minutes as part of your regular class sessions.

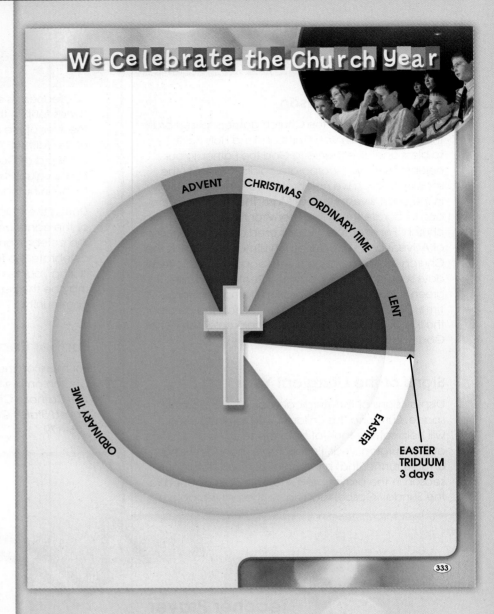

We Celebrate the Church Year

- ADVENT
- CHRISTMAS
- ORDINARY TIME
- LENT
- EASTER
- EASTER TRIDUUM 3 days
- ORDINARY TIME

333

TEACHING TIP

Liturgical Calendar. Make a special effort to mark the important feast days of the Church's year on a classroom calendar or bulletin board. These should include: the Immaculate Conception (December 8), Christmas (December 25), Solemnity of Mary, the Holy Mother of God (January 1), Ascension (forty days after Easter or the Seventh Sunday of Easter), Assumption (August 15), and All Saints (November 1). Also enter children's birthdays on the calendar, as well as any special days your parish celebrates; for example the patron Saint of the parish. Pray for those children and pray to those patron Saints whose day is to be celebrated during the upcoming week. On the last day of the year, pray for the children who celebrate their birthdays during the summer or off time.

The Liturgical Year

The Church celebrates her faith all year long in prayer and worship. The seasons of the Church year are called the liturgical year.

Check (✔) your favorite season or time of the Church year. Why is it your favorite?

Advent
Advent begins the Church year. We get our hearts ready to remember the birth of Jesus.

Christmas
At Christmas, the Church celebrates the birth of Jesus, God's Son. We praise and thank God the Father for sending us his Son, Jesus.

Lent
Lent is the time of the Church year when we remember Jesus died for us. We make sacrifices to help us remember our love for God and others. We prepare for Easter.

Easter
During the fifty days of the Easter season, we celebrate that Jesus was raised from the dead. Jesus gave us the gift of new life.

Ordinary Time
Ordinary Time is the longest time of the Church year. We learn to live as followers of Jesus.

334

Focus

▶ Second graders have a limited understanding of the liturgical year. They are most familiar with the celebrations of Advent and Christmas, and Lent and Easter.

▶ At the beginning of the year, take a few minutes and lead the children through the seasons and times of the year using the liturgical calendar on the page. Point out the starting point at the beginning of Advent.

▶ Help them to notice the colors and ask if they have noticed that the priest's vestments and Church banners change from time to time.

Teach

▶ Use the text on page 226 to describe the major seasons and Ordinary Time.

▶ Ask the children to check the seasons or times that they know the most about. Ask volunteers to tell why they made their choices.

▶ Tell the children that they will be celebrating each season with their class during the coming year.

▶ As you study the various Saints and holy persons in the regular chapters of the child's book, you may wish to add their feast days to your classroom calendar or to a large liturgical calendar. In this way, the children can begin to celebrate these feast days as well.

Exaltation of the Holy Cross

Preparation: Before the students arrive, place a cross on your classroom prayer table.

Focus

Read the Faith Focus question to the students. Ask them what the word *honor* means. If they have difficulty responding to the question, remind them that we honor God by praying to him, we honor our parents by obeying them, and we honor one another by being helpful and kind. Invite the students to share other examples of showing honor to God, our parents and families, and one another.

Discover

▶ Remove the cross from your classroom prayer table and, in silence pass the cross from student to student. When it is his or her turn to hold the cross, encourage each student to look at it closely. When the cross is returned to you, hold it before the class and ask the students to describe what they see.

▶ Read page 335 of the student text aloud to the students. Have them follow along as you read, and ask them to underline the word *cross* each time they hear or see it within the text. *(The word cross appears eight times.)*

▶ Read again the focus question to the students. Invite their responses. Accept all reasonable replies.

Faith Focus
Why do we honor the Cross?

The Word of the Lord
This is the Gospel reading for the Feast of the Exaltation of the Holy Cross. Ask your family to read it with you. Talk about the reading with them.

Gospel
John 3:13–17

Exaltation of the Holy Cross

On the Feast of the Exaltation of the Holy Cross, we honor the Cross of Jesus. We remember that, on the Cross, Jesus sacrificed himself for us. We celebrate how, on the Cross, Jesus was the Savior of the entire world.

Saint Paul wrote,

Jesus is God's Son, but he did not act as God. Jesus became man. He became a servant. He loved us and died for us on the cross. That is why God the Father has honored Jesus so highly, blessed his name, and made him Lord of heaven and earth.

Based on Philippians 2:5–10

The Cross reminds us that Jesus, both God and man, is now Lord of Heaven and Earth. That is why we honor the Cross. That is why the Cross is the great sign of who we are as followers of Jesus.

(335)

TEACHING TIP

Catch the Students Acting with Love. As you work with the students, notice both how they show concern for one another and the good of the entire class. You might say to them, "I see you enjoy helping one another!" "What a good neighbor you are!" "That was a loving action!" "Thank you for being so caring!" Whenever you see the students helping others, use those opportunities to reinforce their being people of the cross by acting loving and caring followers/disciples of Jesus.

The Cross of New Life

The Cross was once a sign of sin and death. Now it has become a sign of reconciliation and new life. Honor the cross by decorating it with words and signs of new life.

MY FAITH CHOICE

This week, I will honor the Cross. I will

_____

_____

Pray, "Jesus, by your holy Cross, you give us new life. Help me to honor that life and share it with others. Amen."

336

TEACHING TIP

A Hands-on Cross. Fashion a large cross of paper. Fasten it to a wall. Have the students:

- Trace their hand on a sheet of colored construction paper
- Cut out the tracing,
- Write the My Faith Choice—the way they plan to show that they are a person of love—and their name on the cut out
- Use tape or glue to post the hands on the cross
- Display the hands-on cross prominently in the classroom.
- Consider leaving the cross displayed throughout the year, adding appropriate symbols and decorations during each liturgical season.

Respond

▶ Read aloud The Cross of New Life and explain the directions to the related activity. Afterward, invite the students to share with a partner the words and signs of new life they chose to decorate their cross.

▶ Read aloud My Faith Choice and have the students complete it. If time allows, have the students share their responses with a partner.

Pray

Gather the class for prayer. Pray together the prayer printed at the bottom of page 336, omitting the Amen. Repeat the prayer (continuing to omit the Amen) several times, again passing the cross from student to student. When the cross is returned to you, conclude the prayer by slowly and reverently making the Sign of the Cross.

Solemnity of All Saints

Focus

Read the Faith Focus question to the class. Tell them saints are people who follow Jesus, the Son of God.

Discover

▶ Write the word *model* on the board. Ask the students to tell you what it means when it refers to a person. Explain to the class that a model is someone we imitate because of the goodness they do.

▶ Write the word *Saint* on the board. Draw a line connecting the two words on the board.

▶ Read the text on the page to the class. Have them follow along. Ask them to underline the word *Saint* in their text whenever they see it.

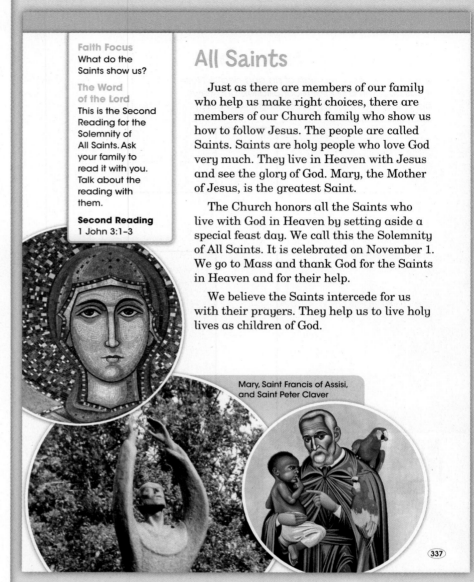

Faith Focus
What do the Saints show us?

The Word of the Lord
This is the Second Reading for the Solemnity of All Saints. Ask your family to read it with you. Talk about the reading with them.

Second Reading
1 John 3:1–3

All Saints

Just as there are members of our family who help us make right choices, there are members of our Church family who show us how to follow Jesus. The people are called Saints. Saints are holy people who love God very much. They live in Heaven with Jesus and see the glory of God. Mary, the Mother of Jesus, is the greatest Saint.

The Church honors all the Saints who live with God in Heaven by setting aside a special feast day. We call this the Solemnity of All Saints. It is celebrated on November 1. We go to Mass and thank God for the Saints in Heaven and for their help.

We believe the Saints intercede for us with their prayers. They help us to live holy lives as children of God.

Mary, Saint Francis of Assisi, and Saint Peter Claver

337

TEACHING TIP

Disciples, Models, Saints. Remind the class that people who follow Jesus are disciples. The Saints throughout history were disciples and their holy lives continue to serve as models for us though they are in Heaven. The Saints help us follow Jesus and teach us that everyone can live holy lives. Invite the students to print the name of a favorite Saint on a slip of paper. Ask volunteers to identify the Saint they chose and explain why they admire the Saint. Have the students save their paper slips for the closing prayer.

Following Jesus

The Saints show us how to live as followers of Jesus. Draw yourself next to the Saint below. Draw a line along the path that will take you to Jesus.

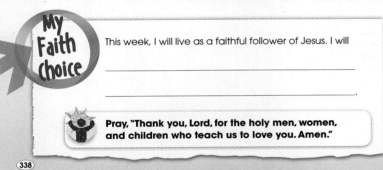

My Faith Choice

This week, I will live as a faithful follower of Jesus. I will

_____

_____

Pray, "Thank you, Lord, for the holy men, women, and children who teach us to love you. Amen."

338

SACRED TRADITION

Holiness. Every member of the Church is called to holiness in the same way that God called the Israelites to holiness: "you shall be holy because I am holy" (*Leviticus 11:45*). Holiness is a mark of the Church, and made possible through the work of the Holy Spirit. "The Church is holy. Jesus, the founder, is holy and makes his holiness available through his Death and Resurrection. The Holy Spirit imparts holiness to us, especially through the Sacraments. The Church's holiness shines in the saints, and most especially in the Blessed Virgin Mary" (*United States Catholic Catechism for Adults*, p. 138). Whenever possible reinforce with the children that holiness is possible for all the baptized through the grace of God.

Respond

▶ Have a volunteer re-read the Faith Focus question. Ask the students to respond in their own words. Affirm all appropriate responses. Ask all disciples of Jesus to raise their hands. Raise yours as well.

▶ Read aloud, or have a volunteer read, the Following Jesus section. Tell the children that the Saints want to help us imitate Jesus. They want to walk with us and help us make right choices.

▶ Invite the students to complete the activity. Help those who need help to finish the activity. When they are finished, help them complete the My Faith Choice section.

▶ Pray together the prayer at the bottom of the page.

Pray

▶ Play reflective background music. If you are using the Teaching Tip on page 470, have the students come to the prayer space, one at a time, to place their slips of paper on the prayer table.

▶ After making the Sign of the Cross, ask the class to listen as you pray:

"God our Father, you gave light to your Church by the example and teaching of your Saints. Grant that we may learn your truth and practice it in charity. Amen."
(Based on the Collect from the Memorial of Saints Basil the Great and Gregory Nazianzen, *Roman Missal*).

Advent

Focus

Read the Faith Focus question aloud. Share with the class that in this lesson they will learn about a season of the Church's year called Advent.

Discover

▶ Invite volunteers to tell how they wait and prepare for days that are special to them.

▶ Point out that Advent is the time during the Church's year that we prepare for the coming of Jesus at Christmas. Ask the students to listen carefully to find out how Advent helps us prepare to welcome Jesus into our lives. Read aloud the text on the page.

▶ Ask the class to look at the picture and describe what they see. *(an Advent wreath)*

▶ Write the words *Jesus is the Light of the world* on the board, and then have the students read them aloud after you.

Faith Focus
How does celebrating Advent help us to welcome God into our lives?

The Word of the Lord
These are the Gospel readings for the First Sunday of Advent. Ask your family to read this year's Gospel reading with you. Talk about the reading with them.

Year A
Matthew 24:37–44

Year B
Mark 13:33–37

Year C
Luke 21:25–28, 34–36

What You See
The Advent wreath is made of evergreens. There are three purple candles and one pink candle. The candles stand for the four weeks of Advent.

Advent

Every year, you get excited about your birthday coming. Your family gets ready to celebrate. In Advent, we get ready to celebrate the birth of Jesus. We also celebrate that Jesus is always with us. We celebrate that he will come in glory at the end of the world.

Advent has four Sundays. On these Sundays, we gather in our parish church. Together we get our hearts ready to welcome Jesus. We may sing "O Come, O Come, Emmanuel." *Emmanuel* means "Messiah" or "Savior."

During Advent, we remember that Jesus asks us to do good things. We pray. We try to be extra kind. We help people who need our help.

339

TEACHING TIP

Making an Advent Chain. Tell the class that they are going to make an Advent chain at home, representing the 24 days that we prepare for Christmas Day. Give each student an envelope that contains 24 six-inch strips made from purple construction paper, which are individually numbered 1 through 24. Tell the students to make and connect the links one at a time each day during Advent. Suggest that they write on each link either a short prayer or one way they can prepare for Christmas. Also give the students star stickers to put on the numbered links for December 6 (Saint Nicholas), December 8 (Immaculate Conception), and December 12 (Our Lady of Guadalupe). These stars represent special feast days, helping us to remember them during Advent.

We Welcome Jesus

Think about ways you can get ready to welcome Jesus.
Write something you can do each day this week.

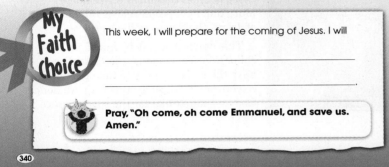

Sunday ⎯⎯ Use the Advent wreath at dinnertime. ⎯⎯

Monday ⎯⎯⎯⎯⎯⎯⎯⎯⎯⎯⎯⎯⎯⎯⎯⎯⎯

Tuesday ⎯⎯⎯⎯⎯⎯⎯⎯⎯⎯⎯⎯⎯⎯⎯

Wednesday ⎯⎯⎯⎯⎯⎯⎯⎯⎯⎯⎯⎯

Thursday ⎯⎯⎯⎯⎯⎯⎯⎯⎯⎯⎯⎯⎯

Friday ⎯⎯⎯⎯⎯⎯⎯⎯⎯⎯⎯⎯⎯⎯⎯

Saturday ⎯⎯⎯⎯⎯⎯⎯⎯⎯⎯⎯⎯⎯

My Faith choice

This week, I will prepare for the coming of Jesus. I will

⎯⎯⎯⎯⎯⎯⎯⎯⎯⎯⎯⎯⎯⎯⎯⎯⎯⎯⎯⎯⎯

⎯⎯⎯⎯⎯⎯⎯⎯⎯⎯⎯⎯⎯⎯⎯⎯⎯⎯⎯⎯⎯.

Pray, "Oh come, oh come Emmanuel, and save us. Amen."

340

Respond

▶ Ask the class how the Church prepares to welcome Jesus at Christmas. *(Affirm appropriate responses.)*

▶ Have the students brainstorm what they might do to get ready to welcome Jesus.

▶ Explain the We Welcome Jesus activity to the class.

▶ Give the class time to complete the activity. If they do not complete the activity during the session, encourage them to complete it at home with their families.

▶ Next have the students complete the My Faith Choice section. Encourage the children to put the choice that they made into practice each day this week by asking them to silently read the prayer at the bottom of the page.

Pray

▶ Gather the students in the prayer area around an Advent wreath which you have set up in advance.

▶ Read this year's Gospel reading for the first week of Advent. Have the class respond "Come, Lord Jesus! Come!"

LITURGY CONNECTION

Songs of the Season. Each time you have Religion class with the students during Advent, teach them a few lines of a Christmas carol, such as "Silent Night" or "Joy to the World." This will prepare the students to sing along with the assembly as these songs are sung at Mass on Christmas Day and throughout the Christmas season. Appropriate music for all the liturgical seasons can be found at *BeMyDisciples*.com.

Immaculate Conception

Focus

Read the Faith Focus question to the class. Tell them that in this lesson they will learn about the special gift God gave to Mary, the Mother of Jesus.

Discover

▶ On the board write the words *Should I or Shouldn't I*. Invite the students to create a list of choices they could make every day. Get them started by writing a few choices on the board, like help a friend or say my prayers. Write their ideas on the board to create a list.

▶ Invite several volunteers to read aloud the text on the page. Have students circle the word that means God's help. *(grace)*

▶ Ask the students to explain grace in their own words. *(God sharing his life with us; God helping us to make good choices to live as his children.)*

▶ Have the students look at the lists created earlier in the session. Emphasize that Mary faced many choices every day, just as they do. Point out that Mary avoided sin by always making good choices. Explain that God also helps us to make good choices but, if we sin, God will always forgive us in the Sacrament of Penance and Reconciliation if we are truly sorry.

Faith Focus
How does the Church celebrate her special love for Mary, the Mother of God?

The Word of the Lord
This is the Gospel reading for the Solemnity of the Immaculate Conception of the Blessed Virgin Mary. Ask your family to read it with you. Talk about the reading with them.

Gospel
Luke 1:26–38

Immaculate Conception

God has a very special love for Mary. The Church has a special love for Mary too. God chose Mary to be the Mother of Jesus, the Son of God. God prepared Mary to be Jesus' mother in a very special way.

God gave Mary a very special grace, or gift. Mary was always free from sin. Mary was born without sin. Mary received God's help all through her life so she would never commit a sin. We call this help from God, "grace."

The angel Gabriel came to Mary to tell her that God had chosen her to be the Mother of his Son. The angel said,

"Hail, favored one! The Lord is with you."

LUKE 1:28

We call this special grace the Immaculate Conception of Mary. We celebrate the Solemnity of the Immaculate Conception of the Blessed Virgin Mary every year on December 8. We honor Mary and her special role as the Mother of Jesus, the Savior of the world.

This day is also a holy day of obligation. This means that Catholics have the responsibility to take part in the celebration of Mass. In this way, we honor God and thank him for the special grace he gave Mary.

(341)

TEACHING TIP

A Mural of God's Gifts. Many second graders are preparing for or have already celebrated the Sacrament of Penance and Reconciliation. Help them to recall that they have learned that God is loving and merciful. Remind them that God will always forgive us when we express sorrow for our sins. Emphasize that grace and forgiveness are two of the gifts that God gives us. Explain that God also gives us Jesus and Mary to show us how to live. Using a roll of white shelf paper, roll out enough for each child to have work space to draw images that represent God's gifts. Display the mural in a place where the students and their parents can admire their work.

Thank You, Mary

In this space, create a thank-you card to Mary. Write a message. Draw a picture. Thank Mary for saying yes to God. Thank her for her prayers and for helping you make good choices.

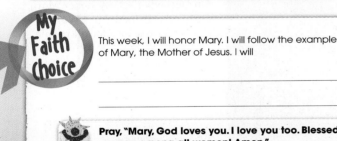

My Faith Choice

This week, I will honor Mary. I will follow the example of Mary, the Mother of Jesus. I will

_____

_____

Pray, "Mary, God loves you. I love you too. Blessed are you among all women! Amen."

342

Respond

▶ Ask the students how they celebrate special occasions with their family. Point out that the Church is the Family of God.

▶ Ask a volunteer to read the Faith Focus question again. Encourage students to respond in their own words. *(Accept all appropriate responses, such as going to Mass or praying to Mary.)*

▶ Tell the class that it is always important to be grateful for the gifts we receive. Ask them if they've ever written a thank you note to someone. Read aloud the Thank You, Mary section. Explain the directions for completing the activity. Ask volunteers to share their work.

▶ Remind the students that Mary loves them and prays for them. Encourage them to ask Mary for her prayers when they are faced with difficult choices. Explain that we express gratitude through our actions as well as our words.

▶ Give the students an opportunity to complete the My Faith Choice section.

▶ Invite the children to silently pray the words at the bottom of the page.

Pray

▶ Gather the students in the prayer area. Encourage them to call to mind some of the choices they made this day.

▶ Ask them to echo each sentence of the following prayer after you:
  Dear God, I thank you for today. Keep me safe throughout the night. Thank you for all the good I did today. I am sorry for what I have chosen to do wrong. Bless my family and friends. Amen.

Our Lady of Guadalupe

Focus

Read the Faith Focus to the class. Tell them that this lesson will help them learn that the Blessed Virgin Mary, the Mother of Jesus, has the title of Our Lady of Guadalupe.

Discover

▶ Invite volunteers to read the text on the page aloud.

▶ Encourage the students to imagine they were there with Juan Diego when Mary appeared and spoke to him. Invite them to share what they would have seen and felt.

▶ Write the numbers 1–4 under one another on the board.

▶ On the board, write the events of the story of Our Lady of Guadalupe out of order. Invite the students to the board to number the events in the correct order. Example: 1. The Blessed Virgin Mary appears to Juan Diego.

Faith Focus
Who is Our Lady of Guadalupe?

The Word of the Lord
This is the Gospel reading for the Feast of Our Lady of Guadalupe. Ask your family to read it with you. Talk about the reading with them.

Gospel
Luke 1:39–48

Celebration to the Virgin of Guadalupe, Hilary Simon

Our Lady of Guadalupe

Many years ago, Mary appeared to Juan Diego. Juan belonged to the Aztec people who lived in Mexico. Mary asked Juan to go to the bishop of Mexico and ask him to build a shrine. The shrine would be a sign of the love of Mary for all people.

The bishop first asked Mary for a sign. She sent Juan Diego to pick roses from the hill. It was winter, a time when roses did not grow. Juan Diego found the roses. He wrapped them up in his cloak and brought them to the bishop.

When Juan opened his cloak, he and the bishop saw an image of Mary. She was dressed as an Aztec princess. The image of Mary is kept safely in the shrine the bishop built. It is named in her honor as Our Lady of Guadalupe. On December 12, we honor Mary, Our Lady of Guadalupe. We remember her love for all people.

343

TEACHING TIP

Brothers and Sisters. One of the many messages of Our Lady of Guadalupe was unity. Mary wants all people to be united as brothers and sisters in Christ. Remind the students that Mary, the Mother of God, is Mother to all children in the world. Explain that Mary has appeared in many countries to encourage people everywhere to pray and do penance. She wants to lead people everywhere to her son, Jesus. Place a small globe on the prayer table. Ask the students to name different countries. Use the countries they identify to create petitions for a litany to conclude today's session. For example, "For the people of Mexico, we pray . . ."

Mary, Our Mother

Color the roses in beautiful colors. Under the roses, write one thing you could do to honor Mary.

My Faith Choice

This week, I will honor Mary, Our Lady of Guadalupe. I will show my love for all people. I will

_____

_____

Pray, "Mary, Our Lady of Guadalupe, thank you for your love. Help me love all people as your Son, Jesus, did. Amen."

344

SACRED TRADITION

To Christ through Mary. Throughout the centuries there have been innumerable apparitions of Mary in countries around the world. Only a very few number of these have been approved by the Church on some level. Guadalupe is considered the first apparition of modern times. It is also one of the first Marian apparitions resulting in the establishment of a sanctuary having worldwide influence on the devotional life of the faithful. Sites of other approved apparitions include Paris, LaSalle, Lourdes, and Pontmain, all in France; Knock, County Mayo, Ireland; Fatima, Portugal; and Beauraing and Banneux, Belgium.

Respond

▶ Restate the Faith Focus question. Invite the students to respond. Ask: "What are some of the other titles for Mary?" Explain that many churches are named after the Blessed Mother. Offer some examples.

▶ Read aloud the directions to the Mary, Our Mother activity.

▶ Invite the students to share their ideas.

▶ Read the My Faith Choice section to the students and help them complete it.

▶ Invite the students to ask Mary's help in living their faith choice by praying the prayer at the bottom of the page.

Pray

▶ Gather the students in the prayer area. Allow them a few moments to become quiet. Remind them they are in the presence of God.

▶ Lead them in prayer, saying: We remember that the Blessed Virgin Mary has appeared to people all over the world asking them to pray and do penance out of love for her son, Jesus.

▶ Using the titles for Mary that you listed with the class, pray them as a litany. Invite the students to respond, "Be with us, Mary," to each petition.

▶ Conclude by praying the Hail Mary.

Christmas

Focus

Ask a volunteer to read the Faith Focus question aloud. Tell the class that the angels had a very special message from God to deliver to shepherds.

Discover

▶ Ask if anyone can tell you why we put statues of shepherds in the Christmas creche. *(Accept appropriate responses, such as, The shepherds visited Jesus and Mary in Bethlehem after the angels told them about the birth of Jesus.)*

▶ Read aloud or have volunteers read to the class the text on the page.

▶ Write the word *angel* on the board. Explain that *angel* means "messenger from God."

▶ Invite a volunteer to read aloud What You See to help the students learn more about the Christmas tree as a sign of God's everlasting love for us.

Faith Focus
Why did the angels visit the shepherds?

The Word of the Lord
This is the Gospel reading for Mass on Christmas. Ask your family to read it with you. Talk about the reading with them.

Years A, B, and C
Luke 2:1–14 (Mass at Midnight)

What You See
The Christmas tree is made up of evergreens. It reminds us that God always loves us.

Christmas

Sometimes people tell us good news. Angels told good news to shepherds. They told the shepherds the good news of the birth of Jesus.

The angels praised God for this good news. They sang,

"Glory to God in the highest and on earth peace to those on whom his favor rests."

LUKE 2:14

At Mass, we sing this great song of the angels. We call it the "Gloria." We use their words to sing, "Glory to God in the highest, and on earth peace to people of good will."

(345)

TEACHING TIP

Prayer Center. Have the students help you decorate the prayer center so it reflects the Christmas season. Cover the prayer table with a white cloth and, if possible, place evergreens and appropriate flowers in the prayer space. The students can make cutout figures for a manger scene. Have them place a Bible opened to Luke's account of the birth of Jesus on the center of the prayer table (see Luke 2:1–7).

Give Glory to God

Color in the letters of this prayer. Pray the prayer each day of the Christmas season when you wake up. Pray it again at bedtime.

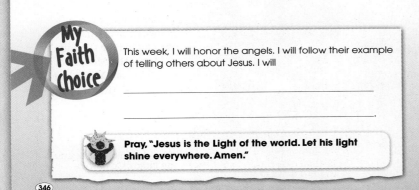

My Faith Choice

This week, I will honor the angels. I will follow their example of telling others about Jesus. I will

_____

_____

Pray, "Jesus is the Light of the world. Let his light shine everywhere. Amen."

(346)

LITURGY BACKGROUND

The Gloria. The singing of the Gloria at Mass recalls the angels' visit to the shepherds and announcement of the joy of Christmas. Print the opening words from the Gloria on the board; leave out some of the main words, such as *God, peace,* and *people.* Read the words of the hymn out loud. Stop at the blank spaces and have the students fill in the missing words. After repeating this activity a few times, the students will become more familiar with this traditional hymn. This will enhance their participation in the liturgy.

Respond

▶ Invite the students to use the picture on page 345 and talk about the part that the angels and shepherds played in the Gospel account of the Christmas story.

▶ Reread aloud Luke 2:14 on page 345. Ask if any of the students have heard those words prayed aloud or sung. (*Accept appropriate responses, such as: They are sung during Mass.*)

▶ Read the directions to the Give Glory to God activity and let the children color the prayer. Give them a few minutes to show one another their artwork.

▶ Invite the students to complete the My Faith Choice. Afterward encourage them to live their choices by reading the prayer at the bottom of the page.

Pray

▶ Practice singing the first line of the Gloria, using the melody most frequently sung at Mass in your parish, or the first verse of "Hark! the Herald Angels Sing."

▶ Gather the students in the prayer area. Ask them to stand, raise their arms to the sky, and joyfully sing the Gloria or "Hark! the Herald Angels Sing."

Mary, the Holy Mother of God

Focus

Read the Faith Focus question to the class. Share that the Church honors Mary and the Saints with special celebrations on particular days of the year.

Discover

▶ Write the word *honor* on the board. Give the students an opportunity to explain what it means. Clarify that we honor people by respecting them and praising them. Ask the students to share reasons why we honor certain people.

▶ Read to the students, or have volunteers read the text on the page aloud. Remind the students to listen for the answer to the Faith Focus question.

▶ Explain to the class that one of the ways we honor Mary is by following Jesus and doing what Jesus taught us.

Faith Focus
How does the Church honor Mary, the Mother of God?

The Word of the Lord
This is the Gospel reading for the Solemnity of Mary, the Holy Mother of God. Ask your family to read the Gospel reading with you. Talk about the reading with them.
Gospel
Luke 2:16–21

Mary, the Holy Mother of God

Mother's Day is a special day set aside to honor our mothers. We make a special effort to let our mothers know how much we love them. Sometimes we make our moms special cards. We want to thank our moms for loving us.

During the Christmas season, on January 1, we honor Mary. On this day, we celebrate that Mary was blessed by God. She was chosen to be the Mother of Jesus, God's Son. Through the power of the Holy Spirit, the Blessed Virgin Mary became the Mother of Jesus.

We honor Mary, the Mother of God, by going to Mass. We praise God for the gift of Jesus, his Son. We thank God for the gift of Mary, the Mother of God. We ask Mary, our Blessed Mother, to pray for us.

Mary Mosaic. Cartagena de Indias, Colombia

(347)

LITURGY BACKGROUND

Marian Feasts. Following the Annunciation, Mary went to visit her cousin, Elizabeth, who proclaims her to be the "mother of my Lord." Mary responds, "All generations will call me blessed." Since then, all generations have honored the Blessed Virgin Mary who became the Mother of God through the power of the Holy Spirit. Mary leads us in love to her son, Jesus Christ, and devotion to the Holy Trinity. "The liturgical feasts dedicated to the Mother of God and Marian prayer, such as the Rosary, an 'epitome of the whole Gospel,' express this devotion to the Virgin Mary" (*Catechism of the Catholic Church* 971). Some of the feasts include: January 1, Solemnity of Mary, the Holy Mother of God; March 25, Annunciation; May 31, Visitation; August 15, Assumption; September 8, Birth of Mary; December 8, Immaculate Conception; December 12, Our Lady of Guadalupe.

We Thank You, Mary!

Create a Mother's Day card for Mary. Address the card and ask Mary for her help and guidance. Remember to sign your name!

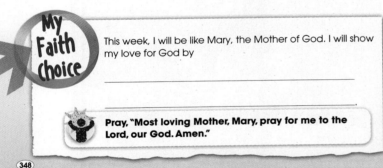

My Faith Choice

This week, I will be like Mary, the Mother of God. I will show my love for God by

_____

_____

Pray, "Most loving Mother, Mary, pray for me to the Lord, our God. Amen."

348

Respond

▶ Ask the students to answer the Faith Focus question. Remind them that we celebrate this feast during the Christmas season. Mary is at the heart of the season because her "yes" to God gave us Jesus, the Son of God.

▶ Read aloud the section We Thank You, Mary! Explain the directions to create the card for Mary.

▶ Write some sample responses as a starting point. When the cards are completed invite the students to share the ways in which they asked Mary for help and guidance.

▶ Review the My Faith Choice section with them. Discuss some of the ways they might choose to be like Mary.

▶ Invite the students to resolve to live their choices by silently praying the prayer at the bottom of the page.

Pray

▶ Gather the students in the prayer area. Ask them to listen reverently while you read the Gospel for the Solemnity of Mary: Luke 2:16–21.

▶ Close by using your own words to thank Mary for her gift of love.

TEACHING TIP

A Calendar for Mary. Duplicate calendar pages with squares for every day of the new year for each child. Arrange two months on a page so that the calendar can be folded in half, with one month appearing at the top of the page and the second month at the bottom. Tell the students that from ancient times, the Church has honored the Blessed Mother by celebrating special feast days and holy days throughout the year. List on the board the feasts and dates found in the Liturgy Background box on the previous page. Have the students find each date on their personal calendars and draw a heart on the date, along with the name of the celebration. Invite the students to fold their calendars and decorate the covers.

Epiphany

Focus

Write the Faith Focus question on the board. Explain to the class that this session will help them understand that God sent his Son, Jesus, as Savior of the world.

Discover

▶ Ask the students to think back to Christmas and remember why they were so excited. Invite them to share how they felt that day.

▶ Encourage the students to talk about why gifts make them happy. Look for opportunities to remind them that gifts are a sign of love.

▶ Read aloud the text on the page.

▶ Invite the students to circle the names of the Magi's gifts in their texts. *(gold, frankincense, myrrh)*

▶ Remind all that Jesus welcomes everyone who comes to him.

Faith Focus
How did the Magi honor Jesus?

The Word of the Lord
This is the Gospel reading for the Solemnity of the Epiphany of the Lord. Ask your family to read it with you. Talk about the reading with them.

Years A, B, and C
Matthew 2:1–12

Epiphany

We all like to receive gifts. When someone gives us a gift, they are showing us they love us. Long ago, some wise people called Magi gave special gifts to the newborn Jesus.

The Magi saw a bright star in the night sky. They believed that the star was telling them about the birth of a newborn king. The Magi left their homes. They followed the star and traveled many miles to Bethlehem. There they found Jesus with Mary and Joseph. Bowing low, they gave Jesus gifts of gold, frankincense, and myrrh.

The Magi came a long way to honor Jesus. The Gospel story of the Magi reminds us that Jesus welcomes everyone who comes to him.

349

TEACHING TIP

Infancy Narratives and Childhood of Jesus. The Gospel accounts of the birth of Jesus and events of his infancy and childhood are only recorded in Matthew's Gospel (see Matthew 1:18-25) and Luke's Gospel (see Luke 2:1-7). These are favorite stories of the children. You might read these stories to the students from a children's Bible, many of which are beautifully illustrated. The illustrations will help the students deepen their understanding of the mystery of the Incarnation.

The Savior of the World

Pretend you are with the Magi on their journey. Follow the maze to Jesus. What gift would you bring to Jesus? What would you say to Jesus when you give your gift to him?

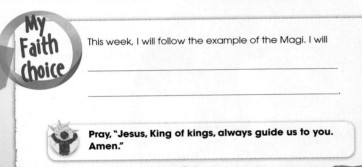

My Faith Choice

This week, I will follow the example of the Magi. I will

_____

_____

Pray, "Jesus, King of kings, always guide us to you. Amen."

Respond

▶ Ask the students to describe how the Magi honored Jesus. *(They bowed their heads and gave him gifts.)*

▶ Introduce The Savior of the World activity. Afterward, ask volunteers to respond to the questions. *(Accept all appropriate responses.)*

▶ Direct attention to the My Faith Choice for this lesson. Offer suggestions, if necessary, to help them choose how they will follow the example of the Magi. Then invite the students to silently pray the prayer at the bottom of the page.

Pray

▶ Gather the students for prayer. Ask them to think of something for which they are grateful. After giving them time to think, invite volunteers to name one of the gifts they thought of.

▶ Conclude by inviting the students to offer a prayer of thanksgiving in the silence of their hearts.

TEACHING TIP

Guests in Our Homes. Remind the class that the Magi, the three kings in the Gospel story, represent people from all over the world who came to honor Jesus. Emphasize that this Gospel story teaches that Jesus is the Savior of all people. Emphasize that this points out God's love for all people. Connect this story to the students' everyday life. For example, discuss the importance of welcoming relatives and friends into our homes. Help the students discover and learn words or actions of hospitality that they can use to welcome guests into their homes.

Ash Wednesday

Focus

Read the Faith Focus question to the class. Tell the students that Lent is the time when we prepare our hearts and minds for Easter, when we celebrate Jesus Christ rising from the dead to new life.

Discover

▶ Ask if anyone can share an experience of Baptism with the class. Explain that Baptism is the Sacrament that unites us to Jesus and makes us members of the Church.

▶ Read aloud to the class the text on the page.

▶ Invite the students to share their memories of receiving ashes at the start of Lent.

▶ Explain that the ashes are a sign of God's mercy. His mercy helps us have clean hearts so we can make good choices.

Faith Focus
How do we begin the celebration of Lent?

The Word of the Lord
This is the Gospel reading for Ash Wednesday. Ask your family to read it with you. Talk about the reading with them.

Gospel
Matthew 6:1–6, 16–18

Ash Wednesday

Easter is the celebration of the Resurrection. We celebrate the rising of Jesus from the dead to new life. At Baptism, we receive new life in Jesus too. We share in his Resurrection.

During Lent, we prepare our hearts and minds to celebrate Easter. We remember our Baptism. We make choices to live our Baptism better. Ash Wednesday is the first day of Lent.

We prepare for Easter during Lent by fasting, praying, and doing good things for others. When we go to church on Ash Wednesday, we pray, "A clean heart create for me, O God." We ask God to help us make good choices to live our Baptism. We pray so our hearts will be ready for Jesus.

On Ash Wednesday, the Sign of the Cross is made with ashes on our foreheads. Catholics all over the world wear this cross to show they love God and want to live their Baptism. They want to live as good and faithful disciples of Jesus.

351

TEACHING TIP

Blessed are the clean of heart. In the Sermon on the Mount, Jesus preaches the Beatitudes, a way of happiness that includes the qualities and actions of those blessed by God. The Beatitudes include, "Blessed are the clean of heart, for they shall see God" **(Matthew 5:8)**. You may want to read this Scripture verse to the students. Relate it to the prayer given in their text that we pray on Ash Wednesday, "A clean heart create for me, God" **(Psalm 51:12)**. Explain to the students that the clean of heart keep God first in their lives. Discuss what actions show that we are placing God first, and invite the students to share examples. In addition to the activity on page 242 of their texts, you may wish to have them create and decorate bookmarks on strips of art paper with these words on them.

Prayer for Forgiveness

In the Act of Contrition, we tell God we are sorry for our sins. Praying this prayer is one way we can ask for God's forgiveness.

Fill in the blanks to complete the prayer.

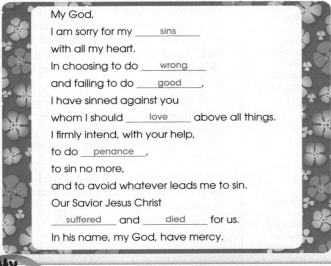

My God,
I am sorry for my ___sins___
with all my heart.
In choosing to do ___wrong___
and failing to do ___good___,
I have sinned against you
whom I should ___love___ above all things.
I firmly intend, with your help,
to do ___penance___,
to sin no more,
and to avoid whatever leads me to sin.
Our Savior Jesus Christ
___suffered___ and ___died___ for us.
In his name, my God, have mercy.

My Faith Choice

This week, I will try to memorize the Act of Contrition and ask my family for help. Circle the time you will pray.

† Every morning
† Every afternoon
† Every evening

Pray, "Help me during Lent, Lord, to become more like Jesus. Amen."

352

Respond

▶ Ask the students how we prepare for Lent. *(Accept appropriate responses that relate to prayer, fasting and doing good for others.)*

▶ Read aloud the directions to Prayer for Forgiveness.

▶ Read aloud the Act of Contrition with the class. When you come to a blank space, ask a volunteer to supply the missing word. Write the words on the board and have the students copy them into the blank spaces in their books.

▶ Read aloud the My Faith Choice and have the students complete it. Then invite them to resolve to live their choice by silently praying the prayer at the bottom of the page.

Pray

Gather the students for prayer. Lead them in praying the Act of Contrition. Remind them to ask their parents' help in memorizing this prayer.

SACRED TRADITION

Lenten Disciplines. Prayer, fasting, and almsgiving (or doing good for others) are the three Lenten disciplines practiced for our spiritual growth. Children under the age of fifteen are not required to undertake the discipline of fasting, which includes abstinence from meat. However, they should be encouraged to practice doing small things with great love. Write the three Lenten disciplines on the board. Explain them to the children. Have the students develop lists under each of the disciplines that would reflect doing small things with great love. To help them, use examples like a small snack given up after meals, or saying thank you to someone every day.

Lent

Focus

Ask a volunteer to read the Faith Focus question aloud. Point out that the students will begin to find out the answer to the question in this lesson.

Discover

▶ Read aloud the text on the page. Pause after each paragraph to make sure the students are adequately grasping what is being taught.

▶ Summarize by connecting the first and last paragraphs on the page. This will help the students establish the relationship between Lent and Easter.

Faith Focus
How does celebrating Lent help us to get ready for Easter?

The Word of the Lord
These are Gospel readings for the First Sunday of Lent. Ask your family to read this year's Gospel reading with you. Talk about the reading with them.

Year A
Matthew 4:1–11

Year B
Mark 1:12–15

Year C
Luke 4:1–13

What You See
During Lent the Church uses the color purple or violet. The colors purple and violet remind us of sorrow and penance.

Lent

Sometimes a special day seems far away. But we can do many things to get ready for that day.

During Lent, we do many things to get ready to celebrate Easter. Lent is forty days long. It begins on Ash Wednesday. During Lent, we turn to God and pray each day. We make sacrifices by giving up some things. This helps us to show our love for God and others.

Lent is the special time of the year the Church prepares new members for Baptism. It is the time members of the Church prepare to renew the promises we made at Baptism.

We do all these things during Lent to help us to prepare for Easter. Easter is a special day for all Christians. It is the day of Jesus' Resurrection.

353

TEACHING TIP

Signs of Lent. Take the time to decorate your prayer space with colors and symbols that represent the Lenten season. For example, cover the prayer table with a purple runner, and place a crucifix and a bowl of holy water on the table. The students will notice that the prayer space has been freshly decorated. This can be a good lead-in to share with them the meaning of the Lenten season.

Prepare for Easter

Pick a partner. Take turns answering each question.
Decide how to keep Lent and prepare for Easter.
On the lines, write your answers to each question.

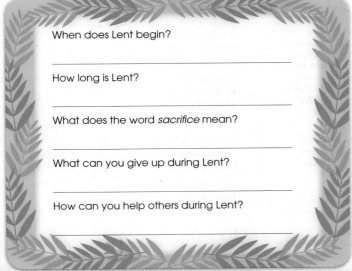

When does Lent begin?

_____

How long is Lent?

_____

What does the word *sacrifice* mean?

_____

What can you give up during Lent?

_____

How can you help others during Lent?

_____

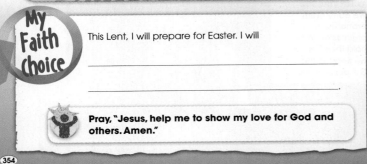

My Faith Choice

This Lent, I will prepare for Easter. I will

_____

_____

Pray, "Jesus, help me to show my love for God and others. Amen."

354

LITURGY CONNECTION

Lenten Prayer Service. Precut slips of purple paper, and print the words "I will" on each slip of paper. Place a basket on the prayer table. Share with the class that Lent is a time to prepare for Easter by thinking about our Baptism and naming ways that we can better live as children of God. Distribute the strips to the students. Ask the students to write or draw one way that they can prepare for Easter during Lent. Have the students place their paper strips in the basket on the prayer table. After all of the students have placed their slips in the basket, pray together, "Dear Jesus, we will grow in your love. Amen."

Respond

▶ Ask the students to describe how Lent helps us get ready for Easter. Have them look for the answer on page 353 and underline or highlight it. *(During Lent we turn to God and pray each day. We make sacrifices, or give up some things.)* Then have them look at the picture on page 353 and connect it to their responses.

▶ Introduce the Prepare for Easter activity and have the students work in groups to complete it.

▶ Have each group share their responses with the whole class.

▶ Have the students make their My Faith Choice. Invite them to pray the prayer at the bottom of the page as a sign of their commitment to live their faith choice.

Pray

▶ Invite the students to gather in the prayer area. Point out that the table is decorated with a purple runner, and then read aloud What You See on page 353 to explain why the Church uses purple during Lent.

▶ Lead the students in prayer. Tell them to repeat each line of the prayer after you.

> Lord God,
> as we begin the Lenten season,
> help us to prepare for Easter.
> Remind us to pray each day and
> help us to make a sacrifice
> that will show our love for you
> and others. Amen.

Palm Sunday of the Passion of the Lord

Focus

Ask a volunteer to read the Faith Focus question aloud. Share with the class that Palm Sunday of the Passion of the Lord is the beginning of Holy Week.

Discover

▶ Tell the class that Holy Week is the week of the year during which the Church remembers and celebrates the events of Jesus' entrance into the city of Jerusalem and his Passion, Death, and Resurrection.

▶ Select a student to read aloud the first paragraph of the text on the page.

▶ Ask a volunteer to describe why the Church calls the day it celebrates this event in the life of Jesus Palm Sunday of the Passion of the Lord. *(Accept all appropriate responses, such as, The people waved palm branches to greet Jesus.)*

▶ Then have the students read the rest of the text on the page silently to discover how the Church remembers and celebrates this event.

▶ Use the What You See section to raise the students' awareness of an important way they can take part in celebrating the liturgy for Palm Sunday of the Passion of the Lord.

Faith Focus
How do we begin our celebration of Holy Week?

The Word of the Lord
These are the Gospel readings for Palm Sunday of the Passion of the Lord. Ask your family to read this year's Gospel reading with you. Talk about the reading with them.

Year A
Matthew 26:14–27:66 or Matthew 27:11–54

Year B
Mark 14:1–15:47 or Mark 15:1–39

Year C
Luke 22:14–23:56 or Luke 23:1–49

What You See
We carry palm branches in procession. We hold them as we listen to the Gospel reading.

Palm Sunday of the Passion of the Lord

When friends come to visit, we welcome them. Once when Jesus came to visit Jerusalem, many people came out to welcome him. They spread cloaks and branches on the road to honor him. The Church remembers and celebrates that special time on Palm Sunday of the Passion of the Lord. It is the first day of Holy Week. Holy Week is the week leading up to Easter.

At Mass on Palm Sunday, we honor Jesus. We hold palm branches and say, "Hosanna to the Son of David. Blessed is he who comes in the name of the Lord!" We welcome Jesus as the people welcomed him to Jerusalem.

355

LITURGY CONNECTION

Celebrating Palm Sunday of the Passion of the Lord. Explain to the class that red is the color used to celebrate Palm Sunday of the Passion of the Lord. The priest wears red vestments. Banners and other decorations are made from red cloth. Tell the students that we use red on this day to remember Jesus' Passion (suffering) and Death. It reminds us that Jesus gave his life for us. Point out to the students that on this first day of Holy Week, the liturgy begins with the blessing of palms, which often takes place outside the church, and the procession of palms into church for the celebration of the Mass. Encourage the students to take part in the Palm Sunday procession at Mass.

We Honor Jesus

People sometimes carry banners in processions. Sometimes we hang banners in our church. Banners in our church help us to remember the liturgical season or feast we are celebrating. Decorate this banner.

"Blessed is he who comes in the name of the Lord!"

My Faith Choice

This Holy Week, I will welcome Jesus. I will

_____

_____

Pray, "Blessed are you, Lord Jesus. Hosanna! Amen."

356

TEACHING TIP

Making Crosses from Palm Branches. Many Christians have the custom of making crosses, using the palm branches that they receive on Palm Sunday of the Passion of the Lord. Invite someone from the school or parish who knows how to weave the palm fronds into designs of crosses to visit with the students and teach them to weave the palms into simple cross shapes. The students will enjoy participating in this custom and sharing it with their families.

Respond

▶ Ask volunteers to describe how the Church begins her celebration of Holy Week. *(Accept all appropriate responses, such as: We celebrate Palm Sunday of the Passion of the Lord. We carry palm branches.)*

▶ Introduce and explain the directions to the We Honor Jesus activity and invite the students to complete it.

▶ Allow time for the students to complete the My Faith Choice. Help them resolve to put their choices into practice. Invite them to silently pray the prayer at the bottom of the page.

Pray

▶ Invite the students to gather in the prayer center.

▶ Proclaim Mark 11:1–10, the Gospel account of Jesus entering Jerusalem, to the group.

▶ Conclude by leading the class in praying aloud,

Hosanna to the Son of David. Blessed is he who comes in the name of the Lord! Amen.

Triduum/ Holy Thursday

Focus

Ask a volunteer to read the Faith Focus question aloud. Explain that Holy Thursday is the first day of the three-day celebration of the Easter Triduum.

Discover

▶ Have the students look at the word *Triduum* at the top of the page. Explain that the word *triduum* means "three."

▶ Tell the class that the three days that make up the Easter Triduum celebrated by the Church are Holy Thursday, Good Friday, and Easter Vigil/Easter Sunday.

▶ Ask the class to listen carefully to discover what the Church celebrates on Holy Thursday as you read aloud to them the text on the page.

▶ Ask the students to explain what the Church celebrates on Holy Thursday. *(We remember and celebrate what happened at the Last Supper, Jesus giving us the Eucharist, the call to serve others, and so on.)*

▶ Ask the students to look at the picture on page 357 and describe what is happening. *(washing of feet)*

▶ Read aloud the What You See on page 357 to make the connection between this event at the Last Supper and the Evening Mass of the Lord's Supper.

Faith Focus
How does celebrating Holy Thursday help us to grow as followers of Jesus Christ?

The Word of the Lord
These are the Scripture readings for the Mass of the Lord's Supper on Holy Thursday. Ask your family to read one of the readings with you. Talk about the reading with them.

First Reading
Exodus 12:1–8, 11–14

Second Reading
1 Corinthians 11:23–26

Gospel
John 13:1–15

What You See
The priest washes the feet of members of the parish. This reminds us that we are to help others as Jesus taught us.

Triduum/Holy Thursday

Many things happen at a family meal. We prepare and cook food. We set the table. We clean up. When we do all these things, we are serving one another.

On Holy Thursday evening, we remember how Jesus showed his love by serving his disciples. Before Jesus and his disciples ate the meal at the Last Supper, he washed their feet. After he finished, he told them to serve others as he served them.

On Holy Thursday evening, we remember all Jesus did at the Last Supper. We especially remember that Jesus gave us the Eucharist.

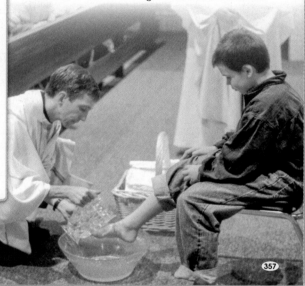
357

LITURGY BACKGROUND

The Evening Mass of the Lord's Supper. Holy Thursday is the first day of the Triduum. This day of the Triduum begins with the evening celebration of the Mass of the Lord's Supper. At this liturgy we remember and celebrate what happened at the Last Supper at which Jesus gave us the Eucharist, the gift of his Body and Blood. We listen and learn what it means to serve as Jesus did as we witness the reenactment of the washing of the feet.

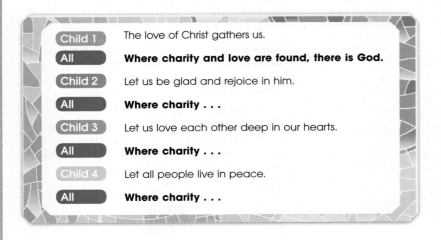

Prayer for Holy Thursday

The hymn "Where Charity and Love Are Found" is sung in many churches on Holy Thursday evening. The words of this hymn remind us that God is love. We are to love one another as Jesus loved us. Pray this prayer with your class.

Child 1	The love of Christ gathers us.
All	**Where charity and love are found, there is God.**
Child 2	Let us be glad and rejoice in him.
All	**Where charity . . .**
Child 3	Let us love each other deep in our hearts.
All	**Where charity . . .**
Child 4	Let all people live in peace.
All	**Where charity . . .**

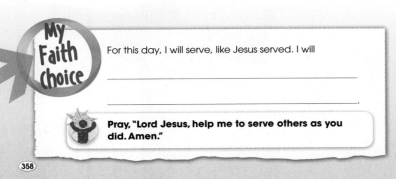

My Faith Choice

For this day, I will serve, like Jesus served. I will

_____

_____

Pray, "Lord Jesus, help me to serve others as you did. Amen."

358

Respond

▶ Have the students suggest ways they can serve others as Jesus taught us to do at the Last Supper. Encourage them to share their suggestions with the whole group.

▶ Invite the students to complete the My Faith Choice. Then pray together the prayer at the bottom of the page.

Pray

▶ Prepare for the prayer service on the page by selecting five students to take the "Child" roles in the prayer. Practice reciting the response in unison with the class.

▶ Invite the students to gather in the prayer center and lead them in the prayer service.

TEACHING TIP

Making a Triduum Triptych. Send a note home encouraging families to spend time on each of the three days of the Easter Triduum with their children. Suggest that they fold a piece of drawing paper or construction paper into three equally spaced horizontal panels. Title the top panel "Holy Thursday," the middle panel "Good Friday," and the bottom panel "Easter Vigil/Easter." Have families work with their children to draw the events in the life of Jesus that are remembered and celebrated on these days.

Triduum/ Good Friday

Focus

Ask a volunteer to read the Faith Focus question aloud. Share with the class that the second day of the Triduum is Good Friday.

Discover

▶ Invite the class to look at the picture of the cross and describe how seeing a cross reminds them of Jesus. *(Accept all appropriate responses, such as, Jesus died on the Cross.)*

▶ Summarize the students' responses by reading aloud the first paragraph on the page.

▶ Ask volunteers to read the rest of the page and have the students listen for how celebrating Good Friday helps us grow as disciples of Jesus.

Faith Focus
How does celebrating Good Friday help us to grow as followers of Christ?

The Word of the Lord
These are the Scripture readings for Good Friday. Ask your family to read the readings with you. Talk about each reading with them.

First Reading
Isaiah 52:13–53:12

Second Reading
Hebrews 4:14–16, 5:7–9

Gospel
John 18:1–19:42

Triduum/Good Friday

Sometimes something happens to us that brings us suffering. We call this a cross. On Good Friday, we remember that Jesus died on the Cross. We listen to the story of his Passion and Death. We pray for everyone in the world.

On Good Friday, we honor the Cross by kissing it or by genuflecting or bowing deeply in front of it. Our celebration of Jesus' Passion and Death ends with Holy Communion. We walk in procession to the altar and share in the Eucharist. We receive the Body of Christ.

At home we think about how Jesus suffered and died on this day. Our prayers help us to get ready for the joy of Jesus' new life at Easter.

(359)

LITURGY BACKGROUND

The Passion of Our Lord Jesus Christ. The liturgical rites for Good Friday are different from the Sunday liturgy. The altar is bare without cloth, candles, or cross. Ministers silently process into the church and prostrate themselves or kneel in silent prayer. The priest prays aloud the Prayer. A longer version of the Prayer of the Faithful , the Solemn Intercessions, concludes the Liturgy of the Word. The Cross of Christ is adored. Then the altar is covered with a white cloth, the Blessed Sacrament is brought to the altar, and the liturgical rite of Holy Communion is celebrated. The priest prays the Prayer After Communion. The priest then prays over the people and dismisses the assembly, and everyone leaves in silence.

Prayers for the Whole World

On Good Friday, the Church prays a special Prayer of the Faithful. Pray this prayer of the faithful together.

Child 1   May God guide our Church and gather us in peace.

All   **Amen.**

Child 2   May God help the Pope to lead us as God's holy people.

All   **Amen.**

Child 3   May God help those who will soon be baptized to follow Jesus.

All   **Amen.**

Child 4   May God bless our government leaders and help them keep us safe and free.

All   **Amen.**

Child 5   May God fill those in need with faith and hope.

All   **Amen.**

BASED ON THE SOLEMN INTERCESSIONS,
THE PASSION OF THE LORD, *ROMAN MISSAL*

My Faith Choice

On this day, I will honor the Cross. I will

_____

_____

  Pray, "We adore you, O Christ, and we bless you. Amen."

360

SACRED TRADITION

Good Friday Silence. There is a long-standing Christian practice of making the three hours of 12:00 noon to 3:00 p.m. on Good Friday quiet or silent time. Remind the children's families of the importance of spending some quiet time in prayer on Good Friday. The family might gather to read the Passion and Death of Jesus in one of the four Gospels. Point out that they might visit *BeMyDisciples*.com for some ideas on ways to share with their families their faith in the meaning of Jesus' Passion and Death.

Respond

▶ Ask the students to describe how taking part in the celebration of Good Friday helps us grow as followers of Christ. *(Affirm all appropriate responses, such as: We listen to the story of Jesus' suffering and Death. We show our love for Jesus by adoring the Cross. We pray for others. We receive Holy Communion.)*

▶ Work with the students and draw up a list of people for whom they wish to pray. Explain that they can include groups of people, such as priests, people who are sick, and so on.

▶ Read aloud the introduction to the My Faith Choice. Allow time for the students to decide how they will honor the Cross. Then pray together the prayer at the bottom of the page.

Pray

▶ Tell the students that at the liturgy on Good Friday the Church prays a special Prayer of the Faithful called the Solemn Intercessions.

▶ Introduce and explain the directions for Prayers for the Whole World. Select five volunteers for the "Child" parts. Explain that everyone will answer "Amen" to each petition. Allow time for the five volunteers to practice their parts.

▶ Have the students bring their books and gather in the prayer center. Lead them in prayer. Begin with the Sign of the Cross. After the last "Amen," conclude with the Sign of the Cross.

Triduum/Easter

Focus

Ask a volunteer to read the Faith Focus question. Point out that Easter, the greatest feast of the Church, is the third and final day of the Triduum.

Discover

▶ Have the students look at the picture on the page. Ask them why they think we place flowers around the altar on Easter. *(They are signs of new life.)* Ask what other signs of new life we see in the spring. *(Accept all appropriate responses.)*

▶ Read aloud the first paragraph. Allow volunteers to respond to the questions in the paragraph.

▶ Ask the students to read silently the rest of the page to find out why Easter is the best day of all for Christians. Invite volunteers to share what they have learned.

Faith Focus

Why is Easter the most important season of the Church year?

The Word of the Lord

These are the Gospel readings for Easter Sunday. Ask your family to read the Gospel reading for this year with you. Talk about it with them.

Year A
John 20:1–9
or Matthew 28:1–10
or Luke 24:13–35

Year B
John 20:1–9
or Mark 16:1–7
or Luke 24:13–35

Year C
John 20:1–9
or Luke 24:1–12
or Luke 24:13–35

Triduum/Easter Sunday

What is the best day of your life? Why do you say it is the best day you remember? For Christians, Easter is the best day of all days. On this day, God raised Jesus from the dead.

During Easter, we remember that we are one with Jesus Christ, who is risen. For Christians, every Sunday is a little Easter. Sunday is the Lord's Day. It is the day on which Jesus was raised from death to new life.

Easter and every Sunday are days of joy and celebration. On these days, we remember that through Baptism, we share in Christ's new life now and forever.

361

LITURGY CONNECTION

Decorating with Signs of Life. Easter is a season of new life in Christ. Easter celebrates both the Resurrection of Jesus and our Baptism into new life in Christ. Decorate your prayer area with a variety of signs of life. Cover the prayer table with a flowing white cloth, put a bowl of holy water on the table to remind the students of their Baptism, and place green plants and candles in the prayer area. Have the students create Easter banners and display them throughout your learning space.

Celebrating Our New Life

The Earth is filled with signs that remind us of the gift of new life in Christ we receive in Baptism. Find and color the signs of new life in this drawing. Talk with your family about what the signs you discover tell about Easter.

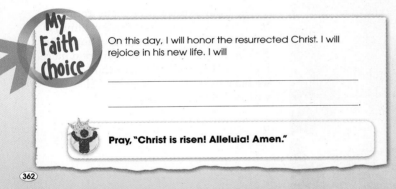

My Faith Choice

On this day, I will honor the resurrected Christ. I will rejoice in his new life. I will

_____

_____.

Pray, "Christ is risen! Alleluia! Amen."

362

Respond

▶ Ask the students to explain why Easter is the most important time of the Church's year. *(Easter is the day on which Jesus rose from the dead.)*

▶ Introduce and explain the Celebrating Our New Life activity to the class.

▶ Give the students time to find and color the signs of the new life of Easter in the activity.

▶ Invite volunteers to talk about what the signs of new life in the picture tell about Easter.

▶ Encourage the students to stop and think of the Resurrection of Jesus and give thanks and praise to God the Father when they see signs of new life, such as flowers, a rising sun, and so on.

▶ Have the students complete the My Faith Choice. Invite them to proclaim their faith choices in prayer, ending with "Christ is risen. Alleluia."

Pray

▶ Gather the students in the prayer area. Have them quiet themselves, close their eyes, and imagine they are with the disciples who went to the tomb three days after Jesus was buried.

▶ Proclaim Matthew 28:1–10 to the children and pause after the Gospel reading.

▶ Tell the students to open their eyes and echo this prayer after you: "This is the day the Lord has made; let us rejoice and be glad."

TEACHING TIP

Understanding Cultural Traditions. A wide variety of ethnic and family customs are used to celebrate Easter. If your school includes specific cultural traditions in the celebration of Easter, such as the blessing of Easter foods, talk about that celebration so that all the students in your group can understand its significance. You might also send a note home asking families who celebrate Easter using specific cultural traditions to visit with the class during the Easter season and share those traditions with the class. The Easter season is fifty days long, so there is plenty of time for the students to share and to learn from one another.

Ascension of the Lord

Focus

Read aloud the Faith Focus question. Assure the students that they will be able to answer the question correctly after they finish this lesson.

Discover

▶ Invite volunteers to share their experiences of moving away from home or having a close friend or relative move away. How did they feel? How did they stay close to the person after the move?

▶ Read to the class or invite volunteers to take turns reading the text. Discuss the following questions:

— Where was Jesus going? *(to his Father in Heaven)*

— What did Jesus promise? *(to send the Holy Spirit)*

— What was the Holy Spirit going to do? *(help them to share his teachings with others)*

— What do we call Jesus' return to his Father? *(the Ascension)*

— When do we celebrate the Ascension? *(forty days after Easter or on the Seventh Sunday of Easter)*

Faith Focus
What is the Ascension?

The Word of the Lord
This is the Gospel for the Solemnity of the Ascension of the Lord. Ask your family to find the reading in the Bible. Read and talk about it with them.

Gospel
Luke 24:46–53

The Ascension of the Lord

After Jesus rose from the dead, he continued to teach his Apostles. He reminded them that soon he would leave them to be with his Father in Heaven. Jesus promised the Apostles that he would send the Holy Spirit to them.

Forty days after Easter, Jesus and the Apostles were in the countryside. He told them that the Holy Spirit would help them to share his teachings with people all over the world.

> [Jesus] raised his hands, and blessed them. As he blessed them he parted from them and was taken up to heaven. They did him homage and then returned to Jerusalem with great joy, and they were continually in the temple praising God.
>
> Luke 24:50–53

The Church celebrates Jesus' return to his Father in Heaven on the Solemnity of the Ascension of the Lord, forty days after Easter. Jesus promised to prepare a place for us in Heaven. We rejoice that one day we too will share in the glory of Heaven with Jesus and all the Saints.

363

SACRED TRADITION

Sharing Gospel Stories. Every time we hear a good story retold, we seem to learn something new. It is amazing how often we hear something we did not hear the last time we listened to the story. The Easter story has been told and retold for centuries. It is "the story" that we need to hear over and over again. It is "the story" that we need to *share* over and over again. The Holy Spirit will open our hearts and minds to hear something new each and every time.

An Ascension Prayer

When Jesus rose from the dead and returned
to his Father, he showed us the way to Heaven.
We rejoice in the Resurrection and the Ascension.

Child 1	Jesus, you rose from the dead.
All	**We celebrate your new life. Alleluia!**
Child 2	Jesus, you promised to send the Holy Spirit.
All	**You are with us always. Alleluia!**
Child 3	Jesus, you ascended to your Father in Heaven.
All	**You will come again in glory to bring us to our heavenly home. Alleluia!**

My Faith Choice

I can prepare for everlasting life in Heaven by living as a disciple of Jesus. I will

_____

_____

Pray, "Jesus, show us the way to Heaven. Alleluia! Amen."

364

TEACHING TIP

Word Web. Print the word *Heaven* on the board and draw five lines extending from it. Divide the class into small groups and have them copy the incomplete word web onto blank paper. Ask the students in each group to work together to print five words that describe Heaven for them on the lines. When finished, ask each group to share their work with the class.

Respond

▶ Invite the students to respond to the Faith Focus question. Help them to appreciate that Jesus' return to his Father is Good News for all of his followers. It means that if we follow Jesus' example and teachings, we too will share happiness forever in Heaven.

▶ Encourage volunteers to role play the Ascension. Have one student take the part of Jesus. The remainder of the class can act as the Apostles. Retell the story. You may want to incorporate Acts 1:9–12 into the story and ask two of the students to take the parts of the men dressed in white garments.

▶ Afterward, discuss with the class what the Apostles might have felt and what they think Jesus' friends said to one another when Jesus was taken up into Heaven.

▶ Read aloud the My Faith Choice and have the student complete it. Encourage them to resolve to live their decision by praying the prayer at the bottom of the page.

Pray

▶ Choose three students for the reading parts of the prayer service.

▶ Introduce the prayer using the opening text for an Ascension Prayer.

▶ Practice the responses to each invocation with the students by having them read each one aloud or echoing the words after you.

▶ Conclude by signing together an Alleluia. (See page 187 in the student text to review the signs with the students.)

Pentecost

Focus

Remind the class that at Baptism they received the gift of the Holy Spirit. Then ask a volunteer to read the Faith Focus question aloud.

Discover

▶ Read the first paragraph and have the students answer the questions. *(Accept all appropriate responses.)*

▶ Invite a volunteer to read the next paragraph.

▶ Then have the students silently read the rest of the page. Tell them to highlight or underline the name of the day on which the Holy Spirit came to Saint Peter the Apostle and the other disciples. *(Pentecost)*

▶ Write the word *Pentecost* on the board and invite several volunteers to tell why Pentecost is such an important day for the Church. *(Accept all appropriate answers, such as, Saint Peter the Apostle began the work Jesus told the disciples to do.)*

Faith Focus
Who helps us to live as followers of Jesus?

The Word of the Lord
These are the Scripture readings for Pentecost Sunday. Ask your family to read one of the readings with you. Talk about the reading with them.

First Reading
Acts 2:1–11

Second Reading
1 Corinthians 12:3–7, 12–13

Gospel
John 20:19–23

Pentecost Sunday

What do you do when you have to do something that is very difficult? How do you feel when someone helps you?

Jesus knew it would not be easy for his disciples to do the work he gave them. So he promised that the Holy Spirit would come and help them.

On the day of Pentecost, the Holy Spirit came to Peter the Apostle and the other disciples as Jesus promised. Peter was filled with courage. He told a crowd from many different countries that God had raised Jesus to new life. Everyone was amazed by what Peter was saying. Over 3,000 people became followers of Jesus that day.

The Holy Spirit is our Helper and Teacher too. The Holy Spirit helps us to tell others about Jesus and teaches us to live as followers of Jesus.

365

LITURGY CONNECTION

Prayer to the Holy Spirit. The traditional prayer of the Church to the Holy Spirit, which comes from the liturgy of Pentecost, begins with the words "Come, Holy Spirit, fill the hearts of your faithful." Write the words on the board for the students to copy, or write the words in advance on pieces of paper to give to the students. Help the students learn the words to the prayer by heart and encourage them to pray this simple prayer each day.

Come, Holy Spirit

The Holy Spirit helps us to live as followers of Jesus. Unscramble the scrambled words in each sentence of this prayer. Write the missing letters of the words on the lines under each sentence. Pray the prayer to the Holy Spirit together.

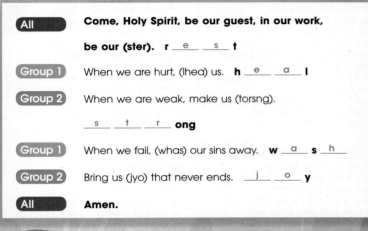

All   **Come, Holy Spirit, be our guest, in our work, be our (ster).**   r <u>e</u> <u> </u> s <u> </u> t

Group 1   When we are hurt, (lhea) us.   h <u>e</u> <u>a</u> l

Group 2   When we are weak, make us (torsng).

<u> </u> s <u> </u> t <u> </u> r **ong**

Group 1   When we fail, (whas) our sins away.   w <u>a</u> s <u>h</u>

Group 2   Bring us (jyo) that never ends.   j <u> </u> o <u> </u> y

All   **Amen.**

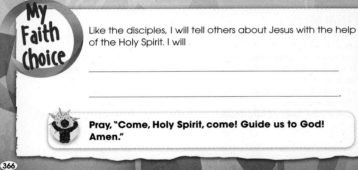

My Faith Choice

Like the disciples, I will tell others about Jesus with the help of the Holy Spirit. I will

_____

_____

Pray, "Come, Holy Spirit, come! Guide us to God! Amen."

366

Respond

▶ Ask the students to share how the Holy Spirit helps Christians today. *(The Holy Spirit helps us to tell others about Jesus and teaches us to live as followers of Jesus.)*

▶ Ask the students to name the people who tell them about Jesus. *(Accept all appropriate responses.)*

▶ Then ask the students to name some of the ways the Holy Spirit can help them live as disciples of Jesus. List their responses on the board. Encourage everyone to choose one or two of the things on the list and do them this week with their families.

▶ Direct attention to the My Faith Choice. Have the students complete this section and resolve to live their choices by praying the prayer at the bottom of the page.

Pray

▶ Have the students prepare for the prayer by working in pairs to unscramble the words in the Come, Holy Spirit prayer and write the words in their books.

▶ Gather the students in the prayer area. Have them form two groups and slowly pray the prayer.

Catholic Prayers and Practices

This section contains some of the major traditional prayers and practices of the Catholic Church. Refer to these pages during your sessions and integrate them into your presentations and your prayer time with the children. Encourage families to use them with their children as an aid to developing the children's Catholic identity.

Memorization

The memorization of prayers facilitates our ability to pray them spontaneously. Use the prayers in this section regularly throughout your sessions. Encourage the children to pause throughout the day and spontaneously pray. This will deepen their awareness that God is always with them as their divine Companion and Friend.

Latin Prayers

You will notice that the prayers on this page also appear in the right column in Latin. Point out these Latin prayers to the children and tell them that Latin is the official language of the Catholic Church. It is not expected that most children will memorize the prayers in Latin at this age, but the U.S. Bishops encourage us to make the children aware of them from the beginning of their formal faith formation. The children also may have noticed that at times, certain Mass parts are sung in Latin—for example, the Lamb of God. This tradition reminds us of the history of sung prayer in the Church.

Catholic Prayers and Practices

Sign of the Cross
In the name of the Father,
and of the Son,
and of the Holy Spirit. Amen.

Our Father
Our Father, who art in heaven,
hallowed be thy name;
thy kingdom come,
thy will be done
on earth as it is in heaven.
Give us this day our daily bread,
and forgive us our trespasses,
as we forgive those who trespass
   against us;
and lead us not into temptation,
   but deliver us from evil.
Amen.

Glory Be (Doxology)
Glory be to the Father
and to the Son
and to the Holy Spirit,
as it was in the beginning
is now, and ever shall be
world without end. Amen.

The Hail Mary
Hail, Mary, full of grace,
the Lord is with thee.
Blessed art thou among women
and blessed is the fruit of thy
   womb, Jesus.
Holy Mary, Mother of God,
pray for us sinners,
now and at the hour of our death.
Amen.

Signum Crucis
In nómine Patris,
et Fílii,
et Spíritus Sancti. Amen.

Pater Noster
Pater noster, qui es in cælis:
sanctificétur nomen tuum;
advéniat regnum tuum;
fiat volúntas tua,
   sicut in cælo, et in terra.
Panem nostrum cotidiánum
   da nobis hódie;
et dimítte nobis débita nostra,
sicut et no dimíttimus debitóribus
   nostris;
et ne nos indúcas in tentatiónem;
sed líbera nos a malo. Amen.

Gloria Patri
Glória Patri
et Fílio
et Spirítui Sancto.
Sicut erat in princípio,
et nunc et semper
et in sǽcula sæculórum. Amen.

Ave, Maria
Ave, María, grátia plena,
Dóminus tecum.
Benedícta tu in muliéribus,
et benedíctus fructus ventris tui,
   Iesus.
Sancta María, Mater Dei,
ora pro nobis peccatóribus,
nunc et in hora mortis nostræ.
Amen.

367

Nicene Creed
(From the *Roman Missal*)

I believe in one God,
the Father almighty,
maker of heaven and earth,
of all things visible and invisible.

I believe in one Lord Jesus Christ,
the Only Begotten Son of God,
born of the Father before all ages.

God from God, Light from Light,
true God from true God,
begotten, not made,
   consubstantial with the Father;
through him all things were made.
For us men and for our salvation
he came down from heaven,

(At the words that follow up to and including and became man, *all bow.)*

and by the Holy Spirit
   was incarnate of the Virgin Mary,
and became man.

For our sake he was crucified under
   Pontius Pilate,
he suffered death and was buried,
and rose again on the third day
in accordance with the Scriptures.
He ascended into heaven
and is seated at the right hand of
   the Father.
He will come again in glory
to judge the living and the dead
and his kingdom will have no end.

I believe in the Holy Spirit, the Lord,
   the giver of life,
who proceeds from the Father and
   the Son,
who with the Father and the Son is
   adored and glorified,
who has spoken through the prophets.

I believe in one, holy, catholic and
   apostolic Church.
I confess one Baptism
   for the forgiveness of sins
and I look forward to the
   resurrection of the dead
and the life of the world to come. Amen.

Apostles' Creed
(From the *Roman Missal*)

I believe in God,
the Father almighty,
Creator of heaven and earth,
and in Jesus Christ, his only Son,
   our Lord,

(At the words that follow, up to and including the Virgin Mary, *all bow.)*

who was conceived by the Holy Spirit,
born of the Virgin Mary,
suffered under Pontius Pilate,
was crucified, died and was buried;
he descended into hell;
on the third day he rose again from
   the dead;
he ascended into heaven,
and is seated at the right hand of
   God the Father almighty;
from there he will come to judge the
   living and the dead.

I believe in the Holy Spirit,
the holy catholic Church,
the communion of saints,
the forgiveness of sins,
the resurrection of the body,
and life everlasting. Amen.

Apostles' Creed

The word *creed* comes from two Latin words which together mean "I give my heart to." They have been joined together to form one word that means "I believe." In the creed we express our belief in, or give our hearts to, God. The Apostles' Creed is one of the earliest creeds of the Church. It is called the Apostles' Creed because the teachings in this creed date back to the main beliefs that the Church has professed since the days of the Apostles. Read the words of the Apostles' Creed one line at a time, and have the children echo, or repeat, the words after you.

Nicene Creed

The Nicene Creed, or, more correctly, the Nicene-Constantinople Creed, is the creed often professed during Mass on Sundays. For this reason it is important to guide your second graders to become familiar with its words so that they can join in professing the creed during Mass. You might slowly integrate the use of this creed into your lessons.

Rhythm of Prayer

▶ Praying is to the spiritual life as breathing is to our physical life. Saint Paul the Apostle captures the truth of this adage when he admonishes us to pray always.

▶ Guide the students to pray always by helping them develop the habit of prayer, or a rhythm to their prayer life.

▶ Make the students aware of and teach them to incorporate prayer into their daily lives.

Morning Prayer

Dear God,
as I begin this day,
keep me in your love and care.
Help me to live as your child today.
Bless me, my family, and my friends
   in all we do.
Keep us all close to you. Amen.

Grace Before Meals

Bless us, O Lord,
and these thy gifts,
which we are about to receive
from thy bounty,
through Christ our Lord.
Amen.

A Vocation Prayer

God, I know you will call me
for special work in my life.
Help me follow Jesus each day
and be ready to answer your call.
Amen.

Evening Prayer

Dear God,
I thank you for today.
Keep me safe throughout the night.
Thank you for all the good I did today.
I am sorry for what I have chosen
   to do wrong.
Bless my family and friends. Amen.

Grace After Meals

We give thee thanks,
for all thy benefits, almighty God,
who lives and reigns forever. Amen.

Act of Contrition

My God,
I am sorry for my sins
   with all my heart.
In choosing to do wrong
and failing to do good,
I have sinned against you
whom I should love above all things.
I firmly intend, with your help,
to do penance,
to sin no more,
and to avoid whatever leads me
   to sin.
Our Savior Jesus Christ
suffered and died for us.
In his name, my God, have mercy.
Amen.

369

The Rosary

Catholics pray the Rosary to honor Mary and remember the important events in the lives of Jesus and Mary. There are twenty mysteries of the Rosary. Follow the steps from 1 to 5.

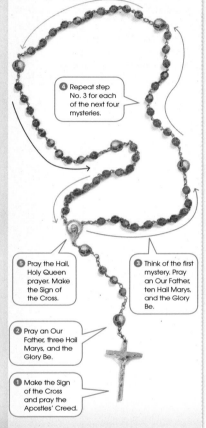

④ Repeat step No. 3 for each of the next four mysteries.

⑤ Pray the Hail, Holy Queen prayer. Make the Sign of the Cross.

③ Think of the first mystery. Pray an Our Father, ten Hail Marys, and the Glory Be.

② Pray an Our Father, three Hail Marys, and the Glory Be.

① Make the Sign of the Cross and pray the Apostles' Creed.

Joyful Mysteries
1. The Annunciation
2. The Visitation
3. The Nativity
4. The Presentation in the Temple
5. The Finding of the Child Jesus After Three Days in the Temple

Luminous Mysteries
1. The Baptism at the Jordan
2. The Miracle at Cana
3. The Proclamation of the Kingdom and the Call to Conversion
4. The Transfiguration
5. The Institution of the Eucharist

Sorrowful Mysteries
1. The Agony in the Garden
2. The Scourging at the Pillar
3. The Crowning with Thorns
4. The Carrying of the Cross
5. The Crucifixion and Death

Glorious Mysteries
1. The Resurrection
2. The Ascension
3. The Descent of the Holy Spirit at Pentecost
4. The Assumption of Mary
5. The Crowning of the Blessed Virgin as Queen of Heaven and Earth

Hail, Holy Queen
Hail, holy Queen, Mother of mercy:
Hail, our life, our sweetness,
   and our hope.
To you do we cry, poor banished children
   of Eve.
To you do we send up our sighs,
mourning and weeping
   in this valley of tears.
Turn then, most gracious advocate,
your eyes of mercy toward us;
and after this our exile
show unto us the blessed fruit
   of your womb, Jesus.
O clement, O loving, O sweet
   Virgin Mary.

370

Devotion to Mary

The Blessed Virgin Mary has a favored and unique place in God's loving plan of Salvation for the world. The twenty mysteries of the Rosary summarize Mary's role in God's plan as intrinsically related to the mysteries of the life of Christ.

Connect the Rosary with your sessions. For example, when a chapter talks about a mystery from the life of Mary and Jesus—the Annunciation, the Nativity, the Crucifixion, the Resurrection, the Ascension, the descent of the Holy Spirit on Pentecost, and so on—make the connection with the Rosary. Introduce the children to the praying of the Rosary.

Use the information on this page to demonstrate to the children how the Rosary is prayed. Point out the centrality of praying the Hail Mary as part of the Rosary.

Living Our Life in Christ

This page offers a brief summary of God's Law of Love. It makes a concrete connection for the children showing that living the Ten Commandments is a way of living the Great Commandment. Use this page to:

▶ Introduce the students to Unit 5, providing the big picture of what it means to live as a child of God.

▶ Reinforce the teaching of chapters 18 through 20 and prepare the students for the Unit Review.

The Ten Commandments

1. I am the LORD your God: you shall not have strange gods before me.
2. You shall not take the name of the LORD your God in vain.
3. Remember to keep holy the LORD's Day.
4. Honor your father and your mother.
5. You shall not kill.
6. You shall not commit adultery.
7. You shall not steal.
8. You shall not lie.
9. You shall not covet your neighbor's wife.
10. You shall not covet your neighbor's goods.

BASED ON EXODUS 20:2–3, 7–17

Precepts of the Church

1. Participate in Mass on Sundays and holy days of obligation, and rest from unnecessary work.
2. Confess sins at least once a year.
3. Receive Holy Communion at least during the Easter season.
4. Observe the prescribed days of fasting and abstinence.
5. Provide for the material needs of the Church, according to one's abilities.

The Great Commandment

"You shall love the Lord, your God, with all your heart, with all your soul, and with all your mind. . . . You shall love your neighbor as yourself." MATTHEW 22:37, 39

The Law of Love

"This is my commandment: love one another as I love you." JOHN 15:12

371

The Seven Sacraments

Jesus gave the Church the Seven Sacraments. The Seven Sacraments are signs of God's love for us. When we celebrate the Sacraments, Jesus is really present with us. We share in the life of the Holy Trinity.

Baptism
We are joined to Christ. We become members of the Body of Christ, the Church.

Confirmation
The Holy Spirit strengthens us to live as children of God.

Eucharist
We receive the Body and Blood of Jesus.

Penance and Reconciliation
We receive God's gift of forgiveness and peace.

Anointing of the Sick
We receive God's healing strength when we are sick or dying, or weak because of old age.

Holy Orders
A baptized man is ordained to serve the Church as a bishop, priest, or deacon.

Matrimony
A baptized man and a baptized woman make a lifelong promise to love and respect each other as husband and wife. They promise to accept the gift of children from God.

372

The Seven Sacraments

This page presents an overview of the Seven Sacraments of the Church. Use the information as:

▶ An overview during the lesson when you introduce the students to the Seven Sacraments in Chapters 9–12.

▶ A reinforcement tool during each session that deals with the Sacraments individually.

We Celebrate the Mass

▶ Use this section of the students' book to help the group participate fully and actively in the celebration of the Mass.

▶ This section of the students' book includes photos that will help the children identify with the rites of the Mass and prayers and responses that are used during the Mass.

▶ Integrate these pages into your presentation of Chapters 13–16.

We Celebrate the Mass

The Introductory Rites

We remember that we are the community of the Church. We prepare to listen to the Word of God and to celebrate the Eucharist.

The Entrance

We stand as the priest, deacon, and other ministers enter the assembly. We sing a gathering song. The priest and deacon kiss the altar. The priest then goes to the chair where he presides over the celebration.

Sign of the Cross and Greeting

The priest leads us in praying the Sign of the Cross. The priest greets us, and we say,

"And with your spirit."

The Penitential Act

We admit our wrongdoings. We bless God for his mercy.

The Gloria

We praise God for all the good that he has done for us.

The Collect

The priest leads us in praying the Collect. We respond,

"Amen."

373

The Liturgy of the Word

God speaks to us today.
We listen and respond to God's Word.

The First Reading

We sit and listen as the reader reads from the Old Testament or from the Acts of the Apostles. The reader concludes, "The word of the Lord." We respond,

"Thanks be to God."

The Responsorial Psalm

The song leader leads us in singing a psalm.

The Second Reading

The reader reads from the New Testament, but not from the four Gospels. The reader concludes, "The word of the Lord." We respond,

"Thanks be to God."

The Acclamation

We stand to honor Christ, present with us in the Gospel. The song leader leads us in singing **"Alleluia, Alleluia, Alleluia,"** or another chant during Lent.

374

The Liturgy of the Word

Here are some suggestions on how you can incorporate these pages into your teaching.

▶ Have the students examine the photographs of the Mass on these pages.

▶ Relate what is happening in the photographs with the prayers and explanations.

▶ Point out that although there may be some differences in the way each parish celebrates Mass, the main rites of the Mass—the responses, prayers, and actions—always remain the same.

Additional Suggestions

▶ Review the parts of the Mass in relationship to each other. This will help the students see that all the parts of the Mass fit together as one whole prayer.

▶ Integrate the *Be My Disciples* music, which contains appropriate songs for parts of the Mass. Be sure to incorporate hymns from the CD in each chapter. The CD also has a hymn that is recommended for each unit. The hymns included are all appropriate choices for liturgy. There are also two sung Mass parts included on your Grade 2 CD.

The Gospel

The deacon or priest proclaims, "A reading from the holy Gospel according to (name of Gospel writer)." We respond,

"Glory to you, O Lord."

He proclaims the Gospel. At the end he says, "The Gospel of the Lord." We respond,

"Praise to you, Lord Jesus Christ."

The Homily

We sit. The priest or deacon preaches the Homily. He helps the people gathered to understand the Word of God spoken to us in the readings.

The Profession of Faith

We stand and profess our faith. We pray the Nicene Creed together.

The Prayer of the Faithful

The priest leads us in praying for our Church and her leaders, for our country and its leaders, for ourselves and others, for those who are sick and those who have died. We can respond to each prayer in several ways. One way that we respond is,

"Lord, hear our prayer."

375

The Liturgy of the Eucharist

We join with Jesus and the Holy Spirit
to give thanks and praise to God the Father.

The Preparation of the Altar and Gifts

We sit as the altar is prepared and the collection is taken up. We share our blessings with the community of the Church and especially with those in need. The song leader may lead us in singing a song. The gifts of bread and wine are brought to the altar.

The priest lifts up the bread and blesses God for all our gifts. He prays, "Blessed are you, Lord God of all creation. . . ." We respond,

"Blessed be God for ever."

The priest lifts up the chalice of wine and prays, "Blessed are you, Lord God of all creation. . . ." We respond,

"Blessed be God for ever."

The priest invites us, "Pray, brethren (brother and sisters), that my sacrifice and yours may be acceptable to God, the almighty Father."

We stand and respond,

"May the Lord accept the sacrifice at your hands for the praise and glory of his name, for our good and the good of all his holy Church."

The Prayer over the Offerings

The priest leads us in praying the Prayer over the Offerings. We respond, **"Amen."**

376

▶ Take the students on a visit to the parish church. Show them the things that are used in the celebration of the Mass. See the Visit to Church on pages 513 and 514 in this Teacher Guide.

▶ Have the students examine the photographs of the Mass on these pages.

▶ Relate what is happening in the photographs with the prayers and explanations.

▶ Explain the prayers, responses, and actions of the Mass so that the children understand what is happening throughout the Mass.

▶ Again, point out that although there may be some differences in the way each parish celebrates Mass, the main rites of the Mass— the responses, prayers, and actions – always remain the same.

Additional Suggestions

▶ Review the rites of the Mass in relationship to each other. This will help the students begin to see that all the parts of the Mass fit together as one whole prayer.

▶ Integrate *Be My Disciples* music as appropriate.

Opening Dialogue and Preface

The priest invites us to join in praying the Church's great prayer of praise and thanksgiving to God the Father.

Priest: "The Lord be with you."
Assembly: "And with your spirit."
Priest: "Lift up your hearts."
Assembly: "We lift them up to the Lord."
Priest: "Let us give thanks to the Lord our God."
Assembly: "It is right and just."

After the priest sings or prays aloud the Preface, we join in acclaiming,

**"Holy, Holy, Holy Lord God of hosts.
Heaven and earth are full of your glory.
Hosanna in the highest.
Blessed is he who comes in the name of the Lord.
Hosanna in the highest."**

The Eucharistic Prayer

The priest leads the assembly in praying the Eucharistic Prayer.

We call on the Holy Spirit to make our gifts of bread and wine holy so that they become the Body and Blood of Jesus. We recall what happened at the Last Supper. The bread and wine become the Body and Blood of the Lord. Jesus is truly and really present under the appearances of bread and wine.

The priest sings or says aloud, "The mystery of faith." We respond using this or another acclamation used by the Church,

"We proclaim your Death, O Lord, and profess your Resurrection until you come again."

The priest then prays for the Church. He prays for the living and the dead.

Doxology

The priest concludes the praying of the Eucharistic Prayer. He sings or prays aloud,

"Through him, and with him, and in him,
O God, almighty Father,
in the unity of the Holy Spirit,
all glory and honor is yours,
for ever and ever."

We respond by singing, **"Amen."**

377

The Communion Rite

The Lord's Prayer
We pray the Lord's Prayer together.

The Sign of Peace
The priest invites us to share a sign of peace, saying, "The peace of the Lord be with you always." We respond,
"And with your spirit."
We share a sign of peace.

The Fraction, or the Breaking of the Bread
The priest breaks the host, the consecrated bread. We sing or pray aloud,
"Lamb of God, you take away the sins of the world, have mercy on us.
Lamb of God, you take away the sins of the world, have mercy on us.
Lamb of God, you take away the sins of the world, grant us peace."

Communion
The priest raises the host and says aloud,
"Behold the Lamb of God, behold him who takes away the sins of the world.
Blessed are those called to the supper of the Lamb."

We join with him and say,
"Lord, I am not worthy that you should enter under my roof, but only say the word and my soul shall be healed."

The priest receives Communion. Next, the deacon, the extraordinary ministers of Holy Communion, and the members of the assembly receive Communion.

The priest, deacon, or extraordinary minister of Holy Communion holds up the host. We bow, and the priest, deacon, or extraordinary minister of Holy Communion says, "The Body of Christ." We respond, **"Amen."** We then receive the consecrated host in our hands or on our tongues.

If we are to receive the Blood of Christ, the priest, deacon, or extraordinary minister of Holy Communion holds up the cup containing the consecrated wine. We bow, and the priest, deacon, or extraordinary minister of Holy Communion says, "The Blood of Christ." We respond, **"Amen."** We take the cup in our hands and drink from it.

The Prayer After Communion
We stand as the priest invites us to pray, saying, "Let us pray." He prays the Prayer After Communion. We respond, **"Amen."**

(378)

Receiving Holy Communion

Review with the students your parish's or school's directions for receiving Holy Communion.

▶ Reverently walk in procession to the altar, singing the communion song, to receive Holy Communion from the priest, deacon, or the extraordinary minister of Holy Communion.

▶ You may receive Holy Communion either in your hand or on your tongue.

▶ The consecrated bread, or host, is offered to you with the words, "The Body of Christ." You respond, "Amen."

▶ If you choose to receive Holy Communion in your hand

- Place one hand underneath the other hand.
- Hold your hands out with palms facing up.
- Bow reverently and receive the consecrated bread in the palm of your hand.
- Step to the side and briefly stop.
- Slowly and reverently take the consecrated bread from the palm of your hand and put the consecrated bread in your mouth.
- Chew and swallow the consecrated bread, the Body of Christ.

The Concluding Rites

▶ Identify the three parts of the Concluding Rites with the students. Read aloud each rite.

The Sacrament of Penance and Reconciliation

Identify the rite of Penance and Reconciliation that the students will be celebrating. Take the students to church to walk them through the rite so they can see where and how they will participate. Show the students where they will sit and where the priest will sit.

The Concluding Rites
We are sent forth to do good works, praising and blessing the Lord.

Greeting
We stand. The priest greets us as we prepare to leave. He says, "The Lord be with you." We respond, **"And with your spirit."**

Final Blessing
The priest or deacon may invite us, "Bow down for the blessing."
The priest blesses us, saying, "May almighty God bless you, the Father, and the Son, and the Holy Spirit."
We respond, **"Amen."**

Dismissal of the People
The priest or deacon sends us forth, using these or similar words, "Go in peace, glorifying the Lord by your life."
We respond, **"Thanks be to God."**
We sing a hymn. The priest and the deacon kiss the altar. The priest, deacon, and other ministers bow to the altar and leave in procession.

The Sacrament of Penance and Reconciliation

Individual Rite
Greeting
Scripture Reading
Confession of Sins and Acceptance of Penance
Act of Contrition
Absolution
Closing Prayer

Communal Rite
Greeting
Scripture Reading
Homily
Examination of Conscience, a Litany of Contrition, and the Lord's Prayer
Individual Confession and Absolution
Closing Prayer

379

A Visit to Church

Catholic churches are built in many styles and sizes. Some Catholic churches are older and some are newer. Some are big and some are small. But, all churches are places where people worship God.

Baptismal Font

As you enter a Catholic church, you may see a baptismal font. The baptismal font is the pool of water used for the Sacrament of Baptism. Water is used to remind us of new life.

Ambo

The ambo is the special place from where the Word of God, the Scriptures, is read. The lector is the person who reads the first and second readings during Mass. The deacon or priest reads the Gospel.

Paschal Candle

During the Easter Season, the Paschal candle, also called the Easter candle, is placed near the baptismal font. It reminds us of Jesus, the Light of the world.

Assembly

The assembly is the people gathered for Mass. The pews are the seats where the people sit.

(380)

A Visit to Church

Use this section in conjunction with the text when the items appear for the first time. Use it independently as a learning session, or integrate its use with the We Celebrate the Mass section.

Use of Photos

Read aloud Baptismal Font. Then have the students look at the photo of the baptismal font on page 380 of their books and share a description. Invite a volunteer to tell where the baptismal font or baptismal pool is in the church. After a brief sharing, move on to the Paschal Candle, then the Assembly and continue the process.

A Visit to Church

Take the students to the church and show them the things that are used in the celebration of the Mass. Let the students see and touch the vestments, books, vessels, and other items used for the celebration of Mass. Allow the students to stand at the altar, the ambo, and the presider's chair so that they can experience the church from that perspective. Remind them to be reverent and respectful during their tour of the church.

The Book of the Gospels Lectionary

The Book of the Gospels contains the Gospel readings we listen to at Mass. The first two readings are read from the Lectionary.

Crucifix

You will see a crucifix or cross that might be carried in procession by one of the servers. Or, it might be a crucifix or cross hanging from the ceiling or hung on the wall.

Tabernacle

The tabernacle is the place in the church where the Eucharist or Blessed Sacrament is kept. Some churches have a chapel where people can pray. When the candle next to the tabernacle is lit, it means that the Blessed Sacrament is in the tabernacle.

Altar

The altar is where the Liturgy of the Eucharist is celebrated at Mass. It reminds us of the Last Supper and that Jesus died for us. It is the table from which Jesus shares his Body and Blood with us.

It is very important to remember that through the Church, Christ continues to be with us in the world. The Church is every one of us, the People of God.

381

Key Teachings of the Catholic Church

The Mystery of God

Divine Revelation

Who am I?

You are a person created by God. God wants you to live in friendship with him on earth and forever in Heaven.

How do we know this about ourselves?

God knows and loves all people. God wants us to know and love him too. God tells us about ourselves. God also tells us about himself.

How did God tell us?

God tells us in many ways. First, all the things God has created tell us about him. We see God's goodness and beauty in creation. Second, God came to us and told us about himself. He told us the most when he sent his Son, Jesus Christ. God's Son became one of us and lived among us. He showed us who God is.

What is faith?

Faith is a gift from God. It helps us to know and to believe in God.

What is a mystery of faith?

A mystery of faith can never be known completely. We cannot know everything about God. We only know who God is because he told us about himself.

What is Divine Revelation?

God wants us to know about him. Divine Revelation is how he freely makes himself known to us. God has told us about himself and his plan for us. He has done this so that we can live in friendship with him and with one another forever.

What is Sacred Tradition?

The word *tradition* means "to pass on." The Church's Sacred Tradition passes on what God has told us. The Holy Spirit guides the Church to tell us about God.

Sacred Scripture

What is Sacred Scripture?

Sacred Scripture means "holy writings." Sacred Scripture are writings that tell God's story.

What is the Bible?

The Bible is God's word. It is a holy book. The stories in the Bible teach about God. The Bible tells the stories about Jesus. When you listen to the Bible, you are listening to God.

What does it mean to say that the Bible is inspired?

This means that the Holy Spirit helped people write about God. The Holy Spirit helped the writers tell what God wants us to know about him.

What is the Old Testament?

The Old Testament is the first part of the Bible. It has forty-six books. They were written before the birth of Jesus. The Old Testament tells the story of creation. It tells about Adam and Eve. It tells about the promise, or Covenant, between God and his people.

What is the Covenant?

The Covenant is the promise that God and his people freely made. It is God's promise always to love and be kind to his people.

382

What are the writings of the prophets?

God chose people to speak in his name. These people are called the prophets. We read the message of the prophets in the Bible. The prophets remind God's people that God is faithful. They remind God's people to be faithful to the Covenant.

What is the New Testament?

The New Testament is the second part of the Bible. It has twenty-seven books. These books were inspired by the Holy Spirit. They were written during the time of the Apostles. They are about Jesus Christ. They tell about his saving work.

What are the Gospels?

The Gospels are the four books at the beginning of the New Testament. They tell the story of Jesus and his teachings. The four Gospels are Matthew, Mark, Luke, and John.

What are the letters of Saint Paul?

The letters of Saint Paul are in the New Testament. The letters teach about the Church. They tell how to follow Jesus. Many of these letters were written before the Gospels.

The Holy Trinity

Who is the Mystery of the Holy Trinity?

The Holy Trinity is the mystery of One God in Three Persons—God the Father, God the Son, and God the Holy Spirit.

Who is God the Father?

God the Father is the First Person of the Holy Trinity.

Who is God the Son?

God the Son is Jesus Christ. He is the Second Person of the Holy Trinity. God the Father sent his Son to be one of us and live with us.

Who is God the Holy Spirit?

The Holy Spirit is the Third Person of the Holy Trinity. God sends us the Holy Spirit to help us to know and love God better. The Holy Spirit helps us live as children of God.

Divine Work of Creation

What does it mean to call God the Creator?

God is the Creator. He has made everyone and everything out of love. He has created everyone and everything without any help.

Who are angels?

Angels are spiritual beings. They do not have bodies like we do. Angels give glory to God at all times. They sometimes serve God by bringing his message to people.

Why are human beings special?

God creates every human being in his image and likeness. God shares his life with us. God wants us to be happy with him forever.

What is the soul?

The soul is the spiritual part of a person. The soul will never die. It is the part of us that lives forever. It bears the image of God.

What is free will?

Free will is the power God gives us to choose between good and evil. Free will gives us the power to turn toward God.

383

What is Original Sin?

Original Sin is the sin of Adam and Eve. They chose to disobey God. As a result of Original Sin, death, sin, and suffering came into the world.

Jesus Christ, Son of God, Son of Mary

What is the Annunciation?

At the Annunciation the angel Gabriel came to Mary. The angel had a message for her. God had chosen her to be the Mother of his Son, Jesus.

What is the Incarnation?

The Incarnation is the Son of God becoming a man and still being God. Jesus Christ is true God and true man.

What does it mean that Jesus is Lord?

The word *lord* means "master or ruler." When we call Jesus "Lord," we mean that he is truly God.

What is the Paschal Mystery?

The Paschal Mystery is the Passion, Death, Resurrection, and Ascension of Jesus Christ. Jesus passed over from death into new and glorious life.

What is Salvation?

The word *salvation* means "to save." It is the saving of all people from sin and death through Jesus Christ.

What is the Resurrection?

The Resurrection is God's raising Jesus from the dead to new life.

What is the Ascension?

The Ascension is the return of the Risen Jesus to his Father in Heaven.

What is the Second Coming of Christ?

Christ will come again in glory at the end of time. This is the Second Coming of Christ. He will judge the living and the dead. This is the fulfillment of God's plan.

What does it mean that Jesus is the Messiah?

The word *messiah* means "anointed one." He is the Messiah. God promised to send the Messiah to save all people. Jesus is the Savior of the world.

The Mystery of the Church

What is the Church?

The word *church* means "those who are called together." The Church is the Body of Christ. It is the new People of God.

What does the Church do?

The Church tells all people the Good News of Jesus Christ. The Church invites all people to know, love, and serve Jesus.

What is the Body of Christ?

The Church is the Body of Christ on Earth. Jesus Christ is the Head of the Church and all baptized people are its members.

Who are the People of God?

The Church is the People of God. God invites all people to belong to the People of God. The People of God live as one family in God.

What is the Communion of Saints?

The Communion of Saints is all of the holy people that make up the Church. It is the faithful followers of Jesus on earth. It is those who have died who are still becoming holier. It is also those who have died and are happy forever with God in Heaven.

What are the Marks of the Church?

There are four main ways to describe the Church. We call these the four Marks of the Church. The Church is one, holy, catholic, and apostolic.

Who are the Apostles?

The Apostles were the disciples whom Jesus chose. He sent them to preach the Gospel to the whole world in his name. Some of their names are Peter, Andrew, James, and John.

What is Pentecost?

Pentecost is the day the Holy Spirit came to the disciples of Jesus. This happened fifty days after the Resurrection. The work of the Church began on this day.

Who are the clergy?

The clergy are bishops, priests, and deacons. They have received the Sacrament of Holy Orders. They serve the whole Church.

What is the work of the Pope?

Jesus Christ is the true Head of the Church. The Pope and the bishops lead the Church in his name. The Pope is the bishop of Rome. He is the successor to Saint Peter the Apostle, the first Pope. The Pope brings the Church together. The Holy Spirit guides the Pope when he speaks about faith, and about what Catholics believe.

What is the work of the bishops?

The other bishops are the successors of the other Apostles. They teach and lead the Church in their dioceses. The Holy Spirit always guides the Pope and all of the bishops. He guides them when they make important decisions.

What is religious life?

Some men and women want to follow Jesus in a special way. They choose the religious life. They promise not to marry. They dedicate their whole lives to doing Jesus' work. They promise to live holy lives. They promise to live simply. They share what they have with others. They live together in groups and they promise to obey the rules of their community. They may lead quiet lives of prayer, or teach, or take care of people who are sick or poor.

Who are laypeople?

Many people do not receive the Sacrament of Holy Orders. Many are not members of a religious community. These are laypeople. Laypeople follow Christ every day by what they do and say.

The Blessed Virgin Mary

Who is Mary?

God chose Mary to be the Mother of his only Son, Jesus. Mary is the Mother of God. She is the Mother of Jesus. She is the Mother of the Church. Mary is the greatest Saint.

What is the Immaculate Conception?

From the first moment of her being, Mary was preserved from sin. This special grace from God continued throughout her whole life. We call this the Immaculate Conception.

What is the Assumption of Mary?

At the end of her life on Earth, the Blessed Virgin Mary was taken body and soul into Heaven. Mary hears our prayers. She tells her Son what we need. She reminds us of the life that we all hope to share when Christ, her Son, comes again in glory.

Life Everlasting

What is eternal life?

Eternal life is life after death. At death the soul leaves the body. It passes into eternal life.

What is Heaven?

Heaven is living with God and with Mary and all the Saints in happiness forever after we die.

What is the Kingdom of God?

The Kingdom of God is also called the Kingdom of Heaven. It is all people and creation living in friendship with God.

What is purgatory?

Purgatory is the chance to grow in love for God after we die so we can live forever in Heaven.

What is hell?

Hell is life away from God and the Saints forever after death.

Celebration of the Christian Life and Mystery

Liturgy and Worship

What is worship?

Worship is the praise we give God. The Church worships God in the liturgy.

What is liturgy?

The liturgy is the Church's worship of God. It is the work of the Body of Christ. Christ is present by the power of the Holy Spirit.

What is the liturgical year?

The liturgical year is the name of the seasons and feasts that make up the Church year of worship. The main seasons of the Church year are Advent, Christmas, Lent, and Easter. The Triduum is the three holy days just before Easter. The rest of the liturgical year is called Ordinary Time.

The Sacraments

What are the Sacraments?

The Sacraments are the seven signs of God's love for us that Jesus gave the Church. We share in God's love when we celebrate the Sacraments.

What are the Sacraments of Christian Initiation?

The Sacraments of Christian Initiation are Baptism, Confirmation, and Eucharist.

What is the Sacrament of Baptism?

Baptism joins us to Christ. It makes us members of the Church. We receive the gift of the Holy Spirit. Original Sin and our personal sins are forgiven. Through Baptism, we belong to Christ.

What is the Sacrament of Confirmation?

At Confirmation, we receive the gift of the Holy Spirit. The Holy Spirit strengthens us to live our Baptism.

What is the Sacrament of Eucharist?

In the Eucharist, we join with Christ. We give thanksgiving, honor, and glory to God the Father. Through the power of the Holy Spirit, the bread and wine become the Body and Blood of Jesus Christ.

Why do we have to participate at Sunday Mass?

Catholics participate in the Eucharist on Sundays and holy days of obligation. Sunday is the Lord's Day. Participating at the Mass and receiving Holy Communion, the Body and Blood of Christ, when we are old enough, are necessary for Catholics.

What is the Mass?

The Mass is the main celebration of the Church. At Mass, we worship God. We listen to God's Word. We celebrate and share in the Eucharist.

What are the Sacraments of Healing?

The two Sacraments of Healing are the Sacrament of Penance and Reconciliation and the Sacrament of the Anointing of the Sick.

What is confession?

Confession is telling our sins to a priest in the Sacrament of Penance and Reconciliation. Confession is another name for the Sacrament.

What is contrition?

Contrition is being truly sorry for our sins. We want to make up for the hurt our sins have caused. We do not want to sin again.

What is penance?

A penance is a prayer or act of kindness. The penance we do shows that we are truly sorry for our sins. The priest gives us a penance to help repair the hurt caused by our sin.

What is absolution?

Absolution is the forgiveness of sins by God through the words and actions of the priest.

What is the Sacrament of the Anointing of the Sick?

The Sacrament of the Anointing of the Sick is one of the two Sacraments of Healing. We receive this Sacrament when we are very sick, old, or dying. This Sacrament helps make our faith and trust in God strong.

What are the Sacraments at the Service of Communion?

Holy Orders and Matrimony, or marriage, are the two Sacraments at the Service of Communion. People who receive these Sacraments serve God.

What is the Sacrament of Holy Orders?

In this Sacrament, baptized men are consecrated as bishops, priests, or deacons. They serve the whole Church. They serve in the name and person of Christ.

Who is a bishop?

A bishop is a priest. He receives the fullness of the Sacrament of Holy Orders. He is a successor to the Apostles. He leads and serves in a diocese. He teaches and leads worship in the name of Jesus.

Who is a priest?

A priest is a baptized man who receives the Sacrament of Holy Orders. Priests work with their bishops. The priest teaches about the Catholic faith. He celebrates Mass. Priests help to guide the Church.

Who is a deacon?

A deacon is ordained to help bishops and priests. He is not a priest. He is ordained to serve the Church.

What is the Sacrament of Matrimony?

In the Sacrament of Matrimony, or marriage, a baptized man and a baptized woman make a lifelong promise. They promise to serve the Church as a married couple. They promise to love each other. They show Christ's love to others.

What are the sacramentals of the Church?

Sacramentals are objects and blessings the Church uses. They help us worship God.

Life in the Spirit

The Moral Life

Why did God create us?

God created us to give honor and glory to him. God created us to live a life of blessing with him here on Earth and forever in Heaven.

What does it mean to live a moral life?

God wants us to be happy. He gives us the gift of his grace. When we accept God's gift by living the way Jesus taught us, we are living a moral life.

What is the Great Commandment?

Jesus taught us to love God above all else. He taught us to love our neighbors as ourselves. This is the path to happiness.

What are the Ten Commandments?

The Ten Commandments are the laws that God gave Moses. They teach us to live as God's people. They teach us to love God, others, and ourselves.

The Commandments are written on the hearts of all people.

What are the Beatitudes?

The Beatitudes are teachings of Jesus. They tell us what real happiness is. The Beatitudes tell us about the Kingdom of God. They help us live as followers of Jesus. They help us keep God at the center of our lives.

What are the Works of Mercy?

God's love and kindness is at work in the world. This is what mercy is. Human works of mercy are acts of loving kindness. We reach out to people. We help them with what they need for their bodies and their spirits.

What are the Precepts of the Church?

The Precepts of the Church are five rules. These rules help us worship God and grow in love of God and our neighbors.

Holiness of Life and Grace

What is holiness?

Holiness is life with God. Holy people are in right relationship with God, with people, and with all of creation.

What is grace?

Grace is the gift of God sharing his life and love with us.

What is sanctifying grace?

Sanctifying grace is the grace we receive at Baptism. It is a free gift of God, given by the Holy Spirit.

What are the Gifts of the Holy Spirit?

The seven Gifts of the Holy Spirit help us to live our Baptism. They are wisdom, understanding, right judgment, courage, knowledge, reverence, and wonder and awe.

The Virtues

What are the virtues?

The virtues are spiritual powers or habits. The virtues help us to do what is good.

What are the most important virtues?

The most important virtues are the three virtues of faith, hope, and love. These virtues are gifts from God. They help us keep God at the center of our lives.

What is conscience?

A conscience. is a gift God gives to every person. It helps us know and judge what is right and what is wrong. Our conscience moves us to do good and avoid evil.

Evil and Sin

What is evil?

Evil is the harm we choose to do to one another and to God's creation.

What is temptation?

Temptations are feelings, people, and things that try to get us to turn away from God's love and not live a holy life.

What is sin?

Sin is freely choosing to do or say something that we know God does not want us to do or say.

What is mortal sin?

A mortal sin is doing or saying something on purpose that is very bad. A mortal sin is against what God wants us to do or say. When we commit a mortal sin, we lose sanctifying grace.

What are venial sins?

Venial sins are sins that are less serious than mortal sins. They weaken our love for God and one another. They make us less holy.

Christian Prayer

What is prayer?

Prayer is talking to and listening to God. When we pray, we raise our minds and hearts to God the Father, Son, and Holy Spirit.

What is the Our Father?

The Lord's Prayer, or Our Father, is the prayer of all Christians. Jesus taught his disciples the Our Father. Jesus gave this prayer to the Church. When we pray the Our Father, we come closer to God and to his Son, Jesus Christ. The Our Father helps us become like Jesus.

What kinds of prayer are there?

Some kinds of prayer use words that we say aloud or quietly in our hearts. Some silent prayers use our imagination to bring us closer to God. Another silent prayer is simply being with God.

Glossary

A

almighty [page 52]
God alone is almighty. This means that only God has the power to do everything good.

Ascension [page 92]
The Ascension is the return of the Risen Jesus to his Father in Heaven forty days after the Resurrection.

assembly [page 176]
The assembly is the People of God gathered to celebrate Mass. All members of the assembly share in the celebration of Mass.

B

Baptism [page 134]
Baptism is the Sacrament that joins us to Christ and makes us members of the Church. We receive the gift of the Holy Spirit and become adopted sons and daughters of God.

believe [page 26]
To believe in God means to know God and to give ourselves to him with all our hearts.

Bible [page 14]
The Bible is the written Word of God.

Body of Christ [page 106]
The Church is the Body of Christ. Jesus Christ is the Head of the Church. All the baptized are members of the Church.

C

Communion of Saints [page 108]
The Church is the Communion of Saints. The Church is the unity of all the faithful followers of Jesus on Earth and those in Heaven.

compassion [page 186]
Compassion means to care about others when they are hurt or feeling sad. Having compassion makes us want to help them feel better.

Confirmation [page 146]
Confirmation is the Sacrament in which the gift of the Holy Spirit strengthens us to live our Baptism.

conscience [page 298]
Conscience is a gift from God that helps us to make wise choices.

consequences [page 296]
Consequences are the good or bad things that happen after we make choices.

courage [page 210]
We receive the gift of courage from the Holy Spirit at Baptism. This gift helps us choose to do what is good.

Covenant [page 68]
The Covenant is God's promise to always love and be kind to his people.

covet [page 266]
We covet when we have an unhealthy desire for something.

Creator [page 50]
God alone is the Creator. God made everyone and everything out of love and without any help.

Crucifixion [page 82]
The Crucifixion is the Death of Jesus on a cross.

D

disciples [page 14]
Disciples are people who follow and learn from someone. Disciples of Jesus follow and learn from him.

E

Eucharist [page 200]
The Eucharist is the Sacrament of the Body and Blood of Jesus Christ.

F

faith [page 28]
Faith is a gift from God that makes us able to believe in him.

[page 132]
The virtue of faith is a gift from God. It gives us the power to come to know God and believe in him.

false witness [page 268]
Giving false witness means telling lies.

forgiveness [page 156]
Forgiveness is a sign of love. We ask for forgiveness because we love God. We want everything to be right again. We share God's forgiving love with others when we forgive people who hurt us.

fortitude [page 240]
Fortitude is another word for courage. Fortitude helps us stay strong, to do our best, and to do what is right and good when it's hard to do so. The Holy Spirit gives us the gift of fortitude to live the way that God wants us to.

G

generosity [page 90]
You show generosity when you use the gifts you received from God to help others.

goodness [page 102]
Goodness is a sign that we are living our Baptism. When we are good to people, we show that we know they are children of God. When we are good to people, we honor God.

grace [page 134]
Grace is the gift of God sharing his life with us and helping us live as his children.

Great Commandment [page 244]
The Great Commandment is to love God above all else and to love others as we love ourselves.

H

Heaven [page 288]
Heaven is happiness forever with God and all the Saints.

Holy Trinity [page 38]
The Holy Trinity is one God in Three Divine Persons—God the Father, God the Son, and God the Holy Spirit.

honor [page 48]
When we honor others, we show respect and value them. We honor God because we are proud to be his children.

[page 230]
To honor someone is to treat them with kindness, respect, and love.

hope [page 318]
Hope is trusting that God hears us, cares about us, and will care for us.

hospitality [page 24]
Jesus tells us to treat all people with hospitality. Hospitality helps us welcome others as God's children. It helps us treat others with dignity and respect.

humility [page 282]
Humility helps us to recognize that all we are and all we have come from God. We are humble when we choose to follow God's ways and make them our own.

J

Jesus Christ [page 68]
Jesus Christ is the Son of God. He is the Second Person of the Holy Trinity who became one of us. Jesus is true God and true man.

joy [page 294]

Joy is one of the Fruits of the Holy Spirit. Joy shows that we are thankful for God's love and for all God has made. Joy shows that we enjoy life and delight in making others joyful.

justice [page 264]

We practice justice when we do our very best to always be fair to others.

kindness [page 228]

We act with kindness when we do things that show we care. We are kind when we treat other people as we want to be treated.

Kingdom of God [page 320]

The Kingdom of God is also called the Kingdom of Heaven.

knowledge [page 144]

Knowledge is one of the Gifts of the Holy Spirit. Knowledge helps us better hear and understand the meaning of the Word of God.

Liturgy of the Eucharist [page 200]

The Liturgy of the Eucharist is the second main part of the Mass. The Church does what Jesus did at the Last Supper.

Liturgy of the Word [page 188]

The Liturgy of the Word is the first main part of the Mass. God speaks to us through readings from the Bible.

love [page 174]

Love is the greatest of all virtues. Love gives us the power to cherish God above all things. It also gives us the power to serve people for the sake of God.

Mass [page 176]

The Mass is the most important celebration of the Church. At Mass, we gather to worship God. We listen to God's Word. We celebrate and share in the Eucharist.

mercy [page 66]

Jesus said, "Blessed are people of mercy." Mercy helps us act with kindness toward others, no matter what.

obedience [page 252]

Authority is a gift from God. God gives people authority to help us follow God's Laws. People in authority, such as parents and grandparents, teachers and principals, priests and bishops, deserve respect. The virtue of obedience gives us strength to honor and respect people in authority.

penance [page 162]

Penance is something we do or say to show we are truly sorry for the choices we made to hurt someone.

Pentecost [page 94]

Pentecost is the day the Holy Spirit came to the disciples of Jesus fifty days after the Resurrection.

piety [page 120]

Piety is a Gift of the Holy Spirit. Piety is the love we have for God. That love makes us want to worship and give God thanks and praise.

procession [page 216]

A procession is people prayerfully walking together. It is a prayer in action.

rabbi [page 242]

Rabbi is a Hebrew word that means teacher.

reconciliation [page 162]

Reconciliation means to become friends again.

respect [page 12]

When we pay attention to what others say to us, we show them respect. Listening is a sign of respect and can help us learn well. Respect for others is a way we show God's love.

Resurrection [page 84]

The Resurrection is God the Father raising Jesus from the dead to new life.

Sacraments [page 124]

The Sacraments are the seven signs of God's love for us that Jesus gave the Church. We share in God's love when we celebrate the Sacraments.

sacrifice [page 78]

You sacrifice when you give up something because you love someone. Jesus sacrificed his life for all people. Followers of Jesus make sacrifices out of love for God and for people.

sanctifying grace [page 135]

Sanctifying grace is the gift of God sharing his life with us.

sin [page 158]

Sin is freely choosing to do or say something we know God does not want us to do or say.

soul [page 38]

Our soul is that part of us that lives forever.

spiritual gifts [page 146]

The Holy Spirit gives us spiritual gifts to help us love and serve other people. We use the spiritual gifts to show our love for God.

Ten Commandments [page 254]

The Ten Commandments are the laws that God gave Moses. They teach us to live as God's people. They help us live happy and holy lives.

thankfulness [page 198]

Thankfulness is a big part of who we are as disciples of Jesus. We have received wonderful blessings and gifts. Jesus calls us to be a thankful people.

trust [page 366]

When we trust people, we know we can rely on them. We can depend on them to help us when we are in need.

wise choices [page 284]

Wise choices help us to live as followers of God.

wonder [page 36]

Wonder is a Gift of the Holy Spirit. It helps us see God's greatness and discover more about God. It then moves us to praise him.

worship [page 124]

Worship means to honor and love God above all else.

Index

399

Credits

Cover Illustration: Marcia Adams Ho

PHOTO CREDITS

Frontmatter: Page 6, © KidStock/Getty Images; 6-7, © Paul Aniszewski/Shutterstock.

Chapter 1: Page 11, © JGI/Jupiterimages; 16, © Digital Vision/Jupiterimages; 21, © Ferguson Cate/PhotoEdit; 22, © Design Pics Inc./Alamy.

Chapter 2: Page 23, © Monkey Business Images/Shutterstock; 24, © NA/Jupiterimages; 24, © Steve Skjold/PhotoEdit; 26, © Den Yamauchi/Getty Images; 27, © Purestock/Getty Images; 27, © ktsdesign/Shutterstock; 29, © Andersen Ross/Blend Images/Alamy; 29, © 68/Ocean/Corbis; 30, © Dominic Labbé/Flickr Open/Getty Images; 30, © Bill Wittman; 33, © Visage/Alamy; 34, © Thinkstock Images/Jupiterimages.

Chapter 3: Page 35, © Jose Luis Pelaez Inc/Getty Images; 38, © Ocean/Corbis; 39, © Leander Baerenz/Getty Images; 39, © Bec Parsons/Getty Images; 40, © Myrleen Pearson/PhotoEdit; 40, © Arra Smith; 42, © Deborah Harrison/Getty Images; 42, © BMD Images/Alamy; 45, © Lee Celano/Getty Images; 46, © MIXA/Jupiterimages.

Chapter 4: Page 47, © Monkey Business Images/Shutterstock; 48, © Tim Pannell/Corbis; 48, © JGI/Jamie Grill/Blend Images/Corbis; 49, © Tony Anderson/Jupiterimages; 50, © Tom Brakefield/Getty Images; 50, © Pal Teravagimov/Shutterstock; 50-51, © Tischenko Irina/Shutterstock; 52, © Seqoya/Shutterstock; 52-53, © International Rescue/The Image Bank/Getty Images; 53, © Ambient Ideas/Shutterstock; 54, © Courtney Weittenhiller/iStockphoto; 57, © Orientaly/Shutterstock; 57, © Sherri R. Camp/Shutterstock; 58, © Stockbyte/Jupiterimages; © Michael Newman/PhotoEdit; 60, © JGI/Tom Grill/Blend Images/Corbis.

Chapter 5: Page 66, © The Crosiers/Gene Plaisted, OSC; 67, © Createa/Jupiterimages; 68, © Dennis MacDonald/PhotoEdit; 75, © Digital Vision/Jupiterimages; 76, © Corbis Fl/Alamy.

Chapter 6: Page 77, © MBI/Alamy; 79, © Camille Tokerud/Getty Images; 79, © KidStock/Getty Images; 79, © Fancy Collection/SuperStock ; 84, © Stock Connection/SuperStock ; 87, © Heide Benser/Corbis; 88, © Jose Luis Pelaez Inc/Getty Images.

Chapter 7: Page 89, © Medioimages/Photodisc/Jupiterimages; 90, © Jose Luis Pelaez Inc/Jupiterimages; 90, © Blend images/Alamy; 91, © Hemera/Thinkstock; 91, © KidStock/Getty Images; 91, © Alexander Puell/Getty Images; 96, © Myrleen Ferguson/PhotoEdit; 99, © Anthony-Masterson/Getty Images; 100, © Stewart Cohen/Jupiterimages.

Chapter 8: Page 101, © Richard Levine/Alamy; 104, © Robert Churchill/iStockphoto; 105, © ROBERT DEUTSCH/Staff/Getty Images; 105, © CNS/Paul Haring; 106, © Mike Kemp/Jupiterimages; 106, © Wavebreak Media/Thinkstock; 108, © Tony Freeman/PhotoEdit; 111, © Christopher Futcher/iStockphoto; 112, © Design Pics/SW Productions/Jupiterimages; 113, © Jupiterimages/Getty Images; 114, © iStockphoto/Thinkstock.

Chapter 9: Page 119, © Fancy/Alamy; 120, © Hank Walker/Time & Life Pictures/Getty Images; 120, © Bettmann/Corbis; 124, © Bill Wittman; 125, © Myrleen Pearson/PhotoEdit ; 125, © Bill Wittman; 125, © Texi/Getty Images ; 129, © David Gee 4/Alamy; 130, © Fuse/Jupiterimages.

Chapter 10: Page 131, © Bill Wittman; 134, © Bill Wittman; 135, © Compassionate Eye Foundation/Digital Vision/Tim Pannell/Getty Images; 135, © Chris Amaral/Getty Images; 138, © Bill Wittman; 141, © Ghislain & Marie David de Lossy/Jupiterimages; 142, © Jupiterimages/Getty Images.

Chapter 11: Page 143, © Lori Adamski Peek/Getty Images; 146, © Ableimages/Thinkstock; 150, © Bill Wittman; 153, © Laura Doss/Corbis; 154, © Maria Teijeiro/Jupiterimages.

Chapter 12: Page 155, © 501443/Jupiterimages; 158, © Benn Mitchell/Getty Images; 162, © Bill Wittman; 165, © PhotoAlto/Michele Constantini/Getty Imges; 166, © Fuse/Jupiterimages.

Chapter 13: Page 168, iStockphoto/Thinkstock; 174, © iStockphoto/Patty_c; 177, © Bill Wittman; 178, © The Crosiers/Gene Plaisted, OSC; 180, © Tony Freeman/PhotoEdit; 183, © Tony Freeman/PhotoEdit; 184, © SW Productions/Jupiterimages.

Chapter 14: Page 185, © Polka Dot/Jupiterimages; 186, © H. MARC LARSON/AP WideWorld Photos; 186, © Myrleen Pearson/PhotoEdit; 188, © Pitu Cau/Alamy; 188, © Tonis Valing/Shutterstock; 190, © Mirek Weichsel/AgStock Images/Corbis; 190, © iStockphoto/Thinkstock; 192, © Bill Wittman; 195, © Sue McDonald/Alamy; 196, © Tom Merton/Jupiterimages.

Chapter 15: Page 197, © Bill Wittman; 198, © Bob Mullen/The Catholic Photographer; 198, © Rick Friedman/Corbis; 200, © Bill Wittman; 204, © Bill Wittman; 207, © Myrleen Ferguson Cate/PhotoEdit; 208, © Inmagine/Alamy.

Chapter 16: Page 209, © Peter Dazeley/Getty Images; 211, © The Crosiers/Gene Plaisted, OSC; 211, © Bettmann/CORBIS; 211, © The Crosiers/Gene Plaisted, OSC; 212, © Bill Wittman; 213, © The Crosiers/Gene Plaisted, OSC; 216, © Bill Wittman; 219, © John Lund/Sam Diephuis/Blend Images/Corbis; 220, © Tony Freeman/PhotoEdit; 221, JGI/Jamie Grill/Blend Images/Corbis; 221, Spencer Grant/PhotoEdit; 222, Steve Debenport/Getty Images.

Chapter 17: Page 227, © Terry Vine/Blend Images/Corbis; 228, © AP Photo/Archdiocese of Detroit/ASSOCIATED PRESS; 229, © Jupiterimages/Thinkstock; 229, © Masterfile; 229, © Juice Images/SuperStock ; 230, © Comstock/Getty Images; 232, © Alexey Stiop/Shutterstock; 234, © Stockbyte/Jupiterimages; 234, © ERproductions Ltd/Jupiterimages; 234, © Frank Gaglione/Getty Images; 237, © DAJ/Getty Images; 238, © Bridget Taylor/Jupiterimages.

Chapter 18: Page 239, © ERproductions Ltd/Blend Images/Getty Images; 241, © Diane Collins and Jordan Hollender/Getty Images ; 241, © Comstock/Thinkstock; 241, © KidStock/Jupiterimages; 245, © Masterfile; 246, © Digital Vision./Getty Images; 246, © Lito C. Uyan/CORBIS; 246, © Stockbyte/Getty Images; 249, © Compassionate Eye Foundation/Getty Images; 250, © Tony Freeman/PhotoEdit.

Chapter 19: Page 256, © Sung-Il Kim/Corbis; 256, © Myrleen Ferguson Cate/PhotoEdit; 256, © Myrleen Ferguson Cate/PhotoEdit; 262, © Beau Lark/Corbis/Jupiterimages.

Chapter 20: Page 263, © Kevin Fitzgerald/Getty Images; 264, © Bob Daemmrich/PhotoEdit; 264, © Design Pics/SW Productions/Getty Images; 266, © Randy Faris/Corbis; 266, 273, © Myrleen Ferguson Cate/PhotoEdit; 274, © Fuse/Jupiterimages; 275, Wavebreak Media/Thinkstock; 275, © Inti St Clair/Blend Images/Corbis; 275, © 2A Images/Getty Images; 276, © Tyler Edwards/Getty Images.

Chapter 21: Page 281, © Varina Patel/Alamy; 282, © The Crosiers/Gene Plaisted, OSC; 285, © apply pictures/Alamy; 285, © Big Cheese Photo LLC/Alamy; 286, © Corbis Premium RF/Alamy; 286, © Bon Appetit/Alamy; 286, © Fancy/Alamy; 288, © Gideon Mendel/Corbis; 288, © Masterfile; 291, © Borderlands/Alamy; 292, © Radius Images/Jupiterimages.

Chapter 22: Page 296, © MBI/Alamy; 298, © moodboard/Corbis; 300, © SW Productions/Photodisc/Getty Images; 303, © Somos Images/Alamy; 304, © JGI/Jupiterimages.

Chapter 23: Page 305, © Fuse/Jupiter Images; 306, © Fuse/Jupiterimages; 306, © Catholic News Service; 307, © Design Pics/SW Productions/Getty Images; 307, © Image Source/SuperStock ; 307, © Larry Mulvehill/Corbis; 308, © Digital Vision./Getty Images; 309, © Grove Pashley/Jupiterimages; 310, © Bill Wittman; 312, © Jurgen Magg/Alamy; 315, © The Crosiers/Gene Plaisted, OSC; 316, © View Stock/Alamy.

Chapter 24: Page 317, © James Shaffer/PhotoEdit; 318, © VINCENZO PINTO/AFP/Getty Images; 318, © Bill Wittman; 319, © Jacek Chabraszewski/Shutterstock; 319, © ifong/Shutterstock; 319, © Masterfile; 319, © Steve Debenport/Getty Images; 320, © image100/Alamy; 321, © Blend Images/Alamy; 322, © Arra Smith; 322, © Andrew Penner/; E+/Getty Images; 323, © Purestock/Getty Images; 327, © Corbis Premium RF/Alamy; 328, © Comstock/Jupiterimages; 329, David Leahy/Getty Images; 330, Myrleen Pearson/PhotoEdit.

Liturgical Seasons: Page 333, © Design Pics Inc./Alamy; 335, © iStockphoto/Thinkstock; 337, © The Crosiers/Gene Plaisted, OSC; 337, © The Crosiers/Gene Plaisted, OSC; 337, © The Crosiers/Gene Plaisted, OSC; 339, © Beneda Miroslav/shutterstock; 341, © The Crosiers/Gene Plaisted, OSC; 343, © The Bridgeman Art Library International; 345, © The Bridgeman Art Library International; 347, © Jannis Werner/Alamy; 349, © The Crosiers/Gene Plaisted, OSC; 349, © The Crosiers/Gene Plaisted, OSC; 351, © LUIS ACOSTA/AFP/Getty Images; 353, © Myrleen Ferguson Cate/Photo Edit; 355, © Prisma Bildagentur AG/Alamy; 357, © The Crosiers/Gene Plaisted, OSC; 359, © The Crosiers/Gene Plaisted, OSC; 361, © The Crosiers/Gene Plaisted, OSC; 363 © The Crosiers/Gene Plaisted, OSC.

Backmatter: Page 367, © Fuse/Jupiterimages; 369, © Blend Images/Alamy; 372, © Bill Wittman; 373, © Bill Wittman; 374, © Bill Wittman; 375, © Bill Wittman; 376, © Bill Wittman; 377, © Bill Wittman; 379, © Bill Wittman.

ILLUSTRATION CREDITS

Listed from Top to Bottom; Left to Right

Chapter 1: Page 9, Carol Liddiment; 12, Q2A Media; Page 14-15, Carol Liddiment 16, Q2A Media.

Chapter 2: Page 25, Jamie Pogue; 28, Carol Liddiment;

Chapter 3: Page 35, Q2A Media, 41, Q2A Media, 43, Q2A Media.

Chapter 4: Page 55, Q2A Media.

Chapter 5: Page 63, Carol Liddiment; 65, Carol Liddiment; 69, Kristin Sorra; 70, Carol Liddiment; 71, Jamie Pogue; 72, Carol Liddiment ; 73, Natalia Vasquez.

Chapter 6: Page 78, Natalia Vasquez; 80, Carol Liddiment; 81, Jamie Pogue; 81, Natalia Vasquez; 82-83, Carol Liddiment

Chapter 7: Page 92, Carol Liddiment; 94, Carol Liddiment; 95, Jamie Pogue.

Chapter 8: Page 102, 103, 107, Estudio Haus.

Chapter 9: Page 117, Carol Liddiment; 121, Jomike Tejido; 122, Carol Liddiment; 126, Jamie Pogue.

Chapter 10: Page 132, Q2A Media; 136, Carol Liddiment; 139, Q2A Media.

Chapter 11: Page 144, Q2A Media; 145, Natalia Vasquez; 148, Carol Liddiment.

Chapter 12: Page 156, Q2A Media; 157, 161, Natalia Vasquez; 159, Q2A Media; 160, Carol Liddiment; 167, Jamie Pogue.

Chapter 13: Page 171, Carol Liddiment; 173, Carol Liddiment; 176, Carol Liddiment.

Chapter 14: Page 189, Q2A Media; 187, 191, Jomike Tejido.

Chapter 15: Page 201, Q2A Media; 202, Carol Liddiment.

Chapter 16: Page 210, Estudio Haus; 214, Carol Liddiment.

Chapter 17: Page 225, Carol Liddiment; 231, Carol Liddiment; 235, Q2A Media.

Chapter 18: Page 240, Q2A Media; 242, Carol Liddiment; 244, Carol Liddiment.

Chapter 19: Page 249, Carol Liddiment; 251, Carol Liddiment; 252, Q2A Media; 254, Carol Liddiment; 258, Carol Liddiment; 261, Q2A Media.

Chapter 20: Page 265, Jomike Tejido; 268, Carol Liddiment; 270, Carol Liddiment.

Chapter 21: Page 284, Carol Liddiment; 287, Q2A Media.

Chapter 22: Page 293, Carol Liddiment; 294, Q2A Media; 301, Remy Simard.

Chapter 24: Page 324, Jomike Tejido.

Liturgical Seasons: Page 338, Jomike Tejido; 350, Jomike Tejido; 362, Burgundy Beam.

Guide Credits

Cover Illustration: Marcia Adams Ho